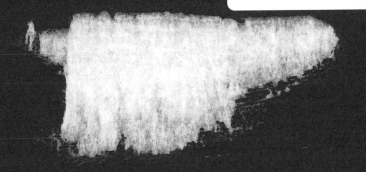

FRENCH OPERA

VINCENT GIROUD

FRENCH OPERA

A SHORT HISTORY

YALE UNIVERSITY PRESS
NEW HAVEN AND LONDON

Published with assistance from the foundation established in memory of Oliver Baty
Cunningham of the Class of 1917, Yale College

For information about this and other Yale University Press publications, please contact:
U.S. Office: sales.press@yale.edu   www.yalebooks.com
Europe Office: sales @yaleup.co.uk   www.yaleup.co.uk

Set in Minion Pro by IDSUK (Data Connection) Ltd
Printed in Great Britain by TJ International Ltd, Padstow, Cornwall

Library of Congress Cataloging-in-Publication Data

Giroud, Vincent.
    French opera : a short history / Vincent Giroud.
       p. cm.
    ISBN 978-0-300-11765-3 (cl : alk. paper)
1. Opera—France.   I. Title.
    ML1727.G57 2010
    782.10944—dc22

                                                                        2009039205

A catalogue record for this book is available from the British Library.

10 9 8 7 6 5 4 3 2 1

To Robert Pounder

CONTENTS

ILLUSTRATIONS

ACKNOWLEDGMENTS

The present book came into being thanks to John Ryden, former director of Yale University Press; now that more than six years have passed, it is a pleasure to have the opportunity to convey my gratitude to him in print at last. I am no less grateful to Robert Baldock and his colleagues at the London office of the Press for shepherding this project to completion. Let me thank, in particular, Tami Halliday and Rachael Lonsdale, as well as Richard Mason for his careful editing.

David Lloyd-Jones, a great lover of French music and no mean expert on it as in many other fields, encouraged this project from the start and at every stage, for which I am deeply grateful, as well as to his wife Carol.

I wish to thank the staff of the libraries where I conducted most of my research, especially the Département de la musique and the Bibliothèque-musée de l'Opéra, both part of the Bibliothèque nationale de France, Paris; the New York Public Library for the Performing Arts, Dorothy and Lewis B. Cullman Center; the library of the École normale supérieure, Paris; the Blegen Library of the American School of Classical Studies, Athens; and the Vassar College Library, Poughkeepsie, New York. As always, Jacques Tchamkerten, at the library of the Conservatoire de musique in Geneva, was exceptionally helpful with illustrations. The same applies to Andrea Cawelti of the Houghton Library, Harvard University. I also wish to thank, among many others, Annette Fern and Pamela Madsen (Harvard Theatre Collection), Lisa Vick (Loeb Music Library, Harvard University), Laurie Klein (Beinecke Rare Book and Manuscript Library, Yale University), as well as to Philippe Garnier and Alain Schmidt. I am deeply grateful to my old friend and former colleague Stephen Parks and to the Elizabethan Club of Yale University for their support.

This book has benefited enormously from the assistance received over the years – at times in the form of a small favor or short conversation, in some cases after a decade or more of fruitful exchanges – from more people than I can remember. Among them I am particularly indebted to my friend and collaborator Jean-Christophe Branger. Let me also mention Cécile Auzolle, Philippe Blay, Leon Botstein, Francis Claudon, Gérard Condé, Damien Colas, Alessandro Di Profio, Yves Gérard, Francine Du Plessix Gray, Denis Herlin, Steven Huebner, Jean-Christophe Keck, Nizam Peter Kettaneh, Hervé Lacombe, Hugh Macdonald, Michela Niccolai, Paul Prévost, Ransom Wilson, and Richard and Adene Wilson. I am aware that the list should be much longer and I hope anyone I have unwillingly forgotten will accept my apologies.

My longtime companion, Robert Pounder, was my first reader and an invaluable mentor throughout the writing of this book. The dedication is a very small token of my gratitude.

INTRODUCTION

As this book hopes to show, French opera is second only to Italian opera in the length, breadth, and diversity of its history. Yet most people, if asked to come up with titles, would mention only a handful – *Carmen, Faust, Pelléas et Mélisande, Manon, Werther, Samson et Dalila, Dialogues des carmélites*. They are indeed works that are regularly staged by opera houses worldwide and have never left the repertory since they were premiered. But they constitute a small number and a relatively short time span – 1859 to 1957 – for an operatic tradition that officially began in 1671 and is still very much alive. Would this suggest that one does not spontaneously think of French opera in terms of a historical continuum, from Lully to Messiaen and beyond? Or does French opera suffer from an identity problem, compared, say, to Czech, Russian, English, or American opera?

Perhaps one ought to start with a simple question: what exactly do we mean by French opera? An obvious answer, which would certainly apply to all the operas listed above, while matching the criteria of the "national" traditions just mentioned, would be: an opera set to music by a French composer on a libretto written in French. Yet this definition immediately strikes one as too narrow. It presupposes a neat equivalence between a cultural form (opera), a national identity (France), and a language (French). But these categories do not coincide, and the subtle relations between them have shifted considerably over the ages – and, as history keeps reminding us, continue to do so. France was not the same country in 1689, 1789, 1889, and 1989. In the course of three centuries, French has evolved from being the language of the educated classes of Europe to having lost this status to English, yet remaining an international language spoken by a much wider range of people around the world than in earlier eras – being now the official language of nearly 30 countries. But should we even restrict our definition to native French speakers? Would it occur to anyone to exclude *Les contes d'Hoffmann*, a work that could easily have been part of our original list, because its composer, Offenbach – though he became a naturalized French citizen – was

German-born? One broader reason for rejecting a narrow definition of our field is that opera is a theatrical as well as a musical genre: the language it is set in, and the dramaturgy it follows, are indicators that are at least equal in importance to the composer's mother tongue and the musical tradition from which he or she may originate. We will therefore use as our working definition of French opera, any opera set originally to a French text: although the nationality of the composer (or librettist, for that matter) may affect their work in all kinds of ways, such differences are components of the genre rather than limits to its definition.

A constant feature of French opera throughout its history is, indeed, its cosmopolitan character. Lully, the first major figure in this history, who exerted such influence on the genre that the model he had introduced remained in place for more than a century, was Florentine. The true creator, in the 1750s, of that so-called "eminently French" genre of *opéra-comique*, Egidio Duni, was from Lucania, then part of the Kingdom of Naples. French opera during the period immediately preceding the Revolution was dominated by figures such as Gluck, Sacchini, Salieri, and Piccinni – none of them French or native French speakers – and by that of Grétry, born in present-day Francophone Belgium. During the Romantic age, *grand opéra*, another quintessentially French genre, linked to the Paris Opera, where it was born, was exemplified by non-French composers – Rossini, Meyerbeer, Donizetti, Verdi – with at least as much éclat as by the French-born Auber and Halévy. It is fair to say that French opera, more than any other operatic tradition, has always thrived, and continues to thrive, on foreign imports. In addition to the aforementioned examples from Austria, Germany, and Italy, musicians who have contributed to it have come from Bulgaria, England, Finland, Greece, Hungary, Ireland, Poland, Romania, Russia, Spain, and what is now the Czech Republic – not to mention French-speaking countries like Belgium, Canada, and Switzerland.

"French" should thus not be understood to mean simply "from France" or "pertaining to France." Gluck, for one, had his first French operas performed in Vienna long before he set foot in Paris. In more recent times, French operas have been mounted in Brussels, Geneva, Monte Carlo, and Montreal that have not been seen in France and may never be. On the other hand, one should not deny or minimize the role France plays in all "French" cultural matters, and most of the following narrative will take place there. Paris, in particular, at various times in this survey, will be seen as a magnet, or a trendsetter, a benevolent – or negligent – foster-parent. Perpetually challenged by other French-speaking capitals, or, more timidly, by the leading French provincial theaters, its supremacy, since the seventeenth century, has never been in question. Although this is not a history of opera in France, let alone in Paris, much of our story takes place in the French capital.

One peculiar character of French culture, from the earliest times, has been its ties with political power. The reasons for this are rooted in French history: the French monarchy slowly established its hegemony, in the sixteenth and seventeenth centuries, by creating a central State that gradually monopolized forms of cultural patronage previously held by the great feudal families. As their power declined, these families became, instead, participants in elaborate court rituals which Versailles, as of the 1680s, came to symbolize, providing a much-admired image that other European monarchies began to imitate. Writers, artists, and musicians were required to play a role in glorifying the king – the source and incarnation of the national identity. This system, which tried to maintain a subtle balance between a centralized administration and regional particularities, was in theory abolished by the French Revolution. But it was in fact replaced, under Napoleon and his successors, by an even more centralized one, in which culture was either put at the service of the State for propaganda purposes or otherwise viewed with suspicion. Beginning in 1830, admittedly, the political power gradually relinquished part of its control over cultural matters. Yet French culture remained – and to a large extent still remains, the French Republic having inherited some features of the French monarchy – influenced by a model whereby the State provides cultural guidance as well as subsidies, while it exercises, in exchange, subtle forms of control. French opera, from its very beginnings to the recent period, has illustrated those tendencies better than any other French artistic form.

This book is a history, and a short one at that. Its ambitions are by definition modest. Our aim is to survey the evolution of the genre by focusing on its actors and their achievements – who wrote what in what context, and how it was received. We cannot hope to begin to do justice to questions that, in any event, have been extensively covered by musicological studies of particular periods or particular composers. The central one, which the limited scope of this book allows us to touch on only briefly, is, of course, the peculiarities of French as an operatic language. One does not have to go so far as to question its very suitability for singing – as Jean-Jacques Rousseau famously did in the mid-eighteenth-century – to note that French is a challenging language, both for composers to set and for singers to project. Unlike Italian, opera's native language, it is largely unstressed (save for a weak tonic stress on the last syllable) and its predominance of "closed" vowel sounds gives the voice fewer opportunities to open up. Its "nasal" vowels (*un, an, on, in*) can have a disagreeable effect on certain timbres, while the ubiquitous "e mute," never elided in classical prosody, is another pitfall. These characteristics, combined with the long-standing preference of French opera for a complex, recitative-like type of declamation over the more lyrical, overtly vocal forms favored by the Italians, have often given French singing – and French opera – a bad reputation: as early as the eighteenth-century, Italian visitors to the Paris Opera began referring to what became proverbially known as the *urlo francese* – French screaming. Beyond such stereotypes, composers have responded in a great variety of ways to those challenges. At times – Spontini and Meyerbeer being prime examples – they put the music first and creatively twisted the rules of prosody to make the text fit their musical requirement. In other examples, such as Gounod and Bizet, the melodic curves seem to derive from the "natural" delivery of the spoken text; and this is usually true of a non-native composer like Offenbach, who developed an innate sense for the language of his adopted country.

Another specificity of French opera that will emerge from this panorama is the relationship between spoken and sung passages in the opéra-comique tradition, from its early eighteenth-century beginnings to its gradual disappearance in the first decades of the twentieth century. French opera, to be sure, was not alone in mixing spoken dialogues and sung numbers – the German *Singspiel* did it at the same time – but the opéra-comique came to be seen as so quintessentially a French genre that this sub-genre occupies a more central position in the French tradition than in any other. Nor have we omitted from this survey the origins and development of French operetta. It may come as a special surprise to realize how many "mainstream" opera composers – Delibes, Bizet, Chabrier, Roussel, Honegger – have contributed to this other "eminently French" genre.

The history of music, as Jean Mongrédien has noted, is not simply the history of masterpieces, and this applies with particular force to the history of opera. Without claiming to be comprehensive, we will look at the contributions of lesser-known composers and at the lesser-known works of well-known composers along with works that posterity ranks as undisputed masterpieces. Yet, posterity is not always fair and can be fickle, and our keenest hope is that the curiosity of the reader will be attracted to a number of works that merit more than a passing reference in music history. Recent stagings of Lully's *Atys* and *Persée*, of Rameau's *Les Boréades* and *Les Indes galantes*, have shown what treasures still remain to be discovered in the French baroque repertory. More fragile gems – less resistant perhaps to an adventurous style of production – will be found in works by Monsigny, Philidor, and Grétry. And while Meyerbeer and Halévy are slowly beginning to receive their due, Boieldieu's *La dame blanche*, Hérold's *Le Pré-aux-clercs*, Auber's *Le cheval de bronze* and *Les diamants de la couronne*, Chabrier's *Le roi malgré lui*, Massenet's *Ariane*, Bloch's *Macbeth*, Sauguet's *La chartreuse de Parme*, among many others, are all works that would deserve a place in the repertory.

As our concluding chapter will argue, French opera since the 1980s has begun a kind of renaissance, with more new works by more composers of the younger generation being staged in sold-out houses. This history thus ends on an optimistic note. But it is, obviously, open-ended, and we will not venture any predictions on the future of French opera. We will simply express one final hope. For many opera lovers, opera has become a museum, where one revisits a few cherished works, chiefly with a view to hearing fine voices sing. No one should deny that opera is about singing; but it is also, and above all, the space where music and theater meet. Looking at the past achievements of French opera should make us all the more interested in supporting new ways in which music and the theater may continue to meet, in France or in French, today and tomorrow.

CHAPTER 1

FROM THE ORIGINS TO LULLY

The ballet de cour, forerunner of French opera

Before opera was introduced to France – and even before it came into being in its native Italy – a new genre, mixing dance and singing, appeared at the French court in the 1580s and flourished for about a century.[1] Deriving in part from the lavish entertainments held at the Burgundy and Valois courts beginning in the late Middle Ages, it was also a product of the Renaissance's ambition to achieve a fusion of the arts of a kind practiced, according to a largely idealized conception, in classical antiquity. After several forerunners in the 1570s,[2] *the ballet de cour* came into being when the *Balet comique de la Reyne* ("comique" meaning here "theatrical") was staged at the Petit-Bourbon in Paris in 1581 on the occasion of the wedding of Marguerite de Lorraine Vaudémont, the queen's half-sister, to Henri III's favorite, the Duc de Joyeuse.[3] Lasting about six hours, the *Balet comique* was conceived and choreographed by the Piedmontese violinist and ballet-master Baldassarino di Belgiojoso (*c.*1535–*c.*1587), who was at the French court as of 1555, restyling himself as Beaujoyeulx. The story of the magician Circe, on which the work was loosely based, was treated as a pretext for a series of elaborate "entrées" comprising dances and songs, interspersed with spoken dialogues. The music (now lost) was by two of the royal musicians, Jacques Salmon and Lambert de Beaulieu. At the end, Circe's enchanted palace was stormed by Jupiter, Mercury and others, and her magic wand was presented to the king, after which a general dance concluded the entertainment. Praised as a synthesis between poetry, music, dance, painting (sets, costumes) and even geometry – dancers formed allegorical patterns that could be followed by the spectators seated higher up – Beaujoyeulx's work was widely imitated in the following decades.[4]

More features were gradually added to the ballet de cour. Next to the mythological, allegorical kind, many were based on burlesque or picturesque themes – birds or animals, games, feasts, the four seasons, etcetera. Comical elements were frequently incorporated into the more serious ballets. Secondly, the spectacular element took more and more importance, thanks especially to the arrival of Italian stage machinery and technicians, such as Tommaso Francini, active as of 1600 in Paris, where his brother Alessandro soon joined him. Thirdly, the musical side of ballet de cour was enriched when spoken dialogues, around 1605, began to be replaced by sung recitatives in the manner of the earliest Italian operas: thus the *Ballet de Monsieur de Vendosme* (1610), based on the Alcina episode in Torquato Tasso's *Gerusalemme liberata*. In this work, Pierre Guédron (1565–c.1620), the most notable French composer for the stage in his generation, gave the heroine a series of musical "scenes" of striking novelty. Yet, music in the ballet de cour remained second to spectacle and its expressive possibilities were limited. It was often the work of two or more composers – dance music by one, vocal music by another – and when it has survived, it is usually because some of it was published in anthologies of *airs de cour*.[5]

One peculiarity of the ballet de cour was that its performers included courtiers and princes as well as professional dancers and musicians. Thus the 14-year-old Duc de Vendôme, Henri IV's son by his mistress Gabrielle d'Estrées, participated in the aforementioned ballet named in his honor. The young Louis XIII, who succeeded to the throne after his father's (Henry IV's) assassination in 1610, was trained both as a musician and a dancer.[6] In 1617, he appeared, first as the demon of fire and as the crusader Godfrey of Bouillon at the end, in the *Ballet d'Armide, ou La délivrance de Renaud*, also inspired by Tasso. The ballet de cour could acquire a political significance: in the *Ballet de Tancrède* (1619), the Duc de Luynes, Louis XIII's favorite, is glorified for ridding the kingdom, two years previously, of the detested Concino Concini, the queen mother's protégé.[7] This dimension was magnified in the 1630s by Cardinal Richelieu, who made the ballet de cour an instrument for political propaganda, with titles such as *Ballet des quatre monarchies chrétiennes* (1635) or *Ballet de la prospérité des armes de France* (1641).[8] To mount the latter he invited the Italian stage-machinery designer Giacomo Torelli, who became known in Paris as "the great wizard."

The popularity of the ballet de cour resulted in its dissemination, geographically and socially, far beyond the court itself: ballets were staged in major cities to mark royal visits, in the châteaux of the nobility and in prosperous bourgeois residences. After 1630, they were performed by the troupe of Charles Le Noir in the various theaters it occupied in the Marais district: thus the *Ballet de l'Harmonie* by Guillaume Colletet (one of the original members of the Académie française in 1635 and the leading ballet writer of the period) was first given before the king at the Louvre on 14 December 1632 and repeated twice, on the 15 and 16, at the Marais du Temple.[9] Even a more popular public could get a glimpse of the genre through cruder renderings at the Foire Saint-Germain. The ballet was also taken up by Jesuit schools all over the country, either for end-of-the-year performances or in honor of royal visitors, as in 1622 when Louis XIII and his wife Queen Anne of Austria, together with the queen mother, were treated in Lyons to a ballet based on the battle of Bouvines in 1214.[10]

Although it arguably delayed the emergence of opera in France, the ballet de cour, as Margaret McGowan has noted, should be seen more as a forerunner than a rival.[11] It anticipated many of the features of the future *comédie-ballet* and *tragédie en musique*, and its long-lasting success explains in part the importance of the ballet as a constituent element of French opera for at least two centuries.

Cardinal Mazarin brings Italian opera to Paris

By 1643, when Louis XIV came to the throne, no opera proper had been performed in France. This hiatus is surprising, considering that the first Italian opera, Jacopo Peri's *Euridice*, was staged at the Palazzo Pitti in Florence in 1600 to celebrate the marriage of Marie de Médicis and Henri IV. Was the new queen of France insufficiently impressed with what she saw and heard? Was she more seduced by the ballets de cour she attended in Paris? Their vogue, as we have seen, continued through the reign of her son Louis XIII. The introduction of opera had to wait until the infancy of Louis XIV and was the work of another Italian, Cardinal Mazarin, who succeeded Richelieu as prime minister. Mazarin was fond of the genre, having experienced it in Rome at the palace of his protectors the Barberini family, where Stefano Landi's *Sant'Alessio* had been staged in 1632.[12] Within four years after Mazarin came to power in 1642, Italian musicians were brought to Paris: the composer Marco Marazzoli (*c.*1602–1662), another Barberini protégé, whose allegory *Il giuditio della Ragione tra la Belta e l'Affetto*, mounted at the Palais-Royal in February 1645, was the first opera heard in Paris; the singer Leonora Baroni, who was Mazarin's mistress; the star castrato Atto Melani, whom the Cardinal later used as a secret agent; and the librettist Francesco Buti. Torelli, the stage-machinery wizard, was brought back in 1645. In December 1645, Francesco Sacrati's *La finta pazza* received a lavish production before an invited audience at the Petit-Bourbon theater, near the Louvre. Despite the addition of ballets to conform to the French taste, it did not elicit much enthusiasm. A bigger effect was made by Luigi Rossi's *Orfeo*, set to Buti's text, at the Palais-Royal in 1647, with Melani in the title role. Unlike the previous works it was written especially for Paris, with a prologue glorifying the young Louis XIV in the manner of the ballet de cour, and it received eight performances. Mazarin's numerous enemies, however, were quick to exploit the high costs of the production for propaganda purposes. When the anti-Mazarin revolt known as the Fronde broke out in 1648, led by the Paris Parliament and a section of the nobility, Rossi and Melani fled. The popular Torelli himself was briefly imprisoned.

Once the Fronde was over (1653), Italian opera returned to Paris with a production at the Petit-Bourbon in 1654 of the "comédie italienne en musique"[13]

Le nozze di Peleo e di Theti. This time again, the music of Carlo Caproli (1615?–1692?) impressed less than Torelli's machines and especially the interpolated ballet, in which both Louis XIV and the young Lully danced.

Mazarin's final attempt to acclimatize his beloved Italian opera in France was in connection with the impending wedding in 1660 of Louis XIV and the Infanta Maria Teresa of Spain. The most prominent operatic composer of the day, Francesco Cavalli (1602–1676) – his *Egisto* had been staged in Paris in 1646 – was commissioned to produce a new work, *Ercole amante* ("Hercules in love") to be premiered in a new theater built especially at the Tuileries by Gaspare Vigarani to accommodate spectacular machinery. In the event, the theater was not ready in time for the wedding, and instead of *Ercole amante* Cavalli's 1654 *Xerse* was presented at the Louvre in November 1660, with a ballet by Lully which completely eclipsed the opera itself. A few months later Mazarin died. Despite Torelli's stage effects, *Ercole amante* flopped in February 1662. The new Tuileries theater, or "Salles des machines" as it was called – to this day the biggest ever built in Paris – was too large for comfort[14] and, once again, Lully's ballet stole the long evening. First in a series of foreign operatic composers to be disappointed by the French, Cavalli returned to Venice. Until 1752, virtually no Italian opera was heard in Paris or in France.

The introduction of full-fledged opera in France would thus appear to have been a failure. Yet, it gave playwrights and musicians a stimulus to create a specifically French operatic form, conceived largely in terms of rejection of the Italian model.

From Isaac de Benserade's ballets to the Pastorale d'Issy

In the 1650s and 1660s, while the ballet de cour enjoyed its last efflorescence, several prototypes of French opera appeared concurrently with the performances of Italian operas in Paris: the tragédie à machines, the pastoral and the comédie-ballet.

Less of a musician than his father Louis XIII – though he learned to play the harpsichord and the guitar and was known for his good ear – Louis XIV, in his younger years, was an even more eager dancer (the Duc de Saint-Simon, a grudging admirer, granted that he had "the finest legs in his kingdom"). He made his stage debut in February 1651 at age 13 in the *Ballet de Cassandre*, designed by the playwright Isaac de Benserade who suggested the themes and wrote the texts for most of the court ballets of the decade.[15] Two years later, the young king appeared as the rising sun – which became the symbol of his reign – in the *Ballet de la nuit*, of which eight performances were given at the Petit-Bourbon theater recently redecorated by Torelli.[16] The participation of the king, joined by princes of the blood and members of the aristocracy, gave new prestige to the genre, which continued to combine spoken passages, sung recitatives, airs and dances, as well as lavish costumes and stage effects. The ballets were long (six hours for the *Ballet de la nuit*) and comprised a large number of entrées (43 for *Ballet de la nuit*), each illustrating the general theme. The music of Benserade's ballets was composed by various composers: Jean-Baptiste Boësset (1614–1685), Jean de Cambefort (1605–1661), Michel Lambert (1610–1696) for vocal music; Michel Mazuel (1603–1676), Louis de Mollier (1615–1688), Guillaume Dumanoir (1615–1697) for dance music. In 1655 Lully, having frequently appeared as a dancer, began to collaborate with Benserade as musician, becoming, by 1660, the principal court ballet composer.

The vogue of Torelli's stage wizardry was not without influence on the "straight" theater either. In 1650 Pierre Corneille (1606–1684), the leading French playwright since the triumph of his *tragi-comédie Le Cid* in 1636, accepted Mazarin's commission to write *Andromède*, subtitled "tragedy performed with machines." Staged at the Petit-Bourbon theater, it used the machinery Torelli had devised for Rossi's *Orfeo* three years before. Unlike regular tragedies, which were in alexandrine verse throughout, it was written in a combination of meters.[17] The stage music (now lost), composed by Charles Dassoucy (1605–1679), comprised airs, duets and choruses as well as instrumental passages. The five acts were preceded by a prologue in which Melpomene, muse of tragedy, and Apollo in his chariot praised Louis XIV. When he published the play, Corneille apologized about the use of music in *Andromède*, claiming that it was there "only to satisfy the ear while the eyes are looking at the machines."[18] Yet *Andromède*, although its text was spoken rather than sung, contained many of the structural features of the *tragédie en musique* as Quinault and Lully would perfect it 25 years later. Without rivaling the ballet de cour in popularity, the tragédie à machines became a specialty of the Théâtre du Marais.[19] Corneille himself produced one more, *La conquête de la Toison d'or*, staged in 1660 at the Normandy château of an eccentric, the Marquis de Sourdéac, whose name we will encounter again in the history of early French opera. Corneille also collaborated with Molière (1622–1673), Quinault, and Lully on the *tragédie-ballet Psyché* (1671). Commissioned to reuse Torelli's *Ercole* machines, it was staged first in the Salle des machines at the Tuileries but soon transferred to Molière's own Palais-Royal theater.[20]

Another prefiguration of French opera was the vogue of pastorals in the 1650s and 1660s – plays set in a rural setting but also involving a supernatural, mythological element.[21] Deriving from classical models – notably Virgil and Longinus – pastoral was reinvented in sixteenth-century Italy. Its two most famous representatives, Tasso's *Aminta* (1581) and Giovanni Battista Guarini's *Il pastor fido* (1589), were, in turn, major influences on the earliest Italian operas. In seventeenth-century France, the pastoral genre was associated especially with *L'Astrée* (1607–24), the enormously popular novel by Honoré d'Urfé, which has been called "the first best-seller of modern French literature,"[22] and with the scarcely less famous play *Les bergeries* by Honorat de Racan, staged at the Hôtel de Bourgogne theater in 1620. The first pastoral sung throughout was *Le triomphe de l'amour sur les bergers et bergères* by Charles de Bey (1610–1659), a playwright and actor who may have been part of Molière's troupe. The music has not survived. Its author, Michel de La Guerre (1606–1679), a reputed lutenist, was organist at the Sainte-Chapelle in Paris. The work was first heard in 1655 at the Louvre and fully staged at the Palais-Royal two years later in the presence of the king and the queen mother.[23] Slight though it may have been, it vies for the title of first French opera.[24] A stronger candidate, however, is the play by Pierre Perrin with music by Robert Cambert performed in 1659 and known as the *Pastorale d'Issy*. Its libretto, published in the same year by Ballard, is headed *Première comédie françoise en musique représentée en France*.

In 1881 the music historian Arthur Pougin published a study on Perrin and Cambert entitled *Les vrais créateurs de l'opéra français*. This polemical title clearly betrayed a nationalistic streak characteristic of the post Franco-Prussian War period: the point was to show that French opera was founded by Frenchmen, not, as commonly assumed, by the Florentine Lully. Yet, no matter what his intentions were, Pougin pointed out the importance of two neglected figures who were not so much Lully's rivals as his victims.[25]

The Lyons-born Pierre Perrin (?1620–1675), whom early sources occasionally call "l'abbé Perrin" though he was not ordained, was the author of a translation of the *Aeneid*, the first part of which was published in 1648 with engravings by Abraham Bosse. He also composed religious verse and secular songs to music by various composers such as J.-B. Boësset, Michel Lambert, or Étienne Moulinié. The vicissitudes of his personal life need to be summarized since they came into play with the emergence of opera in France. In 1653, possibly in order to secure the funds to acquire a royal office, he married a rich widow, 30 years his senior, Mme de La Barroire. She died shortly afterwards, Perrin having incurred the enmity of her son by a previous marriage. His life thereafter comprised little but litigation and time spent in debtor's prisons.

Perrin's collaborator Robert Cambert (*c.*1628–1677), a Parisian, was a pupil of the great harpsichordist Jacques Champion de Chambonnières (1601/2–1672) and the organist at the church of Saint-Honoré. In 1657 Cambert set one of Perrin's songs to music, but the *Pastorale d'Issy* was their first major collaboration. In the previous year Cambert had already stated, apropos his elegy for voices *La muette ingrate*, his "longstanding desire to introduce into France *comédies en musique* like those found in Italy",[26] and he may have given Perrin the impulse to join forces with him to achieve this aim.

Compared to the Italian operas mounted in Paris in the 1640s and 1650s, the *Pastorale d'Issy*, known to us only from its libretto since no music survives, was a modest affair, lasting about 90 minutes, with a cast of 7, an orchestra of 13, and no special staging effects. Yet it had a real plot, albeit simple, was sung throughout, and comprised five acts. It was mounted in April 1659 in a specially built theater seating 300 to 400 people at the residence of a royal jeweler, René de La Haye, at Issy (hence the appellation under which it is remembered), then a village to the southeast of Paris. The success was considerable, with carriages trouping down the road to Issy to bring members of the aristocracy as well as rich members of the bourgeoisie – and, one would presume, musicians as well – at each of the eight or ten performances. Word of this success came to Mazarin, who commissioned a court performance at Vincennes in May, while encouraging the authors in their ambitions.

Perrin, in jail, missed the Issy performances, but the document he wrote at the time (dated April 1659) can be considered the first manifesto of French opera. It was in the form of a letter to Cardinal della Rovere, former apostolic nuncio to France and subsequently archbishop of Turin.[27] Perrin's arguments for the establishment of French opera were presented as a critique of Italian operas of the kind heard in Paris in the previous 14 years. These operas, Perrin claimed, were badly put together as plays and their relative lack of success seemed to indicate, he argued less persuasively, that Italian music was not fit for French ears. Italian operas were too long (some, it will be recalled, lasted six, even eight hours). Consisting of long stretches of recitative, they lacked variety, especially in dialogues.[28] They had the additional, and in Perrin's view crucial disadvantage of being in Italian, a language French audiences could not follow, all the more so since Italian poetry, he further argued, was too metaphorical and figurative, compared to the classical French canons of regularity, clarity, and conciseness. Perrin also found fault with the theaters in which operas were performed in Paris, since they were so large that words could not be understood (and he was writing before the Salle des machines was built). Finally, he denounced the use of castrati, "the horror of the ladies the laughing-stock of the men." This abhorrence of castrati was widely shared in France, and in fact French opera never employed them throughout its history.

Pierre Perrin, Robert Cambert, and the Académie d'opéra

As early as 1659, Perrin had several operas planned. Having explored the pastoral genre at Issy, he announced a play in the "comic" vein (meaning in this instance a serious one with a happy ending), *Ariane, ou Le mariage de Bacchus*, and a tragedy, *La mort d'Adonis*. More ambitious than the *Pastorale d'Issy*, these two works, even though only their text has survived, may be considered the first full-fledged tragédies en musique. Cambert set to work on *Ariane*, possibly in the hope that it might be mounted for the royal wedding, but the commissioned *Ercole amante* monopolized official attention. *Ariane* was rehearsed at the Hôtel de Nevers but not mounted.[29] *La mort d'Adonis* was set by Boësset and extracts were played before the king, but no performance followed. Mazarin's death in March 1661 deprived Perrin and Cambert of their most influential patron.

Perrin was not discouraged and in 1666 sent manuscript copies of his works – including *Ariane* and *La mort d'Adonis* – to Jean-Baptiste Colbert, who by then had become the equivalent of a prime minister to Louis XIV. In his cover letter, Perrin developed the arguments already used in his letter to Cardinal della Rovere but gave them a political edge: why would France, "a nation everywhere victorious," be intimidated by "foreigners" (i.e. Italians) when it came to combining poetry and music? Without using the word "opera," he proposed the creation of an "Academy of Poetry and Music," made up of poets and musicians, "or even, if possible, poet-musicians," which would "examine and establish rules" for this new art form.[30] Perrin's proposal is to be understood in the context of the ambitious cultural policies of the French monarchy in the seventeenth century. Begun by Richelieu, continued by Mazarin and finalized by Colbert, they aimed at incorporating writers and artists into a system that would strengthen national unity (an idea implicit in Perrin's use of the term "nation") while fostering artistic creation, albeit within strictly defined rules. The Académie française, established in 1635, had been intended to fix such standards for the French language, so that it could be pure and easily understood by all. Created in 1648, the Académie royale de peinture et de sculpture (later Académie des beaux-arts) had similar aims.[31] In 1663 Colbert – who envisaged a "general academy" overseeing all cultural and scientific matters – had founded the Académie des inscriptions et belles-lettres, which became known as the "Petite académie." And although the Académie des sciences was not officially created until 1699, its original nucleus – a group of scientists meeting regularly in the Royal Library – was established by Colbert in December 1666, the year of Perrin's letter.[32] It is revealing that the institution that became the Paris Opera was originally conceived by Perrin on the same model as the Académie française and its sisters: a state-sponsored collegial structure aimed at inventing and perfecting a national art form.

Colbert evidently approved the idea, since, three years later, on 28 June 1669, letters patent were granted to Perrin for the establishment of "académies d'opéra." The name "académie" remained but, as the plural reveals, it had taken on a different sense, the focus shifting from gathering poets and musicians to mounting operatic performances.[33] Perrin received a 12-year "privilege" – that is, a monopoly – "to establish in Paris and other towns of France music academies to sing plays in public, as is done in Italy, Germany and England."[34] The formulation may seem perplexing: while there were "academies" in Italy, some of them intimately connected to the history of early Italian opera, the term meant assemblies of musicians, artists and men of letters, as in Perrin's initial project; it did not mean, as in Colbert's formulation, opera companies or theaters. As for Germany and England, no institutions of that name were in existence at the time.[35] The letters patent addressed practical and financial matters. Since he was not to receive subsidies from the Crown, Perrin had permission to charge for admission to performances, and no one – members of the nobility included – was exempted from paying. It was specified, on the other hand, that noblemen could participate in opera performances without loss of status – an important distinction at a time when acting was considered immoral by the Church and actors lived under the threat of excommunication. The stipulation put French opera, from the outset, in the ballet de cour tradition rather than that of regular theater.[36]

Perrin and Cambert apparently first planned to stage *Ariane*, which was put into semi-public rehearsal.[37] Looking for financial backing, they formed an association with Alexandre de Rieux, marquis de Sourdéac, and Laurent Bersac, self-styled "sieur de Champeron." Sourdéac's hobby was stage machinery. He had commissioned and staged Corneille's *La conquête de la Toison d'or* in his Normandy château of Neufbourg in 1660. He had, however, a dubious moral reputation and his associate Champeron an even worse one.[38] While relieving Perrin and Cambert of all but their artistic responsibilities, they proceeded to cheat them of any financial rewards.

Ariane, in the event, was displaced in favor of a pastoral, *Pomone*, which Perrin and Cambert wrote quickly in early 1670. In the "Advis au public" accompanying the published libretto, Perrin justified the change by the contemporary taste for pastoral; by the inexperience of the troupe in the heroic style; and by the unavailability of the elaborate machinery required by the tragic and heroic genres.[39] Singers were recruited under Sourdéac's responsibility with a help of an agent, the singer Pierre Monier, who was sent in January 1670 on a talent-spotting mission to the churches of Languedoc. Some of his recruits – the soprano Cartilly (Marie-Madeleine Jossier), the high tenor Bernard Clédière from Béziers, the bass François Beaumavielle – remained members of the Opéra troupe after Lully took over.[40] As for a theater, Sourdéac and Champeron started remodeling an indoor tennis court (of the kind made famous by the 1789 Oath), the Jeu de Paume du Béquet on the rue de Vaugirard – close to the modern site of the Théâtre de l'Odéon – but, having failed to secure the necessary authorization, they chose another *jeu de paume*, known as "la Bouteille," also on the Left Bank, between the present rue de Seine and rue Mazarine.[41]

After being performed privately at Sèvres in June 1670, *Pomone* had its public premiere on 3 March 1671.[42] Subtitled "opéra, ou représentation en musique," and "pastorale," its structure was similar to the future tragédie en musique: five acts preceded by a prologue, set in front of the Louvre, in which the Nymph of the Seine and Vertumnus, god of gardens, glorify Louis XIV, the "new Mars," and Paris, the "new Rome." The plot, interspersed with dances, is devoted to Vertumnus's courtship of Pomona, goddess of fruits. Perrin's verse has traditionally been criticized for its "low," trivial tone (artichokes and truffles are the wedding present) yet is not without its amusing moments and even a certain freedom ("Let us on the green ferns / Taste love's sweet fruit"). What survives of Cambert's music, though not of the same caliber as Lully's, is lively and tuneful.[43]

The success of *Pomone* was prodigious, with an unprecedented 146 continuous performances over nearly eight months.[44] It was a popular success, as
evidenced by scuffles caused by servants trying to get into the theater without
paying.[45] Yet neither Perrin nor Cambert benefited from the receipts. There
being no formal agreements between poet and composer and their business
associates, Sourdéac and Champeron appropriated the earnings, not even
bothering to pay the singers. Lawsuits ensued, while Perrin himself was
imprisoned again in June 1671 at his former stepson's request. The hapless
writer sold the royal privilege to one of his creditors and fellow musician Jean
de Granouilhet, sieur de Sablières (1627–c.1700), in August, and, a second
time, to more creditors, including his stepson. Amidst this legal imbroglio, and
while performances of *Pomone* continued, Sablières hastily composed an
opera of his own, *Les amours de Diane et d'Endymion*, which was performed at
Versailles in November 1671.[46] Its librettist Henry Guichard, attached like him
to the household of the Duke of Orleans, the king's brother, was later one of
Lully's most implacable enemies. In a final attempt to retain artistic control of
the Opéra, Perrin, still imprisoned, entered into a new arrangement with
Sablières and Guichard, which divided the benefits equally between them.
Meanwhile, Sourdéac and Champeron hoped to capitalize on the success of
Pomone with a new work, *Les peines et les plaisirs de l'amour*, a five-act
"pastorale héroïque" with a prologue by Cambert on a libretto by Gabriel
Gilbert (1620?–1680?), which was published with a dedication to Colbert and
premiered in January 1672.[47] Its run was short. Lully, sensing that his time had
come, visited Perrin at the Conciergerie, bought him out, obtained a new royal
privilege in March, and had the Jeu de Paume de la Bouteille shut down by the
police on 1 April.[48]

Having traded his privilege for his freedom, Perrin died three years later.
Cambert moved to England in 1673, entering the service of Charles II. A
revised and expanded version of his *Ariane*, staged at the Theatre Royal, Drury
Lane, in March 1674, was the first French opera performed outside France.[49]
Cambert died in 1677.

The beginnings of Jean-Baptiste Lully

Lully has already come up several times in this story and will be mentioned
many more, his importance in French operatic history extending far beyond
his lifetime. Whereas he cannot be considered the sole inventor of the tragédie
en musique, the genre to which his name is forever linked, he carried it to a
point of perfection. He made it, as his contemporaries and succeeding generations agreed, into an unsurpassable model to which musicians and critics
alike kept referring. Like those of Corneille, Molière, and Jean Racine
(1639–1699), his works achieved the status of classics in his lifetime. Like
them, he became a repertory author – the first, in fact, in operatic history. But

he also shone in at least two other genres that contributed to the shaping of French opera: the ballet de cour and the comédie-ballet.

Giovanni Battista Lulli – as the name was originally spelled – was born in Florence on 28 November 1632.[50] His father Lorenzo was not a poor miller, as satirical accounts subsequently suggested, but a reasonably prosperous member of the lower bourgeoisie. The young Giovanni Battista probably received his musical education from a Franciscan monk, learning to play the violin at an early age. In 1646 he was recruited by Roger de Lorraine, chevalier de Guise, who had returned from an expedition to Malta and was looking for a young Italian who could provide conversation in Paris with his niece Anne-Marie-Louise d'Orléans, duchesse de Montpensier, better known as the "Grande Mademoiselle," first cousin of Louis XIV. In Paris, Lully received additional musical training[51] and became an accomplished dancer. He made the acquaintance of the singer and composer Michel Lambert (whose daughter Madeleine he later married in 1662) and Lambert's sister-in-law Hilaire Dupuis, also a celebrated singer. In 1652 Lully took part – both as dancer and composer – in a ballet she staged at the Tuileries, the *Mascarade de la Foire Saint-Germain*. Later in the same year, he left the service of "Mademoiselle", who had been exiled by her cousin the king because of her role in the Fronde. In February–March 1653 he appeared, alongside Louis XIV, in the *Ballet royal de la nuit*. Appointed as composer to the royal chamber – one of the three departments of the king's music, along with the *Chapelle* (for church services) and the *Écurie* (for royal hunts) – Lully continued to appear in the ballets that were the young king's favorite pastime, while contributing dance music to them. By 1656 he had his own orchestra, the "petits violons." The danced *intermèdes* he supplied to *Xerse* in 1660, mounted as part of the celebrations of Louis XIV's wedding to Maria Teresa of Spain, and to *Ercole amante* two years later, all but eclipsed Cavalli's music. In 1661 he was named *surintendant* of the king's chamber music.

Lully's collaboration with Molière began with *Le mariage forcé* in 1664. Three years before, Molière had, in his own words, "sewn together" a comedy and a ballet in his play *Les fâcheux*, premiered at Vaux-le-Vicomte during the lavish festivities that Comptroller General Nicolas Fouquet gave to Louis XIV – only to be arrested a few days later on charges of embezzlement. The music to *Les fâcheux* was chiefly by Pierre Beauchamps but included a courante composed by Lully. *Le mariage forcé*, a royal commission, was brilliantly successful and led the two "Baptistes," as Molière and Lully were soon called,[52] to produce together a series of works in which music came to play an increasing role: *La princesse d'Élide*, performed at Versailles in 1664 as part of *Les plaisirs de l'île enchantée*, the fête Louis XIV hosted over several days for his mistress Louise de La Vallière; *L'amour médecin*, premiered at Versailles in 1665; the *Pastorale comique* and *Le Sicilien*, both inserted in the *Ballet des Muses* given at Saint-Germain-en-Laye in 1667; *George Dandin*, performed as part of a *Grand divertissement royal* at Versailles in 1668; *Monsieur de Pourceaugnac*, premiered at Chambord in 1669; *Les amants magnifiques*, in which Louis XIV was announced but eventually declined to appear (Saint-Germain-en-Laye, 1670);[53] *Le bourgeois gentilhomme*, the only work by Molière and Lully to be actually published under the appellation "comédie-ballet" (Chambord, 1670); *Psyché* (1671), written in collaboration with Corneille and Quinault; and *La comtesse d'Escarbagnas*, first performed at Saint-Germain-en-Laye in December 1671 as part of a *Ballet des ballets*.

As the above list shows, the works on which Molière and Lully collaborated were of different kinds. Some – the *Pastorale comique, Les amants magnifiques* – remained close to the world of the *ballet de cour*. *Psyché*, as noted previously, came closest to the nascent tragédie en musique. Full-fledged plays like *Monsieur de Pourceaugnac* and *Le bourgeois gentilhomme*, in which the musical element is intimately connected to the plot, are genuine musical comedies and can be viewed as prefigurations of the opéra-comique. Their novel, experimental character is further evidenced by the fact that, despite their enormous popularity, they found no imitators after Molière's death in 1673.[54]

Lully and the Académie royale de musique

Before 1672, Lully was not at the forefront of the attempts to adapt opera to a French context. He presumably saw it as an essentially Italian form, as opposed to the indigenous genres, in which he excelled, of the ballet de cour and the comédie-ballet. According to Sébastien de Brossard's admittedly late testimony, Lully considered that "the French language was not appropriate for large-scale pieces."[55] The triumph of *Pomone*, the success at court of Sablières's *Diane et Endymion*, convinced him otherwise.

Colbert, probably alarmed by the legal troubles Perrin had brought upon himself, is reported to have favored letting several opera companies operate in competition, but Lully proved so insistent with Louis XIV, "who could not do without this man in his *divertissements*," that he had his way.[56] Not only did the letters patent signed by the king in March 1672 transfer to Lully the privilege of Perrin, they granted him, for his lifetime and to his sons after him, effective control of music theater throughout the country: theaters other than the Académie royale de musique (the institution's new name, which it kept until the Revolution) were not allowed to perform more than two airs or use more than two musicians. There was immediate outcry. Molière – whose theatrical activities were under threat – obtained a loosening of the restrictions on the number of musicians and dancers allowed. Looking for a theater, Lully leased the Jeu de Paume du Béquet near the Palais du Luxembourg (which had been Sourdéac and Champeron's initial choice) and had it refashioned by his compatriot Carlo Vigarani (Gaspare's son).[57] There, on 11 November 1672 Lully's first opera, *Les fêtes de l'Amour et de Bacchus*, a pastoral in three acts with a prologue, was premiered and ran successfully until the following spring. It was a hastily assembled patchwork in which Lully had gathered music he had previously composed for the *Pastorale comique, George Dandin, Les amants magnifiques,* and *Le bourgeois gentilhomme,* reusing Molière's texts, with additional lyrics by Quinault.[58] Meanwhile, Quinault and Lully set to work on their first tragédie en musique, namely *Cadmus et Hermione,* which was premiered in mid-April 1673. Louis XIV attended the performance on 27 April, consecrating Lully's triumph.

Lully's rise did not stop there. Molière having died on 17 February 1673 – he collapsed on stage at the end of the fourth performance of *Le malade imaginaire* – Lully obtained from the king his theater at the Palais-Royal.[59] Remodeled by Carlo Vigarani, it was to remain the home of the Paris Opéra until it burned down in 1763. It opened in January 1674 with Lully's and Quinault's second tragédie en musique, *Alceste ou le triomphe d'Alcide,* public rehearsals of which had been held at Versailles during the fall. In Paris, however, *Alceste* found as many enemies as admirers. Quinault's free adaptation of Euripides – embellished with additional characters and picturesque incidents, such as the siege and capture of a city in Act 2 – was severely criticized (by Racine among others); even Lully's music was satirized. But Lully held on to royal favor. In July 1674 *Alceste* was performed at Versailles as part of festivities celebrating the conquest of Franche-Comté,[60] and Lully's subsequent operas were treated to a court premiere before being staged in Paris: *Thésée* in January 1675, *Atys* in January 1676, and *Isis* in January 1677. Yet, whereas *Atys* was an unqualified success both at court and in Paris, *Isis* caused a scandal of a different kind. Quinault's libretto, dealing with Jupiter's pursuit of the nymph Io, was interpreted as an allusion to Louis XIV's dalliance with Marie-Élisabeth de Ludres, while Mme de Montespan (the principal royal mistress) found herself compared to the opera's Juno. *Isis* was not revived in Lully's lifetime and Quinault suffered temporary disgrace. Lully did not lack enemies: one of them, Henry Guichard, Sablières's former associate and the librettist of *Les amours de Diane et d'Endymion,* had obtained in 1674 a privilege for an "Académie royale des spectacles," officially to perform carousels, tournaments, races, wrestling matches, animal games, fireworks, and "anything that could imitate the ancient games of the Greeks and Romans."[61] In 1675, as the "Affaire des poisons" was brewing, following the arrest of the Marquise de Brinvilliers, Guichard was accused by a former mistress of his, a singer at the Opéra, of having attempted to poison her. Lully brought the charge to the king's attention, only to be sued for libel as a result. During the ensuing trial, which lasted until Guichard was sentenced to a nine-year exile in 1678, grave accusations were exchanged and Lully's homosexuality, already notorious at the time of his marriage, came to the fore.[62]

Momentarily deprived of Quinault's services, Lully, with the help of Thomas Corneille and his nephew Fontenelle, transformed his 1671 *Psyché* from a tragédie à machines into a tragédie en musique, and staged it at the Palais-Royal in April 1678. The same librettists also supplied the text of his next work,

Bellérophon. Premiered in Paris in January 1679, it was one of Lully's greatest popular successes. It was revived at court for the Carnival of 1680, when the reunited team of Quinault and Lully also gave *Proserpine.* In the same year Lully returned to the ballet de cour with *Le triomphe de l'amour,* which celebrated the marriage of the Dauphin to Marie-Anne de Bavière. In 1681 he reached the pinnacle of royal favor when, after appearing with success as the Mufti in a revival of *Le bourgeois gentilhomme* at Saint-Germain-en-Laye, he requested and obtained from Louis XIV a position as royal secretary.

Lully's collaboration with Quinault continued with *Persée,* premiered in Paris in April 1682 and reprised at court in July, and *Phaéton,* premiered at Versailles in January 1683 and subsequently so well received in Paris that it was dubbed "l'opéra du peuple" (as *Atys,* a favorite with Louis XIV, had been called "l'opéra du roi" and *Isis,* because of its musical refinement, "l'opéra des musiciens"). His association with Carlo Vigarani having come to an end in 1680, Lully had a new designer in Jean Berain.[63] *Amadis,* premiered in Paris in January 1684, was not, like all Lully's previous works, drawn from classical mythology but rather from the late Renaissance romance by Garci Rodríguez de Montalvo, *Amadís de Gaula,* first published in Saragossa in 1508 and popular in French translation. Also departing from classical mythology, *Roland* was adapted by Quinault from Ludovico Ariosto's epic *Orlando Furioso.* It was Lully's last work to be premiered at court, in January 1685, just when a scandal erupted over his open liaison with his page Brunet, who was arrested and confined for two years at the Saint-Lazare prison. As we know from the memoirs of the Duc de Saint-Simon and the correspondence of the king's sister-in-law Princesse Palatine and also from satirical literature, homosexuality was widespread at Versailles – beginning with Louis XIV's brother the Duc d'Orléans. But Lully had seemingly gone too far in the increasingly devout climate of the court (1685 was the year of the revocation of the Edict of Nantes). Reportedly pardoned, he never recovered the monarch's good graces.[64]

Still, Lully remained powerful and popular. In the summer of 1685 he set Racine's *Idylle sur la paix,* their only collaboration, which was staged in the manner of a mini-opera when Colbert's son, the Marquis de Seignelay, entertained the king at his Sceaux estate. Later in the same year, the Dauphin – whose great passion was music – commissioned the ballet *Le temple de la Paix,* which was performed first at Fontainebleau, then at Versailles. In February 1686, his last tragédie en musique and last collaboration with Quinault, *Armide,* after Tasso's *Gerusalemme liberata,* triumphed at the Opéra but was not performed at court. Lully's last work, *Acis et Galatée,* a "pastorale héroïque," was performed at Anet, Diane de Poitiers's château near Dreux, then the residence of Louis-Joseph, duc de Vendôme, and his brother Philippe, Great Prior of France, on the occasion of a fête they gave in honor of the Dauphin in September 1686.[65] The librettist, Jean Galbert de Campistron (1656–1723), was Vendôme's secretary.[66]

The circumstances of Lully's death are well known. In January 1687, as he was rehearsing his *Te Deum*, which was to be sung at the church of the Feuillants on the rue Saint-Honoré, as part of the celebrations marking Louis XIV's recovery after surgery for a fistula, the composer accidentally struck his foot with the cane he used to conduct. Gangrene spread and the composer died on 22 March. According to Jean-Laurent Le Cerf de la Viéville, he acceded to his confessor's demand to burn the opera he had begun to compose on a libretto by Campistron, *Achille et Polyxène*, of which he nonetheless retained a copy. Completed by his assistant and disciple Pascal Collasse (1649–1709), the work was performed in November of that year.

The tragédie en musique according to Lully

Produced between 1673 and 1685, Lully's 13 tragédies en musique established a genre that, much like Racine's tragedies, is an expression of French classicism as it took root at the apogee of Louis XIV's reign.[67] Like French classical tragedy, which it resembles in terms of literary diction, it was governed by a set of conventions. Yet these rules differed substantially from the spoken theater. Perhaps for this reason, and in order to emphasize the differences between plays and operas, music historians and theoreticians, beginning in the second half of the eighteenth century, favored the phrase "tragédie lyrique."[68] In Lully's days, however, they were called simply "tragédies." And it should be noted that, although they unquestionably owed their popularity to his music, Lully's works were generally appraised at the time – whether in positive or negative terms – on theatrical rather than musical grounds. Musical beauties were noted, to be sure – and Lully was given full credit for the works' authorship – but what was discussed above all was the treatment of the story, the literary style, the staging. The question of the primacy of the literary text and the spectacular elements, as opposed to musical or vocal considerations, were to remain – well into the nineteenth century – a recurrent debate in French opera.

Lully was fortunate in having as his chief collaborator a man of the theater of the stature of Quinault, whose libretti, criticized by his contemporaries at first, gradually came to be regarded as models. The son of a Parisian baker, Philippe Quinault (1635–1688) was well versed in all theatrical genres.[69] His first comedy *Les rivales* was staged at the Hôtel de Bourgogne when he was just 18. Between 1653 and 1673 when he wrote *Cadmus et Hermione*, his first tragédie en musique, he produced comedies, pastorals, tragi-comédies (in seventeenth-century theatrical terminology, serious plays without a tragic ending) and tragedies. Launched in 1667–8 with the "eclogue in music" *La grotte de Versailles*,[70] his collaboration with Lully occupied him exclusively after that date, and he retired after completing the libretto for their last joint work, *Armide* (1685).

Quinault's tragédies en musique retain some features of French classical tragedy, such as its organization in five acts – to which they add, however, a prologue. The prologue seldom actually introduces the plot of the opera; in most instances, its sole dramatic purpose appears to be the glorification of the king, in connection or not with a topical event (military victory or peace treaty). The play proper shares the preference of classical tragedy for subjects drawn from classical antiquity, though usually of a different kind: French classical tragedies feature heroes and heroines but not, as a rule, gods, and goddesses, who, conversely, frequently appear on the operatic stage. That preference for ancient subjects is not exclusive: three of Lully's operas (*Amadis*, *Roland* and *Armide*) are derived from Renaissance Italian epics and Spanish romances – sources reportedly suggested by Louis XIV himself.[71] The operatic subject matter, in any event, is always drawn from legend, rather than history: even if *Armide* is set in the context of the First Crusade, we remain in a mythological world. This differentiates the tragédie en musique both from the world of classical tragedy – at least four of Racine's plays (*Alexandre*, *Britannicus*, *Bajazet*, and *Mithridate*), and many more by Pierre Corneille, are drawn from history – and from that of contemporary Italian opera as well: one has only to think of Cavalli's *Xerxe* (1654), heard in Paris in 1660, and the now more famous *L'incoronazione di Poppea* (1643) of Claudio Monteverdi.

Another notable difference from classical tragedy is a preference for happy endings. Only two of Quinault's 13 libretti end tragically: in *Atys* the goddess Cybele, jealous of the love of her priest Atys for Sangaride, renders him temporarily insane, so that he kills his beloved and commits suicide afterwards; in *Phaéton*, Apollo's son is fatally struck by Jupiter and precipitated from the sun's chariot borrowed from his father – a spectacular stage effect conceived by Berain.[72] All other libretti end in triumph and celebration, often a wedding (Cadmus and Hermione, Aeglea and Theseus, Bellerophon and Philonoe, Pluto and Proserpina, Perseus and Andromeda, Amadis and Oriane, and Corisande and Florestan in *Amadis*) or, in the other cases, an apotheosis (Hercules, Isis, Psyche) or a deliverance (Roland's from insanity, Renaud's from Armida). Even the tragic denouement of *Acis et Galatée* – Acis's savage murder by Polyphemus, Galatea's despair – is mitigated when Neptune resurrects Acis in the form of a river and reunites the lovers. This predominance of happy endings makes the world of tragédie en musique generally closer, in terms of French classical theatrical categories, to tragi-comédie than to tragedy. From a musical standpoint, it provides opportunities for glorious choral ensembles, such as the 15-minute chaconne that closes *Amadis*.

The principal law that French classical tragedy was expected to respect was unity of plot, place, and time: the play was to focus on one particular story, without indulging in subplots; it was supposed to have one setting, at most two or three different rooms in the same palace; and the story had to unfold in a time sequence as close as possible to the actual duration of the play, at most 24 hours. Telling was generally preferred to showing – a classic example being, in Act 5 of Racine's *Phèdre*, Téramène's account of Hippolytus's fatal encounter with the sea monster. However, the tragédie en musique, being above all a spectacle, shows as much as it tells. Its chief ingredient is the marvelous, itself closely connected to the use of stage machinery.[73] Multiple sets are called for, at times within the same act: Act 4 of *Alceste* begins on the banks of the Acheron river and ends in the palace of Pluto; Act 2 of *Bellérophon* begins in a "delightful garden" and moves to a "horrible desert"; at the very end of Act 5 of *Persée*, set in the unspecified place ("lieu") where the wedding of Perseus and Andromeda is held, the palace of Venus appears on stage, like a set within a set. Three of the five acts of *Thésée* call for set changes. Stage machinery, argued Jean de La Bruyère in a passage from his *Caractères* (1688) devoted to the differences between opera and spoken plays, "heightens and embellishes the plot, and sustains in the audience a sweet illusion that is an essential element of theatrical pleasure."[74] Accordingly, magic – another factor contributing to illusion – is a recurring theme of the plots of tragédies en musique as well as a pretext for staging effects. Medea in *Thésée*, Urgande and Arcabonne in *Amadis*, Logistille in *Roland*, Armide are all magicians, while ancient god and goddesses are endowed with magical powers and make liberal use of them: Pallas (i.e. Athena) petrifies giants into statues in Act 4 of *Cadmus et Hermione*; Juno changes Hierax into a bird of prey in Act 3 of *Isis*; Act 1 of *Phaéton* ends with five successive metamorphoses of Proteus. Apparitions are another manifestation of magic, such as in the dream sequences, showing the character asleep on stage as well as the subject of his dreams, which became one of the most admired and popular features of the tragédie en musique. The earliest and most celebrated one occurs in Act 3 of *Atys*, when the hero is visited by dreams, in turn pleasant and threatening, promising him happiness if he yields to Cybele's love – and grief if he betrays her. The participation of dancers, the presence on stage of a small group of musicians, reinforced the haunting quality of the scene, verifying La Bruyère's definition of opera, in the passage just quoted, as an art form whose purpose "is to keep the mind, eyes and ears in a constant state of enchantment."[75] Dances, obviously, contributed in great measure to this visual and aural enchantment. The plots of most of Lully's tragédies en musique are fashioned in such a way as to include a "divertissement" in the prologue and each act, as often as not deriving directly from the dramatic situation. Thus, in *Amadis*, the prologue features dances for attendants of the sorceress Urgande; Act 1, a kind of danced tournament in honor of Princess Oriane; Act 2, set in an enchanted forest, dances for demons and monsters; Act 3, dances for the freed captives of the magician Arcabonne; Act 4, dances for Urgande's attendants; and Act 5, an extended chaconne danced by "heroes and heroines" in honor of Amadis's triumph.

Different in so many respects from classical tragedy, the tragédie en musique nonetheless obeys some of the same rules. Although not subject to the unity of place or time, it was expected to observe the unity of plot, a matter that was taken seriously – *Alceste* was thus found wanting in this respect. Such issues were debated at the Académie des inscriptions et belles-lettres (the "Petite académie"), and Quinault is known to have submitted his libretti to a committee of its members.[76] Similarly, unity of tone was demanded. The earliest two tragédies en musique, *Cadmus et Hermione* and *Alceste*, contained buffo elements: a dispute between Hermione's confidante Charite and her nurse in the former; a trio of subaltern lovers, Admetus's elderly father, the antics of Charon, and the barking of Cerberus providing comic relief in the latter. This light-hearted side was criticized and eliminated in all subsequent libretti. In addition to unity of tone the tragédie en musique, as Catherine Kintzler has noted, was also subject, within its own magical world, to the same rules of verisimilitude, dramatic necessity, and propriety as the straight theater: only they were applied differently, according to the specific logic of the *merveilleux*. The opera librettist, in dealing with a mythological plot, was not allowed to contradict conventional accounts of the story or its characters, by making, say, Juno docile or Medea modest; but he was allowed to extenuate certain aspects of the ancient myth if these offended contemporary sensibilities. Similarly, a certain amount of mythological decorum was to be respected: thus, a superior divinity was not meant, except under unusual circumstances, to have direct contacts with mortals, and could only connect with them via a divinity of lesser rank; nor could lesser-ranking divinities challenge the actions of superior ones.[77] This attention to the niceties of mythological etiquette remained in place in French opera until the days of Gluck and beyond. Offenbach makes fun of it in *Orphée aux enfers*.

Quinault's poetic form also set standards that remained in place during the entire history of the tragédie en musique. Already Perrin had argued that the alexandrine verse, the 12-foot meter adopted by French classical theater, needed to be combined with shorter meters better suited to sung texts.[78] In his libretti Quinault followed this principle with a flexibility that, at its best, sustains comparison with the virtuosity of his contemporary La Fontaine. The librettist was particularly fond of mixing even and odd meters: a characteristic pattern, in airs organized in an ABA structure, is to use heptasyllables (7-foot lines) for the A sections and alexandrines for the B section – Cybele's air "Espoir si cher et si doux" at the end of Act 3 of *Atys* and Arcabonne's air "Amour, que veux-tu de moi?" in Act 2 of *Amadis* are typical examples. An even more remarkable instance – among many – is the chorus "Tout mortel doit ici paraître," in Act 4 of *Alceste* (set in Hell), where the lines, in seemingly random order, have three, four, five, six, seven, eight, and nine feet. One can wonder to what extent the choice of meter, especially in airs and choruses, was not, in fact, dictated by Lully himself. According to certain traditions, he wrote the music first and sent it to his librettist with words of his own, leaving it to Quinault to adjust them.[79] It is indeed likely that Lully's controlling personality prompted him to get involved in all aspects of the opera, and it is a measure both of Quinault's good nature and his genius that the final result was seamless.[80]

By one of the earliest paradoxes in the history of French opera, an Italian, versed in Italian compositional techniques, became the creator of a musical style that was immediately adopted, and long remained identified as the French style. Lully is traditionally thought to have invented the "ouverture à la française" heard before the prologue and the first act of all his tragédies en musique. Recent scholarship has suggested that other composers before him had experimented with the form, which appeared in ballets de cour (notably those with music by Lully) in the early 1650s.[81] But Lully refined this type of overture and generalized its use. It is immediately recognizable, with its slow opening, with dotted rhythms, and its faster section in the manner of a fugue, at times (as in *Alceste*) with a repeat of the opening section at the end.[82] Lully's instrumentation, in a tradition that survived him for about a generation, is in five parts: violin (called *dessus*) and bass violin for the treble and bass parts, and three viola parts (*haute-contre*, *taille*, and *quinte*).

Even more closely associated with the French style are the recitatives, which Lully made into a distinct feature of the tragédie en musique. This feature of the genre is possibly the most disconcerting to a listener familiar with the main features of Italian baroque opera. It would barely be an exaggeration to suggest that, in fact, the two genres are musically antithetical. In Italian opera, at least in the Scarlatti-Vivaldi-Handel tradition, the *secco* recitatives, however lively, serve as bridges between developed arias, where the main musical interest and vocal excitement reside. In the tragédie en musique, which as its name indicates is first and foremost a play, the recitatives matter as much as anything else. They are the site of the interaction between characters, which is what a play is about. Yet, by another contrast with the *secco* recitative style, French classical recitatives are couched in a semi-melodic style and blend naturally, at times imperceptibly, into more openly lyrical passages, some very short, that constitute the "airs" and "duets." In the earlier tragédies en musique – from *Cadmus et Hermione* through *Isis* – they are of the kind referred to as "ordinary" or "simple" recitatives, which simply follow the natural rhythm of the declamation, with fluctuating meters, limited or no ornamentation (save for occasional flourishes on words such as "gloire" and "victoire"), and instrumental support provided by the continuo. In moments of heightened dramatic tension, the recitative will be sustained by a small instrumental ensemble comprising a few strings, theorbos, and harpsichord, known as the "petit choeur."[83] Beginning with *Bellérophon*, Lully, for the sake of greater expressiveness and variety, introduced so-called "accompanied" (or "measured") recitatives, supported by the entire string section or "grand choeur." More lyrical in character, set in regular meter, they are reminiscent of the Italian arioso, while deriving their much-admired suppleness from their close adherence to the flow of the text.

Airs, by contrast, can be strikingly brief (a few measures at times) and simple, both in their unadorned vocal style and their popular melodic form, which made many of them immediately famous: "Il faut passer tôt ou tard," Charon's scene in *Alceste*, "Quand le péril est agréable" from *Atys*, and "Bois épais" from *Amadis* are only three of the most famous examples. "Air" – rather than duet – was also applied to passages where two characters join their voices, often singing similar or parallel texts: thus Alceste's "Admète, vous pleurez" to Admetus's "Alceste, vous mourez." Like the recitatives, airs were accompanied by the "petit choeur" in Lully's earlier works. In his later tragédies en musique, he introduced extended monologues often requiring the participation of the full orchestra. Duets, short and generally treated in recitative mode in the earlier operas, gain in importance in the later ones, which also feature trios and even, in *Atys*, a quartet.

The vocal distribution of Lully's works, compared to Italian operas at the time, sounds rather "modern": no castrati, tenor voices for the young hero, basses for kings or villains. Beginning with *Proserpine*, Lully had in his troupe one of the first French operatic stars, Marie Le Rochois (*c.*1650–1728). She premiered some of his major female roles and appeared in revivals of earlier works; she was, especially, a famous Armide.[84] For this role Lully wrote as many as four monologues. The one in Act 2 of Armide, "Enfin, il est en ma puissance," in the course of which the heroine realizes she is falling in love with the captive Renaud, came to be considered the very model of Lullian declamation. *Armide* also ends, unusually, with a monologue by the heroine rather than with a divertissement.

Choral interventions play a major role in Lully's operas from *Alceste* on. They reach great expressive heights in passages such as the funereal pomp of the heroine in Act 3 of *Alceste* and the lamentation that follows Atys's death in Act 5, the dark invocations of Amisodar's magicians in Act 2 of *Bellérophon*, or the prison scene in Act 3 of *Amadis*. The famous "shivering chorus" of *Isis*, a scene which epitomizes Lully's sense of the picturesque, so impressed Henry Purcell that he imitated it in *King Arthur*.

Dances, as previously noted, occupy an important part in Lully's tragédies en musique, especially in the three operas premiered at court (*Thésée*, *Atys*, and *Isis*). They are of different kinds, slow (courante, loure, sarabande) or fast (gigue, passepieds, canaries), with a predominance of the minuet among the latter. Equally notable are the large-scale dance forms based over a ground bass pattern: the chaconne – *Roland* and *Amadis* both end with developed ones – and the passacaille, as in *Phaéton* and *Armide*. Dance numbers often include solo vocal or choral interventions – especially to proverb-like texts that have earned them the term "maxim airs." This feature remained in eighteenth-century tragédies en musique.

Staged at the Paris Opéra into the 1770s – though in versions increasingly remote from the originals – Lully's operas thereafter virtually disappeared from the repertory until the revival of baroque performance practice that began in the 1970s. Since then, they have demonstrated that they still can, to paraphrase La Bruyère, enchant the mind, eye, and ear. No one who saw Jean-Marie Villégier and William Christie's production of *Atys* in the late 1980s would disagree.

CHAPTER 2

FROM LULLY TO RAMEAU

French opera after Lully's death

Lully had secured a monopoly on opera performances in France beyond his lifetime. In his will he entrusted the direction of the Opéra to his widow, to be aided by his assistant and closest disciple Pascal Collasse. In the event, Madeleine Lully transferred her duties to her son-in-law Jean-Nicolas de Francine, grandson of the Florentine stage-machinist Tommaso Francini.[1] But Lully's ghost continued to haunt French operatic life for several decades.

The home of the Opéra remained at the Palais-Royal until it burned down in 1763. It had by then outlived its use and was considered "the plainest and smallest opera house, not only in Europe, but even in the entire kingdom."[2] Though figures vary from source to source, it seems that it could accommodate an audience of 1,500 at most, including 600 or so standing in the parterre. There were two tiers of boxes, above which a cheaper level, nicknamed "paradis," was furnished with plain benches. Behind the parterre was an amphitheater, where the most expensive seats faced the stage at about the same level. The demand was such that Lully eventually had two extra tiers of boxes erected on both sides of the stage. Performances took place four days a week, on Sunday, Tuesday, Thursday, and Friday (except during the summer when there were no Thursday performances). They began at 4 p.m. on weekdays – a time pushed back to 5:15 in 1714 – and at 6 p.m. (that is, after Vespers) on Sunday. The season ran from January to December, except on religious festivals and with a 23-day interruption during Lent, averaging between 150 and 200 performances a year at the end of Louis XIV's reign (1715). Contemporary testimonies suggest that, though costing twice as much as the theater, the opera drew a fairly wide section of the Parisian population, which by 1706 numbered more than 850,000 people.[3] The generally unsympathetic La Fontaine, in his verse epistle "À Monsieur de Niert sur l'opéra," mentioned priests, soldiers, office clerks, women of fashion, civil servants, and shop-keepers, in addition to the flow of carriages moving down the rue Saint-Honoré, and we know from other sources that high-ranking servants were also keen to get in to the Opéra.[4] Foreign visitors unfailingly commented on the quality of the orchestra, reputed the finest in Europe, and comprising 43 musicians by 1704. We also know from one illustrious visitor, Joseph Addison, that Parisian audiences customarily enjoyed singing along with the chorus in the more popular passages.[5]

Other opera companies appeared in France in the mid-1680s. In 1684 Lully had signed an arrangement with Pierre Gautier, allowing him to perform operas in Marseilles. Gautier inaugurated his company the following year with an opera of his own, Le triomphe de la Paix. In 1686 he staged Phaéton and Armide, and in 1687 Atys and Bellérophon. Phaéton and Armide were seen in Avignon in 1687, while Lyons opened its first opera house in January 1688 with no fewer than 100 performances of Phaéton.[6] By the 1690s Lully's operas had been mounted in Montpellier, Grenoble, Dijon, Chalon-sur-Saône, Toulouse, Bordeaux, Rennes, Rouen, Lunéville, Nancy, Metz, Dijon, Lille, and Strasbourg. They were also staged abroad: Brussels saw Thésée and Persée in 1682 (and several more works in 1683–4), London Cadmus in 1686, Regensburg Isis in 1683, Wolfenbüttel Proserpine, Psyché, and Thésée in 1685–7. Acis et Galatée was performed in Hamburg in 1689 and at Stuttgart in 1698. Lully's operas were also staged at the court of Ansbach and in The Hague, Amsterdam, Modena, and Rome.[7]

Remarkably, no operas by composers other than Lully were performed in Paris between 1673 and the year of his death, 1687. He was not able, in 1681, to prevent performances at Fontainebleau of Paolo Lorenzani's Nicandro e Fileno – the only full-fledged Italian opera performed in France between 1662 and 1752[8] – and, also at Fontainebleau, of Boësset's Alphée et Aréthuse in 1686, by which time he was in semi-disgrace. The situation changed after 1687, but Lully's followers suffered from comparison with the master, whose works were being regularly revived at the Académie royale. Among his followers were his sons Louis (1664–1734) – whose dissolute life had caused him to be nearly disinherited by his father – and Jean-Louis (1667–1688), who was meant to succeed Lully senior at court. Zephire et Flore, the pastoral that the Lully siblings produced in 1688 to a text by the obscure Michel Duboullay, was probably written in large part by their collaborator Pierre Vignon;[9] a succès d'estime, it was subsequently revived. But Louis's own Orphée, set to a text by the same librettist, was received with hisses and whistles in 1690.

By contrast with Lully's reign, the tenure of Francine, plagued from the outset by financial difficulties and spiraling debts and deficits, was marked, artistically, by more failures than successes; nor did the situation improve, once he had stepped down in 1704, under Pierre Guyenet's more imaginative management.[10] The audience's negative reactions to most of the tragédies en musique premiered during that period, which affected works of such undisputed merit as Marc-Antoine Charpentier's *Médée* (1693), may be partly explained by the feeling of nostalgia conveyed by the epigram that circulated in 1690 after the failure of Collasse's *Énée et Lavinie*:

Quelle pitié que l'opéra
Depuis qu'on a perdu Baptiste . . .[11]

Another, seemingly contradictory factor was the public's growing appetite for new forms of lyric theater. The success of works like André Campra's *L'Europe galante* (1697) and *Les fêtes vénitiennes* (1710), apart from their musical worth, can thus be explained by their formal and thematic novelty – being neither *tragédies en musique* nor mythological – and by their noticeable adoption of Italianate vocal forms. It was in this context that the Abbé François Raguenet, returning from Rome, published his *Paralèle des Italiens et des François, en ce qui regarde la musique et les opéra* (1702). While praising Lully, he expressed strong preferences for Italian music, claiming even that castrati were indispensable in opera (Perrin must have turned in his grave).[12] This prompted a response from Le Cerf de La Viéville, whose *Comparaison de la musique italienne et de la musique françoise* appeared in Brussels in 1704–6. Le Cerf defended the French style on grounds of clarity, naturalness and, above all, good taste.

Collasse's career typifies the predicament of opera composers following Lully's death.[13] As Lully's secretary, and son-in-law of his stage decorator Berain, he had thoroughly assimilated the style of the *tragédie en musique* (especially since his duties involved completing the instrumentation of Lully's works, the composer often supplying only the treble and bass lines).[14] On his own, he scored an unqualified success with *Thétis et Pélée* (1689), on a libretto by Fontenelle. The work is notable for containing, in Act 2, an instrumental depiction of a storm, the prototype of many subsequent, more celebrated operatic "tempêtes." Six years later Collasse proved equally forward-looking with the *Ballet des saisons*, which heralded the new genre of the *opéra-ballet*. The Abbé Pic's libretto consists of four autonomous mythological "mini-operas" loosely tied together by the theme of the seasons: Zephirus and Flora (spring), Vertumnus and Pomona (summer), Bacchus and Aridane (fall), Boreas and Orithyia (winter).[15] But the work was eclipsed, two years later, by Campra's *L'Europe galante*, which went further, not being based on mythological subjects at all. Collasse's other works were dismal failures, from *Astrée* (1692), on La Fontaine's libretto after d'Urfé's famous pastoral novel, to *Polyxène et Pyrrhus* (1706). His career was not helped by accusations of plagiarism of Lully's music suffered not only from the composer's heirs but even from his own librettist Jean-Baptiste Rousseau after the failure of their *Jason, ou La Toison d'or* (1696). Titon du Tillet's report that Collasse died "poor and half-insane," although not verified, is wholly believable.[16]

Unflatteringly assessed by comparison to Lully, the operas of his successors also suffered from Louis XIV's disaffection for opera in the last 20 years of his reign. Apart from a few minimally staged performances at Fontainebleau and Trianon – particularly of works by André-Cardinal Destouches – little support was then provided for a genre frowned upon by the powerful Mme de Maintenon, the king's morganatic wife as of 1685. Furthermore, vigorous attacks on the theater in general, and on the opera in particular, were launched by Catholic theologians. They were led by the bishop and preacher Jacques Bénigne Bossuet, then the most powerful figure in the French clergy, on the occasion of the publication in 1694 of a volume containing the works of the playwright Edmé Boursault with a prefatory letter defending the theater on theological grounds. This text was immediately attributed to the Theatine priest Francesco Caffaro. Within months Bossuet issued his *Maximes et réflexions sur la comédie*, in which Lully's works were condemned as spreading immorality, all the more dangerously for doing so in beautiful music.[17]

The five opera composers who came to prominence in this unfavorable climate – Charpentier, Marais, Campra, Desmarets, and Destouches – will be discussed below. Others include the first French woman opera composer, Élisabeth-Claude Jacquet de La Guerre (1665–1729), a highly regarded harpsichordist and former protégée of Mme de Montespan.[18] Despite its considerable merit, her one tragédie en musique, *Céphale et Procris* (1694), on a libretto by Joseph-François Duché de Vancy (1668–1704), was a failure. The same Duché de Vancy provided the libretto to Theobaldo Gatti's *Scylla* (1701), adapted from Ovid, which contains a complete Italian aria in the Italian style, "Per vincer pugando" – an indication of a growing interest in Transalpine music in the post-Lully period. Known in France as Théobalde, Gatti (*c*.1650–1727), possibly a Florentine, played the bass viol in the Opéra orchestra. Louis Lacoste (1675–1750), also a musician at the Opéra, where he sang in the chorus before being promoted to conductor in 1713, scored a modest success with his *Aricie* (1697), published with the subtitle "ballet" but actually closer to a pastoral; his *Philomèle* (1705) was well received and entered the repertory, but his later works, perhaps on account of their gory subjects (*Télégone*, 1725; *Biblis*, 1732), were not well received.[19] One of the few, if ephemeral, successes of the period was François Bouvard's *Médus, roi des Mèdes* (1702), on the libretto by François-Joseph Lagrance-Chancel. As Medea (the hero's mother), it starred the famous Mlle Maupin (1670–1707), the most prominent singer of the Regency period and considered the first genuine mezzo-soprano in operatic history.[20] In this version, like Semiramis in Voltaire's play of that name (and the opera Rossini derived from it), Medea falls in love with Medus, not realizing he is her son. It was the character's third appearance in French opera after Lully's *Thésée* (1675) and Charpentier's eponymous work (1693). A further indication of the fascination Medea continued to exert was the success of Joseph-François Salomon's *Médée et Jason* in 1713. Charles-Hubert Gervais (1671–1744), like

Charpentier, was close to Philippe d'Orléans, the future Regent, and collaborated with him on two operas, *Penthée* (1703) and *Jérusalem délivrée* (1704), the
latter presented as a continuation of Lully's *Armide*. Gervais's own operatic
career began with a flop, *Méduse* (1697), but his *Hypermnestre* (1716) has been
called by a recent scholar "the best opera of the Regency period."[21] Like Antonio
Salieri's *Les Danaïdes*, it is based on the most ghoulish episodes of Greek
mythology, the massacre of the sons of Aegyptos by their wives, daughters of
Danaus, on their wedding night.

When one examines – or hears – the tragédies en musique premiered
between Lully's death and Rameau's operatic debut, one is, in fact, struck by
their high literary and musical worth. One cannot help feeling that many of the
failures were undeserved and perhaps not due to artistic reasons. Were early
eighteenth-century audiences tired of the genre itself, perceived as derivative
and formulaic, to the point of being blind to the beauties and originality of
many of those new works? A case in point is the recently rediscovered *Ulysse*
(1703), the only opera by Jean-Féry Rebel (1666–1747), who played the harpsichord in the Opéra orchestra. Rebel is remembered both as one of the early
French composers of sonatas and, above all, for his "symphonie" *Les élémens*
(1737–8), a masterpiece of early eighteenth-century French orchestral music.
The librettist of *Ulysse* was Guichard, Lully's old *bête noire*, who was back from
his exile. Though the opera deals with Ulysses's return to Ithaca, the principal
role is given to the magician Circe, who tries to prevent Penelope and Ulysses
from being reunited. Perhaps audiences in 1703 reacted negatively to this
dramaturgy that harks back to early baroque aesthetics (Circe, one recalls, was
the heroine of the *Balet comique de la Reyne*). Yet Rebel's music, heard three
centuries later, comes through as wonderfully inventive and expressive, and it
is hard to believe that the work lay forgotten for so long after its short run of
10 performances.[22]

Marc-Antoine Charpentier

Himself forgotten for two centuries, Marc-Antoine Charpentier (1643–1704)
has now been restored to his due place at the forefront of baroque composers.
Compared to the 450-odd compositions that give him a considerable importance in the history of French religious music, his operatic output is small, but
David et Jonathas and *Médée* suffice to rank him among the great contributors
to that art form in France.

Born in or near Paris – his birth year was misidentified until the 1980s –
Charpentier grew up and was probably educated in the Latin Quarter.[23] He
may have attended the Jesuit Collège de Clermont, the future site of the
premiere of his biblical opera *David et Jonathas*. In the mid-1660s he was in
Rome where, according to tradition, he studied with Giacomo Carissimi
(1605–1674), considered at the time the greatest musician in Italy and famous

for his oratorio *Jephte* (*c*.1648).[24] At a time when a naturalized Italian, Lully, was about to impose on opera a "French style," essentially defined by opposition to Italian traditions, Charpentier, on his return to France, thus found himself in the paradoxical position of a French musician, fully conversant with the Italian style, and eager to accommodate it in the compositions he wrote for the church and for the stage.

Charpentier spent the years 1670–87 at the service of Marie de Lorraine, duchesse de Guise (known as Mlle de Guise), last heiress to this prominent family, and in whose Parisian mansion he resided. In 1672 Molière, after his break-up with Lully, turned to him to compose the music for the Paris performances of his one-act comedy *La comtesse d'Escarbagnas* (as well as new *intermèdes* for *Le mariage forcé* and *Les fâcheux*). Charpentier also wrote the music for Molière's final masterpiece, *Le malade imaginaire* (1673), in which it plays as important a part as in *Le bourgeois gentilhomme*: it included a pastoral prologue, evidently intended for a hoped-for court premiere that did not take place,[25] and three *intermèdes*, the last being the burlesque ceremony in which Argan, the imaginary invalid, is supposedly admitted into the medical profession, and where the blend of spoken text and sung choruses anticipates the world of opéra-comique. When *Le malade imaginaire*, after Molière's death, was revived at the Hôtel Guénégaud, where his troupe performed after the Palais-Royal was requisitioned by Lully, Charpentier had to rescore his music to take into account the drastic limitations imposed by the Florentine composer on the number of musicians allowed in all but his own theaters. Again, in 1675, Lully forced the company to reduce its orchestra in Thomas Corneille's *Circé*, a *pièce à machines* which had considerable success, also set to music by Charpentier. Once Molière's troupe had merged with its rival, the Hôtel de Bourgogne, to form the Comédie-Française in 1680, Charpentier continued to work for this theater, supplying new music for a revival of Pierre Corneille's *Andromède* in 1682.

At Mlle de Guise's, Charpentier wrote two short works in the mid-1680s that were each called an "opéra," though with an additional appellation: "pastorale" (*Actéon*) or "idylle en musique" (*Les arts florissants*). Two other short divertissements dating from the same period, though not so labeled, deserve to be described as little operas as well: *Les plaisirs de Versailles* and *La descente d'Orphée aux enfers*. *Les plaisirs de Versailles* and *Les arts florissants* are both allegories: the former involves personifications of Music, Conversation, and Games; the latter the four liberal arts caught between Discord and Peace, and eventually celebrating their harmony in a chaconne and a sarabande, followed by a final chorus. The remarkably original *Actéon* comprises six scenes, introduced by an overture which departs from the French, Lullian model. The work is based on Ovid's account of the young hunter who surprises Diana and her nymphs as they bathe and is punished by being changed into a stag and devoured by his own hounds. The two great musical moments are Acteon's metamorphosis (scene 4) and the final chorus of lamentation, in turn furious and poignant. Of *La descente d'Orphée aux enfers*, two acts only survive out of a probable three. Act 1 is devoted to Euridice's death and Orpheus's grief; Act 2, set in Hell, corresponds to Act 4 of Monteverdi's *Orfeo*.[26]

Leaving the service of Mlle de Guise shortly before her death in 1688, Charpentier was recruited by the Jesuits for their church of Saint-Louis on the rue Saint-Antoine in the Marais. During that period, he also taught music composition to the Duc de Chartres, the future Regent, who helped him to obtain a position at Sainte-Chapelle, his last appointment, in 1698. *Philomèle*, the tragédie en musique the Duc wrote under Charpentier's supervision, was performed three times at the Palais-Royal in 1694 but is now lost.

At the principal Jesuit establishment in Paris, renamed Collège Louis-le-Grand in Louis XIV's honor in 1683, it had become a tradition in the seventeenth century to stage, both at Carnival time and at the end of the academic year, a Latin tragedy accompanied by danced and sung *intermèdes*, usually but not always on the same subject as the play.[27] Performed by the students, these eventually took on the proportions of genuine operas, involving the participation of court ballet masters and reputed composers, Campra and Collasse among them. These events drew large audiences that included members of the royal family. Charpentier composed two such works for the Collège Louis-le-Grand, *Celse martyr* (1687) and *David et Jonathas* (1688). The music of the former has disappeared, as is the case in nearly all the other Jesuit ballets. Exceptionally, *David et Jonathas*, no doubt on account of its larger scale and signal beauties, has survived; not, unfortunately, in Charpentier's autograph, like nearly all his compositions, but in an imperfect copy made in 1689 by André-Danican Philidor, the royal music librarian.[28] Set to a text by a Jesuit, François Bretonneau (who had already supplied the libretto of *Celse martyr*), the five acts of *David et Jonathas* were performed separately after each act of the Latin tragedy *Saul*, written by another Jesuit, Pierre Chamillart. This unusual combination, added to the fact that no work of comparable scope had been staged at Louis-le-Grand before, gives Charpentier's biblical tragedy a unique place in French operatic history. Among its many original features is the prologue, which is not the usual allegorical and celebratory hors d'oeuvre, but a dramatic exposition of the theme, preceded by an elaborate French-style overture, leading to a confrontation between Saul and the ghost of Samuel, who warns the Hebrew king of his impending fate. Other notable moments of this powerful score are Jonathas's monologue in Act 4, built in the manner of an extended Italian *scena*, and the death of Jonathas in David's arms in Act 5, in which the declamation achieves an emotional intensity seldom previously reached in the French lyric theater.[29]

A similar comment could be made about Charpentier's only tragédie en musique, *Médée*, performed at the Opéra in December 1693. The theme of the enchantress turned infanticide – that Mount Everest of theatrical roles[30] – had been the subject of Pierre Corneille's first tragedy in 1635, the year before *Le Cid*. Medea was also the principal female character of Lully's *Thésée*, whose plot bears no relation to the events described in Charpentier's opera, but which had been revived at the Académie royale as recently as 1688.[31] Thomas Corneille's libretto for *Médée*, while telling the same story, could not be more different from his elder brother's baroque play, so outré in its treatment of this most outré theme that Jason, competing with Medea in cruelty, contemplates the murder of their sons to avenge his fiancée's death.[32] Thomas's version is closer to the decorous world of French classical tragedy in the Racine tradition, where words of irony are the weapon of choice, and a no less efficient one for that. The Medea-Jason-Creusa-Creon quartet is completed by the character of Oronte, Prince of Argos, in love with Creusa. Oronte's wooing of the Corinthian princess is the pretext for the exquisite Act 2 divertissement, which combines French and Italian forms: an aria with chorus sung in Italian is heard in the middle of a chaconne. The drama unfolds during the first two acts in a series of confrontations between the characters – Medea and Jason, Creon and Medea, Medea and Creusa, Creusa and Jason – in which Charpentier shows his mastery of the Lullian-style recitative within a richer harmonic language. In Act 3, despite Jason's hypocritical reassurances, Medea, realizing she has been betrayed, conveys her bitterness in a scene that seems to prefigure the two-part grand aria of romantic opera: a slow, brooding, rondo-form aria in D minor ("Quel prix de mon amour") succeeded, after a short, revelatory dialogue with Medea's confidante Nérine, by a furious resolution in B flat major ("C'en est fait, on m'y force"). As in Lully's works, the *merveilleux*, or supernatural, plays a part: in Act 3, Medea conjures up infernal agents, who assist her in poisoning the festive dress in which Creusa will burn alive in Act 5. The Act 4 divertissement, unusually, is integrated into the plot, showing the first stage of Medea's revenge: turning the tables on Creon, she paralyzes his guards and summons up appari-tions of graceful phantoms, until he loses his reason in a scene that Catherine Cessac rightly likens to the prologue of *David et Jonathas*.[33] Remarkably, though, the gods of Greek mythology, so often present in Lully's world, are absent from this mythological tale[34] – save for a perfunctory appearance of Bellone, goddess of war, in the prologue – and this purely human dimension makes the implacable progression of the final act even more chilling: Creusa imploring Medea for her father's sake; the report of Oronte's death as a result of Creon's murderous rage, followed by the king's own suicide; Creusa's expres-sions of horror and her own agony and death in Jason's powerless presence, a scene rendered by Charpentier with overwhelming sobriety; and Medea's final apparition "astride a dragon in the air," when Jason learns from her mouth that she has killed their sons. After her last words, a "hail of fire" destroys the palace while a brief ritornello concludes the work.[35]

Médée was clearly mounted with great care – and at great expense – by the Opéra's management. The title role, possibly the most demanding in all tragédies en musique, was sung by Le Rochois, the much admired creator of Lully's *Armide*, while the sets and machinery were the work of Berain. The king attended one performance and the music-loving Dauphin four. Yet the work flopped and was not heard in Paris again until the late twentieth century.[36] A single, abortive revival in Lille in 1700 was interrupted by the fire of the theater. Was the failure due in part to the tragic subject, contrasting with Lully's preference for happy, celebratory endings? Contemporary accounts refer to the "altogether novel style" of Charpentier's music, his "sad" – meaning "complex" – harmony, its excess of "science."[37] Rameau, though luckier with audiences than his predecessor, would later be the object of similar criticism.

Marin Marais

Rediscovered in recent decades thanks to baroque musicians – and in some measure to a film[38] – Marin Marais (1656–1728) is a name one rightly associates with viol music, but he was also a prominent opera composer. He was the son of a Parisian cobbler-shoemaker.[39] His musical education was made possible by his uncle, a curate in the royal parish of Saint-Germain-l'Auxerrois, near the Louvre, where Marais was recruited as choirboy. By 1675 he played the bass viol as a member of Lully's orchestra at the Académie royale, even appearing on stage in the dream scene of *Atys* in 1676. Three years later he officially became a court musician as a member of the royal chamber. A warmly received *Idylle dramatique* performed at court in 1686, though probably not a real opera (the music is lost), revealed his ability to write vocal and dance music. In 1693 he collaborated with Lully's eldest son, Louis, on the tragédie lyrique *Alcide*, performed a few months before Charpentier's *Médée*. Campistron's libretto, based on the same episode as Handel's *Hercules*, was criticized, but the music was praised, and the opera was revived in the eighteenth century (as *La mort d'Hercule* or *La mort d'Alcide*). Louis Lully's and Marais's respective contributions remain a matter of conjecture.[40] In 1696 Marais wrote, on his own, another tragédie en musique, *Ariane et Bacchus*, the librettist of which was the otherwise unknown Saint-Jean. The work was unsuccessful and never revived. Yet, as Jérôme de La Gorce has noted, *Ariane* contains "admirable airs and accompanied recitatives, expressive use of melodic line and harmony," and, especially, orchestral innovations, including sleep music in the manner of *Atys*.[41] Around 1705 Marais succeeded Campra as the Opéra's "time-beater," in other words, conductor. The following year came the greatest success of his career – the tragédie en musique *Alcyone*. The libretto by Antoine Houdar de La Motte (1672–1731), collaborator with Campra on *L'Europe galante* (1697), is drawn from Book 11 of Ovid's *Metamorphoses*. Daughter of Eolus, god of the winds, Alcyone loves Céyx but their marriage is thwarted by the magician Phorbas; the lovers are driven to suicide in the last act but Neptune metamorphoses them into halcyons, the legendary birds that supposedly could calm tempests. Apart from its beautiful airs (such as "Trop malheureux Pélée" in Act 1 and "O mer, dont le calme infidèle" in Act 3) and the closing chaconne, *Alcyone* was admired for a magic ceremony in Act 2, its *fête marine* in Act 3, and, above all, the "Tempête" in Act 4, which was both a theatrical feat and a musical tour de force: asleep in the temple of Juno, Alcyone has a dream in which her fiancé is shipwrecked. This event was visible in the back of the stage to the audience, thanks to some complex machinery, while Marais's imitative music – the first passage to feature the double-bass in French opera – brilliantly evokes the tempest, resorting to loosely strung drums in addition to oboes and strings. There had been similar depictions of a storm at sea in previous French operas – in Collasse's *Thétis* (1689), in Campra's *Hésione* (1700), in Desmarets and Campra's *Iphigénie* (1704) – but "Marais's Tempest" became the first instrumental operatic passage to acquire such celebrity. *Alcyone*, which Jérome de La Gorce goes so far as to call "one of the most beautiful scores of the entire French operatic repertory,"[42] was regularly revived at the Opéra between 1719 and 1771, in versions that admittedly had less and less to do with the original.

Three years after the triumph of *Alcyone*, however, Marais's *Sémélé*, set like the previous work to a La Motte libretto, failed – as did every new work performed at the Opéra between 1706 and 1710. A "more learned and more refined" score than *Alcyone*, according to La Gorce, *Sémélé* is equally rich in imitative music, such as the bird songs heard in the accompaniment of the chorus "Secondez-nous, oiseaux" in Act 2 – a device that Rameau was to carry to perfection – or the earthquake announcing the fateful appearance of Jupiter as lord of the storms in Act 5. It was also the second time – after Campra's *Les Muses* in 1703 – that *musettes* (French peasant hornpipes) were assigned a specific part in a divertissement.[43]

Though the failure of *Sémélé* put an end to his operatic production, by the time he died Marais was a famous, prosperous musician, celebrated both as France's greatest viol player and for the achievement of *Alcyone*.

André Campra

The most important French opera composer between Charpentier and Rameau, André Campra (1660–1744) came from an old Provençal family on his mother's side, while his father was a Piedmontese surgeon.[44] He was trained as a choirboy at the cathedral in his native Aix-en-Provence, then he became "maître de chapelle" at Saint-Trophime in Arles from 1681 to 1683 and in Toulouse for the next 11 years. He thus made his reputation, like Charpentier, as a church musician – author of motets, of a *Te Deum* and, especially, of a beautiful *Requiem* dating possibly from the mid-1690s – and was appointed at Notre-Dame in Paris in 1694. This position, from which he eventually resigned in 1700, prevented him from openly acknowledging his first works for the stage. They were given (without fooling anyone) under the name of his younger brother Joseph. He subsequently supported himself by becoming the chief conductor at the Opéra until Marais's appointment in 1705.

L'Europe galante (1697) – the title could be rendered as Europe at Love[45] – has been called the first eighteenth-century French opera:[46] it established a new genre (anticipated two years before by Collasse's *Ballet des saisons*), which remained popular in the following five decades. Called simply "ballet" at the time, it was subsequently called "opéra-ballet" to distinguish it both from the ballet de cour, which included arias and ensembles but had no integrated plot, and the ballet in the modern sense, danced throughout.[47] La Motte, the librettist, was an active proponent of the *moderne* in the aesthetic quarrel that divided the Académie française into two camps at the end of the seventeenth century. His four entrées, preceded by a mythological prologue, form independent one-act plays, each tied to the others by the theme of love: the first is set in France, the second in Spain, the third in Italy, the fourth in Turkey.[48] The stylized characters stand for "types" – the fickle Frenchman, the constant Spaniard, the jealous Venetian, the impetuous Turk. Each story leaves space for a divertissement supposedly in the manner of the country evoked: the Spanish entrée features a serenade in Spanish, the Italian entrée two songs in Italian as well as the first forlane (an old Italian dance in 6/8 time) of French music; the French entrée includes a rigaudon, a passepied, and a sarabande (all quintessential French dances) and the Turkish one a march for the Bostangi Guards. The same model was used by Rameau 35 years later in *Les Indes galantes*, which echoes Campra's title, and whose librettist Louis Fuzelier had in fact collaborated with him on a comédie-ballet, *Les âges* (1718). *Le carnaval de Venise* (1699) was another opéra-ballet, this time set to a libretto by Jean-François Regnard (1655–1709), one of the most successful comic playwrights in the generation following Molière. Its structure is different: after a "theater-within-the-theater" prologue, in which we see the workers preparing the stage for the opera we are about to see, we follow during three acts the fortunes of a Franco-Italian love quadrangle, interspersed with several lively Venetian divertissements.[49] As in *L'Europe galante*, the musical language is overtly Italianate, including a delightful coloratura aria in Italian sung by the heroine in response to a serenade. The final act – another theater-within-the-theater effect, anticipating *Ariadne auf Naxos* – consists in a mini-Italian opera on the theme of Orpheus in the underworld, the French language returning for the chorus of general rejoicing that ends the opera.[50] For the mythological tragédie en musique *Hésione* (1700), considered at the time one of the finest since Lully, Campra worked with the librettist Antoine Danchet (1671–1748), who remained his most constant collaborator.[51] Together they produced what is arguably Campra's masterpiece, *Tancrède* (1702), based on the episode from Tasso's *Gerusalemme liberata* that inspired Monteverdi in 1624 for the work published in 1638 in his book of *Madrigali guerrieri, et amorosi*.[52] The crusader Tancredi loves the proud Saracen princess Clorinda; he is loved by Herminie, a Christian princess, she by Argant, a Saracen knight. United in jealousy, Herminie and Argant, with the help of the magician Isménor, discover the truth. The opera ends with Tancredi's despair after he involuntarily kills Clorinda in an offstage battle. Danchet's taut libretto – its prologue, in praise of Louis XIV at the start of the disastrous War of Spanish Succession (1701–14), sounds almost ironical in the context of the ensuing tragedy – is matched by Campra's musical sobriety and the unusual, sombre vocal coloring: the three male principals are all basses, while the generally low-lying part of Clorinde was written for Mlle Maupin. The divertissements are short (there are none in Act 4) and dramatically in situation. A new, heightened level of expressiveness is reached in the airs and recitatives, such as Herminie's "Cessez, mes yeux" in Act 3, or, immediately afterwards, Tancredi's arrival in the enchanted forest, with the orchestra depicting "moans and laments coming from within the trees."[53] It is significant that Le Cerf de la Viéville's *Comparaison de la musique italienne et de la musique françoise*, set in the form of a dialogue between a count, his wife and a chevalier, begins with a discussion following a performance of *Tancrède*.[54]

Campra and Danchet also collaborated on *opéras-ballets*. In *Les Muses* (1703), each entrée was devoted to a genre (pastoral, satire, tragedy, comedy). In *Les fêtes vénitiennes* (1710), their greatest public success, one of the entrées (entitled "L'opéra") is at once a mini-opera and a parody of a tragédie en musique: the heroine, an Italian singer, is spirited away by her French lover disguised as Boreas, god of winds.[55] Campra's other major tragic work was *Idoménée* (1712), for which Danchet's libretto was itself the source for Giovanni Battista Varesco's text set by Mozart in 1781.[56] Its own source was a 1705 play by Prosper Jolyot de Crébillon, but it was Danchet who introduced Electra into the story. He also changed the name of the heroine, Erixène, into the more euphonious Ilione – Mozart's Ilia. Unlike Varesco and Mozart, Danchet and Campra retained the Greek tragic ending: in an effect reminiscent of the denouement of Lully's *Atys*, Nemesis appears to drive Idoménée into a mad rage and he kills his son.[57] As in Charpentier's *Médée*, the ending reveals a shift away from the tragédie en musique with a happy ending that was the norm in Lully's day.

Yet, like *Médée*, *Idoménée* failed. Two years later, Campra went south to become head of the Marseilles opera house, returning to Paris after the death of Louis XIV in 1715. The music-loving Regent protected him and appointed him "maître de chapelle" at Versailles in 1722 (at first in a triumvirate arrangement with Nicolas Bernier and Gervais), and he devoted himself again principally to religious music. By then a senior figure in the French musical establishment, he returned to the Opéra in 1731 as "Inspecteur de l'Académie royale de musique" (a position previously held by Destouches) and to the stage one last time – still with Danchet – with the tragédie lyrique *Achille et Déidamie* (1735).

André Cardinal Destouches

Throughout his life, André Cardinal Destouches (1672–1749) was plagued with the reputation of being an amateur musician. No doubt this was largely due to jealousy, as he enjoyed exceptional favor at court. He was, not, however, from a musical family, nor did his beginnings point towards a musical career. Born to a prosperous Parisian merchant family, he traveled to Siam in 1687–8 with a Jesuit mission.[58] In 1692 he entered the army as a royal musketeer, but left it four years later to become a musician.[59] A student of Campra, he contributed three airs to his teacher's *opéra-ballet* *L'Europe galante* (1697). La Motte, the work's librettist, was Destouches's cousin and supplied the libretto of his first work, *Issé*. A "pastorale héroïque" in three acts dealing with the love of Apollo (disguised as a shepherd) for a nymph, it received its first performance at court in Fontainebleau in October 1697 – possibly on the recommendation of Prince Antoine de Monaco, who became one of Destouches's key supporters (and a regular correspondent) – and at Versailles, by the Opéra troupe, two months later. *Issé* was the last part that the soprano Le Rochois premiered. The work's success marked a revival of a genre that had failed to arouse interest since the days of Perrin and Cambert – as shown by the failure of Collasse's *Astrée* six years before. *Issé* was no less successful in Paris in late 1697. For its 1708 revival Destouches revised it extensively, expanding it to five acts, with a final divertissement involving "a troup of European men and women, Chinese, American men and women and Egyptian men and women." In this version it was regularly revived in the capital until 1757. It was also heard abroad, with performances at Wolfenbüttel (in German) and The Hague (1710), Brussels (1711), and in private settings: the Marquise du Châtelet, Voltaire's friend, sang the title role at Sceaux in 1746; so did Mme de Pompadour at a private Versailles performance three years later.

Issé, generally considered his masterpiece, put Destouches at the forefront of operatic composers in the post-Lully generation: according to Titon du Tillet, Louis XIV declared to the composer that no music had pleased him as much since Lully's death. His next four works were all set to libretti by La Motte: the tragédies en musique *Amadis de Grèce* (1699), *Marthésie, reine des Amazones* (1699) and *Omphale* (1701), and the opéra-ballet *Le carnaval et la folie* (1703–4). Though they were often satirized, they were better received than many operas of the period. *Omphale*, in particular, was revived several times in the eighteenth century. In 1713, when after years of financial crises, statutes were promulgated by royal letters patent for the management of the Opéra, Destouches was appointed to the newly created position of inspector general, which gave him both artistic and financial oversight. After the Regent's death he was protected by Queen Maria Leszcynska, who married Louis XV in 1725, and he rose to the rank of director of the Opéra in 1728–30.

The finest achievement of Destouches's maturity was the tragédie en musique *Callirhoé*, premiered in December 1712. Pierre-Charles Roy's (1683–1764) libretto, after an episode in Pausanias's *Description of Greece* set in Calydon, deals with a love triangle involving a priest of Bacchus, whose jealousy triggers civil unrest but who eventually kills himself rather than sacrifice his beloved as commanded by an oracle. Revising the work in 1743, Destouches made its conclusion more powerful by removing the final divertissement, ending on the priest's suicide and words of forgiveness.[60] *Télémaque et Calypso* (1714), set to a libretto by Simon-Joseph Pellegrin (1663–1745), was less successful, and Destouches abandoned the tragédie en musique after the failure of *Sémiramis* (1718), whose librettist was Roy. The adolescent Louis XV danced in his opéra-ballet *Les Élémens*, performed at the Tuileries in 1721 – a short-lived return to the court ballet tradition of the youth of Louis XIV. Destouches retired from the stage after the failure of the ballet héroïque *Les stratagèmes de l'amour* in 1726. In addition to being one of the leading opera composers of the early eighteenth century, Destouches also wrote secular cantatas and motets that were sung at court in the 1720s and 1730s, though none of them survives.

Henri Desmarets

By contrast with the royal favor Destouches enjoyed, the ups and downs of the life of Henri Desmarets (1661–1741) make his career one of the most unconventional in music history. He came from a modest Parisian middle-class family.[61] His precocious talents earned him a position as page in the king's chapel until 1678. Trained as a church musician under Pierre Robert and Henry Du Mont, his masters at the royal chapel, he was noticed by Lully, who, according to Desmarets's biographer Titon du Tillet, even prevented him from pursuing his training in Italy for fear that his excellent dispositions for French music might be contaminated there.[62] In 1685 his first tragédie en musique, *Endymion* (text and music now lost), was performed at Versailles in the royal apartments. The second, premiered in September 1693 at the Académie royale, was *Didon*, set to a text by Louise-Geneviève de Saintonge (1650–1718), the first French woman librettist.[63] Performed in the same year as Marais's *Alcide* and Charpentier's *Médée*, Desmarets's work was considerably more successful than either. The greatest operatic triumph since Lully's death, it earned its composer, probably on Charpentier's recommendation, a position as "maître de chapelle" at the Collège Louis-le-Grand, though there is no evidence that he contributed to its operatic activities like Charpentier. In 1694 *Circé*, also set to a text by Mme de Saintonge, was less successful than *Didon*; like Lully's *Atys* – to which it was compared – it contained a sleeping scene for Ulysses in Act 3.

A new librettist, Duché de Vancy, supplied the text for *Théagène et Cariclée*, after the third-century Greek romance by Heliodorus, which was coldly received in 1695, more it seems as a result of the staging and the text (it was dubbed "l'opéra des exclamations")[64] than on account of the music. Later in the same year, Desmarets and Duché de Vancy presented *Les Amours de Momus*. Published and advertised as a "ballet," the work raised characteristic generic questions: unlike the traditional ballet de cour, or the earliest examples of opéra-ballet, it had a unified, if somewhat loose three-act plot, rather than independent entrées; yet its semi-character, non-tragic subject did not entitle the work to be called tragédie en musique, nor even "pastorale héroïque," like Lully's *Acis et Galathée*, which is also in three acts.[65] It was thus a forerunner of operas on comic subjects such as Jean-Joseph Mouret's *Le mariage de Ragonde* (1714) and Rameau's *Platée* (1745).

Desmarets's next work, *Vénus et Adonis*, was a tragédie en musique set to a play by Jean-Baptiste Rousseau (1670–1741), then at the dawn of a distinguished poetic career.[66] The subject is reminiscent of *Atys*: a goddess falls in love with a mortal, who dies as a result – though in this case not because of her jealousy but of the combined jealousies of Mars and Adonis's spurned lover Cidippe. It inspired Desmarets to write what is now considered his finest score – its musical writing both learned (as in the beautiful Act 5 passacaille) and affecting, with expressive accompanied recitatives.[67] The premiere of the work in July 1697[68] was soon followed by a scandal which resulted in Desmarets becoming the first (and so far as one knows, only) French opera composer to have been sentenced to death. Widowed in 1696, Desmarets had fallen in love with the 18-year-old Marie-Marguerite de Saint-Gobert, daughter of a royal officer in Senlis he had befriended. In early 1698, she gave birth to their son and the lovers eloped. Facing arrest, they fled to Brussels in August 1699; tried in absentia the following year, he received a death sentence.

Desmarets went to Spain for the period 1701–6, working for Philip V, Louis XIV's grandson, to whom he had been recommended by his fellow composer Jean-Baptiste Matho (like him a former royal page). He then moved to the court of Leopold, Duke of Lorraine, and remained in Lunéville from 1707 until his death. There he resumed his operatic activities, mounting Lully's operas and reviving his own *Vénus et Adonis* as early as November 1707. Meanwhile in France, exile had interrupted his career as an opera composer but not performances of his works. His unfinished *Iphigénie en Tauride* was completed by Campra. Mounted at the Opéra in 1704, with Mlle Maupin as Diana, it was coolly received, but it triumphed when it was revived in 1711 and gained a respectable place in the eighteenth-century repertory.[69] In 1721 Desmarets – at last – was granted a royal pardon. In March 1722 the Opéra produced his last work, the tragédie en musique *Renaud ou la suite d'Armide*, on a text by Pellegrin. Presented as a continuation of Lully's work, it achieved only seven performances and was never revived, ending the career of one of the most

interesting of Lully's disciples. Desmarets survived by 14 years his beloved
Marie-Marguerite, who died in 1727.

The origins of opéra-comique

Along with the opéra-ballet a new form of lyric theater was born in the decades
following Lully's death. Though, in 1667, Louis XIV had sent back to Italy the
singers and musicians brought by Mazarin, there remained in Paris an Italian
theatrical troupe, led by the Bolognese Domenico Biancolelli (1636–1688), an
unforgettable Harlequin. Since 1680 they had been performing at the Hôtel de
Bourgogne and their comedies, which at times included music, continued to
draw appreciative audiences. In 1697, however, they crossed the line by staging
La fausse prude, which was interpreted – correctly, it seems – as an allusion
to Mme de Maintenon.[70] They were expelled and did not return to Paris in
Louis XIV's lifetime. The void left by their absence was filled by a development
in comic theater in the context of the two large fairs that took place in Paris
at two different moments in the year: the Foire Saint-Germain, held from early
February until Easter Week near Saint-Germain-des-Prés on the Left Bank, and
the Foire Saint-Laurent, held from late July through September in the northern
outskirts of the city, roughly where the Gare de l'Est now stands. Earlier forms
of theatrical life, notably puppet theaters, had been repeatedly thwarted both
by the Comédie-Française, which considered it owned a monopoly on plays
in French in Paris, and by the Académie royale, whose parallel monopoly
severely restricted all forms of public entertainment involving music and
dance – not just in Paris but anywhere in France. Among the most persistent
and successful opponents of these monopolies had been the German-born
acrobat Maurice Vondrebeck who had appeared in Molière and Lully's Psyché
in 1671, and his wife Jeanne. In December 1698 his widow (known as the
"Veuve Maurice") obtained from Francine a 10-year exclusive permit to stage
theatrical spectacles at the two fairs using three actors, three dancers, and
three musicians. This agreement has been called the birth certificate of the
opéra-comique.[71]

The semi-improvised comic entertainments staged at the two fairs took
place in provisional wooden buildings erected near the fairgrounds, but at
times in actual theaters using, like the first French opera houses, remodeled
tennis courts. They attracted diverse audiences, from the Duchesse de
Bourgogne, mother of the future Louis XV, who seems to have preferred those
lighter forms of theater to the grand genre, to popular crowds that would never
have attended the Opéra. Some performances were mythological spectaculars:
Thésée, ou la défaite des Amazones (1701) thus launched the long and prolific
career of Fuzelier, Rameau's future librettist, who also wrote for the Foire
Saint-Laurent Le ravissement d'Hélène in 1705. Increasingly, though, they were
parodies of tragédies en musique: thus, Alain-René Lesage's Arlequin Thétis,

set to music by Jean-Claude Gillier (1667–1737), performed at the Foire Saint-Laurent in 1713, was based on Collasse's *Thétis et Pélée*, which had been revived at the Opéra only a few months previously; and the same authors' *Télémaque*, performed at the Foire Saint-Germain in February 1715, parodied Destouches's 1714 tragédie en musique. The fact that Pellegrin, Destouches's librettist, regularly contributed plays to the fair theaters shows how porous the borders between the two worlds could be. As for Lesage (1668–1747), he was not only the foremost playwright of his generation – his masterpiece, *Turcaret*, a mordant satire of unscrupulous financiers, had caused a scandal at the Comédie-Française in 1708 – but also its most prominent novelist: the first part of his immensely popular and influential *Gil Blas de Santillane* was issued in that same year, 1715. Music consisted mostly, in the early years, of new words set to well-known or recycled tunes: such songs became known as "vaudevilles," "timbres," or "Pont-Neufs" (being often heard on the bridge of that name). The term "vaudeville" was also soon used to describe works that included vaudeville-type songs. Gradually, however, the fair theaters combined arrangements of old airs with original music. Gillier, formerly attached to the Comédie-Française, became their most regular composer as of 1713.[72] That his music to *Télémaque* was performed by a group of 15 musicians – nine strings, including a double-bass, with flute, oboe, bassoon, two horns, and a harpsichord – indicates how effectively the strictures put in place by Lully were by then challenged.[73]

The success of theatrical performances at fairs continued to alarm the Comédie-Française, especially after the privilege granted to the Veuve Maurice was renewed by the Opéra in 1708.[74] The agreement was rescinded in 1710, the fair theaters being forbidden to perform anything containing a text: they responded by having it printed on placards (*écriteaux*) so that the audience itself could sing the words. Finally, new agreements were concluded in 1713, 1714, and 1716 between the Académie royale and the fair theaters, allowing them, against payment of a fee, to continue to perform musical comedies (specifically called "opéras-comiques" as of 1714) with modest forces, and provided they were not sung throughout.[75] One of the first works to use "opéra-comique" as its subtitle was Lesage's *Le tombeau de Nostradamus*, set to music arranged by Gillier and staged at the Foire Saint-Laurent in September 1714.[76]

Little operas

Another type of lyric theater that flourished at the end of the reign of Louis XIV is one that has been called, for lack of a better term, "little opera": in one act or, if organized in several entrées, seldom lasting more than an hour, these works were usually mounted in a private or courtly setting on the occasion of a fête or a celebration. Their size makes them comparable to the short "opéras" Charpentier wrote in the early or mid-1680s. Their structure, however, makes

them closer to miniature pastorals or tragédies en musique in the Lullian tradition.[77] Michel-Richard de Lalande (or Delalande, 1657–1726), principal court
composer after Lully's death – he held positions both in the royal chapel and in
the *chambre* – wrote several for Fontainebleau or Trianon. Other such works
were produced for the royal residence of Marly by Anne-Danican Philidor
(1681–1728), the son of Louis XIV's music librarian. Not all little operas of the
period have survived, since they were not intended for publication. Even when
they have come down to us, generally in manuscript form, we do not always
know the circumstances of their composition or first performance.

A typical work of this type, recently revived and recorded, is *Le triomphe
d'Iris* by Louis-Nicolas Clérambault (1676–1749).[78] A Parisian, Clérambault
worked as an organist and that is how he is simply identified on the manuscript
of this "pastorale," the only such work he evidently wrote. In 1715 he became
music master of Saint-Cyr, the school for young women founded by Mme de
Maintenon, and in 1719 he succeeded his teacher André Raison as organist of
Saint-Sulpice. Like Charpentier before him, he contributed *intermèdes* (all
lost) for Latin tragedies performed at the Collège Louis-le-Grand. His
published oeuvre includes harpsichord pieces (1704), five books of cantatas
(1710–26), and religious music composed, in particular, for Saint-Cyr.

The only information we have about *Le triomphe d'Iris* is the date of 1706 in
the manuscript. The three entrées, without prologue, and preceded by a tripar-
tite overture in the French style, are set in a "delightful grove" and involve two
pairs of shepherds – a fifth, Silvandre, who has the opening air, acts as a sort of
master of ceremonies. All three entrées include a danced divertissement and the
first also contains a three-part coloratura "air italien" – a feature we have encountered in Charpentier and Campra. In the first entrée, Daphnis confesses his love
to Silvie but she claims to be "insensible à l'amour." In the second, Tircis does the
same to Philis, who proves immediately responsive. In the third, Silvie realizes
that she is not indifferent to Daphnis after all and eventually yields to his love. A
"symphonie agréable" is heard, signaling the "descent" of Cupid – an indication
that at least a minimum of stage machinery was involved – who asks all shepherds to join him in praising "Iris," and the work ends in a joyful celebration. It
can be assumed that Iris, rather than Hera's minister and messenger of the gods,
is here a code name for the unidentified commissioner or dedicatee of the work.

Clérambault's altogether exquisite piece could have been performed in a
context similar to the court of Sceaux for which composers like Jean-Baptiste
Matho, Lalande's protégé François Collin de Blamont and, especially, Mouret,
composed works of comparable scale.

Jean-Joseph Mouret

The name of the Avignon-born Jean-Joseph Mouret (1682–1738) is closely associated with the legendary "Grandes nuits" held between July 1714 and May 1715

at Sceaux. They were the last great festivities of the reign of Louis XIV, who died on 1 September 1715. Located 15 miles southwest of Paris, Sceaux was previously owned by Colbert, who had the château rebuilt by François Mansart with grounds designed by André Le Nôtre. After Seignelay, Colbert's son, died in 1690, this little Versailles was acquired from his brother by Louis-Auguste de Bourbon, duc du Maine, the legitimated son of Louis XIV and Mme de Montespan. His glamorous, ambitious wife, born Anne-Bénédicte-Louise de Bourbon-Condé, daughter of the "Grand Condé" and therefore of royal blood herself, gathered around her an artistic and literary court, at a time when Versailles was declining into morose piety, the aging king having gradually restricted his pleasures to hunting and card games.[79] Mouret entered the Maine household in 1708, at first as music teacher to the Duke's children, but he was the principal composer involved in the 1714–15 Sceaux festivities.[80] These were conceived by Nicolas de Malézieu, the Duchess's literary adviser. Between 1702 and 1707 Malézieu had already staged several comedies for the Maine court at his house in close-by Châtenay, set to music (now lost) by Matho. A Breton, Matho (1663–1746) had already had a tragédie lyrique, *Coronis*, performed at Fontainebleau in 1699. He and Mouret found themselves in rivalry at the Opéra in 1714 when two of their works were staged within a few months: whereas Matho's tragédie lyrique *Arion*, set to a Fuzelier libretto, was poorly received in April,[81] Mouret's opéra-ballet *Les fêtes, ou le triomphe de Thalie* (subsequently published as *Les fêtes de Thalie*) on a libretto by Joseph de La Font, opened in August with a success further heightened by scandal: its prologue featured the defeat of Melpomene, the tragic muse, by Thalia, muse of comedy. The implication of this allegory, or so it was felt by part of the public, was that the old tragédie en musique – La Font's text contains specific references to Lully and Collasse – was being dethroned by the new, popular genre of the opéra-ballet. Indeed, no tragédie en musique premiered since Marais's *Alcyone* (1706) had been remotely as successful as Campra's *Les fêtes vénitiennes* in 1710, a state of affairs Mouret was to verify in later years, since his own tragédies lyriques – *Ariane* (1717) and *Pirithoüs* (1723) – similarly failed to please.

The "Grandes nuits" of 1714–15 took place on 15 or 16 occasions – Saint-Simon, who loathed the Duchess (and her husband even more), called them "white nights" – and Mouret made several contributions to them.[82] The most important was the short three-act *Le mariage de Ragonde*, on a text by the playwright Néricault Destouches (1680–1754), performed on the thirteenth night in December 1714. Though called "comédie-ballet," it was sung throughout, unlike those of Molière and Lully.[83] It does, on the other hand, belong to that tradition insofar as it introduced for the first time into French opera an unabashedly burlesque tone, reminiscent of some of Molière's *farces*. Ragonde, its heroine, is a sexagenarian widow bent on marrying the young shepherd Colin, who is tricked into accepting during a mascarade in which fellow peasants disguised as evil spirits threaten to haunt him forever unless he consents. It all ends in a joyful *charivari*. Mouret's music – which we only know from the version published in 1742 under the slightly different title *Les amours de Ragonde* – vividly captures the boisterous, if arguably cruel, subject matter.[84] This 1742 revival, at the Opéra, was hugely successful and the work was subsequently compared to Rameau's *Platée* (1745), which it may have influenced. Mouret did not live to see the triumph of his comic masterpiece: having lost his employment at Sceaux following the death in 1736 of the Duc du Maine, he exhibited symptoms of insanity in 1737 and died shortly after being interned in the Charenton asylum the following year. Thus ended the career of a composer whom Durey de Noinville, writing a decade later, remembered for his endearing appearance, his pleasant voice, his lively conversation, and his charming Provençal wit.[85]

CHAPTER 3

THE AGE OF RAMEAU

French opera under the Régence

Few rulers in history can have been more sympathetic to opera than Philippe d'Orléans, who became regent at the death of Louis XIV in 1715 – Louis XV being only five – until his own death in 1723. He had studied composition with Charpentier and written an opera in collaboration with him and two more with his music master Gervais. He protected Destouches, Bertin de La Doué,[1] Campra, and Baptistin.[2] Pleasure-loving – to excess, his enemies claimed – he shared none of Louis XIV's inclinations to religious devotion. An Italophile, notably in his musical taste, he immediately brought back the Italian Comedians, absent since 1697. Led by Luigi Riccoboni, who used the stage name of Lelio, they reoccupied their old theater in the Marais district, the Hôtel de Bourgogne, and became known as the Comédie-Italienne – an appellation suggesting a status parallel to the Comédie-Française. Their repertory included plays spoken throughout, in Italian or in French – Marivaux, the greatest French playwright of the century, was soon writing for them – as well as comedies with sung and danced *intermèdes*, for which they hired the services of no lesser a composer than Mouret as of 1717. Meanwhile, the Comédie-Française remained suspicious of the fair theaters' competition and succeeded in restricting their operations for two years in 1718–20 and again in 1721–24. A modus vivendi was reached the following year, sanctioning the co-existence of the four theaters – Opéra, Comédie-Française, Comédie-Italienne, and Opéra-Comique. It lasted until 1745, when the Comédie-Française succeeded in forcing the Opéra-Comique to close, once again, for seven years. Also in 1725, a new musical institution appeared in the French capital, the Concert Spirituel. Founded by Anne-Danican Philidor – son of the royal music librarian – its purpose was to perform instrumental and religious music on the days the Opéra was closed, using its orchestra and soloists as well as musicians from various Paris churches; secular vocal music was soon heard there as well and the Opéra ended up taking over the management in 1734.[3]

At the Académie royale, the 18 years between the death of Louis XIV and Rameau's *Hippolyte et Aricie* witnessed no significant changes in the repertory: Lully's works remained its core and continued to please, whereas most new tragédies en musique premiered during that period were ephemeral successes or downright failures, public favor going rather to opéras-ballets on modern or mythological subjects.[4] One of the acknowledged masterpieces of the latter kind was Destouches's *Les élémens*, which also contained music by Lalande, performed at court in 1721 and premiered in 1725 at the Opéra, where it was regularly revived until the 1780s. The young Louis XV, who danced at the court performances, also appeared in two works by Lalande that marked a short-lived renewal of the court ballet, *L'inconnu* (loosely based on a popular comedy by Thomas Corneille) and *Les folies de Cardenio* (adapted from an episode from *Don Quixote*), both staged at the Tuileries in 1720, the latter in the little used Salle des machines.[5] Another popular opéra-ballet of the period was Collin de Blamont's *Les fêtes grecques et romaines* (1723). Labeled "ballet héroïque" by its librettist, Fuzelier, it introduced for the first time in French opera historical – rather than mythical – characters and events: the first entrée was devoted to the Olympic Games and the second ("Les Bacchanales") to the meeting of Antony and Cleopatra. The first tragédie en musique to delve into history – and to feature not just a Muslim hero, but even a mosque in Act 5 – was Rebel and Francoeur's *Scanderberg* (1735), based on a play by La Motte on the fifteenth-century Albanian patriot.[6] The composers François Rebel (1701–1775), son of Jean-Féry Rebel, and François Francoeur (1698–1787), had first collaborated on *Pirame et Thisbé* (1723), one of the few successful tragédies en musique of the period: on account of its authors' youth, it was dubbed "l'opéra des enfants." An unique case of a long-standing musical partnership, Rebel and Francoeur eventually teamed up as Opéra directors between 1743 and 1753 and again from 1757 until 1767.[7]

The orchestra of the Opéra underwent notable changes in the first decades of the century. By 1764, the year of Rameau's death, it was very different from what it had been at the time of Lully's death.[8] Although the division between the "petit choeur," used in most recitatives and some of the airs, and the "grand choeur" still existed, the former was reduced in size. Theorbos were gone as of 1735, while the use of the harpsichord was maintained only until 1776. In 1720 the Opéra orchestra comprised around 45 members. Its largest section was the violins (16), while the *hautes-contres* and *tailles de violons* of Lully's five-part orchestra were reduced to two each, and the *quintes de violon* disappeared altogether around the same time. Similarly, bass viols were gradually replaced by cellos as of the 1730s, supplemented by the double bass, which had appeared around 1700. These modifications resulted, throughout the period, in the slow transition to an instrumentation in four parts as in Italian music. The woodwind section comprised recorders and "German" (i.e. transverse) flutes as well as oboes and bassoons, occasionally played by the same musicians. One of the flutists, Michel Blavet, was a celebrated soloist; another, Jacques Mangot, became Rameau's father-in-law. Horns were an obligatory feature of the hunting scenes in operas by Rameau or Jean-Joseph Cassanéa de Mondonville, while clarinets, imported from Germany, were introduced by Rameau in *Zoroastre* (1749). Trumpets were used frequently but became an integral part of the opera only in the 1740s. Timpani, kettledrums, and snare drums composed the percussion section, while the hornpipe or musette, for which separate parts exist as of 1703 (though its previous use by Lully is documented), remained until the late 1760s the pastoral instrument par excellence.

If the basic structure of the tragédie en musique remained unchanged throughout the period, it gradually accommodated vocal forms that subtly altered its style. Already in the opéras-ballets of Campra and his successors, a new, more developed type of air, called "ariette," had been introduced: far from what the diminutive term would suggest, it was an adaptation of the Italian da capo aria, allowing for a kind of vocal display based on the repetition of certain words, rather than on continued declamation, that had been hitherto absent from French opera. The tragédie en musique gradually incorporated this innovation, though such ariettes are typically found in the middle of divertissements and were not sung by the leading characters.

Under Destouches's management, the Opéra recovered somewhat from the financial troubles it had experienced under Francine and his successors. Shortly before Louis XIV's death, two sets of regulations concerning the administration of the Académie royale were issued, in 1713 and 1714. They covered such matters as royalty payments to composers and librettists; salaries of singers, choristers, and musicians; and pension funds for retired personnel. Despite greater administrative stability, the status of the Opéra was modified in 1749, when the privilege originally held by Lully and his descendants was transferred to the city of Paris, which kept it for the next 35 years.

Although Rameau dominated the French operatic scene for three decades, his importance should not make us forget other significant opera composers of the time, especially Montéclair, Leclair, and Mondonville.

Michel Pignolet de Montéclair

Though his name is known mostly to music historians, Michel Pignolet de Montéclair (1667–1737) occupies a front-rank position in the history of French opera. Not only was his biblical lyric tragedy *Jephté* (1732) the first performed at the Académie royale de musique, it remains one of the greatest, on a level comparable to Saint-Saëns's *Samson et Dalila*.

Montéclair took his name from the ruined fortress in his native Champagne town of Andelot (now Andelot-Blancheville).[9] Educated in nearby Langres,

Diderot's native city, he is known to have spent time in Italy, from where he may have brought back the use of the double bass. He played this instrument in the Opéra orchestra, probably as early as 1701 and certainly in Campra's *Tancrède* (1702); he was still active in the year of his death. He also became a respected teacher, whose pupils included François Couperin's daughters, and wrote several pedagogical treatises. His *Méthode facile pour apprendre à jouer du violon* (1711–12) was the first violin method published in France. He composed religious music (mostly lost), three volumes of cantatas, airs, and instrumental music.

Montéclair's first opera was an opéra-ballet in the manner of Campra, *Les festes de l'été*, premiered in 1716.[10] The librettist, taking as a pseudonym the name of his mistress Marie-Anne Barbier, was one of the principal librettists of the time, Simon-Joseph Pellegrin (1663–1745), generally known as Abbé Pellegrin, whose name has already been encountered: he was to provide Montéclair with the text of *Jephté*.[11] A Marseillais, Pellegrin became a priest more by economic necessity than owing to a religious vocation. After serving as chaplain on Orient-bound galley ships, he devoted himself to literature and, increasingly, to the theater, beginning with an *opéra-comique* for the Foire Saint-Laurent. In addition to being Rameau's first librettist, he collaborated with Destouches and Desmarets as well as with lesser-known composers (Baptistin, Bertin de la Douée, Lacoste, and Salomon).

Producing an opera based on the Old Testament was not a matter of course in 1732. To be sure, biblical plays were regularly performed in religious schools (especially Jesuit houses) in the manner of Italian *sacre rappresentazioni*. Many featured stage music – such as Racine's *Esther* (1689) and *Athalie* (1691), written for Saint-Cyr, Mme de Maintenon's boarding school for girls. Some were short operas without the name – Charpentier's *David et Jonathas* being the greatest example. Even within those confines, however, the genre remained controversial.[12] It was thus a particularly audacious move for Pellegrin and Montéclair to propose to adapt a biblical subject to the canons of the tragédie en musique, all the more so since theologians considered opera even more immoral than the theater.

The episode from the Book of Judges, in which Jephthah is forced to kill his daughter as a result of his imprudent vow to sacrifice the first person he meets, may have been selected by Pellegrin owing to its similarity with the story of Idomeneus, which was treated in 1712 by Danchet and Campra (not to mention echoes of the sacrifice of Iphigenia by her father Agamemnon, though no opera on this subject had appeared yet).[13] In his fascinating preface to the published libretto, Pellegrin details and justifies the changes he made in the biblical story to render it compatible with French operatic decorum.[14] The most significant concerns the denouement: as Jephthah is about to strike his daughter, thunder is heard and Phinée, the high priest, moved by divine inspiration, stops the sacrifice.[15] At the same time, this change of the divine will is cleverly related to the opera's subplot, which makes it more believable as well as more palatable: unlike her utterly innocent (and nameless) biblical counterpart, Iphise, Jephthah's daughter, loves an Ammonite. It would have been unthinkable, Pellegrin argues, to dispense with "profane love" in a genre from which it is inseparable. By the same token, Iphise's remorse and repudiation of her guilty passion for an enemy of her country make God's forgiveness understandable as well as miraculous in the tradition of the operatic *merveilleux*. Pellegrin also took the trouble to justify the presence of dances – "an insuperable obstacle" in the eyes of some – by reference to the Old Testament, from David dancing before the ark to Jephthah himself being met by his daughter with dancing and tambourines. The remarkable allegorical prologue is almost a manifesto for a new genre: it begins inauspiciously with appearances by Apollo and Venus, until Truth appears, driving away the "offspring of imposture" and opening the way to a new kind of theater.

Montéclair rose to the challenge by producing one of the most beautiful scores of the period. Particularly striking are the vocal characterizations, the vigor of the choral writing (notably in the Act 1 ensemble "Tout tremble devant le Seigneur"), the variety and originality of the orchestral accompaniments (such as the exquisite five flutes in Iphise's aria at the start of Act 4), the striking effects of "tone-painting" (such as the parting of the waters of the River Jordan in Act 1), the liveliness of the dances, and the martial music: everything in this opera, rather than echoing Lully, like most of the *tragédies en musique* staged in the previous 45 years, anticipates much of what we admire in Rameau, who reportedly was impressed and influenced by the work.[16] Premiered during Lent – its religious subject making it exempt from the ban on secular theatrical performances in this period of penance – the opera was revived frequently until 1761.

The career of Jean-Philippe Rameau

Jean-Philippe Rameau (1683–1764) was far and away the greatest French opera composer of his century. His works took the genre to a degree of perfection seldom attained since. A man of the theater as well as a musician of consummate learning and refinement, he has not always received his due in the perception of Western musical history – outside France at least – because his works were long absent from opera houses. Fortunately, the rediscovery of authentic baroque performance practice in the past three decades and the collaboration of its finest exponents with imaginative directors have begun to restore him to his place, along with Berlioz and Debussy, as one of the three indisputable geniuses of French music.

Rameau originated from Dijon, the historical capital of Burgundy. Of his first 40 years, little is known.[17] He occupied positions as organist in Avignon, Lyons, and Clermont-Ferrand, where he composed religious music, some of which is lost, and the greater part of his *Traité de l'harmonie*. The most important work of music theory of its time, it first appeared in 1722, the year when he settled permanently in Paris. It earned him immediate celebrity. His first experience in the lyric theater was at the fairs, for which he contributed music to four plays by his fellow Dijonnais playwright Alexis Piron in the 1720s and early 1730s. To the book of harpsichord pieces he had published in 1706, he added a second and a third in 1724 and 1729, and a book of cantatas in 1730. He still occupied positions as organist, at Sainte-Croix-de-la-Bretonnerie and at the Jesuit novitiate, both in the Marais, until 1736–8. In 1741 he published his last masterpiece in the field of chamber music, the *Pièces de clavecin en concert*. He had married a musician and singer, Marie-Louise Mangot, in 1726; they had four children.

Rameau had just turned 50 when his first tragédie en musique, *Hippolyte et Aricie*, opened at the Opéra in 1733. As we saw, the librettist, Pellegrin, had recently collaborated with Montéclair on *Jephté*, which Rameau admired. *Hippolyte* was as controversial as it was successful and the criticism it met continued to plague Rameau for the remainder of his career. Admirers of Lully and partisans of Italian opera, for once in agreement, though for different reasons, were offended by the richness and sophistication of the music. The Lullistes viewed it as a threat to the harmonious balance that characterized the lyric tragedy, in which "natural" declamation was supposed to remain paramount, whereas the Italianists found the subtle, often complex orchestral tissue detrimental to the melody and pure *vocalità* they prized above all in their models. But Rameau had become the man of the hour. Sometime in the mid-1730s, he met Alexandre-Jean-Joseph Le Riche de La Pouplinière, a wealthy tax collector, who remained his patron and benefactor for 20 years. Plans for a biblical opera on the subject of Samson, for which Voltaire wrote the libretto, were dropped owing to censorship threats from the Theology Faculty of the Sorbonne. Rameau's next work for the stage, the opéra-ballet *Les Indes galantes* (its title, which can be rendered as "Love in Exotic Countries", neatly parallels Campra's *L'Europe galante*), written with the experienced librettist Fuzelier, triumphed in August 1735: within weeks, a third entrée ("Les fleurs," set in Persia) was added to the original two. The fourth, "Les sauvages," set in North America, completed the work in March 1736: its final ensemble is based on the harpsichord piece of the same title adapted, according to Rameau's own testimony, from a dance he had seen Indians perform on the Pont-Neuf. Rameau's next tragédie en musique, *Castor et Pollux*, on a libretto by Pierre-Joseph Bernard (known as Gentil-Bernard (1710–1775)), was comparatively less successful when premiered in 1737. A second opéra-ballet, *Les fêtes d'Hébé*, on a libretto by the obscure Antoine Gautier de Montdorge, subsequently revised by Pellegrin and Bernard, was enthusiastically received in the spring of 1739. Rameau's third tragédie en musique, *Dardanus*, on a libretto by Le Clerc de La Bruère (1716–1754), though not a failure when premiered later that year, came under attack both from a dramatic and a musical point of view. For its 1744 revival, the composer recast it substantially; *Hippolyte et Aricie* had also been revised, though far less extensively, in 1742.

The year 1745 marked the pinnacle of Rameau's official recognition. Two new works were commissioned for performance at court on the occasion of the Dauphin's wedding to the Infanta Maria Teresa: the comédie-ballet *La princesse de Navarre*, his second collaboration with Voltaire, and the comic masterpiece *Platée*, a "ballet bouffon" on a libretto by Jacques Autreau (1657?–1745) loosely drawn from Pausanias. Two opéras-ballets were commissioned later in the same year to celebrate the Fontenoy victory. The first, *Les fêtes de Polymnie*, was on a text by Louis de Cahusac (1706–1759), who remained Rameau's most regular librettist; the second, *Le temple de la Gloire*, brought to a close the increasingly less smooth collaboration with Voltaire (who also managed to antagonize Louis XV at the Versailles premiere). Yet Voltaire, still in 1745, agreed to arrange the text of the one-act *Les fêtes de Ramire* to accommodate music from *La princesse de Navarre*. The young Jean-Jacques Rousseau (1712–1778) – who by his own account had taught himself music by reading Rameau's treatise on harmony – was involved in the revision, but his work was found unsatisfactory; the episode inspired in him a lifelong hostility to Rameau.

Rameau's favor with the French court continued throughout the late 1740s and the 1750s. After the death of the first Dauphine, he composed, with Cahusac, the opéra-ballet *Les fêtes de l'Hymen et de l'Amour, ou Les dieux d'Égypte* (1747) to mark the Dauphin's remarriage with Maria Josefa of Saxony (mother of Louis XVI, Louis XVIII, and Charles X). To celebrate the treaty of Aix-la-Chapelle, which ended the War of Austrian Succession in 1748, another opéra-ballet, *Les surprises de l'amour*, on a libretto by Gentil-Bernard, was commissioned and premiered at the Petits-Cabinets, the bijou theater Mme de Pompadour had built in the royal apartments at Versailles; she herself appeared in two of the soprano roles. The "pastorale héroïque" *Daphnis et Églé* (with the poet and lyricist Charles Collé (1709–1783), 1753), the opéras-ballets *La naissance d'Osiris* and *Anacréon* (both with Cahusac, 1754) and *Les Sibarites* (with Jean-François Marmontel (1723–1799), 1757) were all premiered at Fontainebleau.[18] For the Opéra, Rameau produced two works in 1748: the "pastorale héroïque" *Zaïs* (with Cahusac) and the one-act ballet *Pigmalion* (with Ballot de Sauvot, who had helped with last-minute revisions for *Platée*). They were followed, in 1749, by the "pastorale héroïque" *Naïs* and the tragédie en musique *Zoroastre*, both with Cahusac; and, in 1751, by the ballet *La guirlande, ou Les fleurs enchantées* and the "pastorale héroïque" *Achante et Céphise, ou La sympathie*, both on libretti by Marmontel. Rameau's final contributions to the Opéra were, in 1757, a thorough revision of *Castor et Pollux*; and the lyric comedy *Les paladins*, on an anonymous libretto after La

Fontaine (its author has been identified as Duplat de Monticourt). In this second version *Castor* established itself as the most generally admired of Rameau's operas.

By the 1750s Rameau was one of Europe's most celebrated musicians. His appearance at a revival of *Pigmalion* in the spring of 1751, as reported by the quasi-official journal *Le Mercure de France*, conveys a vivid image of his popularity:

> His presence aroused a murmur that began in the stalls and spread rapidly throughout the whole audience. Then suddenly there broke out a general applause and – something that had never been seen before – the assembled orchestra added their rapturous cheers to those of the *parterre* . . . [Rameau] shared with the public the pleasure of an excellent performance.[19]

Having declined to write the musical articles of the *Encyclopédie*, which began to appear in 1751 (and to which his collaborator Cahusac supplied several major entries), Rameau was hurt when he was deprived of the chance to review them, especially Rousseau's essay on "Musique," which was unsympathetic to him. In the last decade of his life he resumed his theoretical writing, attacking the Philosophes in *Erreurs sur la musique dans l'Encyclopédie* (1755), though some, like d'Alembert, were former friends, and others collaborators, like Diderot, who had partially ghost-written Rameau's *Démonstration du principe de l'harmonie*, published in 1750.[20] A final tragédie en musique, *Les Boréades*, on a libretto generally attributed to Cahusac (who had died in 1759), was rehearsed at Choisy, possibly with a view to a performance at court and in Paris in 1763. The fire that destroyed the Opéra that spring may have been the cause of its withdrawal. Preserved in manuscript in the Bibliothèque nationale, the work was first heard in its entirety in a French radio concert performance in 1964 and staged at the Aix-en-Provence Festival in 1982.[21] In that same year, the Bibliothèque nationale, by selling exclusive rights to a music publisher, created an interesting precedent of a mid-eighteenth-century opera now fully protected by copyright until 2052.

Rameau died on 12 September 1764 at his home near the Louvre. The large crowds that attended the memorial services held in Paris and the provinces indicate the reverence in which he was held by people well beyond the ranks of opera-goers.

Rameau and opera

Rameau's libretti – like most libretti – have been unfairly denigrated. Sour remarks were made by the disgruntled Collé over the composer's relationship with his librettists – on whom he admittedly appears to have imposed tough financial conditions.[22] Yet Rameau's collaborators included Voltaire, the foremost French writer of the age – and considered then its foremost play-wright, a claim posterity has not sustained – a major minor writer (Marmontel) and prominent, talented librettists like Pellegrin, Fuzelier, and Cahusac. Their inferiority to Quinault, as we may feel it, may be largely due to the more artifi-cial, stereotyped theatrical diction of the period, which to modern ears often sounds painfully periphrastic (as in "Vous qui d'Hébé suivez les lois," the opening words of *Les Indes galantes*, to mean "You the young"). *Dardanus* has the most problematic plot, hence the drastic revision to which it was submitted between 1739 and 1744. Yet even La Bruère's libretto, in both versions, offers striking dramatic situations: Dardanus, hidden, overhearing Iphise confessing her love for him to the magician Isménor; Dardanus, asleep on the shore, visited by dreams (in the manner of *Atys*); Dardanus's rival Anténor about to be overcome by a sea monster but rescued by Dardanus in disguise. *Zoroastre*, also revised, though less extensively, is on an unusual subject – Persian mythology – while containing clear references to Masonic symbols, in a manner that antici-pates Mozart's *Magic Flute*.[23] Rather than in its conventional love interest, its finest moments are the two contrasting ceremonies, to the sun in Act 2, to the powers of darkness in Act 4; in the 1756 version, a second ceremony to the sun was introduced in Act 3, interrupted by the apparition of the tyrant Abramane.

If less original, since closer to the habitual world of the tragédie en musique, *Castor et Pollux*, in its 1737 and 1754 versions both by Gentil-Bernard – the latter with an entirely new first act, in which Castor is still alive, whereas the former opens with a chorus lamenting his death in battle – can be consid-ered a model of the latter-day tragédie en musique: a Racine-like love quartet (Phoebe loves Pollux, who loves Telaira, who loves Castor); the rescue of Castor from Hell by the chivalrous Pollux, reminiscent of *Alceste* (in this version Pollux is a demi-god but his brother is not, at least until the denoue-ment); and the final assumption of the Dioscuri into constellations, reminis-cent of *Isis*.[24] As for *Hippolyte et Aricie* and *Les Boréades*, which stand at the two extremes of Rameau's operatic career, they are both masterpieces of their kind. *Hippolyte*, in particular, offers a fascinating example of the adaptation of a French classical tragedy – Racine's *Phèdre* (1677), itself contemporary with Quinault's *Isis* – into a tragédie en musique. As the title indicates, the pair of young lovers is given greater prominence. Racine himself had created the char-acter of Aricie to make the character of Hippolytus – a celibate misogynist in Euripides – conform more to seventeenth-century decorum. In Pellegrin's version Aricie is the character we encounter first, while the final scene is devoted to the reunification of the young lovers in the Arician Grove under Diana's tutelage – a further twisting of the classical myth to provide a relatively happy ending. No longer the central figure, Phaedra has nevertheless two great moments: the air "Cruelle mère des amours" in Act 3, and her lament, accom-panied by the chorus, over Hippolytus's death in Act 4, as moving a scene as the end of *Atys*. Theseus, on the other hand, is arguably a more striking figure in the opera than in the play.[25] Making most of the convention that allowed the tragédie en musique to show what the regular tragedy can only tell, Pellegrin sets the entire second act in Hell after the failure of Theseus's ill-advised attempt, with his friend Pirithous, to abduct Proserpina: as Theseus is being set free, Pluto having relented, the Fates – in a trio of such harmonic audacity that it defeated performers at the Opéra in 1733 and had to be cut – warn him that he will find home an even worse hell than the one he is about to leave.[26] Predestination, which in Racine's tragedy was associated with Phaedra's troubled ancestry, is here shifted to Theseus, who becomes the central tragic figure of the drama.

Although by comparison, *Les Boréades*, focusing essentially on a marriage interest, could be described as a mythological tragi-comédie, its subject is surprisingly effective theatrically: the hand of Queen Alphise is promised to a descendant of Boreas, god of the winds, two of whose sons persistently woo her, whereas she loves the unknown Abaris. At the end, and after Alphise has been carried away by a storm unleashed by her furious suitors, Abaris is revealed to be the son of Apollo and a nymph descended from Boreas. The underlying meteorological theme, with its suggestion of a fight between light and darkness, provides both eloquent images and a symbolic background (as in the elaborate ariette "Un horizon serein" at the end of Act 1) as well as opportunities for musical tone-painting – for example in the storm that closes Act 3 and opens Act 4, or the depiction of Boreas's lugubrious kingdom at the start of Act 5.[27]

Beside his five tragédies en musique – he actually wrote a sixth, *Linus*, which was rehearsed in 1752, but the music was lost – the largest part of Rameau's output was in the genre we now call "opéra-ballet," but which then was more frequently called "ballet héroïque" or (if in a single act) "acte de ballet." Only the first, *Les Indes galantes*, is of the non-mythological kind invented by La Motte and Campra. Its four entrées deal respectively with a generous Turk in love with a Provençale captive, whom he releases after her French lover unexpectedly turns up (an anticipation of Mozart's *Abduction from the Seraglio*); a fanatical Inca priest, jealous of the love of his beloved Phani for the conquistador Carlos and who perishes in the volcanic eruption he engineers to frighten her back to him; a masquerade involving four lovers at a Persian flower festival; and the courting of the native American Zima by a French and a Spanish colonizer, both of whom she spurns in favor of her own tribesman Adario. The other opéras-ballets have a Greco-Roman mythological setting, save for *Les fêtes de l'Hymen et de l'Amour*, whose entrées, unusually, have an Egyptian theme. Some are of the allegorical kind launched by Collasse's *Les saisons* in 1695. The three entrées of *Les fêtes d'Hébé* (also known as *Les talens lyriques*) are each devoted to one art form: poetry, represented by Sappho; music, portrayed as more powerful than love and war in the context of legendary Sparta; dance, personified by Églé, a follower of its muse Terpsichore, courted by Mercury disguised as a shepherd. Similarly, the isolated act *Pigmalion* is adapted from the entrée "La sculpture" from La Motte and La Barre's *Le triomphe des arts* (1700). More loosely allegorical is *Le temple de la Gloire*, admission into which provides the unifying theme; unusually, it features a historical character, the emperor Trajan.

The "pastorales héroïques" differ from the opéras-ballets insofar as they have a single plot spread over three or four acts rather than entrées each with its own subject. Thus, *Achante et Céphise* deals with a pair of lovers endowed with magic powers of telepathy and *Naïs* with Neptune's courtship of a Corinthian nymph.

Of Rameau's three comedies, the comédie-ballet *La princesse de Navarre* is not really an opera since it consists, like Molière's and Lully's early works, of three *intermèdes* without much connection to the play. *Platée*, on the other hand, is one of Rameau's most original and effective works and the first full-fledged lyric comedy in the history of opera. The heroine, a high tenor role in travesty, is a ridiculous frog-like nymph who fancies herself the object of Jupiter's love. The work climaxes on a mock-wedding presided over by the allegorical character of Folly. In fact the god is only pretending to fancy Platée to deflect Juno's jealousy. The Aristophanesque verve of Autreau's libretto, with additions by Le Valois d'Orville, disconcerted the original audience at Versailles.[28] It inspired Rameau with some of his most individual music, often bordering on self-parody. The work quickly became one of his most admired – notably by the *Encyclopédistes*. *Les paladins*, by contrast, was long his least successful. Like Beaumarchais's *Barbier de Séville*, it deals with the attempts of the young Atis to abduct his lover Argie, kept under lock and key by her old guardian Anselme, who intends to marry her. The comedy largely revolves on Anselme's servant Orcan who, while guarding Argie, flirts with her maid Nérine – a situation reminiscent, this time, of Osmin and Blondchen in Mozart's *The Abduction from the Seraglio*. Anselme's undoing in the third act conforms to La Fontaine's tale, no doubt familiar at the time to most members of the audience. Its implications are unusually risqué for the eighteenth century: the fairy Manto, a high tenor part, appears to Anselme in the form of a Moorish slave boy and promises him a palace and treasures in exchange for sex ("Tu me plais; je veux ton hommage"), a bargain the covetous Anselme accepts, only to be immediately exposed by his ward.

Zoroastre was the first tragédie en musique to dispense with a prologue. There is none either in the 1754 *Castor et Pollux* or *Les Boréades*: the Lullian model was by then perceived as outdated and unnecessary. When there is a prologue, it is often allegorical rather honorific; in some instances it even functions as an introduction to the opera. The one in *Hippolyte et Aricie* focuses on a dispute between Diana and Cupid: it serves to explain her uncharacteristic support of the young lovers of the tragedy and justify Pellegrin's twisting of his

Greek model. The theme of *Les Indes galantes* is allegorically presented as dictated by the wars that take away the young men of Europe, driving love to faraway lands. In *Les fêtes d'Hébé*, the goddess of youth persuades her attendants to accompany her to the banks of the Seine in order to attend the opera we are about to hear. Subtitled "La naissance de la comédie," the prologue to *Platée* is at once an introduction to the work and a stand-alone mythological representation of the invention of comedy by Thespis under the triple tutelage of Bacchus, Thalia, the comic muse, and Momus, the god of ridicule. Its popularity is attested by performances of it as a separate piece late into the eighteenth century.[29]

Rameau also departed from the Lullian tradition in several of his overtures. Whereas the earlier ones conform to the stately, objective model, the late ones tend to relate to the musical climate of the opera. In some cases (*Platée* for one), they even quote from it. They may also include effects of tone-painting: the overture to *Pigmalion* mimics the strokes of the sculptor's chisel – an effect first noted by d'Alembert; the one to *Zaïs* opens with a musical picture of chaos. Its disjointed harmony having proved too shocking to the original audiences, a new one was substituted.

In the recitatives, Rameau remains superficially closest to Lully's model, yet with a degree of flexibility, variety, and musical sophistication that seems to herald the following century as much as it recalls the previous one. The scene in which Phaedra, almost in a slip of the tongue, reveals her love to Hippolytus, the accompanied recitative that introduces Theseus's great invocation to Neptune in Act 3 of the same opera, are two instances among many. This invocation is one of the earliest of Rameau's great monologue arias, remarkable both for the eloquence of the vocal line and the rich and expressive orchestral accompaniment. Other celebrated examples are Telaira's mournful aria "Tristes apprêts" in *Castor et Pollux* and the imprisoned Dardanus's "Lieux funestes" in the second version of the opera: in both cases the bassoons underline the lugubrious character of the situation. This role of the orchestra, which went far beyond its use by Lully and his successors, was one of the innovations to which Rameau's contemporary critics particularly objected.

From Lully, Rameau also retains the "little airs" that come up, almost unnoticeably, in the middle of the recitative, and the "maxim airs" often heard in the middle of a divertissement, their tune often based on dance movements in which they are inserted. At the same time his operas, in keeping with the evolution of taste since Lully's day, resort to a much greater degree of *vocalità*, though requiring less virtuosity than his contemporaries Vivaldi and Handel. This trend is manifest in the additions made to the role of Castor in 1754, as well as in such interpolations as the Italian aria ("Fra le pupille") that the composer, at an unknown date, introduced into the Persian Act of *Les Indes galantes*.[30]

Rameau had at his disposal two of the finest singers of the day, the high tenor Pierre de Jelyotte (1713–1797) and the soprano Marie Fel (1713–1794).

Jelyotte, who sang small roles (Cupid and one of the Fates) in *Hippolyte et Aricie* in 1733, was the first Dardanus and Zoroastre; he sang the role of Platée in the one performance given at court in 1745 and appeared in all Rameau's leading tenor parts – notably the much expanded role of Castor in the revised version of 1754 – until his retirement in 1765. The high tessitura and florid writing of Mercury in *Les fêtes d'Hébé*, another role he premiered, provide a good indication of the exceptional possibilities of this first star tenor in operatic history.[31] Fel shone in the role of La Folie in *Platée*, which displayed both her coloratura and gift for soft singing. She often partnered Jelyotte, as Amélite in *Dardanus* or Telaira in the revised *Castor et Pollux*. She had a long affair with Cahusac and was also involved with Maurice-Quentin de La Tour, the greatest French portrait painter of the period.[32] Her pupil Sophie Arnould (1740–1802) succeeded her in the same parts after 1758. She was the first Argie in *Les paladins*. Alphise in *Les Boréades*, with its difficult "Storm aria," was in all likelihood intended for her.

Rameau also placed great demands on the Opéra choral forces, which numbered 40 singers at the time of *Zoroastre*.[33] Although nothing in the later operas matches in length and complexity the chorus "Que ce rivage retentisse," in Act 3 of *Hippolyte et Aricie* in which the returning Theseus is greeted by his unsuspecting subjects, his choral writing in them, as has been pointed out, bears comparison with Bach and Handel.[34] The Inca sun-worship and peace-pipe ceremonies of *Les Indes galantes*, the burial, battle, and Hell scenes of *Castor et Pollux*, the temple scenes of *Zoroastre* are splendid examples. In the first entrée of *Les fêtes de l'Hymen et de l'Amour*, the overflowing of the Nile is described in a 10-part double chorus.[35]

Dance – from the beginning, as we have seen, a constituent element of French baroque opera – plays an even more prominent part in Rameau's works than in Lully's.[36] One of the finest contemporary interpreters of Rameau, William Christie, has gone so far as to call him, next to Stravinsky, "the most original dance composer of the last three hundred years." The ballet music is, obviously, the most immediately appealing aspect of his works. Beginning with *Hippolyte et Aricie*, all feature a divertissement in each act or entrée. The old dance forms are rejuvenized and re-energized, such as the impressive instrumental chaconnes that conclude *Hippolyte*, *Les Indes galantes*, *Castor et Pollux*, and the original version of *Dardanus*. Eighteenth-century audiences must also have recognized arrangements of some of Rameau's popular harpsichord pieces, such as "Les niais de Sologne" in *Dardanus*, as they no doubt recognized the "tambourin" from the prologue of *Castor et Pollux* in the *Pièces de clavecin en concert* of 1741. Cahusac, Rameau's chief librettist, was also one of the foremost ballet theorists. Besides covering the subject for the *Encyclopédie*, he published a three-volume treatise on dance in 1754, in which he advocates a closer integration of the danced numbers into the plot of the opera. Finding fault with the "simple dance" (his own phrase) of the traditional, decorative operatic divertissement where, as he puts it, one dances just for the sake of dancing, he argued for what he called the *ballet figuré*, consisting in a danced representation of events connected to the plot.[37] He introduced no fewer than seven such ballets in *Les fêtes de l'Hymen et de l'Amour*. As for his singers, Rameau had at his diposal the greatest dancers of his day: Marie Sallé (*c.*1707–1756), who appeared in *Castor et Pollux* in 1737 and *Dardanus* two years later; Louis Dupré (1697–1774), who reportedly found the dazzling chaconne of *Les Indes galantes* at odds with his customary majestic style;[38] and, especially, Marie-Anne de Cupis de Camargo (1710–1770). Originally from Brussels, she starred, along with Dupré, in *Hippolyte et Aricie* and most of Rameau's works. She was particularly acclaimed as Églé in "La dance" in *Les fêtes d'Hébé*. The ballet troupe of the Opéra numbered 40 dancers around 1750.

Like Lully's operas, and only a handful of those composed since, Rameau's were regularly revived at the Opéra through the 1770s and mounted in opera houses all over France. Unlike Lully, however, Rameau subjected them to constant revision. While the original version of *Hippolyte et Aricie*, including the cuts made before the premiere, may be considered closest to his artistic wishes, most other cases are far from being clear-cut. In those of *Castor et Pollux*, *Dardanus*, and *Zoroastre*, one has to conclude that there exist two autonomous versions which are best treated as such in editions, recordings, or performances.[39]

Rameau's works then suffered after the tragédie en musique and the other genres he had illustrated lost their ability to please. Though his name was not forgotten – he was still known as "le grand Rameau"– his music was confined to respectful ignorance and none of his operas were staged in the nineteenth century.[40] The situation began to change in the late 1890s, when he benefited from a renewal of interest in French music in France, admittedly in a context that can be described as cultural nationalism. An edition of his complete works was launched in 1895, but was interrupted in 1924. *La guirlande*, *Zoroastre*, *Dardanus*, and *Castor et Pollux* were heard in concert at Vincent d'Indy's Schola cantorum, the first two in 1903 and the other two in 1907 and 1908 respectively – *Castor* was enthusiastically reviewed by Debussy. *Hippolyte et Aricie* was staged at the Opéra in 1908 and *Les fêtes d'Hébé* at Monte Carlo in 1914. A lavish production of *Les Indes galantes* was highly successful at the Opéra throughout the 1950s. But Rameau had to wait until the 1980s for productions that did him justice musically and dramatically. As anyone who has had the privilege of seeing them can attest, they reveal that his musical genius was fully equalled by his genius for the theater.

Joseph Bodin de Boismortier

Joseph Bodin de Boismortier (1689–1755) spent his youth in his native Lorraine and his early adulthood in Perpignan, where he had a position involving the distribution of tobacco to the troops, moving to Paris only in 1723. He then embarked on a prolific and lucrative career as a composer of attractive instrumental music, especially dances, but also concertos, motets, and cantatas. Like many others, he was involved with the fair theaters and conducted both at the Foire Saint-Laurent (1743–5) and at the Foire Saint-Germain (1745). His first work for the stage was the "ballet" – that is, opéra-ballet – *Les voyages de l'Amour* (1736), on a libretto by La Bruère which deals with Cupid's vain search for constant love in different settings.[41] A more original and important work, *Don Quichotte chez la duchesse* was premiered at the Opéra in 1743 as part of a double bill with a revival of Mouret's *Les amours de Ragonde*. This "ballet comique" in three acts on a libretto by Charles-Simon Favart (1710–1792) – his Opéra debut – was inspired by an episode in Cervantes's novel that had already been treated by Antonio Caldara in 1727, and in which a duke and his wife stage for their entertainment imaginary fantastic adventures featuring giants, enchanters, and monsters believed by Don Quixote to be real. Fel sang the role of Altisidore (supposedly Queen of Japan), while Camargo appeared in the dances. The work has its serious side – Don Quixote's constancy is recognized and honored at the end – but the music is notable above all for the liveliness and tunefulness that characterize Boismortier's entire production.[42]

Daphnis et Chloé, a pastoral in a prologue and three acts, was also premiered at the Opéra in 1747. It was loosely adapted from Longus's novel by Pierre Laujon (1727–1811), a provider of parodies for the fair theaters and libretti of some little operas performed at court. In this setting, neither Daphnis nor Chloe are actually shepherds: she turns out to be the daughter of the rich Saphir, he of the equally rich Agenor. Jelyotte sang Daphnis, partnered by Fel as Chloe; once again Camargo starred in the dance numbers. Fel's admirers, in particular, must have been grateful to Boismortier for letting her display her gift for expressive singing in the tender aria "Si le rang" and her agility in the final ariette "Vole, Amour, vole." Like *Don Quichotte chez la duchesse*, the work ends with an attractive chaconne.[43]

Boismortier died in 1755 at La Gâtinellerie, the magnificent estate he had acquired two years before in Roissy-en-Brie in the Île-de-France.

Jean-Joseph Cassanéa de Mondonville

Jean-Joseph Cassanéa de Mondonville (1711–1772) was born in Narbonne at whose cathedral, one of the most beautiful in southern France, his father was organist.[44] A violin virtuoso, he made his debut at the Concert Spirituel in 1734. His first published works as composer were violin sonatas, a genre then much in vogue, at which he excelled. His motets, performed at the royal chapel at Versailles as of 1738, were also well received, earning him a high reputation as a religious composer. His operatic debut, the "pastorale héroïque" *Isbé* was

not, however, particularly successful at the Opéra in 1742. His next effort was
the little opera *Bacchus et Érigone*, on a libretto by La Bruère, performed at
Versailles in March 1747, at the Petits-Cabinets, before an invited aristocratic
audience. The Marquise de Pompadour was Érigone and the Duc d'Ayen
Bacchus. Another little opera, *Vénus et Adonis*, on a text by Collé, was also
staged by Mme de Pompadour in 1752 at her Bellevue château in Meudon to
entertain a distraught Louis XV following the death of his daughter Henriette.
By then, Mondonville had scored a success at the Académie royale in 1749
with a "ballet héroïque" by Fuzelier, *Le carnaval du Parnasse*, which received
more than 60 performances in one year, rivaling and eventually eclipsing
Rameau's *Zoroastre*. In 1753, Mondonville's "pastorale héroïque" *Titon et
l'Aurore*, staged at the Opéra at the height of the Querelle des Bouffons (see
pp. 62–64), was hailed as a model of the French style. Its prologue was set to a
previously used text by La Motte, while the libretto of the opera proper – on a
subject suggested by Mme de Pompadour – resulted from a collaboration
between the Abbé de La Marre and the Abbé de Voisenon.[45] The following
year, at Fontainebleau, Mondonville unveiled his most original work, the
"pastorale languedocienne" *Daphnis et Alcimadure*. The text, after Theocritus
via La Fontaine, was written by Mondonville himself in southwestern dialect,
with a prologue in French by Voisenon. The two Opéra stars who headed the
cast, Fel[46] and Jelyotte, both originated from that part of France. D'Alembert
praised the work, calling it an "opéra gascon." In his next work, the opéra-
ballet *Les fêtes de Paphos*, premiered at the Opéra in 1758, Mondonville incorporated the earlier *Vénus et Adonis* and *Bacchus et Érigone* and added
a third entrée, *L'Amour et Psyché*, on a libretto by Voisenon. Though not
otherwise mentioned in the libretto, the title would have been immediately
understood by eighteenth-century audiences as a reference to the legendary
birthplace of Venus on the island of Cyprus. Dance figures prominently in the
work, with as many as 30 numbers. The new entrée, which includes an instrumental "tempête" in the manner of Marais' *Alcyone*, had the most success and
was revived independently in 1760, 1762, and 1777.[47]

   In 1755 Mondonville succeeded Pancrace Royer as director of the Concert
Spirituel, where his works were so popular that they were performed more
than those of any other composer. Yet his career suffered a serious setback in
1765 with the tragédie lyrique *Thésée*, for which he simply reused Quinault's
libretto set by Lully 90 years before – a precedent launched by Antoine
Dauvergne with Collasse's *Énée et Lavinie* and which Gluck and Piccinni were
to follow. Politely received at Fontainebleau, Mondonville's version of the
revered masterpiece was greeted by Parisian audiences, punning on the work's
title, with cries of "Taisez-vous, Mondonville"; after three performances,
Lully's work was restored to the repertory – admittedly in a version hardly
faithful to the original. Mondonville returned to the stage only once more with
the opéra-ballet *Les projets de l'Amour*, on a text by his faithful Voisenon,

performed at Versailles in 1771. It was one of the last examples of the genre born in 1697 with Campra's *L'Europe galante*.

Mondonville's operas contain much enjoyable, at times irresistibly tuneful music. His vocal writing, beyond the obvious influence of the florid Italian and *galant* styles, looks back to Lully – with less imagination, no doubt, in the recitatives, notated in a smooth, but pedestrian triple meter – but his orchestral writing is very much of his time, as can be heard in the lively overture to *Titon et l'Aurore*. Lacking Rameau's powerful originality and sense of the theater, he stood at the end of the classical period, when the genres of the tragédie en musique and opéra-ballet showed signs of fatigue; what he brought to them was his métier and ability to please, which were both considerable.

Jean-Marie Leclair

Jean-Marie Leclair (1697–1764), the greatest composer born in Lyons, began his career as a dancer and a violinist. It was as the latter that he became famous, both as a virtuoso performer – he is considered the father of the French violin school – and the author of four books of sonatas, three of trio sonatas, and 12 concertos. He occupied positions both at the French court in the 1730s and at the Nassau court in Holland, before being hired by a former aristocratic pupil, Antoine-Antonin, duc de Gramont, who had set up his own orchestra. Leclair had separated from his second wife, Louise Roussel, a music engraver (her name appears in some of Rameau's works), and lived by himself on the outskirts of Paris when, a mere five weeks after Rameau's death, his gardener found him mortally stabbed outside his house in the early morning of 23 October 1764. Though the murder was never solved, the prime suspect appears to be his nephew (and fellow violinist) Guillaume-François Vial.[48]

Leclair wrote only one opera, the tragédie en musique *Scylla et Glaucus*, which received 18 performances at the Opéra in 1746. Like Rameau at the time of *Hippolyte et Aricie*, Leclair was nearly 50. He subsequently contributed music, as composer or arranger, to operatic entertainments staged at the Duc de Gramont's mansion in Puteaux, but little of it survives. The prologue of *Scylla et Glaucus* – one of the last of its kind – combines praises of Louis XV and his son with an episode, drawn, like so many French lyric tragedies, from Ovid's *Metamorphoses*, in which Venus turns into stone the impious young women of the city of Amanthus. This episode foretells the denouement of the tragedy proper, also drawn from Ovid, which deals with Circe's revenge on the nymph Scylla, whom she turns into a rock out of jealousy over her unrequited passion for Scylla's lover, the marine deity Glaucus. The libretto by the little-known d'Albaret provides many opportunities for spectacle: Circe appearing in a cloud in Act 3; Mount Etna erupting in Act 4 as Circe invokes Hecate and her demons; Circe riding a dragon in the first scene of Act 5. The final tableau (out of seven) shows the coastal landscape off Sicily with the whirlpool of

Charybdis next to the metamorphosed Scylla while Glaucus laments and Circe gloats. From a dramatic and literary point of view, we are fully in the aesthetic universe created by Quinault and Lully 75 years previously. Yet the work abounds in musical riches that make it one of the most captivating operas composed, as it were, in the shadow of Rameau. Not only does it contain ballet music of a vitality and variety not unworthy of the great master – Leclair's own training as a dancer must be credited for this – but the Act 2 sung passacaille, "Amants dont le prix," Glaucus's brilliant Act 5 ariette, "Chantez, chantez l'amour," and the entirety of Circe's role, show that Leclair was no second-rate opera composer. Yet *Scylla et Glaucus*, despite a cast headed by Fel and Jelyotte in the title roles and Camargo's participation in the dances, only got a respectful reception and was never revived, serving instead as a quarry for the Opéra management to "embellish" repertory works. The reasons for this semi-failure, as Neal Zaslaw has suggested, must be sought in the historical context of its premiere: musically too advanced for the *Lullistes*, too much rooted in the French tradition for the *Italianistes*, too implacably tragic for the *Ramistes*.[49]

The "Querelle des Bouffons"

The mid-eighteenth-century pamphlet war known as the "Querelle des Bouffons" – "Bouffons" referring specifically to Italian opera buffa performers – was one of those public controversies characteristic of French intellectual and cultural life since the late Renaissance. It pitted partisans of the supposedly "pure" French operatic tradition, introduced and imposed by Lully, against those of Italian opera, whose influence had been felt, in more or less overt ways, in the works of nearly every French opera composer from Charpentier to Rameau. Yet, although Italian opera, buffa or seria, was popular all over Europe, hardly any had been heard in Paris since 1662, save for two intermezzi performed at the Opéra in 1729 and for Pergolesi's *La serva padrona*, given at the Comédie-Italienne in 1746 – on the same night as the premiere of Leclair's *Scylla et Glaucus* at the Opéra – apparently without causing any particular sensation.[50] Paradoxically, it was the management of the Opéra, temple of the French tradition, that decided to capitalize on the public curiosity for Italian opera by inviting the troupe of Eustachio Bambini, who had been performing in Strasbourg and Rouen, to produce comic Italian inter-mezzi and *opere buffe* at the Palais-Royal. Remaining in Paris for 20 months, they gave performances of 13 different operas by Latilla, Leo, Pergolesi, Cocchi, Jommelli, Rinaldo di Capua, Sellitto, and Ciampi between August 1752 and March 1754. According to Jean-Jacques Rousseau's polemical testimony in his posthumous *Confessions*, the shock came on August 1 when *La serva padrona* was performed on the same evening as Lully's *Acis et Galatée*:

Sometime before *The Village Soothsayer* [Rousseau's own opera *Le devin du village*] was given, the Italian Bouffons arrived in Paris and were made to play in the Opera theatre, without anyone foreseeing the effect they were going to have there. Although they were detestable and the Orchestra, which was very ignorant at that time, mangled at pleasure the pieces they gave, they did not fail to inflict an injury on French opera which it has never put right. The comparison of these two types of music, heard the same day at the same theatre, unblocked French ears; none of them could endure the dragging of their music after the lively and marked accent of the Italian.[51]

In fact, though *La serva padrona* became an inescapable reference, the Bouffons' greatest success was Ciampi's *Bertoldo in corte*, on a libretto by the Venetian playwright Carlo Goldoni (1707–1793).[52] Besides, the presence of the Italians was not so much the cause as the pretext of the series of tracts attacking or defending French opera – or, more precisely, the tragédie en musique – that appeared in the space of 18 months.[53] Other factors have to be considered: the effervescent intellectual climate created by the publication of the first volumes of the *Encyclopédie* the previous year; the reopening of the Opéra-Comique in February 1752, after a seven-year hiatus; the highly charged political climate, with the Paris Parliament in open conflict with both the king and Church authorities.[54] In January 1752, more than six months before the Bouffons' arrival, the German diplomat Friedrich Melchior von Grimm, then at the start of his brilliant career as a critic (his *Correspondance littéraire*, manuscript copies of which were distributed by subscription all over Europe, was launched the following year), took the opportunity of a revival of Destouches's *Omphale* to publish a pamphlet denigrating the old-style tragédie en musique. Grimm was a friend of Diderot and (at least provisionally) Rousseau. The latter, whose *Le devin du village* was about to be premiered at court, quickly entered the debate with a pamphlet of his own, presented as a response to Grimm's *Lettre sur Omphale*. At this stage Grimm and Rousseau, while heaping scorn on the French recitative and singing style of the tragédie en musique in the Lully tradition, still treated Rameau with reverence. Once the Bouffons started performing at the Académie royale, the focus shifted from a debate between the old-fashioned *Lullistes* and the modern *Ramistes* to a controversy between two national styles. Opposite camps were formed at the Opéra, taking their names from the phrases used to call the two sides of the stage at the Opéra: partisans of the French school were "le coin du roi" and their opponents "le coin de la reine." The "guerre des coins," as the controversy was dubbed, was no mere war of words: Rousseau was hanged in effigy by members of the Opéra's orchestra, while Ballot de Sauvot, librettist of Rameau's *Pigmalion*, was reported to be wounded in a duel with the celebrated Neapolitan castrato Caffarelli (1710–1783), the latter having suggested that the French could do no better than to imitate Italian music.[55] Protected by Mme de Pompadour, Mondonville, rather than Rameau, came closest to being the official French composer. In January 1753 his *Titon et l'Aurore* was hailed as a model of the national genre. As for Rousseau, he was in a paradoxical position: within months of the triumph of his *Devin du village*, first at court, then at the Opéra, he published his *Lettre sur la musique française*, a wholesale attack on French opera and on Rameau in particular. The divorce between the latter and the *Encyclopédistes*, who rallied behind Rousseau, then a friend and collaborator, was complete.

The Querelle proper ended in early 1754 even before the Bouffons' departure. The chief victim of its excesses and prejudices was arguably Rameau, once accused of having an "Italian" harmony, now presented by the intellectual avant-garde as the representative of the outmoded French style. But the controversy was symptomatic of a certain lassitude vis-à-vis the old French forms and of a widely shared need for renewal. It is also revealing of the general restlessness that characterizes the last decades of the Ancien Régime. Although it made Rousseau both famous and infamous, the longest lasting artistic consequence of the Querelle des Bouffons was on the evolution of the opéra-comique, both as a genre and an institution.

Jean-Jacques Rousseau

It is remarkable that one of the pre-eminent writers of the eighteenth century should also figure in French operatic history both as theoretician and composer, and all the more so since Rousseau was in several ways an outsider. He was not from France, but from Protestant Geneva. As a musician, he was largely self-taught. His first operatic projects, of which only the libretti survive, were a mythological "opéra-tragédie" lyrique, *Iphis et Anaxarète*, and a lyric tragedy on a historical subject, *La découverte du nouveau monde*. His stay in Venice in 1743–4 as secretary to a diplomat, Count Montaigu, opened to him the world of Italian opera.[56] Back in Paris, he was introduced into the circle of La Pouplinière, Rameau's patron, at whose home his "ballet héroïque" *Les Muses galantes*, written with some help from François-André Philidor, was rehearsed. Its three entrées were devoted to Tasso (later replaced by Hesiod), Ovid, and Anacreon. Rameau heard it and dismissed it harshly. Rehearsed at the Opéra, it was withdrawn by the author. Nor were the relations between the older composer and his former admirer repaired by the flap over the revision of *La princesse de Navarre* as *Les fêtes de Ramire* in 1745.

Rousseau's great moment came seven years later with his one-act opera *Le devin du village*, which he composed to his own libretto. Set in the countryside – real French countryside, not the mythological pastoral variety – the plot revolves around the lovers' quarrel of two peasants, Colin and Colette, happily reconciled by the village soothsayer. That this reconciliation is achieved, despite the piece's title, not through magic powers but psychological acumen can be seen as a deliberate rejection of the tradition of the operatic *merveilleux*.[57] The music, though hardly refined, is catchy and charming. Rousseau was particularly proud of his style of recitative, closer, he claimed, to the natural rhythm of the language. According to Book 8 of the *Confessions*, the tenor Jelyotte, who premiered the part of Colin opposite Fel's Colette, substituted tamer recitatives for the court premiere at Fontainebleau, but the genuine ones were reintroduced when *Le devin du village* was given in Paris in April 1753, with an overture and a divertissement added. The success was considerable. Soon Mme de Pompadour was producing the work herself privately (as Colin) at her Bellevue residence, while Louis XV could be heard humming Colette's "J'ai perdu mon serviteur" in "the most out-of-tune voice in his kingdom" (Rousseau's words). *Le devin du village* became one of the most often performed eighteenth-century operas, remaining in the Opéra's repertory until 1829.[58]

Radicalized by his sudden rise to fame, Rousseau outlined his views in several pamphlets he wrote during the Querelle des Bouffons, especially the *Lettre sur la musique française* that came out in November 1753 and the entry on opera he contributed to the *Encyclopédie*. Beyond the polemical exaggerations (French singing described as "relentless barking, unbearable to any unprepared ear"), Rousseau's writings on opera, as recent critics have shown, are consistent with the philosophical ideas he expounded in his other works, from the *Discours sur les sciences et les arts* (1750) to *Émile* and the *Contrat social* (both 1762).[59] The superiority of Italian opera comes from its being based on melody. Lully's recitative declamation, Rameau's subtle harmony and refined accompaniments are both rejected as unnatural, inauthentic, intellectual – as obstacles to the transparent state of being where men and women can only hope to retrieve a little of their essential goodness, and experience, even briefly, a sense of happiness as little uncorrupted by civilization as possible. In this respect Rousseau is anticipating by several decades the aesthetics of Romanticism. His operatic ideal recalls, in fact, that of another confirmed Italophile, Stendhal, three generations later. Yet, as Catherine Kintzler has shown, Rousseau's views also look back to the traditional condemnations of the theater on moral or religious grounds from Plato onwards, a condemnation Rousseau embraced in his *Lettre à d'Alembert sur les spectacles* (1758).[60] As Bossuet had argued in his polemic with Caffaro, opera, being a hypersophisticated, more seductive form of theater, was all the more dangerous and condemnable.

Rousseau wrote no opera after *Le devin du village*. He had, in any event, become persona non grata at the Opéra. Yet he made another far-reaching contribution to the lyric theater in the 1760s with his "scène lyrique" *Pygmalion* – based on the same subject as Rameau's "acte de ballet." Rather than being sung, the work is spoken throughout over musical accompaniments.[61] It was performed semi-privately in Lyons in 1770 with music by

Horace Coignet, an amateur local composer, save for two ritornellos by Rousseau himself. Enthusiastically received, it proved enormously influential. Rousseau had, quite simply, invented a new musical form that was quickly imitated, especially in Germany, where it began to be called "melodrama" as of the late 1770s. It also found its way into opera, both in Germany and in France, from Méhul's *Ariodant* to Massenet's *Manon*.[62]

Another indication of Rousseau's ambiguous status – at once reactionary and forward-looking – is his admiration for Gluck. After attending the first and second performances of *Iphigénie en Aulide* in 1774, Rousseau – who had argued in the *Lettre sur la musique française* that the French language was essentially incompatible with melodious singing – complimented the German composer on achieving something he would never have thought possible.[63] Gluck even inspired him to undertake a final operatic project, *Daphnis et Chloé*, based on the same Laujon libretto as Boismortier's 1752 opera; Rousseau left it unfinished at his death in 1778. Charles Burney, admittedly no great admirer of the French operatic tradition, characterized Rousseau's role by stating that he had done more good for music in matters of musical taste and refinement than all other writers put together.[64]

Opéra-comique in the mid-eighteenth century

In 1743 the Opéra sold the Opéra-Comique privilege to Jean Monnet (1703–1785). This colorful figure in eighteenth-century theatrical history came from Condrieu, the wine-making village in the northern Rhône Valley. He led an adventurous life, including imprisonment on libel charges, until he moved to Paris.[65] He surrounded himself with a brilliant team: the librettist Favart, the painter François Boucher (as set designer) and the retired star dancer Dupré as choreographer. The Parisian Favart (1710–92) had actually been recruited by Monnet's predecessor, Boizard de Ponteau. A prolific author, Favart exemplifies the transition from the satirical, popular opéra-comique of the early part of the century – his early production included parodies of Lully and Rameau, and he continued to present similar works – to the more serious, sentimental, "bourgeois" tone, which he introduced in the vaudeville comedy *La chercheuse d'esprit* (1741), and which was to remain a hallmark of the genre.[66] The success of Monnet's first seasons with the Opéra-Comique once again alarmed its rivals – the Comédie-Française and the Comédie-Italienne – who got the Opéra-Comique closed in 1745. After a few wandering years – in the Netherlands, in Lyons, where he briefly directed the opera, and in London, where he struck up a friendship with David Garrick – Monnet returned to Paris in 1751. Securing a new lease from the municipality, to which Louis XV had transferred the Opéra privilege in 1749, he built a new theater in 37 days at the Foire Saint-Laurent; decorated by Boucher, it was considered one of the prettiest of the century.[67]

The Bouffons' productions at the Opéra in 1752–4 presented the Opéra-Comique and the Comédie-Italienne with a new competition, while challenging them to look for French-style equivalents of Italian intermezzi – short, tuneful, and amusing. Monnet turned to Antoine Dauvergne (1713–1797), one of the conductors at the Opéra. Despite his name, he was not from the Auvergne but from Moulins in nearby Bourbonnais. His *Les amours de Tempé*, a "ballet héroïque" in five acts on a text by Cahusac, had been moderately successful in 1752. For a subject, Monnet selected the verse tale by La Fontaine, "Les troqueurs," which Jean-Joseph Vadé (1719–1737) adapted into a libretto. Premiered on 30 July 1753, shortly after the Foire Saint-Laurent opened, Dauvergne's one-act *intermède* was enthusiastically received. As Rousseau had done when submitting *Le devin du village* to the Opéra, Monnet kept the authorship secret at first, letting the audiences assume it was an adaptation of an Italian work. The slight plot of *Les troqueurs* revolves around two peasants, Lubin and Lucas (basses both) about to marry, respectively, Margot and Fanchon, but, having cold feet, they decide to swap (*troquer* in French). They soon realize that the original arrangement suited them better but they first need to overcome the resentment of the swapped fiancées. Dauvergne's music, beginning with a lively, Vivaldi-like overture, demonstrates his assimilation of the style of Neapolitan intermezzi, with a succession of da capo arias, duets and quartets – especially the extended final ensemble – tied together by harpsichord-sustained *recitativo secco*. Rameau himself, according to his biographer Maret, was delighted with the piece.[68] Unusually for a work performed at the Opéra-Comique at the time, it was not only sung throughout but entirely set to original music.[69]

The Bouffons' success also prompted numerous French-language "parodies" – the term meant, in this instance, appropriation of music, adapted to new words, rather than satirical intent – of some of their most popular intermezzi.[70] As early as November 1752, Blavet and Collé had joined forces in *Le jaloux corrigé*, a one-act "opéra-bouffon" first performed privately at the Comte de Clermont's château at Berny and revived the following year at the Opéra (where Blavet was first flutist). The ten "ariettes" used music from *La serva padrona* and the pasticcios *Il maestro di musica* and *Il giocatore*, while Blavet's original recitatives were presented as "imitated from the Italian." No sooner had the Bouffons departed than visitors to the Foire Saint-Germain could applaud *Bertholde à la ville*, a vaudeville comedy by Louis Anseaume (1721–1784) inspired by Ciampi's *Bertoldo in corte*, while Pierre Baurans adapted *La serva padrona* into a two-act spoken "comédie mêlée d'ariettes": this label ("comedy interspersed with Italian-style arias") remained synonymous with opéra-comique until the end of the century. Baurans's Pergolesi adaptation was staged by the Comédie-Italienne in August 1754. The popular *Bertoldo* also inspired Favart's three-act parody *Le caprice amoureux, ou Ninette à la cour*, performed at the Comédie-Italienne in 1755. It starred Favart's wife Marie-Justine, who had been attached to the Hôtel de Bourgogne since 1751. The Favarts enjoyed Mme de

Pompadour's protection and it may be though her intervention, as Andrea Fabiano has suggested, that the Bouffons, too successful in the view of their competitors, were sent back to Italy.[71] Favart was eventually appointed head of the Comédie-Italienne in 1758, while being part of a triumvirate that succeeded Monnet at the Opéra-Comique in that same year.

As the peculiar position of the Favart ménage reveals – having, as it were, one foot in two rival institutions – the Opéra-Comique and the Comédie-Italienne had similar repertories and increasingly competed for the same audiences. After the triumph of *Les troqueurs*, the Opéra-Comique scored another success in 1756 with *Le diable à quatre*, commissioned from Michel-Jean Sedaine (1719–1797), the principal opéra-comique librettist of the next three decades. It combined vaudevilles with original music by Philidor and Laruette. The following year Monnet brought from Italy the composer Egidio Duni (1708–1775), then maestro di cappella of the Duke of Parma, who wrote the music for *Le peintre amoureux de son modèle*. Anseaume's libretto deals with the infatuation of the middle-aged Alberti with the young woman he has hired to pose for him as Venus, while she herself loves Zerbin, one of his young disciples. The work, which repeated the triumph of *Les troqueurs*, can be considered the first example of the new kind of opéra-comique: a full-length play, in two acts, with spoken dialogue in prose or in verse (the latter in this case) mixed with arias and ensembles and set to original or mostly original music. In 1758 Duni collaborated with Favart on the equally successful *La fille mal gardée* for the Comédie-Italienne:[72] the play was loosely based on one of the entrées in Mouret's *Les fêtes de Thalie*, but the music was Duni's own. In 1761 Duni became director of the Comédie-Italienne. As Lully for the tragédie en musique, an Italian composer thus again became the true creator of a genre that came to be considered quintessentially French.

Another Italian had arrived in Paris in 1760. Under both financial and artistic pressure, the Comédie-Italienne had approached the Venetian play-wright Carlo Goldoni with a view to establishing a regular opera season.[73] Duni and Goldoni had collaborated in Parma. In Paris they resumed their collaboration by arranging their 1756 melodramma giocoso *La buona figliuola* into an opéra-comique, *La bonne fille*. Hired on a two-year contract beginning in 1762, Goldoni settled in Paris and never returned to his native country. However, by the time he arrived, the Opéra-Comique and the Comédie-Italienne settled their rivalry, after protracted negotiations, by a royally sanc-tioned merger. The resulting institution, which called itself the Nouveau Théâtre Italien, was in fact an absorption by the Comédie-Italienne of the fair theaters and their repertory. Only five members of Monnet's and Favart's troupe were recruited by the new company, which remained at the Hôtel de Bourgogne and opened its first season with a revival of two one-act opéras-comiques, both on libretti by Sedaine: Philidor's *Blaise le savetier* (1759) and Monsigny's *On ne s'avise jamais de tout* (1761). A new chapter in the history of the genre had begun.

CHAPTER 4

GLUCK TO REVOLUTION

French opera after Rameau

When the English musician and future music historian Charles Burney, whose adaptation of Rousseau's *Le devin du village* was staged at Drury Lane in 1766, visited Paris in June 1770, he went to the opera. After the fire that had destroyed the Palais-Royal theater in 1763, the Académie royale had been provisionally installed in the Salle des machines of the Tuileries, remodeled into smaller proportions by Jacques-Germain Soufflot, the great neo-classical architect, who in 1756 had built the Grand Théâtre in Lyons, and the even more famous Ange-Jacques Gabriel, who designed both the Place de la Concorde and the Petit Trianon. By the time Burney arrived in Paris, the new Palais-Royal opera house, designed by Louis-Pierre Moreau, had opened in January 1770 with Rameau's *Zoroastre*. Burney found the architecture of Moreau's oval-shaped auditorium, which could accommodate an audience of 2,500,[1] "elegant and noble," but he had no praise for what he heard, a revival of Pancrace Royer's 1739 "ballet héroïque" *Zaïde, reine de Grenade*. At a time when new musical fashions were spreading all over Europe, he commented,

> the French, commonly accused of more levity and caprice than their neigh-
> bours, have stood still in music for more than thirty or forty years: nay, one
> may go still further, and assert boldly, that it has undergone few changes at
> the great opera since Lulli's time, that is to say, in one hundred years.[2]

Burney's rueful statement is typical of the prevailing contemporary sense that the grand genre – tragédie en musique, ballet héroïque – had run its course. The directors, Rebel and Francoeur until 1767 and their successors Pierre-Montan Berton and Jean-Claude Trial, continued to depend largely on the old repertory, though often in the form of anthologies ("fragments") or resettings

of old libretti by Quinault or La Motte, such as Mondonville's *Thésée*, an igno-
minious failure in 1767, or Jean-Benjamin de La Borde's *Amadis de Gaule*
(1771). In addition, repertory works were presented in increasingly less recognizable versions, most of them arranged by Berton: when Marais' *Alcyone* was
revived for the last time in 1771, it incorporated music by Berton himself,
Campra, Collin de Blamont, Dauvergne, Desmarets, Destouches, Francoeur,
Granier, Leclair, Rameau, Rebel, Royer, and Salomon in addition to the
little that was left of the original.[3] New works were lukewarm successes at best,
like Berton and Trial's own *Silvie* in 1766 and *Théonis* in 1767; in one instance,
Berton proved a pioneer with *Adèle de Ponthieu* (1772), whose medieval theme
anticipated Grétry (see pp. 78–79) and Sedaine's opéras-comiques of the
following decade.

Burney was not alone in noting what struck him as a form of cultural isolationism, at a time when opera seria was popular all over Europe but conspicuously absent from French stages throughout the eighteenth century.
Returning to the issue at a later stage in his journey, Burney listed five differences that were supposed to set the French lyric tragedy above other operatic
models: superior stage machinery ("those puerile representations of flying
gods and goddesses"); splendid costumes; the large number of singers and
dancers involved; prominent and elaborate participation of the chorus; and the
"union of song and dance." "To all which objections," Burney concludes, rebut-
ting potential defenders of French opera, "a real lover of music would perhaps
say, *so much the better*."[4] As Burney implied, the tragédie en musique was too
much spectacle and not enough music. This critique parallels comments made
by numerous foreign visitors – echoed by Rousseau and others during the
"Querelle des Bouffons" – about what they felt was the unrelieved monotony
of French-style recitatives and the apparent absence of arias. Thus Goldoni's
famous account of an evening at the Opéra:

> I waited for the arias . . . The dancers appeared; I thought the act was over,
> not an aria. I spoke of this to my neighbor who scoffed at me and assured me
> that there had been six arias in the different scenes which I had just heard.
> How could this be, say I, I am not deaf; instruments always accompanied the
> voice . . ., but I took it all for recitative.[5]

Burney's comments quoted above also betray impatience with what he saw
as the excessive role of dance at the Opéra. This peculiarity – which, as we have
seen, went back to the origins of French opera – remained in place. Yet, beginning in the 1770s, the ballet emerged as an autonomous genre – as opposed to
works combining sung passages and divertissements, either in the context of a
continuous action or as separate entrées. The phrase "ballet d'action" was
coined at the time to distinguish the new form – which owed much to the
reform of the ballet carried out by Gluck in Vienna in the 1760s – from what

the French called "ballet," that is an opera including dances. Some of the first "ballets d'action" were, in fact, choreographic adaptations of operatic plots: thus Maximilien Gardel's *La chercheuse d'esprit* (1778), after Favart, and Jean Bercher Dauberval's *Le déserteur* (1785), after Pierre-Alexandre Monsigny (see p. 76).

By contrast with the widely perceived decline of the traditional genres associated with the Opéra, the 1760s and 1770s have rightly been called the golden age of opéra-comique.[6] The term, as we have seen, had been in currency since about 1714, at first describing works based entirely on borrowed tunes. In the mid-eighteenth century it was applied to parodies of Italian buffo works, even when sung throughout, as was the case of Anseaume's *Bertholde à la ville*, which is nothing but a succession of vaudevilles. Beginning with Duni's *Le peintre amoureux de son modèle*, it meant a play with spoken dialogues and original musical numbers. This latest form, which became the norm, was often called "comédie mêlée d'ariettes" until the end of the century. It is a confusing label since, in addition to developed arias in the Italian style (the traditional definition of "ariette"), an opéra-comique also featured French-style strophic songs (*couplets*), as well as ensembles. An important clarification, with long-lasting aesthetic implications, was introduced after the 1762 merger: opéra-comique was supposed to include spoken dialogue, sung recitatives being a prerogative of the Opéra. Nor was the Comédie-Italienne allowed to stage works in Italian, a right the Opéra also retained for itself.

The paradox of opéra-comique was thus that, born largely as a result of the popularity of Italian opera buffa, and adopting Italianate forms, it developed into another national genre, which came to be seen just as quintessentially French as the tragédie en musique or the opéra-ballet. Its vogue paralleled an evolution of the French theater in general, away from the classical tragedy and its mythological or ancient themes, and towards what Diderot (who theorized this change in 1757 in his *Entretiens sur* Le fils naturel) called the "drame bourgeois": serious plays, usually in prose, set in the present, and involving characters with whom a middle-class audience could identify and situations it would recognize. These features characterize Sedaine's comedy *Le philosophe sans le savoir*, which the Comédie-Française premiered in 1765, and most of his early opéra-comique libretti.

Three major opéra-comique composers dominate the period: Philidor, Monsigny, and Grétry. Duni, the true creator of the genre, remained active until 1770. He continued to collaborate with Anseaume, notably in *L'école de la jeunesse* (1765), adapted from George Lillo's 1731 play *The London Merchant* (also known as *George Barnwell*). Its serious, indeed tragic tone – although Anseaume, unlike Lillo, spares his young hero the gallows – is typical of the contemporary shift towards the *drame*. The importance it gives to ensembles (one sextet, two septets) also goes along with a closer integration of music in the theatrical action. Premiered in 1765 as well, Duni's *La fée Urgèle* is, by contrast, a medieval fantasy derived indirectly by its librettist Favart from Chaucer's *Wife of Bath's Tale*. Lavishly staged by the Comédie-Italienne, it proved Duni's longest-lasting success. Unusually for a mid eighteenth-century opéra-comique, it is in four acts. Duni also worked with Favart on *Les moissonneurs* (1768), a modern retelling of the Old Testament story of Ruth and Boaz, and with Sedaine on *Les sabots* (1768) and *Thémire* (1770), his final work.

Other opéra-comique composers who came to prominence during the period include the Bohemian-born Josef Kohaut (1738–1793), the Bavarian-born Jean-Paul Martini (1741–1816), the Veronese Alessandro Fridzeri (1741–1825), and the mysterious Nicolas Dezède (*c.*1740/5–1792), whose name was taken from the initials "D.Z." with which he signed his works. He was illegitimately born and may have been German. As we can see – and not to mention Grétry's Belgian birth – the quintessentially French genre of opéra-comique was illustrated, even more widely than the tragédie en musique had been, by non-French composers. Kohaut scored an early success with *Le serrurier* (1764). Martini's most notable work was *Henri IV, ou la bataille d'Ivry*. Staged in 1774 at the Hôtel de Bourgogne to celebrate the accession of Louis XVI, it was the first work to be labeled "drame lyrique" (its librettist, Barnabé Farmian Durosoy, was a strong believer in Diderot's theories). It climaxed on an instrumental interlude depicting the battle, including drums and cannon, with musketry optional.[7] Born blind, Fridzeri is remembered above all for *Les souliers mordorés, ou La cordonnière allemande* (1776). It was published under the two appellations "opéra bouffon" and "comédie lyrique," a further indication of the uncertainties early opéra-comique composers felt about labeling their works. Dezède's first work was the sentimental comedy *Julie*, on a libretto by the actor and playwright Jacques Boutet de Monvel (1745–1812). Its fame is attested by the fact that Mozart based a set of piano variations (K. 264) on the ariette "Lison dormait dans un bocage." Another Dezède work, *Blaise et Babet*, was the most popular opéra-comique of the 1780s.[8]

One major late eighteenth-century composer made a brief appearance in French opéra-comique history. François-Joseph Gossec (1734–1829)[9] was born in a part of Flanders that was then French and is now Belgian. Moving to Paris in 1751, he became attached, thanks to Rameau's recommendation, to La Pouplinière's private orchestra. His first opera, *Le Périgourdin*, was staged at the Prince de Conti's theater in 1761. At the Comédie-Italienne he presented five works between 1765 and 1769. The most notable was *Les pêcheurs* (1766), which recovered from a poor initial reception to be revived, in its revised form, for several decades.

Given the size of the pit at the Hôtel de Bourgogne, Opéra-Comique composers were limited to modest forces compared to the Opéra: in 1768 the orchestra comprised ten violins, two violas, three cellos, two double-basses, and six wind players (flute, oboe, two bassoons, two horns), with one of the string players doubling as percussionist.[10] The situation improved when the Comédie-Italienne moved into a new theater, designed by Jean-François Heurtier, in 1783. Inaugurated in the presence of Marie-Antoinette, the Salle Favart, as it became known, could accommodate an audience of 2,000 after it was remodeled in 1784. It stood where the current Opéra-Comique building (third on the site) stands. The orchestra could now include twelve violins and five cellos, while the number of flutes and oboes was increased to three each.[11]

The Comédie-Italienne troupe included several stars, whose gifts as singing actors contributed to the rise of the opéra-comique. Jean-Baptiste Clairval (1737–1795), one of the very few members of the old troupe retained in 1762, premiered many leading tenor roles, from Dorval in *On ne s'avise jamais de tout* to Blondel in *Richard Coeur-de-lion*. Officially labeled a tenor, Joseph Caillot (1732–1816) was evidently a high baritone of the kind later known as "baryton Martin."[12] He was praised by Garrick. François-Joseph Fétis notes that, though possessing a beautiful voice, he was more an actor than a singer.[13] Another survivor from the Opéra-Comique troupe, Jean-Louis Laruette (1731–1792), a composer as well as a singer, was the original Alberti in *Le peintre amoureux de son modèle*: the name "laruette" came to mean a particular kind of tenor cast in roles of fathers or older men. Similarly, the name "trial," after the Avignon-born tenor Antoine Trial (1736–1795), brother of the Opéra director, described another type associated with comic roles.[14] Last but not least, Louise-Rosalie Dugazon, born Lefèvre (1753–1821), who debuted as a dancer, became the leading female singer of her generation. Her name was later used to characterize both the kind of lyric and agile parts she sang in her youth and the mother roles she played in her mature years (*mère Dugazon*).

François-André Philidor

François-André Danican Philidor (1726–1795) came from a distinguished musical family. His father, in his mid-70s when his son was born (from a second marriage), had been the royal music librarian and his half-brother, who died when he was two, had founded the Concert Spirituel. As for François-André, he became internationally famous as a chess player and wrote an important treatise on the subject, published in 1749 in London, where he resided for several years.[15] His first work for the theater was at the Opéra-Comique, where he collaborated with Sedaine on the two La Fontaine-based one-acters *Blaise le savetier* and *L'huitre et les plaideurs*, both in 1759, and on *Le jardinier et son seigneur*, a witty piece of social satire, in 1761. That same year he produced his first full-fledged masterpiece, *Le maréchal ferrant*. The first act opens with the eponymous blacksmith, who moonlights as a surgeon, at work, Hans Sachs-like, banging on his anvil and singing in endearingly ungrammatical French ("J'ons courage" instead of "J'ai du courage"). He later gets drunk with the village coachman, who sings a picturesque aria about his own trade. Antoine-François Quétant's (1733–1823) slightly outrageous libretto is delightfully matched by the music. Philidor's chief librettist, Antoine-Alexandre-Henri Poinsinet (1735–1769), supplied the texts of three opéras-comiques: *Sancho Pança dans son île* (1762), another example of the vogue of *Don Quixote* in eighteenth-century France; *Le sorcier* (1764), whose plot recalls Rousseau's *Le devin du village*; and, especially, *Tom Jones* (1765). Henry Fielding's novel, which came out in 1749, had been immediately translated – adapted would be a better description – by Pierre-Antoine de La Place. Poinsinet managed the feat of condensing this long novel into three acts. Disappointed with the initial reception in 1765, Philidor had the libretto revised with Sedaine's help and the work became an international success. Its highlights are Squire Western's Act 1 horn-accompanied hunting aria ("D'un cerf dix cors"), which ends as a boisterous trio; Tom's graceful Act 2 ariette "Vous voulez que je vous oublie"; and the septet at the end of the same act, when Tom is banished from the house. Act 3 opens with an unaccompanied quartet, sung by patrons of Upton Hill, the first such a cappella ensemble in opera. The work ends with a "vaudeville" in the new sense of the word: a finale in which each character sings a short strophe, followed by a general refrain.[16]

Poinsinet also supplied the libretto of Philidor's tragédie lyrique *Ernelinde, princesse de Norvège*. After its lukewarm initial reception at the Opéra in 1767, Philidor revised it three times, the second one with the help of Sedaine, who expanded the original three acts into five. The unusual "Gothic" – more precisely Viking – subject had been treated more than once in Italian opera but was new to the French stage: Sandomir, prince of Denmark, and Ricimer, king of Sweden, vie for the hand of Ernelinde, daughter of Rodoald, king of Norway. Though it remains respectful of the traditional French form (including a final chaconne), Philidor's lyrical, openly Italianate style seems to anticipate Gluck in passages such as Ernelinde's plea on a six-part choral background in the second scene of Act 1, or the jailed Sandomir's monologue, sustained by the offstage chorus of fellow prisoners. Ernelinde's long "récitatif obligé" ("Où suis-je? Quel épais nuage") at the end of Act 2 was also an innovation, with its use of expressive orchestral interventions commenting on the heroine's despair. Decades later, Berlioz singled out the chorus "Jurons sur nos glaives sanglants" for its "terrible énergie."[17] Indeed Julian Rushton, in his preface to a recent reprint, calls *Ernelinde* "probably the most important work staged at the Paris Opéra between Rameau and Gluck."[18] The work's novelty was overshadowed by accusations of plagiarism: Philidor – an "engaging and somewhat naïve personality" according to Rushton – "cited" passages from Gluck, Jommelli, and others. These borrowings were quickly publicized by his enemies.[19] His other attempts at tragédie lyrique were not successful: *Persée* (1780) had a libretto adapted from Quinault by Marmontel; *Thémistocle*, premiered at Fontainebleau in 1785, went no further than three performances at the Opéra the following year. Nor did the remainder of Philidor's opéra-comique production match the success of his earlier work, with the exception of *Les femmes vengées* (1775), his last collaboration with Sedaine. He divided the rest of his life between Paris and London. Caught in the British capital when England and Revolutionary France were at war, he died there without being able to return to Paris.

Pierre-Alexandre Monsigny

Unlike Philidor, Pierre-Alexandre Monsigny (1729–1817) did not come from a musical background. He was from northern France, where he received his initial training before moving in 1749 to Paris, where he held a position in the household of the Duke of Orléans, a situation that compelled him to publish his works anonymously.[20] At the 1759 Foire Saint-Germain he presented an *intermède*, *Les aveux indiscrets*, based on La Fontaine like so many early opéras-comiques.[21] *Le cadi dupé* (1761), which combined original music and *timbres*, was set on the same libretto by Pierre-René Lemonnier (1731–1796) (after the *Arabian Nights*) as Gluck's Viennese version of the same year. It brought Monsigny to the attention of Sedaine, with whom he formed a long-lasting partnership, beginning with *On ne s'avise jamais de tout*, premiered at the 1761 Foire Saint-Laurent. Based on La Fontaine's tale after a medieval source, the plot is the proverbial story, familiar from the *Barber of Seville*, of the young lover resorting to several disguises to win the hand of a girl from her guardian and would-be suitor (a laruette part). Monsigny's music combines a sentimental strain (as in Dorval's opening ariette) with a comic verve which culminates in a buffo quartet, followed by an equally lively quintet. The work ends with a vaudeville, the refrain of which is the motto that serves as the opera's title. The opera's popularity was such that a court performance was immediately arranged. *Le roi et le fermier* (1762), three years before Philidor's *Tom Jones*, launched the fashion for opéras-comiques drawn from English literature – in this case Robert Dodsley's "dramatick tale" *The King and the Miller of Mansfield* (1737). Sedaine's libretto for this three-act "comédie mêlée de morceaux de musique" – a comedy remarkably devoid of comic elements – tones down the original, in which Jenny, the farmer's fiancée, is seduced by the aptly named courtier Lurewell. In his foreword to the published libretto, Sedaine also hints at the difficulties he encountered over putting a king on stage – even a medieval one (the action is supposedly set under Henry VI's reign in the fifteenth century).[22] Musically, the work is dominated by the scenes in the forest of "Chéroud" (Sedaine's rendering of Sherwood) at the beginning of Act 2, and by the Act 3 septet in the course of which the king's identity is revealed. Another original effect in Act 3 is the trio in which Jenny, Betsy, and the mother join their voices while actually singing three independent songs.

The one-act *Rose et Colas* (1764), by contrast, returns to the traditional world of village opéra-comique, as popular chansons alternate with more elaborate ariettes. The Rousseau-like moral of the final vaudeville is "Il faut seconder la nature/Puisqu'elle nous fait la loi." Two years later, Sedaine and Monsigny made a highly successful debut at the Opéra with *Aline, reine de Golconde*, with Sophie Arnould in the title role. The plot revolves around the love between Saint-Phar, French ambassador to the Indian kingdom of Golconda, and its queen, who appears to him disguised as a shepherdess. The work remained in the Opéra repertory until 1782, but Monsigny never composed for the Académie royale again.

Monsigny and Sedaine's longest-lasting triumph was *Le déserteur* in 1769. It was not labeled "comédie" but, significantly, "drame," in keeping with the darker elements of the plot. Inspired by a true story, it is a perfect illustration of Diderot's views on the theater. Alexis, the hero, deserts from the army after being the victim of a cruel, if improbable, practical joke – he witnesses the mock-wedding of his fiancée Louise and her semi-retarded cousin Bertrand.[23] Sentenced to death, he is rescued *in extremis* when Louise obtains his pardon from the king. The final tableau is an extended ensemble with chorus (an unusual feature of opéra-comique at the time, since the Comédie-Italienne had no permanent chorus) set in the public square where the execution is scheduled. The overture, based on the main theme of this finale ("Oublions jusqu'à la trace"), is the first of this kind in French operatic history. Alexis, a part premiered by Caillot, is a virtuoso high-baritone role requiring both vocal agility (trill included) and histrionic ability. It mixes pathos and burlesque elements – the latter involving Alexis's interaction with Montauciel, a fellow soldier, whose spelling difficulties are the subject of a bravura aria.[24]

Monsigny's collaboration with Sedaine, interrupted in 1773 when he set Favart's comédie-féerie *La belle Arsène*, resumed one last time in 1777 with *Félix, ou L'enfant trouvé*. Called "drame" like *Le déserteur*, the work anticipates many features of early nineteenth-century melodrama. When he retired from composition, partly because of declining eyesight, Monsigny was only 48 and had another 40 years to live. Fétis, who knew him, recalls his exceptional sensitivity, suggesting he occupied a position in operatic history similar to Greuze in the visual arts.[25]

André-Modeste Grétry

Though few of the operas of André-Modeste Grétry (1741–1813) are occasionally revived, his current reputation does no justice to his importance in French operatic history.[26] His native town of Liège, where his father was a professional violinist, was then an independent principality ruled by the city's bishop. He received his musical education there, then in Rome, where he spent the years 1760–66. Encouraged by Voltaire, he settled in Paris in 1767. The following year, the Comédie-Italienne premiered his two-act opéra-comique *Le Huron*, adapted by Marmontel from Voltaire's *L'Ingénu*. Published anonymously in 1767, this philosophical tale had been banned at once on religious and political grounds. As in *Candide* (the two titles convey one same message), Voltaire used a "naïve" hero to denounce political abuse and attack established religion. It was a bold choice for a subject, even though the libretto obviously had to expunge the tale's most controversial passages. Grétry's next work, *Lucile* (1769), also on a Marmontel libretto, is a sentimental comedy revolving around a social issue: the heroine's marriage to Dorval (the name of Diderot's *fils naturel*) is compromised when, on her wedding-day, she learns that she is not the daughter of a rich bourgeois but of a working-class man. The quartet "Où peut-on être mieux qu'au sein de sa famille?", sung at the dinner table by Lucile, her putative father, and her fiancé and his father, attained a proverbial celebrity.[27] Also in 1769, Grétry collaborated with Anseaume on *Le tableau parlant*, in which he showed that his gifts extended to farce: the elderly guardian, realizing that he is being duped, spies on the young lovers by introducing himself behind his portrait, with the face cut out. The work remained in the Opéra-Comique repertory until the 1860s.

Grétry returned to Marmontel, and to a sentimental and moral strain, with *Sylvain* (1770), adapted from Salomon Gessner's *Erast*: estranged from his father for having married below his class, the eponymous hero is reconciled with him after convincing him of his and his wife's goodness of heart. The couple's two young daughters also have sung parts. The piece was contemporary with Grétry's affair with Jeanne-Marie Grandon and preceded the birth of their daughter Jenny; another daughter, Lucile (1772–1790), became a composer and collaborated with her father on two operas (one of them a sequel to his *Richard Coeur-de-lion*).[28]

A token of Grétry's high standing, two of his operas were premiered at Fontainebleau during the festivities marking the wedding of the future Louis XVI and Marie-Antoinette in 1770: the opéra bouffon *Les deux avares* and the "comédie mêlée d'ariettes" *L'amitié à l'épreuve*, the latter, dedicated to the new Dauphine, on a Favart libretto. Several of Grétry's next operas also received a court premiere: *L'ami de la maison* and *Zémire et Azor*, both on Marmontel libretti (1771), the sentimental pastoral *La rosière de Salency* (1773), and, also in 1773, the ballet héroïque *Céphale et Procris, ou L'amour conjugal* (the subject previously treated by Élisabeth de La Guerre), given at Versailles in honor of the wedding of the Comte d'Artois (later Charles X). On her accession as queen in 1774, Marie-Antoinette appointed Grétry her private music director. By then he had become the leading French opéra-comique composer.[29]

The comédie-ballet *Zémire et Azor*, drawn by Marmontel from Jeanne-Marie Leprince de Beaumont's "Beauty and the Beast" tale (but borrowing the names Zémire and Azor from Nivelle de la Chaussée's play *Amour pour amour*), was also influenced by Favart and Duni's popular fairy opera *La fée Urgèle*, as David Charlton has pointed out.[30] The action is reset in Persia, where the rich merchant Sander and his Papageno-like slave Ali, shipwrecked – the storm is pictured in the overture, leading directly into the opera – find refuge in the palace of Azor, a prince once changed into a beast by an evil fairy. Having angered Azor, Sander offers one of his daughters in exchange for his life. Zémire, the youngest, sacrifices herself, and, through her love, rescues Azor from the spell. The work's most celebrated moment occurs in Act 3, when the captive Zémire, thanks to Azor's magic power, is able to see her despairing father and sisters, despite the distance, in a "magic picture"; an offstage wind sextet underlines the supernatural effect. Another delicate musical intervention occurs in Act 4, set in Azor's wild garden, when Zémire's distant calls are accompanied by offstage horns and flutes. Vocally, the opera offers more variety than any of Grétry's previous works, as soft, tender passages alternate with Italianate virtuoso displays, such as the "Fauvette" aria Zémire sings to Azor in Act 3. Dedicated to Louis XV's last mistress, the Comtesse du Barry, *Zémire* became extremely popular in France and internationally and was regularly revived until the 1860s.[31]

Relations between Grétry and Marmontel cooled off after *Céphale et Procris*. They collaborated only once more in *La fausse magie* (1775). An even more fruitful partnership began between Grétry and Sedaine with *Le Magnifique* (1773), based on a play by La Motte after La Fontaine. Set in Renaissance Florence, the work opens with a programmatic overture describing a procession of captives whom the heroine and her governess are watching. It quotes the popular tune "Vive Henri IV" and also includes an extraordinary irruption of offstage trumpets.[32]

The two medieval works that Grétry composed to Sedaine texts occupy a prominent position in his oeuvre. *Aucassin et Nicolette* (1779) was inspired by a popular thirteenth-century tale revolving around the hidden identity of the heroine, deemed by Aucassin's father unworthy of marrying his son until she turns out to be of noble origin. Grétry imbued his music with what he himself calls a "Gothic" flavor to match the deliberate archaisms of Sedaine's verse. As the composer recalls in his memoirs, this attempt to evoke a distant past, beginning with the overture, which depicts a battle, was found ludicrous at the court premiere. The first Paris performances in 1780, featuring Dugazon as Nicolette, were not an unequivocal success either. Sedaine and Grétry recast the work from four into three acts, but this landmark in musical antiquarianism never became one of Grétry's most popular works.

Richard Coeur-de-lion, conversely, triumphed in 1784 at the Salle Favart (the new home of the Comédie-Italienne), becoming among Grétry's most widely staged operas: it totaled more than a thousand Parisian performances by the end of the nineteenth century, but was eclipsed during the Revolution when its royalist theme made it unpopular – even though its theme recalls the so-called "rescue plays" in vogue at that time. Rather than relying on uniform musical archaism as *Aucassin* does, it modulates the style from character to character: the imprisoned Richard the Lionheart and his beloved Marguerite, Countess of Flanders, thus sound more "modern" than Richard's squire Blondel, disguised as a blind troubadour, while the peasants' words and music are in a more popular idiom (as in the onomatopeic song "Eh zig, et zog, eh fric et froc . . ."). More remarkably, *Richard Coeur-de-lion* was the first opera to be based on a recurring musical theme, in other words a leitmotif. The song "Une fièvre brûlante," supposedly composed by Richard for Marguerite, is heard no fewer than nine times throughout the work. It functions as a symbol, both in the original Greek sense – a sign of recognition – and, in the modern sense, a musical representation of Richard's and Marguerite's love. Decades before Richard Wagner, a French opéra-comique was thus based on a musical cell functioning, in Grétry's own words, as "the pivot around which the whole play revolves."[33]

Other than Marmontel and Sedaine, Grétry's most significant collaborator as librettist was Thomas Hales (*c*.1741–1780), an Englishman (or possibly Irishman) who settled in Paris and gallicized his last name as "d'Hèle." The mythological comedy *Le jugement de Midas*, premiered at the Comédie-Italienne in 1778, develops into a musical parody, which, as David Charlton points out, anticipates Wagner's *Die Meistersinger*: like Beckmesser, Apollo's antagonists, Pan and Marsias, express themselves in an immediately recognizable old-fashioned style (that of baroque recitative), aping the mannered kind of singing in fashion at the Opéra.[34] Premiered at Versailles, also in 1778, *L'amant jaloux* was adapted by Hales from Susanna Centlivre's popular 1714 comedy *The Wonder: A Woman Keeps a Secret*. With its extended finales, which have been compared to the ones in Acts 2 and 4 of Mozart's *Le nozze di Figaro*.[35] In *Les événements imprévus* (1779), Hales's third and last libretto, the tone of moral and social satire is more pronounced – Charlton suggests a parallel with the Marquis de Sade and Choderlos de Laclos' near-contemporary *Liaisons dangereuses* (1782).[36] Clairval, the star tenor of the Comédie-Italienne, where he was the original Blondel, was cast this time as a rake who seduced and abandoned a Countess by borrowing a friend's identity.

Grétry's career was not one of uninterrupted successes. Set in ancient Greece, the "drame lyrique" *Les mariages samnites*, adapted by Durosoy from Marmontel (1776), did well in the provinces but was poorly received in Paris.[37] A tragédie lyrique, *Andromaque*, premiered at the Opéra in 1780, got Grétry into trouble with the Comédie-Française, which tried to block it, since Louis-Guillaume Pitra's (1736–1818) libretto reused lines from Racine's tragedy. Despite a new third act, it was not revived after 1781. It was Grétry's first attempt – before *Richard Coeur-de-lion* – to give each of the principal characters a musical "signature." The mythological comedy *L'embarras des richesses*, whose hero is Plutus, god of wealth, failed in 1782. Grétry's only undisputed triumph at the Académie royale was, in fact, the orientalist opéra-ballet *La caravane du Caire* in 1784, which remained in the repertory well into the following century.[38] According to a well-established tradition – uncorroborated by Grétry's memoirs, written during the Revolution and by necessity prudent on such topics – the Comte de Provence (Louis XVI's brother and the future Louis XVIII) had a hand in the libretto. The plot centers on the love between two captives, the Frenchman Saint-Phar (the same name as the hero of Monsigny's *Aline*) and the Indian-born Zéline. Onstage camels figured in Act 1, while the Act 2 divertissement, capped by a brilliant coloratura Italian ariette, is set in the Cairo bazaar. Grétry may have benefited from the same royal collaboration for the "comédie lyrique" *Panurge dans l'île des lanternes* (1785), the first opera based, albeit loosely, on François Rabelais. According to the composer, it was the first French comic work to enter the Opéra repertory – a puzzling claim, since *Platée* and *Les amours de Ragonde* had long been part of it. Another comedy, *Amphitryon*, adapted by Sedaine from Molière's mythological play, flopped at the Opéra in 1788 after failing to please the court two years before.

Yet Grétry could also transform failure into success. Thus *L'épreuve villageoise* (1784), a reworking of the poorly received *Théodore et Paulin*, was still in the Opéra-Comique repertory in the late 1880s. A peasant comedy in the tradition of Rousseau and Grétry's own *Rosière de Salency*, its language contrasts the popular, ungrammatical diction of the rural lower classes – Denise, the heroine, is illiterate – with the "correct" language spoken by the city fop La France, whose attempts to woo her are ultimately foiled.

Two other notable works that Grétry presented at the Comédie-Italienne before the Revolution are *Le comte d'Albert* and *Raoul Barbe-bleue*. The former, premiered at Fontainebleau in 1787, was dedicated to the court painter Élisabeth Vigée-Lebrun. It is unusually structured: Acts 1 and 2 deal with the count's unjust arrest and imprisonment, followed by his escape arranged by a working man whose life he had saved. The third and last act, set on his estate near Brussels after his return, is so different in tone that Sedaine treated it as an independent work entitled *Suite du comte d'Albert*. The main character is the countess, a part premiered by Dugazon, by then specializing in roles of mothers. She also starred, a mere four months before the fall of the Bastille, as Isaure in *Raoul Barbe-bleue*, adapted by Sedaine from Charles Perrault's famous 1698 tale. The brutality of the subject appalled some contemporary critics, one of whom pointed out that tragedy was "forbidden at the Théâtre Italien."[39] Sedaine's libretto is, in fact, one of his strongest, and Grétry's music matches it in vigor. One of its inventive twists is the reappearance in Act 2 of Isaure's former fiancé Vergy – a tenor role – in women's clothes, as he pretends to be her sister Anne. The score's finest moment is the Act 3 trio, "Vergy, ma soeur," in which Isaure anxiously asks the disguised young man whether help is on its way, while Blue-Beard's offstage voice orders her into the secret room where he is ready to execute her.

In its abundance and variety, Grétry's operatic career before 1789 was unparalleled in the history of French opera. Even if the Revolution, as we shall see, affected his later production in diverse ways, he had by then made an irreplaceable contribution to opéra-comique.

Christoph Willibald Gluck and French opera

The involvement of Christoph Willibald Gluck (1714–1787) with French opera preceded his Parisian years of 1774–9 by nearly two decades.[40] From 1758 to 1764 he was music director of the French theater in Vienna, which had been in operation at the Burgtheater since 1752 and remained active until the death of Emperor Francis I, Maria Theresa's husband, in 1765.[41] Their repertory included opéra-comique, especially after the Genoese Count Giacomo Durazzo became superintendent of Viennese theaters in 1754. Gluck's first contributions, in 1758, were two vaudeville comedies by Anseaume, *La fausse esclave* and *L'île de Merlin*. The first combined original numbers and arrangements, but the second was entirely original. *Le diable à quatre* (1759), on the Sedaine text, mixed arrangements of pre-existing tunes and new music, including a "snuff aria" quoted by Josef Haydn in his contemporary Symphony no. 8 ("Le Soir").[42] *Cythère assiégée* (1759) was adapted from *Le pouvoir de l'amour, ou Le siège de Cythère*, Favart's parody of Lully's *Armide*. In 1760 Gluck composed music for two La Fontaine-based opéras-comiques, Vadé's *L'arbre enchanté* and Anseaume's *L'ivrogne corrigé*, his most ambitious French-language work to date. *Le cadi dupé* (1761) was composed within months of Monsigny's. The Baghdad setting of Lemonnier's play prompted Gluck to introduce local color through the use of "Turkish" percussion. This was also the case of his eighth and last opéra-comique for Vienna, *La rencontre imprévue* (1764). Its original libretto by the actor-playwright Louis Hurtaut Dancourt was an adaptation from Lesage and d'Orneval's *Les pèlerins de la Mecque* – a title Dancourt and Gluck had initially retained. The plot, set in Cairo, ends with an act of clemency that recalls Mozart's *Die Entführung aus dem Serail*, though here, as Bruce Alan Brown has noted, the beneficiaries, Rezia and Ali, are Muslims not Christians.[43] The work also features a ridiculous character, a French painter called Vertigo. It enjoyed considerable success, in Vienna and beyond, and its libretto, in an Italian adaptation, was reset by Haydn as *L'incontro improvviso* in 1775.[44]

By 1762 Gluck and his librettist Ranieri de' Calzabigi (1714–1795), partnered by the choreographer Gasparo Angiolini, had also launched his reform of Italian opera with *Orfeo ed Euridice*. Against the artificiality of opera seria, they advocated simpler vocal lines and greater theatrical urgency and authenticity. Exceptionally for a non-French work, the full score of *Orfeo*, through Favart's agency, was published in 1764 in Paris, where it was shown to Duni, Mondonville, and Philidor (the last named making "creative use" of one passage in *Le sorcier*).[45] There may have been plans to have it staged in the French capital, but they were thwarted by the fire of the Palais-Royal theater.

Following the ecstatic reception of Gluck's second "reform opera," *Alceste* (1767), and despite the lukewarm reaction to its successor, *Paride ed Elena* (1770), Gluck was approached by a French diplomat posted in Vienna, François Leblanc Du Roullet (1716–1786), who offered him his libretto based on Racine's *Iphigénie en Aulide* (1674). Unlike Iphigenia in Tauris, the subject had never been treated in a tragédie en musique. Diderot, for one, had singled it out as ideally suited for operatic purposes. So had Francesco Algarotti, whose *Saggio sopra l'opera in musica* (1755) advocated some of the principles illustrated by Gluck's reform: Algarotti's treatise even included a prose synopsis for a hypothetical operatic treatment. According to Burney, who visited Gluck in Vienna at the time, the work was completed by September 1772. Du Roullet had already entered into negotiations with the Opéra, headed since 1763 by Dauvergne, via an open letter which appeared in the *Mercure de France*.[46] Gluck, whose flair for publicity was acute, entered the debate with a letter published in the same periodical. Citing Rousseau's critique of the tragédie en musique, he suggested that the great man might help him achieve his objective, which was "to do away with the ridiculous differentiation between national musical styles" (i.e. the French and the Italian) by:

> seeking a type of melody which is noble, expressive, and natural, and declaimed exactly according to the prosody of each language and the character of each nation.[47]

Gluck also sought the protection of Marie-Antoinette, who had taken harpsichord and singing lessons with him in Vienna. Faced with this well-orchestrated public relations campaign, Dauvergne accepted *Iphigénie*, provided Gluck write six more operas for Paris.

Gluck arrived in Paris in late 1773. Despite much-publicized stormy rehearsals, pitting the Bohemian composer against librettist, singers, and orchestra, the premiere, on 19 April 1774, in the presence of the Dauphin and the Dauphine, was a triumph.[48] "You have brought about that which up to this moment I thought impossible," wrote Rousseau to the author.[49] In keeping with Gluck's stated intentions, *Iphigénie* was seen by the philosophical camp as an ideal synthesis between the tragic grandeur the subject demanded and the natural style of declamation they had been advocating. It respected many of the conventions of French opera, including a lengthy divertissement in Act 2. There are still "little airs" in the French style, mixed with virtuoso Italianate ariettes. The work's summits, however, are the two great monologues for Agamemnon: the first at the beginning of Act 1 (its opening repeating the music heard at the start of the overture), the second at the end of Act 2.

The death of Louis XV in May 1774 closed the theaters, interrupting *Iphigénie* after five performances. Gluck's next Parisian opera, which opened in August, was a French adaptation of *Orfeo* as *Orphée et Eurydice*.[50] Castrati being unwelcome on French stages, the title role was rewritten for a tenor.[51] Its mercilessly high tessitura, tailored for Joseph Legros, who had sung Achille in *Iphigénie*, and taking the voice to C and even D (in "Laissez-vous toucher" in Act 2), has been detrimental to the work's fortunes in recent times.[52] In concession to the French taste for Italian virtuosity, Act 1 ended with a florid aria, "L'espoir renaît dans mon âme," which Gluck was subsequently accused of having lifted from Ferdinando Bertoni's 1767 *Ifigenia in Tauride*.[53] Among the new passages were the trio "Tendre amour" in the last scene (recycling music from *Paride*) and additional dance numbers, notably the D minor section, with flute solo, of the "Dance of the Blessed Spirits" and the extended chaconne that, in the manner of Lully and Rameau, concludes the work. Changes were also made in the orchestration, with a more prominent role given to wind instruments. The public reception was enthusiastic – Rousseau once again expressed his admiration[54] – and Gluck considered settling permanently in Paris. Yet no offer of a position came from the Opéra or court.

Having returned briefly to Vienna, Gluck presented a revised version of *Iphigénie en Aulide* in January 1775, which modified the denouement. Du Roullet's libretto departed from Racine by eliminating the character of Ériphile (Racine's invention), whose suicide at the end turned out to be a divinely acceptable substitute for Iphigenia's sacrifice. Without her, the gods' sudden change of heart at the end of the opera had been found too abrupt by critics. In 1775 it was clarified by an apparition of Diana. Other changes were made in the divertissement, which had also been criticized.[55]

While Gluck had returned to Vienna, where he fell ill, *Cythère assiégée*, a reworking of his 1759 opéra-comique into an opéra-ballet, got a poor response in August 1775. He was back in Paris in the spring of 1776 and the French version of *Alceste* was unveiled on 23 April, with Marie-Antoinette and the king's brothers in attendance; the event followed by two days the death, in Vienna, of the composer's beloved niece Nanette. The third act was criticized and Gluck and Du Roullet, author of the French text, recast it at once, adding the character of Hercules, as in Euripides as well as in Lully's tragédie en musique on the same subject. Despite the revision, *Alceste* provoked controversy (as Lully's own *Alceste* had a century before), though it gradually recovered to become one of Gluck's most admired works.

Summarizing the many changes between the Viennese and Parisian versions of *Alceste* cannot be adequately attempted within the scope of this book.[56] They are essentially two different operas, and it would be pointless to try to establish a "hybrid" text, as has traditionally been done with *Orfeo/Orphée*. Act 1 is recognizably the same – a long mourning ceremony while Admetus is dying, leading to Alcestis's resolution to sacrifice herself to save his life – though significantly abridged in the Paris version. Evander, Admetus's confidant, loses most of his music, and Ismene, who had a scene with him at the end of the act, disappears altogether. The act now concludes with Alcestis's aria "Divinités du Styx" (where the relation between words and accompaniment is also considerably altered). Act 2, which in Vienna began with a long scene where Alcestis confronted the gods of the underworld, now took place entirely in Admetus's palace. The divertissement, which in the Viennese version did not involve Alcestis's presence, takes on an unusual ironic dimension: Admetus is blissfully unaware of the reason for his recovery and Alcestis knows she is doomed. The end of the act is based on the same music as the Italian version, but with extensive cuts. As for the new Act 3, it is in three tableaux, the middle one, set at the entrance to the underworld, based on music from Act 2 in the Viennese *Alceste*, but with important modifications. A long divertissement concludes the Paris version; three of its six numbers (but not the final chaconne) were composed, or at least arranged, by Gossec.

Inevitably, the acclaim Gluck won at the Opéra aroused jealousy. Even before the *Iphigénie* premiere, the Comtesse du Barry, who disliked Marie-Antoinette, had sided with the opposition. In 1776 Gluck was invited to compose a *Roland*, based on Quinault's libretto like the *Armide* on which he was already working. Hearing that Niccolò Piccinni had been approached with a similar proposal, he publicly withdrew. The anti-Gluck camp was headed by Marmontel, an ardent partisan of Italian opera, who in 1777 issued his *Essai sur les révolutions de la musique en France*, and by the Neapolitan ambassador Domenico Carraccioli. *Armide*, premiered in September 1777, provided new fodder for controversy, which actually helped the work recover from an initially cool reception. Set on Quinault's text (minus the prologue), with few alterations, it incorporates music from earlier works by Gluck, notably *Telemaco* (1765), which features Circe, mythological forerunner of Armida, and from even earlier *opere serie* and opéras-comiques: thus the encounter with Hatred in Act 3 borrows music from *L'ivrogne corrigé*.[57] This composite character notwithstanding, *Armide* contains many powerful passages, such as the vengeful chorus of the Damascenes at the end of Act 1 and the monologues of Armida in Act 2 and Act 5. In the former ("Enfin, il est en ma puissance"), Gluck had to measure himself against one of Lully's most admired passages, producing a "récitatif obligé" where the expressive orchestral commentary denies the heroine's hate-filled words. In fact the Kundry-like figure of Armida[58] stands next to Alcestis and the Tauris Iphigenia among Gluck's great female roles.

After attending the premiere of Piccinni's *Roland* in 1778, Gluck (who seems to have borne his rival no grudge) returned to Vienna to work on his next and, in the event, final two operas, *Iphigénie en Tauride* and *Écho et Narcisse*. *Iphigénie* had been projected with Du Roullet, but the libretto Gluck had projected this second Iphigénie with Du Roullet as early as the mid-1770s, but one libretto he eventually set was by Nicolas-François Guillard (1752–1814). Unbeknownst to him the new director of the Opéra,

Anne-Pierre-Jacques de Vismes, hoping to generate publicity, offered Piccinni a different libretto on the same subject – the common source, rather than Euripides, being a 1757 tragedy by Claude Guymond de La Touche – even promising the Italian composer that his opera would be mounted before Gluck's. As it turned out, Gluck was ready long before Piccinni. Rehearsed amidst considerable excitement, *Iphigénie en Tauride* was premiered, on 18 May 1779, in the queen's presence. From the outset it received unqualified approbation.

Generally considered Gluck's finest achievement, *Iphigénie en Tauride* recycled music from previous works – like *Armide*, if to a lesser extent. The prelude depicting a storm, which leads directly into the opera, was thus adapted from *L'île de Merlin*. Even Iphigenia's Act 2 lament, "Ô malheureuse Iphigénie" – one of the work's most stirring moments – derives from Sesto's aria in Gluck's Neapolitan opera seria of 1752, *La clemenza di Tito*. Yet Gluck, who evidently had a hand in fashioning the libretto,[59] achieved possibly a closer rapport between words and music than ever before. Among the work's most discussed and admired passages is the Act 2 monologue, especially the moment when the palpitating, syncopated viola figuration contradicts Orestes's words of self-reassurance: "Le calme rentre dans mon coeur!"[60] Departing from the sacrosanct French tradition, *Iphigénie en Tauride* dispensed with the obligatory divertissement: whereas Act 1 contains two brief dances for the Scythians, the apparition of the Furies in Act 2 is fully integrated into the play – a pantomime rather than a divertissement, along the lines of the "ballet figuré" advocated by Cahusac.

Écho et Narcisse, a "drame lyrique" based on Ovid's *Metamorphoses* by a new librettist, the Metz-born Baron Ludwig Theodor von Tschudi (1734–1784), lasted only 12 performances at the Opéra in the autumn of 1779. The libretto, especially, was found lacking in dramatic interest. The piece itself, a step back compared to *Iphigénie en Tauride*, seemed to retreat into the old-fashioned world of the pastorale héroïque. Gluck suffered a stroke during rehearsals and returned to Vienna in October. Despite revisions, the work had only five more performances in 1780, though it was favorably received when staged in a smaller theater the following year. Sporadic attempts were made to revive it in the early nineteenth century, but its reputation has never matched that of Gluck's other Parisian operas.[61]

Though remaining in touch with his Parisian contacts over operatic matters, Gluck never returned to the French capital, nor did he forgive the Opéra for what he thought was a constant atmosphere of cabal around his works. He spent his remaining years in Vienna, where he died on 15 November 1787 after a final stroke.[62]

Gluck's influence on French opera was enormous and could be felt throughout the nineteenth century. Instinctively a man of the theater, he was not, paradoxically, a gifted linguist. His native language was Czech and, according to contemporary testimonies, his German, Italian, and French were not pedantically correct.[63] Yet he could set a French text as eloquently as any of his predecessors and he rejuvenated the moribund tragédie lyrique. By another paradox, this non-French composer, who grew out of the world of *opera seria*, came to be gradually identified as a representative of the grand French tradition, free from Italian influence, that ran from Lully to Berlioz.

Niccolò Piccinni

Piccinni was not Gluck's only foreign competitor in the French capital. Vismes, the enterprising Opéra director, commissioned a French work in the summer of 1778 from Johann Christian Bach (1735–1782), Johann Sebastian's youngest son. It was yet another remake of Lully, *Amadis*, pruned by Vismes's own brother down to three acts. Johann Christian Bach visited Paris, where he saw Mozart one last time, in August 1778, and returned one year later to supervise the preparations. Premiered in late December, with Legros and Rosalie Levasseur in the title roles, *Amadis de Gaule* only lasted seven performances, in spite – or perhaps because – of its musical refinement.[64] There was apparently no room for a third man in the well-publicized "war" between Gluckists and Piccinists.

Niccolò Piccinni (1728–1800), who came from Bari, belonged to a family of musicians (he was Gaetano Latilla's nephew).[65] After studying at the Naples Conservatory, he began his career as an opera buffa composer. *La bona figluola* (1760), based on Goldoni's play previously set by Duni, established his reputation. He was enormously prolific, both in the buffo and the seria genre,[66] but his popularity was beginning to decline when ambassador Carraccioli recommended him in 1774 as a possible rival to Gluck. Arriving in Paris on 31 December 1776, without speaking French, Piccinni is reputed to have exclaimed (presumably in Italian) "Does the sun ever shine in this country?"[67] Coached by his librettist, Marmontel, Piccinni set to work on the tragédie lyrique *Roland*, loosely adapted from Quinault but reduced to three acts. Premiered in February 1778, the work, almost to the composer's surprise, became a big hit (Mozart, then in Paris, heard it). Like Gluck's *Iphigénie* and *Orphée*, but with less theatrical urgency and more emphasis on lyricism, it offered an attractive compromise between traditional French dramaturgy and a modern, Italianate musical idiom. The three demanding leading roles were taken by the singers who sang Gluck's *Iphigénie en Tauride* the following year: Levasseur as Angélique; Legros in the high-lying, florid part of Médor; and, as Roland (who gets a bravura mad scene in Act 3), the baritone Henri Larrivée, the Agamemnon in *Iphigénie en Aulide*.[68]

Vismes had taken the opportunity of Piccinni's presence to mount Italian works for the first time since the Bouffons' visit in 1752–4. Thus, *opere buffe* by Anfossi, Sacchini, Traetta, Paisiello, Salieri, Galuppi, and Piccinni himself were successfully staged under the composer's supervision.[69] It was also Vismes who tricked Piccinni into competing with Gluck on an *Iphigénie en Tauride*. Meanwhile, Piccinni's second tragédie lyrique, *Atys*, was also adapted from Quinault by Marmontel, who, as in *Roland*, cut it down to three acts. The absence of the Dream Scene, the highlight of Lully's work, typifies the evolution of taste since the baroque age. By contrast, the most memorable passage in Piccinni's work is the Act 3 quartet for Cybele, Atys, Sangaride, and Coelenus. Not as successful as *Roland* – Marmontel was compared unfavorably with Quinault – *Atys* is rated more highly by modern scholars.[70] A happy ending was introduced at the 1783 revival.

When Piccinni's *Iphigénie en Tauride* was finally mounted in January 1781, it suffered from the parallel with Gluck.[71] Like Goethe in his *Iphigenia auf Tauris*, Alphonse Ducongé Dubreuil's (1734–1801) libretto introduces a new twist with Thoas's plans to marry Iphigenia; superficially similar to Guillard's libretto in other respects, it is inferior in dramatic intensity; accordingly, despite beautiful moments, such as the Act 3 trio, the music lacks tension. With Larrivée and Legros as the male principals, the work had an honorable reception but was dropped from the repertory after 1790.[72]

Piccini's reputation was by now secure in France. His *Adèle de Ponthieu* (a subject previously treated by Berton) opened the new Opéra in October 1781. Built in less than three months by the architect Lenoir, on a site near the Porte Saint-Martin previously used by the Opéra as a warehouse, the new theater replaced the second Palais-Royal theater, which a fire had destroyed in June. Piccinni also had three opéras-comiques performed at the Salle Favart: *Le dormeur éveillé* (1783), with Marmontel, and *Le faux lord* (1783) and *Lucette* (1784), both to libretti by his son Giuseppe.

Piccinni's greatest success, *Didon*, was premiered at Fontainebleau in October 1783 and at the Opéra on 1 December. By 1826 it had received 250 performances in that theater.[73] Unlike *Roland* and *Atys*, Marmontel's libretto was independently drawn from Virgil and bore no relation to the one Mme de Saintonge provided Desmarets for his 1693 tragédie en musique. It is also very different from Berlioz's later version: Aeneas's decision to leave for Italy, made early in the second act, is treacherously revealed to Dido by Iarbe (Iarbal), a character mentioned but not present in *Les Troyens*. As Dido, the soprano Antoinette-Cécile de Saint-Huberty made a powerful impression.

Success deserted Piccinni after *Didon*. Both *Diane et Endymion* (1784) and *Pénélope* (1785), the latter on a Marmontel libretto and with Saint-Huberty in the title role, were tepidly received. The Revolution put Piccinni in a difficult financial situation. He returned to Italy, first to Naples, then to Venice, where he was placed under house arrest in 1794 because of his daughter's marriage to a Jacobin. Recalled to Paris by Bonaparte and appointed inspector at the recently created Conservatoire in 1800, he died in the same year.

Because of Piccinni's half-hearted involvement in an artistic polemic from which Gluck emerged victorious, his contribution to French opera has been unjustly neglected. Once the dust had settled, as Berlioz perspicaciously noted, one could see that the two composers were more similar than dissimilar in their approaches.[74]

Antonio Salieri

Antonio Salieri (1750–1825) played in French opera a brief part that reveals another side of the theatrical mores of the period.[75] Brought from his native Veneto to Vienna in 1766, he had become a friend and disciple of Gluck. At the age of 24 he was appointed head of the Italian theater in the imperial city; four years later his *Europa riconosciuta* inaugurated the newly built Scala opera house. In 1782 Gluck, toying in his retirement with the idea of returning to Paris, turned his attention again to an abandoned project, a tragédie lyrique on a libretto by his collaborators Du Roullet and Tschudi, adapted from an earlier libretto by Calzabigi, *Ipermestra o Le Danaidi*. Tired and in poor health, Gluck, without withdrawing his name, entrusted Salieri with the composition of *Les Danaïdes*. The suspicious Opéra directorate accepted the work only after pressure from Emperor Joseph II, Salieri's protector, and possibly from the emperor's sister Marie-Antoinette as well, and on the assurance that the opera was mostly by Gluck. This claim was maintained until after the premiere in April 1784, following which an indignant Calzabigi protested at not being properly credited as author of the libretto. Gluck then published a statement to the effect that the music had been composed by Salieri, who confirmed it while acknowledging Gluck as an "inspiration." The truth seems to be that Salieri, in John A. Rice's words, had begun the work "not as composer but as Gluck's amanuensis," and only misgivings about his disciple's abilities had dissuaded the Bohemian composer from acknowledging at least partial authorship of the work.[76]

Set in five acts, somewhat unusually for a late eighteenth-century tragédie lyrique, *Les Danaïdes* is based on one of the most gruesome episodes of Greek mythology, already set by several Italian composers and, in France, by Gervais: the wedding-night massacre of the 50 sons of Aegyptus by their wives, daughters of Aegyptus's brother and enemy Danaus. Separating herself from her sisters, Hypermnestra spares her beloved Lynceus. The feigned reconciliation at the beginning and ensuing wedding ceremony provide opportunities for choruses and divertissement, but the climax of Salieri's work is the final tableau, showing the Danaids and their father being tortured in Hell. From the overture, in which festive sounds are interrupted by gloomy premonitions, to the final scene, Salieri makes full use of the large orchestral forces he had at his disposal, with expressive use of trombones, trumpets, and timpani. Premiered with Larrivée as Danaus and Saint-Huberty as Hypermnestra, the work achieved more than 125 performances until it was dropped from the repertory in the late 1820s. It impressed Berlioz when he saw it on his first evening at the Opéra in 1822.[77] It also fascinates Honoré de Balzac's character Lucien de

Rubempré on *his* first night at the Opéra in *Illusions perdues*, which is set at about the same time.[78]

Salieri was rewarded for the success of *Les Danaïdes* with two commissions. The first, *Les Horaces*, was adapted by Guillard, Gluck's collaborator for *Iphigénie en Tauride*, from Corneille's tragedy. A dismal failure, it disappeared from the repertory after three performances in December 1786. The second, *Tarare*, had Beaumarchais, no less, as a librettist. The playwright had intended *Le barbier de Séville* as an opéra-comique, and his *Mariage de Figaro* (which Mozart and Da Ponte set to music within three years of its 1784 premiere) contained songs and ended with a vaudeville. *Tarare*, however, was his first and only opera libretto proper. He prefaced it with a manifesto entitled "Aux abonnés de l'Opéra qui voudraient aimer l'opéra." It is both a critique of opera libretti and a plea for the restoration of the primacy of the "poem" vis-à-vis the music (contrary to Salieri's own *Prima la musica, e poi le parole*, staged in Vienna in 1786). Beaumarchais also advocated oriental subjects in preference to mythological or historical ones. Drawn accordingly (without acknowledgment) from James Ridley's *Tales of the Genii* (1764), *Tarare* is set in Ormus on the Persian Gulf. The kingdom – where, oddly, Hinduism appears to be the religion – is ruled by the evil sultan Atar, a quasi-anagram of the hero's name. Tarare himself – his name a nonsense word which may also bear a connotation with Everyman – is, by contrast, the person-ification of virtue. Atar and Tarare's rivalry over Astasie, whom Atar has abducted, ends with the tyrant's suicide, after a final confrontation with strongly phrased lines about kings not being above the law. A lighter element is provided by the chief eunuch, Calpigi, presented as a castrato "trained in the chapels of Italy," while his wife Spinette is a Neapolitan prima donna.[79] The work, as if to advocate a return to Quinault, opens with an allegorical prologue featuring Nature and the genius of Fire, who both reappear at the end of the work. Salieri's music combines oriental color with the same kind of orchestral splendor he had displayed in *Les Danaïdes*, notably in the Act 3 divertissement, a "fête européenne." Beaumarchais' direct involvement in the musical side is apparent from the (then) unusual expressive directions to the singers printed in the score, which tend to emphasize simplicity and variety in the declamation.[80]

Thanks to Beaumarchais' sense of publicity, *Tarare* opened to much public excitement in June 1787. Like *Les Danaïdes*, it earned a respectable place in the repertory through the 1820s. Salieri reworked *Tarare* with Da Ponte into an Italian *dramma tragicomico*, *Axur re d'Ormus*, which was premiered in Vienna in January 1788 and subsequently performed all over Europe.[81] The Revolution had ended Salieri's career as a French opera composer.

Antonio Sacchini

Like Piccinni, the Florentine Antonio Sacchini (1730–1786) was trained at the Naples Conservatory. Like him, he achieved prominence both in the comic and the serious genre. His opera seria *Olimpiade*, on a libretto by Pietro Metastasio (1698–1782), was ecstatically received in 1763. Brought to London in 1772, he was highly in favor at first but his reputation had declined by the time he moved to Paris in 1781.[82] Initially well received there by the Piccinist clan, he was recommended to the Opéra by Marie-Antoinette, who, while protecting Gluck, was artistically open-minded and appears to have been genuinely fond of Italian opera. Sacchini's first tragédie lyrique, *Renaud*, modeled by its librettist Jean-Joseph Le Boeuf (1730?–1799?) on Pellegrin and Desmarets's 1722 work, and reusing music from Sacchini's own *Rinaldo* (1780), failed in February 1781, largely, it seems, because of a cabal from the Piccinists, who now viewed Sacchini as a dangerous rival. *Chimène*, Sacchini's next work, was adapted by Guillard from Corneille's classic *Le Cid*, a subject new to the French operatic stage, though treated several times in Italian opera, once by Sacchini himself.[83] Premiered at Fontainebleau in November 1783, a month after Piccinni's *Didon*, it remained in the Opéra repertory until 1808. The following year, Sacchini set Guillard's revision of La Bruère's libretto for Rameau's *Dardanus*. The work, unsuccessful at first but subsequently revised, got a respectable reception in its new, shortened form and was kept in the repertory in the next two decades.

Sacchini's main triumph, however, was to be posthumous. His tragédie lyrique *Œdipe à Colone*, which was also his first entirely original French work, had its premiere delayed by technical problems when, in January 1786, it inaugurated the new opera theater opened in Versailles by Mlle Montansier. Born Marguerite Brunet, Montansier (1730–1820) was a protégée of the queen, who in 1775 had appointed her as head of the court theaters. Marie-Antoinette, after being publicly besmirched in connection with the Necklace Affair, which had erupted the previous year, was now also openly criticized for unduly favoring foreign composers. Having promised Sacchini that his work would be staged again at Fontainebleau, she had to break the news to him on 3 October that Jean-Baptiste Lemoyne's *Phèdre* would be mounted instead. Sacchini died three days later. Having triumphed at the Porte Saint-Martin on 1 February, *Œdipe* was acclaimed as the composer's masterpiece and remained in the Opéra repertory until the 1840s, by which time it had received 600 performances.

Adapted directly from Sophocles's tragedy, Guillard's libretto does not feature the encounter between Oedipus and Creon and eliminates the character of Ismene. On the other hand, it introduces the character of Eriphyle, daughter of Theseus and promised to Polyneices – a pretext for a divertissement in Act 1. This hors d'oeuvre postpones the appearance of Oedipus guided by Antigone – which so movingly opens Sophocles's play – until Act 2. By another striking departure from the Greek original, but in keeping with contemporary *sensibilité*, the opera ends with the reconciliation of father and son. In a trio "Où suis-je? Mes enfants!" whose sweetness and "simple yet insidious melody" reduced the young Berlioz to tears when he heard it at the Opéra,[84] Oedipus withdraws his curse on Polyneices, and the opera ends, not with Oedipus's death, but in general harmony and rejoicing after a thunderbolt has signaled the gods' approval. Despite its many theatrical concessions to contemporary taste, *Œdipe à Colone* is a strong work on its own terms, remarkable, as Julian Rushton has pointed out, for its melodic finesse, dramatic ensembles, and fine choral writing.[85]

At his death Sacchini was working on *Arvire et Evelina*, also on a libretto by Guillard dealing, this time, with the fight between Romans and Celts in ancient Britain. Completed by Jean-Baptiste Rey (1734–1810), the work was premiered in 1788 and was successful enough to remain in the repertory until 1821.

Nicolas-Marie Dalayrac and pre-Revolutionary opéra-comique

Nicolas-Marie Dalayrac (1753–1809) was the leading opéra-comique composer to emerge in the 1780s, eventually rivalling Grétry in popularity. He was born in the Languedoc in the medieval city of Muret and was educated in nearby Toulouse.[86] By 1774 he was in Versailles, where his noble background – his original name was d'Alayrac – earned him a position in the personal guard of the Comte d'Artois. His earliest published compositions were string quartets. After the favorable reception of two privately staged short works, his "comédie mêlée d'ariettes" *L'éclipse totale* (one more opéra-comique based on La Fontaine) was performed at the Comédie-Italienne in 1781, thanks to Marie-Antoinette's support and Grétry's encouragement. In May 1786 in that same theater, *Nina, ou la folle par amour*, with Dugazon in the title role, was one of the biggest successes of the decade and a key moment in the history of pre-Revolutionary sensibility. Benoît-Joseph Marsollier's (1750–1817) one-act libretto, based on an episode, presented as a true story, from François de Baculard d'Arnaud's *Les délassements de l'homme sensible*, is set in a garden. The heroine, whose engagement to Germeuil has been broken by her father in favor of a richer suitor, has lost her reason. Simply dressed in white, her hair artfully disheveled, she sings a romance, "Quand le bien-aimé reviendra" – a moment beautifully captured in a 1787 painting by Antoine Vestier.[87] It was this aria, recycled as a religious hymn, that Berlioz was to recall as his earliest musical experience on the day of his first communion.[88] Later in the work, Germeuil reappears and Nina recovers her sanity. *Nina* both looks back to the pastoral tradition and contains elements foretelling Romantic opera, like the melancholy oboe tunes supposedly played by a shepherd in scene 9 to entertain the distracted heroine, or the slow process of painful recollection Nina – a forerunner of Bellini's Amina and Donizetti's Linda – goes through in the final scene. Dalayrac's contemporaries responded to the elegiac charm and studied naivety of his music. Immensely popular in Paris, *Nina* was staged throughout Europe and was revived at the Opéra-Comique until the 1850s. It was the basis for Giovanni Paisiello's equally popular *Nina, o sia la pazza per amore* (1789).

Two more of Dalayrac's pre-1789 works deserve mention. *Renaud d'Ast* (1787), a two-act comedy after La Fontaine's tale "L'oraison de saint Julien," contains in Act 2 an extended aria for the main female character Céphise ("Viens à ma voix, douce espérance"), which contains the most difficult coloratura written in French opera so far; it has been compared to the second aria of Mozart's Queen of the Night in *Die Zauberflöte* but goes even higher (to high G).[89] In the same opera, the romance "Vous qui d'amoureuse aventure" was later adapted, to different words, as the Bonapartist anthem "Veillons au salut de l'Empire." *Les deux petits Savoyards* (1789), to a libretto by Marsollier, exploits another sentimental vein: the chief characters are two young orphan boys (soprano trouser-roles), wearing the Savoy costume and speaking the local patois. The work's popularity, which lasted until the 1840s, shows that once again Dalayrac and his librettist had touched a sensitive cord.

Another new name in the opéra-comique world of the 1780s was the Marseilles-born Stanislas Champein (1753–1830), who in 1781 scored a success at the Comédie-Italienne with *La mélomanie* (1781), a farce-like satire of the contemporary passion for Italian music: Lisette's father having decided she will marry a certain Fugantini, her lover impersonates the latter. The work was performed in several European countries and its libretto was reset, in Russian, by Martin y Soler in 1790.[90]

Italian opera – in the original language or in the form of French parodies – was indeed welcome in Paris again. Besides Vismes's *opera buffa* seasons at the Opéra in 1778–80, Montansier mounted Italian operas with success in Versailles beginning in the late 1770s.[91] As of 1786, she produced works by Domenico Cimarosa and Paisiello at her new theater, drawing large audiences among which the queen was not the least appreciative. In 1787 a buffo troupe performed at court in Versailles and Saint-Cloud. A further step was taken in 1788 with the decision to establish in Paris a new, permanent theater for the staging of opera buffa with Italian singers. It was officially placed under the protection of the Comte de Provence. Marie-Antoinette herself was involved (her hairdresser, the famous Léonard, was the nominal manager). The "Théâtre de Monsieur"[92] opened in January 1789 with a performance of Giacomo Tritto's (1733–1824) *Le vicende amorose*. Endowed with a first-rate orchestra recruited by Léonard's associate, the violinist Giovanni Viotti, it was first installed in the remodeled Salle des machines at the Tuileries.[93] From the outset it began to compete with the Comédie-Italienne by presenting original opéras-comiques and disguising them as parodies: Champein's *Le nouveau Dom Quichotte*, premiered in May 1789, was thus announced as the work of a non-existent Zaccharelli.[94]

CHAPTER 5

REVOLUTION TO ROMANTICISM

Opera and the Revolution

The French Revolution is remembered above all for its excesses and, especially, for the period known as the Terror, which lasted from June 1793 until the fall of Maximilien Robespierre in July of the following year. But the Revolution went through several phases. The initial one was essentially liberal, favoring free enterprise by reaction against the controls and monopolies put in place by the absolute monarchy. A law was thus passed by the National Assembly on 13 January 1791 that allowed theaters to operate freely. Not only did it permit new theaters to open but for the first time it let them choose their repertory. As far as opera was concerned, this ended, for a brief period, a situation that had lasted since the privileges granted to Perrin, and then Lully, in 1669 and 1672, whereby the Académie royale controlled all matters relating to opera in France. Even censorship was abolished for a brief period, though it was reintroduced in other forms as the political situation deteriorated in early 1792. The new state of affairs resulted, in Paris, in a proliferation of smaller institutions, many of them situated along the northern boulevards, near the Porte Saint-Martin where the Opéra had been housed since 1783. These "boulevard theaters" drew more popular audiences, performing vaudeville plays and opéras-comiques in addition to regular plays. Provincial opera houses were similarly liberated from the tutelage of the Académie royale.

The change made life more difficult for the Opéra. It lost both its privileged status and a source of income – the fees it had previously charged other French opera houses just for permission to perform. The word "royale" was dropped from its title, first in June 1791 after the arrest of Louis XVI and his family at Varennes as they were attempting to leave the country, and again in August 1792 – this time until 1814 – when the monarchy was abolished. In 1794 the Opéra, once more under the authority of the city of Paris, moved from the

Porte Saint-Martin to a recently confiscated theater. Built for Montansier in 1791 by Victor Louis (architect of the handsome Grand Théâtre in Bordeaux) on a site roughly across the street from the entrance of the Bibliothèque nationale on the rue Richelieu, it remained the Opéra's home until 1820. The company first took the name of Théâtre des Arts, becoming Théâtre de la République et des Arts in 1797.

The repertory was not different at first from what it had been before 1789: tragédies lyriques on ancient subjects, such as Grétry's *Aspasie*, whose lackluster reception in the summer of 1789 may have been an indirect consequence of the Fall of the Bastille; or on medieval ones, like Lemoyne's *Louis IX en Égypte* (1791); resettings of famous libretti, like Pierre-Joseph Candeille's *Castor et Pollux* (1791), based on Gentil-Bernard's text for Rameau; opéras-ballets, like Jean-Baptiste Rochefort's *Bacchus et Ariane* (1791); and repertory works by Gluck, Piccinni, Salieri, and Sacchini replacing the now unfashionable Lully and Rameau. However, as political tensions rose, the Opéra was put under pressure – and, during the Terror, obligation – to mount occasional pieces best described as propaganda. Typical of these offerings was in September 1792 Gossec's *L'offrande à la liberté*, to a text by Marie-Joseph Chénier (1764–1811), younger brother of the poet André Chénier. With nearly 150 performances in the next five years and revivals until 1848,[1] it was Gossec's first stage triumph: his *Sabinus* (1774), the first French opera to feature trombones, had been moderately received and his sentimental comedy *Rosine* (1786) flopped. He, along with Étienne-Nicolas Méhul, became the leading French Revolutionary composer. As a symphonist, he was ranked on a par with Haydn.[2] He further collaborated with Chénier on *Le triomphe de la République, ou le camp de Grandpré*, a one-act "divertissement lyrique" celebrating the victory of the French republican army at Valmy a few months before. The premiere took place six days after the execution of Louis XVI on 21 January 1793. Other operas celebrating Revolutionary events at the *ci-devant* Académie royale – there were similar ones in provincial houses – included the "drame lyrique" *Le siège de Thionville* (June 1793), by Louis-Emmanuel Jadin (1768–1853), a composer now esteemed above all for his chamber music; Rochefort's *Toulon soumis* (March 1794), a representation of the siege and capture of the Mediterranean port; and the allegorical "sans-culottide dramatique" in five acts, *La réunion du Dix Août, ou L'inauguration de la République française*, performed 36 times between April 1794 and January 1795 – its title referring to the overthrow of the monarchy in August 1792. The words were by Gabriel Bouquier and Pierre-Louis Moline – author of the French text of Gluck's *Orphée* – and the music by the expatriate Roman composer Bernardo Porta (1758–1832).[3] Grétry, once close to the royal family, made two such contributions to the Opéra, both in one act. *Denys le tyran* (August 1794) shows the exposure and eventual expulsion from Athens of the former "king" of Corinth, concealed under the identity of a schoolmaster (a tyrannical one at that). Incongruously with the ancient setting, it ends with the singing of the *Carmagnole* and the *Marseillaise*. As the work was premiered one month after the Ninth of Thermidor, its political message could be perceived as a celebration of the fall of Robespierre as much as an anti-royalist tract.[4] As *La rosière républicaine, ou la fête de la vertu* (September 1794), it shows a village vicar enthusiastically abandoning his estate and creed to join the ranks of the sans-culottes and believers in the goddess Reason; at the end, nuns take off their veils and dance the *Carmagnole*. The title deliberately echoed *La rosière de Salency*, one of Grétry's popular pre-1789 works. Grétry's librettist on both occasions was Sylvain Maréchal (1750–1803), author of a *Dictionnaire des athées* published in 1800.[5] These topical works were hardly revolutionary from an aesthetic standpoint.[6] In his memoirs, Grétry is understandably reticent on this aspect of his production. He returned to a more conventional mode in 1797 with the tragédie lyrique *Anacréon chez Polycrate*, which remained in the Opéra repertory through the mid-1820s.

Grétry's opéras-comiques staged during the period at the Salle Favart (officially called Opéra-Comique as of 1793) also reflect the escalation of events beyond what the 1789 revolutionaries envisaged. The *Pierre le Grand* he presented in January 1790, with Dugazon in the main female role, was an openly monarchist work: Jean-Nicolas Bouilly's (1763–1842) libretto, by his own admission, was intended as a tribute to Louis XVI as father of the people, easily recognizable behind the idealized picture of Peter the Great.[7] Leaving aside its ideology, the work, as David Charlton has shown, has real musical merit, and was revived in Paris until 1817; it was revived in 2003 in connection with the St Petersburg tercentennial celebrations. Grétry's next work for the Comédie-Italienne, in April 1791, was *Guillaume Tell*, on a Sedaine libretto based on a 1766 tragedy by Antoine-Marin Lemierre. Apart from its exaltation of liberty and the fight against tyranny, the work is musically remarkable, by contemporary opéra-comique standards, for the size of its choral participation. It numbered 82 performances in 10 years, only to be overtaken by Rossini's 1829 work on the same subject.[8] In January 1792, by which time many French priests had dissociated themselves from the Revolution by refusing to swear allegiance to the civil constitution of the clergy, condemned by the Pope in March 1791, Grétry produced *Cécile et Ermancé, ou les deux couvents*, retitled *Le despotisme monacal* in November 1792. It was written partly in collaboration with Claude-Joseph Rouget de Lisle (1760–1834), the composer of the *Marseillaise*. In June 1794, at the height of the Terror, the Salle Favart mounted Grétry's "fait historique" *Joseph Barra*, a tribute to the 14-year-old whose death – exploited by Robespierre for propaganda purposes – also inspired Jacques Louis David's unfinished painting.[9]

Next to Grétry, Dalayrac – despite his aristocratic background – was the most popular composer of the Revolution.[10] He, too, remained active at Favart throughout the period. His "comédie mêlée d'ariettes" *Raoul, sire de Créqui*, on a libretto by Monvel, drawing from the medieval vein launched by Grétry in the 1780s, was greeted warmly at the Comédie-Italienne in October 1789, and was widely staged throughout Europe. Pressed into service in 1794, along with Grétry and 10 others including Luigi Cherubini, for the ephemeral occasional work *Le congrès des rois*, Dalayrac limited his involvement in Revolutionary politics to the "tableau patriotique" *La prise de Toulon* (February 1794) and the "fait historique" *Les détenus* (November 1794), while his *L'enfance de J.-J. Rousseau* marked the solemn transfer of the philosopher's remains to the Panthéon in Paris, May 1794. Dalayrac's most substantial works of the decade, *Camille, ou le souterrain* (1791), on a libretto by Marsollier after Mme de Genlis, and *Léon, ou le château de Monténéro* (1798), on a libretto by the Alsatian François-Benoît Hoffmann (1760–1828), are non-political and belong to the genre of "Gothic horror":[11] the former features a duke who wrongly suspects his wife of being unfaithful and keeps her imprisoned in an underground vault; in the latter, which evokes the world of Ann Radcliffe's *The Mysteries of Udolfo* (1794), young women are abducted and imprisoned in a mysterious castle. Both works' dark themes, alleviated by the presence of comic servant characters, relate them to the nascent melodrama in the modern sense. Musically, they make use of reminiscence motifs, while the vocal writing, recalling the forms and sentimental tone of Dalayrac's earlier work, displays none of the virtuosity one encountered in *Renaud d'Ast*.

Liberation from religious tyranny was a popular subject in Revolutionary theater. As early as February 1790, the Constituent Assembly had passed a law abolishing monastic vows and suppressing convents and monasteries. The ban on the representation of these institutions on stage was thereby lifted, resulting in a series of plays picturing them as dens of arbitrary power, forced reclusion, or (as in the Marquis de Sade's novels) outright debauchery. The most famous of these, Monvel's *Les victimes cloîtrées*, achieved proverbial celebrity from the time of its premiere in March 1791. It was preceded, as early as August 1790, by the "drame lyrique" *Les rigueurs du cloître* by Henri-Montan Berton (1767–1844), son of the composer and Opéra director. First staged at Favart, the work had an extraordinary, if short-lived, success, with performances in many large and mid-size provincial cities.[12]

Joan of Arc, popularized by Voltaire's controversial epic poem *La Pucelle*, was then viewed as a national heroine rather than as a religious figure. She made, as it were, her operatic debut at the Comédie-Italienne in May 1790 in *Jeanne d'Arc à Orléans*.[13] Its composer Rodolphe Kreutzer (1766–1831) – immortalized as the dedicatee in 1805 of Beethoven's famous violin sonata – was born at Versailles to a Swiss father. He also won international acclaim in 1791 for *Paul et Virginie*, after Bernardin de Saint-Pierre's immensely popular 1787 novel, while his *Lodoiska*, also premiered at the Salle Favart, was better received in France than Cherubini's work of the same title, which had preceded it by a mere six weeks. Next to Berton and Kreutzer, mention should be made of the Marseillais composer Dominique Della Maria (1769–1800), a student of Paisiello, who during his short life had two highly successful works performed at Favart in 1798, *Le prisonnier, ou La ressemblance* (after August von Kotzebue's comedy *Der Gefangene*), and the "theater-within-the theater" *L'Opéra-Comique*.

Luigi Cherubini, Étienne-Nicolas Méhul, and Jean-François Le Sueur are the three major French opera composers who emerged during the French Revolution. Whereas Méhul (see pp. 99–101) reserved his works for the Salle Favart and the Opéra, Cherubini (see pp.101–5) and Le Sueur (see pp. 109–10) were attached to the third, and in several respects most important, Paris opera theater operating at the time, the Théâtre Feydeau.

When the royal family was forced to leave Versailles and move to the Tuileries in early October 1789, the Théâtre de Monsieur had to look for a new home. It held performances in the Théâtre des Variétés at the Foire Saint-Germain until a theater was built on rue Feydeau on the Right Bank, a few blocks away from the Salle Favart (near the current location of the Paris stock exchange on Place de la Bourse), where it moved in early January 1791. After the Comte de Provence emigrated later in that year, it changed its name to Théâtre de la rue Feydeau. Still headed by Viotti, with Cherubini as music director as of 1792, it retained its Italian troupe until the summer of 1792. Afterwards its repertory was entirely French.

The Théâtre Feydeau, too, staged its share of propaganda works, such as the "tableaux patriotiques" *L'apothéose du jeune Barra*, by François-Pierre-Auguste Léger, and *Les Montagnards, ou l'école de la bienfaisance*, by Louis-Abel Beffroy de Reigny, in the spring and summer of 1794. Of considerably greater worth, despite its anti-religious flavor, was François Devienne's *Les visitandines*. Its premiere on 7 July 1792 preceded the fall of the monarchy by two months.[14] Born in the Champagne region in 1759, Devienne was first a bassoonist. In 1779–80 he was part of the Opéra orchestra and, in the same capacity, joined the orchestra of the Théâtre de Monsieur in 1789. By then he had become famous as a flutist and a composer of woodwind concertos and chamber music. When the Conservatoire opened in 1795, he was appointed its first professor of flute. Besides *Les visitandines* he wrote ten opéras-comiques, all for the Théâtre Feydeau, but none was comparably successful. For undocumented reasons Devienne was interned in the psychiatric hospital at Charenton in 1803 – one can suspect that such cases of precocious dementia were caused by syphilis – and died there, a few months later, at the age of 43.

A two-act "comédie mêlée d'ariettes" on a libretto by Louis-Benoît Picard (1769–1828), *Les visitandines* opens, like *Iphigénie en Tauride*, with an overture depicting a storm. The plot, set first outside a convent, then within its walls, centers on the attempts of the young Belfort to woo his beloved Euphémie, who, fearing he has abandoned her, is about to pronounce her vows. Burlesque developments involve a drunken gardener and coachman and the arrival of Belfort and his servant Frontin at the convent, disguised as nuns (a twist anticipating Rossini's *Le comte Ory*). Among the work's more serious moments are Euphémie's Act 2 aria, "Ô toi dont ma mémoire," with its elaborate obbligato horn. The part was created by the soprano Julie-Angélique Scio (1768–1807), soon to be Cherubini's first Medea. After the triumph of the initial run, Devienne and Picard revised the opera in three acts. In this new version, the anti-religious note was heightened: as in a Sade novel, the nuns' convent communicates through a secret tunnel with the neighboring Capucin monastery. *Les visitandines*, in its two- or three-act versions, had totaled 435 performances in Paris by 1815 and maintained its popularity even under the religious-minded Restoration – with the setting changed to a boarding school for girls.

A notable success at the Théâtre Feydeau, in October 1793, was *Roméo et Juliette* by the German-born Daniel Steibelt (1765–1822) – once a deserter from the Prussian army – who moved to Paris in 1790. It had an aristocratic librettist, the Vicomte Alexandre de Ségur (1756–1805) (demoted to "Citoyen J.-A. Ségur" in the first printings) and was first intended for the Opéra. In keeping with opéra-comique conventions, a happy ending was introduced, while the politically undesirable Friar Lawrence was replaced by a secular figure. With its rich orchestration and subtle harmony, the work has been compared by Winton Dean to Mozart and Carl Maria von Weber.[15] A disreputable character – the *New Grove* describes him as "extraordinarily vain, arrogant, discourteous, recklessly extravagant and even dishonest"[16] – Steibelt left Paris for London in 1796 under suspicions of fraud.

The Béziers-born Pierre Gaveaux (1760–1825) was both an opera composer of note as well as the leading tenor at the Théâtre Feydeau, where he was the first Belfort in *Les visitandines*. He usually acted himself in the 20 opérascomiques he produced between 1792 and 1800. The most significant was *Léonore ou l'amour conjugal*, a great success at its February 1798 premiere.[17] Bouilly's two-act libretto announced itself as a "fait historique," the events having supposedly taken place, possibly during the Terror, in his native Touraine. Bouilly is known to have been involved in the repression of counter-Revolutionary activities in his capacities as public prosecutor at the Tours tribunal. Whether his libretto – the plot of which is, in any case, transplanted to Spain – was truly based on facts has never been verified. The story and characters – Léonore, disguised as a young boy called Fidélio, Florestan, Pizzaro, Roc, Marceline, and Jacquino – are, of course, familiar from Beethoven's treatment of the same story, to a libretto by Joseph von Sonnleithner. This libretto remains very close to the French original, as does the one that Giovanni Schmidt prepared for Ferdinando Paër's *Leonora* in 1804.[18]

The final years of the Revolution were financially difficult for the Théâtre Feydeau, which even filed for bankruptcy in 1799. In 1801 it merged with the Opéra-Comique (formerly Comédie-Italienne). Limiting itself to French repertory, the company, which took the name Théâtre national de l'Opéra-Comique, nevertheless continued to use the Théâtre Feydeau, which remained its home until 1829. The Salle Favart was given to the new Italian opera buffa troupe which settled in Paris under Napoleon's protection. Thus, as Alessandro Di Profio has noted, at the beginning of the Napoleonic period Paris had returned more or less to the 1789 situation, with three opera houses, each, at least in theory, with a different repertory.[19]

Étienne-Nicolas Méhul

Étienne-Nicolas Méhul (1763–1817) was from Givet, a small city in the Ardennes. He moved to Paris around 1778.[20] There he studied with the Alsatian composer Jean-Frédéric Edelmann (1749–1794), whose Gluckist one-act opera *Ariane dans l'isle de Naxos* had been staged at the Opera in 1782. By 1788 Méhul had written two sets of sonatas for keyboard. In 1785 he began to work on the tragédie lyrique *Cora*. Valadier's libretto, first offered to Gluck, was based on Marmontel's *Les Incas*. It had to wait another six years to be premiered, but despite stage effects that included a volcanic eruption it lasted only five performances at the Opéra in 1791. Méhul's principal collaborator, François-Benoît Hoffmann, was Sedaine's successor as France's leading librettist. He wrote the words of Méhul's *Euphrosine, ou le tyran corrigé*, which had a successful run at the Comédie-Italienne in September 1790. *Stratonice* (1792), *Mélidore et Phrosine* (1794), and *Ariodant* (1799) all premiered at Favart, established Méhul as the most important French-born opera composer of the Revolutionary years. His *Horatius Cocles*, an "acte lyrique" premiered in February 1794 with a strictly male cast, is characteristic of the cult of republican Rome that was promoted at the height of the Terror (one victim of which was his teacher Edelmann, guillotined in Strasbourg). Méhul, at the time, composed the music for the second most popular Revolutionary song after the *Marseillaise*, the *Chant du départ*, to words by Marie-Joseph Chénier. His *Pont de Lody* (1796), a "fait historique mêlé d'ariettes," staged at the Théâtre Feydeau, was an occasional piece marking Bonaparte's recent victory against the Austrians in Lombardy.[21] Yet Méhul was not exempt from political trouble. Originally banned on the eve of its March 1792 Opéra premiere as unpatriotic,[22] *Adrien, empereur de Rome*, loosely based by Hoffmann on Metastasio's *Adriano in Siria*, when mounted in 1799 was withdrawn on the same grounds after a mere four performances; the ban was lifted the following year. Similarly, the openly monarchist *La jeunesse de Henri IV*, composed in 1791 to a libretto by Bouilly, was shelved in early 1792 owing to the unfavorable political climate; revised as *Le jeune Henri*, it was premiered at the Opéra-Comique in 1797 but disappeared after one performance. Its overture, however, based on hunting motifs, became extremely popular as a concert piece entitled *La chasse du jeune Henri*.[23] This and others of Méhul's overtures can be considered, in Winton Dean's words, "the true ancestors of the symphonic poem."[24]

Despite his occasional failures, by the end of the eighteenth century Méhul was close to being a national composer. The first musician to be elected in 1795 a member of the Académie des Beaux-Arts, within the newly incorporated Institut de France, he was appointed inspector to the Conservatoire, created in the same year. In favor with Bonaparte, Méhul dedicated to him his buffo opéra-comique L'irato, ou l'emporté (1801), one of his more popular works,[25] and was rewarded with official commissions as well as membership in the Légion d'Honneur as soon as it was created in 1804. Among his many works of the early 1800s, the opéras-comiques Une folie (1802) and Les deux aveugles de Tolède (1806) and the biblical "drame mêlé de chants" Joseph (1807) were better received than the more experimental Héléna (1803) and the Ossian-based Uthal (1806): Joseph, on a text by Alexandre Duval (1767–1842), was awarded the prize for the best opéra-comique of the decade. For the wedding of the French emperor with Marie-Louise of Austria, Méhul wrote Les troubadours, ou la fête au château (1810), but it was not performed. His career took a downward turn with the failure of Les Amazones at the Opéra in 1811; his Valentine de Milan remained unstaged in his lifetime and Sesostris was left incomplete. The Bourbons' return in 1814 did not put an end to official favor, but he died three years later as a result of the tuberculosis from which he had been suffering since 1810. After the collapse of his marriage, he had been living with the sister of his friend Cherubini's French wife.

Berlioz, in the homage to Méhul he wrote in Les soirées de l'orchestre,[26] praised Méhul's eloquent declamation, his bias towards the truth of expression at the expense of frivolous prettiness, his sense of the theater. The author of four completed symphonies, Méhul was also an innovator in terms of orchestral texture and color and in his harmony, not shying away from expressive dissonance, as in the one-act "comédie lyrique" Stratonice, one of his masterpieces. It delicately portrays a rivalry between father and son (named respectively Antiochus and Séleucus, like the twin brothers in Corneille's Rodogune). The latter suffers from a mysterious illness, under which he disguises his secret love for his father's bride Stratonice (a Dugazon role). The work's climax is a "consultation" scene, a five-movement quartet (beginning as a duet), in which the three principals are joined by the doctor Erasistrate, a high baritone part.[27] Mélidore et Phrosine has an uncommon subject, Jules' incestuous love for his sister Phrosine. "Méhul's most experimental opera," in the words of M. Elizabeth C. Bartlet,[28] it uses recurring motifs and is one of the earliest French works to be based on a unifying harmonic scheme, another anticipation in French opera of the Wagnerian leitmotif technique.[29] The opening of the third act, set on the sea shore, is through-composed in a highly original way, with a mélodrame linking Mélidore's aria with the following recitative with chorus describing a storm and leading to a spectacular theatrical effect when lightning strikes in scene 6. Ariodant, adapted by Hoffmann from Ariosto's Orlando Furioso, also makes use of recurring motives. Focusing on the theme of jealousy, it features an Iago-like character, Othon, a tenor villain (there is also one in *Euphrosine*). The Ossian-based *Uthal*, if a moderate success compared to Le Sueur's *Ossian, ou les bardes*, became famous as "the opera without violins": instead Méhul used divided violas and a reinforced cello section to produce a darker tone. Another original effect was the intervention of Malvina, the heroine, during the overture, in the middle of which she can be heard calling the name of her father Larmor.

Joseph, the only Méhul opera to maintain a place in the repertory throughout the nineteenth century, especially in Germany, resurrected the genre of biblical opera (untouched in France since Montéclair's *Jephté*), while its setting also exploited the fashion for Egypt launched by Napoleon's expedition and the scientific studies accomplished in its wake. In keeping with the return of religion to favor – the Concordat was signed with the Pope in 1802, which was also the year of Chateaubriand's *Génie du Christianisme* – it is an appropriately, but uncharacteristically, austere work, without women's roles (except for the soprano Benjamin), and it looks back to earlier musical styles.[30] Wagner, who admired *Joseph*, ranked Méhul among his mentors.[31]

Luigi Cherubini

Luigi Cherubini (1760–1842) has yet to be given his due as a French opera composer of the first rank. It is especially unfortunate that his masterpiece, *Médée*, the only one of his works to have earned a place in the repertory, is known in a version he had nothing to do with and that does no justice to his original.[32]

The Florence-born Cherubini received his initial training from his father, who played the harpsichord at the Teatro alla Pergola. After serving as assistant to Giuseppe Sarti and writing mostly *opere serie* for various Italian theaters, Cherubini moved to London in 1784 as house composer to the King's Theatre Company. After the failure of *Giulio Sabino*, which had only one performance in 1786, he moved to Paris. His compatriot Viotti, with whom he shared an apartment, introduced him to Marie-Antoinette. His first Opéra commission was *Démophon* (1788), a tragédie lyrique adapted from Metastasio by Marmontel. The librettist had initially entrusted it to Johann Christoph Vogel (1756–1788), but the expatriate German composer's intemperate lifestyle apparently prevented him from meeting deadlines.[33] Blamed for its monotony and poor word-setting – but praised by recent critics for its innovative orchestral writing[34] – *Démophon* disappeared after eight performances. It was eclipsed the following year when Vogel's version was premiered posthumously, though this too failed to gain a foothold in the repertory.

On becoming director of the newly founded Théâtre de Monsieur in 1789, Viotti recruited Cherubini as music director. His task consisted at first in writing substitute arias for the *opere buffe* in its repertory.[35] *Lodoiska*, his first opéra-comique for the Théâtre Feydeau, was premiered in 1791. It pleased Parisian audiences – the work numbers among the unqualified successes of the Revolutionary period – but Kreutzer's opéra-comique on the same subject, premiered in the same year, pleased them even more. In Germany, however, Cherubini's work was favored by both audiences and musicians.

The departure of the Feydeau Italian troupe after the events of August 1792 put Cherubini in a difficult situation, even though he remained in charge of the theater after Léonard and Viotti emigrated to England. He spent most of the Terror period in Normandy at the architect Victor Louis' country home. There he began to compose the music to *Éliza ou le voyage aux glaciers du Mont Saint-Bernard*, premiered at the Théâtre Feydeau in December 1794, and started work on *Médée*. When the Conservatoire opened its doors in 1795, Cherubini was appointed among its inspectors (the others being Gossec, Grétry, Le Sueur, and Méhul).

Premiered at the Théâtre Feydeau in 1797 with Scio in the title role and Pierre Gaveaux as Jason, *Médée*, on a libretto by Hoffmann, lasted a mere 20 performances. It was followed by three lighter opéras-comiques in 1798–9 – the third, *La prisonnière*, in collaboration with Cherubini's student Boieldieu – but none was successful. Cherubini's next work, however, the three-act comédie lyrique *Les deux journées*, triumphed in 1800 with 56 consecutive performances at the Théâtre Feydeau. Performed all over Europe, it earned praise from Goethe and Beethoven, among others, as well as a place in the international repertory until the beginning of the twentieth century.

The incorporation of the Théâtre Feydeau into the Opéra-Comique deprived Cherubini, now married and with children, of part of his income. To make up for the loss, he launched a music publishing venture, the Magasin de Musique, in partnership with Méhul, Kreutzer, and others. His opéra-ballet *Anacréon* flopped at the Opéra in 1804, evidently on account of its unpopular subject (an "old man" in love).[36] Disappointed over the lack of recognition from Napoleon, who found his music "too loud" compared to his favorite, Paisiello,[37] Cherubini went to Vienna the following year. There he met Haydn and Beethoven and attended the premiere of *Fidelio*. His opera *Faniska*, on a libretto based on a melodrama by Guilbert de Pixérécourt, opened at the Vienna Opera in February 1806. After Napoleon occupied the city the following November, Cherubini returned to France, where he went through a period of depression that lasted nearly two years.

Cherubini returned to French opera in 1812 with *Les Abencérages*, premiered at the Opéra in April 1813 with Napoleon in attendance – back from the disastrous Russian campaign and defeat at Leipzig. The work, which prefigures some aspects of *grand opéra*, did not get more than a polite reception.

Though the Bourbon Restoration did not imperil Cherubini's standing, it interrupted his career as opera composer for two decades (save for two occasional pieces performed at court). Along with Le Sueur, he was appointed superintendent of the royal chapel, a position he kept until 1830; his religious music is indeed the finest to have come out of France during the period. In 1822 he was named director of the Conservatoire. He tried in particular to reform the teaching of singing, French methods having come under severe criticism, and recruited Italian teachers to replace some native ones.

Having collaborated on the collective opéra-comique *La marquise de Brinvilliers*, a "drame lyrique" by Eugène Scribe (1791–1861) and Castil-Blaze (1784–1857), performed at the Salle Ventadour in 1831, Cherubini turned to opera one final time with *Ali-Baba, ou les quarante voleurs*, on a libretto drawn by Mélesville (pseudonym of Anne-Honoré-Joseph Duveyrier) and Scribe from the famous *Arabian Nights* episode. Lavishly produced at the Opéra, it received only 11 performances, none of which the composer attended. Some of the music was recycled from *Koukourgi*, an abandoned project from the mid-1790s. Coolly received in Paris despite a first-rate cast, the work was very successful in Berlin two years later.[38]

Described by Fétis as "a musical revolution," *Lodoiska* can be considered the first Romantic opera, combining a dramatic plot and a musical language that drew both from the Italian tradition at its most melodic and Gluck's innovations, albeit within a richer symphonic texture. Claude-François Fillette-Loreaux (1753–1821) based his libretto on an episode from the pre-Revolutionary bestseller, the mildly erotic novel *Les amours du chevalier de Faublas* by Jean-Baptiste Louvet de Couvray (1760–1797), published in parts between 1787 and 1790. Its author, a Girondin politician during the Revolution, having barely escaped the guillotine, was appointed French consul at Palermo and died of tuberculosis on his return. Set in Poland in the 1670s, the plot centers on the fate of the eponymous heroine, held prisoner in the castle of the sadistic Dourlinski, who intends to marry her. Her fiancé Floreski (Louzinski in Louvet's novel) and his servant Varbel introduce themselves into the castle and eventually succeed in freeing her with the help of the Tartar chief Titzikan, who lays siege to the castle, setting it on fire – a much-commented stage effect at the time. Cherubini's vocal writing, described as "austere, almost rarefied,"[39] departs from the melodious and decorative style of Dalayrac or Kreutzer. Its dramatic qualities are particularly suited to ensembles, such as the Act 1 quartet, in two parts, between Floreski, Varbel, Titzikan, and a Tartar; the trio-finale in a same act, with the voice of the imprisoned Lodoiska joining those of Floreski and Varbel; the septet in Act 2, followed by a trio; the dramatic Act 2 finale, in the course of which Dourkinski's emissaries try to poison Floreski and his servant; and the Act 3 quartet that immediately precedes the final battle. The dramatic and musical parallels with *Fidelio* are obvious: Beethoven himself considered Cherubini the greatest living composer.

Another landmark in pre-Romantic opera, *Éliza* is set at the Great St. Bernard Pass between Switzerland and Italy, where Florindo and Eliza, separated by her father, are eventually reunited. This happy ending is delayed by suicidal threats, a storm, and the collapse of a bridge plunging Florindo into a chasm from which he is miraculously rescued. The secondary characters are as picturesque as the setting: the postman Michel, singing in comical patois to a background of *sul ponticello* strings imitating the bells of his mules; Savoyards and mountain guides drinking at the inn; shepherds playing their rustic pipes heard in echo (they are also heard in the overture). A moment of relief is provided by the heroine's lovely Act 2 aria with oboe obbligato, "Je vais revoir tout ce que j'aime."

The timely rediscovery of *Médée* in the 1950s, in Maria Callas's powerful interpretation, took place, sadly, in a 1855 *durch-komponiert* version by the Bavarian composer Franz Paul Lachner (1803–1890). This gave a new lease on life – in Italian translation – to an arrangement that may have been serviceable at the time but is stylistically incongruous and hardly deserved to pass to posterity. To be sure, it later became a standard practice for nineteenth-century opéra-comique composers to substitute sung recitatives for spoken dialogue with a view to foreign performances in translation. With few exceptions, such versions were the work of the composer himself and were not intended to replace the original. The substitution is all the more to be deplored in the case of *Médée*, given the novelty of the original. Cherubini and his librettist had initially intended the work for the Opéra but, after being turned down, opted for the opéra-comique form. What makes *Médée* a landmark is that, for the first time, the spoken/sung combination was applied, not to a comedy or "drame" but to a classical tragedy, while the style of the music fully reflected the innovations introduced by Gluck, beginning with the interplay of a furious theme and a suppliant motive in the overture. Melodrama – hitherto used only in semi-serious works – is used to great effect when Medea and Neris react to the sound of the offstage wedding ceremony in Act 2, scene 7.[40] This challenging work demands singing actors of exceptional versatility, capable of projecting a powerful sung text set in tense vocal lines and of delivering spoken lines of equal intensity.[41] With the possible exception of Charpentier's own Médée, no role in previous French opera matched that of Medea in terms of vocal and dramatic requirements, from her mysterious spoken entrance in Act 1 to the emotional summit of Act 3, during which she commands the stage for half an hour.

As in the case of the Léonore he wrote for Gaveaux, Bouilly presented the plot of *Les deux journées* (the title referring to the duration of the plot) as based on a real story that had occurred during the Revolution.[42] True or not, one can easily see how a post-Revolutionary audience would have identified with it in 1800, even though the action is transposed to 1647, just before the Fronde, under a Cardinal Mazarin who resembles Robespierre much more than his historical self. The Savoyard water-carrier Mikéli, sheltering the aristocrat Armand and his wife Constance (Gaveaux and Scio at the premiere), manages to smuggle them out of Paris by disguising her as his daughter and hiding him in his water barrel. All seems to go well until the next day, when two Italian soldiers notice Constance and threaten to rape her, forcing Armand to come out of his hiding place and face arrest. As in Bellini's *I puritani*, the announcement of a miraculous amnesty saves the situation. Dedicated to Gossec (as *Médée* was to Méhul), the work has an endearing Utopian side, with Mikéli's patois-speaking family affectionately rubbing shoulders with elegant aristocrats, a state of harmony conveyed in the extended, Beethoven-like Act 1 finale. There is remarkable integration of the music into the action, such as in the suspense-filled episode at the city gate in Act 2, treated in a combination of melodrama, sung dialogue, and choral passages. There are more examples of melodrama in Act 3. The work, often under the title *The water-carrier*, was popular in Europe, especially in Germany.[43]

Les Abencérages ou L'étendard de Grenade is set to a libretto by Étienne de Jouy (1764–1846), the leading librettist of the Napoleonic era, whose own life reads like a novel of adventure: military service in French Guiana, a dangerous liaison leading him to jail, a shipwreck, soldiering in the Revolutionary armies, flight to England on counter-Revolutionary charges, marriage to the daughter of the Earl of Malmesbury, a third tenure in the military interrupted by arrest on suspicions of spying. He ended his career as Louvre librarian, after having provided libretti for some of the most important operas of the age.[44] He drew the one for *Les Abencérages* from Jean-Pierre Claris de Florian's popular *Gonzalve de Cordoue, ou Grenade reconquise*, first issued in 1791.[45] Set in the Granada Alhambra in the fifteenth century, the plot revolves on the predicament of the Moorish general Almanzor, who, in the middle of a victorious battle against the Zegris army, loses the battle standard of the city: as it turns out, it was treacherously stolen from him by Alemar, his rival for the love of the Zegris princess Noraïme. Banished, Almanzor returns in slave's disguise to meet Noraïme in the moonlit Alhambra gardens, where he is arrested but saved by the last-minute intervention of the Christian prince Gonzalvo of Cordoba, who exposes Alemar's duplicity. The colorful plot and setting, complete with orientalist ballets, are matched by the opulence of Cherubini's vocal and orchestral writing. The 1813 audiences found the action "slow and cold," according to Fétis, and the music lacking in melody. The cast gathered the three leading Opéra singers of their generation: as Noraïme, the Santo-Domingo-born Caroline Branchu (1780–1850); as Almazor, the tenor Louis Nourrit (1780–1831), a celebrated Orpheus in Gluck's opera and the father of the even more famous Adolphe Nourrit; and as the villain Alemar, Henri-Étienne Dérivis (1780–1856), who for three decades was the Opéra's reigning bass.[46]

Opera under Napoleon Bonaparte

Like Louis XIV before him, Napoleon was keenly aware of the political advantages to be reaped from state intervention in cultural matters.[47] Minimally interested in "pure" music, he viewed the Opéra as an instrument of national prestige and was determined to restore its greatness after the decline it had undergone during the Revolution. As First Consul – after the coup that brought him to power in November 1799 – he put the institution under the authority of his Minister of the Interior, but as of 1802 it was under his direct control. Lavishly subsidized, tightly supervised, it was placed at the top of the theatrical hierarchy by the 1806–7 decrees that regularized the theaters, ending the freedom introduced by the Revolution and drastically limiting their number in Paris and the provinces.

Speaking Italian as well as French, Napoleon was not nationalist in his own musical taste. He enjoyed *opera buffa* and in 1801 encouraged the establishment of a new Italian theater, subsequently named Théâtre de l'Impératrice named in honour of Empress Joséphine.[48] He did not share his compatriots' distaste for castrati: his Tuileries chapel, which he invited his favorite Paisiello to head in 1802, included eight of them, and Cherubini was able to cast the famous Crescentini in his one-act opera *Pimmalione* in 1809 – but for a private court performance only.

Napoleon may have hoped at first that Paisiello might become his Lully and write tragédies lyriques for the Opéra.[49] In the event, the Neapolitan composer produced only a *Proserpine*, set to a libretto by Guillard based on Quinault's 1680 version. Its poor reception at the Opéra in March 1803 annoyed Napoleon, who blamed it on a cabal of French musicians. While appointing Le Sueur to succeed Paisiello when the Italian composer stepped down from his position, the emperor continued to hope to attract major Italian composers to Paris. The Parma-born Ferdinando Paër (1771–1839) was recruited from the court of Saxony and brought to Paris in 1807 to head the Opéra-Comique, later succeeding Gaspare Spontini (see pp.111–14) as director of the Théâtre-Italien. He became the principal court composer and wrote several Italian operas for performance at the Tuileries. Napoleon's protection even extended to Niccolò Antonio Zingarelli (1757–1837), despite his being arrested in Rome for refusing to conduct a Te Deum at St Peter's to celebrate the birth of the emperor's son in 1811. However, the Neapolitan composer, whose *Antigone* had failed at the Académie royale in 1790, declined to return to French opera. Paer, on the other hand, who had debuted that same year with an *Orphée et Eurydice*, with spoken dialogues, for the Francophile court of Parma, eventually wrote one of the most successful opéras-comiques of the post-Napoleonic period, *Le maître de chapelle, ou Le souper imprévu* (1821). Set near Milan at the time of Bonaparte's Italian campaign, it features a certain Barnabé, author of an opera seria entitled *Cleopatra* who tries to coach his French cook Gertrude to sing its love duet with him. This amusing, widely popular work remained in the Salle Favart repertory until the First World War.

Although Le Sueur and Spontini dominate the Opéra repertory of the period, at least two other names deserve mention. The first is the Mannheim-born Peter Winter (1754–1825), Kappelmeister of the Bavarian court in Munich, whose *Tamerlan* was an adaptation by Étienne Morel de Chédeville (1757–1837) of Voltaire's play *L'orphelin de la Chine*. Winter was an experienced opera composer, having set texts in German and Italian: his "heroisch-komische Oper" *Das unterbrochene Opfefest* (1796) has been described as "the most successful German opera in the thirty years between *Die Zauberflöte* and *Der Freischütz*."[50] *Tamerlan* was unusual in having a baritone and a mezzo-soprano in its leading roles, but was thought "too German" in style when staged in 1802 and soon disappeared. It was Winter's one of two attempts to have a Parisian career: the other was *Castor et Pollux* (1806), recycling music from his own *Trionfo dell'amor fraterno* (1804) to fit Gentil-Bernard's libretto for Rameau, revised by Morel de Chédeville, but it also failed.

The shift in public taste from the old-style tragédie lyrique towards more exotic and lavish entertainments is exemplified by the operatic career of Pierre-Simon Catel (1773–1830). Born in Normandy, a student of Gossec and like him an active producer of music for open-air Revolutionary festivals, he was the Conservatoire's first professor of harmony and counterpoint. His first opera, *Sémiramis*, on a libretto by Philippe Desriaux after Voltaire's tragedy, remained dramatically and stylistically close to pre-Revolutionary models, despite its refined musical writing. The work's relative failure in Paris (23 performances) was attributed to a cabal, Catel's reforms at the Conservatoire having earned him enemies.[51] It did significantly better in Vienna. By contrast *Les bayadères* (1810), on a Jouy libretto that is an oriental extravaganza set in Benares, despite containing music more notable for its jollity and elegance than for any particular exotic character, was an unqualified success and by 1818 had reached 100 performances.[52] Leaving much space for dances, it was the first opera performed in Paris featuring the English horn.

Of the composers active during the Revolutionary period, apart from Le Sueur, only Kreutzer pursued a successful career at the Opéra during the Empire. His *Astyanax* (1801) and *Aristippe* (1810) were both revived throughout the Empire. Mythological or Greek subjects were in official favor, Napoleon having, in Robert Pounder's terms, an "almost obsessive interest" in classical antiquity.[53] Kreutzer's *Abel*, first performed before Empress Josephine at her Malmaison château in 1807,[54] was more coolly received when premiered at the Opéra in 1810 but, especially in its 1823 revision as *La mort d'Abel*, gradually matched Méhul's *Joseph* in popularity and earned Berlioz's praise. Berton contributed several ballets to the Académie impériale (including the biblical ballet *L'enfant prodigue* in 1812), but no opera, save for his participation in the one-act pasticcio *Le laboureur chinois* in 1813, in which the music by Haydn, Mayr, and Mozart must have sounded very exotic indeed in a Chinese context.

As during the Revolution, the Opéra was pressed into staging propaganda works, especially to mark Napoleon's military victories.[55] In October 1807 his return from Prussia was celebrated with *Le triomphe de Trajan*, a three-act tragédie lyrique on a libretto by Joseph Esménard (1767–1811). Officially credited to the sole Louis-Luc Loiseau de Persuis (1769–1819), the music was partly written by Le Sueur. Unusually for such an occasional piece, it had reached its hundredth performance by 1814 and, its political message notwithstanding, maintained a place in the repertory even under the Bourbons.[56] That was not the case of *L'Oriflamme*, commissioned in haste in 1814 as a desperate morale-boosting effort in the face of foreign invasion, shortly before the regime collapsed. Its libretto was the work of two *bien en cour* writers, the playwright Charles-Guillaume Étienne (1777–1845) and Pierre-Marie-Louis Baour-Lormian (1770–1854), the leading poet of the Napoleonic period, the music being the result of a collaboration between Berton, Kreutzer, Méhul, and Paër.[57]

The restoration of the Opéra to its previous prestige did not go along with a decline of the Opéra-Comique. The 1806–7 decrees on the theater reaffirmed both its national status and the obligation to perform works including spoken dialogue. Unlike Grétry produced no work of consequence after *Lisbeth* (1797) and *Élisca ou l'amour maternel* (1799), Dalayrac remained active until his death in 1809. After the one-act *Adolphe et Clara ou Les deux prisonniers* (1799), one of his major successes to date, he scored an even bigger triumph the following year with *Maison à vendre*, set to a libretto by Duval (author of Méhul's *Joseph*), in which the composer's usual graceful style is applied to a lighter form of comedy, centered on comic misunderstandings and their sentimental consequences. It was performed all over Europe and was still in the Opéra-Comique repertory in the 1930s. By contrast *Léhéman, ou La tour de Neustadt* (1801) returned to the romantic deliverance opera in the manner of Cherubini's *Lodoïska*, which it resembles in its use of a recurrent musical motif; it too became an international, if shorter-lived, success. Among his later work, *Gulistan, ou Le hulla de Samarcande* (1805), on a libretto by Étienne in collaboration with Ange-Étienne-Xavier de La Chabeaussière, contributed to the fashion for exoticism.

While Boieldieu and Nicolo (Nicolas Isouard; pp.119–21) dominate the period, Berton was another pillar of the Opéra-Comique repertory in the early 1800s. His *Montano et Stéphanie* was based on the same episode from *Orlando furioso* as Méhul's *Ariodant*, which it largely eclipsed at the time. When it was first staged in 1799, audiences objected to the third act taking place in a chapel and featuring a priest, forcing the police to put an end to the first run of performances. By 1800 a new third act by Gabriel Legouvé was substituted and the work began a successful run. Berton's one-act *Le délire, ou Les suites d'une erreur*, also premiered in 1799, was popular too and was mounted in theaters as far away as Moscow and Buenos Aires. In 1803 Berton scored an even greater triumph at the Théâtre Feydeau with *Aline, reine de Golconde*, an opéra-comique version by Jean-Baptiste Vial and Edmé-Guillaume-François de Favières of Sedaine's libretto set by Monsigny for the Opéra in 1766. None of Berton's later productions achieved the same success as these three works. In his later years, he championed eighteenth-century French tradition against Italian influences. He published a treatise on harmony in 1815 and, in 1822, a pamphlet against Rossini's music, which he described as "musique mécanique."

Jean-François Le Sueur

The third major opera composer to come of age during the Revolution, Jean-François Le Sueur (1760–1837) was born in Picardy, near Abbeville, to a peasant family.[58] Trained as a choirboy, he became a choirmaster in various cathedral cities and, in 1786, at Notre-Dame in Paris, where his reformist ideas got him dismissed the following year. His first opera, the "drame lyrique" *La caverne*, was mounted at the Théâtre Feydeau in February 1793, less than a month after the execution of Louis XVI. Unquestionably one of the major works staged during the Revolution, it was a hit in France, where it was still performed in the 1840s, and was seen in many other countries, especially in northern Europe.[59] The librettist Paul Dercy (d. 1803), about whom little is known, adapted an episode from Lesage's *Gil Blas de Santillane*, but the subject and subtitle (*Les voleurs*) also evoke Friedrich von Schiller's *Raüber*. The three acts take place in the cave where robbers hold Gil Blas prisoner, along with Séraphine, a noble Spanish lady with whom their chief, Rolando, has fallen in love. Her husband Alphonse, whom she believes killed by the bandits, manages to introduce himself into the cave disguised as a blind old man, arousing her captors' suspicions. They also plot to get rid of the too chivalrous Rolando – who turns out to be Séraphine's long-lost brother Don Juan. All are finally rescued by Gil Blas, who in the meantime had escaped. Le Sueur responded to the originality of the setting with his own unconventional musical style: frequent shifts in dynamics, disjointed vocal lines, appropriately "wild" choruses of robbers, unorthodox harmony and orchestration. The only nod to convention is Séraphine's grand air in two parts at the opening of Act 2.

Le Sueur's next opera, *Paul et Virginie* (1794), was found to be no match for Kreutzer's work on the same subject, nor was the more traditional *Télémaque dans l'île de la Calypso* (1796), which had been more than 10 years in the making, a lasting success. But Le Sueur's reputation was firmly established. He was among the first inspectors appointed at the Conservatoire in 1795 – though after repeated clashes with Bernard Sarrette, its director, he resigned in 1802.

Le Sueur's five-act *Ossian, ou Les bardes* was the first work staged, in July 1804, at the newly renamed Académie impériale. It was also the first opera based on James Macpherson's Gaelic epic. This in itself is surprising, given the phenomenal fame of the Ossian poems, initially published in 1760 and

popular in France through Le Tourneur's 1777 version.[60] Le Sueur had
begun working on the project in the late 1790s, and originally intended it for
the Théâtre Feydeau (thus with spoken dialogue). After Dercy's death in 1803,
the libretto was completed by Jean-Marie Deschamps. Departing freely from
its source, it is based on the rivalry between the Scandinavian tribe of
Duntalmo (bass), who has invaded Scotland, and the Caledonian tribe of
Hydala (tenor). Duntalmo intends his son Mornal to marry Rozmala
(soprano), who is betrothed to Ossian (tenor). Eventually, as Ossian, Rozmala,
and her father Rozmor are about to be sacrificed, the Caledonians rescue
them, killing Duntalmo and his son. The concluding chaconne (marked
Allegro pomposo fiermamente) celebrates the triumph of the Caledonians and
the Scandinavians' capture. The work's greatest moment is the imprisoned
Ossian's dream at the end of Act 4, where a "simphonie fantastique" – Le
Sueur's coinage – with chorus and pantomime, describes his Valhalla-like
vision of virgins and warriors, ending, "as in Ossian's poems," in a "fog-like"
pianissimo. This dream episode, which does not figure in Macpherson's epic,
was itself the source of Jean-Auguste-Dominique Ingres's 1813 painting *Le
songe d'Ossian*.[61] Throughout the work, Le Sueur proves an innovator both in
his individual approach to vocal declamation and his sense of orchestral
color – including the use of no fewer than 12 harps.

Ossian, along with classical antiquity, being Napoleon's passion, Le Sueur's
work became the quintessential Empire opera. Le Sueur had by then been
appointed to succeed Paisiello as head of the Tuileries chapel, a position he
kept through the Restoration, sharing it then with Cherubini. His next and last
opera, *La mort d'Adam, et son apothéose*, on a libretto by Guillard was partly
based on Friedrich Klopstock's *Der Tod Adams*. Though the least successful of
the biblical operas of the Napoleonic period – it only lasted a few performances – Le Sueur's work has nonetheless been described by Winton Dean as
"one of the most interesting works of its age."[62] Too static, no doubt, for the
operatic stage, it ends on a Miltonesque epilogue – the apotheosis of the title –
in which God, represented by an offstage heavenly choir, and Satan vie over
Adam's soul.[63]

As of 1817 Le Sueur taught composition at the Conservatoire, where he
trained some of the most important composers – and especially opera
composers – of the younger generation, Berlioz, Gounod, and Ambroise
Thomas among them. At his death Le Sueur left a completed opera, *Alexandre
à Babylone*, on a libretto by Baour-Lormian. It was never performed.

As Jean Mongrédien has noted, Le Sueur's operatic production is marked by
the eclecticism characteristic of many French musicians of his generation.[64]
Powerful and original at his best, he was also criticized for his faulty compositional technique. Interestingly, his student Berlioz would later be similarly
praised and blamed.[65]

Gaspare Spontini

Gaspare Spontini (1774–1851), another leading French opera composer of the Empire and Restoration, came from the small town of Majolati in the March of Ancona, a region which, along with most of the Papal States, was incorporated by Napoleon into a republic and, as of 1808, the short-lived Kingdom of Italy. He received his musical training in Naples and between 1796 and 1802 had ten *opere buffe* and one *opera seria* premiered in various Italian theaters (including Palermo, where the court of the Two Sicilies sought refuge in 1798). In 1803 he moved to Paris, where his *dramma giocoso La finta filosofa* was well received at the Théâtre-Italien. His first three French works, *La petite maison*, *Milton*, and *Julie, ou Le pot de fleurs* were staged in less than a year in 1804–5. *Milton*, a one-act "fait historique" – one of the last appearances of this Revolutionary appellation – was unusual in having a writer as its subject, though Rousseau had first experimented with the idea in *Les Muses galantes*. Its climax is a quintet in which the blind poet dictates *Paradise Lost* to his daughter, who plays the harp on stage.[66] Jouy, the work's co-librettist, then offered Spontini the libretto of *La vestale*, previously turned down by Méhul, Cherubini, and Boieldieu. Thanks to the patronage of Empress Josephine – for whose court Spontini arranged a vaudeville, *Tout le monde a tort*, in 1806 – the work was a triumph at the Opéra in December 1807.

Jouy's main source was *Éricie ou la vestale*, a tragedy published in 1768 by Jean-Gaspard Dubois-Fontanelle and banned at once, as it was (correctly) perceived as an attack on monastic vows. The Comédie-Française finally accepted it in 1789. Another source, acknowledged by Jouy when he published the libretto (with a dedication to Empress Josephine) was Johann Winckelmann's *Monumenti antichi inediti*. A precautionary warning against an anti-religious reading of the plot – Napoleon had just concluded an arrangement with the Vatican – Jouy stressed the historical ambitions of the work in a way that could only please his archeologically-minded audience, while appealing to the taste for the antique that characterizes the Napoleonic period. Set in Rome in the third century BC, *La vestale* departs from the previous operatic tradition in that the love story is inseparable from the historical pomp and pageantry that surrounds it. In Act 1, which takes place on the Roman Forum, we are introduced to the main characters – Licinius, the young victorious general returning from Gaul, and Julia, his former beloved, who became a vestal against her will while he was gone – and we witness the long solemnity of Licinius's triumph. At the end of Act 2, after Julia has let the fire go out when Licinius was with her, we are shown the details of her degradation by the Pontifex Maximus. Set in the Field of Execration, the final act begins with Licinius's desperate efforts to save Julia and shows the procession and rituals leading to her being buried alive. By superimposing an intense personal drama on a painstakingly reconstructed historical context, *La vestale* thus anticipates some aspects of the *grand opéra* world of Halévy and Meyerbeer, though its choice of an ancient subject and archeological bent are also forerunners of Verdi's *Aida*. Admittedly, the plot distorts historical evidence on a crucial point: vestals were chosen when they were little girls, so Julia could not have become one in her adolescence during the absence of her beloved. Jouy also departs from Winckelmann's account by sparing Julia (Georgia in the source) at the end, in the spirit of the eighteenth-century tragédie lyrique. Interestingly, though, the question of divine intervention, de rigueur in a tragédie en musique, is carefully left vague: unlike the superstitious Romans on stage, we are free to believe that the rekindling of the sacred fire by the storm is purely accidental.

Spontini's music rose to the originality of the subject. To be sure, he embraced some of the Opéra conventions, giving dance more than its due with a divertissement in Act 1 and a second one at the very end. For his lifelong admiration for Mozart, Spontini, as a composer, was more indebted to Gluck and Piccinni. Like the former, he is not a memorable melodist, but the work makes up for its relative lack of tunefulness by its theatrical sweep and sense of contrast. This is especially true of Act 2, in which Julia's forebodings, the lovers' anxious reunion, the panic following the catastrophe, while angry crowds can be heard offstage, and the horror of Julia's public exposure and sentencing, are conveyed in what Berlioz described as a "gigantic crescendo"[67] without precedent in French opera, ending with a concertato finale that, though common in French *buffo* works, was a novelty in the serious genre. Spontini also had larger forces at his disposal: with two flutes, two oboes, two clarinets, two bassoons, four horns, two trumpets, three trombones, and timpani, his instrumentation, objected to by some for its loudness, made full use of orchestral resources that can be described as modern.[68]

The success of *La vestale* was considerable, perhaps not as much in Paris, where it totaled 200 performances by 1830, as internationally – including stagings in French in New Orleans and Philadelphia in 1828.[69] In addition to Berlioz, the work impressed Schubert, Weber, Meyerbeer, and Wagner.[70] Along with Méhul's opéra-comique *Joseph*, it was considered the best opera of the decade.

In 1808 Napoleon invaded Spain and it was evidently at his instigation that the official poet Esménard, author of *Le triomphe de Trajan*, was asked to write a libretto on the subject of Hernán Cortés's conquest of Mexico, with strict instructions to stress the Aztec priests' obscurantism. Assisted by Jouy, Esménard adapted a 1744 tragedy by Alexis Piron.[71] *Fernand Cortez, ou La conquête du Mexique* was premiered in November 1809. The staging, even costlier than that of *La vestale*, betrayed a similar obsession with historical reconstitution: because Cortés had conquered Mexico with 17 cavalrymen, so 17 horses were paraded on the stage of the Académie impériale, earning the work the nickname "opéra Franconi" after the circus impresario whose services were recruited for Act 2. In the event, the propaganda backfired, with audiences soon cheering the Spaniards not for the intended reasons but as victims of the Napoleonic invasion. The authorities reacted by having the work withdrawn after 13 performances. Spontini and his librettists drastically recast it in 1817, and it is in this new version, in which the original order of the first two acts was reversed, that the opera has generally been performed since, though Spontini revised it at least twice more in later years.[72]

The plot, in both 1809 and 1817, takes liberties with the events of 1520 – let alone Mexican geography. It involves, in addition to Cortés (tenor), his brother Alvar (another tenor), who together with a group of Spaniards is held prisoner by the Aztecs; Cortés's native girlfriend Amazily (soprano), niece of the Aztec king Montezuma (bass); and her brother Télasco (a third tenor). The opera is dominated by the figure of Amazily, torn between her love for Cortés and her family loyalties. In the temple scene (Act 1 in the 1817 version), she confronts the priests in the aria, "Dieu terrible, prêtre jaloux," faces her brother in a duet in three parts, and takes part in a quartet with chorus in which she is joined by Telasco, Montezuma, and the High Priest. Act 2, set in Cortés's camp, climaxes with the Spanish leader silencing a mutiny of his troops by shaming them – a scene admired by Berlioz. In between, Amazily has a second aria and joins Cortés in a duet, while a long Mexican ballet takes place in honor of Telasco's embassy. The first scene of Act 3, set in view of Mexico City, opens with Telasco's eloquent aria "Ô patrie, ô lieux pleins de charmes," followed by a trio for Amazily, Cortés, and Cortés's confidant Moralès, accompanied by an offstage chorus. The set then changes in open view to Montezuma's palace. "Ce monde est à vous," Cortés tells the Spaniards, ominously, while effusively assuring Montezuma of his friendship and peaceful intentions. The blatant colonialist overtones and martial character of the music may not make *Fernand Cortez* the most appealing candidate for revival. But the work, even more so than *La vestale*, displays Spontini's breadth of vision, with long, through-composed tableaux in which solos, ensembles, and choruses follow each other without leaving room for applause.

Showered with honors by Napoleon, Spontini, who by his marriage in 1810 became related to the Érard piano manufacturers, was appointed music director of the Théâtre de l'Impératrice in the same year. In this capacity he added *opera seria* to the repertory and arranged the Paris premiere of Mozart's *Don Giovanni* in its original version. But he was fired in 1812, evidently over irregularities in his management, and Paër was named as his successor.[73] Spontini greeted the return of the Bourbons in 1814 with the two-act *Pélage, ou Le roi et la paix*, on a text by Jouy, a gross piece of flattery in which Pélage (Louis XVIII) is driven into exile by the Moors (the Revolutionary rabble) along with his devoted niece Favila (the Duchesse d'Angoulême, Louis XVI and Marie-Antoinette's daughter). Unsurprisingly, the work was not revived after its four performances.[74]

Spontini's final French opera, the tragédie lyrique *Olimpie*, was one of the last major works of the period to be based on an ancient subject, and its relative failure in 1819–20 indicates that the genre itself was now out of favor. The source of Charles Brifaut and Michel Dieulafoy's libretto was Voltaire's 1762 tragedy, already adapted by Guillard as a libretto set by Christian Kalkbrenner in 1798.[75] The intricate plot is set in Ephesus 15 years after the death of Alexander the Great, and involves his generals Cassander (tenor) and Antigonus (bass), rivals for the hand of Amenais (soprano) who favors the former. As the action unfolds, Cassander is accused of having murdered Alexander, while Amenais turns out to be Alexander's daughter Olympia and the High Priestess Arzane (soprano) is revealed to be Statira, Alexander's widow and Olympia's mother. In the original version, which more or less followed Voltaire, Cassander slew Antigonus, and Statira and Olympia both committed suicide, to reappear, transfigured, at Alexander's side in the palace of immortality. The 1819 Paris premiere, mounted with the same care for historical verisimilitude as *La vestale*,[76] had an exceptional cast: Olympie was the young Laure Cinti (later Cinti-Damoreau 1801–1863), future creator of many important roles in the Romantic repertory. She was partnered by Branchu (Statira), Louis Nourrit (Cassandre), and Dérivis (Antigone). Disappointed by the reviews, Spontini withdrew the work after seven performances and revised it. In this second version, Antigonus, mortally wounded in battle by Cassander, reveals that it was he who murdered Alexander, and the lovers can marry. The triumphal march featuring onstage trumpets, horns, trombones, ophicleide, and percussion, which opened Act 3 in 1819, is now heard at the end, just before the concluding ballet. This new version was successfully staged in Berlin in 1821, in a German translation by E.T.A. Hoffmann, and unveiled in Paris in 1826, but *Olimpie*, despite being held in high esteem by Berlioz and others for the grandeur and nobility of its orchestration, never gained a foothold in the repertory. For its old-fashioned subject, it is even more forward-looking than *Fernand Cortez* in its symphonic approach, which Spontini was to carry even further in his German opera *Agnes von Hohenstaufen* (1827). Spontini remained in Berlin until 1842. Embittered by the intrigues that plagued his final years in the Prussian capital, jealous of Meyerbeer's Parisian successes, he devoted his last years to philanthropic work, of which his native city, where he died in 1851, was the chief beneficiary. It was appropriately renamed Majolati Spontini in 1939.

Adrien Boieldieu

The fact that *La dame blanche*, the masterpiece of Adrien Boieldieu (1775–1834), was the single most performed opera in nineteenth-century France – 1,500 showings at the sole Opéra-Comique by 1875 – is sufficient indication of the place he occupies in French operatic history.[77] Born in Rouen to a lower middle-class family, he was instructed by local musicians, especially the Rouen cathedral organist Charles Broche (unjustly depicted as an unsavory character in Maurice Ourry's 1834 opéra-comique *L'enfance de Boieldieu*). Little "Boiel" – a nickname he retained throughout his life – began his career as an organist. His first exposure to opera was at his native city's Théâtre des Arts, where works by Grétry, Dalayrac, and Méhul were popular. He made his own stage debut there in 1793 with the sentimental opéra-comique *La fille coupable*, set to a libretto by his father. He also acquired a reputation as a composer of *romances* and piano sonatas. Moving to Paris in 1797, he had three one-act opéras-comiques performed in 1797 at the Théâtre Feydeau and Salle Favart. In 1798, his breakthrough year, he was appointed piano teacher at the Conservatoire while his three-act *Zoraïme et Zulnar*[78] had much success at the Opéra-Comique. The subject, adapted from Florian's *Gonzalve de Cordoue*, is roughly similar to the one that Cherubini – the work's co-dedicatee along with Méhul – subsequently derived from the same source in *Les Abencérages*. The cast included two singers who were to be particularly associated with Boieldieu's works. One, the tenor Jean-Baptiste Elleviou (1769–1842), became the leading male opéra-comique singer of the Napoleonic decade. The other, the high baritone – or low tenor – Jean-Blaise Martin (1768–1837), has given his name to this unusual, and specifically French vocal type, halfway between baritone and tenor.[79] In June 1800 the Salle Favart staged Boieldieu's three-act *Béniowski, ou Les exilés du Katchamtka*, adapted by Duval from Kotzebue's melodrama *Graf Benjowsky*, itself based on the memoirs of the Polish general Maurycy August Beniowski. Set in Siberia, and revolving on a conspiracy of Polish captives against their Russian captors, complicated by the fact that their leader marries the daughter of the Russian governor, it is a typically dark work in the mode popularized by Cherubini's *Lodoïska*, with patriotic choruses ("Ciel, tremblez tyrans") and touches of exotic color. Three months after *Béniowski*, the one-act *Le calife de Bagdad* firmly established Boieldieu's reputation. Staged more than 175 times at the Opéra-Comique by 1812, it was soon performed in theaters around the world and remained one of his most popular works. The plot by Claude de Saint-Just (1768–1826) is slight: the caliph, disguised as a simple subject, wins the heart of Zétulbe over the misgivings of her mother (one of Dugazon's last roles) before revealing his identity. It is set in a manner already characteristic of Boieldieu at his most winning: a sparkling overture, followed by arias in turn tender and witty, like the one sung by the servant Késie ("De tous les pays pour vous plaire") with samples of various European vocal styles. The work throughout is characterized by a lightness of touch that in this case can be described as art hiding art.[80]

Ma tante Aurore, ou Le roman impromptu nearly collapsed at its Théâtre Feydeau premiere in January 1803, on moral rather than musical grounds: the original plot involved children supposedly born out of wedlock. Recast at once from three to two acts, the work recovered three weeks later and was soon a favorite with French and European audiences. Like Jane Austen's contemporary *Northanger Abbey*, it satirizes the contemporary craze for Gothic novels in the person of a female Don Quixote. To persuade the reluctant, unmarried Aurore to let her niece Julie wed Edmond, insufficiently heroic in her eyes, romantic episodes are staged by the lovers, until the aunt relents. The score is remarkable both for its Mozartian grace and the verve of its ensembles, such as the Act 1 quartet "Toi par qui l'on fait des romans," during which the lovers and their servants Marton and Frontin decide on a course of action.[81]

Boieldieu's career took an unexpected turn in 1803 when he accepted an appointment from the court of St Petersburg, where he remained until 1810. The move was prompted by Boieldieu's estrangement from his wife, the dancer Clotilde Mafleurai, whom he had married the previous year. French opera, especially opéra-comique, was popular in St Petersburg, where a French company had first been established in 1764.[82] Boieldieu became its director as well as the court composer, succeeding Sarti, who had left his position shortly before his death in 1802. Some of Boieldieu's work in Russia consisted in resetting pre-existing libretti, such as the ones for Le Sueur's *Télémaque* and Berton's *Aline, reine de Golconde*.[83] His most important original work for Petersburg was the two-act opéra-comique *Les voitures versées* – the phrase for "car accident" in pre-automobile parlance – premiered in 1808 at the Hermitage Theater. The amusing libretto, based on a contemporary play by Emmanuel Dupaty, is about a bored, snobbish provincial, Dormeuil, who deliberately neglects to maintain the road going through his estate: as a result he can play host to stranded travelers whenever passing coaches break down. In the lively opening sextet, we discover that a victim of the accident is a tenor who fears the consequences for his voice; in Act 2, there is debate on the comparative merits of Italian and French music – Grétry, Méhul, and Dalayrac are duly mentioned – leading to variations on "Au clair de la lune," fitted to Italian words, and a singing lesson that develops into a three-voice canon. Boieldieu revised the piece for the Opéra-Comique in 1820 and it too became a popular favorite.

In 1810 Boieldieu left St Petersburg – his successor was Steibelt – and returned to the French capital, where his *Jean de Paris* was staged to great acclaim at the Opéra-Comique in 1812. It marked a return to the light medieval genre launched by Grétry in the 1780s. One of Elleviou's last roles, the eponymous character in Saint-Just's libretto is the future King John II, son of Philip VI, founder of the Valois dynasty. Taking the identity "Jean de Paris," he has come incognito to the inn of Pedrigo to get to know the Navarre princess he is to marry; it turns out that she was warned of this ruse. In the Act 1 finale Boieldieu inserted an aria for the princess, "Ah! Quel plaisir d'être en voyage," for which he reused music from *Télémaque*. Weber, who conducted the work in Prague in 1814, praised Boieldieu's "flowing and well proportioned melodies" and the "excellence and finish of his instrumentation."[84] *Jean de*

Paris remained popular in Europe throughout the nineteenth century, earning the admiration of Robert Schumann and even Wagner.[85]

The qualities highlighted by Weber are also in evidence in Boieldieu's next two works. The plot of *Le nouveau seigneur de village* (1813) anticipates some aspects of Nikolai Gogol's *Government Inspector* (the village lord's servant successfully impersonates his master), while *La fête du village voisin* (1816) has a plot resembling Marivaux's *Le jeu de l'amour et du hasard*: a young widow and her maid, disguised as peasant girls, flirt with two peasants at the village ball, unaware that these are actually the heroine's disguised suitor and his servant. The overture, the Act 1 trio where the two women are instructed on how to behave at a country fair, the quintet at the opening of Act 2 ("Ne craignez rien, laissez-moi faire") – there are two more – are among the gems of the work, which was regularly revived until the 1890s.

Boieldieu's standing as the foremost opéra-comique composer of his generation was confirmed by an appointment at the Bourbon court in 1815. He succeeded Méhul both at the Académie des Beaux-Arts in 1817 and as professor of composition at the Conservatoire in 1820. In 1818 he produced one of his most accomplished works, the fairy opera *Le petit chaperon rouge*, loosely derived by Emmanuel Théaulon (1787–1841) from Perrault's "Little Red Riding Hood" tale. The work opens with Boieldieu's only programmatic overture, a musical retelling of the tale. The heroine, Rose d'amour, is courted both by the chivalrous Count Roger (tenor), disguised as a shepherd, and, in the wolf's part, the lecherous Baron Rodophe (baritone).[86] In Act 2, lost in the forest, she falls asleep and a dream sequence follows, showing her being crowned as countess to the accompaniment of echoing choruses on and offstage, after being wooed by Roger in a ravishing 20-measure, high-C capped cavatine. The last act is set in a hermitage, where Rodolphe takes the hermit's place and nearly succeeds in his designs until he learns that Rose is his niece.

Apart from revising *Les voitures versées* in 1820 and *Béniowski* in 1824, Boieldieu wrote little between 1818 and 1825. He collaborated with Berton, Cherubini, Kreutzer, and Paër on *Blanche de Provence* (1821), an occasional piece celebrating the birth of the king's grand-nephew the Duc de Bordeaux; and with Berton and Kreutzer on *Pharamond* (1825),[87] marking, this time, Charles X's coronation – the event that inspired Rossini's contemporary *Viaggio a Reims*. These were Boieldieu's single contributions to the Opéra.

The libretto of *La dame blanche*, first entitled *La dame d'Avenel*, was offered to Boieldieu in 1821. Scribe, its author, who had already collaborated with Carafa, Kreutzer, and Auber, was quickly establishing himself as the leading librettist of his generation. In *La dame blanche*, he capitalized on the tremendous vogue enjoyed in France (as all over Europe) by the novels of Walter Scott. Scribe and Boieldieu were not the first to exploit the resulting vogue for Scottish subjects: in 1817 Catel, a close friend of the composer and his neighbor in the country, had the "opéra-héroïque" *Wallace, ou Le ménestrel écossais* premiered with success at the Opéra-Comique. *La dame blanche* freely combines elements from both *Guy Mannering* and *The Monastery*.[88] By the time Boieldieu set it to music, he had heard *Der Freischütz*, given in Paris in 1824 in Castil-Blaze's absurd adaptation as *Robin des bois*, and the work's atmosphere betrays a subtle influence of Weber's masterpiece. Yet, behind its Scottish setting and fantastic elements – both treated with some irony – *La dame blanche* must have touched a personal resonance in the Restoration audience. "Georges" Brown, the hero, like a French émigré, returns to his ancestral land.[89] By the end of the opera he is revealed to be the legitimate heir to the Avenel castle. This restoration is also an initiation. Georges is unaware at first of his past and status; one of the work's most beautiful passages is the slow recovery of his identity in Act 3 with the help of the song *Robin Adair*, which he gradually remembers from his childhood. He has to prove himself worthy of being restored to his privileges. Act 1 shows his good humor and benevolence; Act 2 his bravery, gentlemanliness, and even entrepreneurial gutsiness – without a penny to his name, he outbids his rival Gaveston at the onstage auction which concludes the act and is one of the great tours de force in all French opera. Gaveston, by contrast, the upstart trying to gain possession of Avenel, reveals his unworthiness – an everyday version of the villain in Revolutionary "tyrant operas." As for the fantastic element, its treatment by Boieldieu and his librettist reflects the shift in opéra-comique fashion from high drama to semi-serious comedy. The White Lady of the title, presented in Act 1 as a supernatural agent, both protective and threatening – the refrain of Jenny's ballad is "Prenez garde! La dame blanche vous regarde !" – turns out to be a clever impersonation by Anna, the orphan reared by the late Avenels and Georges's childhood sweetheart.

The most anthologized parts of *La dame blanche* are Georges's three arias – the dazzling rondo "Ah! Quel plaisir d'être soldat" in Act 1, ostensibly in praise of military life, with subtle ironical touches;[90] the limpid invocation to the White Lady, "Viens, gentille dame" in Act 2; and the more free-form "air écossais" in Act 3. The role is indeed one of the most demanding lyric tenor parts in early Romantic opera, requiring virtuosity (there are Rossini-like roulades in the Act 1 "Fear duet") as well as acting gifts. Even more impressive are the ensembles, such as the auction scene, or the extended trio "Grand Dieu! Que viens-je d'entendre" at the end of Act 1, which builds up into a storm.

The eagerly awaited premiere of *La dame blanche* on 10 December 1825 was the apogee of Boieldieu's career. Pressed for time, he was assisted for the composition of the overture, a sparkling pot-pourri, by his students Adolphe Adam and Théodore Labarre, who completed it on the day before the dress rehearsal. Most Parisian reviewers extolled *La dame blanche* as a French retort to Rossini. In fact, the two composers admired each other and were on the friendliest terms. Rather, as Damien Colas has perspicaciously argued, *La dame blanche* shows how well Boieldieu had assimilated the Rossinian style –

just as some of the new music Rossini soon afterwards wrote for *Le comte Ory* might be described as Boieldian.[91] Soon staged all over Europe, *La dame blanche* earned ecstatic praise from Weber, among others. A more unexpected enthusiast, Wagner, called it "a unique work, incomparable in its way," declaring a propos the auction scene, "a model of what the French spirit can produce," even adding: "In comparison to that we are a nation of drunken artisans."[92]

Though he had eight more years to live, Boieldieu composed little after *La dame blanche*. He toyed with the idea of an opéra-comique based on Goethe's *Faust* but gave it up on hearing that Scribe had embarked on a similar project with Meyerbeer.[93] His last work, *Les deux nuits*, on a libretto by Bouilly retouched by Scribe, was well received in 1829 but the success did not last. Set in Ireland, its intricate plot, old-fashioned for the time, involves the substitution of a bride for another to rescue her from a loveless match. Its weaknesses compromised from the start the career of a work that Georges Favre nonetheless considered one of Boieldieu's "most endearing opéras-comiques."[94] The composer, who was finally able to marry his longtime girlfriend Jenny Phillis Bertin after his wife's death in 1826, spent much of his last years in his Île-de-France estate of Jarcy, where he died in October 1834. At his funeral, the band played – as he had requested – the melancholy spinning-song of Dame Marguerite which opens Act 2 of *La dame blanche*.

Nicolo (Isouard)

The Maltese Nicolò Isouard (1773/5–1818) was Boieldieu's principal rival at the Opéra-Comique before and after the latter's stay in St Petersburg.[95] Educated in Paris in the mid- to late-1780s, he returned to his native island after the Revolution broke out, then moved to Sicily and, eventually, Naples, where he completed his musical education. Between 1794 and 1798, he had eight *buffo* and one serious Italian operas performed in Florence, Leghorn, and, after 1796, Malta – including versions of *Il barbiere di Siviglia* (after Paisiello) and *Renaud d'Ast* (after Dalayrac). He signed them "Nicolo" not to expose the name of his prosperous mercantile family, which originally came from Marseilles. In 1800 he moved back to Paris. His first work for the Opéra-Comique, the one-act *Le petit page* (1800), was written jointly with Kreutzer, with whom he collaborated again on *Flaminius à Corinthe* (1801). From then on, Nicolo – who continued to sign his work with his first name in preference to his surname[96] – produced at least one opéra-comique annually – at times two, and even three in 1805 and 1806 – except in the politically volatile year 1815. Most of them were of the one-act variety popular at the time, but he also composed works in two and three acts. His librettists included Hoffmann, with whom he produced one of his best-known works, *Les rendez-vous bourgeois*, in 1807; Marsollier (*Léonce, ou Le fils adoptif*, 1805); Bouilly, for *L'intrigue aux fenêtres* (1805) and *Cimarosa* (1808); and, especially, beginning with *Un jour à Paris, ou La leçon singulière* (1808), Étienne, with whom he produced his finest work. This included the opéra-féerie *Cendrillon* (1810), one of the major successes of the Napoleonic period, and two three-act opéras-comiques that are considered his masterpieces: *Joconde*, staged at the Théâtre Feydeau in February 1814, shortly before the Empire's collapse; and *Jeannot et Colin*, mounted during the Bourbons' first return in October of the same year. Étienne also supplied the text to his last work – and his single departure from the genre of opéra-comique – the five-act opéra-féerie *Aladin, ou La lampe merveilleuse*, completed by Angelo Maria Benincori and lavishly staged in 1822 at the Opéra, with gas lighting being used for the first time.

A comparison between the output of Nicolo and Boieldieu is inevitable. It reveals interesting differences, apart from the fact that their once good relations deteriorated after the latter's return from Russia – if Castil-Blaze is to be trusted, they even publicly came to blows when Grétry's furniture was auctioned in 1813.[97] Both remained essentially faithful to opéra-comique conventions, applying to them their wit and inventiveness rather than attempting to renew the genre as Méhul, Le Sueur, and Cherubini had tried to do. *Les rendez-vous bourgeois*, Nicolo's longest-lasting success before *Cendrillon*, is a typically light-hearted drawing-room comedy of the post-Revolutionary years: a contemporary setting on the outskirts of the robber-infested Bondy forest; a gullible, easily frightened father; the two girls arranging rendez-vous with their lovers; the lovers turning out to be the unexceptional young men the father had in mind for them to begin with. With its graceful and memorable tunes, often based on simple, jaunty dance rhythms, the work delighted Opéra-Comique audiences well into the first half of the twentieth century.[98] More original perhaps are the three works based on artists and musicians: *Michel-Ange* (1802), *Cimarosa*, and *Lully et Quinault, ou Le déjeuner impossible* (1812), all containing amusing expressive effects or musical quotations.

Cendrillon has been eclipsed by Rossini's *Cenerentola*. Yet Nicolo's version of Perrault's tale remained popular for several decades. Étienne's libretto served, in fact, as a model for Rossini's work, with Alidor, the prince's tutor, replacing the traditional fairy-godmother. Musically, Rossini's and Nicolò's works could not be more dissimilar, Nicolo being firmly grounded in the tradition of Grétry. His *Cendrillon*, unlike her Rossinian sister, is characterized by simple, lyrical singing, which contrasts with the coloratura displays of her sisters, who are more individual presences (each has a solo) than in Rossini's opera. A nice touch in the opening quartet, the ditty sung by Cendrillon to Clorinde and Thisbe's exasperation is the popular children's song, "Il était un p'tit homme," familiar – now as then – to everyone who grew up in France, and which Nicolo delightfully combines with the sisters' lines.[99]

Joconde, ou Les coureurs d'aventures was Nicolo's principal contribution to the neo-medieval style in the manner launched by Grétry. Based on a La

Fontaine tale, the plot, which echoes Mozart's *Cosi fan tutte*,[100] features the disguised troubadours Robert (tenor) and Joconde (baritone) outwitted by their fiancées and the peasant girl Jeannette, whom they try to court. The music is enlivened by occasional flashes of Provençal color. The title role long remained one of the staples of the baritone repertory – the first version in English was, in fact performed by the great English baritone Charles Santley (1834–1922), who sang it with the Carl Rosa Company in 1876. Only the lack of such a star role can explain why the Voltaire-based *Jeannot et Colin*, arguably a more refined work, had a shorter lifespan. It shows, as Hervé Lacombe has argued, that Nicolo was Grétry's true heir, as well as an important transitional figure in the history of pre-Romantic opéra-comique.[101]

Gioachino Rossini in Paris

Though *Guillaume Tell* (1829) is the only entirely original opera that Gioachino Rossini (1792–1868) composed to a French text, his creative years in Paris (1823–9) are a capital episode in French operatic history. Moreover, the other three French works that he derived in part from earlier ones – *Le siège de Corinthe* (1826), *Moïse et Pharaon, ou Le passage de la Mer Rouge* (1827), and *Le comte Ory* (1828) fully belong to a history of French opera.[102]

Negotiations between Rossini and the Opéra were already underway by 1818. *L'Italiana in Algeri* had failed the previous year at the Théâtre-Italien, headed by his rival Paër, but *Il barbiere di Siviglia* triumphed in 1819, followed by more productions that provoked both excitement and controversy. When he first visited Paris in November 1823 with Isabella Colbran, his wife since the previous year, Rossini was 32. With 34 operas already to his credit, he was the musical sensation of Europe. Though he spoke little French as yet, a good number of his works were based on French sources: besides the well-known case of *Il barbiere di Siviglia* (1816), *Tancredi* (1813) and *Semiramide* (1823) were adapted from Voltaire tragedies and *Ermione* (1819) from Racine's *Andromaque*; *La gazza ladra* (1817) from a 1815 French melodrama *La pie voleuse, ou La servante de Palaiseau*; and there were several more. Rossini was furthermore familiar with the budding genre of *grand opéra*, having overseen the first production of Spontini's *Fernand Cortez* at the Teatro San Carlo in Naples in 1820.

In April 1824 a French biography and critical study of Rossini by his enthusiastic admirer Stendhal – who compared him to Napoleon – was published in Paris.[103] In November of that year, Rossini was appointed music director of the Théâtre-Italien to succeed Paër. The first original work he wrote for Paris, *Il viaggio a Reims*, was performed in that theater in June 1825 to celebrate the coronation of Charles X. The expectation, however, was that Rossini would contribute works in French, both for the Opéra and the Opéra-Comique. The first, *Le siège de Corinthe*, which triumphed at the Opéra in October 1826, was a reworking of *Maometto II*, premiered in 1820 at the Teatro San Carlo in Naples.[104] Rossini and his librettists, Luigi Balocchi (1766–1832) (house poet of the Théâtre-Italien) and Alexandre Soumet (1788–1845), were prompted by the outpouring of sympathy for the Greeks in their ongoing war of independence against the Turks. Only two years before, Lord Byron, whose poem *The Siege of Corinth* (1816) was echoed in the title of the new work, had died at Missonlonghi. Balocchi and Soumet retained most of the substance of Cesare della Valle's Italian libretto for *Maometto*, moving its setting from the Venetian colony of Negroponte to fifteenth-century Corinth, leaving it to the audience's imagination to see references to current events. The final tableau – the fire and collapse of the catacombs of the city, after the heroine has stabbed herself so as not to fall into the hands of the conqueror – was a kind of an operatic equivalent of Eugène Delacroix's *Massacre at Chios* (1824). This denouement was in the original, but with a less spectacular impact in the context of a rousing cabaletta for the soprano. In reworking his score – modified from two into three acts – Rossini observed some of the French operatic conventions. A ballet was added in Act 2, while the part of the young general Calbo, the heroine's unhappy suitor – Néoclès in *Le siège de Corinthe* – was rewritten from contralto to tenor (trouser roles on French stages being generally reserved for children and pages). The vocal writing, especially the bass role of Mahomet, was simplified,[105] but Pamira, the heroine, still requires agility as well as a gleaming high C for the third act Prayer. Act 1 preserves only an abbreviated version of the "terzettone" between Anna, her father, and Calbo – this number was the most impressive in *Maometto II*. On the other hand, the majestic scene in Act 3, in which Hieros (bass), keeper of the tombs, blesses the doomed Greek warriors, invoking Marathon and Leonidas, has no equivalent in the Italian source and anticipates many similar moments in Romantic grand opera. "Considerably more conservative formally" than *Maometto II*, in Philip Gossett's words, *Le siège de Corinthe* was nonetheless an important date in what can be termed the Italianization of French opera in the Romantic age.[106] The cast of the premiere included Cinti as Pamira; Dérivis, then at the close of his career, as Mahomet; Louis Nourrit, in his last role, as Cléomène; and, as Néoclès, his son Adolphe Nourrit (1802–1839), who had debuted in 1821 as Pylade in Gluck's *Iphigénie en Tauride* and was on his way to becoming the leading French tenor of the age. Rossini was rewarded for his success with an appointment as royal composer and inspector general of singing.

With *Moïse*, premiered in March 1827, Rossini competed on the stage of the Académie royale with Kreutzer's *La mort d'Abel*, the one other biblical opera in the repertory, last heard there in 1826.[107] Rossini's own "azione tragico-sacra" *Mosè in Egitto* (1818) had been performed there once in 1822 (with Giuditta Pasta as Elcia) before being staged at the Théâtre-Italien. Balocchi and Jouy expanded the opera into four acts – the third leaving room for a ballet, largely borrowed from *Armida*. The plot remained basically unchanged, even though some of the characters are renamed: Elcia becomes Anaï, Osiride (Pharaoh's son) Aménophis, and Amaltea (Pharaoh's wife) Sinaïde, while Aaron, for prosodic reasons, is renamed Eliezer. (Confusingly, Amenofide was Elcia's mother in *Mosè* – changed into Marie – while Osiride is now the high priest of Isis, a new character.) Rossini revised the work as extensively as in the case of *Le siège de Corinthe*: arias are cut or – in one case – transferred from one character (Elcia) to another (Anaï), and in a different context. The chorus has a significantly larger role: indeed, surprisingly for a work of its kind (often referred to by Rossini himself as an "oratorio"), *Mosè* did not make an exceptional use of the chorus, even by Rossini's standards.[108] Among the new music in *Moïse* is a beautiful aria for Anaï, "Quelle horrible destinée," at the beginning of Act 4. Its florid writing and extended range (up to E natural) is evidence of the capacities of Laure Cinti, the Parisian creator of the role. The younger Nourrit partnered her in the high-lying part of Aménophis, while Nicolas Levasseur (1791–1871), Dérivis's sucessor as the Opéra's star bass, repeated his Moses from the 1822 French premiere. As in the case of his previous Parisian opera, Rossini created a masterpiece in its own right, which, without supplanting the earlier work, conquered a place in the French operatic repertory. *Moïse* was even more successful than *Le siège*, totaling 187 performances until it was last revived in 1865.[109]

Rossini's third Parisian work, *Le comte Ory*, is unique in the history of the Opéra in the nineteenth century for its unabashedly comic character: its only genuine antecedent would be Rameau's *Platée*, and one looks in vain for an equivalent work premiered on the same stage until the present day, its real successors – on a different stage, and with considerably smaller orchestral forces – being Jacques Offenbach's *buffo* operas of the 1850s and 1860s. The libretto was derived by Scribe from a one-act vaudeville comedy, identically titled, which he had co-authored with Charles-Gaspard Delestre-Poirson. Mounted by one of the boulevard theaters in 1816, it was subtitled "Anecdote du XIe siècle"; the eponymous hero, a kind of medieval Don Giovanni, taking advantage of the absence (on a crusade) of the Comte de Formoutiers, tries to gain the favors of his sister Adèle by disguising himself as a nun – the original medieval ballad went much further, with the count and his companions impregnating an entire convent[110] – but is outwitted by the countess's page (and cousin) Isolier, whom she loves.[111] Scribe toned down the original – the nuns become female pilgrims – and invented a first act in which the count makes a first and equally unsuccessful approach, posing, this time, as a hermit. Whereas most of the music of the first act was recycled from *Il viaggio a Reims*, including the irresistible finale, most of Act 2, save for two numbers, is original – save for one of the drinking songs for the would-be nuns in the château's cellar, based on the medieval ballad tune. The work's gem, one of Rossini's finest inspirations, is the long trio "À la faveur de cette nuit obscure," in which the somewhat scabrous situation – Ory (still in female pilgrim's disguise) and

Isolier alone with the countess in her bedroom – is handled with incomparable grace and vocal and orchestral refinement. Labeled simply "opéra," *Le comte Ory* was enthusiastically received at the Opéra in August 1828. The cast was headed by the younger Nourrit, who had a hand in the libretto, and Cinti as Adèle, while Levasseur sang Ory's tutor. The work remained part of the Opéra repertory for more than five decades. In modern times, it was one of the first lesser-known Rossini operas to be rediscovered, when the Glyndebourne Festival programmed it in the mid-1950s.

Guillaume Tell, Rossini's first completely original French work, nonetheless offers similarities with *Le siège de Corinthe* and *Moïse*: in all three cases the plot revolves on the fight of a community against an oppressor – victoriously in the case of *Moïse* and *Tell*, tragically in that of *Le siège* (even though the moral advantage is made clear). In this context, *Tell* emerges as even bolder, as an essentially secular quest for liberation and independence ("Ou l'indépendance ou la mort") which resonated only too well in post-Napoleonic Europe, making the work undesirable in certain countries.[112] Napoleon's own censors had banned Grétry's opéra-comique on the same subject, staged at the Comédie-Italienne in 1791 (and revived at the Opéra-Comique, rescored by Berton, in 1828). Yet the source of Sedaine's libretto, Lemierre's 1766 tragedy, was rather innocuous compared to Jouy's for Rossini – Friedrich von Schiller's last completed play, staged in Weimar in 1804. Even before completing the work, the composer gave indications that he intended it to be his last opera, and one to which he attached enormous importance.[113] Changes to the libretto were made, with Jouy's approval, by Hippolyte Bis (and probably others, including Nourrit), and the music was written mostly at the country house of a friend, the banker Alexandre Aguado, dedicatee of *Le comte Ory*. Adjustments and cuts were imposed on the reluctant composer during rehearsals, especially to meet the choreographer's demands (there are divertissements both in Act 1 and in Act 3). The premiere, in August 1829, was a triumph for Rossini and his cast, especially Nourrit as Arnold, partnered by the baritone Henri-Bernard Dabadie as Guillaume.

Apart from the fact that it is cast in four acts and ends happily, *Guillaume Tell* exhibits all the features of grand opéra: passions of a heroic nature on a spectacular historical – or, in his case, pseudo-historical – background which offers scope for lavish sets, touches of local color, and abundant opportunities for choral singing. To the love interest – Arnold, son of the Swiss patriot Melcthal, killed by the Austrians, is in love with Mathilde, a Habsburg princess – is attached the most openly Italianate music, such as the three-part Act 2 duet between the lovers, a real archetype of the form, or Arnold's two-part aria "Asile héréditaire" in Act 4. Guillaume Tell himself has no such showy scena, but his Act 3 aria, "Sois immobile," accompanied by a solo cello, is a much more original piece, admired (by Wagner, for one) as a model of expressive declamation, and widely imitated. The historical, patriotic episodes, on the other hand, are treated in the grander, dignified style particular to the Opéra and recalling similar passages in Spontini's *Fernand Cortez* or Rossini's own *Siège de Corinthe*. That is especially the case of the second half of Act 2, where the trio sung by Arnold, Tell, and Walther is succeeded by the meeting on Rütli Heights of the representatives from the cantons of Unterwalden, Uri, and Schwyz. The arrival of the confederates, the swearing of the oath of allegiance, are moments that came to be identified – in the view of Berlioz, among others – with the Romantic notion of the sublime. Equally powerful is the long crescendo at the end of the work, when principals and chorus of the Swiss greet the reappearance of the sun after the storm and their newborn freedom.

Admiration was mixed with criticism. The character of Mathilde, stooping to conquer a Swiss patriot of lower social standing, was objected to. The opera's length – four and a half hours – was also considered excessive, and an abbreviated version in three acts was introduced in Paris in 1831. It became customary to stage Act 2 on its own, generally billed with a ballet. Gilbert Duprez (1806–1896), who made his Opéra debut as Arnold in 1837, performed the work, in the three-act version, with a new finale in which his *grand air* ended the evening: he could thus steal the show with the chest-produced high C he had perfected. Nevertheless, *Guillaume Tell*, restored to its four acts in 1856, remained a staple of the Opéra repertory – and that of the leading provincial theaters – until the First World War and often beyond.[114]

CHAPTER 6

THE AGE OF GRAND OPÉRA

Introduction

The 1825–70 era was a golden age for opera in general and French opera in
particular. During that period, Paris enjoyed unprecedented cultural prestige,
becoming, in Walter Benjamin's phrase, the "capital of the nineteenth
century."[1] The Opéra was then Europe's principal lyric theater. Having a work
successfully staged there, for French and non-French composers alike, was a
consecration avidly sought by the leading opera composers of the age.
Although it partly eluded the greatest two, Verdi and Wagner, who had to wait
several decades to gain full acceptance in France, their eagerness to conquer
Parisian audiences, with works either written or revised specifically for Paris,
reveals how important the stakes were in their own perception.

Three Parisian companies were active throughout the period – the Opéra,
the Opéra-Comique and the Théâtre-Italien. They were joined in 1847 by a
fourth, equally important one, the Opéra-National, which reopened as the
Théâtre-Lyrique in 1851–2.

The Académie royale (rebaptized Théâtre de la Nation in 1848, then
Académie impériale in 1852) operated on new premises. The assassination in
February 1820 of the Duc de Berry, the king's nephew, as he was leaving
the Opéra, resulted in the demolition of the theater it had occupied since the
Revolution on the rue Richelieu. The company shared the Salle Favart with the
Théâtre-Italien for a few months, performed at the Salle Louvois for a few
weeks, and moved in August 1821 to newly built premises it occupied until a
fire destroyed them in October 1873. Known as the Salle Le Peletier after the
street on which it stood – a few blocks to the northeast of the Palais Garnier
site – it had a spacious auditorium accommodating about 1,900 spectators. By
contrast with the Napoleonic and Restoration periods, when the Opéra was
directly administered by the government, the more liberal July Monarchy gave

more freedom to its directors, being content with stipulating official requirements via a "Cahier des charges" and having their management overseen by a
committee. Louis Véron, a prosperous pharmaceutical entrepreneur and
founder of *La Revue de Paris* in 1829, ran the theater from 1831 to 1835 with
a business acumen that made it profitable – by contrast with the Restoration
period. Charles Duponchel, his successor until 1840, although not his match
as a financier, was directly involved in the staging of the operas produced
during his tenure. He was in turn succeeded by Léon Pillet until his
resignation in 1847.

Although the tragédie lyrique – essentially represented by a handful of
works by Gluck, Sacchini, and Spontini – retained a hold in the repertory, no
new ones were produced and the genre was considered dead by the mid-1820s.
One of the last, Berton's *Virginie, ou Les décemvirs*, premiered in 1823,
achieved a respectable 32 performances before disappearing in 1827. The
following year, the triumph of Daniel-François-Esprit Auber's *La muette de
Portici* (see pp. 135–7) inaugurated the reign of grand opéra.[2]

The phrase "grand opéra" predates the period we are discussing: in the eighteenth century it was applied to the tragédie lyrique, especially works by Gluck,
Piccinni, and their contemporaries.[3] By the 1830s, however, it designated the
genre that supplanted the tragédie lyrique, flourished through the 1860s and
survived until the mid-1880s.[4] Many of its characteristics were already in
place by 1809 in Spontini's *Fernand Cortez*: subjects drawn from medieval,
Renaissance, and at times even modern history, rather than mythology or
ancient history;[5] multiple sets and lavish *mise en scène*; and a musical structure
giving at least equal importance to imposing tableaux, with large choral participation, as to arias, duets, and trios. In *Olimpie*, Spontini had tried to graft
these elements onto what was essentially a tragédie lyrique, but the attempt
was unsuccessful. After his departure from Paris, Rossini's *Le siège de Corinthe*
and *Guillaume Tell* were defining milestones. They went further than Spontini
in their incorporation of Italianate vocal forms. An *aria di bravura* like
Arnold's "Asile héréditaire" in *Guillaume Tell*, with its opening recitative, cavatine, transitional passage (known as *tempo di mezzo*) including choral interventions, and a brilliant cabaletta, was something altogether new in French
opera. Such moments, where the dramatic interest gives way to pure vocal
excitement, are usually limited to one instance in most grands opéras, and
often reserved to the heroine – thus Isabelle at the start of Act 2 of Meyerbeer's
Robert le diable (1831), or Marguerite de Valois at the same spot in his *Les
Huguenots* (1836), whereas the tenor lead, in these works, has no cabaletta to
sing.[6] Solo numbers, instead, tend to follow simpler French forms, like the
romance, ballade, or strophic song (known as *couplets*). Duets, on the other
hand, usually follow the extended, Italianate form introduced by Spontini in
La vestale and by Rossini in *Guillaume Tell*: three magnificent examples are
found in *Les Huguenots*.

Structurally, unlike most of late eighteenth-century tragédies lyriques, which are set in three acts, or occasionally four – the five acts of Salieri's *Danaïdes* being an exception – most examples of grand opéra are in five acts, and can include (as does Meyerbeer's *Le prophète*) seven or more tableaux. Also unlike most tragédies lyriques, a grand opéra usually ends tragically, *Guillaume Tell, Robert le diable* being notable exceptions: the three main characters are shot in the last scene of *Les Huguenots*, and when the final curtain falls on *Le prophète* no one is alive. As in the tragédie lyrique, dance is *de rigueur*: most examples of grand opéra feature two divertissements, though almost never in Act 1, the *balletomanes* being notorious latecomers – a rule Wagner ignored at his peril in *Tannhaüser*.[7] *Les Huguenots* includes three divertissements, in Acts 2, 3 and 5. Most of the time, however – with the exception of *La muette de Portici* – the link between dance and the plot is minimal. To paraphrase Cahusac, in grand opéra, one dances for the sake of dancing. At best the scene depicts a ball (as in *Les Huguenots* or *Gustave III*), or peasants dancing (as in *Le prophète*). In many cases – *La Juive, La favorite, Don Carlos* – the action simply stops and the characters on stage become an audience watching a ballet.[8]

Dramatically, grand opéra owes much to the French Romantic theater, called for by Stendhal in *Racine et Shakespeare* (1825) and theorized by Victor Hugo in the preface to his historical drama *Cromwell* (1827). The discovery of Shakespeare, known to the French in bowdlerized versions until Charles Kemble's troupe first performed in Paris in 1827, was from this point of view as important as the acclimatization of Italianate vocal forms.[9] One element Hugo particularly admired in Shakespeare and promoted in his advocacy of the modern *drame* was the combination of "sublime" and "grotesque" elements – a mixing of tones forbidden in French classical tragedy. Likewise, in grand opéra, subaltern characters are often used for effects of contrast – a contrast frequently mirrored in the character of the music. The unheroic Raimbaud in *Robert le diable* – cowardly, greedy, not unlikeable perhaps but certainly an unpromising fiancé for Alice – is typical of this diversification of tone. Another example is the "Trio bouffe" sung in Act 3 of *Le prophète* by Oberthal and the Anabaptists Zacharie and Jonas, all three of whom cut sinister figures in the rest of the opera. Hugo himself followed the principle in his one opera libretto, *La Esmeralda*, adapted from his novel *Notre-Dame-de-Paris*, which characteristically mixes low-life jollity and a tragic love story ending in death. Its music was composed by Louise Bertin (1805–1877) and the cast was headed by Adolphe Nourrit and Cornelie Falcon, but the work, reportedly the victim of a cabal directed at the composer's father, head of the powerful *Journal des débats*, was withdrawn after six performances.[10]

The aesthetics of grand opéra are indebted to an even greater extent to popular theater, particularly melodrama, a genre born during the Revolution and which flourished in the Boulevard theaters during the Empire and the

Restoration.[11] A strong influence, as we have seen, on the "serious" opéra-comique of the Revolutionary and post-Revolutionary period – the founding father of melodrama, Pixérécourt, directed the Théâtre Feydeau between 1815 and 1827 – it was no less so on Romantic opera and Romantic drama. In Karin Pendle's words, "by the mid-1830s, French Grand Opera had absorbed all the most progressive and characteristic features of boulevard entertainments and had assimilated them with such skill and on such scale that they had come to be identified less with the popular theaters than with the Opéra itself."[12] Melodrama is essentially a non-literary theater: its style is simple, at times crude. Yet the characteristics of melodrama permeate the literary plays of more canonical writers like Hugo and Alexandre Dumas. In their plays melodrama combined tragic and comic elements, but put a greater emphasis on spectacle, including pantomime and ballet.[13] Romantic melodrama, indeed, made much use of stage music: among the composers active at the Porte Saint-Martin and Gaîté theaters, where the plays of Victor Ducange, Anicet Bourgeois and Auguste Maquet were performed, was Alexandre Piccinni, the composer's grandson.

The spectacular element had been prominent in French opera from the earliest days of the tragédie en musique. But in grand opéra – as in the visual arts of the Romantic period – the taste for the *merveilleux*, still alive in Gluck's days, and of which there are still traces in the last act of *La vestale*, was replaced by the cult of the picturesque, both geographical and historical. Pierre-Luc-Charles Ciceri, stage designer at the Opéra from 1824 until 1847, whose contribution to grand opéra was considerable, traveled to Switzerland to prepare the sets for *Guillaume Tell*. Unlike the sumptuous, but fanciful, Greek or Roman palaces of the tragédie lyrique, his historical tableaux – fifteenth-century Konstanz in *La Juive*, the Pré-aux-Clercs in August 1572 in Act 3 of *Les Huguenots* – aimed at historical reconstitution. Technical innovations – gas lighting, first used in Nicolo's *Aladin* in 1822; electricity, introduced for the sunrise over the frozen lake in Act 3 of *Le prophète* (1849) – were also put at the service of the overall effect. When Ferdinand Hérold (see pp. 132–4) wrote that the ending of a five-act opera ought to be "in the hands of the set designer, the *machiniste*, or the director,"[14] he was not abdicating his artistic responsibilities: he was simply acknowledging the fact that grand opéra was a collaborative work, in which the composer was only first among equals.[15] From this perspective, grand opéra was both returning to the original traditions of French opera and attempting to create a "total work of art" in a sense parallel to the Wagnerian concept of the *Gesamtkunstwerk* – and one should not minimize the influence of grand opéra on the Bayreuth master.[16]

The restoration of the Opéra to a dominant position, after several decades when the Opéra-Comique had had the artistic edge, was obviously a challenge for the latter company. In 1829 it left the by then decrepit Théâtre Feydeau and moved to the smaller premises of the Salle Ventadour on the street of the same

name, a few blocks away from the Palais-Royal; and, in 1832, to the Salle de la
Bourse on rue Vivienne, where it remained until 1840. It was then transferred
to the second Salle Favart, a fire having destroyed the original one in 1838. Its
auditorium was of the same size as the Salle Le Peletier, while the pit could
accommodate more than 50 musicians, a respectable size if no match for the
Opéra's 85 musicians.

The age of grand opéra was also a period of considerable vitality for the
Opéra-Comique. While Boieldieu and Nicolo remained popular, the next generation was dominated by Hérold, Auber, Fromental Halévy (see pp. 150–5) and
Adolphe Adam (see pp. 147–50), succeeded in turn by Félicien David, Victor
Massé, and Ambroise Thomas. As in earlier times, non-French composers
continued to enrich the repertory. The Turin-born Felice Blangini (1781–1841),
whose career began with the completion of *La fausse duègre*, the opera of the
opéra-comique left unfinished by Della Maria at his death, wrote 30 opéras-
comiques of his own between 1803 and 1833. The Neapolitan Gioseffo Catrufo
(1771–1851) had 10 French works premiered on the same stage between 1813
and 1832. His aristocratic compatriot Michele Carafa (1787–1872), who moved
to Paris in 1821, had a brilliant Opéra-Comique career, from *Jeanne d'Arc à
Orléans* (1821) and *Le solitaire* (1822) to *Thérèse* (1838). His four-act "drame
lyrique" *Masaniello, ou Le pêcheur napolitain* (1827) preceded by three months
Auber's grand opéra on the same subject.[17] Carafa collaborated with Scribe
on *La prison d'Édimbourg* (1833), adapted from Walter Scott's *The Heart of
Midlothian*.[18] The Spanish composer José Melchor Gomis (1791–1836), who
lived in France as a political refugee as of 1823, gained attention in 1833 with *Le
revenant*, another Scott-based opéra-comique, this time based on *Redgauntlet*.
Le portefaix, for which Gomis collaborated with Scribe, was also well received in
1835. In the following decade, the Irish composer Michael William Balfe
(1808–1870), also working with Scribe, scored a major success with *Le puits
d'amour* in 1843, the same year that his masterpiece *The Bohemian Girl* (which
has a French source) was premiered in London. Balfe composed two more
French operas, the opéra-comique *Les quatre fils Aymon* (1844) and the grand
opéra *L'étoile de Séville* (1845), after Lope de Vega's *La estrella de Sevilla*, but
neither had a comparable success.

Eugène Scribe (1791–1861), already mentioned several times, is the central
figure of French opera in the Romantic period. A Parisian, he had already had
several plays staged by the time he graduated in law from the Imperial
University in 1815. Immensely prolific, he wrote an average of eight or nine a
year. His production includes more than a hundred vaudeville comedies,
comedies of manners for the Comédie-Française (*Bertrand et Raton* and *Le
verre d'eau*, staged respectively in 1833 and 1840, remain the most famous),
ballet scenarios and close to 120 opera libretti. Karin Pendle's survey of Scribe's
work for the lyric theater lists 86 opéras-comiques and 30 operas.[19] In addition
to the aforementioned Balfe, Boieldieu, Carafa, Cherubini, Gomis, Halévy,

Meyerbeer, and Rossini, his collaborators included Adam, Donizetti, Gounod, Albert Grisar, Hérold, Massé, Offenbach, Verdi, and especially Auber, to whom he contributed a total of 37 libretti (one third of his output), as well as lesser-known figures: Bertin, Antoine-Louis Clapisson, Fétis, Manuel García, Loïsa Puget, and a dozen others. No librettist in operatic history matches Scribe in quantity and scope.

Scribe's unprecedented success was explained in his day by his ability to fashion "well-made plays."[20] As this supposedly self-evident formulation suggests, his dramaturgy aimed at meeting the expectations of the audience – hence, perhaps, the failure of his dramaturgy to outlive its time. This "triumph of craft over art," to quote Karin Pendle,[21] was achieved through the combination of recurrent dramatic formulas – the same author has identified 21 stock situations in Scribe's opéras-comiques and 19 in his operas (with, naturally, some overlap between the two).[22] But Scribe's success in the operatic world was also a measure of his ability to provide in a short time an endless supply of lively, singable texts that stimulated the musical imagination of the composers he worked with.

A different stimulant to French opera in the Romantic period was provided by the presence in Paris of an exceptional Italian troupe, which remained active until 1870.[23] Regularly staged in Paris since 1800, Italian opera gained in visibility when Rossini became its director in 1824 and his influence remained strong throughout the period. Not only were many new works by Bellini, Donizetti, Giovanni Pacini, and Luigi Ricci mounted there shortly after their Italian premieres, but some new Italian works – notably Bellini's *I puritani* and Donizetti's *Marino Faliero*, within a few weeks in the spring of 1835 – were first given in Paris. The greatest Italian singers performed there. Giuditta Pasta, recruited by Hérold, came to Paris in 1821. In the next decade, the four singers who composed the opening cast of *I puritani* – the soprano Giulia Grisi (1811–1869), the tenor Giovanni Battista Rubini (1794–1854), the baritone Antonio Tamburini (1800–1876), the bass Luigi Lablache (1794–1858) – formed an unparalleled ensemble.

This competition presented a challenge to French singers, whose style and training had repeatedly come under attack during the previous period. Reforming French singing was one of Cherubini's priorities when he became director of the Conservatoire in 1822. Four years later, Rossini was appointed inspector general of singing. Whatever may have actually caused this development, the 1830s and 1840s represented a point of perfection in French singing, especially at the Opéra.[24] We have already encountered the name of the tenor Adolphe Nourrit, who premiered grands opéras by Rossini, Auber, Halévy, and Meyerbeer. His meteoric career ended with his suicide in Naples in 1839, due to a fit of depression partly caused by the success of his rival Gilbert Duprez (1806–1896). Equally at ease in the French and Italian repertories (he was the original Edgardo in Donizetti's *Lucia di Lammermoor*), Duprez himself can be considered the prototype of the modern tenor. Like him, the baritone Henri-Bernard Dabadie (1797–1853) had an international career: he was the first Belcore in Auber's *Le philtre* in Paris and the first Belcore in Donizetti's *L'elisir d'amore* in Milan – the two works based on the same Scribe libretto. Although she lost her voice at the age of 26, Cornélie Falcon (1812–1897), who premiered *La Juive* and *Les Huguenots*, gave her name to a vocal type, characterized by a strong lower register and gleaming top, though seldom required to go above C or C sharp. Laure Cinti-Damoreau (1801–1863), who sang Marguerite de Valois to Falcon's Valentine in *Les Huguenots*, is notable for having had successful careers both at the Opéra – she was the first Mathilde in *Guillaume Tell* – and at the Opéra-Comique, where she sang between 1836 and 1841. At the Opéra-Comique the outstanding male singer was Jean-Baptiste Chollet (1798–1892), who premiered the high, florid tenor parts in Auber's *Fra Diavolo*, Hérold's *Zampa*, and Adam's *Le postillon de Longjumeau*. If French Romantic works – particularly the exceptionally arduous over by Meyerbeer – have failed to retain their share of the modern repertory, it is to some extent because of the lack of singers capable of doing them justice.

Ferdinand Hérold

On a par with Boieldieu, Auber, and Adam, Ferdinand Hérold (1791–1833) is one of the great figures of French Romantic opéra-comique.[25] Born in Paris, he was the son of the Alsacian musician François-Joseph Hérold (1755–1802), a respected piano teacher, whose premature death from consumption deeply affected his son. At the Conservatoire, which he entered at the age of 15, Ferdinand Hérold studied with Louis Adam (father of the composer) and Catel, Kreutzer, and Méhul – the last his professor of composition. He won the Prix de Rome in 1812, but after his first year at the Villa Medici moved to Naples, where he obtained a position at the court of Napoleon's brother-in-law, Joachim Murat. There he made his operatic debut with an Italian work, *La gioventù di Enrico quinto*, which was rapturously received when staged in January 1815. The title role was sung by the tenor Manuel García, father of the singers Maria Malibran and Pauline Viardot.[26] On his return trip Hérold stopped in Vienna, where he was kindly received by Salieri but was too shy to use the letter of introduction he had for Beethoven. Back in Paris in the summer of 1815, he was hired as pianist by the Théâtre-Italien, collaborating with Boieldieu on an official commission and winning recognition on his own with the three-act opéras-comiques *Les rosières* and *La clochette*, both in 1817. Then came a string of failures, one of them a resetting of Vadé's libretto for Dauvergne's *Les troqueurs*. Discouraged, Hérold provisionally gave up the theater for a few years, during which he returned to Italy on a prospecting and recruiting mission for the Théâtre-Italien.

Hérold returned to the stage in 1823 with *Le muletier*, whose librettist Paul de Kock (1793–1871) later became a famous popular novelist. Contemporaries admired the grace and wit that Hérold displayed in his setting of the bawdy subject, which came from Boccaccio by way of La Fontaine. After this success, the one-act *Lasthénie*, a comedy set in ancient Athens and featuring Alcibiades as one of the characters, was a mere *succès d'estime* at the Opéra in the same year, despite Nourrit's presence in the cast. Hérold's breakthrough came in 1826 with *Marie*, a three-act opéra-comique on a libretto by Eugène de Planard (1783–1855), which remained in the repertory for several decades and established his international reputation. A serious work, in the tradition of Grétry, Dalayrac, and Boieldieu, it revolves on a social issue reminiscent of Diderot's theories and recalling the contemporary novels of Claire de Duras: Marie, brought up as an orphan by a baron and his wife but in reality the baroness's daughter from a first marriage, is prevented by her situation from marrying the young man she loves and who loves her, while he himself has been promised to Émilie, the baron's daughter. The distraught Marie disappears, and the fear that she might have drowned herself prompts her mother to confess the secret of her birth. But Marie's hiding place is discovered and her stepfather explains to her the situation in a (spoken) scene of surprising subtlety. This "drame bourgeois" plot was perfectly attuned to Hérold's genius. Elegant melodies and lively ensembles alternate with moments of emotion and even power in the second act, while giving vocal virtuosity its due, both in the soprano and tenor roles (one of the latter going up to D flat).

In the fall of 1826 Hérold left his position at the Théâtre-Italien to become singing coach at the Opéra, a position he kept for the remainder of his life. For the Opéra he composed five full-length ballets: one, *La fille mal gardée* (1828), has kept his name alive to this day. His next work for the Opéra-Comique, *L'illusion* (1829) was no match for *Marie* in popularity, but represents an interesting evolution of the genre, since it ends on the heroine's suicide: such a denouement was unprecedented in opéra-comique.

The climax of Hérold's career came in May 1831, when *Zampa, ou La fiancée de marbre*, a three-act opéra-comique on a libretto by Mélesville, triumphed at the Salle Ventadour. Like like Auber's *Fra Diavolo*, which preceded it by a year, it has a "negative" hero: Zampa, a Sicilian nobleman turned pirate, once seduced and abandoned a young girl, who died of grief. Her statue can be seen in the castle where Alphonse, Zampa's long-lost brother, and Camille are about to get married. Zampa, who has designs on Camille, blackmails her out of the wedding. However, he makes the mistake of putting his ring on the statue's finger – a "Gothic" twist that may have been inspired by the Bleeding Nun episode in Matthew Lewis's *The Monk*, and was in turn borrowed by Prosper Mérimée in 1837 for his tale *La Vénus d'Ille*. The denouement unfolds as expected: as Zampa is about to rape Camille, the statue – silent, unlike the one in Mozart's *Don Giovanni* – appears in the alcove and crushes the pirate in its embrace, while Mount Etna erupts in the background. The "dark" character of the plot is tempered by touches of irony and humor, while Hérold's music is alternately graceful and vigorous. With Chollet in the title role,[27] *Zampa* succeeded brilliantly in Paris (694 performances by 1913) and numbers among the most widely performed French operas of the nineteenth century. Besides its unusual plot, it shows Hérold to be an imaginative melodist, a subtle harmonist and a deft orchestrator. Even Berlioz, who did not like the work, nevertheless suggested it was a cross between Rossini and Weber.

Mérimée was all the more entitled to draw his inspiration from *Zampa* since Hérold's final work, and perhaps his masterpiece, *Le Pré-aux-clercs*, was adapted by Planard from his novel *Chronique du temps de Charles IX*.[28] Few opéras-comiques of the period come so close to the world of grand opéra. It anticipates *Les Huguenots*, whose third act is set in this very Pré-aux-clercs, the piece of land along the Seine, across the Louvre, which in the sixteenth century served as the equivalent of a public garden. The plot, however, is not set in 1572 at the time of the St Bartholomew Massacre, as in Mérimée's novel, but 10 years later, under the reign of Henri III. Isabelle, the heroine, a protégée of Marguerite de Valois, Queen of Navarre, is courted both by the Protestant Mergy, Navarre's envoy to the court, whom she loves in return, and the Catholic Comminges, officially her fiancé (both tenor roles). A quarrel between the two young men results in the duel at the Pré-aux-clercs, in the course of which Comminges is killed. This happy ending of sorts – the lovers can marry and return to Navarre – hardly makes the work a comedy; indeed, one of its memorable episodes is the moment when Comminges' corpse is brought back, in a boat, from the scene of the duel. Comic relief – as is often the case in grand opéra as well – is provided by lower-class characters, Girot the innkeeper (bass) and his fiancée Nicette. From the opening fugato of the overture to the taut third act, the work offers a dramatic unity and tension that are barely interrupted by Isabelle's grand air with violin solo ("Jours de mon enfance") at the beginning of Act 2. Rivaling *La dame blanche* as the most frequently performed opéra-comique in nineteenth-century France, *Le Pré-aux-clercs* had been staged nearly 1,600 times at the Salle Favart by 1898. Hérold, too sick to take a curtain call at the triumphant premiere on 15 December 1832, died five weeks later of tuberculosis at the age of 42. His unfinished opéra-comique *Ludovic* was completed by Halévy.

Daniel-François-Esprit Auber

Luckier than Hérold, his friend and rival, Daniel-François-Esprit Auber (1782–1871) had a long, prosperous career which puts him at the forefront of opéra-comique composers of the first half of the nineteenth century.[29] And unlike Hérold, whose dream to write a fully-fledged work for the Opéra was never fulfilled, Auber occupies also an important position in the history of grand opéra.[30] He came from the city of Caen in Normandy but his family moved to Paris at the time of the Revolution. Apart from a short stay in

London in 1802–3, he remained a Parisian all his life. His musical beginnings were as a gifted amateur, and it was in an amateur theater that he made his operatic debut in 1805 with the opéra-comique *Julie*, based on the Monvel libretto already set by Dezède in 1772. At that time, however, Auber studied with Cherubini for three years. His second opera, *Jean de Couvain* (1812), was written for the private theater of the Prince de Caraman-Chimay, his teacher's patron. Like *Julie*, it remained unpublished. Auber made his public debut at the comparatively ripe age of 31 with the one-act *Le séjour militaire*, which achieved 16 performances at the Opéra-Comique in 1816. Only after the death of his father in 1820, which resulted in the bankruptcy of the family art-publishing business, did Auber devote himself fully to composition, turning himself into one of the most prolific opera composers of his age, with nearly 50 works to his credit.

Auber's early successes were *La bergère châtelaine* (1820) and *Emma, ou La promesse imprudente* (1821), both on Planard libretti. *Emma* alone was performed 181 times in Paris. *Leicester, ou Le château de Kenilworth* (1823), after Scott's novel, inaugurated Auber's close collaboration with Scribe.[31] *La neige, ou Le nouvel Éginard* (1823), *Le concert à la cour, ou La débutante* (1824), the Cervantes-based "drame lyrique" *Léocadie* (1824), were all successes, and *Le maçon* (1825) even more so, with more than 500 Opéra-Comique performances in the nineteenth century. Like Rossini's *Le Siège de Corinthe* the following year, it reflects the anti-Turkish feelings generated by sympathy for the cause of Greek independence. On his wedding-day, the eponymous mason is kidnapped and forcibly taken to a château outside Paris where a young Greek woman, Irma, is held captive by a Turk who intends to marry her though she is in love with a young Frenchman, Léon. All ends well thanks to the intervention of the mason, whose first-act *ronde* ("Du courage, les amis sont toujours là") gained enormous popularity.[32]

Auber's first work for the Opéra, in collaboration with Hérold, was the occasional "drame lyrique" in one act, *Vendôme en Espagne*, staged in 1823 to celebrate the French military intervention, under the Duc d'Angoulême, which had restored the Bourbon king Ferdinand VII to the Spanish throne. By contrast with this overt celebration of monarchy, *La muette de Portici* was based by Auber and his librettists, Scribe and Germain Delavigne, on the revolt led in 1647 against Spanish rule by the Neapolitan fisherman Masaniello.[33] The political implications of the work have been much debated by recent scholars. Auber and Scribe were certainly far from harboring any subversive views. Nor did the royal censors object to the theme, which had just been set by Carafa, any more than they tried to stop Rossini from writing the potentially more inflammatory *Guillaume Tell*. *La muette de Portici* was even performed in May 1830 before the visiting King and Queen of Naples. On the other hand, three months later, it was selected as a benefit for the victims of the July uprising which, in the meantime, had driven Charles X into exile.[34] Clearly, the story of a revolution, even a failed one, was in the spirit of the time and Auber and Scribe, however unwittingly, touched a sensitive chord in many audiences. The most celebrated instance occurred on 25 August 1830 when the riot that led to the proclamation of the independence of Belgium began during a performance of *La muette de Portici* at the Théâtre de la Monnaie, precisely at the end of the rousing Act 2 duet "Mieux vaut mourir que rester misérable" – the words of its refrain, "Amour sacré de la patrie," borrowed from the text of the *Marseillaise*.[35]

Political ambiguity is not the only distinctive feature of *La muette de Portici*. Its mute heroine was not an unknown device in contemporary melodrama. It had been introduced into French opéra-comique by Dalayrac in *Deux mots, ou Une nuit dans la forêt* (1806) – another operatic instance being the eponymous heroine of Weber's *Silvana* (1810), based on Karl von Steinsberg's *Das Waldmädchen*. Auber and his librettists took it even further by making their heroine, Fenella, manifestly deaf and dumb[36] and giving the role to a ballerina: this integration of dance – or more precisely pantomime – in the structure of an opera is highly uncommon in the history of the genre.[37] Fenella – her name comes from the dumb heroine in Scott's *Peveril of the Peak* – has been seduced and abandoned by Alphonse, son of the Spanish viceroy. Having escaped from the jail into which she was thrown by his father, she denounces him publicly on the day of his marriage with the Spanish princess Elvire. Fenella then reveals the facts – though not the identity of her seducer – to her brother Masaniello. The rebellion begins in the third act, on the market square, when Fenella and Masaniello are threatened with arrest. From the melancholy barcarolle that introduces him in Act 2 to the haunting berceuse he sings in Act 4 to console his sister, Masaniello comes off as a pessimistic, doomed hero. Another original feature of the work is that neither of its tenor roles (the other being the remorseful Alphonse) is particularly heroic. Horrified by revolutionary violence, Masaniello finds himself having to extend his protection to Alphonse and Elvire, arousing the hatred of his fellow conspirator Pietro – his partner in the patriotic duet. As the sedition faces defeat, Masaniello is massacred by his partisans. While Mount Vesuvius erupts in the distance (this circumstance had actually occurred in 1631, not in 1647), Fenella throws herself from the terrace of the viceroy's palace.[38] Auber's score reaches impressive heights in the depiction of Masaniello's madness, with strains of the Barcarolle and the Act 3 revolutionary music providing motivic unity. In the 1828 production, designed by Ciceri, Masaniello was sung by Nourrit, while Louise Noblet (1801–1852) danced the part of Fenella. Within the next decades, *La muette de Portici* was staged in many countries around the world. It maintained itself in the Opéra repertory until 1882, having by then achieved more than 500 performances. It was especially popular in Germany. Wagner, an unexpected champion, praised the work's "unaccustomed concision and drastic compactness of Form" (it is indeed by far the shortest grand opéra) and

Auber's "brilliant instrumentation" and "striking colour", as well as "the sureness and audacity of his orchestral effects." He considered it, in fact, the highest point of perfection so far attained in French opera.[39]

Though not matching the success of La muette, the "opéra historique" Gustave III ou Le bal masqué (1833), describing events that had occurred a mere four decades before, was one of Scribe and Auber's finest achievements.[40] Its wide success did not extend to Sweden, however, where it was unwelcome. Today it is remembered – if at all – for having served as a model for Verdi and his librettist Antomo Somma in Un ballo in maschera (1859). Anyone familiar with Somma's text will be struck by how closely it follows Scribe – with the important difference that censorship forced Verdi to change the setting from eighteenth-century Stockholm to seventeenth-century Boston.[41] Based on the same vocal distribution as Verdi's, Auber's work is notable for its ensembles and duets, especially the one in Act 3 between the king and Amélie (sung by Nourrit and Falcon in 1833), its slow section built on a beautiful chromatic, soaring phrase. Audiences of 1833 were impressed above all by the splendor of the final ballroom scene with 300 people on stage.[42]

None of the other works Auber gave to the Opéra (all on texts by Scribe) belong to the grand opéra category. Le dieu et la bayadère (1830) is an opéra-ballet, based on Goethe's ballad Der Gott und die Bayadere. As in La muette de Portici, the heroine is a danced and mimed role. Le philtre (1831) and Le serment (1832) are comic operas (not opéras-comiques according to the terminology of the period, however, since they are sung throughout). The former is a two-act peasant comedy on a libretto which, two years later, Felice Romani adapted for Donizetti as L'elisir d'amore. Ultimately supplanted by its Italian rival, Le philtre is nonetheless a delightful work and had achieved nearly 250 performances by the mid-1860s. Le serment deals with a young soldier who chances upon a group of counterfeiters and is spared his life provided he swears not to reveal their identity – an oath that comes back to haunt him when his sweetheart is promised by her father to the gang leader. As the title indicates, Le lac des fées (1839) is a fairy opera set in medieval Germany, a cross between Swan Lake and The Little Mermaid. It also features a Jewish usurer, possibly inspired by Shakespeare's Shylock. Moderately successful in Paris, it was staged in several countries and did well in Germany. With L'enfant prodigue (1850), Scribe and Auber produced a biblical opera, a genre last illustrated in Paris by Rossini in Moïse (1827).[43] Acts 2 to 4 are set in Egypt and are the pretext for colorful, exotic music. As for Zerline, ou La corbeille d'oranges (1850), a romantic comedy set in Renaissance Palermo, it was written as a vehicle for the star coloratura contralto Marietta Alboni (1826–1894). In the manner of many Italian operas of the period, but unusually for Auber, it ends with a flashy aria for the heroine.

Most of Auber's output was reserved for the Opéra-Comique, where he and Scribe had an almost uninterrupted string of successes, from La fiancée (1829), the Tyrolienne of which served as the motif for a Grande Fantaisie by Franz Liszt, to *La Circassienne*, premiered in the year of Scribe's death (1861). *Fra Diavolo, ou L'auberge de Terracine* (1831) belongs to the genre of "brigand opera" launched by Le Sueur in *La caverne* (1793) – and, much later, parodied by Offenbach in *Les brigands* (1869).[44] Based on a historical character hanged in Naples in 1806, but without any pretense to factual accuracy, *Fra Diavolo* features the bandit disguised as an aristocrat and trying to rob a hilarious if rather improbable English couple, Lord Kokbourg (i.e. Cockburn) and his slightly dotty wife "Milady," until he is captured by the carabinieri. Set in Auber's most high-spirited, tuneful manner, Scribe's libretto has an endearing tongue-in-cheek quality[45] that clearly accounts for the popularity of the work worldwide. It is, in fact, the only Auber work to have remained in the repertory, especially in German-speaking countries (hence the existence of several complete recordings in German).[46] The work was also widely disseminated in an Italian version premiered in London in 1857, and to which Auber added a brilliant coloratura aria for Zerline, the soprano heroine, in whose father's inn the action is set.

After *Lestocq* (1834), set in Russia at the time of Empress Elizabeth – Wagner conducted the work at Magdeburg in 1836 – Auber and Scribe produced one of their most accomplished works with *Le cheval de bronze* in 1835. Set in a legendary China, it combines various subplots loosely linked by the theme of a magical bronze horse that transports whoever mounts it to the planet Venus, which has an entirely female population. In the final act – a witty inversion of the Orpheus myth[47] – the main female character, Péki, resorts to the horse to go there herself to rescue her lover Yanko, changed into a statue for having babbled about his Venusian experience. From its joyful opening chorus, which also closes the work, *Le cheval de bronze* has a vitality and wit that characterize Auber's best works.[48] It was later revised for the Opéra in the form of an opéra-ballet.

The heroine of *L'ambassadrice* (1836) is a prima donna called Henriette, a transparent allusion to its model, the German soprano Henriette Sontag (1806–1854). The role was premiered by Cinti-Damoreau, hitherto star of the Opéra, who had just transferred to the Opéra-Comique. The 417 performances the work achieved in Paris pale by comparison with the more than 1,200 Parisian showings for *Le domino noir* (1837), Auber's most popular work in France – its only competitors, before 1914, were *La dame blanche* and *Le Pré-aux-clercs* – and in the rest of Europe. Set in Madrid on Christmas Eve, Scribe's libretto rests on an unapologetically absurd premise: the night before she is supposed to become abbess of her convent, Angèle d'Olivarès (another Cinti-Damoreau part) escapes to attend a masked ball, dressed in a black domino. There she encounters Horace, the young man she had met the previous year under similar circumstances and, naturally, falls in love with him again. In the second act, she follows him to a Christmas party, claiming to be the niece of the host's housekeeper, freshly arrived from Aragon (the pretext for a virtuoso Aragonese song). Set in the convent, the third act is a gently satirical picture of intrigues and jealousies, happily resolved when Angèle cheerfully leaves the position of abbess to her rival and marries Horace. Among the work's gems are the strophic song of the convent's porter Gil Perez, "Nous allons avoir, grâce à Dieu," which parodies Gregorian chant; and the Act 3 chorus of chattering nuns, "Ah! quel malheur pour nous."[49]

Another highlight of the Scribe-Auber collaboration, *Les diamants de la couronne* (1841), set in Brazil, returns to the "bandit" theme, complicated by a bizarre twist: not only is the head of the bandits a woman, with whom the hero Henrique duly falls in love in Act 1, but she turns out to be the new queen of the country. As often in Auber's opéras-comiques, the dramatic and musical culmination is the Act 2 finale, when the situation – worthy of a Feydeau comedy – reaches utmost confusion.[50]

By contrast with Auber's previous opéras-comiques, *Haydée, ou Le secret* (1847) is remarkable for its lack of comical elements. The heroine's name comes from Byron's *Don Juan*, but by way of Alexandre Dumas' *Le comte de Monte Cristo* where, under the spelling "Haidée," she is, as in Scribe's libretto, a Greek slave of noble birth. The plot hinges on a circumstance derived from Mérimée's tale, *La partie de tric-trac*, with the action transposed to Renaissance Dalmatia and Venice and a second act – like Act 3 of Meyerbeer's *L'Africaine* – set on a boat.[51] The secret of the subtitle is that the hero, Loredano, a Venetian general, once cheated at a game of dice, causing the ruin and suicide of a senator. Captain Malipieri, Loredano's enemy, gets hold of the incriminating document and blackmails him until Haydée, who is in love with Loredano, buys it back from Malipieri by agreeing to marry him.[52] The situation is saved at the last minute by the senator's son, who kills Malipieri, while Loredano becomes Doge. *Haydée* is among Auber's strongest scores, totaling close to 500 Paris performances in the nineteenth century. One memorable moment is the end of Act 1, when a sleeping Loredano, as in a trance, reveals his secret in Malipieri's presence. The text breaks off on an unfinished word – the first syllable of the word "amours" – followed by an unconventional chromatic coda.[53]

Auber's *Manon Lescaut* (1856) was the first operatic adaptation of the Abbé Prévost's famous story, preceded only by a ballet on a libretto by Scribe and with music by Halévy, staged at the Opéra in 1830. Compared to Massenet's and Puccini's subsequent treatments, the opéra-comique's libretto considerably softens the character of Manon, whose foibles amount to little more than coquetry and sauciness. As in Prévost and Puccini (and unlike Massenet's heroine), she dies in Louisiana, but it is made clear that her transportation resulted from a false accusation. Scribe adds characters not present in the original, such as Manon's friend Marguerite and her fiancé Gervais: we encounter them again in Louisiana, where they have conveniently emigrated. Another is the Marquis d'Hérigny, Manon's would-be "protector" (a more petulant version of Massenet's Brétigny), who gets two elegant, florid arias. The part was written for Jean-Baptiste Faure, the greatest French baritone of the period, while Manon herself was the Belgian coloratura soprano Marie Cabel (1827–1885). Among the work's finest moments are its ensembles: the Act 1 and Act 2 finales (the famous "Bourbonnaise," Manon's Laughing Song, is part of the former); and, in Act 3, the quartet "Du courage! Dieu nous regarde!" and the last duet, which, however, does not end the opera, since Gervais and Marguerite reappear, "along with a group of black slaves," to announce that Manon has been pardoned. But Manon has died. Unlike Kreutzer and Le Sueur (and their librettists), who had introduced a happy ending into their respective versions of *Paul et Virginie*, Scribe and Auber, by 1856, were unwilling to distort the denouement of a well-known literary work to satisfy opéra-comique convention.[54]

Auber was 74 when *Manon Lescaut* was premiered in 1856 but his activity had barely diminished with age. Before that, in 1842 he had succeeded his teacher Cherubini as head of the Conservatoire. Furthermore, on his accession as emperor in 1852, Napoleon III had appointed Auber his maître de chapelle, and he fulfilled his duties by composing religious music. In his eighties he produced three more opéras-comiques in three acts: *La fiancée du roi de Garbe* (1864); the enchanting *Le premier jour de bonheur* (1868), which was performed 175 times in five years; and *Rêve d'amour* (1869), an eighteenth-century "paysannerie" in the tradition of Grétry.

Sadly, now that Auber's works have virtually disappeared from the repertory, his importance in operatic history is usually ignored. As Herbert Schneider's thematic catalogue of his works shows,[55] he was one of the most published and performed composers of his age – on a level comparable to Rossini – with many of his works popularized worldwide in every possible kind of arrangement. Among his successors, only Offenbach and Massenet were to match him in this respect.

Giacomo Meyerbeer in Paris

As his self-chosen identity indicates, Giacomo Meyerbeer (1797–1864) had made his name as an Italian opera composer. He became, however, a byword for Parisian grand opéra, while making two notable contributions to French opéra-comique.[56] His two principal Italian works had French sources: his first major success, *Margherita d'Anjou* (1820), was based on a popular 1810 melodrama by Pixérécourt; the even more successful *Il crociato in Egitto* (1824), the last opera featuring a castrato, was based by its librettist Gaetano Rossi on an obscure play by Jean Antoine Marie Monperlier, H. Albertin, and Jean-Baptiste Dubois.[57] However, when the Théâtre-Italien staged it in 1825, under the composer's supervision, the castrato role was sung by Pasta. *Margherita d'Anjou* was seen in Paris, in French, at the Odéon the following year, in a version in which Meyerbeer probably had no hand.

Even before *Il crociato* triumphed in Venice, the Opéra authorities, as with Rossini, were trying to lure the rising star to write a French opera. The first, *Robert le diable*, was, however, first planned to be written with Scribe in late 1826 for the Opéra-Comique – that is, with spoken dialogue and without a ballet – as a result of a commission from Pixérécourt, then head of the Feydeau company. Shelved when he resigned, it was reconceived for the Opéra in the fall of 1829. From then on Meyerbeer, who, largely because of the frail health of his wife Minna, retained his native Berlin as his primary residence, paid regular and prolonged visits to the French capital, usually staying at the Hôtel des Princes on the rue Richelieu.

Robert le diable, which caused a sensation in November 1831, was the first production of the Véron régime.[58] Meyerbeer reportedly contributed 60,000 francs of his own money to make sure that the Opéra's resources would be utilized in full.[59] Duponchel directed, Ciceri designed the sets, Philippe Taglioni was choreographer (with his daughter Marie as prima ballerina). The cast was headed by Nourrit and Levasseur, while Julie Dorus-Gras (1805–1896) sang Alice and Cinti-Damoreau sang Isabelle. The biggest success of the decade in Paris, it reached its 100th performance in less than 30 months. Within five years, *Robert le diable* was staged in practically every French city possessing a theater and an orchestra – often under considerably less than ideal artistic conditions to be sure – while its popularity spread throughout the world.[60] It was almost universally praised by critics, writers, and musicians as well. Berlioz was particularly impressed by the orchestration, but the theatrical aspects of the work clearly also attracted him (he subsequently worked on the Scribe adaptation of *La nonne sanglante*). Joseph d'Ortigue, the influential critic of the *Revue et Gazette musicale*, viewed it as the answer to his prayers for the opera of the future, a synthesis of Italianate vocal forms with the harmonic and orchestral refinement of the German school.[61]

The source of *Robert le diable* came from the same kind of popular literature as *Le comte Ory*. Legends that had accumulated around the unmarried Robert I, Duke of Normandy (*c.*1002–35) – father of William the Conqueror – had been disseminated beyond medieval times in a type of chapbook known as the "Bibliothèque bleue."[62] Scribe and Meyerbeer combined this crude model with elements that spoke to the Romantic imagination: an ambiguous hero vacillating between the forces of good – represented by his dead mother and, *in loco parentis*, his foster-sister Alice – and the forces of evil – represented by Bertram, his unknown father; damned nuns re-enacting their lives of sin in the archetypal Gothic setting of a ruined convent;[63] a colorful, pseudo-historical Sicilian setting, with a tournament in Act 2 and, at the end of Act 5, the interior of Palermo Cathedral.[64]

Rather than the indecisive, gullible Robert, the work is dominated by the figure of Bertram, a brooding, Miltonesque devil, whose evil designs on

Robert are mitigated by paternal love. His centrality to the work is indicated musically from the beginning of the prelude, which opens with the theme of his invocation to the nuns in Act 3. Although Robert remains unaware of his father's identity until Act 5, the audience is, naturally, informed of it sooner: his first appearance is underlined by the motif of an opéra-comique-style ballad just sung by Raimbaut and retelling the legend of Robert's sinister birth.

The excitement the work generated in 1831 (and which it can still generate under the right conditions)[65] was not due simply to spectacle. Meyerbeer had written four star roles. Even Isabelle, who appears only in two acts, has several opportunities to shine: a two-part aria, a duet with Robert, brilliant roulades in the Act 2 finale, and a beautiful Act 4 cavatine ("Robert, toi que j'aime"). Audiences also responded enthusiastically to Robert's rousing patriotic duet with Bertram in Act 3. Modern listeners will be more impressed by the two trios for Alice, Robert, and Bertram – the first a cappella in Act 3, the second, concluding Act 5, a long crescendo at the end of which Alice succeeds in wrenching Robert's soul away from his diabolical father. But the excitement was equally due to novel effects, some related to Meyerbeer's orchestral writing – his highly personal use of the bassoon, unusual sound combinations (harp and solo English horn), the exposition by the timpani of the motif associated with the devilish Prince of Grenada. Meyerbeer was also an innovator in resorting to spatial effects, notably the offstage chorus of devils, amplified by megaphones, which accompanies Bertram's Act 3 "Valse infernale." Last but not least, the ballet of the damned nuns can be considered the ancestor of the moonlit episodes in the Romantic ballet – from Adam's *Giselle* (1841) to Ludwig Minkus's and Marius Petipa's *La bayadère* (1877).

Nearly four and a half years went by until Meyerbeer's next opera, *Les Huguenots*, was premiered.[66] The delay reflects Meyerbeer's fastidiousness, from the fashioning of the libretto, in which he was intimately involved, to details of the production, which he also directly supervised. Unlike *Robert le diable*, *Les Huguenots* is devoid of fantastic elements. It was, rather, an ambitious attempt to reconstitute a famous event in French history – the St Bartholomew Massacre on 24 August 1572. There were precedents in French opera – especially opéras-comiques[67] – but none on such a scale. Scribe's source – also the inspiration for Hérold's *Le Pré-aux-clercs* – was Mérimée's *Chronique du règne de Charles IX*. At odds with Scribe over the libretto, Meyerbeer provisionally broke his contract – at a cost of 30,000 francs that he subsequently recouped – and had some passages redrafted in Italian by Gaetano Rossi, his collaborator on *Il crociato in Egitto*, and translated into French by Émile Deschamps.

Conceived from the outset as a grand opéra (unlike *Robert le diable*), *Les Huguenots* made even broader use of the facilities of the Salle Le Peletier, with opulent sets (the château of Chenonceaux in Act 2, the crowded Pré-aux-clercs in Act 3) and large choral participation: the beginning of Act 3 thus pits against each other differentiated and conflicting groups (passers-by, Protestant soldiers, hymn-singing Catholic women, students).[68]

By contrast with *Robert le diable*, which ends happily for all but Bertram, the denouement of *Les Huguenots* is grim: the chivalrous Nevers is killed by fanatic Catholics, and the three main characters – Valentine, Raoul, and Marcel – are shot by a posse headed by Valentine's own father. The message is neither religious nor metaphysical, but essentially political. A practicing Jew, Meyerbeer strongly identified with this plea for religious toleration, even though the opera shows its defeat – the sense of powerlessness being eloquently conveyed by Queen Marguerite's horrified, but mute apparition at the very end. Perhaps the plot's chief weakness is that the misunderstanding separating the lovers could have been easily explained away in the next act.

Of the seven principals only Raoul de Nangis, the Protestant hero, appears in every scene. Sung by Nourrit in 1836, the role has two solos: a rapturous romance ("Plus blanche que la blanche hermine") in Act 1, to which the viola obbligato lends a "Renaissance" color; and the breathless "À la lueur de leurs torches funèbres," when he rushes in, interrupting the Act 5 ballet. Marguerite de Valois (Dorus-Gras at the premiere) gets a fully-fledged grand air in three parts at the beginning of Act 2. Marcel has solos in Act 1: a brief statement of the Luther Chorale ("Ein fester Burg"), which takes the voice to a low E, and the humorous "Chanson huguenote." The page Urbain does have a cavatine but it is inserted in the Act 1 finale.[69] Valentine, a role created by Falcon and clearly tailored for her opulent voice, has no solo, but takes part in two extended duets – with Marcel in Act 3, with Raoul in Act 4 – which are among the musical summits of the work. Another is the large scale ensemble known as the "Blessing of the daggers" in Act 4, a powerful musical description of fanaticism, in which the sinister interventions of three monks are underlined by unconventional harmonic progressions,[70] The final trio, built on the motif of the Luther Chorale, is dominated by Marcel, literally transfigured from his faintly comical Act 1 appearances to preside over Valentine's conversion and her union with Raoul at the hour of death. Marcel was, significantly, the character with whom Meyerbeer most closely identified, and it can be presumed that he imbued him with his own religious faith.[71]

Les Huguenots was, in the long run, even more popular than *Robert le diable*. By 1906 it had been performed at the Opéra a thousand times and left its repertory only in 1936. Because of its political resonance, the setting was frequently modified in Catholic countries: it thus appeared as *Die Anglicaner und Puritaner* in Munich in 1838, as *Die Gibellinen in Pisa* or *Die Welfen und die Gibellinen* in Vienna in 1839, as *I Guelfi ed I Ghibellini* in St Petersburg in 1850, and as *Renato di Croenwald* in Rome as late as 1864.[72]

Scribe and Meyerbeer began plans for *Le prophète* shortly after completing *Les Huguenots*, but the project came to fruition many years later.[73] Scribe drew his inspiration from a passage in Voltaire's *Essai sur les moeurs* (1756) on the revolt of the sixteenth-century Anabaptist sect, which established a short-lived theocracy in the Westphalian city of Münster in 1534–5. Its leader was a

25-year-old Dutch tailor from Leyden named Johann Buckholdt, who was eventually betrayed by his followers, captured, and gruesomely executed. The plot centers on a mother-and-son relationship: Jean (not a tailor but a tavern-keeper, an alternative suggested by Voltaire) is driven to revolutionary action when Berthe, his fiancée, is abducted by the neighboring landlord, whose soldiers threaten to kill his mother Fidès, putting Jean in the position of having to choose between his mother and Berthe. The work climaxes in Act 4, scene 2: Jean, suddenly recognized and apostrophized by his long-lost mother in the middle of his coronation, forces her to retract herself and publicly claim she does not known him. In the final act Berthe kills herself on learning about the prophet's identity, and mother and son, reconciled, decide to blow them-selves up with the Anabaptists during a banquet. Fidès – whose name means faith – dominates the work emotionally, but Jean, a conscious impostor, is also a fascinating dramatic creation, comparable to Dimitri in *Boris Godunov*.[74]

The composition of *Le prophète* was interrupted in 1841 owing to difficul-ties with Pillet, the Opéra co-director, who, against Meyerbeer's wishes, intended to cast his mistress Rosine Stoltz (1815–1903) as Fidès.[75] Work was resumed after Pillet's departure in 1847, and involved changes to both libretto and music. As for *Les Huguenots*, Deschamps was recruited – this time by secret contract – to make further changes that Meyerbeer wanted: they resulted in emphasizing Jean's fanatical aspects at the expense of his more human side.[76] The completion of this opera dealing with a revolutionary uprising coincided with the 1848 Revolution which brought down Louis Philippe. After a much-publicized rehearsal period, *Le prophète* was premiered to enormous acclaim in April 1849. The title role, initially intended for Duprez, was sung by Gustave Roger (1815–1879), who found the demanding part a challenge. An even more arduous one,[77] Fidès was sung by Pauline Viardot (1821–1910) née García, Maria Malibran's sister, for her Opéra debut (she had previously appeared at the Théâtre-Italien). Fidès became one of her greatest roles, which she sang more than 200 times. Hailed as a masterpiece, though ultimately less popular than *Les Huguenots*, *Le prophète* totaled more than 500 performances by the time it left the repertory of the Paris Opera in 1912.

Meyerbeer considered *Le prophète* his best work. The Cathedral Scene, introduced by a Coronation March which is the one part of the work that has retained genuine popularity, uses unprecedented orchestral forces, in the pit and onstage – including 16 saxhorns and organ – and unusual effects, such as otherworldly children's voices (an effect Wagner may have remembered when he wrote *Parsifal*). But *Le prophète* includes many other memorable moments: the Anabaptists' chorale "Ad nos, ad salutarem undam" (Meyerbeer's inven-tion), which recurs throughout the opera, like a dark, foreboding equivalent of "Ein feste Burg" in *Les Huguenots*; Jean's first encounter with the three Anabaptists, to whom he reports a prophetic dream (which quotes some of the music later heard in the Coronation Scene); Fidès' Act 2 arioso "Ah! mon fils," introduced by an expressive solo cello; the boisterous Skaters' ballet in Act 3; in the same act, the taming of the Anabaptists' mutiny and the triumphant March Song, "Roi du ciel"; and Fidès' two-part "grand air" in Act 5, and the following duet between mother and son.

When Meyerbeer was commissioned to write an opera for the opening of the rebuilt Berlin Hofoper after its destruction by fire in 1843, he asked Scribe for a scenario. *Ein Feldlager in Schliesen* was premiered in December 1844 with the famous Swedish coloratura soprano Jenny Lind. The opera was based on the life of Frederick the Great, but owing to the censors' requirement, he never appears on stage. The work was rewritten for Vienna in 1847 as *Vielka*, still as a vehicle for Lind, and with the Prussian king changed into an anonymous duke.[78] The musical material was recycled yet again for Meyerbeer's next Parisian project, and his first opéra-comique, *L'étoile du nord*, for which Scribe wrote the text.[79] The hero, this time, was the young Peter the Great. The plot, a distant echo of Grétry's *Pierre le Grand*, deals with his courtship of his wife and future successor Catherine I. Act 1 shows him living in a Karelian village under the fictitious identity of "Péters." In Act 2 Catherine, disguised as a *cantinière*, follows him to the army and is able to foil a plot to kill him. But the strain of the situation temporarily clouds her reason and in Act 3 she is rescued from temporary insanity when Peter recreates before her in his palace the village happiness of Act 1. The opera's great "tune," famous in our times by Constant Lambert's incorporation into his Meyerbeer-based ballet *Les patineurs*, is first heard in Act 1 when Catherine recalls – in melodrama form – her mother's prediction that she will become the "northern star" of the title. It is heard again in the next two acts. Premiered at the Opéra-Comique in February 1854, *L'étoile du nord* was performed a hundred times in its first year and was last revived there in 1887, after more than 400 performances. For the 1855 Covent Garden premiere (in Italian), Meyerbeer wrote sung recitatives to replace the spoken dialogues, as was customary for performances of opéra-comique in translation.

Meyerbeer's second opéra-comique, *Le pardon de Ploërmel*, was premiered, also at the Salle Favart, in April 1859. Scribe, to his annoyance, was dropped in favor of Jules Barbier (1825–1901) and Michel Carré (1819–1872), who had come to prominence the month before as the librettists of Gounod's *Faust* (a collaboration Barbier remembered as being much easier than the one with the tyrannical Meyerbeer).[80] "Pardon" refers to the traditional Marian pilgrimages in Brittany, where the town of Ploërmel is located. The heroine Dinorah, a gypsy, has lost her mind after being abandoned by her husband Hoël, an obsessive treasure-hunter. In Act 2, caught in the middle of a storm, Dinorah leaps into a torrent but is rescued by her repentant husband. The couple are reunited in Act 3 as the Pardon ceremony unfolds – a symbol of Dinorah's own forgiveness. Meyerbeer's most pastoral work, with picturesque touches of local color, it is essentially an opera with two characters – the third, the shepherd Corentin (tenor), is little more than a comprimario. The brilliant coloratura part of Dinorah was written for Cabel (Auber's Manon three years before), while Faure sang the first Hoël. Like many opéras-comiques of the 1850s, and to a greater extent than *L'étoile du nord*, which retained buffo elements, this opéra-comique is without comedy – favoring, rather, moments of emotional intensity. A stronger, more original work than its predecessor, it was not as successful in Paris in the long term (though revived until 1912), but it was particularly popular in its Italian version with recitatives, retitled *Dinorah*, and first heard at Covent Garden in 1859.

L'Africaine, Meyerbeer's final opera, was planned as early as 1837. When the composer died in Paris on 2 May 1864, its eagerly anticipated premiere was announced for the following year.[81] Few operas in history have had such a long genesis. The earliest version, based by Scribe on a 1770 play by Lemierre that had already inspired Louis Spohr's *Jessonda* (1823), dealt with the hopeless love of the African princess Sélika for Fernand, a Spanish naval commander. The first two acts were set in Seville, the third on a ship bound for Africa, and the last two in an unnamed African country. Meyerbeer completed the vocal score in early November 1843.[82] But the project – already much discussed in the press – was set aside. When Meyerbeer wrote Fidès' Act 5 cavatine "Ô toi qui m'abandonnes," a late addition to *Le prophète*, he used music he had composed for Selika's "La haine m'abandonne" in Act 5 of the 1843 *L'Africaine*.[83] Then in 1849 Scribe suggested transposing the action from Africa to India and making the hero the Portuguese explorer Vasco da Gama – whose name became the opera's new working title. This entailed a complete recasting of the first two acts, now set in Lisbon. Meyerbeer worked on the opera sporadically in the 1850s and resumed it in earnest after the premiere of *Le pardon de Ploërmel*. Then Scribe died in 1861. The composer asked the popular German playwright Charlotte Birch-Pfeiffer, assisted by a Paris-based German scholar, Joseph Duesberg, to make more changes to the text. But when Meyerbeer himself died, the opera, though technically finished, was not ready for performance. Meyerbeer's widow hired Fétis, then in his eighties, to supervise the musical side, while Mme Scribe appointed a literary team to oversee the literary side. If ever an opera was the result of committee-work, *L'Africaine* is the one. At long last the premiere took place, to considerable *réclame*, on 28 April 1865.

One of Fétis' decisions was to revert to the original title, understandably since it was in that form that the work had been announced and was expected. Fétis and his team tried to reconcile this with the new setting by suggesting that Selika's kingdom is Madagascar, but inconsistencies remained – the most glaring being the natives boarding the ship at the end of Act 3 while invoking Brahma and Vishnu. Yet *L'Africaine*, which touches upon such topics as slavery, colonization, and the clash of cultures, is a powerful work. Its Portuguese characters, though neatly drawn – Vasco's fiancée Inès, the devious Don Pédro who blackmails her into marrying him instead and is eventually massacred by the natives, Vasco himself – pale by comparison with the two "African" heroes: Sélika, who, failing to win the heart of Vasco, commits suicide by breathing the deathly perfume of the manchineel tree; and the proud warrior Nélusco (Faure at the premiere), driven by his hatred for Christians and his desire for vengeance but humanized by his unrequited love for Sélika.

Musically, *L'Africaine* is not inferior to Meyerbeer's earlier masterpieces. More intensely lyrical, more refined in its orchestration, more intimate in its effects, as many critics have noted, it combines familiar grand opéra ingredients – historical pageantry, spectacular staging, touches of (here exotic) local color – with a quasi-Wagnerian concern with dramatic and musical unity. However, as John H. Roberts has noted, it is to be hoped that the work will some day be available in a performing edition closer to the composer's intentions: this would affect its most famous number, Vasco's Act 4 aria "O paradis," which, far from being a blatant colonialist statement as in the version issued by Fétis and his collaborators ("Ô paradis . . . tu m'appartiens"), was originally a melancholy farewell to life as the explorer was about to be sacrificed by the natives ("Ô doux climat . . . brillez au loin").[84] Notwithstanding these major textual issues and formidable casting and staging difficulties, *L'Africaine* has proved the one Meyerbeer opera not to have completely left the repertory.[85]

Adolphe Adam

The operas of Adolphe Adam (1803–1856) have unjustly suffered from the enduring popularity of his ballet *Giselle* (1841).[86] The son of one of the first piano teachers at the Conservatoire, whose pupils included Hérold, Adam studied composition with Anton Reicha and Boieldieu (whom he later assisted with *La dame blanche*), but gave up on the Prix de Rome after finishing second in 1825. After supplying music to more than 25 vaudeville plays staged in boulevard theaters, he made his own Opéra-Comique debut in 1829 with *Pierre et Catherine*, a one-act version by Saint-Georges of the story of Peter the Great's courtship of his wife, the inspiration for Meyerbeer's subsequent *L'étoile du nord*. A curtain-raiser to Auber's *La fiancée*, *Pierre et Catherine* was performed 80 times.

While continuing to write for boulevard theaters, Adam began a prolific Opéra-Comique career. *Le châlet*, premiered in September 1834, was his most enduring success and the most regularly performed single-act French opera.[87] Adapted from Scribe and Mélesville from Goethe's 1771 Singspiel *Jery und Bätely*, it is set, like the original, in the Swiss Alps but the names of the male characters are modified and the action is transposed to the time of Napoleon's campaigns. The slight but delightful plot deals with a ploy by the village inhabitants to persuade a semi-reluctant Bettly to marry the rich and personable

Daniel (tenor) by enlisting the help of her brother Max (bass), who joined the army 15 years before and whom, of course, she does not recognize. As Karin Pendle has noted, Scribe has improved on Goethe's original in several respects.[88] The piece displays Adam's melodic gift, notably in Max's "Mountain Song," prompted (a device that recalls *La dame blanche*) by his hearing in the distance a folksong he remembers from his youth.[89]

Adam scored another major success in 1836 with *Le postillon de Lonjumeau*. Initially entitled *Une voix*, Léon Brunswick and Adolphe de Leuven's libretto, set during Louis XV's reign, pays homage to the world of eighteenth-century opéra-comique, which Adam knew well: he revised works by Monsigny, Grétry, and Dalayrac for court performance. On the day of his wedding, Chappelou, postilion in the southern Île-de-France village of Longjumeau (as it is now spelled), sings a song about his trade, capped by a ringing D natural. The Opéra manager, who happens to be there, in desperate search for a tenor, spirits him away. The next two acts take place 10 years later. Chappelou has become a star under the name Saint-Phar (an allusion to both Monsigny's *Aline, reine de Golconde* and Grétry's *La caravane du Caire*). He falls in love with a Mme de Latour, not recognizing in her the wife he abandoned, and marries her. He then faces the accusation of bigamy and the threat of the gallows but is saved when her identity is revealed. The absurd plot does not take itself too seriously and Adam's score, full of references to the world of eighteenth-century music, abounds in charm and wit. Not quite as popular as *Le châlet* in Paris – where it nevertheless achieved 500 performances by 1873 – it was a favorite in other countries, especially Germany.[90]

Brunswick and Leuven also collaborated with Adam on *Le brasseur de Preston* (1838), another light-hearted comedy based on a series of comical misunderstandings involving twins (played by the same tenor). Adam himself conducted it – in a German version – in St Petersburg when he visited Russia in 1840 and dedicated the score to Czar Nicholas I. The same librettists worked with him on *Le roi d'Yvetôt*, inspired by Pierre-Jean de Béranger's famous satirical song of 1813, and treated by Adam with a verve that prefigures Offenbach.

At the Opéra, where Marie Taglioni had appeared in Adam's ballet *La fille du Danube* in 1836, and Carlotta Grisi triumphed in *Giselle* five years later, he was less successful as a lyric composer: the three-act *Richard en Palestine* (1844), the one-act *La bouquetière* (1847), and the two-act *Le fanal* (1849) were all failures. By then, however, Adam was involved in an ambitious venture, the creation of a new opera company. Having quarreled in 1844 with Alexandre Basset, the new Opéra-Comique director, he applied in 1846 for permission to open a "popular lyric theater," with a view to staging works by younger French composers as well as attracting an audience more socially diversified than in the other three Parisian opera houses. The Opéra-National opened in November of the following year, using the 2,400-seat, renovated Cirque-Olympique on the boulevard du Temple. The work performed was

Aimé Maillart's *Gastilbelza, ou Le fou de Tolède*, preceded by a curtain-raiser, *Les premiers pas*, with music by Auber, Carafa, Halévy, and Adam himself. Adam's promising plans were dashed when the revolution that broke out in February 1848 temporarily diverted public interest away from the arts. The theater closed the following month, leaving him debt-ridden. In the last eight years of his life, Adam deployed an astonishing energy to restore his finances. He became a music critic to two major papers, taught composition at the Conservatoire, and resumed his own compositional activities, producing 15 operas and four full-length ballets.

Purportedly written in six days, *Le Toréador, ou L'accord parfait* was staged at the Opéra-Comique in 1849. The saucy libretto by Thomas Sauvage (1794–1877), set in Barcelona, involves three characters: Don Belflor, a retired torero; his wife Coraline, a part premiered by the soprano Delphine Ugalde (1829–1910); and Coraline's flute-playing lover Tracolin. The subtitle, a pun on "perfect chord" and "perfect agreement," underlines the "immoral" denoue-ment, which suggests that Coraline's adulterous arrangement is working perfectly – a theme also underlined throughout Adam's witty score by clever musical jokes. There are also, as in *Le postillon*, musical references to the style of eighteenth-century opéra-comique, culminating in variations on the song "Ah! vous dirai-je maman."[91]

The following year Adam resumed his collaboration with Scribe with *Giralda, ou La nouvelle Psyché*, a comedy of intrigue, also set in Spain. Its virtuous heroine survives travails of all kinds until her noble birth is revealed, allowing her to marry the man who has rescued her from bandits. Adam's score, once again, was praised for its melodic invention and deft orchestration.

The Opéra-National reopened in September 1851 in a different building (the Théâtre-Historique, also on the Boulevard du Temple). It was renamed Théâtre-Lyrique in April 1852. Adam was no longer associated with its management but several of his last works were staged there. The most successful, both in 1852, were *La poupée de Nuremberg*, a three-act fairy opera on a libretto by Brunswick and Leuven, which was performed in many European opera houses, and *Si j'étais roi*. The latter, on a libretto by Adolphe Dennery (or d'Ennery) (1811–1899) and Jules Brésil (1818–1899) adapted from the Kismet episode in the *Arabian Nights*, is a version of the "king for a day" story, set in this case in an imaginary Indian setting. Adam displayed once again his melodic gifts in the arias and, in the ensembles, his ability to translate humor and emotion into subtle musical terms. The work long remained a favorite in France and in other European countries. An unusual touch is the return of the hero's Act 1 romance "J'ignore son nom" as a duet in Act 2 and as the final Act 3 trio.

Four days before an exhausted Adam died in his sleep in May 1856, his last work, the one-act opéra-comique *Les pantins de Violette*, was staged at the Bouffes-Parisiens, Offenbach's theater, in a double bill with Offenbach's own *Le thé de Polichinelle.* It was fitting that the career of the finest heir to the lighter vein of eighteenth-century opéra-comique should have been associated with the composer who became Adam's match in wit and invention – and thus his true heir.

Fromental Halévy

Along with Auber and Meyerbeer, Jacques Fromental Halévy (1799–1862) remains associated with grand opéra, but he also made an important, if now neglected, contribution to opéra-comique. He was born in Paris to a German Jewish father, Elias Levy, originally from Fürst in Bavaria, who gallicized his name as Halévy in 1808, and in 1817–19 founded and edited the first French-language Jewish periodical, *L'Israélite français*; the composer's mother was from a Jewish family in Lorraine.[92] Fromental's younger brother Léon Halévy (1802–1883) was to become a classical scholar and man of letters – as well as the father of Ludovic, future collaborator with Offenbach and co-librettist of Bizet's *Carmen*. Having entered the Conservatoire in 1809, Fromental studied composition with Cherubini and became his favorite pupil. He also took instruction from Berton and Méhul. Awarded the Prix de Rome in 1819, he spent the next two years at the Villa Médicis. He returned by way of Vienna, where he met Beethoven. In 1827 he became a professor of harmony at the Conservatoire (where he subsequently taught counterpoint and fugue and, as of 1840, composition). The same year, following several rejections, his one-act opéra-comique *L'artisan* was staged at the Salle Feydeau with Chollet in the principal role. Saint-Georges, the librettist of *L'artisan*, was to become one of Halévy's regular collaborators. In 1828 the Théâtre-Italien, where Halévy worked as vocal coach for three years, mounted his "opera semiseria" *Clari*, with Maria Malibran in the title role.[93]

Halévy's first major success was *Le dilettante d'Avignon* (1829) at the Salle Ventadour, the Opéra-Comique's new home. The libretto by the veteran F.-B. Hoffmann (who died in 1828) was completed by the composer's brother Léon. The subject is a satire of the fashion for Italian opera (in France the word "dilettante" then meant partisan of Italian opera and especially Rossini). Having made his Opéra debut with the ballet *Manon Lescaut*, Halévy completed Hérold's unfinished *Ludovic*. It was well received – and staged internationally – but did not gain a footing in the repertory.

It was thus to a promising but hardly an established composer that Scribe, in 1833, offered the libretto of *La Juive*, which Meyerbeer (Halévy's senior by only two years) had rejected. As Diane Hallman has shown, it is clear that Halévy personally responded to a plot based on anti-Semitic persecution. It takes place in Constance at the time of the 1414–15 Council, remembered above all for its condemnation and treacherous arrest of Jan Hus. Rachel, daughter of the goldsmith Eleazar, has been seduced by a young man she believes to be Samuel, a Jewish painter, whereas he is actually Leopold, son of the Holy Roman Emperor Sigismund[94] and the fiancé of Princess Eudoxie. The first act sets the menacing atmosphere surrounding Rachel and her father, who are twice threatened by the crowd but rescued through the intervention of Cardinal Brogni, a dignitary of the Council. In the second act Rachel discovers that her lover is an impostor – not a Jew but a Christian – and confronts him, first alone, then joined by her father. Only in Act 3 does she realizes his true identity, at which point she denounces him publicly, which leads to her and Eleazar's arrest. Yet, in a situation somewhat reminiscent of the denouement of Verdi's *Rigoletto*, she eventually sacrifices herself by exculpating her lover. Refusing to convert, she walks to her death – consisting of being plunged alive into a boiling cauldron – while Eleazar reveals to Brogni that Rachel was, in fact, his long-lost daughter.

Unlike other grands opéras, *La Juive* is characterized by a relentlessly dark atmosphere, almost without any light elements (if one excepts the obligatory Act 3 ballet). Originally conceived for the bass Levasseur, Eleazar was written as a tenor role for Nourrit, who helped to fashion the text (Levasseur himself sang the impressive, low-lying part of Brogni). Despite the appeal for religious toleration, the character is in some respects a Shylock-like caricature, driven by a fanatical hatred for Christians. Even Rachel, the only fully lovable character in the opera, is not without stereotypical elements.[95] As Diana Hallman has shown, the portrayal of Jews in the opera reflects Halévy's own ambiguities. A thoroughly assimilated but practicing Jew, he lived in a country and a milieu where anti-Semitism was not unusual. Though his score eschews local color earning in this and other respects the praise of Wagner, the Seder led by Eleazar at the beginning of Act 2, and in which the harp plays a noticeable part, is influenced, more than had been traditionally recognized, by Halévy's own interest in synagogal music. It is one of the many paradoxes of late nineteenth-century France that in the context of widespread anti-Semitism that preceded, and influenced the Dreyfus Affair, one of the cornerstones of the country's operatic repertory was entitled *La Juive*. However, the work was not performed in Paris between 1894 – when the Affair started – and 1907 – one year after it ended.[96]

La Juive established itself, after *Les Huguenots*, as the second most performed grand opéra and a model of the genre. Its success in 1835 was due to the dramatic power of Scribe's libretto, which can be considered his masterpiece; to brilliant vocal performances from Falcon, Nourrit, and Levasseur; to the pageantry of the staging, especially Sigismund's solemn entrance into Constance at the end of Act 1; and most of all to Halévy's compositional skills, manifest above all in his ensemble writing and sense of orchestral color. Eleazar's poignant Act 4 aria "Rachel, quand du seigneur" long enjoyed a celebrity among French tenor arias that was matched only by Faust's cavatine and Don José's "La fleur que tu m'avais jetée" from Bizet's *Carmen*.[97]

None of Halévy's subsequent grand opéra work matched the achievement of *La Juive*. *Guido et Ginevra, ou La peste de Florence* (1838), starring Stoltz and Duprez, was admired for its originality and unusual orchestral effects, but was criticized for Scribe's macabre subject, six years after the devastating 1832 cholera epidemic, which had killed Prime Minister Casimir Périer among others.[98] *La reine de Chypre*, premiered in 1841 with the same principals, was based by Saint-Georges on the story of Caterina Cornaro.[99] It, too, was praised by Wagner, who realized the piano-vocal reduction.[100] He particularly admired the Act 5 quartet between Catarina, her lover Gérard, her dying husband Lusignan, and the traitor Mocenigo. Halévy's second most successful grand opéra, it achieved more than 100 performances in Paris.

Charles VI (1843), on a libretto by the Delavigne brothers (Germain (1790–1868) and Casimir (1793–1843)), deals with the madness of the French king during the Hundred Years War, while his wife Isabelle of Bavaria allied herself with the English, represented in the opera by the Duke of Bedford. Remarkably for a grand opéra, the work lacks any love interest. Instead, the main female role (premiered by Stoltz) is the Joan-of-Arc-like figure of Odette, a peasant girl who partially succeeds in reawakening the king's sanity.[101] Charles VI himself, a part sung by the Italian-trained baritone Paul Barroilhet (1810–1871), is a pathetic, Lear-like figure, whose first words are "J'ai faim." The work includes a medieval ballet, comprising a pavane, a "mascarade," and a bourrée, and shows the Hotel Saint-Pol in the Marais in Act 3. In the short final act, set in the basilica of Saint-Denis, north of Paris – traditional burial site for the French royal family – Odette predicts the coming of Joan of Arc while the dying Charles VI passes on the torch to his Dauphin. The patriotic, anti-English tone of the work is said to have annoyed Prime Minister François Guizot, who was then forging a military and diplomatic alliance with England.[102]

Le Juif errant (1852) was adapted by Scribe and Saint-Georges, with much simplification, from Eugène Sue's 1845 bestseller, a retelling of the legend of the accursed Ahasvérus, condemned to eternal wandering for having denied Christ on the road to Calvary.[103] Set at the time of the Crusades, the work achieved 49 performances in little more than a year but was never revived. Also set in the Middle Ages, like all Halévy's grand operas, *La magicienne* (1858) tells the story of the crusader René de Thouars, seduced by the Armida-like enchantress Melusina, who convinces him that his wife is unfaithful. At the end Mélusine forsakes Satan, represented in the opera by the necromancer Stello, and becomes a Christian before she dies.

In the same year as, 1835, *La Juive* Halévy had an Opéra-Comique success with *L'Éclair*, on a libretto by Saint-Georges and Planard, which was widely performed in the nineteenth century.[104] Though a fully-fledged work in three acts, it features only four characters and no chorus, prompting a modern critic to describe it as a "chamber opera."[105] Set outside Boston, it features a young hero who is blinded by lightning as he was about to sail to Europe. Falling in love with Henriette, who nurses him, he mistakes her pretty aunt for her on recovering his vision. The misunderstanding – a regular ingredient of the "well-made play" – is happily solved at the end. The part of Lionel, premiered by Chollet, includes a long two-part aria ("Partons, la mer est belle") and takes the singer up to D in his Act 2 duet with Henriette.

By contrast with the Napoleonic period, the 1830s in France were a period of anglophilia, reflected in the choice of opéra-comique subjects. Scribe and Halévy's *Le shérif* (1839) shows us Camilla, daughter of Sir James Turner, Sheriff of the City of London, being courted by Edgard Falsingham, a young "corsair captain," and by the ridiculous (and improbably named) Amabel d'Invernesse, an "Irish nobleman." Equally important to the plot are the two lower-class figures of Yorik, Edgard's factotum, and Keatt, the Sheriff's cook – premiered by Cinti-Damoreau in a character role. (Halévy further demonstrated his anglophilia when he wrote *La tempestà*, a three-act Italian adaptation of Shakespeare's play, staged in 1850 at Her Majesty's Theatre.)

Le guitarrero (1841) was the first hit at the Opéra-Comique after it moved back to the Salle Favart. Scribe's semi-serious libretto derives from Hugo's 1838 drama *Ruy Blas*. Unlike *Ruy Blas*, however, it does not take place at the Spanish court but in Portugal and it ends happily. Spurned by Zarah, Marchioness of Villareal, Don Alvar de Inigo disguises the young guitar player Riccardo, who is secretly in love with her, as a fictitious Juan de Guymarens. Public dishonor is averted at the end when Juan, having proved his valor, is named Marquis of Santarem.[106]

Les mouquetaires de la reine (1846), on a Saint-Georges libretto, is unrelated to Dumas' hugely popular novel, published two years before, but obviously capitalized on its fame. The hero, Olivier d'Entrague, is in love with Cardinal Richelieu's niece Athénaïs de Solange. Arrested for dueling in the middle of a masquerade – the arrest itself is treated in melodrama form – Olivier is rescued by Athénaïs who announces he was with her at the time of the duel. This revelation leads to a misunderstanding, since the man Athenaïs thought was Olivier was another musketeer, his friend Hector. Halévy once again showed how congenial the semi-serious historical genre was to him, and the work remained popular at the Opéra-Comique.

Even more successful, both on account of its picturesque music and exotic locale, was *Le Val d'Andorre*, premiered in November 1848, shortly before the first French presidential election, which brought to power Louis Napoléon Bonaparte, Napoléon I's nephew and the future Napoleon III. Set in the Pyrenean principality of Andorra during the reign of Louis XV, the plot hinges on the plight of the young hunter Stephan, who deserts when selected as one of the 15 men that Andorra is supposed to supply to the French army. When his beloved Rose puts up the money to buy him out, she is accused of having stolen it from a rich widow, Theresa, who is also in love with Stephan – and turns out to be Rose's mother. Once again, melodrama is used for the dramatic final revelation. Touches of local color include a Basque song, which Berlioz singled out for praise.

After *La Fée aux roses* (1849), an exotic fairy opera, on a libretto by Scribe and Saint-Georges, Scribe and Halévy collaborated once more with *La dame de pique* (1850), a free adaptation of Aleksandr Pushkin's tale, which had appeared in French the year before in Mérimée's translation. In their version, which preceded Tchaikovsky's by 40 years, the elderly, hunchbacked princess who reveals the secret of the three cards to the young officer she loves, Nelikoff, eventually turns out to be young and beautiful, having had to hide her identity. While this happy ending is hardly faithful to Pushkin, the work does not lack dramatic, colorful moments, especially the final card game, which Massenet may have had in mind when he composed Act 4 of *Manon* and which is also treated partly as a melodrama.

Halévy's predilection for exotic subjects and original themes was confirmed with *Le Nabab* (1853) the first act of which is set near Calcutta and the last two in Wales.[107] The hero of Scribe and Saint-Georges's libretto is an unhappily married young Englishman, Lord Evendale. At the suggestion of his friend Cliffort, a doctor, Evendale, to cure his depression, seeks employment in a Welsh factory under a false identity.[108] There he falls in love with Cora, an orphan he once protected in India. All ends well with Evendale's unhappy marriage being dissolved. The score abounds in picturesque elements. Act 2 opens with an aria in praise of tobacco sung by Toby, Dora's uncle, who also has a song in which he imitates a violin, with the baritone voice going up to a falsetto B natural. Act 3 features a hunting song, with a bagpipe-like orchestral accompaniment and the chorus imitating dogs barking. At the Opéra-Comique, Cora was sung by the 26-year-old Caroline Miolan-Carvalho, while Toby was Romain Bussine, the future co-founder of the Société nationale de musique.

One last notable work among Halévy's neglected opéras-comique is *Jaguarita l'Indienne* (1855), his single contribution to the Théâtre-Lyrique. Adapted from a novel of adventure by Eugène Sue, the libretto by Saint-Georges and Leuven is about colonization, like Meyerbeer's yet unfinished *L'Africaine*. *Jaguarita* is set in 1772 in Dutch Guyana, where the heroine, a member of the Anacota tribe, falls in love with Maurice, a soldier in the Dutch colonizing army. She offers him her hand and the throne of her country, but he refuses the latter. Instead, Jaguarita agrees to follow him to Holland. Berlioz, for one, praised the work's dramatic originality.[109]

Halévy's standing in French music after 1835 was considerable. Elected to the Académie des Beaux-Arts in 1836, he became its permanent secretary in 1854. After living for several years with an Opéra chorister by whom he had three children,[110] in 1842 he married Leonie Rodriguez, a member of a prominent Sephardic banking family from Bordeaux. His daughter Geneviève subsequently married Bizet, who completed *Noé*, the biblical opera Halévy was working on when he died.[111]

Gaetano Donizetti in Paris

Rossini's Parisian successes and the presence of contemporary Italian opera at the Théâtre-Italien were strong incentives for the Paris Opéra and Opéra-Comique managements to lure more Italian composers to write original works, or adapt some of their previous Italian works, for the French stage.[112] Bellini would no doubt have done so if he had not suddenly died of dysentery in Puteaux at the age of 33, eight months after the Parisian premiere of *I puritani*. In 1839 the Milanese composer Marco Aurelio Marliani (1805–1849), whose opéra-comique *Le marchand forain* had been staged at the Théâtre de la Bourse in 1834, thus presented *La Xacarilla*, a one-act opera on a Scribe libretto, set in Cadiz and – in anticipation of *Carmen* – featuring smugglers.[113] Premiered by Dorus-Gras and Stoltz in a travesti role, the work was given more than 110 times until 1866. But the prominence of Gaetano Donizetti (1797–1848) among Italian opera composers after Bellini's death made him the chief candidate for an invitation, especially after his problems with Italian censors and his failure to be confirmed as head of the Naples Conservatory after Zingarelli's death convinced him that his future was abroad. In May 1838 Duponchel commissioned from him two works for the Opéra. Donizetti moved to the French capital in October, living at first in the same building as Adolphe Adam.[114] His first project was not an original production for the Opéra but a French version of *Lucia de Lammermoor*, which in its original language had been enthusiastically received in 1837 at the Théâtre-Italien. Staged in August 1839 by a new company, the Théâtre de la Renaissance – its original sponsors were Hugo and Dumas – which used the former home of the Opéra-Comique at the Salle Ventadour, the French *Lucie* differs at several points from the Italian original. A phenomenal success, in Paris and in the provinces, it was eventually staged at the Paris Opéra in 1846.[115]

Donizetti's first Paris Opéra commission was not an entirely original work either. It derived from an abortive project, suggested by the tenor Nourrit, to adapt as an Italian opera Pierre Corneille's Christian tragedy *Polyeucte* (1642). Traditionally considered one of the playwright's masterpieces, it was a staple of the Comédie-Française repertory.[116] Its subject is the conversion and martyrdom of a prosperous local imperial dignitary in third-century Armenia, whose wife Pauline was once in love with the Roman official who has to deal with the situation once Polyeucte disturbs an official religious ceremony. Polyeucte's steadfastness wins the conversion of his wife and father-in-law, and the respect of his rival. *Poliuto*, on a libretto by Salvatore Cammarano (1801–1852), was completed in the spring of 1838 and about to go on rehearsal at the San Carlo Theater when the king forbade the stage representation of

Christian martyrs. His depression no doubt aggravated by this failure, Nourrit threw himself from a balcony of the Barbaia Hotel at Naples in March of the following year.[117] Once Donizetti had moved to Paris, Scribe was put in charge of preparing a French version. Entitled *Les martyrs* – not Corneille's title but rather that of a famous novel by Chateaubriand dealing with a similar theme – he expanded the work from three to four acts. Introducing some of Corneille's original lines,[118] he also made room for a divertissement in Act 2. Scribe also brought the libretto closer to its well-known French source by removing any suggestion of marital jealousy on Polyeucte's part. As for the music, only one-fourth of *Les martyrs* was original, which admittedly results in a hybrid work, Italianate in its core moments, *Vestale*-like in the ceremonial and spectacular music.[119] Premiered in April 1840 with Duprez as Polyeucte – highlighting his high register, the role rises to high E in the Act 3 cabaletta[120] – the work was well received by both critics and audiences, but lasted only 20 performances. It was the first opera on a Roman subject premiered in Paris since Berton's *Virginie* 17 years before, and its relative failure shows that subjects from antiquity were still a long way from returning to fashion.

Though *Les martyrs* was Donizetti's first Parisian commission, its premiere was preceded at the Opéra-Comique by *La fille du régiment* on 11 February 1840.[121] An altogether original work, on a libretto by Jean-François-Alfred Bayard (1796–1853) and Saint-Georges, it became the most popular opéra-comique set by a non-native composer – its 1,000 performances by 1914 putting it in the same league as *La dame blanche*, *Le Pré-aux-Clercs*, and *Le domino noir*. This popularity is understandable: for his first genuinely French work, Donizetti – a fluent French speaker, as his correspondence shows – could not have found a more Gallic theme than this comedy, in turn sentimental and irrepressibly funny, about a *vivandière* (female supplier of provisions to troops) separated from her comrades-in-arms when she is revealed, improbably, to be the natural daughter of a Tyrolian marquise and a captain in the French Revolutionary army. Eventually, of course, she gives up an aristocratic marriage to wed her beloved Tonio, the local peasant who has enlisted in the French army for her sake. The year 1840 in France was marked by nationalist agitation, culminating with the return of Napoleon's remains from St Helena and their solemn burial in the Invalides in Paris on 15 December.[122] The militarism of *La fille du régiment* was in the spirit of the time: in turn, it made its mark on French military music since the march heard in the overture (and again in Marie's Act 1 aria "Chacun le sait") was adopted by the French army and is known, to this day, by people who may never have heard of Donizetti.[123]

Donizetti was well aware of the musical challenges that an Italian composer faced when setting a French text. In a much-quoted letter he wrote to his teacher Simone Mayr, he explained that "the music and the poetry of French opera have a cachet all their own, to which each composer must adapt, whether in recitatives or in set pieces." In a French opera, he added, one had to avoid Rossini-type crescendos, "the usual cadences felicità, felicità, felicità," and "lazy" solutions such as the mere repetition of the same lines between two statements of the cabaletta.[124] Donizetti also embraced French musical forms, such as Tonio's strophic Act 2 romance "Pour me rapprocher de Marie," which the composer, significantly, left out of the Italian version he prepared for its Scala premiere a few months later. Berlioz, in the negative review he wrote for the *Journal des débats* in February 1840, could thus blame Donizetti for aping the French style instead of remaining faithful to his Rossinian roots.[125] Yet the work shows that Donizetti was capable of irony and humor vis-à-vis his French sources, such as in the Act 2 singing lesson – the opera's musical gem – in which the Italian composer, rather than quoting a genuine song by Garat as suggested in the libretto, produced a witty pastiche, which contrasts even more amusingly with the military rhythms of the "rantaplan." Despite its topicality (and an initial run of 55 performances), *La fille du régiment* disconcerted audiences and critics initially. The first Tonio was the tenor Mécène Marié de L'Isle (1811–1879), whose daughter Célestine was to premiere *Carmen* 25 years later. By the 1850s the work had become one of Donizetti's most popular, prompting in turn several parodies and imitations by Offenbach and others.

Following the success of *Lucie de Lammermoor*, the Théâtre de la Renaissance commissioned from Donizetti a three-act opera, *L'ange de Nisida*, on a libretto by Alphonse Royer (1803–1875) and Gustave Vaëz (1812–1862), authors of the French version of *Lucie*. But the theater went bankrupt in April 1840. Donizetti had also started working on a four-act grand opéra on a Scribe libretto, *Le duc d'Albe* (originally intended for Halévy). At that point Pillet, the new director of the Opéra, stepped in, suggesting that a modified version of *L'ange de Nisida*, rewritten by Scribe, be produced first, and stipulating that Stoltz, his mistress, should be cast in the principal role. The result was *La favorite*, premiered with great success in December 1840 with Duprez and Barroilhet (his debut role at the Opéra) partnering the mezzo-soprano heroine.[126] Critics complained that Donizetti's musical style was not French enough – or, conversely, that he followed Halévy or Meyerbeer too closely. Yet *La favorite*, along with *La fille du régiment*, became popular in France. By the time it left the Paris Opéra repertory in 1918, it had been performed nearly 700 times. When Pathé issued its original series of complete opera recordings on 78rpm discs in 1911–12, *La favorite* was one of them.[127]

Despite its impressive stylistic unity, *La favorite* actually recycled several theatrical and musical sources. The main one, the unperformed *L'ange de Nisida*, dealt with the secret love affair between a young soldier and a woman who is actually the mistress of Ferdinando, king of Naples. It was itself partly based on an earlier project, *Adelaide*, adapted from François de Baculard d'Arnaud's play *Les amants malheureux, ou Le comte de Comminge*. Published in 1765 but never performed owing to its religious setting, it takes place in a monastery, where a monk discovers that the woman he once loved has joined him under male disguise – the same situation as in Act 4 of *La favorite*.[128] To write the music, Donizetti plundered previous works, among them the abandoned *Le duc d'Albe*, from which he lifted the tenor's Act 4 romance "Ange si pur."[129] The libretto, published under the names of Royer, Vaëz, and Scribe, is set in Fourteenth-century Spain under the reign of Alfonso XI, king of Castile. The opening tableau and last act take place in the monastery of St James of Compostella, where Fernand, a novice, confesses to Balthazar, his Father Superior (premiered by Levasseur), that he has fallen in love with an unknown woman and asks to leave the monastery. Unbeknownst to him, the woman, with whom he has a secret assignation on the island of Leon in the following scene, is Leonora de Guzman, the king's favorite. The second act, set in the gardens of the Alcazar in Granada, opens with a mellifluous cavatine for Alphonse (the most "French" of Donizetti's baritone roles) and ends with a solemn denunciation of the king's morals by Balthazar (who has improbably traveled across the country for this purpose). In between is the divertissement. In Act 3 the king, who, while Fernand was covering himself with glory in the royal army, finds out that Leonora is in love with him, arranges for her and the unsuspecting Fernand to get married. The message sent by Leonora to Fernand to inform him of her situation having been intercepted, it is left to the indignant courtiers to tell Fernand about his misfortune. Renouncing all the honors that have been heaped upon him, he hastens back to the monastery. In the stark, concise final act Leonora appears disguised as a novice, just as Fernand pronounces his vows, and obtains his pardon before she dies.

The religious setting and references – not to mention the heroine's status as a "fallen woman" – were acceptable in France but bound to be obstacles in the eyes of Italian censors, who demanded major modifications when *La favorite* was premiered in Italy, first in Padua in 1842, under the title *Leonora di Guzman*. The action was moved to the times of the Crusades and the setting changed to a Templar Hospital; absurdly, Balthazar, from Father Superior, became the *father* of *both* Fernand and Leonora. Though the original title and setting were subsequently restored, the Italian version, which not only alters the composer's word-setting but also tampers with the music (most conspicuously at the very end), has, regrettably, eclipsed the original French.

Having gone back to Italy, where his melodrama semiserio *Adelia* was given in Rome in 1841, Donizetti returned to Paris in the summer of 1841 and, while waiting for the libretto of a Scala commission, composed a one-act opéra-comique on a Vaëz libretto, *Rita, ou Le mari battu*. This light-hearted farce, more Italianate in spirit and style than *La fille du régiment*, remained unperformed until 1860, when it was finally staged at the Salle Favart.[130] In spite of the success of this original version, it is now only known in Italian translation.[131]

After completing *Maria Padilla* (1841) for Milan, *Linda de Chamounix* (1842) and *Maria di Rohan* (1843) for Vienna, and *Caterina Cornaro* (1844) for Naples – all four works based, incidentally, on French sources – Donizetti was ready to tackle another major commission for Paris. In 1842 he was elected a corresponding member of the Institut de France,[132] and in January 1843 his buffo masterpiece *Don Pasquale* received its world premiere at the Théâtre-Italien with a splendid cast (Grisi, her husband Mario, Tamburini, and Lablache). The unfinished *Le duc d'Albe* was once again put aside – only the first two acts were set[133] – in favor of a fully-fledged grand opéra in five acts, *Dom Sébastien de Portugal*, Donizetti's final masterpiece and his greatest contribution to French opera.[134]

Adapted from a play of the same title by Hugo's brother-in-law Paul Foucher, *Dom Sébastien* is based on the story of the 24-year-old Portuguese king who perished in 1578 in the disastrous battle of Alcazarquivir that he rashly fought against the Moroccan king, Ahmed Mohammed. Subsequently, as in the case of the Czarevich supposedly murdered by Boris Godunov, legends spread about his having survived, prompting the apparition of impostors. Scribe's libretto – one of his finest – begins as the Portuguese army is about to sail for Morocco, while the Grand Inquisitor (the opera's villain, sung by Levasseur) plots to deliver the country to Philip II of Spain in his master's absence. Having rescued a Moorish girl, Zayda, who was about to be burned at the stake, Sebastian – like the departing Igor in Alexander Borodin's opera *Prince Igor* – is warned of impending disaster when the sky suddenly darkens, an omen commented upon by the poet Luis de Camoens (who in reality did not participate in the expedition).[135] Act 2 is set in Morocco, where Zayda, who has fallen in love with the Portuguese king, is promised by her father to the Arab chieftain Abayaldos. The second scene shows the defeated Portuguese army and poignantly ends (unusually for a grand opéra) with Sebastian's elegiac aria "Seul sur la terre." In Act 3 we are back in Lisbon, where Camoens recognizes the king, whom everyone believes dead and whose funeral is being celebrated, to the sound of the uncannily Mahler-like march already heard in the opera's prelude. When Sebastian reveals his identity, he is denounced as an impostor by the jealous Abayaldos. Act 4 shows Sebastian's trial by the Inquisition, ending with a death sentence for him and Zayda, who has risen to his defense. The act culminates on what William Ashbrook has described as "arguably the finest of Donizetti's great concertatos."[136] In the short, tragic, last act, Camoens tries to rescue Sebastian and Zayda and provides them with ropes for them to escape from prison, but they are shot as they begin their descent.

Despite the lavish *mise-en-scène* and a cast that, in addition to Stolz, Duprez, and Levasseur, included Barroilhet as Camoens, the 1843 audiences were disconcerted by the unrelieved gloom of the story.[137] As for the critics, rather than praising Donizetti's mastery in assimilating the French style of declamation, they favored the score's more openly Italianate moments, such as the Act 4 ensemble. The work left the repertory of the Opéra in 1845 after 32 performances, to be revived only once in 1849.[138] Despite the relative oblivion into which it has fallen and difficulties posed by its staging, *Dom Sébastien* is among Donizetti's neglected masterpieces the most deserving of rediscovery.

Dom Sébastien was Donizetti's last completed work. A legend spread subsequently was that the trouble Stoltz gave him during rehearsals caused so much strain that it hastened his demise.[139] The fact is that the composer – who had dealt with *prime donne* (and *primi uomini*) throughout his career, and besides was familiar with the difficulties inherent in the preparation and staging of a large-scale work – was entering the final stages of syphilis. His condition gravely deteriorated in 1845 when he returned to Paris following the Vienna premiere of *Dom Sébastien*. In early 1846, suffering from dementia and paralysis, he was forcibly interned in a sanatorium at Ivry, the southern Parisian suburb. It took his nephew Andrea nearly 20 months to get him released and bring him back to his native city of Bergamo, where he died on 8 April 1848.

CHAPTER 7

FRENCH OPERA UNDER
THE SECOND EMPIRE

Second Empire opera

Born of Louis Napoléon's coup d'état on 2 December 1851 – "legalized" by refer-
endum the following year – the Second Empire ended in disgrace when the
French were ignominiously defeated by the Prussians at Sedan in September
1870. It has, understandably, been judged harshly as a result, even in the
aesthetic sphere. Reynaldo Hahn could write in 1925: "The Second Empire was
an essentially anti-musical period. Its music resembled its furniture: it was ill-
assorted, mediocre, and heavy, comprising elements of every genre and every
period; its style consisted of a total lack of style."[1] Admittedly, the 1850s and
1860s are no match for the following four decades for French chamber or
symphonic music. Regarding opera, though, Hahn might have granted that the
age of Gounod and Offenbach – and why not add Ambroise Thomas? – and of
Bizet's and Massenet's debuts can hardly be dismissed as mediocre. And even if
works by Berlioz, Verdi, and Wagner that are now rightly considered masterpieces were half-successes or failures in Paris, they too belong to the history of
the period.

Underlying Hahn's attack is the accusation of eclecticism – a characterization
applied to many late nineteenth-century composers. Eclecticism was actually, at
the time, a doctrine defined by the quasi-official philosopher Victor Cousin,
author of *Du vrai, du beau, du bien* (1853), who presented it as an alternative to
sterile, intolerant systems. One should add that, despite its authoritarian beginnings and a short period of repression following Felice Orsini's failed attempt
on Napoleon III's life in 1858, the Second Empire was remarkably liberal in its
outlook. This affected opera houses, which the 1864 law on the liberty of
theaters made free to choose their repertory from any genre they pleased.

Arguably the most significant figure in Second Empire opera was Léon
Carvalho (1825–1897). Born Léon Carvaille on the island of Mauritius (then

called Île de France), he entered the Conservatoire as a singing student and began a modest career as a baritone in the Opéra-Comique troupe. In 1853 he married its rising star, the Marseilles-born Caroline Miolan (1827–1895), known thereafter as Miolan-Carvalho. Two years later he was hired by the Théâtre-Lyrique, which he directed in 1856–60 and again in 1862–8. He made it the most enterprising Parisian opera house of the period.[2] Its prominence was manifested in 1862 when, forced to leave its premises on the boulevards when they were demolished as part of Baron Haussmann's renovation of the city, it moved to a new theater which still stands on the Place du Châtelet, though the theater was rebuilt after the fire that destroyed it during the Commune in 1871.[3] Throughout the Second Empire, the Théâtre-Lyrique staged an impressive 137 works (against the Opéra's 52).[4] Premieres included Charles Gounod's *Le médecin malgré lui, Faust, Mireille,* and *Roméo et Juliette*; Berlioz's *Les Troyens à Carthage*; and Bizet's *Les pêcheurs de perles.* Carvalho also expanded the repertory from contemporary opéra-comique to revivals of works by Gluck, Grétry, Méhul, Mozart, Rossini, and Weber. His successor, the conductor Jules Pasdeloup (1819–1887) mounted Wagner's *Rienzi* in 1869. Like its predecessor the Opéra-National, the Théâtre-Lyrique, especially during its days on the boulevards, appealed to a broader section of the population; Berlioz, unkindly, made fun of its *blouse*-clad "working-class dilettanti."[5] Less lucky financially than artistically – only in 1864 did the money-losing operation begin to receive state subsidies – the Théâtre-Lyrique finally went bankrupt in 1872. An attempt to revive it at the end of the decade was short-lived.[6]

Carvalho's counterpart at the Opéra and the Opéra-Comique during the Second Empire was Émile Perrin (1814–1895), who also directed the Théâtre-Lyrique in 1854–5. At the Salle Favart, which he ran from 1848 until 1857 and again briefly in 1862, he welcomed Meyerbeer and launched the careers of Thomas and Massé. He was succeeded by the team of Eugène Ritt and the librettist Adolphe de Leuven.[7] At the Opéra, Perrin presided over the long-delayed premiere of Meyerbeer's *L'Africaine* and that of Verdi's *Don Carlos*. However, the most momentous event of the period at the Opéra – not concerning a French opera, but with consequences for the evolution of French opera – was the fiasco of *Tannhaüser* in 1861.[8]

As a young conductor at Würzburg and, later, Magdeburg, Wagner was familiar with works by Auber, Boieldieu, Cherubini, Hérold, Méhul and Meyerbeer, among others. Profoundly influenced, especially but not only in his early work, by the aesthetics of grand opéra[9] – to which, as we have seen, his concept of the *Gesamtkunstwerk*, or "total work of art", can be related – Wagner's ambition was to succeed in Paris. Between 1839 and 1861 he visited the French capital seven times. During his initial, unhappy stay in 1839–42 he vainly tried to obtain a commission and ended up selling to the Opéra his *Flying Dutchman* scenario: versified (in two acts) by Foucher and Henri Revoil, set by the conductor Pierre-Philippe Dietsch (1808–65), *Le vaisseau fantôme ou Le maudit des mers* lasted only 11 performances in 1842. When Wagner arrived in Paris for his extended final visit in 1859 – having by then composed more than half of *Der Ring des Nibelungen* and just completed *Tristan und Isolde* – he understood the need to surround himself with a group of influential friends from the world of politics, literature, and the arts who would promote his cause. They included the opposition leader Émile Ollivier, who became Napoleon III's last prime minister in 1869 and whose wife Blandine, daughter of Liszt and Marie d'Agoult, was the sister of Wagner's future wife Cosima von Bülow; Princess Pauline Metternich, wife of the Austrian ambassador, who successfully lobbied Napoleon III in Wagner's favor; and, most impressively in retrospect, Charles Baudelaire, the poet of *Les fleurs du mal* (1857). Baudelaire approached Wagner in 1860 after hearing him conduct his music at the Salle Ventadour. In 1861 he published in the *Revue européenne* the essay "Richard Wagner et *Tannhäuser* à Paris," which reads like one of the earliest manifestos of modernism. Several people were involved in the preparation of the French text of *Tannhäuser*. The final version was arranged by Charles Nuitter, the recently appointed archivist of the Opéra, and Wagner himself, who adapted the vocal lines to the French text. To the first act – rather than to the act in the Warburg, which could easily have accommodated it – he added the Venusberg ballet. This antagonized members of the Jockey Club (among others), entrenched in their habit of arriving at the opera after the first act to applaud the ballerinas, some of whom were their mistresses besides.[10] These members disturbed the first performance on 13 March 1861, in the presence of the emperor, and the next two, after which Wagner withdrew the work, which had had a record 164 rehearsals. Unhappy with Dietsch, the conductor, he had nothing but praise for the singing of the Elisabeth, the Belgian soprano Marie Sasse (1834–1907), who four years later was the first Sélika in *L'Africaine*.

Besides Gounod, Massé, Berlioz, and Thomas, several notable opéra and opéra-comique composers flourished during the period. Antoine-Louis Clapisson (1808–1866) is remembered mostly for gathering the collection of historical instruments he sold to the Conservatoire in 1861. Born in Naples, where his father played in King Murat's band, he became a violinist but also, in his day, a successful opéra-comique composer, with whom Scribe collaborated six times, notably on *Jeanne la folle*, a five-act grand opéra which was tepidly received at the Académie nationale in November 1848. His finest work, *La Fanchonnette*, on a libretto by Saint-Georges and Leuven, was the first hit of Carvalho's tenure at the Théâtre-Lyrique in 1856, thanks to Miolan-Carvalho's performance in the title role.

The Provençal Félicien David (1810–1876), an active member of the Utopian Saint-Simonian movement in the 1830s, came to prominence in 1844 with his symphonic ode *Le désert*, inspired by his missionary trip to the Middle East with fellow Saint-Simonians in 1832–5. *Le désert* was performed throughout the world.[11] Exoticism also characterizes his opéra-comique *La perle du Brésil*, staged at the Opéra-National in November 1851. The work is familiar – at least to collectors of historical recordings – for the haunting Mysoli song, in which the voice of Zora, the soprano heroine, is doubled by a flute. Originally planned for the Théâtre-Lyrique, the four-act *Herculanum*, on a libretto by Joseph Méry (future co-librettist of *Don Carlos*) and T. Hadot, was eventually staged at the Opéra in 1859. Like *Les martyrs*, it is an unusual case of a work based on a classical subject that can still be described as a grand opéra. Audiences may have found the presence of Satan in the plot disconcerting but were thrilled by the spectacular eruption of Mt Vesuvius. Performed 74 times until 1868, it was one of the more successful Second Empire operas. David's masterpiece, however, was *Lalla-Roukh*, performed at the Opéra-Comique in 1862. Adapted by H. Lucas and Michel Carré from Thomas Moore's 1817 poem, set in Kashmir and Samarkand, its theme is the proverbial tale of the king who disguises himself in order to find out whether he is loved for his own sake. The work's delicate exoticism anticipates later works such as Bizet's *Djamileh* and Rabaud's *Mârouf, savetier du Caire*. Auber, uncharitably, commented: "I wish he'd get off his camel."[12] Disappointed by the failure of another opéra-comique, *Le saphir*, based on Shakespeare's *All's Well that Ends Well*, David retired from the stage. A member of the Institut, where he succeeded Berlioz, he nonetheless retained to the end of his life some of the radicalism of his younger days. At his non-religious funeral, the officer commanding the military detachment sent to render honors expressed his disapproval by dismissing the soldiers; the resulting outrage led to the resignation of the prime minister and the war minister.[13]

A fellow Provençal, the Marseilles-born François Bazin (1816–1878), who won the Prix de Rome in 1840 and taught at the Conservatoire as of 1844 (Léo Delibes was among his pupils) came to prominence with the one-act opéra-comique *Maître Pathelin* (1856). Based by Leuven and Ferdinand Langlé on the well-known medieval farce, it remained popular well into the twentieth century and the tenor aria is still periodically recorded. A more substantial piece, *Le voyage en Chine* (1865) owed its wide popularity, in France and internationally, to the witty libretto by Eugène Labiche (1815–1888), the greatest French play-wright between Musset and Feydeau. The third act, perhaps hinting at *L'Africaine*, premiered a few months before, is set on a boat off Cherbourg harbor, on board which a stubborn Breton and his family are held hostage by another stubborn Breton until the former agrees to let his daughter marry the latter. The trip to China is, of course, only a threat – but also the pretext for musical allusions to Auber's *Cheval de bronze*. The press greeted the return of sheer comedy to the stage of the Opéra-Comique, largely dominated in the previous two decades by semi-serious works. Bazin's last, less successful, work was *L'ours et le pacha* (1870), on a posthumous libretto by Scribe and Saintine.

Aimé Maillart (1817–1871), another southerner, has already been mentioned (see Chapter 6, p. 149): his "drame lyrique" *Gastibelza, ou Le fou de Tolède* had opened Adam's Opéra-National in 1847. A student of Halévy at the Conservatoire, he won the Prix de Rome in 1841. His name remains linked to the perennially popular *Dragons de Villars*. Rejected by Perrin for the Opéra-Comique owing to the failure of Maillart's previous two works, *Le moulin des tilleuls* (1849) and *La croix de Marie* (1852), it was produced at the Théâtre-Lyrique in 1856 and became one of the most successful works in its repertory. By the time the Opéra-Comique reclaimed it in 1868, it had been mounted in Algiers, Basel, Madrid, New Orleans, New York, Prague, Riga, Stockholm, and many other cities. Eugène Cormon (1810–1903) and Lockroy's (pseudonym of Philippe-Joseph Simon, 1803–1891) libretto, set at the time of the crackdown on Protestants in southwestern France towards the end of Louis XIV's reign, features one of the most positive female characters in opéra-comique, Rose Friquet, who compromises her marriage in her effort to hide Protestant fugitives from the dragoons. The chief of these, Belamy, is, however, a debonair figure, and the work remains lighthearted throughout, as does Maillart's tuneful, attractive score. His next work, *Les pêcheurs de Catane*, another "drame lyrique" (1860) was not nearly as successful. As for the Byron-based *Lara* (1864), it launched the career of Célestine Galli-Marié, the future Carmen, in the role of a young woman who disguises herself as a slave. The work itself did not last, but the composer's by then solid reputation ensured that it was staged in several countries.

Non-French composers who had a Parisian career during the Second Empire include the Antwerp-born Albert Grisar (1808–1869), a student of Reicha. Of his 20-odd opéras-comique in the style of Boieldieu, whom he venerated, the most successful was *La chatte merveilleuse* (1862). Based by its librettists, Dumanoir and Dennery, on Perrault's "Puss in Boots" tale, it starred Marie Cabel and was the biggest hit of the Théâtre-Lyrique during the two years when Charles Réty replaced Carvalho as its director. Another forgotten figure, Józef Poniatowski (1816–1873) was the great-nephew of the last Polish king and the nephew of one of Napoleon's marshals. Endowed with a tenor voice described by Berlioz as "one of the most entrancing [he had] ever heard,"[14] he was born and trained in Rome and his early operatic career took place in Italy. Appointed by Napoleon III as a member of the French Senate, he had a respectable success at the Opéra with *Pierre de Médicis* (1860), on a libretto by Saint-Georges and Émilien Pacini, which ran for 47 performances, and another at the Théâtre-Lyrique with a one-act work, *Au travers du mur* (1861), also on a Saint-Georges libretto. In 1862 he became director of the Théâtre-Lyrique. Following Napoleon III in his exile, he died a few months after him at Chislehurst, the emperor's residence in Kent, as he himself was about to leave for the United States to pursue a career as conductor.

The two outstanding singers of the period have already been encountered in the previous chapter. Following her success in *Le prophète*, Pauline Viardot (1821–1910), the exceptionally gifted sister of Maria Malibran, launched

Gounod's operatic career. At the Théâtre-Lyrique she sang Fidelio and Gluck's Orphée, in Berlioz's 1859 arrangement. Particularly associated with this role, she also revived *Alceste* at the Opéra in 1861. A teacher, a pianist, a composer of romances and chamber operas (such as the enchanting *Cendrillon*),[15] a close friend of George Sand among many writers and artists, Viardot features among the leading cultural personalities of her age. As for Jean-Baptiste Faure (1830–1914), he premiered the three major baritone parts of the 1860s – Nelusko, Posa, and Hamlet. He also sang at the Opéra Gounod's Mephistopheles – nowadays entrenched in the bass repertory. Remarkably, Faure was an early collector of Édouard Manet (who painted him as Hamlet) and Impressionist painters – an unexpected connection between Second Empire opera and the artistic avant-garde.

Giuseppe Verdi in Paris

Even before Donizetti sank into dementia in the mid-1840s, Verdi was poised to inherit the position of leading Italian opera composer. In this capacity he was bound to be attracted to Paris. The Théâtre-Italien staged *Nabucco* in 1845, and *Ernani* (retitled *Il proscritto* to placate Hugo) and *I due Foscari* in 1846. By 1844, as Verdi was considering the subject of Attila – his opera on this subject was premiered at La Fenice, Venice, in 1846 – he suggested to the Parisian music publisher Léon Escudier that it could be made into a grand opéra for Paris.[16] In 1847, when Escudier was able to arrange an invitation to him from the Opéra, Verdi decided instead to revise his fourth opera, *I Lombardi alla prima crociata* (1843), in the same way as Rossini had recast *Maometto secondo* into *Le siège de Corinthe*. Royer and Vaëz, Donizetti's former collaborators, wrote the libretto of the new work, which was now entitled *Jérusalem*.

   Retaining the historical frame – the first crusade of 1095–9 – Royer and Vaëz refashioned the work into four acts, making it more "French" thematically and structurally, adding a ballet and giving more prominence to the tenor, who in *I Lombardi* did not appear until Act 2. In this new setting he is Gaston de Béarn, in love with Hélène, daughter of Count Raymond de Toulouse, the historical leader of the first crusade (a baritone role, whereas his fictional equivalent in *I Lombardi*, Arvino, was a tenor). As in the Italian original, Act 1 of *Jérusalem* climaxes on a tragic case of mistaken identity: the Count's brother Roger, consumed by an incestuous passion for his niece, has his brother assassinated (so he thinks) instead of his rival, letting Gaston stand unjustly accused of the crime. In the following acts all the characters including the Count – who survived the assassination attempt – are in the Holy Land, where Gaston is exculpated by the repentant Roger, who has become a hermit. Before then Gaston has been publicly sentenced and stripped of his arms by the Papal Legate in a dramatic scene in Act 3, the role's great moment. As Gilles de Van has pointed out, the work gains in unity and clarity by the transforma-tion of the tenor role from the son of the tyrant of Antioch to a French crusader.[17] The vocal highlights of *I Lombardi* are preserved: the soprano's beautiful "Salve Maria" in Act 1; the tenor's Act 2 cavatina "La mia letizia infondere," now set to the words "Je veux entendre encore" (transposed up and rising twice to high C in deference to Duprez's abilities); the two stirring choruses of the crusaders in Acts 3 and 4; and the trio between soprano, tenor, and bass, rewritten without the violin obbligato. *Jérusalem* is unquestionably more refined musically than *I Lombardi*, more subtly harmonized and orches-trated;[18] it was also the first time that a new type of brass instruments, called saxhorns after their inventor Adolphe Sax, were heard at the Opéra. Yet it is essentially a hybrid work and may seem to be lacking the irresistible, if at times crude, excitement of its predecessor *I Lombardi*, which, despite the positive reception of *Jérusalem* in 1847, it has never been able to displace.[19]

Verdi's first visit to Paris in 1847 was followed by many more, some of them for extended periods: Alessandro di Profio numbers them at about 25 until 1894.[20] Ten of his operas – a smaller number but a larger percentage than Donizetti's – are based on French sources, not counting unrealized projects. He also revised several of his works for performance in French. These revi-sions consisted at times of the addition of a ballet – even for *Otello* in 1894 – but they could involve substantial modifications. When *Il trovatore* was staged (as *Le trouvère*) at the Opéra in 1857, eight numbers were rewritten; the revisions to *Macbeth* for the Théâtre-Lyrique in 1865 were extensive.

After the positive reception of *Jérusalem*, Verdi was scheduled to write an original French work, but the revolutionary events of 1848 in Italy took him home. The project was resumed in 1852, Verdi receiving generous terms. Royer and Vaëz had approached him about a possible adaptation of Schiller's *Don Carlos*,[21] but Verdi insisted on Scribe as librettist: he clearly intended to measure himself against Auber's, Halévy's, and Meyerbeer's masterworks. His great point of reference was the Coronation Scene in *Le prophète*, a moment he described as "miraculous."[22] Scribe offered Verdi the old libretto of *Le duc d'Albe*, which had previously gone through the hands of Halévy and Donizetti, agreeing to recast it in a Mediterranean setting. Holland became Sicily, the four acts became five, and the result was *Les vêpres siciliennes*, as the 1182 uprising of the Sicilians against Anjou rule was known.[23] Like *Les Huguenots*, it ends with a massacre in which all the principals save the villain perish. The most dramatic moment occurs when Montfort, head of the French, will only pardon the Sicilian plotters if Henri, his natural son by a Sicilian woman, will publicly acknowledge him – a transposition of the mother-son situation in *Le prophète*, congenially for Verdi, who was always more interested dramatically in the father's side of parental relations. On the other hand, as Verdi himself ruefully commented before the premiere of *Les vêpres siciliennes*, it was a strange subject to choose for the Opéra, since the French occupiers of Sicily are unflatteringly pictured; nor was it fair to the historical figure of Giovanni da Procida, revered as a patriot in his home country, but treated by Scribe as "a common conspirator with a dagger in his hand."[24]

While exhibiting many of the outward characteristics of grand opéra à la Meyerbeer – a historical setting, a sumptuous ballet ("The Four Seasons") in the context of a masked ball, a tragic and spectacular denouement – *Les vêpres siciliennes* is even more remarkable in the ways it steers away from the tradition, as Anselm Gerhard has noted. It is as if Verdi, who had set out to fight Meyerbeer on his own terrain, had decided instead to appropriate the form to create his own brand of grand opéra.[25] As shown by the revisions he demanded to the libretto, Verdi was less interested in the political dimension of the conflict – calling for public scenes and large ensembles – than in the personal relationships between his characters: hence the prominence of the duets, of which there are four large-scale ones (two between father and son, two between the young lovers); hence also the relative sobriety of the denouement – the massacre lasts 20 seconds and without interventions from the principals. Musical unity is provided by the presence throughout of the anapestic rhythm (two shorts, one long) heard in the first measures of the overture, a rhythm that at various points in the opera stands for the humiliation and desire for revenge of the occupied Sicilians, or, even more subtly (as in the baritone's Act 2 aria), as an ill-defined motif that critics have associated with death.

Delayed by various factors, including the disappearance of the prima donna, Sophie Cruvelli (she had eloped with a nobleman, who later married her), *Les vêpres siciliennes* was premiered on 13 June 1855, coinciding with the first Paris Universal Exposition. The public and critical reception was favorable. Berlioz praised the work's "grandeur" and "sovereign majesty."[26] There were 62 performances through to 1865. At the 1863 revival with Marie Sasse as Hélène, Verdi wrote an alternative aria for the tenor in Act 4 but clashed with the orchestra and its conductor, Dietsch – Wagner's nemesis. Then the work disappeared from the Opéra repertory. In Italy, owing to censorship, it was mounted under a different title (*Giovanna de Guzman*), the story being moved to seventeenth-century Portugal under Spanish domination. The translation, which remains the basis of the standard performing version, has been characterized by Julian Budden as "one of the worst ever perpetrated."[27] Its most obvious flaw cannot even be blamed on the translator: once the Sicilian setting is restored, the heroine's name, Elena in Italian, scans differently from the French Hélène, with the result that "Arrigo" can only address her as "O donna"! Only when *Les vêpres siciliennes* is given in the form in which Verdi conceived it will this "noble, thoughtful, and often exciting work," to quote Budden again, be appreciated.[28]

Verdi's third Opéra commission was *Don Carlos*. *King Lear* – a project that haunted him at various stages throughout his life – had been considered and rejected. The task of adapting Schiller's play was entrusted to Méry, who died when the work was in progress, and Camille du Locle, Perrin's son-in-law.

Verdi was actively involved at all stages.[29] Though the libretto remains generally faithful to its source, two important elements were introduced. The first,
the mysterious monk in the monastery at St. Just, is probably Charles V,
though this is never made absolutely clear, even when he reappears at the end
to rescue his grandson. The second is the tableau of the *auto da fé*, set in front
of Valladolid Cathedral, which is also the site of the ballet. This ballet, entitled
"La Peregrina," was devoted to the story of a diamond once owned by Philip II
and then in the possession of the Empress Eugénie.[30]

Grands opéras can be very long, *Don Carlos* being no exception. It required
a record 270 rehearsals and 8 dress rehearsals. By the last one, five passages had
been amputated from the work. On opening night, 11 March 1867, more cuts
were made, including the impressive Fontainebleau woodcutters' chorus at the
beginning of Act 1. By the second performance, the end of Act 4 was also
shortened. In this truncated state, the original version was performed 43 times
at the Opéra until 1869, making the work a respectable success, but hardly a
triumph, and it was not revived. The reviews were mixed. The main complaint
was that Verdi was not true to his old self and had become "Wagnerian" (an
accusation that was to plague every French opera composer for the remainder
of the century).[31] Admittedly, Verdi had never written such a "symphonic"
work or one in which recurrent musical themes – a technique found, in any
event, in French opéra-comique – played such a prominent role. The main two
are the one associated with the doomed love between Carlos and Elizabeth and
the one attached to the friendship between Carlos and Posa. A third, heard at
the start of Act 2 and again at the very end, stands for Charles V in his new
incarnation as a monk.

It is no disparagement of French grand opéra to suggest that *Don Carlos*
may be the greatest of them all. More successfully than *Les vêpres siciliennes* –
and more in keeping therefore with the grand opéra tradition – it achieves a
powerful synthesis of the political and personal dimensions. The conflict
between an imperialist, clerical, intolerant power, on the one hand, and the
fight for intellectual freedom and the Flemish cause on the other, is played out
against the relationships between five strongly characterized personalities. The
Grand Inquisitor, labeled "first bass" (though the scheduled singer, feeling he
was not given enough to do, stormed out of the cast), is an even more effective
presence for not appearing until Act 4 for his great scene with the king and
only for two brief moments afterwards. The French censors weighed possible
objections to this personification of religious intolerance but let it stand; for
the Roman premiere in 1868 the Inquisitor was restyled "Grand Chancellor."
As for the seventh character,[32] its unclarified identity and role of "deus in
machina" left Verdi unsatisfied, even though it was retained in the work's
subsequent revisions.

As Budden points out, "Don Carlos was conceived from the start as a French
opera, conditioned by French prosody and traditional French verse metres."[33] It

is misleading to suggest, as is occasionally done, that there is a French version and an Italian version. There are several French versions, in five or four acts and with passages cut or entirely revised, and for which the French text was translated for performances in Italy or other countries where the work was performed in Italian (London being the first city that heard it outside France). The revisions were conducted with the assistance of Nuitter (Wagner's collaborator on the French *Tannhaüser*). They resulted in a five-act version, first performed in Naples in 1872, for which the Philip-Posa duet in Act 2 was rewritten and the Act 5 duet between Carlos and Elizabeth modified; the four-act version, as mounted at La Scala in 1884, incorporating further changes; and an alternative five-act version, unveiled at Modena in 1886, which restored the Fontainebleau act while remaining faithful to the 1884 text. As with so many nineteenth-century operas, which took shape gradually through trial and error, it is pointless to imagine there is only one authoritative version. There can be no doubt, on the other hand, about the superiority of the original French, providing singers of the right caliber can be found who will do justice to the language, making it possible to hear this masterpiece as Verdi conceived it.

Victor Massé

Victor Massé (1822-1884) came from the Breton port of Lorient. He entered the Paris Conservatoire in 1834, studying with Halévy and winning the Prix de Rome in 1844.[34] He made his Salle Favart debut in 1850 with the one-act *La chanteuse voilée*, on a text by Scribe and Leuven. Two years later *Galathée* propelled him to the front rank of the younger generation of French opéra-comique composers. Barbier and Carré's two-act libretto is a witty mythological comedy. In their version of the Pygmalion story – previously treated by Rameau and Rousseau – the Cypriot sculptor (Faure's debut role) obtains from Venus that his beautiful creation be endowed with life. But Galathée (premiered by Delphine Ugalde) turns out to be both capricious and flirtatious. To Pygmalion, to the rich collector Midas who also courts her, she prefers Midas's slave Ganymede (tenor) and tries to elope with him during a banquet. Pygmalion, exasperated, begs Venus to change Galathée back into a statue. This opera without chorus combines graceful strophic songs (the most famous, in praise of laziness, sung by Ganymede at the beginning of Act 2) and moments of virtuosity for both soprano and baritone, notably Galathée's "Cup aria" in Act 2, while the quartet gathering the principals in Act 2 is treated with Offenbach-like verve.[35]

Massé's longest-lasting success was the one-act peasant comedy *Les noces de Jeannette*, written by the same team of Barbier and Carré. Premiered in 1853, it reached its thousandth Opéra-Comique performance in 1895 and remained popular in Paris and in the provinces well into the twentieth century. Like other opéra-comique composers at the time, Massé also supplied recitatives for performances abroad. There are only two singing characters, Jean (tenor) and his fiancée Jeannette (soprano). On the morning of their wedding-day, Jean has cold feet, gets drunk, and misbehaves, but Jeannette wins him back by a combination of wit and persuasion. The simple plot anticipates the naturalism of the last decades of the century (Jeannette sets the table and trims the lettuce). Massé produced a wholly enchanting score, combining melodies of exquisite freshness (an especially winning spinning song) with a vocal virtuosity of the kind associated with the role's creator, Caroline Miolan – who married Carvalho that year.[36] Wagner is reported to have said that the work touched him more than any other he had heard at the Salle Favart.[37] He also had kind words for the composer when Massé directed the Opéra chorus at the time of the *Tannhaüser* premiere.

Miolan-Carvalho, having followed her husband to the Théâtre-Lyrique, starred in Massé's *La reine Topaze* in 1856. Featuring a set of dazzling variations on an original Italian tune known as "le Carnaval de Venise,"[38] it was performed 170 times in the following decade.[39] Massé fared less well at the Opéra. *La mule de Pédro* lasted only three performances in 1863, despite a cast headed by Faure and Pauline Gueymard, for whose brilliant mezzo-soprano voice Verdi tailored the part of Eboli in *Don Carlos*. *Fior d'Aliza*, after a novel by Alphonse de Lamartine, was no more successful in 1866. Named professor of composition at the Conservatoire, Massé returned to the stage with *Paul et Virginie*, staged at the Théâtre-Lyrique in 1876 with the tenor Victor Capoul in the principal role. Adapted by Barbier and Carré from the ever popular Bernardin de Saint-Pierre novel, the work exhibits Massé's melodic gifts with an additional touch of exoticism, notably in the symphonic interlude depicting the tropical forest.

Massé's final work, *Une nuit de Cléopâtre*, based on the tale by Théophile Gautier, was premiered posthumously at the Opéra-Comique in 1885, with the same principals (Marie Heilbronn, Jean-Alexandre Talazac, Alexandre Taskin, Max Bouvet) who had premiered Massenet's *Manon* the year before.

Hector Berlioz

The status of Hector Berlioz (1803–1869) as the greatest musical genius in nineteenth-century France – a status parallel to Rameau's in the previous century – is now secure, but it was only in recent decades that his due place in French operatic history has been fully recognized.[40] A profoundly original and creative individual, he failed to get recognition in his day on the stage for reasons that are still debated, now that *Les Troyens*, long reputed impossible to stage, can finally be viewed as his towering achievement.

By contrast with most successful French opera composers of his day, Berlioz never taught at the Paris Conservatoire, nor did he ever have a position at the Opéra or the Opéra-Comique. Instead, he was a successful conductor, receiving invitations from as far away as St. Petersburg (plans for a US visit never materialized). A first-rate writer, he became a renowned music critic – in which capacity, however, he made more enemies than friends.[41] His training and beginnings could have destined him for a conventional route. At the Conservatoire he studied with Le Sueur, the leading Empire opera composer along with Spontini, and with Reicha, who had had a more modest opéra-comique career. Before winning the Prix de Rome in 1830, Berlioz had completed a first opera, *Estelle et Némorin* (1823), which he destroyed, and begun another, *Les francs-juges*, several extracts from which (including the well-known overture, published in 1833–6) were performed in 1828.[42]

The subject of the first of Berlioz's three completed operas, *Benvenuto Cellini*, was suggested to him by Alfred de Vigny, one of the leaders of the French Romantic movement.[43] For a librettist, Vigny recommended Léon de Wailly (1804–1878), translator of Matthew Lewis and Robert Burns, who recruited as his collaborator the poet and fellow translator Auguste Barbier (1805–1882).[44] Initially planned with spoken dialogue, the work was turned down by the Opéra-Comique in 1834 but – despite the unusual absence of a ballet – accepted at the Opéra when Duponchel succeeded Véron in 1835, at which point Vigny assisted with revisions. Labeled "opéra semi-seria," *Benvenuto* was ostensibly inspired by the Florentine sculptor's colorful autobi-ography, but the libretto is actually little indebted to this source. The papal treasurer Balducci is a historical character, but Benvenuto's wooing of his daughter is imaginary. As for the statue of Perseus, the casting of which is the culmination of the opera, it was not commissioned by Pope Clement VII for Rome but by Cosimo de' Medici for Florence (where it still stands). Begun in 1834, the score was written mostly in 1836–8. The overture was completed last, but shortened for the premiere. Censors objected to the presence of the Pope on stage: he was changed to a cardinal. Other pre-premiere revisions inter-vened, such as the replacement of Teresa's poetic romance "Ah! que l'amour une fois dans le coeur" by the more showy, conventional two-part *grand air* "Entre l'amour et le devoir."[45] For Stoltz, who sang the page Ascanio, Berlioz added a second aria in Act 2. The cast also included Duprez, Dorus-Gras, and Dérivis as Balducci. Two decades later, Berlioz recalled the rehearsals in his *Memoirs* as a "horror." The Opéra orchestra was put off by the originality and difficulty of Berlioz's brilliantly orchestrated score. At the premiere on 10 September 1838, only the overture and Ascanio's second aria were unqual-ified successes. The reviews were mixed and, despite cuts, the public reception did not improve at the next two performances. Duprez having left the cast, the fourth performance[46] took place with a different tenor, and Berlioz withdrew the work in March 1839.[47]

Liszt, a tireless advocate of Berlioz's music, resurrected *Benvenuto* in March and November 1850 at Weimar, where it was performed seven times in German. During this run Berlioz revised and shortened it. In this version but in Italian (and with the Roman Carnival overture added as an entracte), the opera was staged in 1853 at Covent Garden, in the presence of Queen Victoria and Prince Albert, with the famous Enrico Tamberlick in the title role. Conducted by Berlioz himself, the performance was a complete disaster and once again he withdrew the work.[48] Apart from two further performances at Weimar in 1856, and despite abortive plans to mount it at the Théâtre-Lyrique in that same year, it was not staged again in Berlioz's lifetime.[49] Looking back on it in early 1856, he noted: "Never again will I recapture such verve and vitality."[50]

The failure of *Benvenuto* may explain why Berlioz's next operatic project, *La nonne sanglante*, was set to a more conventional grand opéra libretto adapted by Scribe from the famous episode in Matthew Lewis's Gothic novel *The Monk*. The gruesome subject, though toned down by Scribe, must have appealed to the imagination of the author of the *Symphonie fantastique*, who greatly admired the Ballet of the Nuns in *Robert le diable*. He composed some of the music for the first two acts in 1841–2 but abandoned the project in 1847. The memory of the *Benvenuto* flop may also explain why his next completed lyrical compositions, *Roméo et Juliette* (1839) and *La damnation de Faust* (1846–54), were published under the respective labels "symphonie drama-tique" and "légende dramatique." However, when the latter was premiered at the Opéra-Comique in 1846 (unsuccessfully), it was advertised as an "opéra de concert," which suggests that the composer viewed it as something else than an oratorio – and indeed a revision was planned (with Scribe) for a London staging in 1848.[51] The work also marked an important step insofar as Berlioz wrote most of the libretto himself.

The project of a large-scale opera based on Virgil's *Aeneid* took shape in 1855–6.[52] It was encouraged by Princess Carolyne Sayn-Wittgenstein, Liszt's mistress, whom Berlioz visited at Weimar at that time. The libretto was ready by June 1856. The music was not composed in sequential order: after finishing Act 1 in February 1857, he proceeded to Act 4 before writing Acts 2, 3, and 5. The work was completed in April 1858, with further revisions in 1857–60. Although the *Aeneid* is the main inspiration (the score is dedicated to "the divine Virgil"), Berlioz also drew from Aeschylus's *Agamemnon* for his depic-tion of Cassandra, whom Virgil hardly mentions. There is also a strong Shakespearian influence – literal in the case of the Act 4 love duet, the words of which are taken from the scene between Lorenzo and Jessica in Act 5 of *The Merchant of Venice*. The end of Act 5 was conceived at first as a pantomime-like epilogue featuring great figures of Roman history and Virgil himself.[53] Viardot's lack of enthusiasm prompted Berlioz to modify it to the dying Dido's prediction of the coming of Hannibal and the ultimate glory of Rome while her subjects curse the Trojans to the sound of the *Marche troyenne*.

Lasting 4 hours and 26 minutes by the composer's own reckoning, *Les Troyens* did not exceed in length *Les Huguenots* or *L'Africaine* (let alone Wagner's yet unwritten *Götterdämmerung*), but Berlioz realized that attempts to stage it would be fraught with difficulties. Ancient subjects were unfashionable in the 1850s: Donizetti's *Les martyrs* had left the repertory; Gounod's *Sapho* had been tepidly received; and David's *Herculanum* largely owed its vogue to the spectacular final tableau. Yet Carvalho, having already staged at the Théâtre-Lyrique Berlioz's version of Gluck's *Orphée*, expressed interest in mounting *Les Troyens* as early as 1860. However, he left the direction of the theater the following year. Alphonse Royer then accepted it for the Opéra – sensing that the work might arouse interest as a French, "Mediterranean" answer to *Tannhaüser* – but Perrin, his successor, withdrew the offer. Finally, Berlioz agreed to divide the work into two parts, entitled respectively *La prise de Troie* and *Les Troyens à Carthage*. The latter was premiered at the Théâtre-Lyrique in November 1863 in a version the composer described as "mutilated." Further cuts were made after the first night, the most grievous being the symphonic interlude with pantomime and chorus, "Chasse royale et orage," which depicts the moment when Dido and Aeneas, driven by a storm into a cave, become lovers.[54] Despite these mutilations, the 21 performances were very well received.[55]

Of *La prise de Troie* Berlioz only heard two fragments in concert. Performed in its entirety by Pasdeloup in 1879, it was first staged at Karlsruhe under Felix Mottl in 1890. It was the first time the entire *Troyens* was heard, though the two parts were heard on consecutive evenings. The work was staged at Covent Garden in 1957 under Rafael Kubelik, but for a really complete version one had to wait until the Scottish National Opera production of 1969, based on Hugh Macdonald's critical edition. Finally available in a complete recording conducted by the Berlioz pioneer Colin Davis, with Jon Vickers as Aeneas and Josephine Veasey as Dido, the work's reputation increased to such an extent that it is now possible to claim it as Berlioz's ultimate masterpiece – a view that would hardly have been shared by most Berliozians a few decades ago. It is significant that the opening production at the new Bastille Opera in 1990 was not *Faust* or *Carmen* but a complete (or nearly complete) *Troyens*.[56]

As music critic, Berlioz wrote harsh words about opéra-comique as a genre, but hardly had he completed *Troyens* than he himself made a splendid contribution to it with *Béatrice et Bénédict*, his own adaptation of Shakespeare's *Much Ado About Nothing*.[57] Though it was his last major composition, it was envisaged as early as 1833. The project took shape when he received a commission in 1860 from the director of the casino at the Black Forest spa of Baden-Baden, where a new theater was being built – its small size explaining the relatively small orchestral forces the work calls for. Completed in February 1862, it was premiered in August of that year with the composer conducting, and starring as Beatrice the soprano Anne Chartron-Demeur who was to sing Dido at the Théâtre-Lyrique the following year. Berlioz describes the work in his *Memoirs* as "one of the liveliest and most original things I have done," yet wrote to a correspondent that because of its humor it was more difficult to perform than

Les Troyens. Berlioz conducted *Béatrice et Bénédict* in Weimar in 1863, and again at Baden-Baden that summer. In Paris, save for a pre-dress rehearsal at the Théâtre-Lyrique in 1862,[58] it was not heard until the Opéra-Comique staged it in 1890.

By focusing the action on the relationship between Benedick and Beatrice – who cannot stand each other until they fall in love with each other – Berlioz eliminated the play's dark, disturbing moments. As a result the characters of Claudio and Hero become secondary, while Don John, the villain of Shakespeare's comedy, disappears altogether. Beatrice, on the other hand, gains in human complexity and verisimilitude, and her aria of self-realization in Act 2, "Il m'en souvient," is the musical summit of the work, along with the beautiful "duo-nocturne" sung by Hero and her attendant Ursula in Act 1, scene 16. The character of Berlioz's invention is the Kapellmeister Somarone (literally "Big donkey"), whose pompous musical ways have been interpreted as a satire of Spontini (whom Berlioz genuinely admired), Cherubini, and Rossini (both *bêtes noires* of his), but there is an element of self-parody.[59] Among the opera's many felicitous touches is the return of the music of the overture in the final duettino between the eponymous characters.

Berlioz's neglect by his contemporaries – a mere 25 complete performances of his operas in France during his lifetime[60] – is all the more vexing in retrospect since, as Hugh Macdonald has pointed out à propos *Les Troyens*, the operas are "anything but revolutionary."[61] Each fits within the French operatic tradition: *Benvenuto*, featuring a more positive hero than most operas of the time, is a flamboyant Renaissance comedy centered on a creative artist; *Les Troyens*, as the historical genre was on the wane, marked a return to the classical tradition of Gluck and Spontini; and *Béatrice et Bénédict* expunges the dark side of Shakespeare's comedy to make it conform to the happier world of opéra-comique.

Charles Gounod

If Berlioz's operas failed to make their mark in nineteenth-century France, Charles Gounod (1818–1893), by the end of the Second Empire, was a prophet in his own country. His career, however, was far from being a series of uninterrupted triumphs; indeed failures far outnumbered successes.[62] But he came to be viewed as the leader of a kind of French operatic renaissance following a period when the Italian influence had been predominant, and his own influence on the following generation was enormous.

The Paris-born Gounod lost his father at a early age. His mother supported herself by teaching the piano. After receiving private tuition from Reicha, Gounod entered the Conservatoire in 1836. There he studied with Berton, Halévy, Le Sueur, and Paër, winning the Prix de Rome in 1839. In the Italian city, he was drawn especially to traditional religious music, especially Giovanni da Palestrina, and fell under the spell of the charismatic Dominican preacher Henri Lacordaire, a leader of the nineteenth-century Catholic revival in France. He also became acquainted with Fanny Mendelssohn and visited her brother Felix in Leipzig on his return journey; his influence on Gounod (especially as a song writer) is not negligible. Back in Paris in 1843, Gounod took a position as *maître de chapelle* to the Foreign Mission seminary, even taking steps towards joining the priesthood.

The decisive factor in Gounod's life was the protection he enjoyed from Viardot. Fresh from her triumph in *Le prophète*, she used her influence at the Opéra to procure him a commission. She also found him a librettist in the person of Émile Augier (1820–1889), then at the dawn of a successful, if highly academic, career as a playwright. With *Sapho* he produced a three-act lyric tragedy on a classical subject, a genre unpopular at the Opéra since the 1820s. The theme, treated by Pacini in 1840, was the mythical life of the Lesbian poet. In Act 1 she wins a singing contest but, treacherously outwitted by her rival Glycère, is abandoned by her lover Phaon and throws herself into the sea. Gounod gave his benefactress opportunities to shine in two arias, both adapted from earlier mélodies: the Act 1 prize song "Héro, sur la tour solitaire" and the final *stances* "Ô ma lyre immortelle." From its opening chords, recalling the beginning of Haydn's "London" Symphony, the work is characterized by an appealing, uncompromising, neo-classical flavor. It culminates with an especially beautiful third act, the tragic tone of which is relieved only by an exquisite shepherd's song. Gounod's innate sense of prosody, his melodic gift, his feeling for orchestral color were already in evidence. Yes, the work was not a success: seven performances at the Opéra in the spring of 1851, one (in Italian) at Covent Garden in August, two more, without Viardot, in Paris in December. Revised versions in 1858 (in two acts) and 1884 (in four, with ballet added) similarly failed to gain the work a place in the repertory. *Sapho*, however, brought Gounod to the attention of critics such as Berlioz, and one can see why Camille Saint-Saëns described it as a milestone in French operatic history.

In April 1852 Gounod married Anna Zimmermann, daughter of the well-known professor of piano at the Paris Conservatoire. This alliance made the composer a member of the musical establishment. It provoked a rift with Viardot, under circumstances that do little credit to his tact. A resulting casualty was a projected collaboration with her friend George Sand.[63] Gounod's second operatic project was a setting of Scribe's *La nonne sanglante*, which, initially offered to Meyerbeer, had been turned down, following Berlioz's withdrawal, by Halévy, Verdi, Grisar, Clapisson, and David. Though it only received 11 performances and was never revived, the work – Gounod's closest approach to Romantic grand opéra à la Meyerbeer or Halévy – was not an outright failure, earning Gounod praise from Berlioz, among others, while most negative comments were reserved for the libretto, widely considered one of Scribe's weakest.[64]

The *Faust* project dated from Gounod's years at the Villa Médicis (1839–1843) and had remained with him since.[65] In 1855 he became acquainted with Barbier and Carré, the latter the author of a "drame fantastique," *Marguerite et Faust*, for a boulevard theater. This source explains why the resulting opera owes as much to the aesthetics of French Romantic melodrama as to Goethe, notably in the characterization of Mephistopheles and the focus on the plight of Marguerite as a "fallen woman." Turned down by the Opéra, the work was accepted by Carvalho in 1856 but temporarily shelved when another Faust adaptation by Dennery was announced at the Porte Saint-Martin. To this postponement we owe one of the masterpieces of French opéra-comique, *Le médecin malgré lui*, adapted by Barbier and Carré from Molière's 1666 farce (an unusual choice in the 1850s). The libretto uses Molière's text for spoken dialogues, adding lyrics based on the play and on other sources.[66] An obstacle arose when the Comédie-Française, claiming copyright on Molière's works, tried to stop the project, but the intervention of Princess Mathilde, Napoleon III's first cousin, cleared the way for the January 1858 premiere. A work of irrepressible charm and wit – its climax the Act 2 sextet in which Sganarelle, pretending to be a doctor, examines Lucinde, who is pretending to be dumb – *Le médecin malgré lui* was performed 142 times at the Théâtre-Lyrique before entering the Salle Favart repertory in 1872. Though revivals have been few, it has always been admired, especially by composers such as Debussy and Stravinsky – whose own neo-classicism has affinities with Gounod's. For a revival as part of the 1924 Ballets russes season at Monte Carlo, Serge Diaghilev commissioned from Erik Satie additional music to replace the spoken dialogues.[67]

The success of *Le médecin malgré lui* revived the *Faust* project, and the premiere was planned for November 1858. Ugalde was the initially choice for Marguerite, while Faust was promised to the tenor Guardi (real name Hector Gruyer), a pupil of Bizet's father, whose baritone color explains some of the role's low-lying phrases. In the event, to Georges Bizet's grief, Guardi went hoarse during the rehearsals and had to be replaced, while Miolan-Carvalho took the part of Marguerite – a surprising move for a coloratura soprano associated with florid roles like *La reine Topaze*. The work premiered on 19 March 1859 differed in important aspects from the version performed today.[68] It included spoken dialogues as well as melodramas.[69] It also differed from Gounod's original version, passages from which had to be cut: a trio between Faust and his students Wagner and Siebel in Act 1; a duet between Marguerite and her brother in Act 2; an additional aria for Siebel in Act 4. Mephistopheles's Golden Calf song was now a Song of the Beetle.[70] The love duet in the garden in Act 3 and the prison duet in Act 5 were both longer.[71] Act 4 began with the now seldom heard Spinning Scene, followed by the death of Valentin, followed by the Church Scene (which at first worried the censors); only later did it become standard practice to put Valentin's death after the Church Scene.

As for the Soldiers Chorus, it was lifted, apparently at Ingres' urging, from an abandoned *Ivan le terrible*. For the Strasbourg premiere in 1860 Gounod added recitatives, which the Théâtre-Lyrique finally adopted in 1866; a model of their kind, they blend so naturally with the musical numbers that it is now difficult to imagine the work without them. The Milan and London premieres (the latter at Her Majesty's Theatre, in Italian) cut the Walpurgis Scene and reverted to the longer versions of the duets. For the Covent Garden premiere (July 1863) Gounod threw in an aria for Siebel, "Quando a te lieta" ("Si le bonheur") in the Spinning Scene. When the work was revived in 1864 at Her Majesty's Theatre, as a friendly gesture to the baritone Charles Santley, Gounod added Valentin's Act 2 cavatine, set to Chorley's words "Even bravest heart may swell" (rendered in French as "Avant de quitter ces lieux") on the F major tune heard in the opening prelude. Gounod was never happy with this addition – which now makes the theme an anticipation of Valentin's aria rather than the unique appearance of a symbolic "redemption" motif. It was not included in any of Choudens' editions of the piano-vocal score and was not part of the standard performing version in Paris until the second half of the twentieth century.

When a bankrupt Carvalho left the Théâtre-Lyrique in 1868 – *Faust* had by then been performed more than 300 times – Perrin negotiated with Gounod the transfer of the work to the Opéra, where it was premiered the following year, with Christine Nilsson (and subsequently Miolan-Carvalho) as Marguerite. The last addition to the work was thus the ballet, which a recalcitrant Gounod tried to get Saint-Saëns to write in his place, though, in Paris at least, its popularity quickly supplanted Faust's drinking song in the Walpurgis Scene. No work has been performed more often at the Opéra (more than 2,000 times by 1975).

Some aspects of the work clearly look back to the opéra-comique tradition. That is particularly the case of the arias: Faust's lyrical cavatine, Marguerite's florid Jewel Song, Mephistopheles's strophic songs in Acts 2 and 4. Many other passages, on the other hand, defy characterization: the long monologue of Faust at the beginning of Act 1, a kind of mini-cantata with arioso-style recitatives blending into short arias, punctuated by offstage choral interventions; the Kermis Scene, especially the waltz with chorus framing the encounter between Faust and Marguerite – a short exchange which Gounod made into one of the score's memorable moments; the Garden Quartet and ensuing love duet; the Prison Scene, with its moving quotations of snatches from the previous acts as the delirious Marguerite recollects past happiness. Massenet was to replicate the effect in *Manon* – as would Puccini in *La bohème*.

Gounod's next opera, *Philémon et Baucis*, originated from a commission for Baden-Baden which Carvalho, sensing another star vehicle for his wife, rerouted for the Théâtre-Lyrique, where it was premiered in February 1860. Barbier and Carré adapted a verse tale by La Fontaine, based on Ovid's

Metamorphoses, dealing with the old couple, touchingly devoted to each other and kindly hospitable to a disguised Jupiter accompanied by Mercury. In the opera Mercury became Vulcan, a more obviously droll character, whose Act 1 strophic aria, "Au bruit des lourds marteaux d'airain," became the work's most famous number. Expanding the story in Offenbach-like fashion, Barbier and Carré imagined that Jupiter restored his hosts to their youthful shapes and promptly proceeded to fall in love with Baucis, who eventually begs him to change her back into an old woman. A second act, not part of the original design, depicts the sinful festivities of the city nearby – a tableau based on Thomas Couture's celebrated painting *Les Romains de la décadence* – and their annihilation by Jupiter. This additional act was removed when the work entered the Opéra-Comique repertory in 1876. Not successful at first (15 performances), *Philémon et Baucis* was praised for its melodic charm and the refinement and pastoral coloring of its orchestration. It was in its two-act version that the work was also staged in a number of theaters internationally and it long remained in the Opéra-Comique repertory.

To make up for the withdrawn *Philémon et Baucis* Gounod offered Baden-Baden the short, two-act opéra-comique *La colombe*. A kind of chamber opera, it has four principals (one of them a soprano *en travesti*) and no chorus. It is also based on a La Fontaine tale, "Le faucon," this time after Boccaccio. It is the story of a poor young Florentine who, having to entertain the countess he loves, is ready to sacrifice his favorite bird to serve it as a main dish – unaware that she is about to ask him for the bird as a present. Fortunately, it turns out that a different bird was substituted at the last moment and all ends well. The four Baden-Baden performances in August 1860 were highly successful, but *La colombe* remains one of the least performed of Gounod's operas, despite the existence of a version with recitatives by Francis Poulenc – like *Le médecin malgré lui* a Diaghilev commission for Monte Carlo in 1924.

Gounod returned to the Opéra in February 1862 with *La reine de Saba*, a four-act opera inspired by an episode from the "Nuits de Ramazan" section from Gérard de Nerval's *Voyage en Orient*. The work centers on a love triangle between Solomon, here called Soliman (baritone), who loves Balkis, the Queen of Sheba. But she loves Adoniram, the Temple's architect, and is loved in return. In the meantime he is involved in a labor dispute with three of his workers, who denounce him to Soliman and in the end murder him. Despite its undeniable beauties – the arias for Adoniram ("Inspirez-moi, race divine") and Balkis ("Plus grand dans son immensité") are Gounod at his most seductively eloquent – the work was a fiasco that deeply affected the composer. As Steven Huebner has pointed out, *La reine de Saba* was probably the first French opera to be plagued with indiscriminate accusations of Wagnerism, no doubt prompted in its case by the use of recurrent themes, or recurrent motifs, at key moments in the opera.[72]

Hardly had *La reine de Saba* been completed than Gounod embarked on an opera based on the Provençal verse epic *Miréio* which eventually earned its author, Frédéric Mistral, a share in the 1904 Nobel Prize for Literature. The story of the 15-year-old daughter of a rich farmer, who walks all the way to the Saintes-Marie-de-la-Mer to join her lover Vincent, son of a poor basket-maker, and dies of a sunstroke on arrival, was adapted by Carré under Mistral's supervision. The libretto, in fact, retains some lines from Mistral's own prose translation of the poem published in the first, bilingual edition of 1859: "Chantez, chantez, magnanarelles," "Saint Jean le moissonneur, saint Jean l'ami de Dieu," "Les ailes de l'amour et le vent de la foi" – these familiar lines from Gounod's work are all Mistral's. Gounod sought his inspiration in Provence, moving to Saint-Rémy for three months in the spring of 1863 and visiting the sites featured in the opera: imbued with Provençal melodies and rhythms, the score is his most atmospheric. One might even argue that of all his works, *Mireille* has the subject matter most attuned to his genius. Reality, however, intervened in the person of Miolan-Carvalho, who had urged the composer to write "brilliant, brilliant, brilliant," whereas Gounod's instinct, already much in evidence in *Faust*, was towards a highly personal form of lyricism that could happily dispense with vocal virtuosity; with Mireille he created, in fact, a demanding lyric soprano role that exceeded Miolan-Carvalho's capacities. Despite last-minute compromises, the March 1864 premiere was far from successful, prompting modifications that departed further from the composer's intentions. One objection was the heroine's death at the end. By the time of the London premiere in July (in Italian, as usual), Gounod, while adding the required recitatives, had substituted a happy denouement – Vincent and Mireille are allowed to get married and live happily ever after. When the work reappeared at the Théâtre-Lyrique in December, it was reduced to three acts, ended happily, and Mireille was gratified with a prepos-terous "Valse-ariette" at her Act 1 entrance. In this version the work lasted for 41 performances. When transferred to the Opéra-Comique in 1874 (with spoken dialogue), *Mireille* had four acts. They became three in 1889, and five again in 1901, in a version conducted by André Messager which, despite a few cuts, largely restored Gounod's original intentions. Yet, in 1939, a new edition was published, credited to the team of Hahn and the composer-conductor Henri Busser, which misleadingly presented itself as a return to "the true *Mireille*." Admittedly, it eliminated the Valse-ariette and remained faithful to the original, tragic denouement. But it has problems of its own. It is sung throughout – despite Gounod's attachment to the opéra-comique form – and Act 4, far from respecting Gounod's intentions, follows the truncated, rearranged version that had been forced on him as a result of the inadequacy of his 1864 cast. In the original libretto, as in Mistral, Mireille, about to cross the Crau on her way to the Camargue, encountered the young shepherd Andreloun (a mezzo part, not a tenor as Hahn and Busser would have it), who warned her against crossing the plain in the midday sun. In the 1939 text, this enchanting episode is moved to the previous tableau, which takes place miles away on the previous evening. Mireille now embarks on her grand air immediately after the prelude, and since the two keys hardly match, any listener can tell that something is missing.[73]

Gounod's greatest and sole undisputed triumph occurred in April 1867, still at the Théâtre-Lyrique, with *Roméo et Juliette*. Along with *La grande-duchesse de Gérolstein*, it was the chief operatic attraction of the second Universal Exposition in Paris. Unlike Gounod's previous work for that company, it was sung throughout – though the composer unsuccessfully fought for an alternative version with spoken dialogues. Miolan-Carvalho was obviously cast as Juliette, and this time Gounod preempted her objections by giving her "brilliant" singing in Act 1 (the waltz-song "Je veux vivre dans le rêve"), after which the role is more in keeping with his stylistic preferences. Barbier and Carré treated Shakespeare's play more faithfully than when tackling the admittedly much more challenging *Hamlet* for Ambroise Thomas. The one exception is that Juliet awakens before Romeo dies: this variant had a precedent in Garrick's version, popular beyond the eighteenth century. From the outset *Roméo et Juliette* was admired for the variety and beauty of its four love duets – an unprecedented figure – in every act save for Act 3. This one is arranged in two scenes: the first, the wedding scene, gives us a whiff of Gounod the composer of sacred music, earnest and slightly bombastic; the deaths of Mercutio and Tybalt and subsequent banishment of Romeo lead to an imposing choral finale. Musical unity is provided by one recurrent theme, symbolizing Romeo and Juliet's love: it is initially exposed on the cellos at the end of the prologue, recurs when Romeo first sees Juliet, and is heard again during three of their duets.

After its initial run of 120 performances in 1867–8, *Roméo et Juliette* was performed 300 times at the Théâtre-Lyrique. In 1873 it was transferred, under Bizet's supervision, to the Opéra-Comique: it was the first entirely sung work staged there. Finally, in 1888 it entered the Opéra, Gounod supplying a ballet for the second scene of Act 4. Unlike the one in *Faust*, it adds nothing to his reputation.[74]

Following *Roméo*, Gounod went through a period of depression and spiritual crisis. He began to work on *Polyeucte*, after the Corneille tragedy that had already inspired Donizetti for *Poliuto* and *Les martyrs*. Like Scribe, Barbier and Carré kept lines from the original, notably the hero's famous *stances* at the beginning of Act 4. They outdid Scribe in emphasizing the contrast between the pagan and Christian worlds – allowing for exotic musical effects – and giving more prominence to the public scenes, referred to but not shown in Corneille's tragedy. Although Gounod, who grew more and more religious in his later years, claimed it was his best work, *Polyeucte* was coolly received when it was finally – and lavishly – staged at the Opéra to coincide with the 1878 Exposition. It disappeared from the repertory after a modest 29 performances.

The long delay that separated the composition and staging of *Polyeucte* was due to Gounod's prolonged stay in England, where he took his family when the Franco-Prussian War was declared in 1870. Instead of returning to Paris after the Commune, he remained in London, having fallen under the spell of one of the more curious characters to have emerged from Victorian England, the amateur singer Georgina Weldon (1837–1914). From the period of their entanglement, a bizarre episode in the composer's biography,[75] dates the tantalizing project of an opéra-comique based on Molière's *George Dandin*, the musical numbers set directly to the original text of the play. If completed, it would have been the first French opera on a prose libretto, two decades before Massenet's *Thaïs*, but Gounod abandoned it. The surviving full-score manuscript, most of its pages with Georgina Weldon's angry signature across the page, is preserved in the Frederick R. Koch Collection at Yale.[76]

Carvalho having become director of the Opéra-Comique after Du Locle went bankrupt in 1876, Gounod, for the first and only time, had a work premiered in that theater. Labeled "opéra dialogué" – an unusual appellation characteristic of the gradual blurring of the operatic categories under the Third Republic – *Cinq-Mars* was based by his librettists, Paul Poirson (1836–19?) and Louis Gallet (1835–1898), on Alfred de Vigny's celebrated historical novel inspired by the 1642 conspiracy against Cardinal Richelieu, which resulted in the execution of Louis XIII's young friend (and, according to contemporary sources, lover) the Marquis de Cinq-Mars, together with his friend François de Thou. Despite the excitement created by a new work from a musician considered by then France's national composer,[77] the opera only lasted a few months. Audiences and critics were apparently put off by the grand opéra features of a work whose musical language – noticeably in the exquisite Act 2 divertissement – was more in keeping with the classical style of *Le médecin malgré lui*.

After giving up a projected *Maître Pierre* on the subject of Héloïse and Abélard set to a libretto by Poirson and Gallet, the co-librettists of *Cinq-Mars*, Gounod returned to opera once more with *Le tribut de Zamora*, premiered at the Palais Garnier in 1881 with a cast headed by the famous Gabrielle Krauss (who had sung Pauline in *Polyeucte*) and the baritone Jean-Louis Lassalle. Initially intended for Verdi, Dennery and Jules Brésil's libretto is a medieval melodrama set in Oviedo and near Cordoba under Moorish rule. The mad heroine, held captive by the Arabs, recovers her sanity upon recognizing her long-lost daughter who has also been abducted by the chieftain Ben-Saïd. The work lasted 50 performances until 1885 and was staged in several countries (and several languages) but, owing mostly to an unanimously negative press, soon disappeared from the repertory – although an opera dealing with Christian and Arab relations might seem to be an intriguing candidate for revival in the early twenty-first century.[78]

1 This engraving is the only visual testimony we have of the 1671 production of Cambert and Perrin's *Pomone*, the first full-fledged French opera.

2 Lully's *Alceste* as performed at Versailles in 1674 as part of the celebrations of the conquest of Franche-Comté, engraving by Jean Lepautre.

3 Alain-René Le Sage's *Télémaque* (1715), a parody of Destouches's opera of the same title with music arranged by Jean-Claude Gillier, was one of the earliest opéras-comiques. From *Le théâtre de la foire, ou L'opéra-comique* (Paris, 1721–37).

4 Jean Monnet (1703–85), one of the key figures in the history of opéra-comique. Engraved frontispiece to Jean Monnet, *Supplément au Roman comique* (London [i.e. Paris] 1772).

5 Charles-Simon Favart (1710–92), the true creator of opéra-comique, after whom the Opéra-Comique theater was named. Frontispiece to Favart's *Théâtre, ou Recueil des comédies* (Paris, 1763).

6 The soprano Marie Fel (1713–94), who premiered many important parts in operas by Rameau and Mondonville (as well as Colette in Rousseau's *Le devin du village*). Pastel by Maurice Quentin de La Tour (one of Fel's lovers).

7 Rosalie Dugazon in the title role of Dalayrac's *Nina, ou La folle par amour* (1787), oil painting by Antoine Vestier (1740–24). The soprano is portrayed singing her Act 1 romance, "Quand le bien-aimé reviendra." Long attributed to Élisabeth Vigée-Lebrun, the original is currently in a private collection. Reproduced from Louis Hautecoeur, *Madame Vigée-Lebrun* (1914).

8 The "Magic Picture" scene in Act II of Grétry's *Zémire et Azor* (1771), in which Azor ("The Beast") shows Zémire ("Beauty") her father and sisters mourning her absence.

9 Frontispiece by D. Delaroche to the 1882 printing of the piano-vocal score of Jean-François Le Sueur's *Ossian ou Les bardes* (1804), showing the Dream Scene which inspired Ingres's 1813 celebrated painting, except that in the painting Ossian, asleep and ageless, is a far cry from the dashing tenor pictured here.

10 Built in a few months in 1821, the Salle Le Peletier was the home of the Paris Opéra until a fire destroyed it in 1873. Most French grands opéras were premiered there, from Auber's *La muette de Portici* to Verdi's *Don Carlos*.

11 "A Box at the Opéra," print by H. Robinson after Eugène Lami's 1842 painting. What can be seen of the stage in the background suggests a production of *La Juive* by Fromental Halévy.

12 Caroline Miolan-Carvalho (1827–95), star of the Opéra-Comique, and then of the Théâtre-Lyrique, who premiered, among many roles, Gounod's Marguerite, Mireille, and Juliette.

Théâtre-Lyrique : Madame Miolan-Carvalho , d'après une photographie de Numa Blanc.

13 Contralto Pauline Viardot towards the end of her life. The sister of Maria Malibran, she premiered Meyerbeer's *Le prophète* and was instrumental in launching the careers of Gounod and Massenet.

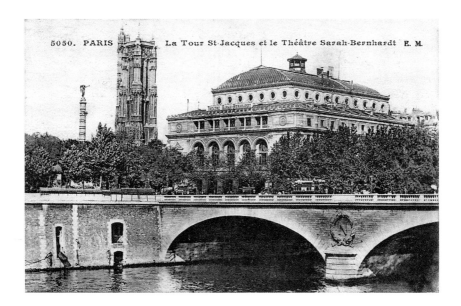

14 The second home of the Théâtre-Lyrique, on the place du Châtelet, was inaugurated in 1862. It burned down during the Commune and was rebuilt. Between 1887 and 1898 it was occupied by the Opéra-Comique and eventually became the Théâtre Sarah-Bernhardt. It hosted the premieres of Gounod's *Mireille* and *Roméo et Juliette*, Berlioz's *Les Troyens à Carthage* and Bizet's *Les pêcheurs de perles* and *La jolie fille de Perth* and – when it hosted the Opéra-Comique after the 1887 fire – Massenet's *Esclarmonde* and Bruneau's *Le rêve* and *L'attaque du moulin*.

15 The Théâtre de la Gaîté, inaugurated in 1862, still stands on the Square des Arts-et-Métiers. In the 1870s it was briefly run by Offenbach, whose *Orphée aux enfers* was revived there in its revised version (1874), and it housed the ephemeral Opéra-National-Lyrique and Opéra populaire.

16 The Grand-Théâtre in Lyons in the mid-nineteenth century. After 1870, it hosted several important premieres, such as Saint-Saëns's *Étienne Marcel* (1884) and the French premiere of Reyer's *Sigurd* (1885). Wagner's *Die Meistersinger*, among other works, was first seen here before being staged in Paris. After 1945, and especially in the mid-1960s, it became the leading provincial French opera house.

17 The third Salle Favart, home of the Opéra-Comique from 1898 to the present day, was built following the fire that destroyed its predecessor in May 1887, and on the same site off the boulevard des Italiens.

18 Massenet in 1906 at his country home at Égreville, the estate near Fontainebleau he purchased in 1899. Photograph by F. et C. published in the journal Musica.

19 A scene from Act II in the original production of Gustave Charpentier's *Louise* at the Salle Favart in 1900, showing, on the right, the bass Léon Rothier as the Tinker. Photograph by Carle de Mazibourg published in *Le théâtre*.

20 Lucien Fugère, who premiered Louise's father, had an exceptionally long career, which extended from the mid-1870s onwards.

21 The Grotto Scene (Act II, scene 3) in the original production of Debussy's *Pelléas et Mélisande* at the Opéra-Comique in 1902, with Mary Garden as Mélisande and Jean Périer as Pelléas. Photograph published in *Le théâtre*.

22 Mary Garden (1874–1967) as Mélisande. The Scottish-American soprano, who made her Opéra-Comique début as Louise, also premiered Massenet's *Chérubin* and Erlanger's *Aphrodite*. Photograph by Reutlinger published in *Le théâtre* in 1902.

Mᵐᵉ LUCIENNE BRÉVAL
DE L'ACADÉMIE NATIONALE DE MUSIQUE

23 Lucienne Bréval (1869–1935), the Swiss dramatic soprano who premiered several Massenet roles. She was also the first Lady Macbeth in Bloch's opera and the first Pénélope in Fauré's. Photograph by W. Histed published in *Le théâtre*, September 1903.

24 Soprano Germaine Lubin (1890–1979) and tenor Thomas Salignac (1867–1945) in Ropartz's *Le pays*, in which they appeared at the Opéra-Comique premiere in 1913. Both singers were later compromised during the Nazi Occupation. Photograph by Bert published in *Le théâtre*.

LE THÉATRE

Photo Bert   VÉAL   SALUDE
              (M. Salignac)   (Mᵐᵉ Lubin)
THÉÂTRE NATIONAL DE L'OPÉRA-COMIQUE. — *LE PAYS*

Ambroise Thomas

Few French opera composers have elicited from their contemporaries more contemptuous comments than Ambroise Thomas (1811–1896). "There is good music, bad music, and music . . . by Ambroise Thomas," Emmanuel Chabrier famously declared.[79] Was this due, as Georges Masson has suggested, to the length of the career of a man who could have met Beethoven – whom he idolized – and was still alive when Maurice Ravel wrote his first piano pieces?[80] Fortunately, posterity has been less unkind lately to a musician who ranks among the finest opera composers of the period.

Thomas was from Metz where his father, who taught him music, played the violin at the city theater. When his father died in 1823 Ambroise and his elder brother Charles moved to Paris, where Charles was hired as a cellist by the Opéra orchestra. Five years later Ambroise entered the Conservatoire, where he studied composition with Le Sueur. He also studied the piano with Zimmermann and Kalkbrenner. He was awarded the Prix de Rome in 1832 and spent several happy years at the Villa Médicis, where had friendly relations with Ingres, the new director. His first opéra-comique, the one-act *La double échelle* (1837) set to a libretto by Planard, lasted 247 performances. Other well-received works followed, notably *Le panier fleuri* in 1839. At the Opéra, where Thomas debuted in 1839 with the ballet *La gypsy* starring Fanny Elssler, the three-act Venetian comedy *Le comte de Carmagnola*, on a Scribe libretto, was withdrawn after eight showings in 1841. *Le guerrillero*, a two-act work capitalizing on the vogue for Spanish subjects, was better received the following year.

Le caïd (1849) established Thomas' reputation. This "opéra-bouffon" in two acts is set in Algeria, which the French had colonized in the course of the previous two decades. Fatma, daughter of Aboul-y-far, the eponymous kaid (the village leader), has fallen for Michel, the French drum-major.[81] Yet her father, fearing beatings by his constituents over high taxes, promises her to the wily Birotteau, a young *colon* newly arrived with his fiancée Virginie. Embarrassing though the patronizing portrait of the locals in Sauvage's libretto may be to modern audiences, *Le caïd* remains a fascinating period piece. Despite its exotic locale – the muezzin's call to prayer is heard in Act 1, while the second is set in the kaid's own house – the music is not particularly orientalist and does not depart from the Italianate opéra-comique style of the period. The work was enormously successful in France and abroad.

Le songe d'une nuit d'été (1850) is not, as the title might suggest, based on *A Midsummer Night's Dream*. Instead, Rosier and Leuven's libretto is an allegorical representation of Shakespeare's life. Its chief characters are the playwright himself and Queen Elizabeth, who rescues him from a life of debauchery (Falstaff, improbably, figures among his drinking companions) and persuades him that his calling is to become England's great national poet. Without matching *Le caïd*'s 400 performances at the Opéra-Comique, the work was well received and was later revived with, as Shakespeare, the baritone Victor Maurel, Verdi's first Iago and Falstaff.[82]

Thomas, by now considered the heir to Auber and Halévy at the Opéra-Comique, was less successful with *Raymond, ou Le secret de la reine* (1851), inspired by the Man in the Iron Mask enigma; only its overture has remained famous. In the same year he succeeded Spontini at the Académie des Beaux-Arts and in 1852 was appointed professor of composition at the Conservatoire, where Massenet was his pupil. None of the six opéras-comiques he produced in the following eight years was a lasting success, though they were not lacking in musical qualities. Among them was the mythological comedy *Psyché* (1857), which in the 1870s was recast into a full-fledged opera. Premiered in 1855 with Miolan-Carvalho, the recently rediscovered *La cour de Célimène*, a picture of love in eighteenth-century France in which buffo elements alternate with a more sentimental tone, also shows Thomas at his most individual.[83]

After a six-year gap, Thomas returned to the Favart stage with *Mignon* (1866), drawn by Barbier and Carré from Goethe's novel *Wilhelm Meisters Lehjahre*. Along with Gounod's *Faust* and *Roméo et Juliette*, it proved in the long run the most successful Second Empire opera:[84] by 1870 it had been performed more than 500 times in Paris, and by 1900 more than 1,200 times.[85] As with *Faust*, Thomas' librettists, who had first offered the work to Meyerbeer, have been accused of trivializing their source. The main reproach concerns the ending in which Mignon becomes Wilhelm's wife, while the actress Philine, her rival for his affection, consoles herself by marrying her admirer Frederick. When premiered in November 1866 the work actually ended, as in Goethe, with Mignon's death.[86] This tragic ending was coolly received by Opéra-Comique audiences – as *Mireille*'s had been two years before – and the authors resigned themselves to altering it. Few opéras-comiques before *Carmen* – Auber's *Manon Lescaut* being the main exception – could get away with the death of the heroine.[87] As for the Wilhelm adapted by Barbier and Carré, he inevitably lost in complexity as he was transformed into an operatic character; his is nonetheless among the most beautiful lyric tenor roles of the period. Mignon herself, the long-lost daughter of Count Lothario and abducted as a child by gypsies, is also a watered-down version of Goethe's asexual, androgynous creation. Yet, the character retains some bohemian traits that make her a distant cousin of Carmen – a kinship reinforced by the fact that the two roles were premiered by the same Galli-Marié – and her melancholy, almost otherworldly side is subtly, tellingly conveyed by Thomas.

The success of *Mignon* in France prompted Thomas to revise the work for performances abroad: Weimar, Goethe's own city, and Vienna both staged it in 1868. For this version, Thomas wrote sung recitatives to replace spoken dialogues and melodramas; he also reinstated the tragic denouement. For the 1870 London premiere, in Italian, he rewrote the part of Frederick (originally a second tenor) for a mezzo, fleshing out the role with a rondo-gavotte ("In veder l'amata stanza"). In was in this sung- through version that *Mignon* remained popular all over the world well into the twentieth century, when most lyric tenors – from Tito Schipa to Alain Vanzo – and lyric mezzo-sopranos – from Conchita Supervia to Frederica von Stade – had Wilhelm and Mignon in their repertory, while no self-respecting coloratura soprano would turn down an opportunity to shine in Philine's Polonaise (the theme of which is first heard in the Allegro section of the overture). Even in France, where the opéra-comique version remained in favor, the sung recitatives were adopted at the Opéra-Comique in 1963 and most recent revivals have preferred a "compromise" version, using the Weimar denouement and sung recitatives except for the melodramas, where the original version was, justifiably, retained.[88]

Thomas' *Hamlet*, premiered in March 1868, was the Opéra's answer to Gounod's *Roméo et Juliette* at the Théâtre-Lyrique the previous year.[89] An undeniable success, it did not, in the end, rival the Gounod work nor did it prove as successful as *Mignon*, despite 300 performances in 30 years and a number of stagings abroad – beginning with London, in Italian, in 1869. More than *Mignon*, the work was blamed, from day one, for trivializing its source. Faced with the daunting task of reducing an exceptionally long play into manageable proportions – yet with the addition of a ballet, demanded by the Opéra director – Barbier and Carré did, in fact, no worse than most librettists who have adapted Shakespeare to the operatic stage, and in some respects better than many. Warned by the *Mignon* precedent, they substituted for the Parisian premiere a happy ending, in which Hamlet, having killed Claudius, is proclaimed king of Denmark;[90] an alternative denouement, faithful to the original, was written for London.[91] In keeping with operatic convention, the plot focuses on Hamlet and Ophelia. The former, planned initially as a tenor role, was rewritten for Faure; it is one of the most arduous roles in the baritone repertory. The latter, premiered by the 25-year-old coloratura Swedish soprano Christine Nilsson, who took it around the world, culminates on a long, atmospheric mad scene. Whether Thomas consciously meant to respond to the Wagnerian challenge, or, more probably, took as his model the French opéra-comique tradition, the work is built on a series of recurrent motifs. The whole piece is permeated by an "unreal and poetic atmosphere"[92] – an atmosphere beautifully conveyed by Thomas' orchestration, which includes saxophones in addition to saxhorns. Sadly neglected in France since the Second World War, *Hamlet* has, fortunately, been maintained in the international repertory thanks to baritones (Sherrill Milnes, Thomas Hampson, Simon Keenlyside) who have periodically demonstrated its viability.

Thomas' operatic career practically came to an end with the Second Empire. Auber's successor as director of the Paris Conservatoire in 1871, he kept the position until his death. His final work, *Françoise de Rimini*, premiered at the Opéra in 1882, was drawn by Barbier and Carré – who first intended it for

Gounod – from the episode in Dante's *Divine Comedy* that had already inspired Liszt and Tchaikovsky. A prologue – much admired at the time by critics like Arthur Pougin and Ernest Reyer – features Dante (baritone) and Virgil (contralto), who also reappear in the epilogue at the end of which Beatrice, accompanied by a choir of angels, forgives the doomed lovers. The work was performed 40 times until 1885 but was never revived.

Though *Mignon* remained popular in France until the 1960s, Thomas' reputation has declined in his home country, where the modernist musical establishment remembered him above all as the reactionary Conservatoire director who was hostile to César Franck and blocked the appointment of Gabriel Fauré.

Hervé and the origins of French operetta

Another reason why the Second Empire is an important period in the history of French opera is the emergence of operetta – a new genre promised to a long future if one considers that the modern musical largely derives from it. Admittedly, the term "opérette," in common use by 1855[93] and popularized the following year by Offenbach's competition, was applied retrospectively to a variety of works originally staged and published under other appellations – opéra-bouffe, vaudeville-opérette, comédie-opérette, or even opéra-comique.[94] Indeed Second Empire operetta, with its emphasis on parody, marked a return to the origins of opéra-comique. And although Offenbach made the greatest contributions to the genre, he was actually preceded by the now less famous Hervé.[95]

Hervé was the pseudonym of Louis-Auguste-Florimond Ronger (1825–1892).[96] Born in the northern city of Houdain to a French father and a Basque Spanish mother, he was trained as a choirboy in the fashionable parish of Saint-Roch while receiving private tuition from Antoine Elwart (1808–1877), who taught harmony at the Conservatoire, as well as from Auber. At a young age he became organist at the mental asylum of Bicêtre. A pioneer of music therapy,[97] he staged his first work *L'ours et le pacha* (1842), a "vaudeville opérette" based on Scribe's 1820 comedy, using hospital patients as his cast and audience. In 1845 Hervé was appointed organist at the old prestigious parish of Saint-Eustache. For the next nine years, he kept this position while moonlighting as singer, conductor, and comic-opera composer under his pseudonym – a schizophrenic existence he later dramatized in his best-known work, *Mam'zelle Nitouche* (1883), in which Célestin, organist of a fashionable religious school for girls, writes risqué operettas on the side under the name Floridor. *Don Quichotte and Sancho Pança*, the two-character "tableau grotesque" in which Hervé starred with the popular singer known as Désiré, was launched in small theaters before being staged at the Opéra-National in 1848, just before it closed, and subsequently revived in other houses. In 1851

Hervé was appointed music director of the Théâtre du Palais-Royal.[98] While on rehearsal his *Folies dramatiques* (1853), a vaudeville by Clairville and Philippe Dumanoir that contained hilarious parodies of Italian opera, caught the attention of Napoleon III's half-brother the Comte de Morny, who had it premiered at the Tuileries. Later that year Hervé acquired his own theater on Boulevard du Temple, which he named "Folies-Concertantes" (Folies-Nouvelles as of 1854),[99] recruiting a small troupe of singer-actors who typified the new kind of comic performer associated with operetta. There Hervé, who resigned from his church position and soon gave up his administrative duties to devote himself entirely to composition, gave a series of works such as *Le compositeur toqué* (literally "the loony composer"), where he appeared with his sidekick Joseph Kelm,[100] or *La caravane de l'Amour* which, four years before *Orphée aux enfers*, featured Cupid and Mercury. He also hosted the premieres of Offenbach's first operetta, *Oyayaye, ou La reine des îles* (1855), in which he appeared in the title role, and of Delibes' *Deux sous de charbon* (1856).[101]

Hervé's career, interrupted by a prison sentence on charges of pedophilia,[102] was resumed in 1861 when he opened a new theater, the Délassements-Comiques, which he soon abandoned for an Egyptian tour. In 1863 Hortense Schneider (1833–1920), the future heroine of *La belle Hélène* and *La grande-duchesse de Gérolstein*, starred in his *Toréadors de Grenade* at the Palais-Royal. On the same stage Hervé presented a parody of Berlioz's recently premiered *Les Troyens à Carthage*, entitled *Les Troyens en Champagne*. It was followed by a Roman extravaganza, *Le joueur de flûte* (1864), which was highly successful. In 1864–5 he moved his activities to the Eldorado, a "café-concert" – launching a different, more popular kind of music that was not yet called "music-hall" – and wrote songs for its leading chanteuses, Thérésa, and Suzanne Lagier.

Challenged by the success of Offenbach's large-scale works, Hervé responded with a three-act opéra-bouffe, *Les chevaliers de la table ronde*, premiered to great acclaim in 1866 with Ugalde and Kelm. It was followed by three parodies staged at the Folies-Dramatiques, which are among Hervé's best-known works: *L'oeil crevé* (1867), an irresistibly zany spoof on *Guillaume Tell* and an international success; *Chilpéric* (1868), a medieval comedy inspired by the extraordinary vogue, since 1834, of Augustin Thierry's *Récits des temps mérovingiens*, with Hervé in the title role; and, coinciding with the entrance of Gounod's masterpiece into the Opéra repertory, *Le petit Faust* (1869), also with Hervé as Faust. Like *L'oeil crevé*, it was performed around the world.[103]

In September 1870 Hervé was in London, where *Chilpéric* was given in the presence of the Prince of Wales. In the following two decades he divided his activities between Paris and the British capital. Like Offenbach's, his career suffered from the collapse of the regime with which his work was associated. *La veuve du Malabar* flopped in 1873,[104] despite Hortense Schneider and Marie Heilbronn in the cast; so did *Alice de Nevers* in 1875. In 1878 Hervé appeared as Jupiter in the revival of Offenbach's *Orphée aux enfers* at the Théâtre de la Gaîté. His greatest and most enduring success – 212 consecutive performances – was the "comédie-opérette" *Mam'zelle Nitouche*, on a libretto by Henri Meilhac and Albert Millaud (assisted anonymously by Ernest Blum), premiered in 1883 with Anna Judic (1850–1911) in the title role. The story of the convent-school boarder who goes AWOL, steps in for a capricious operetta star, and finishes the night in a military barracks in soldier's disguise, is the real ancestor of the modern musical comedy. It also anticipates it in its musical language, which favors simple tunefulness and an effective if often crude orchestration, and above all absolute clarity of words.[105] Its humor has aged better than that of other Hervé works, which, like all parodies, depend on familiarity with what they parody. But it has in common with them an almost unparalleled sense of the absurd which was and remains their author's most remarkable, endearing quality.

Jacques Offenbach

The music of Jacques Offenbach (1819–1880) has become synonymous with a particular Parisian tone of gaiety and satirical verve to such an extent that one has to remind oneself that he was German.[106] Unlike Meyerbeer, though, he fully adopted France and its capital – which did not, however, make him immune from vicious xenophobic and anti-Semitic attacks during his life and afterwards.

Offenbach grew up in Cologne, where his father Isaac was a cantor at the synagogue; he had taken the name of his native town when asked to choose one in keeping with the provisions of the Napoleonic Code (Cologne being under French domination from 1794 until 1814). After learning to play the violin, the young Jacob became an excellent cellist and his first compositions were for this instrument. In 1833 his father brought him to Paris together with his elder brother Julius. Cherubini was sufficiently impressed to let him enroll in the Conservatoire, where he only remained one year. In 1834–8 he played the cello in the orchestra of the Opéra-Comique, where he thoroughly assimilated the style of Adam, Auber, Hérold, and Halévy. The last named became a mentor but Offenbach's own musical style was much more influenced by the first three. He first became reputed as a composer of dance and salon music as well as a cellist (appearing with Liszt in 1843). His stage debut was *Pascal et Chambord*, a vaudeville comedy by Anicet Bourgeois performed at the Palais-Royal in 1839. In 1844 he converted to Catholicism to marry Herminie d'Alcain, daughter of a Basque Spanish officer.

Offenbach's beginnings were fraught with difficulties. In 1847 an Opéra-Comique production of *L'alcôve* was announced but did not take place; he arranged a concert performance instead, getting favorable notices. The following year, the collapse of the Opéra-National brought down with it the scheduled production of *La duchesse d'Albe*.[107] In 1850 he became musical director at the Comédie-Française. He left this position in 1855, the year of the International Exposition, which marked his real breakthrough: while Hervé premiered *Oyayaye* at the Folies-Nouvelles, Offenbach opened a summer theater just off the Champs-Élysées with a view to staging "pantomime and operettas limited to three characters" and named it the Bouffes-Parisiens; he soon rented another theater on the Passage Choiseul for winter performances (featuring up to five singers), where he subsequently transferred all his activities.[108] Staging one-act comic works by Offenbach and others (including Adam and Delibes), the Bouffes-Parisiens turned into a prodigiously successful venture, with Offenbach himself doubling as theater director and composer and his brother Jules leading the orchestra. Also in 1855 began his collaboration with Ludovic Halévy (1834–1908), son of Fromental's brother Léon: in December they produced their first comic masterpiece, the one-act "chinoiserie musicale" *Ba-Ta-Clan*: the characters, after an irresistibly funny quartet in would-be Chinese (they all turn out to be French) and an equally hilarious parody of a Bellini duet, gather to sing the eponymous "Ba-Ta-Clan," where Offenbach displayed the kind of comic frenzy for which he remains unequaled. The work ran for more than 150 performances at the Bouffes-Parisiens. In 1856 the premiere of Adam's final work, *Les pantins de Violette*, marked the start of another important partnership: it starred Hortense Schneider, who would become Offenbach's greatest interpreter.

Having introduced a chorus and expanded the number of characters in *Mesdames de la Halle* in March 1838 (the opening a memorable musical depiction of the atmosphere of the famous Parisian covered market), Offenbach ended the year with his first great coup, *Orphée aux enfers*. Mythological comedy was not a novelty, but Halévy and his collaborator Hector Crémieux (1828–1892) – encouraged by Offenbach, who took an active part in the fashioning of the libretto – went far beyond their predecessors, Massé's *Galathée* for one, in combining parody of grand opéra and social satire. In a country where education and culture were largely dominated by the classics, the work was considered sacrilegious, or even unpatriotic, by some; the first attacks on Offenbach – at times openly anti-Semitic – date from this period.[109] Audiences, however, flocked to the Bouffes-Parisiens and the work began its triumphant career (346 performances until 1861).

Orphée was succeeded by the risqué medieval comedy *Geneviève de Brabant* (1859), which revolves around the impotence of the heroine's husband; like *Orphée* it indulges in burlesque anachronism, such as a reference to the newly built Gare du Nord at the end of Act 1. The public and critical response was far from matching the enthusiasm *Orphée* that had inspired. Offenbach revised the work in 1867 and again in 1875.[110]

In 1860 Offenbach became a French citizen and made his Opéra-Comique debut with *Barkouf*, a three-act opéra-bouffe on a Scribe libretto. This pseudo-Indian story of a dog crowned king fell victim to a press campaign, directed both at the libretto and the composer; Berlioz, never at his best when discussing opéra-comique, took part in the fray. Despite the success of *Le pont des soupirs* (1861), on a libretto by Halévy and Crémieux, which parodied romantic melodramas with a Venetian setting, Offenbach had to resign his Bouffes-Parisiens directorship in early 1862. One of his last works performed under his tenure, *Monsieur Choufleury restera chez lui le . . .*, had a libretto by the Comte (and soon afterwords Duc) de Morny, using the pseudonym Saint-Rémy. A hilarious satire of the fashion for Italian opera, it climaxes on a mock salon concert supposedly given by Henriette Sontag, Giovanni Battista Rubini, and Antonio Tamburini, impersonated by Choufleury, his daughter, and her suitor.

Based on a short play by Cervantes – hence the Spanish flavor of the music – *Les bavards*, premiered at Bad Ems and revived in Vienna (where Offenbach's works had become as popular as in Paris) before its Parisian premiere in 1863, demonstrated that Offenbach could blend boisterousness with musical refinement. In 1864 came two important premieres. *Les fées du Rhin*, a romantic opera in the manner of Heinrich Marschner, set to a French text by Nuitter, was premiered in Vienna in German translation. The work contains the first apparition of the tune that Offenbach later reused as the Barcarolle of the *Tales of Hoffmann*. In December of the same year *La belle Hélène* opened at the Théâtre des Variétés, Offenbach being by then on bad terms with the management of his old theater. Halévy wrote the libretto with his new collaborator Henri Meilhac (1831–1897), with whom, in the same year, he had collaborated on the ballet *Néméa* for the Opéra. As the original title *La prise de Troie* suggests, *La belle Hélène* may have been intended by its authors as a satire of Berlioz, whose *Les Troyens à Carthage* had been staged in the previous year. The censors' objections focused on Calchas, an obvious satire of the clergy, but critics were more concerned with the overt sensuality conveyed by the character of Helen (a triumph for Schneider) and her affair with Paris. The latter, a difficult, high-lying role, was premiered, like other similar Offenbach tenor roles, by José Dupuis. Once again, Offenbach's music combines irresistible dance rhythms and parodies of the serious genre (quoting, for instance, the patriotic trio of *Guillaume Tell* in Act 3). Less controversial than *Orphée*, the work was even more successful, with 273 performances in its first run. It marked the beginning of the most brilliant part of Offenbach's career, which for the next six years was intimately tied to both the Théâtre des Variétés and his winning team of librettists. Works premiered elsewhere, written with other collaborators, did significantly less well: *Les bergers* (libretto by Crémieux and Philippe Gille) had a short career following its Bouffes-Parisiens premiere in 1865; *Robinson Crusoé* (libretto by Cormon and Crémieux) was a mere *succès d'estime* at the Opéra-Comique in 1867–8, with Galli-Marié as a travesti Man Friday.

By contrast, the Offenbach-Meilhac-Halévy collaboration produced a string of triumphs: *Barbe-Bleue*, a corrosive adaptation of the Perrault tale, starring

Schneider and Dupuis, in February 1866; *La vie parisienne*, mounted at the Palais-Royal, the theater of Offenbach's debut, in October 1866, a few months before the opening of the International Exposition, an opera that reveals a picture of Paris that nearly a century and a half later has lost little of its drollery and appeal (265 performances by August 1867); *La grande-duchesse de Gérolstein*, another success for Schneider and Dupuis in a satire of the army, which drew to the Théâtre des Variétés many visitors to the Exposition. *La périchole*, an ebullient yet occasionally grim adaptation of Mérimée's 1828 play *Le carosse du Saint-Sacrement*, set in Peru, was not a success in the same league when premiered in 1868,[111] while *Le château à Toto* (1868) and *La diva* (1869) got only a lukewarm reception – as if Offenbach's star had be on the wane while Hervé's shone at its brightest. But in December 1869 *Les brigands*, a high-spirited parody of Auber's *Fra Diavolo* – among other works – succeeded brilliantly, its cast headed by Dupuis and Zulma Bouffar, the other leading female interpreter of Offenbach (and one of his many mistresses).

The relationship between Offenbach's great operettas of the 1860s and the regime of Napoleon III has long been a disputed topic, especially after the publication in 1937 of Siegried Kracauer's *Jacques Offenbach und das Paris seiner Zeit*.[112] Was Offenbach, as Kracauer suggested, a kind of "court jester," compromised with a regime whose repressive policies it secretly served? The facts, as analyzed by Jean-Claude Yon in his richly documented biography of the composer, are kinder both to the composer and to the Second Empire – a period that for understandable reasons, as we have indicated, has persistently suffered from unfair appraisals. Napoleon III – not a great connoisseur of music – is said to have enjoyed Offenbach almost more than any other composer. Yet it is clear that official censors were often troubled both by the subject matter and its treatment by Offenbach and his librettists. They occasionally asked for cosmetic changes: thus the fanciful Gérolstein, borrowed from Sue's *Les mystères de Paris* (and mentioned nowhere in the operetta), was a last-minute addition to protect the susceptibilities of grand duchesses visiting the Exposition. Usually, the censors somewhat uneasily let the words and the music speak for themselves, even though they were aware that the moral tone and, occasionally, political undertones of, say, *La vie parisienne* or *La périchole* were too cynical – or, to put it more positively, too richly ambiguous – for conservative tastes. Offenbach's operettas of the 1860s confirm, if anything, that the liberal tendencies of the final years of the regime were genuine.[113]

Offenbach's fortunes were certainly imperiled by the Franco-Prussian War of 1870–71 and subsequent regime change. As early as August 1870 Empress Eugénie, in her capacity as regent, crossed out his name from the list of nominees for promotion in the Légion d'Honneur.[114] A German-born French Jew, he was viciously attacked by Wagner in his satirical comedy *A Capitulation*, published in 1873.[115] Offenbach was all but accused by French nationalists of causing the defeat by ridiculing the French army in *La grande-duchesse de Gérolstein*, a work "tacitly banned"[116] from French stages until 1878. Those attacks reached a hysterical climax in Édouard Drumont's anti-Semitic pamphlet *La France juive*, which came out in 1886, six years after Offenbach's death.

Yet the 1870s were for Offenbach a period of intense creativity, featuring 30 new works and revisions of earlier ones: thus *Orphée aux enfers*, transformed into an "opéra-féerie" in 1874 – a reflection of the taste of the period for escapist fantasies rather than mordant satire. On the other hand *Boule-de-Neige*, recycling music from *Barkouf*, failed in 1871. Similarly, despite its high musical qualities, *Fantasio*, based on Alfred de Musset's poetic prose play of 1834, and starring Galli-Marié in the trouser title role, lasted only 10 performances at the Salle Favart in 1872. But *Le roi Carotte*, an "opéra-bouffe-féerie," ran for 195 performances in 1872–3. Based by its librettist Victorien Sardou (1831–1905) on E.T.A. Hoffmann's "Kleinzach" tale (the subject of the song in Act 1 of *The Tales of Hoffmann*), it launched the career of Anna Judic, who starred as Cunégonde along with Zulma Bouffar as the Puck-like genii Robin-Luron.

In 1873 Offenbach moved to the Théâtre de la Gaîté, where *Le roi Carotte* had been premiered, staging works by others as well as his own. His new creations were also seen in other theaters: the delightful one-act *Pomme d'api* and the three-act *La jolie parfumeuse* (1873), at the Renaissance;[117] *Madame l'archiduc*, an eighteenth-century fantasy in the spirit of Charles Lecocq's operettas of the 1870s, at the Bouffes-Parisiens (1874); *La boulangère a des écus*, with Meilhac and Halévy once again, at the Théâtre des Variétés (1875); *La Foire-Saint-Laurent* (1877) and *Madame Favart* (1878), both homages to the world of eighteenth-century opéra-comique, at the Folies-Dramatiques; and, at the Royal Alhambra Theatre in London, *Whittington*, premiered (in English) in 1875.

Offenbach faced new financial difficulties as a result of the high costs of the revised *Orphée*, compounded by the flop of Sardou's medieval drama *La haine*, for which he wrote stage music. Resigning the Gaîté directorship in 1875, he sailed the following spring for the United States, where he was invited on the occasion of the 1876 Centennial Exhibition, conducting 30 concerts in New York and Philadelphia. On his return *Le docteur Ox* (1877), after Jules Verne, and *Maître Péronilla* (1878), to Offenbach's own libretto, got no more than a polite reception. But *La fille du tambour-major*, premiered at the Folies-Dramatiques in December 1879, was one of the biggest successes of his career, with 195 consecutive performances. Its charm is undeniable, but it can be seen as a concession by the author of *La grande-duchesse de Gérolstein* to the *Revanche*-bound Third Republic patriotism: set in Lombardy at the time of Napoleon's Italian campaigns, it ends with a tableau showing the entrance of the French troops into Milan, to the strains of Méhul's *Chant du départ*, cleverly incorporated into Offenbach's score.

Offenbach died at his home in Saint-Germain-en-Laye on 5 October 1880 as his longtime project, the opéra-comique *Les contes d'Hoffmann*, was scheduled for performance at the Salle Favart.[118] Mentioned as early as 1873, it was planned as an adaptation of an 1851 *drame fantastique* by Barbier and Carré, an imaginary portrait of the German Romantic writer and composer in the form of an adaptation of four of his tales, with borrowings from several more. The three central acts – set respectively in Nuremberg, Munich, and Venice – are framed by a prologue and an epilogue, set in Luther's tavern in Nuremberg while a performance of Mozart's *Don Giovanni* is in progress. Hoffmann, obsessed with the soprano singing Donna Anna, sees in her another embodiment of the woman he believes to have loved in three different incarnations – a lifelike animated doll, a consumptive singer, and a diabolical Venetian courtesan. Carré having died in 1872, Barbier alone wrote the libretto. The work was initially destined for the Gaîté. From the outset Offenbach intended the four women to be sung by one singer – a coloratura soprano. Hoffmann, first a baritone role, was rewritten for a tenor once Carvalho, Du Locle's successor at the Opéra-Comique in 1876, convinced Offenbach to let him stage the work, while the impresario Franz Jauner obtained the rights to the Vienna premiere. Large extracts of the music were heard at a concert given at Offenbach's home in the spring of 1880, with Carvalho and Jauner in attendance, and with members of his family singing in the chorus. The reception was enthusiastic and Offenbach, though by then seriously ill, devoted himself to finishing the task. At his death the music of the first four acts had been completed in short score; only the end of the epilogue, for which several options were considered by the composer, remained unsettled. Nor was the work orchestrated.

In agreement with Offenbach's family, Carvalho entrusted the orchestration and musical preparation to Ernest Guiraud, a pupil of Halévy, who had supplied the recitatives for *Carmen*. As was customary, Guiraud prepared recitatives for *Hoffmann* to replace the spoken dialogue at the Vienna premiere; he is almost certainly also the author of the short opening prelude, since there exists no short-score manuscript in Offenbach's hand.[119] During the rehearsal process Carvalho began to cut much music out of the Venice act. In the end he removed it altogether, transferring some of the music (including the Barcarolle) to the other acts. These manipulations before the premiere resulted in the accidental dispersion of Offenbach's manuscript – with Guiraud's orchestration – causing everyone to believe, for more than a century, that Offenbach had left the Venice act unfinished.

Despite a text that thus departed from Offenbach's intentions, the posthumous Parisian premiere of *Les contes d'Hoffmann* was an immense success on 10 February 1881, as was the premiere of *Hoffmanns Erzählungen* in Vienna on 7 December in the same year. However, the disastrous fire that destroyed the Ringtheater at the second performance the next day, killing 400 people and causing Jauner's imprisonment and subsequent suicide, appeared to cast a

curse on a work whose text remained problematic. The first edition of the
piano-vocal score published by Choudens in 1881 included the Venice act, but
in the cut, rearranged version prepared by Carvalho for the premiere. It also
placed it before the Antonia act – musically richer, to be sure, since much
Venice music was left out: this mistaken order has usually prevailed to this day.
When Raoul Gunsbourg, director of the Monte Carlo Opera, decided to stage
the work in 1904, he obtained from the Offenbach family all the material cut
at the 1881 Parisian premiere. Perhaps unaware that these manuscripts
contained the music missing from the Venice act, he fleshed it out, instead,
after his own fashion. To replace Dapertutto's aria "Tourne, tourne, miroir"
(moved by Carvalho, reset to different words, to the Coppélius act), he asked
the composer André Bloch (1873–1960) to arrange a new aria, "Scintille,
diamant," to words supplied by Barbier's son, and set to a tune borrowed from
the overture to Offenbach's 1875 "opéra-féerie" *Le voyage dans la lune*.
Furthermore, Bloch was asked to provide a big concertato – a sextet with
chorus – reusing the Barcarolle motif. Those two accretions, incorporated in
the new edition of the score Choudens issued in 1907, became two of the
work's best-known numbers, though they had nothing to do with Offenbach.
Fritz Oeser's 1982 edition, which includes recovered music from manuscripts
held by the composer's descendants, complicated the issue by adding arrangements that are clearly Oeser's own. The reappearance of Gunsbourg's manuscripts, found in his Burgundy château of Cormatin and sold at Sotheby's,
London in 1984 – minus the very end of the act, which reappeared subsequently – has finally made it possible to reconstitute the work in a version as
close as possible to Offenbach's intentions.[120]

The story of *Les contes d'Hoffmann* highlights the paradoxical situation of
Offenbach, a composer both famous and misunderstood. His works, which
often exist in several versions, are seldom treated with the textual respect they
deserve, and a vast amount of his enormous production, including masterpieces like *Fantasio*, is still waiting to be rediscovered. The misunderstanding
has been exacerbated by the popularity of Manuel Rosenthal's 1938 ballet *Gaîté
parisienne*, arranged for the Ballets russes de Monte Carlo, and which hardly
deserved to be passed on to posterity. It perpetuates the simplistic, slightly
coarse image of a composer of cancan – which came into being after his
death – whereas this theatrical and musical genius, heir to Auber and Adam,
created miracles of musical wit infinitely more refined than Hervé's, setting for
French operetta standards that few since have equaled and none surpassed.

CHAPTER 8

FROM *CARMEN* TO *PELLÉAS*

French opera after 1870

The defeat of 1870–71 by Prussia was one of the worst catastrophes France had known. Its human cost – an overall demographic deficit of 600,000 – was high. In Paris, the horrors of the siege were compounded by a civil war – the Commune – crushed with extraordinary severity. The humiliation caused by the capitulation and the annexation of three eastern *départements* by the newly born German Reich resulted in feelings of wounded patriotism. The insouciant cosmopolitanism of the Second Empire was now viewed as one of the root causes of the military disaster. This moral and intellectual crisis had far-reaching cultural consequences. Appeals were made, almost at once, for an "intellectual and moral reform," to cite the title of Ernest Renan's influential 1871 essay. This regeneration, it was felt, called for a rediscovery or redefinition of French cultural identity. It was in this context that a Société nationale de musique was established in February 1871. Founded by Saint-Saëns and the singer Romain Bussine, it had fruitful effects on the development of French symphonic and instrumental music. Fauré, Franck, Massenet were among its first members. In the field of opera, the most noticeable evolution involved the virtual disappearance, in the following decades, of French works by foreign, or at least non-Francophone composers. Verdi's *Don Carlos* turned out to be the final episode in that glorious series. French operas were now operas written by French nationals or native French speakers. One of the rare exceptions premiered at the Opéra-Comique in 1894, César Cui's (1835–1918) *Le flibustier* on a libretto by Jean Richepin (1849–1926), ran for a modest nine performances – and it should be added that the Russian composer, on his father's side, was half French.

In apparent contradiction with this new state of affairs, the period that came to be known as the *fin-de-siècle* was dominated – in literature as much as in opera – by the figure of Wagner. Despite the support received from Napoleon III, he appeared untainted by ties with the Second Empire: the *Tannhaüser* debacle in 1861 even gave him the enviable prestige, in the French intelligentsia, of an *artiste maudit*. After Baudelaire, who had died in 1867, Verlaine, Mallarmé, Huysmans, Villiers de l'Isle Adam were all fervent Wagnerians. They contributed to the *Revue wagnérienne* (1885–8), whose influence extended well beyond music. Even the nationalist riots that interrupted the scheduled run of performances of *Lohengrin* at the Éden-Théâtre in 1887 and disturbed the premiere of the same work at the Opéra in 1891, far from hurting Wagner's cause, advanced it.[1] Whenever a new French opera or opéra-comique was reviewed during the period, the reference to Wagner was always present – composers being either blamed or praised for following his model or rejecting it.

The Third Republic, as it became known after hopes for a restoration of the monarchy vanished for good, inherited a building planned by the previous regime and intended as its crown jewel. Built by the Parisian architect Charles Garnier (1825–1898) – his first commission – the Opéra's new home was inaugurated in January 1875 after 14 years of work. Its conspicuous location, splendid façade, luxurious public spaces, comfortable size (2,000 seats), and up-to-date facilities seemed to translate into architectural terms the position of the city as opera capital during the Second Empire. Ironically, the preeminence of Paris in the world of music was beginning to wane. A parallel decline affected the genre of grand opéra that had been associated with the city, and which the new Opéra seemed to be made for. Indeed, while Meyerbeer and Halévy (whose busts adorned its façade) continued to be revived, though less and less frequently by the 1890s, few of the 41 works premiered at the Opéra between 1870 and 1914[2] can be called grand opéra in a strict sense – the closest being Massenet's *Le roi de Lahore* (1877), Saint-Saëns's *Henry VIII* (1883), and Émile Paladilhe's *Patrie!* (1886). The influence of the grand opéra model continued to prevail, though challenged, especially after 1890, by the alternative model of the Wagnerian "drame lyrique." This new appellation was, admittedly, used rather indiscriminately. Works as different as Saint-Saëns's *Proserpine* (1887), Benjamin Godard's *Le Tasse* (1891), Rodolphe Lavello's *Marie Stuart* (1895), Augusta Holmès's *La montagne noire* (1895), and Albert Cahen's *La femme de Claude* (1896) were all labeled "drame lyrique." Of their composers only the Franco-Irish Holmès (1841–1903), who wrote her own libretto, would have identified herself as Wagnerian;[3] the other works are grands opéras without the name (*Marie Stuart*, a work premiered in Rouen), Renaissance costume dramas (*Proserpine*, *Le Tasse*), and "drame bourgeois" adapted by Louis Gallet from the 1873 play by Alexandre Dumas fils (*La femme de Claude*).[4] The one thing they have in common is that they are sung throughout.

Compared to the Second Empire, there were fewer permanent opera companies in Paris. The Théâtre-Italien disappeared as a permanent institution in 1878 – another symptom of the turning away from cultural cosmopolitanism.[5] The Théâtre-Lyrique, which for two decades had dominated the operatic landscape, went bankrupt in 1872. Auguste Vizentini briefly tried to resurrect it in 1876–8 as the Opéra National Lyrique. An attempt to establish an "Opéra Populaire" similarly failed in 1879–80. By contrast, the Opéra-Comique, which had suffered from the Théâtre-Lyrique's competition, entered what may be its most brilliant period ever. Not only did it premiere the two works mentioned in the title of this chapter, but in fact most of the important or significant French operas of the age – by composers of the caliber of Massenet, Delibes, Alfred Bruneau, Édouard Lalo, Saint-Saëns, Chabrier, and Gustave Charpentier – were first staged at the Salle Favart. For most of the period, the company was headed by Carvalho, who stepped in after Du Locle's bankruptcy in 1876. On 25 May 1887, under Carvalho's tenure, a disastrous fire that began ten minutes into the first act of Ambroise Thomas's *Mignon*[6] destroyed the second Salle Favart, with major loss of life.[7] Rendered responsible, Carvalho was fined and even imprisoned briefly, though eventually acquitted. Within four years he returned to the helm of the company, which for the next decade and while a new theater was being built, relocated itself to the former Théâtre-Lyrique on the Place du Châtelet.[8] Carvalho remained director until his sudden death in December 1897. Another strong personality, his successor Albert Carré (1852–1938), came from the "straight" theater; he hired André Messager as his music director.

A corollary to the diminution of the supremacy of Paris was the rise in importance of other operatic centers, both in France and outside the French borders. Baden-Baden and Karlsruhe (where the entire *Troyens* was first heard) have already been mentioned. Saint-Saëns's *Étienne Marcel* (1879) received its first performance in Lyons and his *Samson et Dalila* its first French performance in Rouen. The posthumous premieres of César Franck's *Hulda* (1894) and *Ghiselle* (1896) both took place at Monte Carlo – in the elegant theater built by Garnier next to the casino – as did that of Lalo's *La Jacquerie* (1895), also posthumous. Massenet's *Werther* was first heard (in German) in Vienna in 1892 and his *Navarraise* (in French) at Covent Garden, London in 1894. A remarkable number of important French premieres took place at the Théâtre de la Monnaie in Brussels: Massenet's *Hérodiade* (1881), Reyer's *Sigurd* (1884) and *Salammbô* (1890), Chabrier's *Gwendoline* (1885), d'Indy's *Fervaal* (1897), Chausson's *Le roi Arthus* (1903). Whereas, in the first decades of the nineteenth century, Paris had acted as a magnet to non-French composers, prompting them to write French operas, now other cities than Paris premiered operas by prominent French composers.

French operetta, born during the Second Empire, continued to flourish, with Hervé and Offenbach contributing significantly to it in the later stages of their careers, along with composers of the following generation (Edmond Audran, Charles Lecocq, Robert Planquette, Louis Varney and, subsequently, André Messager). At the Opéra-Comique, meanwhile, the tone and the form of new works underwent a notable evolution, to the extent that the genre of opéra-comique itself gradually lost its identity. Semi-serious, serious, even tragic subjects, instead of being exceptions – and often meeting with resistance, as we have seen in the cases of *Mireille* and *Mignon* – were now considered not just acceptable but normal. Apart from *Carmen*, works premiered at Salle Favart or on Place du Châtelet between 1880 and 1893 that end tragically include *Les contes d'Hoffmann* (at least the Antonia act), *Manon*, *Lakmé*, *Le rêve*,[9] *Werther*, and *L'attaque du moulin*. Even more strikingly the Opéra-Comique, beginning, as previously mentioned, with *Roméo et Juliette* in 1873, started to perform works sung throughout. Of those just mentioned, two – *Le rêve* and *L'attaque du moulin* – include no spoken dialogues at all, while the spoken interventions in *Werther*, telling though they are, are the briefest (at the end of Act 1 and when Albert calls his wife's name twice towards the end of Act 3). Lamented by some critics, who felt that the Opéra-Comique was abandoning its traditional mission, this evolution was sanctioned in 1881 when Carvalho obtained the removal from his *cahier des charges* of the stipulation that works mounted at the Salle Favart had to include at least a few spoken exchanges.[10] By the time of *Louise* (1900) and *Pelléas* (1902), the evolution was no longer questioned. It went along with the gradual acceptance, both at the Opéra and the Opéra-Comique, of works that were no longer a succession of autonomous "numbers" (arias, duets, ensembles, choruses, and finales) but through-composed. Carvalho went further in abolishing the difference between the Opéra and the Opéra-Comique by giving dance – hitherto the preserve of the Opéra – a role at the Opéra-Comique: beginning with Gounod's *Cinq-Mars* (1877), many works of the period, from *Lakmé* (1883) to *Cendrillon* (1899), include a full-fledged ballet. Carré confirmed this trend by recruiting the Spanish dancer Mariquita as choreographer.

Although Bizet, Delibes, Massenet, Saint-Saëns, Franck, Lalo, Chabrier, Reyer, Chausson, Bruneau, d'Indy, Charpentier and Debussy obviously deserve separate treatment in this exceptionally rich period of French opera – as do the operetta composers referred to above – several lesser names deserve at least a passing mention. At the Opéra-Comique, Ferdinand Poise (1828–1892), like his teacher Adam or Grisar in the previous generation, gave several works inspired by the eighteenth century: *La surprise de l'amour* (1877) is one of the very few operatic adaptations of Marivaux and *Jolli Gilles* (1884), premiered a few months after *Manon*, is a witty and poetic evocation of the world of Italian comedy. Preceding the Italian composer Ermanno Wolf-Ferrari, Poise also wrote an opéra-comique based on Molière's *L'amour médecin* (1880).

Remembered above all for the recitatives he wrote for *Carmen* as well as his completion of *Les contes d'Hoffmann*, Ernest Guiraud (1837–1892) was an opera composer in his own right. He was born in New Orleans where his father, himself a composer, was established. At 15 Ernest's first work, *Le roi David*, was staged there. After studying with Halévy, he won the Prix de Rome in 1859 (two years after Bizet, with whom he developed a close friendship). He built his reputation in Paris with the opéra-comique *Madame Turlupin* (1872) and the Sardou-based *Piccolino* (1876). In 1880 he became professor of composition at the Conservatoire, where Debussy and Dukas were among his pupils. His medieval grand opéra *Frédégonde*, completed by Dukas under Saint-Saëns's supervision, was posthumously premiered in 1895, with limited success.

Another friend of Bizet, Émile Paladilhe (1844–1926) was, at the age of 16, the youngest composer ever to win the Prix de Rome. After a one-act opéra-comique, *Le passant* (1872), based on François Coppée's play and starring Galli-Marié, he made an impressive Opéra debut in 1886 with *Patrie!*, adapted from Sardou's historical drama set in Brussels under Philip II. The libretto, which Sardou wrote with Louis Gallet, is a gripping account of a conspiracy against the Spanish rule, denounced by the heroine Dolorès (Gabrielle Krauss at the premiere) in the vain hope of saving her lover, and implacably repressed by the Duke of Alba. Third Republic audiences predictably responded to this nationalist tale of resistance and betrayal, efficiently set by Paladilhe in a style that looked back nostalgically to the grand opéra of the 1830s and 1840s. One of the undisputed successes of the period, it was performed 93 times until 1919.[11]

Victorin Joncières, whose real name was Félix-Luger Rossignol (1839–1903), had debuted at the Théâtre-Lyrique with an orientalist grand opéra, *Sardanapale* (1867), which ran for 16 performances (Nilsson as the female lead). He followed this two years later with *Le dernier jour de Pompéi*, adapted by Nuitter and Beaumont from Edward Bulwer-Lytton's novel, which was seen 13 times. His most original work, praised by Chabrier among others, was *Dimitri*, a grand opéra in five acts and seven scenes, based not on Pushkin's *Boris Godunov* but on Schiller's unfinished *Demetrius*. Mounted by Vizentini at the Gaité in 1876, it was revived at the Opéra-Comique in 1890. At the Palais Garnier *La reine Berthe* (1878) was a failure, and both *Le chevalier Jean* (1885) at the Opéra-Comique and *Lancelot* (1900) at the Opéra got a lukewarm reception. An early supporter of Wagner, Joncières found himself accused of Wagnerism in his early works, while his late ones, despite the label "drame lyrique," were criticized as prisoners to tired formulas.

More attuned to the spirit of the times – though wholly impenetrable to Wagnerian influences – Benjamin Godard (1849–1895), who came from a prosperous Jewish background, was a precocious, gifted musician whose piano compositions have undeniable charm. His opera *Jocelyn*, after Lamartine's verse novel about a priest, was premiered in Brussels in 1888. Its lullaby survives in historical recordings by several stars of the period. Suffering from lung disease, Godard died before the premiere of *La vivandière* at the Opéra-Comique, starring the 20-year-old Marie Delna, who had been catapulted to fame two years before as Dido at the revival of Berlioz's *Les Troyens à Carthage*. Set during the Revolution, the work is an unabashed hymn to political reconciliation in the name of patriotism and the cult of the army, with snatches from the *Marseillaise* at appropriate moments. Its widely successful career all over

France up to 1914 makes it, like *Patrie!*, one of the emblematic operas of the post 1870-period.

Georges Bizet

The preeminence of *Carmen* – which by the 1930s had overtaken Gounod's *Faust* as the most performed French opera (and is indeed the most performed opera in all categories) – has put its author on a pinnacle he never approached in his short life, during which he justifiably felt he was a constant prey to bad luck. The opera has also cast a shadow on the rest of his works, several of which qualify as masterpieces in their own right.

Georges Bizet (1838–1875) was the son of a Parisian singing teacher. His maternal uncle, François Delsarte, was a singer and a teacher with a reputation as an eccentric.[12] A precocious child, Bizet was admitted to the Conservatoire at the age of 9 in 1848. He studied the piano with Marmontel and Zimmermann (through whom he later became acquainted with Gounod) and composition with Halévy. In 1856 he entered Offenbach's operetta competition, sharing the first prize with Lecocq for *Le docteur Miracle*, for which the libretto was supplied by Léon Battu (1829–1857) and Halévy. When the two settings were performed at the Bouffes-Parisiens, Bizet's was generally viewed as the more musically refined, while showing his gift for comedy – notably in a hilarious "Omelette Quartet."

Having won the 1857 Prix de Rome, Bizet spent three happy years in Italy, from December of that year until September 1860. Contemporary Italian opera did not attract him: of Verdi's works he liked only *Rigoletto* and *La traviata* – and, later, *Aida*. But he loved Rossini, the main inspiration for *Don Procopio*, the two-act Italian opera buffa he composed at the Villa Médicis, on a libretto by Carlo Cambiaggio (1798–1880) which recalls *Don Pasquale*. In one of its numbers Bizet reused the second theme from the finale of the Symphony in C he wrote at the age of 17 and which remained undiscovered until 1933, while a serenade was subsequently reused in *La jolie fille de Perth*. *Don Procopio* was posthumously staged at Monte Carlo in 1906.

Recommended by Gounod to Carvalho, Bizet received a commission from the Théâtre-Lyrique in April 1863. After planning a work with a Mexican setting, the librettists Cormon and Carré shifted it to Ceylon, drawing from a recently published travel book. The music was quickly written in the summer, with sung recitatives replacing spoken dialogues at a late stage, and *Les pêcheurs de perles* opened on September 30 to public acclaim. Yet the press – save for Berlioz – was cool and the opera was performed only 18 times. In this exceptionally attractive score Bizet made the most of a conventional plot, taking advantage of the setting to introduce delicate exotic touches in the manner of Félicien David, and making the theme of friendship between the two men the work's musical center thanks to the memorable tune of their opening duet, which recurs at key moments throughout the work. As Hervé Lacombe has pointed out,[13] the device was probably borrowed from Halévy, but contemporary critics, put off besides by Bizet's masterly orchestration, inevitably accused him of being Wagnerian. Forgotten during more than two decades, *Les pêcheurs de perles* was rediscovered in the wake of the success of *Carmen* and revived for the first time in Italian in Milan in 1886, reaching Paris again in 1889 (also in Italian) until Carvalho revived it at the Opéra-Comique in 1893. The version published and disseminated by then differed substantially from Bizet's original – this even affected the work's best-known number, the duet "Au fond du temple saint" – and supplanted it, despite the dubious authenticity of the second version. The denouement, in particular, was tampered with: Zurga, whose fate is not mentioned in the original libretto, being alternatively burned at the stake or stabbed in the back.

After the half-success of *Les pêcheurs de perles* Bizet returned to an earlier project, *Ivan IV*, a grand opéra in five acts initially intended for Gounod. The music, calling for large orchestral forces, was composed in 1862–3 and revised in 1864–5, but Bizet abandoned the work after the Théâtre-Lyrique declined to stage it, as planned, and the Opéra also rejected it. An enchanting march found its way into the four-hand piano suite *Jeux d'enfants* (1871). Completed and rearranged in four acts by Busser, *Ivan IV* was first staged at Bordeaux in 1951.[14]

Despite the deterioration of his relations with Carvalho,[15] Bizet signed a contract in 1866 for an opera based on Walter Scott's *Fair Maid of Perth*. The convoluted libretto by Saint-Georges and Jules Adenis (1823–1900) has found few admirers,[16] but Bizet's score – called "opera" and without spoken dialogue – compensates for its weaknesses, especially in the first three of its four acts. Rather than attempting to create á Scottish local color, it includes, instead, touches of musical exoticism associated with the gypsy character of Mab. The part of Catherine Glover, the most florid role Bizet wrote, was intended for Christine Nilsson, who did not take part in the production, and was offered to Miolan-Carvalho, who declined. "Henri" Smith, notwithstanding his exquisite serenade, lifted from *Don Procopio*, is a fairly conventional tenor hero, but the other male roles – Ralph, the drunken apprentice, Catherine's father Simon, and the flirtatious Duke of Rothsay, are neatly characterized. Less audacious harmonically than *Les pêcheurs de perles*, the work is brilliantly orchestrated and its second act was Bizet's finest overall achievement to date. At the long-delayed premiere in late December 1867, the most popular number was the famous Gypsy dance (in recent times occasionally interpolated in Act 2 of *Carmen*). Like *Les pêcheurs de perles*, *La jolie fille de Perth* was performed only 18 times. Lacking the unity of its predecessor, it has never matched its popularity despite sporadic revivals, which often disfigured the work with cuts and rearrangements.[17]

While *La jolie fille de Perth* was awaiting its premiere, Bizet became engaged to Geneviève Halévy, younger daughter of his composition teacher. Naturally hypersensitive, greatly affected by the deaths of her father in 1862 and her sister

Esther two years later, she suffered from a mental instability inherited from her mother.[18] The engagement was broken at the family's insistence in 1868, but Georges and Geneviève were married (in a civil ceremony) in June 1869. Bizet devoted the rest of the year to completing Halévy's biblical opera *Noé*, but plans to stage it at the Théâtre-Lyrique were canceled. He also worked on *La coupe du roi de Thulé* for a competition launched by the Opéra. The winner was the amateur composer Eugène Diaz de la Peña, a pupil of Massé, with Massenet the runner-up.[19] Of Bizet's music, tantalizingly, only fragments survive. Three more abortive projects – *Calendal*, after Mistral; *Clarisse Harlowe*, after Richardson; *Grisélidis*, with Sardou[20] – occupied him in 1869–71.

In 1871 the Opéra-Comique directors, Du Locle and Leuven, commissioned from Bizet a one-act opera adapted from Alfred de Musset's poem "Namouna". Gallet's libretto is set in Cairo. The pleasure-seeking Prince Haroun (tenor) is about to acquire a new slave as his mistress, as he does at the end of each month, but the incumbent Djamileh, with the complicity of Haroun's henchman Splendiano, presents herself in disguise, forcing Haroun to relent and yield to her love. On this tenuous and improbable plot, Bizet has composed a hauntingly atmospheric score, from the opening evoking the sunset on the Nile (with offstage chorus), to the "Ghazel" in which Djamileh (a mezzo-soprano role) sings of Nour-Eddin, king of Lahore; she also has a poignant lamento. This masterpiece of nineteenth-century exoticism, *Djamileh*, hampered by casting problems, lasted a disappointing 11 performances in 1872. Benefiting from Bizet's posthumous popularity, it was staged all over Europe at the end of century but had to wait until 1938 for a Paris revival.[21]

Djamileh made effective use of the technique of melodrama, as did Bizet's next work, the stage music he wrote to Alphonse Daudet's drama *L'Arlésienne*. Premiered in September 1872 without much success at the Théâtre du Vaudeville (of which Carvalho was the director), it made a deep impression on Massenet, who used the device extensively in his own work. The most developed melodrama occurs in Act 4 as the music known as the Intermezzo (from the second suite, arranged by Guiraud) is played softly by a string quartet during the dialogue between the old shepherd Balthazar and Renaude, the woman he loved in his youth and has not seen since.

Despite the relative failure of *Djamileh*, Bizet was commissioned a three-act opéra-comique to be written in collaboration with Henri Meilhac and Ludovic Halévy. He also worked in 1873 on a *Don Rodrigue*, set to a libretto by Gallet and Édouard Blau (1836–1906) after Corneille's *Le Cid*, intended for Faure and the Opéra. He nearly completed the work in short score, but the fire that closed the Opéra in September 1873 brought the project to a halt.

Halévy's memoirs credit Bizet with the idea of adapting Mérimée's *Carmen*, first published in 1845 in the *Revue des deux mondes*.[22] Halévy also reports the reaction of Leuven, appalled by the immorality of the subject and hostile to the idea of an opéra-comique with a tragic ending; shortly afterwards, he resigned his directorship. By May 1873, the first act was composed. Bizet was involved in the writing of the libretto: thus the texts of "L'amour est enfant de Bohème" and the card scene are his.[23] Chosen for the title role, Galli-Marié asked Bizet for a tessitura closer to Marguerite in *Faust* rather than to Mignon, which lay too low for her – an interesting indication, considering that one usually thinks of Carmen as a mezzo-soprano part. She also played a key role in Bizet's decision to jettison the traditional opéra-comique entrance aria he had first composed in favor of the Habanera, adapted from Sebastián Yradier's popular song *El Arreglito*.[24]

As this direct musical borrowing indicates, *Carmen*, especially compared to earlier opéras-comiques inspired by Spain, makes extensive use of local color. Its Spanish tone is infinitely more pronounced than in works with a Spanish setting such as *Le toréador*, or even *Le domino noir*. A less famous forerunner was Théophile Semet's *Nuits d'Espagne*, performed 47 times at the Théâtre-Lyrique in 1856–7: it featured both a chorus of toreadors and a heroine named Carmen.[25] As for the use of recurrent themes – the Death/Carmen motif heard at the end of the prelude and throughout the work, the theme associated with both Micaëla and José's mother, the Toreador song – it is indebted more to the French opéra-comique tradition than to Wagner, a composer Bizet admired but with whom he felt no affinity.[26] Remarkably, José has no theme of his own – a suggestion that he is acted upon rather than acts, torn between his lover and his mother.

Carmen went into rehearsal in October 1874. The Opéra-Comique players found Bizet's refined orchestration a challenge. Other difficulties arose with the chorus, put off by the unusual demands, especially in terms of characterization. The fight in the cigar factory in Act 1 was a kind of choral participation the Opéra-Comique had never seen before. The censors, no doubt placated by the introduction of Micaëla, a character invented by the librettists Meilhac and Halévy, raised no serious objections. Du Locle, on the other hand, got cold feet and tried in vain to have the denouement changed at the last minute. The premiere, on 3 March 1875, was attended by many composers, singers, and writers. The first two acts were well received (despite the "strange harmonies" of the Flower Song), but only Micaëla's aria was applauded in Act 3, and Act 4 was icily received. Many reviews, though not all, were tepid to hostile. Yet audiences came: there were 35 performances by mid-June, when the Opéra-Comique closed, and 48 by February 1876 when Du Locle's resignation interrupted the initial run. Contrary to popular opinion, *Carmen* – similar in this respect to Debussy's *Pelléas* – was not a flop. The first foreign production was in Vienna in German, with Guiraud's recitatives (and a ballet added to Act 4) in October 1875. *Carmen* was then heard in 1876 in Brussels, Antwerp, and Budapest; in St. Petersburg, Stockholm, London, Dublin, New York, and Philadelphia in 1878; in Melbourne and Naples in 1879; in Hamburg, Prague, Berlin, and Geneva in 1880. In the French provinces, it was seen in Marseilles,

Lyons, and Bordeaux in 1878. At the Opéra-Comique a reluctant Carvalho, who shared his predecessors' moral scruples, revived it in 1883 with Adèle Isaac (creator of the coloratura soprano roles in *The Tales of Hoffmann*), until Galli-Marié, who had sung the part in Italy and Belgium, was finally allowed to repeat the role that made her name immortal. By 1891 the work had been heard 500 times in Paris; the 1,000th performance took place in 1904. At the Opéra-Comique and in the provinces, the opera continued to be performed in its original opéra-comique form.[27] Only when *Carmen* was transferred to the Palais Garnier in 1959 were the Guiraud recitatives adopted. This decision was unfortunate: although we know for a fact that Bizet himself was planning to supply recitatives to be used in foreign productions[28] (as Thomas did for *Mignon*), the ones Guiraud composed are not his, not to mention their relative banality. It is when *Carmen* is heard in its original form that one can truly appreciate the unique combination of traditional opéra-comique numbers, such as the opening chorus or the brilliant Act 2 quintet, and the exhilarating novelty of the Carmen-José duets, where the musical declamation matches the dramatic intensity.

Bizet died at his Bougival house three months to the day after the *Carmen* premiere. Plagued by depression, quinsy, and acute rheumatism, which a swim in the Seine on 30 May probably exacerbated, he suffered two heart attacks and died early in the morning of 3 June 1875. One wonders how many among the thousands who attended his funeral at the Trinité church two days later realized that they were burying the greatest living French composer.

Léo Delibes

Justly famous for *Lakmé* and his marvelous ballet scores, Léo Delibes (1836–1891) is otherwise curiously neglected as an opera composer.[29] Born in the wine-making village of Saint-Germain-en-Val, now a suburb of La Flèche, between Le Mans and Angers, he received musical instruction from his mother and uncle, the organist Édouard Batiste (1820–1876). At the Conservatoire he studied with Adam, whose refined, stylish works resemble his own. From 1853 onwards, he combined functions as church organist and accompanist and eventually chorus master at the Théâtre-Lyrique and (as of 1864) at the Opéra. Hervé – another organist doubling as operetta composer – staged his "lyric asphyxiation" *Deux sous de charbon, ou Le suicide de Bigorneau* in 1856. Until 1870 Delibes had 15-odd similar, short comic works staged, mostly at the Bouffes-Parisiens. One of them, *L'omelette à la Follembuche* (1859) was on a play by Labiche; others, including *Le serpent à plumes* (1864) and *L'Écossais de Chatou* (1869) were in collaboration with Philippe Gille (1831–1901), future co-librettist of *Lakmé*. Despite their small scale, they all display an elegance and melodic invention that put Delibes at the forefront of light opéra-comique composers. His one more ambitious work of the period, the one-act *Le jardinier et son seigneur*, on a libretto by Théodore Barrière (1825–1877) after the La Fontaine fable (previously treated by Philidor), despite a modest 11 performances at the Théâtre-Lyrique in 1863, was praised – notably its enchanting overture.

The turning-point in Delibes's career was his ballet *Coppélia*, which triumphed at the Opéra in May 1870. His next opera, *Le roi l'a dit*, was a full-fledged opéra-comique on a libretto by Edmond Gondinet (1828–1888) first intended for Offenbach. The plot is set toward the end of Louis XIV's reign. A father of four girls, needing a son to present at court, grooms in the role the lover of his servant girl Javotte. Requiring a fairly large cast of 14, the work pastiches the French classical baroque style in a manner reminiscent of Gounod's *Le médecin malgré lui*. Delibes's first international success, it was sporadically revived in Paris until the early 1960s. The same features characterize the slightly less successful *Jean de Nivelle* (1880), a more serious work on a libretto by Gondinet and Gille. In the same year Delibes was appointed professor of composition at the Paris Conservatoire.

Lakmé was premiered at the Opéra-Comique in April 1883 with Talazac – the first Hoffmann – as Gérald and, in the title role, the American coloratura soprano Marie Van Zandt (1858–1919), who had a meteoric Salle Favart career between 1880 and 1885. Gondinet and Gille's libretto was inspired by Pierre Loti's novel *Le mariage de Loti*, one of the literary sensations of 1880.[30] Moving the setting from Polynesia to India, they placed the work in the tradition of *Les pêcheurs de perles*. The theme of the impossible marriage between East and West also anticipates Puccini's *Madame Butterfly* (itself indirectly derived from Loti). Delibes's score owes part of its appeal to the subtle characterization of the two worlds, the Indian side treated with a discreet use of modal writing, the British side more diatonic and closer to traditional opéra-comique forms – such as the delightful quintet in Act 1, one of the work's gems.[31] Posterity has isolated highlights such as the Bell Song – nowadays rivaled in popularity by the Flower Duet between Lakmé and Mallika – and Gérald's "Fantaisie aux divins mensonges." However, when heard as a whole, the work impresses for its musical continuity, its dramatic tension – especially the feeling of menace towards the end of the Market Scene, before Gerald is stabbed by Lakmé's father – and the sharpness of its characterizations. Praised by Delibes's contemporaries for the refinement of its writing, *Lakmé* was also influential on such unlikely admirers as Debussy and Ravel. It reached its 1,000th Opéra-Comique performance in 1931.

At his death Delibes left a "drame lyrique," *Kassya*, completed but not orchestrated. Meilhac and Gille's libretto is based on a story by Leopold von Sacher-Masoch. Massenet finished it and oversaw its posthumous production in 1893, but it disappeared from the repertory after eight performances.

Jules Massenet

If Jules Massenet (1842–1912) had died, like Bizet, at the age of 36, he would be a minor name in operatic history. If Bizet, on the other hand, had lived, he would no doubt have found in Massenet his most formidable rival. In any event, Massenet became the leading French opera composer of the late nineteenth century. Yet, in France at least, the importance of his achievement has not always been fully acknowledged.

Massenet – who detested his given name and eventually stopped using it, signing with his initial or "M." for Monsieur – was born in a suburb of the mining town of Saint-Étienne, but his family, of Alsatian origin on his father's side, moved to Paris in 1848.[32] Having learned the piano with his mother, he entered the Conservatoire in 1853. There he studied composition with Ambroise Thomas, winning the Prix de Rome in 1863. While in Italy he met a pupil of Liszt, Louise-Constance de Gressy, known as Ninon, whom he married in 1866. Recommended by Thomas, he made his Opéra-Comique debut with the one-act *La grand' tante*, performed in 1867 with the star tenor Victor Capoul and Marie Heilbronn, who, 17 years later, would be the first Manon. It achieved 17 performances, but Massenet had to wait five years to have a work staged again. In the meantime, he gave piano lessons and made his name as a composer of mélodies, notably song cycles clearly influenced by Schumann.[33] His second opera, *Don César de Bazan*, is named after a colorful, Quixotic character in Hugo's *Ruy Blas*, which had inspired a play by Adolphe Dennery and Guillaume Dumanoir. Composed quickly in the summer of 1872 – the music had initially been commissioned from Jules Duprato[34] – the work anticipated the Spanish color of *Carmen*, three of the principals of which were in its cast: Galli-Marié, the tenor Paul Lhérie (the first José), and the baritone Jacques Bouhy (the first Escamillo). Perhaps due to insufficient preparation, it only had 13 performances in November–December 1872, but was later staged in Vienna and Stockholm. The orchestral material later disappeared in the fire of the Opéra-Comique. Massenet then reconstituted the orchestration, recasting the work from three into four acts. This new version was unveiled at Geneva in 1888.

Once again, nearly five years elapsed before Massenet returned to Parisian stages. His real breakthrough occurred in 1873, when his sacred oratorio *Marie-Magdeleine* was given on Good Friday with Viardot in the title role. Earlier that year he had also contributed stage music to Leconte de Lisle's version of the Electra story, *Les Érinnyes*, where he made prominent use of the melodrama technique.

Massenet's orientalist grand opéra *Le roi de Lahore*, premiered at the Opéra in April 1877, was the second new work presented at the Palais Garnier – following Auguste Mermet's *Jeanne d'Arc*, a complete failure, in 1876. Gallet's libretto, in five acts and six tableaux, is set in India at the time of the Muslim invasions. As Joël-Marie Fauquet has noted, this military background – and the fact that the hero, despite is bravery, is defeated in Act 2 – was likely to appeal to post-1870 audiences. But the opera then takes us back to the *merveilleux* of the world of the tragédie lyrique: once in paradise, Alim is allowed by the god Indra to return to earth as a simple mortal – though in the end it is only in death that he is reunited with his beloved Sita. With opulent vocal writing for the three principals (especially Scindia, the baritone villain), rich choral interventions, and a spectacular scene in paradise, where the ballet is set, *Le roi de Lahore* firmly established Massenet's reputation. Performed 57 times at the Opéra until 1879, it was heard in Turin in early 1878 (with a new scene for the soprano) and staged, within a few years, as far as Argentina and Chile. It earned its author an appointment as professor of composition at the Paris Conservatoire, where for the next 18 years he taught most of the French opera composers of the following generation.

The success of *Il re di Lahore* in Italy prompted the commission of *Hérodiade* from Ricordi for La Scala. Brussels, however, heard it first in December 1881, the Milan premiere taking place two months later, with the young Puccini an enthusiastic member of the audience.[35] The libretto, loosely adapted from Gustave Flaubert's tale "Hérodias" by Paul Milliet (1848–1924) and Henri Grémont (pseudonym of the music publisher Georges Hartmann, 1843–1900), launched the long series of Massenet operas titled after their heroine. The vocal honors are actually nearly stolen from Hérodiade by Salomé, who in this version is not aware – until the very last minute – of her mother's identity. A very different character from the one portrayed by Oscar Wilde and Richard Strauss, Massenet's Salomé is a cousin of his Mary Magdalen – a *grande amoureuse*, more sinned against than sinning – a parallel reinforced by the audacious Christ-like portrayal of John the Baptist.[36] The suggestion that he is not insensitive to Salomé and hesitates between love and duty duly raised ecclesiastical eyebrows.[37] Featuring impressive choral tableaux as well as a ballet (unusually placed in the last act), the work is, however, less recognizably a grand opéra than *Le roi de Lahore*; nor, with its emphasis on the love interest, does it qualify as a biblical opera in the manner of Saint-Saëns's *Samson et Dalila*. Its blend of mysticism and eroticism was well attuned to a positivist age, when, even before Sigmund Freud, religion was frequently explained as a form of neurosis. Between 1881 and 1884, when it was finally heard in Paris (in Italian) – the French premiere having taken place in Nantes – the work went through several revisions and is thus, textually, one of the more complex of Massenet's works.

Having vainly hoped to get *Hérodiade* staged at the Opéra-Comique – which by then was open to works without spoken dialogue – Massenet signed a contract for a new opera.[38] The subject of Manon Lescaut was suggested by Carvalho in early 1882, when Auber's centenary was marked by a performance of the final duet from his *Manon Lescaut*. Though having the heroine die en route to Le Havre rather than in Louisiana, Massenet's librettists, Meilhac and

Gille, are much more faithful than Scribe to the spirit of the Abbé Prévost's novel. Manon does betray her Chevalier in Act 2 – the music makes it clear that she has made up her mind even before her emotional farewell to the "petite table" – and the secondary characters – the venal, duplicitous Lescaut, the fatuous, cruel Guillot, the unscrupulous Brétigny, even the conventional, unsympathetic Comte des Grieux – are not flattered. Des Grieux, on the other hand, is more virtuous than in Prévost's novel: there is no indication that he actually cheats in the gambling scene. Yet, for his goodness of heart, he emerges mostly as an example of human frailty – a kind of eighteenth-century Don José. Indeed, despite its occasional high spirits, the work is no less tragic than *Carmen* or *Roméo et Juliette*. Like the latter, it features four duets for the lovers – the last of which further resembles Gounod by quoting passages from the previous acts. Whereas his early opéras-comiques were unexceptional from a formal point of view, Massenet here approached the genre in a highly innovative way: arias are relatively few, on the short side, and often free of form, such as Manon's "Je suis encore tout étourdie" at her entrance; a discreet pastiche of eighteenth-century music – but in such a way that we never forget that this is the eighteenth century of the nineteenth century; a complex web of recurring musical motifs expressing the characters' various moods (some heard only within a single act, others throughout the work); and, perhaps most remarkably, no free-standing spoken dialogues, but instead melodramas throughout, a feature that makes *Manon* a unique case in opéra-comique history.[39] Though Massenet reset those melodramas as sung recitatives for foreign-language productions, it is notable that (unlike *Carmen* or *Les contes d'Hoffmann*) it is the original version that has prevailed.[40]

Premiered in January 1884 with Heilbronn and Talazac, *Manon* was quickly staged internationally. For the London premiere (1885), Massenet added the famous sung Gavotte ("Obéissons quand leur voix appelle") to the Cours-la-Reine tableau. He had previously modified the end of the last act, with the *ff* restatement of the "N'est-ce plus ma main" theme – an effect previously used by Gounod at the end of the Garden Scene in *Faust*, and which Puccini was to replicate in *La bohème* and *Tosca*. Heilbronn's premature death in March 1886 interrupted the Salle Favart performances. The following year, at Ruggero Leoncavallo's urging, Massenet heard the young Californian soprano Sybil Sanderson (1865–1903).[41] Fascinated by her exceptionally high and agile voice, he modified the role of Manon for her by introducing alternative vocal lines that changed the basically lyrical character of the role as initially conceived: great Manons since then have been either lyric sopranos (Victoria de los Angeles, Ileana Cotrubas) or coloraturas (Beverly Sills). In 1898 Massenet finally wrote an alternative to the Cours-la-Reine Gavotte, the "Fabliau," premiered by Georgette Bréjan-Gravière (later Bréjan-Silver),[42] and he sanctioned a few cuts. By 1905 *Manon* had been performed 500 times in Paris. By the late 1930s it came second to *Carmen* only in popularity at the Opéra-Comique.

After *Manon*, Massenet completed *Le Cid*, premiered at the Opéra in 1885 with the star Polish tenor Jean de Reszke (1850–1925) in the title role and his brother Édouard (1853–1917) as Don Diègue. The libretto was fashioned by Gallet, assisted by Dennery and Blau, from the *Don Rodrigue* he had written for Bizet. Whereas some scenes remain close to Corneille's original, from which entire lines are cited, others are added, providing more spectacle – there are as many as ten tableaux – and bringing the work close to the aesthetics of grand opéra.[43] This hybrid character may have harmed its career in the long run: highly successful at first, with 100 performances by 1900 – the first opera premiered at the Palais Garnier to reach this figure[44] – *Le Cid* has been more anthologized than revived since. Its ballet – a brilliant bouquet of Spanish dances – and Chimène's aria "Pleurez, mes yeux," an example of Massenet's vocal writing at its most eloquent, remain its best-known numbers.

Werther, completed in 1887, had to wait five years to be staged. In the meantime, Massenet contributed to the 1889 International Exposition festivities with *Esclarmonde*, an "opéra romanesque" written for Sanderson – it climaxes on a high G, dubbed the "sol Eiffel" in honor of the recently erected tower. Adapted from a French medieval romance – a trend advocated by contemporary French critics as a suitable alternative to the Nordic mythology of Wagner's operas[45] – the work centers on a Byzantine princess endowed with magic powers. Having fallen in love with a knight errant, she spirits him off to a magic island – a rapturous intermède depicting their lovemaking – but, in a reversal of the Psyche myth, insists that he should not see her face. Massenet's luscious score, which contemporary critics found Wagnerian, was heard more than 100 times at the Opéra-Comique in its first year but – no doubt because it was so associated with one particular singer – was not widely staged and was forgotten until Richard Bonynge resurrected it in the 1970s as a vehicle for his wife Joan Sutherland.[46]

Le mage (1891), an orientalist work set to a libretto by Jean Richepin, based on the figure of Zoroaster, was a relative failure at the Opéra, where it was performed only 31 times. The following year *Werther* was finally premiered in Vienna, in German, starring the Belgian heldentenor Ernest Van Dyck, before being staged in Paris in January of the following year with, as Charlotte, the 18-year-old Marie Delna. Massenet had toyed with the idea of setting Goethe's epistolary novel at least since 1880[47] – thus even before *Manon*. The libretto was prepared by the *Hérodiade* team of Milliet and Hartmann (using his own name this time) in collaboration with Blau. As the label "drame lyrique" suggests, the work was Massenet's first attempt to write a through-composed opera. Indeed, although there are identifiable arias and duets – though, in this essentially intimate work without chorus, no ensembles in a traditional sense – they blend into a continuous musical discourse, leaving few opportunities for applause in the middle of the acts, save perhaps for Charlotte's "Letters" aria and Werther's Ossian Lied, the work's only real "numbers." This feeling of continuous music is reinforced by the absence of interruption between the last two acts – they are even treated as one in the first edition. The work's novelty is perceptible also in the use of recurrent themes, more subtly and flexibly than in *Manon*,[48] and in the greater freedom of vocal forms: compared to the four *Manon* duets, still indebted to the traditional Italian form, the four scenes between Charlotte and Werther – from the Act 1 "Clair de lune," based on the simplest melodic formula, to the long final scene (an episode not in Goethe) – are treated in the mode of musical conversations. Similarly, the airy orchestration emphasizes the intimate quality of the opera, with delicate moments suggestive of chamber music.

Quickly mounted around the world, *Werther* took a while to establish itself as Massenet's second most popular work in Paris. There, its reputation took off only as of the 1903 revival at Salle Favart with the outstanding Léon Beyle and, as Charlotte, Jeanne Marié de l'Isle (Galli-Marié's niece). By 1938 the work had received its 1,000th Opéra-Comique performance.[49]

Three new Massenet works were premiered in 1894. The one-act *Le portrait de Manon* shows the aging Des Grieux, opposed at first to the marriage of his nephew (a travesti role) to Aurore, the niece of his best friend Tiberge (an important character in Prévost's novel, eliminated by the *Manon* librettists). He eventually consents after she appears to him dressed like Manon at their first meeting. Musical reminiscences echo the earlier work. *Le portrait de Manon* was the last work Massenet called an "opéra-comique." Contrasting with this quiet, nostalgic vignette, or "épisode lyrique," *La Navarraise*, premiered at Covent Garden in June 1894 with Emma Calvé (1858–1942), a famous Carmen, is a violent drama set in Spain at the time of the Carlist wars. A "hysterical woman" as described by contemporary psychologists, the half-demented heroine, Anita, commits a crime in order to raise the money she needs to marry the soldier she loves. Horrified, he spurns her and is killed in battle, while Anita goes into a hallucinatory trance before breaking down. *La Navarraise* was compared at the time to Pietro Mascagni's *Cavalleria rusticana* – Calvé being a celebrated Santuzza – but the differences are more striking than the similarities, Massenet preferring small, almost miniature vocal forms and creating an intensely atmospheric tension, relieved only by an exquisitely scored intermezzo.

Massenet's preoccupation with self-renewal – the dominant feature of his creative maturity, which earned him the reproach of eclecticism – is particularly in evidence in *Thaïs*, premiered in March 1894.[50] Adapted by Gallet from Anatole France's faintly scandalous novel published four years before, it had, for the first time, a libretto in prose, a prose described by the author as "mélique" – literally "musical," that is, rhythmical though not rhymed.[51] The story of Athanaël, a monk in fourth-century Egypt, who succeeds in converting Thaïs, a glamorous Alexandrine courtesan, but in the process realizes he loves her and loses his faith, was no less shocking than *Hérodiade*'s

Christ-like John the Baptist wavering between love and duty. Despite Sanderson's performance, the work was too original for 1894 audiences. In particular, the ballet *La tentation*, in which Athanaël, in his cell, is visited by impure dreams, soon had to be cut, as was a symphonic interlude depicting the story of Venus and Adonis. Four years later Massenet revised *Thaïs* drastically, cutting the ballet and interlude, adding a new, conventional ballet as well as an additional scene between Thaïs and Athanaël in the oasis near the nunnery where she will end her days. This new scene ends with a repeat of the "Méditation religieuse" initially heard between the two tableaux of Act 2 (with a choral intervention unfortunately often cut in performances and even recordings). The Méditation also recurs in the powerfully concise final scene, one of Massenet's greatest achievements: rather than a love scene, it is a "divergent duet" (to borrow a phrase usually applied to baroque opera) in which the delirious, dying Thaïs, who cannot hear Athanaël's desperate declaration, rises twice to an ecstatic high D – a moment where vocal brilliance and psychological intensity are beautifully matched. The irony of the situation justifies the puzzling label "comédie lyrique" that Massenet gave to the work. In its revised version *Thaïs* became one of his most frequently performed operas, especially after the 1907 performances with the Italian soprano Lina Cavalieri.

Massenet's "pièce lyrique" *Sapho* was based on another famous contemporary novel by Alphonse Daudet, this time with a contemporary setting, published in 1884 and made into a play the following year. Henri Cain's (1859–1937) libretto is an effective retelling of the story of Fanny Legrand, a bohemian woman – nicknamed Sapho because she posed for a statue of the Lesbian poet by her former lover Caoudal – who hopes to start a new life with the young, naïve Provençal Jean Gaussin. Maliciously apprised of her past by her former friends, he breaks up with her, then returns, but in the end it is she who slips away. The realistic story – Massenet's contribution to the naturalist school illustrated by his students Alfred Bruneau and Gustave Charpentier – partly recalls *La traviata* (while its ending anticipates Puccini's *La rondine*). Massenet treated it powerfully, yet with great economy of means. With Calvé in the title role, the work was well received in November 1897, shortly before Daudet's death.[52]

Cendrillon was Massenet's last work performed in the nineteenth century. Adapted by Cain from Charles Perrault's fairy tale, it was one of the first successes of the Carré regime when premiered at the Opéra-Comique in 1899. The label "conte de fées" given to the opera suggests an opera for children in the manner of *Hansel und Gretel* (a work Massenet esteemed).[53] Like Humperdinck, he produced a score of considerable refinement. By making Prince Charming a travesti role, Massenet drew enchanting timbre combinations in the Act 2 duet with Cendrillon and, perhaps especially, in the Act 3 trio where lyric soprano and mezzo-soprano are joined by a coloratura soprano (the Fairy Godmother), anticipating by 12 years the Richard Strauss of *Der Rosenkavalier*.[54] The heroine's stepmother, Madame de la Haltière, and Cendrillon's father Pandolphe, with whom she sings a lovely duet in Act 3, are also sharply characterized.

By the end of the century, Massenet had an enviable – and envied – status in France. Though his career had been far from an uninterrupted string of successes, he had become, with Verdi – whom he genuinely admired – the most performed contemporary opera composer. He was also influential, not so much in France at that point as on Italian composers of the *verismo* generation, who learned much from his vocal and orchestral writing. Well aware of their indebtedness towards him, Massenet was thus practically alone in his generation in France in refraining from making disparaging remarks about Mascagni, Puccini, and their contemporaries.

Charles Lecocq

French operetta, as we have seen, was a daughter of the Second Empire. If the collapse of the regime did not cause it to decline, its character was affected. It became less satirical, more sentimental, with a predilection for subjects set in the eighteenth century in the tradition launched in 1866 by Aimé Maillart's *Dragons de Villars*, an opéra-comique which, significantly, came to be placed in the operetta category. Examples of this change have already been noted in the late career of Offenbach, but Lecocq is even more characteristic of this evolution.

Charles Lecocq (1832–1918) came from a modest Parisian background and suffered from a further disadvantage by being physically handicapped (he walked with crutches). At the Conservatoire, he studied with Bazin and Halévy but economic reasons forced him to abandon his studies without competing for the Prix de Rome. He came to public attention in 1856 when his setting of *Le docteur miracle* shared the first prize with Bizet at Offenbach's operetta competition. Following a few ephemeral compositions at operetta theaters, his first major success was the three-act Japanese opéra-bouffe *Fleur-de-Thé*, on a libretto by Henri Chivot (1860–1897) and Alfred Duru (1829–1889), staged at the Athénée in 1868 – a topical subject in the year when Japan opened itself to the West. From that point his career took off and his production of the 1870s matched Offenbach in quantity and quality. Having temporarily settled in Brussels, Lecocq had some of his biggest successes premiered there before they were transferred, with equal success, to Paris. Following *Les cent vierges* (1872), *La fille de Madame Angot* in the same year became Lecocq's most popular work. This was due both to a clever libretto by Clairville, Paul Siraudin, and Victor Koning, set during the Revolution and featuring the historical characters of the pamphleteer Ange Pitou and the actress Mlle Lange, and to the charm and personality of Lecocq's music, which brilliantly modeled itself on the style of Revolutionary songs.[55] *Giroflé-Girofla* (1874), also premiered in

Brussels, also has an extremely funny libretto by Eugène Leterrier (1843–1884) and Albert Vanloo (1846–1920) the story of twin girls, one of whom is abducted by pirates as she is about to wed a particularly aggressive suitor, prompting the parents to try a substitution. This kind of risqué element was becoming a clear difference between operetta and opéra-comique (even though *La fille de Madame Angot* officially carried the latter appellation). The same element is present in other Lecocq works, especially *La petite mariée* (1875) and *Le jour et la nuit* (1882), where the music elegantly clothes the suggestive jokes. Lecocq collaborated with Meilhac and Halévy with *Le petit duc* (1878), one of the composer's freshest scores – set in the eighteenth century and with a soprano as the hero – and with *Janot* (1881). The following year *Le coeur et la main* (1882), Lecocq's final success, starred the soprano Marguerite Vaillant-Couturier, whom Massenet considered at the time for the part of Manon. The more serious *Plutus* (1886) failed at the Opéra-Comique and Lecocq's production declined thereafter, though the perennial success of at least a half-dozen of his works was enough to keep his name alive. In 1918, the year of his death, *La fille de Madame Angot* triumphantly entered the repertory of the Opéra-Comique. Although the French Revolutionary flavor of the work was no doubt to the taste of First World War audiences, it also canonized a work hitherto performed in lesser, more popular theaters, and by singers specializing exclusively in operetta, a division that appeared at the time of Offenbach and was to last through the first half of the next century.

Other operetta composers

If Lecocq was the most productive and successful operetta composer of the 1870s and early 1880s, others illustrated the genre with works of comparable style. Of the 24 operettas written by Robert Planquette (1848–1903), a Parisian and a student of Duprato at the Conservatoire, posterity has retained *Les cloches de Corneville*. In his native country at least, his name is also linked to "Le régiment de Sambre-et-Meuse," a famous French military march. Like Hervé, Planquette had a career at the café-concert, until *Les cloches de Corneville*, on a libretto by Clairville and Charles Gabet (1793–1860), ran for 400 consecutive performances at the Folies-Dramatiques in 1877. The plot, which has obvious similarities with *La dame blanche*, deals with an aristocrat returning to claim his ancestral, haunted château from a miserly upstart. The virtually unknown Planquette supplied a tuneful score, from which the "Legend of the Bells" became the most popular number. It was particularly well received in London. As a result *Rip Van Winkle* was commissioned by the Comedy Theatre, Planquette setting directly in English H.B. Farnie's (1836–1889) libretto after Washington Irving; Meilhac and Gille subsequently adapted it for the French premiere. The same Farnie anglicized *Surcouf* (1887), which dealt with a French corsair fighting the British, into a more palatable *Paul Jones* (1889).

Like Planquette, Louis Varney (1848–1910) is remembered today for one work. Born in New Orleans, he was the son of the conductor Alphonse Varney, a regular collaborator of Offenbach at the Bouffes-Parisiens. It was in this theater that *Les mousquetaires au couvent*, on a libretto by Paul Ferrier (1843–1920) and Jules Prével (1835–1889), opened in the spring of 1880. Adapted from an 1835 vaudeville-comedy, the plot, set in the era of Cardinal Richelieu, deals with two musketeers who, disguised as monks, visit a convent to rescue two young women condemned to the veil for political reasons. This leads to highly comical situations, especially an irresistible Act 2 finale led by the Porthos-like character of Brissac, one of the would-be monks, by then now in his cups, preaching on the subject of love. After the success of the initial run, Varney revised the work, expanding Brissac's part to make it a genuine opéra-comique baritone role. Of the remainder of his vast production (40-odd operettas), one of Varney's most successful was *Fanfan-la-tulipe*, also on a libretto by Ferrier and Prével, premiered at the Folies-Dramatiques in 1882.

The Lyons-born Edmond Audran (1840–1901), son of the Opéra-Comique tenor Marius Audran, also achieved celebrity thanks to one work, *La mascotte*, an opéra-comique on a libretto by Chivot and Duru, premiered at the Bouffes-Parisiens in December 1880. Set in seventeenth-century Italy, it is remembered chiefly for the adorably silly Act 1 farmyard love duet between Bettina (the mascot in question) and her lover Pippo – she imitating her turkeys, he his sheep. In less than five years *La mascotte* had been seen more than 1,000 times in Paris, and by 1897 had reached 1,700 performances – which makes it the greatest success of the period. Without approaching this record, Audran's other successful works included *La cigale et la fourmi* (Gaîté, 1886), *Miss Helyett* (Bouffes-Parisiens, 1890), and *La poupée* (Gaîté, 1896).

The name of Louis Ganne (1862–1923) also survives mostly thanks to a single work, *Les saltimbanques*, premiered in Paris in 1899. Its theme is the life of a circus, with a *Mignon*-like twist, the troupe's star turning out to be the long-lost daughter of an aristocrat. Born in a small mining town in central France, Ganne received the most orthodox training from Théodore Dubois[56] and César Franck at the Conservatoire, where he also studied with Massenet, but he decided to specialize in light music. He wrote, in particular, for the Folies-Bergère (founded in 1869) and the Casino de Paris (established in 1880). His other notable success was *Hans, le joueur de flûte* on the subject of the Pied Piper, premiered at Monte Carlo in 1906.

Ernest Reyer

Ernest Reyer was the pseudonym of the Marseilles-born Louis-Étienne-Ernest Rey (1823–1909).[57] After spending his adolescence in recently colonized Algeria, he moved to Paris in 1848 and became closely acquainted with Théophile Gautier, who provided the inspiration for his earliest musical compositions, the oriental symphony *Le sélam* (1850), the opéra-comique *Maître Wolfram* (1854), which had 21 performances at the Théâtre-Lyrique, and the ballet *Sacountalâ* (1858). His 1861 opéra-comique *La statue*, adapted by Jules Barbier and Michel Carré from the *Arabian Nights* and initially entitled *Les ruines de Balbeck*, was – after *Faust* and *Roméo et Juliette* – the third most successful work premiered at the Théâtre-Lyrique.[58] Reyer later revised *La statue* when it entered the repertory of the Opéra-Comique in 1878 and he supplied sung recitatives when it was transferred to the Opéra in 1903. His next opera, *Érostrate*, a mythological work premiered at Baden-Baden in 1862 (it tells the story of how Venus de Milo lost its arms), was also revived at the Opéra but had only two (disastrous) performances in 1871.

In 1866 Reyer succeeded Joseph d'Ortigue, himself the successor of Berlioz (a composer Reyer venerated), at *Le journal des débats* and for the next three decades was among the sharpest and most respected Parisian music critics, in this and other journals. He had started working on his magnum opus, *Sigurd*, on a libretto by Du Locle and Alfred Blau (18??–1896) after the Scandinavian *Edda*, and completed it in the early 1870s.[59] The similarity with Wagner's *Siegfried* and *Götterdämmerung* may be a coincidence: Reyer maintained he was unaware of the *Ring* tetralogy when he began his own opera. Its heavy reliance on recurrent motifs, unusual for the late 1860s in France, could also be mistaken for a Wagnerian device, but it was primarily indebted to the French tradition.[60] An ambivalent Wagnerian himself, Reyer never visited Bayreuth – or, after the Franco-Prussian War of 1870–71, Germany.

Sigurd took a long time to reach the stage. It was finally mounted in Brussels in 1884, with the great French dramatic soprano Rose Caron (1857–1930) as Brunehilde (as the name is spelled in the score). After Lyons stole the honor of the French premiere in January of the following year, it was staged in June 1885 at the Opéra for Caron's Paris debut.[61] Heard more than 250 times at the Palais Garnier until 1935, as well as in many French provincial theaters, it was never particularly popular abroad, no doubt because of its similarity to Wagner's operas. In fact, as Joël-Marie Fauquet has pointed out,[62] it is unfair to dismiss it as a poor man's *Ring*. Unlike Wagner, Reyer treats the legend for its narrative, picturesque, decorative elements, not for its symbolic or philosophical implications. The nine tableaux take us from the palace of Gunther in Worms to the apotheosis of the dead Siegfried and Brunehilde as they enter Valhalla – in other words the very ending Wagner first intended, then rejected in keeping with his new Schopenhauerian humanism. With its martial rhythms and melodic simplicity, Reyer's music has its crude, repetitive side, but it also contains moments of beauty and individuality, as anyone who has heard Georges Thill's recording of "Le bruit des chants s'éteint" or Régine Crespin in Brunehilde's awakening can attest.[63]

Salammbô, Reyer's last opera, based on Flaubert's novel about Hamilcar's daughter and Mathô, the chief of the revolted slaves who falls under her spell, was in the planning from the book's publication in 1862 (although Flaubert reportedly had Verdi in mind first). After Gautier's death in 1872 Catulle Mendès and Barbier were approached to write the libretto, which in the end, as for *Sigurd*, was supplied by Du Locle.[64] Begun before Flaubert died (1880), the composition was completed only after the premiere of *Sigurd* and, like it, *Salammbô* was premiered in Brussels, to great acclaim in 1890. It was lavishly staged at the Opéra in 1892, conducted by Édouard Colonne. Caron, for whose voice the title role was written, sang it both in Brussels and in Paris. The work was heard nearly 200 times at the Palais Garnier until 1943. Its seven scenes are through-composed, as in *Sigurd*, and it makes the same systematic use of recurrent motifs. *Salammbô* was blamed by critics, Paul Dukas among them, for its rudimentary effects. Others were more sensitive to Reyer's sense of color and to the sweep of the work's great moments, such as the Act 4 duet in Mathô's tent.[65]

Largely self-taught, Reyer was a highly respected figure in French music by the time he died at his summer house in Le Lavandou, near Marseilles. When *Sigurd* was revived for his centenary in 1923, the president of the republic was in attendance, as was Caron, who laid a wreath on the composer's bust on the stage of the Palais Garnier.

Édouard Lalo

Reyer's senior by a few months, and like him a partly self-taught musician, Édouard Lalo (1823–1892) studied the violin, the cello, and composition in the Conservatoire of his native Lille, moving to Paris in the late 1830s.[66] A founding member of the Armingaud Quartet, he had composed chiefly chamber music by the time he worked on his first opera, *Fiesque*, on a libretto by Charles Beauquier (1833–1916) after Schiller's play. Both opponents of the Second Empire, Lalo and his librettist – himself the author of a *Philosophie de la musique* (1865) – treated the theme of Giovanni Luigi Fiesco's unsuccessful attempt to overthrow the Doria family in sixteenth-century Genoa as a republican manifesto. Submitted anonymously at an official opera competition in 1867, the work placed third. The Théâtre de la Monnaie accepted it in 1871 but the production never materialized and, though published in piano-vocal score by Durand in 1872 (with the label "grand opéra"), *Fiesque* remained unperformed in Lalo's lifetime.[67]

Having become famous with the *Symphonie espagnole*, which Pablo de Sarasate premiered in 1875, Lalo immediately began work on *Le roi d'Ys*, adapted by Édouard Blau from Breton folklore – the legend of the submerged city of Ys. The overture, a kind of symphonic poem (with discreet echoes of the *Tannhaüser* pilgrim march), was performed as early as 1876. Yet Vizentini turned down the work in 1878, as did the Opéra the following year. Finally, *Le roi d'Ys* was at last premiered at the Opéra-Comique in 1888, after being thoroughly revised by the composer. It was highly successful and was soon staged abroad. When the Metropolitan Opera in New York finally produced it in 1922, it was with a cast headed by Frances Alda, Rosa Ponselle, and Beniamino Gigli. In 1941, after nearly 500 performances at the Salle Favart, it was transferred to the Opéra repertory, as had been the composer's wish.[68]

Wary of his Wagnerian propensities – he once declared that Germany was "his true musical homeland"[69] – Lalo opted for a compromise.[70] The work is organized in recognizable, discrete numbers, but other features evoke a through-composed "drame lyrique." Unlike many of his contemporaries, Lalo refrains from using recurrent themes, relying instead on his melodic gift and individual sense of rhythm. Initially subtitled "Légende des guerres bretonnes au Ve siècle," it was simply called "Légende bretonne" a setting that naturally accommodates an element of Christian *merveilleux*, with two apparitions of the local saint Corentin. Local color there is too, except that some of it is invented: only two of the motifs are actual Breton themes (another, which appears in the Act 3 marriage ceremony, is a Christmas carol from the Île de France). Despite the work's title, the king himself is not at all the central figure. There are two contrasting couples – a "white" couple formed by Rozenn and Mylio, a "dark" couple consisting of Margared and Karnac. The obvious similarities with Wagner's *Lohengrin* is reinforced by the similar vocal typology: soprano-tenor on the one hand, mezzo-soprano and baritone on the other. Rozenn and Mylio (a part premiered by Talazac) both have exceptionally beautiful music, notably Rozenn's act 2 aria (encored twice at the premiere) and the love duet "À l'autel, j'allais rayonnant" (its melody recycled from *Fiesque*). Yet the work is dominated by the powerful figure of Margared – next to Dalila the great dramatic mezzo part in the late nineteenth-century French repertoire. Lalo conceived it for his wife, the contralto Julie de Maligny (1843–1911), herself of Breton origin, although the role was premiered by Blanche Deschamps.

At his death Lalo left an incomplete opera, *La Jacquerie*, based on the peasant revolt in fourteenth-century France. Finished by Arthur Coquard, it was premiered at Monte Carlo in 1895 and at the Opéra-Comique later in the same year, though without much success.

Camille Saint-Saëns

Although *Samson et Dalila* had achieved permanent repertory status in Saint-Saëns's lifetime and remains one of the most regularly staged French operas worldwide, its composer was disappointed not to see any other of his 12 stage works win a comparable position. Massenet's senior by seven years, he bitterly resented the younger composer's success, which he attributed to intrigue and publicity, though, being unusually self-critical, he must have sensed that it was due above all to Massenet's superior sense of the theater.

A Parisian, Camille Saint-Saëns (1835–1921) was famous as a pianist from his early teens and remained a celebrated performer throughout his life.[71] At the Conservatoire, which he entered in 1851, he studied composition with Halévy. He failed to get the Prix de Rome in 1851, being considered too young, and again in 1864, by which time he was thought to be too old. At 22 he was appointed organist at the church of Madeleine in Paris and held this position for 20 years. A man of considerable intellectual curiosity, he was an early admirer of Wagner – attending the first season of the Bayreuth Festival in 1876 – but took a firm stance against the "Wagnerolatry" that swept French avant-garde musical milieus in the final decades of the century. Instead, he extolled the tradition of Gluck and Rameau, spearheading editions of both.

Saint-Saëns's first completed opera was *Le timbre d'argent*, an "opéra fantas-tique" on a libretto by Barbier and Carré, commissioned for the Théâtre-Lyrique. A cross between *Faust* and *The Tales of Hoffmann*,[72] it is a long dream sequence during which Conrad, the hero, receives from the devil-like Spiridion a silver bell which will procure him all the gold he wants, but at the expense of a human life.[73] Like Auber's *La muette de Portici*, the work features a silent character played by a ballerina. The projected premiere capsized when Carvalho resigned in 1868. Saint-Saëns revised it for the Opéra-Comique and again, as a sung-through "drame lyrique," for the Opéra, where the projected production fell victim to a press campaign. When eventually premiered at the Opéra-Lyrique-National (in the version with dialogues), the work only lasted 18 performances.

Saint-Saëns's first staged opera was the one-act *La princesse jaune*, premiered at the Opéra-Comique in 1872 – some performances double-billed with Bizet's *Djamileh*. Gallet's libretto is an orientalist fantasy set in Holland: the Japan-obsessed, opium-loving hero confuses in his dreams the yellow princess of his lacquer screen for his cousin Lena. The witty score abounds in humorous and exotic musical effects (pentatonic scale, unusual percussion instruments). Moderately successful at the time, it was admired by Debussy and Ravel.

Paradoxically, in the light of its eventual fame, *Samson et Dalila* took longer to be staged in Paris than any other of Saint-Saëns's operas. It was planned as an oratorio as early as 1857. The second act, written first, was performed sepa-rately, but responses were not encouraging. Biblical opera, despite the Rossini and Auber precedents, was not popular. The music was completed in 1873 and published in 1876, but with no Parisian production forthcoming, it was left to Liszt to have *Samson* premiered (in German) at the Grand-Ducal theater in Weimar in December 1877. Rouen staged it in 1890 before it was heard in Paris at the Éden-Théâtre later in the same year with Talazac – the original Hoffmann and Des Grieux, thus a lyric, not heroic tenor. Further perform-ances followed in the French provinces before the Opéra took it on in 1892. By 1922 it had reached 500 performances.

Though the style of Ferdinand Lemaire's (18?–1879) libretto has been criti-cized, its structure allows for great dramatic variety. A church musician –

though agnostic – Saint-Saëns achieved an effective blend of the religious and the profane, notably in Act 1, which seamlessly progresses from the opening fugue of the lamenting Hebrews to Dalila's sensuous "Printemps qui commence." The composer's admiration for Wagner is perceptible in the resolutely "through-composed" structure of each act and his energetic use of recurrent themes, notably in the great Act 2 duet, where the orchestra depicts the storm raging as tension mounts between the characters. Yet the influence of Berlioz and Gounod is equally clear, the latter notably in the Act 3 Bacchanale, so well integrated in the work's structure that a performance without it is unthinkable. Vocally, although Samson is one of the great tenor roles in the French repertory, the honors go to the opulent dramatic mezzo role of Dalila, who along with Carmen is the quintessential *femme fatale* in all opera.

Saint-Saëns turned to French medieval history with *Étienne Marcel*, a four-act opera on a libretto by Gallet based on an episode during the Hundred Years War, pitting the Parisian bourgeoisie against the Dauphin, the future Charles V (a mezzo-soprano role).[74] After its successful premiere at Lyons in 1884, the work was staged in Paris at the Gaîté (then Opéra Populaire) in 1884, but was never mounted at the Opéra: perhaps the subject matter, intended to be a homage to the city of Paris, also brought with it embarrassing memories of the Commune.

The libretto of *Henry VIII* (by Léonce Détroyat (1829–1898) and Armand Silvestre (1837–1901)) had been turned down by Gounod, who may have felt that its blend of love and history was too close to the now *passé* world of grand opéra.[75] The plot, in fact, takes many liberties with historical truth. Its primary source was, in any event, not a historical study but Pedro Calderón de la Barca's 1627 play *La cisma de Inglaterra*. It deals both with the repudiation of Catherine of Aragon and the synod at which the king broke with Rome, which forms the substance of Act 3. Anne Boleyn (here Anne de Boleyn) is portrayed as an ambitious schemer ("Je vais donc enfin te connaître, ivresse du pouvoir") who is secretly in love with the Spanish ambassador, while Catherine, magnanimously, refuses to divulge the proof of Anne's duplicity and dies of grief at the end. A planned fifth act was dropped that was to show the wedding of Henry and Anne. Though consisting of discrete musical numbers, *Henry VIII* is remarkable for being essentially based, more than any other of Saint-Saëns's works, on a system of recurrent motifs – the first such work to be heard at the Palais Garnier.[76] The one representing the Schism, and heard both in the prelude and in Act 3, was on a sixteenth-century theme that Saint-Saëns found in the British royal collections. Other touches of local color, however anachronistic, occur in the Act 2 ballet, which makes use of genuine Scottish melodies. Marking Saint-Saëns's belated Opéra debut in 1883, with Gabrielle Krauss as Catherine, *Henry VIII* was his second most popular work. It was revived at the Palais Garnier until 1919, though often, to the composer's annoyance, in a version amputated of Act 3.

Of Saint-Saëns's subsequent stage works, several were highly successful but none was to enter the repertory. *Proserpine*, which despite the similarity of its title with Lully's tragédie en musique is not a mythological work but deals with a vengeful Florentine courtesan during the Renaissance, was well received in the spring of 1887 but the fire at the Opéra-Comique interrupted its career. *Ascanio*, premiered at the Opéra in 1890, was liked by the audience but poorly treated by critics; it was subsequently revived for Saint-Saëns's eightieth birthday during the First World War – he was by then treated as the national composer – and in 1921, the year of his death. Its principal characters are Benvenuto Cellini and his pupil Ascanio – as in Berlioz's opera, but with a different vocal distribution (bass and tenor). The female lead, named Colombe, starred the American soprano Emma Eames. The setting is the court of Francis I at Fontainebleau, and Saint-Saëns introduced archaic colors in the divertissement. The mythological farce *Phryné*, with Sanderson in the title role, was a hit at the Opéra-Comique in 1893 and was mounted in several countries before disappearing from sight.[77] *Frédégonde*, on the other hand, Saint-Saëns's completion (assisted by Dukas) of Guiraud's unfinished opera on a macabre Merovingian subject, barely lasted nine performances at the Opéra in 1895–6. Originally intended for the open-air Roman theater at Orange, the "tragédie lyrique" *Les barbares*, a one-time collaboration with Sardou, was eventually premiered at the Opéra with a fine cast in 1901 and received 28 performances but was never revived in its entirety.[78] Saint-Saëns's last three works, like several of Massenet's, were staged at Monte Carlo. *Hélène* (1904), a one-act "pièce lyrique" to the composer's own libretto, was premiered with Nellie Melba in a double bill with Massenet's *La Navarraise*.[79] It was heard with Mary Garden at the Opéra-Comique the following year and eventually mounted at the Opéra in 1919. Another American star of the period, Geraldine Farrar, premiered *L'ancêtre* (1906), a somber Corsican drama of vendetta, and one of Saint-Saëns's least popular works. *Déjanire* (1911) was a reworking of an earlier work, a tragedy by Louis Gallet on the death of Hercules with stage music. Saint-Saëns had conducted it before an audience of 10,000 at the open-air Béziers arena in 1898. The composer himself rewrote the text of the newly composed parts. The Russian-born dramatic soprano Félia Litvinne (1860–1936) sang the title role at Monte Carlo and repeated it at the Opéra, where *Déjanire* achieved a modest 17 performances; on the same stage *Samson* had by then been seen more than 350 times.

César Franck

César Franck (1822–1890) is not usually thought of as an opera composer.[80] Yet the Belgian-born musician, who moved permanently to Paris in 1836, worked on four operatic projects. A student of Henri-Montan Berton at the Conservatoire, he wrote in his late teens *Stradella*, based on Émile

Deschamps and Émilien Pacini's libretto for Louis Niedermeyer's work (a flop at the Opéra in 1837).[81] In 1851–3, with a view to a Théâtre-Lyrique production that never happened, Franck composed *Le valet de ferme* on a libretto by Royer and Vaëz, set in Ireland in the 1690s.[82] Franck later disowned the work, which has remained unpublished; the manuscript has survived but was recently dispersed.

By the time Franck turned to opera again in the 1870s, he was the famous organist of the church of Sainte-Clotilde (since 1858) and organ professor at the Paris Conservatoire (since 1872). Championed by a group of fervent disciples, headed by Henri Duparc and Vincent d'Indy, soon joined by Ernest Chausson, he was hailed by them as a French answer to Beethoven and Wagner – a misleading image, as Joël-Marie Fauquet has pointed out, for someone who was above all influenced by Liszt and whose musical taste encompassed Boieldieu and boisterous operettas like *La fille de Madame Angot*.

Franck composed *Hulda*, the first opera of his maturity, between 1879 and 1885. Subtitled "légende scandinave" (an appellation that recalls the subtitle of *Le roi d'Ys*), the libretto by Charles Grandmougin (1850–1930) is based on *Halte Hulda* by the Norwegian playwright Bjoernsterne Bjoernson, itself drawn from the Völsung Saga.[83] In the prologue Hulda, part magician part *femme fatale*, is abducted by Gudleik, chief of the rival Aslak tribe. Two years later, as Gudleik is about to marry her, he is killed by his rival Eiolf, who has abandoned his own fiancée Swanhilde. The next act consists mostly of a long duet between the lovers. Yet Eiolf returns to Swanhilde, and Hulda arranges for him to be killed. Cursed by the Aslaks but having satisfied her desire for revenge, she throws herself into the sea. Like Lalo in *Le roi d'Ys*, Franck has included a few popular Norwegian themes, while the rich and refined orchestration underlines the exotic character of the setting.

Hulda having been turned down by the Opéra, Franck vainly tried to have it premiered in Brussels. Yet Belgium, where many important French works of the period had been premiered, failed to acknowledge its greatest living composer. Only the allegorical ballet on the theme of winter and spring, detached from the penultimate act, was performed in Franck's lifetime. The opera was finally staged at Monte Carlo in 1894, with Blanche Deschamps in the title role; Lhérie, the original Don José in *Carmen* but by then turned baritone, sang Gudleik. Both text and music had been subjected to cuts and rearrangements, and in that mutilated version the work was mounted in a few theaters. Only in 1994, in London, was the opera heard in its original version, as produced by University College Opera.

Franck was not discouraged by his failure to get *Hulda* accepted. One of his last projects was the drame lyrique *Ghiselle*, inspired (like Guiraud and Saint-Saëns's *Frédégonde*, with which it shares the same heroine) by an episode from Augustin Thierry *Récits des temps mérovingiens*, adapted into an opera by Thierry's own nephew.[84] The short score draft was completed by the fall of

1889, but the orchestration, contemporary with the composition of Franck's String Quartet, was unfinished when he died in November 1890. His son entrusted the completion to Franck's student Arthur Coquard, assisted by other disciples – d'Indy, Chausson, Pierre de Bréville, and Marcel Samuel-Rousseau. In this somewhat heterogeneous form – and the second act merged into the second scene of Act 3 – the work was premiered at Monte Carlo in 1896 but has not been heard since.

Emmanuel Chabrier

The colorful personality of Emmanuel Chabrier (1841–1894), vividly conveyed by his correspondence,[85] is endearingly reflected in his music, making him one of the most popular late nineteenth-century French composers. Furthermore, his originality as a harmonist and orchestrator have earned him the admiration of his peers, from Debussy, Ravel, and Poulenc to Stravinsky. His contribution to opera, long neglected, is gradually being recognized as equally original.

A son of the Auvergne city of Ambert (producer of one of France's most delicious cheeses), Chabrier received his musical education first in Clermont-Ferrand, then in Paris, where his main professor of composition was Théophile Semet, composer of *Nuits d'Espagne* and *La petite Fadette*. Chabrier did not enter the Conservatoire, nor did he embrace a musical career from the outset. A law graduate, he took a position as civil servant with the Ministry of the Interior. Parallel to this conventional status, he frequented bohemian literary circles. His friends included Richepin, whose ribald *Chanson des gueux* got him imprisoned for a month in 1876, and Paul Verlaine, who came to prominence as the author of *Poèmes saturniens* (1866) and *Fêtes galantes* (1869) before embarking on his scandalous affair with Arthur Rimbaud. Chabrier's first operatic projects, in 1864, were two satirical operettas on texts by Verlaine, *Vaucochard et Fils Ier* and *Fisch-Ton-Kan*, an absurdist chinoiserie (the title a pun on the colloquialism for "get lost") in the manner of Offenbach's *Ba-Ta-Clan*. Neither was completed.[86] Chabrier's friendship with his future librettist Mendès, an early Wagnerite, also dates from that period. Chabrier's avant-garde interests extended to the visual arts: he became a friend of Manet, acquiring *Un bal aux Folies-Bergères*, one of the painter's masterpieces (now at the Courtauld Institute Galleries, London).

In 1875 the recently married Chabrier was introduced by the painter Gaston Hirsch to Leterrier and Vanloo, librettists of several of Lecocq's works. The result was the two-act operetta *L'étoile*, which was accepted at the Bouffes-Parisiens, Offenbach's old theater, then headed by his son-in-law Charles Comte. After an unusual 41 rehearsals (the orchestra was taxed by Chabrier's orchestral writing), *L'étoile* was performed 47 times in 1877–8, with Paola Marié (sister of Galli-Marié) in the trouser role of Lazuli. Though a disappointed Chabrier later spoke of a flop,[87] it was more than a half-success for a work that counts among the most sparkling comedies of its age. The unapologetically wacky libretto deals with a poor peddler about to be publicly executed when an astrologer predicts that his and King Ouf's fate are linked. In the end Lazuli wins the hand of Princess Laoula. Chabrier's inventive score, where poetic moments – Lazuli's "O ma petite étoile" a discreet homage to Wolfram's "O du mein holde Abendstern" in *Tannhaüser* – alternate with duets and ensembles of irrepressible verve. Though the work, incomprehensibly, was not seen again in his lifetime, the Opéra-Comique staged it for the Chabrier centenary in 1941, reviving it periodically until 1968, but it was only in the 1980s that it entered the international repertory.[88]

Chabrier collaborated with the same librettists for his next work, also an operetta, the one-act *Une éducation manquée*. Set in the eighteenth century, it is a kind of *jeu d'esprit*: Gontran (a trouser part), about to get married to Hélène, upbraids his preceptor Pausanias (bass) for teaching him everything but the facts of life – which eventually Gontran and Hélène, with the help of a storm, discover by themselves. This witty score, admired by Stravinsky,[89] received one private performance in Chabrier's lifetime, in 1879. Its public premiere took place only in 1912 at the Théâtre des Arts in Paris. Diaghilev revived it at Monte Carlo in 1924 with recitatives by Darius Milhaud replacing spoken dialogues.

Having quit his job as a civil servant in 1880, Chabrier embarked on his most ambitious project, which he completed in 1883 – the year when his orchestral fantasy *España* triumphed at the Concerts Lamoureux. *Gwendoline*, on a three-act libretto by Mendès,[90] is Chabrier's single completed "serious" opera, and, ostensibly, a thoroughly Wagnerian work. An ardent Wagnerian, Chabrier was bowled over when he heard *Tristan* in Munich in 1880 and the *Ring* in London in 1882. Despite Mendès's own admonition to French composers, whom he urged to choose subjects rooted in their own heritage, *Gwendoline* has a Saxon-Scandinavian early medieval setting. The plot takes place on the British coast in the eighth century. Harald, a young Danish warrior, having overpowered the Saxons led by Armel, falls in love with Armel's daughter Gwendoline. Seeing an opportunity for revenge, Armel acquiesces to the wedding, but plots a massacre of the unsuspecting Danes during the wedding banquet (a situation recalling *Les Danaïdes*). In the final scene, Harald and Gwendoline die together while the Danish ships are set ablaze. The Nordic setting notwithstanding, Chabrier was far too individual a composer to ape Wagner's musical style. The leitmotifs themselves – such as the big tune familiar from the overture – could never be mistaken for anyone else's music. Having failed to get the work accepted at the Opéra, Chabrier had highlights performed in concert. The stage premiere took place in Brussels in April 1886 (in sets recycled from previous productions ranging from *Sigurd* to Massé's *Paul et Virginie*).[91] Success seemed clear, but the bankruptcy of Henry

Verdhurt, director of the Théâtre Royal de la Monnaie, interrupted the run after two performances. Three years later, thanks to the intercession of Chabrier's friend the tenor Ernest Van Dyck, Felix Mottl agreed to champion the work at Karslruhe. Hermann Levi (who had conducted the premiere of *Parsifal* at Bayreuth) did the same in Munich in 1893. The French premiere took place in Lyons in 1893, the year when finally the Opéra also mounted it, yielding to pressure from Countess Greffuhle. By then in the last stages of the syphilis that killed him soon afterwards, Chabrier could barely enjoy the consecration he had long hoped for in vain.[92]

For the many fine moments in *Gwendoline*, Chabrier, however, was aware that his genius lay above all in comedy, and he produced what is arguably his greatest masterpiece in 1887 with the opéra-comique *Le roi malgré lui*. Adapted by Émile de Najac and Paul Burani (the latter an operetta librettist) with behind-the-scenes help supplied by Richepin, from an 1836 romantic comedy of the same title by Virginie Ancelot,[93] it deals with the short and unhappy reign of Henri de Valois after he was elected King of Poland in 1572, until the death of his brother Charles IX gained him the French throne. In the opera the reluctant king, taking the identity of his friend Nangis, joins a conspiracy against himself, involving Alexina, with whom he once flirted in Venice (under a different disguise), now married to the fatuous Italian duke Fritelli. Nangis, meanwhile, is in love with the gypsy slave Minka. Henri almost succeeds in fleeing the country but the plan fails and he has to stay put for the time being. Beginning with the startling opening chords of the prelude, Chabrier's music is so consistently fresh and subtle that the obscurities of the plot are forgotten. Among the work's many delights are the celebrated "Fête polonaise," in which the Polish dance is combined with a deliberately "naughty" French waltz; Minka's gypsy song, alternating between melancholy and brilliance; the great conspiracy ensemble, some of the music of which is first heard in the overture; and the duet for Minka and Alexina in the last act, worthy of Berlioz's similar pages in *Les Troyens* and *Béatrice et Bénédict*.[94]

Premiered at the Opéra-Comique on 18 May 1887, to mostly positive reviews, with a cast headed by Adèle Isaac and including the great buffo bass Lucien Fugère,[95] *Le roi malgré lui* had its career torpedoed by the fire that destroyed the theater one week later. After 20 performances in 1887–8, it disappeared from the repertory. Mottl conducted it at Karlsruhe in 1890, and there were stagings in Dresden and Cologne. In 1929 Albert Carré decided that a complete rewriting of the libretto might help. Unfortunately this version introduced more confusion of its own. One can only hope that, as in the case of Berlioz's long-misunderstood masterpieces, *Le roi malgré lui* will eventually find its rightful place in the French repertory.

After *Le roi malgré lui* Chabrier considered subjects from Shakespeare, Pushkin, Hugo, Richepin, and even Sardou. He eventually settled on *Briséis*, based on an adaptation of Goethe's *Die Braut von Korinth* by Bernard Lazare, who later became famous as Alfred Dreyfus's first champion, and Ephraïm Mikhaël (1866–1890), a gifted poet who died of consumption at 24. The latter wrote the libretto together with Mendès. Chabrier himself only completed Act 1. Despite its ancient theme – the spreading of Christianity in Greece at the time of Emperor Hadrian – it is the most Wagnerian of Chabrier's works, with its tense vocal writing, rich orchestral web, and dense system of leitmotifs.[96] In its truncated form, the work was premiered by Lamoureux in 1897 and staged for the first time in Berlin two years later under Richard Strauss. Attempts to get Georges Enesco or Ravel to complete it led nowhere. Such as it is, the opulent vocal and orchestral writing is an additional testimony to Chabrier's versatile genius.

Ernest Chausson

Although he wrote only one opera, Ernest Chausson (1855–1899) deserves a major place among *fin-de-siècle* French opera composers.[97] From a well-to-do Parisian family and privately educated in a highly cultured milieu, he devoted himself to music only after graduating as a lawyer in 1877. At the Conservatoire he studied with Massenet, who was deeply impressed with his capacities, and with Franck, of whom he became an enthusiastic disciple. A devoted Wagnerian, he attended the first performance of *Parsifal* at Bayreuth in 1882, returning, on his honeymoon, the following year.

As early as 1875 Chausson, whose personal library was rich in medieval literature and history, had immersed himself in the Arthurian legend, which inspired his symphonic poem *Viviane* in 1882. He toyed with other subjects for an opera: Hugo's *Notre-Dame-de-Paris* in 1880; Alfred de Musset's dark comedy *Les caprices de Marianne* (which, much later, was set by Sauguet) in 1882–4; *Hélène*, a drame lyrique after Leconte de Lisle's version of the Greek myth, in 1883–4.[98] Like his contemporary and friend d'Indy, his fellow secretary of the Société nationale de musique in 1886, he decided to write the text himself, a Berliozian as well as a Wagnerian gesture. The libretto of *Le roi Arthus*, which was innovative in combining rhythmic prose and verse, was drafted in 1885–6. Possibly inspired in part by Tennyson's *Idylls of the King*,[99] it focuses on the love affair between Guinevere (Genièvre in Chausson's version) and Lancelot; Arthur's discovery of the adultery, denounced to him by the treacherous Mordred; and Arthur's disillusionment and death. Chausson's initial draft, on which he sought advice from Duparc,[100] differs substantially from the text he set. In rewriting it, he removed some elements that recalled *Tristan* too closely – such as Guinevere collapsing on the dead Lancelot in the presence of her husband. In the final version there is no confrontation between the king and the adulterous lovers. Guinevere initially ended her days in a convent, as in the medieval source. In the finished libretto she strangles herself with her own hair, remaining defiant until the end, while the remorseful

Lancelot voluntarily seeks death on the battlefield. A principled, slightly aloof personality with mystical leanings, Chausson clearly identified strongly with his idealistic hero. Lancelot, racked by guilt, is also portrayed sympathetically. On the other hand, as Steven Huebner has pointed out,[101] Guinevere is a more ambiguous figure, open to misogynistic interpretation – yet so strongly projected that a modern director could make much of her opposition to the values of what is otherwise an entirely male world.

The composition of *Le roi Arthus* occupied Chausson for more than six years. Though by 1886 he had expressed the wish to "dewagnerize" himself, the Wagnerian influence can be felt keenly in the first act, composed in 1888–9, especially in the love duet between Lancelot and Guinevere in the second scene: the situation and the music both strongly recall the garden scene in Act 2 of Wagner's *Tristan*. Lancelot's squire Lyonnel watches like Wagner's Brangäne, while Mordred is a Melot-like figure. The influence of Berlioz – obvious in the opening fanfares of Act 1 – is equally clear.[102] This influence is also in evidence in Act 2, composed between 1888 and 1892, with a two-year interruption in 1889–91; the haunting, mock-medieval song heard in the first scene, on the other hand, anticipates the atmosphere of Debussy's *Pelléas*. At the end of the act Merlin appears to Arthur, prophesying, Erda-like, the end of the Round Table and Arthur's death. In Chausson's first version of Act 3, Arthur's death resembled a suicide; in the final one, it is a veritable apotheosis, the king being brought away in a boat while celestial voices are heard in the sunset, proclaiming his spiritual victory: musically, this moment is very much Chausson's own.

Having completed *Le roi Arthus* in 1895, Chausson spent the next four years vainly trying to get it staged.[103] After Chausson died in a cycling accident in June 1899, d'Indy approached the Théâtre de la Monnaie, which agreed to produce it, not without having extracted from Chausson's widow the large sum of 15,000 francs. Premiered in November 1903 with a strong cast headed by the French heroic tenor Charles Dalmorès (1871–1939) as Lancelot and, as Arthur, the Dutch baritone Henri Albers (1866–1926), the work was well received but was given only 13 performances. Only in the last decades of the twentieth century did it begin to be given its due as a powerful, stirring opera, surprisingly effective dramatically, and the greatest legacy of a deeply individual composer.[104]

Vincent d'Indy

For the historical importance of Vincent d'Indy (1851–1931) in late nineteenth-century and early twentieth-century music, none of his four operas has gained a permanent footing in the repertory nor is it likely to be staged. Yet this respected, individual voice deserves more than a passing mention.[105] He belonged to an aristocratic family with roots in the Vivarais region of the Cévennes mountains, to which, despite his Parisian birth, he was deeply attached. His father Wildrid d'Indy was a minor opéra-comique composer and salon musician. Attracted first to a military career, Vincent d'Indy became a law student but eventually settled on a musical career. He took private tuition with the pianist Louis Diémer, the musicologist Albert Lavignac (an active champion of Wagner in France), and, at Duparc's urging, Franck, whose Paris Conservatoire organ class d'Indy joined in 1874–5. The following year he attended the first *Ring* at Bayreuth. His first major work, the dramatic legend *Le chant de la cloche*, was awarded the Prix de la Ville de Paris in 1885. An active participant in the activities of the Société nationale de musique, he became a competent choral conductor. His dissatisfaction with the Conservatoire led him, with Alexandre Guilmant and Charles Bordes, to found a rival school in 1894, the Schola Cantorum.

D'Indy's first operatic projects included adaptations of George Sand's regionalist novel *Les maîtres sonneurs* and Chateaubriand's novel *Le dernier des Abencérages*, which, like Cherubini's opera on a related source, deals with the conflict between the Muslim and Christian worlds. In 1882 the Opéra-Comique produced, with moderate success, his uncharacteristically unambitious *Attendez-moi sous l'orme*, a single act drawn from a comedy by the early eighteenth-century playwright Jean-François Regnard. D'Indy then contemplated adapting the drama *Axel* by the Swedish playwright Esaias Tegnér, which instead developed into *Fervaal* for which he wrote his own libretto, completing it in 1888. An "action dramatique" – a departure from the prevailing "drame lyrique" appellation – the work is set in a legendary past in the mythical kingdom of Cravann in d'Indy's beloved Cévennes. The eponymous hero – whose name recalls *Parsifal*, d'Indy's favorite Wagner opera,[106] while connoting the idea of religious fervor – is a Celtic knight of semi-divine origin, torn between his attraction towards Guilhen, a Saracen princess who looked after him when he was wounded in battle, and his calling for absolute purity, enforced by his mentor the druid Arfagard. Despite the Erda-like warnings of the mother-goddess Kaito, Fervaal leads his people to battle but is defeated. Forced to choose between Guilhen and Arfagard, he kills the druid, but the young woman dies in his arms. In his own final moments Fervaal has a vision of the "new Cravann" and the Christian world due to replace Celtic paganism. Carrying Guilhen's body, he ascends the mountain, to the sound of the Gregorian hymn *Pange lingua*.

D'Indy's symbolic work is indebted to Wagner both dramatically and musically. It is built on a leitmotiv system (12 of them according to the composer), with *Tristan*-like use of chromaticism, and the vocal declamation, especially in the scenes featuring the Kundry-like Guilhen, is often reminiscent of Wagner. However, the frequent expressive recourse to dissonance is very much d'Indy's own. Similarly his rich orchestration, which includes four saxophones, differs from Wagner's fusion of instrumental timbres, emphasizing instead their individuality and variety. The piano-vocal score was published in 1895 and the premiere took place two years later in Brussels. With the same principals, the work was produced in 1898 at the Opéra-Comique, where it lasted 10 perform-ances. It was performed twice at the Opéra in 1912, under André Messager, with the great Swiss dramatic soprano Lucienne Bréval (1869–1935).

Conceived soon after the completion of *Fervaal*, *L'étranger*, a similarly styled "action musicale," was intended as a more accessible, even popular work.[107] Set in a fishing village on the Basque Atlantic coast, d'Indy's libretto owes much, however, to Tegnér, while some of its elements, as Steven Huebner has pointed out, recall Henrik Ibsen's *Brand* and *The Woman from the Sea*. Vita ("life"), the heroine, is engaged to a customs official, André (after the Greek for "man"), but falls under the spell of a mysterious, older stranger/foreigner (*étranger* can mean either), endowed with special powers, symbolized by the green emerald he wears in his cap. Yet the stranger, while reciprocating her feelings, decides to go, entrusting his green emerald to Vita, who throws it into the sea. When a tempest arises, she follows him into his boat and they are both engulfed in the ocean. In an effect recalling *Fervaal*, the ending quotes the plainchant hymn "Ubi caritas," suggesting that the story – for all the echoes of Wagner's *The Flying Dutchman* – is essentially a Christian allegory of love. Also like *Fervaal*, the work is built on a series of leitmotifs, but it uses smaller orchestral forces. It was also premiered in Brussels, in January 1903, with Claire Friché as Vita and Albers as the Stranger, before being staged at the Opéra in December of the same year, with Bréval as Vita and Francisque Delmas as the Stranger. It was revived in 1916, 1934 (with Germaine Lubin), 1944, and 1951 (with the young Régine Crespin), totalling 39 performances at the Palais Garnier.

D'Indy's political views, always firmly rooted in the right, were radicalized during the Dreyfus Affair, when his nationalism and anti-Semitism became more pronounced. After the turn of the century, he developed paranoid views on operatic history, according to which a perverse Jewish influence had been at work, not just in the form of Meyerbeer, Halévy, and Offenbach, but Rossini, Auber, and, in his own times, Massenet – whom he wholeheartedly despised – and Richard Strauss. (To be fair, he held Paul Dukas, who *was* Jewish, in high esteem, dedicating to him his Second Symphony.) Those conceptions came into play in his final opera, *La légende de Saint-Christophe*, composed mostly in 1908–13 but premiered only in 1920 at the Opéra, where it was seen 19 times and never revived.[108] This "drame sacré" – a label reminiscent of *Parsifal* – was also, in the composer's own words, an "anti-Jewish drama." A retelling of the story of St Christopher, it features allegorical characters such as the King of Gold (conceived as an anti-Semitic caricature) and the evil "Sathanaël," a portmanteau name linking Satan and Athanaël, by reference to *Thaïs* (one more jab at his nemesis Massenet). Snatches of music also satirize various modern composers, from Strauss to Ravel. Unsurprisingly, the work's heavy-handed ideology has compromised prospects for future revivals.

Alfred Bruneau

Until *Louise* and *Pelléas* brought Charpentier and Debussy to the fore, Alfred Bruneau (1857–1934) was generally seen as the most "modern" opera composer of his generation.[109] He was the son of a Parisian violinist who played in the orchestra of the Théâtre-Italien. Trained as a cellist, Bruneau studied this instrument at the Conservatoire before enrolling in Massenet's composition class in 1880. His first opera, *Kérim*, on a libretto by Milliet and Henri Lavedan (1859–1960) lasted only three performances at the Opéra Populaire (as the Théâtre du Château d'eau was briefly called) in 1887. An exotic tale with atmospheric moments recalling Bizet's *Djamileh* (such as the Act 3 prelude with wordless chorus), it was partly based on authentic oriental tunes. The following year Bruneau's life took a new turn when he was introduced to Émile Zola, by then a famous and successful author. Bruneau asked him for permission to adapt his novel *La faute de l'abbé Mouret*. But the rights had been reserved by Massenet (who never completed the project)[110] and Zola entrusted Bruneau instead with his latest work, *Le rêve*. For the libretto Bruneau turned to Gallet, and their drame lyrique in four acts and eight tableaux – the first Zola novel to receive an operatic treatment – was premiered in 1891 at the Opéra-Comique. Within two years it was seen in London, Brussels, Königsberg, and Hamburg (under Gustav Mahler), as well as in several French provincial theaters.

Considered the first French naturalist opera, *Le rêve*, paradoxically, is based on the least realistic of all Zola's Rougon-Macquart novels. But the author's naturalism always includes a strong symbolic element. The foundling Angélique, brought up by Hubert and Hubertine in their house next to a cathedral, leads a secluded life, lost in her *Golden Legend*-fed dreams while making liturgical embroidery. She falls in love with Félicien, son of the bishop Jean d'Hautecoeur (who joined the priesthood after he lost his wife) but he is opposed to the marriage. He relents when Angélique falls desperately sick, but, on the day of the wedding, she collapses under the porch of the cathedral – the implication being that she lived only in a world of dreams and can no longer live once her dream becomes reality. A serious opera with a contemporary setting was not common in 1891, and Bruneau emphasizes the modernity of the work with his musical discourse, which combines Wagnerian leitmotifs, quotations from plainchant and folk tunes (Act 2, set at a public festival, is built on a "vieille chanson française"), a style of musical conversation that anticipates some of the characteristics of Debussy's yet unwritten *Pelléas*, and harmonic audacities that make *Le rêve* Bruneau's most avant-garde work.[111] As so often in the history of the Opéra-Comique, the tragic ending disconcerted audiences, and the final tableau was soon cut – thereby distorting the work's meaning.[112]

Two years after *Le rêve*, Bruneau returned to Zola with *L'attaque du moulin*, based on a novella first published in Russian translation in 1877 and included in 1881 in the collective volume *Les soirées de Médan*.[113] Contrasting with the prevailing nationalist tone of the period, this tale of the Franco-Prussian war shows in moving and eloquent terms how the life of a miller's daughter is shattered after her father and her Belgian fiancé, unwillingly drawn into the mêlée, are both killed, while the destruction of the mill takes on a powerful symbolic significance. The transformation of the story into an opera provides a fascinating example of the compromises required by the passage to a different genre. Although Zola had played a limited role in the libretto of *Le rêve*, he took an active part in the fashioning of *L'attaque du moulin*, though Gallet alone got credited: Zola thus wrote the words of the score's most anthologized passage, Dominique's farewell to the forest in Act 2. The denouement was modified: whereas the miller is summarily executed by the retreating Prussians, Dominique survives – a note of optimism not present in the original. Zola added the character of Marcelline, the miller's old servant,[114] who acts as a sort of Greek chorus: in an impassioned arioso at the end of Act 1, she denounces the evils of war, and has the last word of the opera. It is she, not Françoise as in the original novella, who falls into conversation with the enemy sentinel – an exchange made all the more poignant when Dominique, shortly afterwards, stabs the young German when making his escape. An even more telling departure from the source is that explicit references to the Franco-Prussian War of 1870–71 have been removed. The Prussian captain is called simply "the enemy captain," a distancing gesture reinforced in the original staging when the action was set during the French Revolution.[115] In 1907, after Zola's death, Bruneau consented to more compromises when the work was revived at the Gaîté: he agreed to a radical modification of the ending, where, without the music being altered, the miller was saved in extremis and the enemy captain was shot instead. Zola's widow never forgave Bruneau for what she considered a betrayal of the work's message, which was further altered by an additional aria for Marcelline (set to the composer's own text). Thus, what was a pacifist opera in the post-1870 years had been transformed, in the tense international climate of the pre-1914 period, into a patriotic work.[116]

L'attaque du moulin, which until the Second World War rivaled *Le rêve* in popularity among Bruneau's operas, was followed by *Messidor*, for which Zola wrote the libretto on his own – giving it a title obviously recalling his novel *Germinal*.[117] Whereas *L'attaque du moulin*, in theory at least, had a contemporary setting and (though entirely sung) marked a return to some of the opéra-comique traditions, *Messidor* is a full-fledged drame lyrique on a prose libretto, with a strong symbolic element. Each of the four acts takes place in a different season, in an unspecified period. The setting is a mountain village whose inhabitants are deprived of their means of subsistence when Gaspard, the local capitalist, diverts a stream to operate his gold-producing factory. By the end Gaspard himself is ruined, while his daughter Hélène marries the villager Guillaume. At the center of the work is an allegorical ballet, "La légende de l'or."

Like *Le rêve*, but even more so, the opera is built on a web of leitmotifs. Its premiere shortly preceded Zola's involvement in the Dreyfus Affair. Bruneau joined him wholeheartedly, even acting as a kind of bodyguard to the writer at the time of his trial after the publication of his manifesto *J'accuse* in January 1898.

Symbolic elements similarly pervade Bruneau's *L'ouragan*, premiered at the Opéra-Comique in 1901. Zola's prose libretto is set in a fishing village on the mythical island with the Breton-sounding name of Goël – a setting that recalls d'Indy's yet unperformed *L'étranger*, while some elements of the story may have been influenced by *Le roi d'Ys*. Like *Messidor*, it is a tale of destruction and renewal. Two brothers once were in love with the same woman, Jeannine, whose sister Marianne loved Richard, the elder. Richard went away, letting his younger brother Landry marry Jeannine, whom he mistreats. On his return, Richard saves Jeannine from his brother's fury and plans to elope with her. In the third act, while the hurricane raging outside mirrors the psychological turmoil of the characters, the jealous Marianne, having tried in vain to recapture Richard's heart, delivers him to his brother's vengeance, but at the last moment stabs Landry herself. In the last act, Jeannine and Richard realize that death has created between them an insuperable obstacle, and Richard leaves with Lulu, the childlike young woman he brought with him from his travels. Dominated by the dramatic mezzo role of Marianne, a part written for Marie Delna, *L'ouragan* is the most openly Wagnerian of Bruneau's operas, both in its use of "organic" leitmotifs[118] and in its heroic style of declamation. Debussy was among the admirers of this work, which was only a *succès d'estime*.[119]

After Zola's mysterious death by carbon monoxide poisoning in 1902,[120] Bruneau completed their last project, *L'enfant-roi*, set in contemporary Paris: Act 1 takes place in a bakery shop, Act 2 at the Tuileries, Act 3 at the flower market at the Madeleine. A "comédie lyrique" on a serious theme, but a happy ending – the heroine's husband accepts the existence of a child, which she has been keeping secret – it evokes the world of *Louise*, with its mixture of musical conversation and moments of intense lyricism. Mounted at the Opéra-Comique in 1905, the work only lasted for 12 performances.

Deprived of Zola's collaboration, Bruneau became his own librettist in two more Zola adaptations:[121] *Naïs Micoulin*, premiered at Monte Carlo in 1907, and *Les quatre journées*, a "conte lyrique" whose structure recalls that of *Messidor*, premiered at the Opéra-Comique in 1916.[122] His works after the First World War – among them the mythological comedy *Le roi Candaule* (1920) and the "comédie lyrique" *Virginie* (1931) – were lighter in character.

It is a pity that Bruneau's association with Zola has not encouraged modern opera directors to revive his works. *Le rêve* and *L'ouragan* are the prime candidates, though *L'attaque du moulin*, *Messidor*, and even *L'enfant-roi* lack neither dramatic interest nor musical beauties.

Gustave Charpentier

More than any of his musical contemporaries, Gustave Charpentier (1860–1956) remains the composer of one major work – *Louise*.[123] The son of a modest baker, this quintessential Parisian was nevertheless born in Lorraine, which his family fled before the Prussian invasion in 1870 to settle in Tourcoing. After beginning studies at the Lille Conservatoire, Charpentier was able to enter the Paris Conservatoire in 1879 thanks to a pension from the Tourcoing town council, and he settled in Montmartre, which he made his permanent home. A bohemian individualist, possibly with anarchist leanings,[124] he developed a reputation as an enfant terrible at the Conservatoire. Yet he was an excellent student in Massenet's composition class, winning the Prix de Rome in 1887. From his Italian years date the first sketches of *Louise* as well as the autobiographical "symphonie-drame" *La vie du poète*, from which he was later to extract most of the material for his second and last opera, *Julien, ou la vie du poète*.

Charpentier made the clear decision at an early stage that he would be his own librettist. He did seek advice from writer friends, notably Camille Mauclair and the Symbolist poet Saint-Pol-Roux, but their input – which, to be sure, may partly explain the high literary quality of the text of *Louise* was essentially of a stylistic nature.[125] As we have previously noted, it was unusual for operas with a serious theme to be set in the contemporary period – Massenet's *Sapho* being a notable exception. It was even more unusual for operas to feature working-class characters except in small parts often verging on caricature – the exception here being Bruneau's *Le rêve*, which, however, is not strictly a realist work.[126] In *Louise*, for the first time, we are shown intimate scenes from the life of a lower middle-class family – eating their dinner in silence, reading the newspaper, exchanging jokes, arguing; street scenes involving greengrocers, rag-pickers, homeless people; a seamstress's workshop full of chattering young women, with real sewing machines; a spontaneous popular festival featuring Louise being crowned queen of Montmartre (an episode drawn from Charpentier's separate work, *Le couronnement de la muse*, his first major success in 1897). Equally importantly, the characters express themselves in prose, and even at several points in argot, with dropped "e mute" and other popular touches. This intensely picturesque décor, fully justifying the subtitle "roman musical," provides a vivid frame for the opera's main theme, the love story between Louise and the poet Julien and her break with her parents. Though the audience is obviously meant to be on Louise's side, the parents are portrayed with sensitivity, especially the father, whose final confrontation with his daughter is the work's emotional summit. His final gesture – cursing the city that has taken Louise away from him – suggests that Paris, on a symbolic level, is the real subject of the opera. Musically, Charpentier, who uses a vast number of recurrent themes,[127] is indebted above all to Massenet (who genuinely admired the work). But he also looked back to Berlioz, especially with his rich, imaginative orchestral texture, while there are also numerous flashes of Wagnerian color. Like Massenet, Charpentier freely and effectively mixes sung and spoken passages – notably in ensemble scenes.

It took Charpentier several years to have his work accepted at the Opéra-Comique. Carvalho detested the subject matter. Carré, conversely, must have sensed that Charpentier's modern setting was exactly what could appeal to a Belle Époque audience. He made it the first new production of the year 1900, which coincided with another international exhibition. The first Louise, Marthe Rioton – a ravishing heroine, judging from photographs – was part-nered by the Belgian tenor Henri Maréchal as Julien. Taken ill during a performance, she was succeeded by the virtually unknown Scottish-American soprano Mary Garden (1874–1967), who made her reputation in the role. By 1914 *Louise* had been staged in the world's main opera houses, not to mention places as distant as Algiers and Johannesburg. By the mid-1930s it had reached 1,000 performances at the Opéra-Comique.

Eagerly awaited, Charpentier's second opera *Julien, ou la vie du poète* was unveiled in the spring of 1913 – six days after the scandalous premiere of Stravinsky's *Le sacre du printemps*. As suggested by the subtitle, *Julien* was little more than a reprise of Charpentier's 1892 work, with little new musical mate-rial.[128] Nor was it really a sequel to *Louise*, the heroine herself appearing only in a few scenes and very much as a secondary character – a setback, considering Charpentier's success in making Louise such a memorable character of a modern young woman. Lacking the Parisian color that had done much for the popularity of the earlier work – only the final tableau is set in Montmartre – *Julien* empha-sized instead symbolic elements that, 20 years later, had lost their novelty and might even seem heavy-handed. It was never revived. Nor was the projected *L'amour au faubourg*, possibly a third installment in the *Louise* trilogy, ever completed. But Charpentier's place in the French operatic repertory was secure.

Claude Debussy

Like the composer of *Louise* – a work he loathed – Claude Debussy (1862–1918) combined a bohemian side with the most orthodox musical training.[129] He was born and grew up in the town of Saint-Germain-en-Laye to the west of Paris, where his father Manuel ran a china shop. In 1871 the elder Debussy was sentenced to four years of imprisonment for joining the Commune – a sentence commuted after one year to temporary loss of civil rights. In 1872 Debussy entered the Conservatoire, where he eventually joined the composition class of Guiraud, becoming his favorite pupil and winning the Prix de Rome in 1884 with the cantata *L'enfant prodigue*.

After his return from Italy in 1887, Debussy frequented avant-garde literary and artistic milieus, including that of Mallarmé. Like all French Symbolists, he developed a lifelong passion for Edgar Allan Poe. Unlike them, and although he went to Bayreuth in 1888 and 1889, he soon became wary of the influence of Wagner. His musical friends included Chausson and Dukas.

After toying with the project of an operatic version of Flaubert's *Salammbô* in the early 1880s, Debussy, while at the Villa Medici, worked on an adaptation of the play *Diane au bois* by the Parnassian poet Théodore de Banville.[130] In the late 1880s he became interested in *Axël*, Villiers de l'Isle-Adam's Symbolist drama. By 1890 he was engaged in *Rodrigue et Chimène*, a version of the Cid story prepared in 1879 by Mendès, who drew from early Spanish sources more than from Corneille.[131] Debussy's willingness to tackle a subject so alien to his literary and artistic sensibility – and furthermore preempted by the success of Massenet's *Le Cid* (1885) – has been attributed to Mendès's offer to help financially with the publication of the *Fantaisie* for piano and orchestra. Over the next two years, Debussy more or less completed three acts (out of four) but by the summer of 1893 had abandoned the project for good. Completed by Richard Langham Smith and orchestrated by Edison Denisov, *Rodrigue et Chimène* was heard for the first time at the Lyons Opera in 1993.[132]

The Belgian playwright Maurice Maeterlinck, Debussy's exact coeval, had published his first play *La princesse Maleine* in 1889, and Debussy first considered setting it. He probably read Maeterlinck's *Pelléas et Mélisande* (published in 1892) even before attending its stage premiere by Aurélien Lugné-Poë's troupe at the Bouffes-Parisiens in May 1893 (with Lugné-Poë himself as Golaud), which convinced him of the play's theatrical viability.[133] The play's Symbolist outlook and language – as different from historical melodrama as from Naturalist theater – obviously appealed to his aesthetic sensibility. He must also have equally responded to the style of Maeterlinck's poetic prose, which invited the kind of natural melodic declamation he was looking for – neither aria nor recitative, as well as eschewing both unison and ensemble writing. In August 1893 he approached Maeterlinck via the poet Henri de Régnier, and obtained his permission to set his text directly to music. He first drafted the love scene in Act 4 (at the end of which Pelléas is killed by Golaud). He then visited the Belgian playwright and secured his advice and authorization for possible cuts. In the event, Debussy cut four short scenes altogether, notably the opening scene of Act 1, which shows the servants washing the steps of the château. Minor cuts (and textual changes) were also made in the scenes he set. The music of Acts 1, 3, 4, and 5 was written between December 1893 and June 1895; Act 2 – which he considered the most complex – was composed last, and finished in August 1895.[134]

Several years went by before *Pelléas* was accepted by a theater.[135] Prompted by André Messager, Carré, newly appointed director of the Opéra-Comique, accepted it "in principle" in the spring of 1898, but no commitment was made until three years later. Debussy then revised Acts 4 and 5 before the vocal score was engraved by his publisher Fromont and issued before the premiere.

The orchestration was realized rapidly while the work was already in rehearsal.

Maeterlinck had assumed the leading role would be offered to his mistress Georgette Leblanc (1875–1941). He was enraged when discovering that it was being offered instead to Mary Garden, whom *Louise* had propelled to fame. On the eve of the premiere, he published a letter in *Le Figaro* disavowing the opera. The part of Pelléas, evidently written with a tenor in mind (it is always in the G clef in Debussy's manuscripts), is rather low-lying in the first two acts, but uncomfortably high for a baritone in Acts 3 and 4. In the event it was offered to the baritone Jean Périer (1869–1954), from whom accommodations were made; but it has remained the work's "problem part." Golaud was the Belgian baritone Hector Dufranne (1871–1951), while Félix Vieuille (1872–1953) premiered the role of Arkel. Debussy was actively involved in the rehearsals, urging the cast "to forget, please, that you are singers."[136] Difficulties in finding a suitable boy for the part of Yniold forced the removal of the "Scène des moutons" in Act 4, while censors demanded a modification in the scene where Yniold is coaxed into spying on Pelléas and Mélisande at the end of the previous act. The most significant alteration, necessitated by scene changes, was the lengthening of the interludes in Acts 1, 2 and 4 – a necessity of which Debussy arguably made virtue by adding music of great beauty, even though recent productions have advocated a return to the work's previous state as closer to his intentions.[137]

Messager, who conducted, referred to the dress rehearsal on 28 April 1902 as a disaster. Garden herself maintained that Maeterlinck was responsible for the cabal – a cabal that backfired, since most of the laughs seem to have been directed at the text. The premiere, two days later, if not an unqualified triumph, was a success. Although conservative critics were predictably perplexed by the work's novelty, the perceptive d'Indy was the first to point out its debt to Wagner,[138] while describing it, equally perceptively, as a return to the lyrical recitative of early Italian opera. *Pelléas* was revived in almost every season until 1914. By 1970 it had been seen at the Opéra-Comique 437 times.[139] Perhaps on account of the opera's idiosyncratic character, foreign productions were relatively slow in coming: Brussels and Frankfurt (1907); New York, Milan (under Arturo Toscanini), Prague, Munich, and Berlin (1908); Rome and London (1909).

Pelléas et Mélisande, in France at least, quickly became a "cult" opera, which inevitably triggered reverse reactions – a conductor is quoted as dismissing the work in the 1930s as one "enjoyed only by snobs and pederasts."[140] Its very nature, which, like a modern tragédie en musique, appears to favor above all the clarity of the text and uncompromisingly rejects all elements of vocal exuberance, can reinforce that impression of elitism. Like Alban Berg's *Wozzeck*, which it resembles in this regard, it is a resolutely modernist work, one that demands from its audience the kind of concentration that more traditional operas may give the impression of sparing their listeners. Almost from the outset, it was perceived as a defining moment in French operatic history. It offered, in the most positive terms, a response to the challenges that the Wagnerian drame lyrique had posed to French composers of the post-1870 period. In this respect, Debussy positioned himself as a French Wagner: from then onward there would be a pre-*Pelléas* and a post-*Pelléas* era.

Pelléas was the first and only opera Debussy completed. There were other projects – including a *Tristan* based on Joseph Bédier's reconstitution of the legend. The ones that retained Debussy's attention for the longest period were two Poe adaptations.[141] In 1903 he signed a contract with his publisher Jacques Durand for an adaptation of *The Devil in the Belfry*, drafting a synopsis and a few sketches. In 1908 – by which time, having divorced his first wife, and living expensively on the Avenue du Bois, he was in perpetual need of money – he sold first performance rights to Giulio Gatti-Casazza, the new manager of the Metropolitan Opera in New York. The arrangement also concerned the other Poe project, *The Fall of the House of Usher*, for which he *did* compose much of the music. Three different stages of the libretto – Debussy's own – survive, drafted respectively in 1908–9, 1909–1910, and 1915–16. Most of the surviving music dates from this latest period, when the rectal cancer that was to kill him two years later was in remission. As Robert Orledge has shown, the work presented obvious similarities with *Pelléas*: the sickly Lady Madeline dying away; the oppressive, doomed atmosphere; the haunted, Golaud-like figure of Roderick Usher. As the same scholar has also argued, Debussy's musical inspiration may have been hampered by the unrelieved gloom of the story. The "slow, mostly sinister music"[142] he wrote, for all its impressive beauty, may lack theatrical variety, though its dramatic tension leading to the spectacular denouement (the collapse of the house following Madeline's ghostly reappearance) offers staging possibilities of which the composer was no doubt well aware. Two reconstitutions of the existing music were unveiled, both in 1977, one by Carolyn Abbate, the other by Juan Allende-Blin. More recently, Orledge wrote a completed version of *La chute de la maison Usher*, which received its first performance at the 2006 Bregenz Festival.

CHAPTER 9

FROM THE BELLE ÉPOQUE TO THE ANNÉES FOLLES

Belle Époque opera

The period known as the Belle Époque, which began with the Paris Universal Exposition of 1900 and ended with the start of the First World War, was ushered, in the field of opera, by the double sensation of *Louise* in 1900 and *Pelléas* two years later. Each represented a different kind of operatic avant-garde. With *Louise*, Charpentier, like a "painter of modern life" to borrow Baudelaire's phrase, produced the most accomplished example of French operatic Naturalism, a homegrown response to Italian *verismo*. In a parallel way, with a more radical musical language, *Pelléas*, unlike previous French "drames lyriques," appeared to have broken free from the paralyzing influence of the *maître de Bayreuth*.

Wagner and *verismo* both loomed large on French opera stages during the Belle Époque. By contrast with the nationalist demonstrations that had derailed the first Paris production of *Lohengrin* in 1887, Wagner had become widely accepted as well as commercially successful when his operas were staged at the Opéra or in provincial theaters. *Die Walküre* was produced at the Opéra in 1893; *Die Meistersinger* was seen in Lyons in 1896 and in Paris the following year; Paris heard *Tristan* whole in 1899, under Lamoureux (after Aix-les-Bains in 1897, and Nice earlier in 1899); *Das Rheingold* was performed in concert by Lamoureux in Paris in 1901 and staged in Nice in 1902; 1902 witnessed the Paris premieres of *Siegfried* at the Opéra (Rouen had mounted it two years before) and *Götterdämmerung*, under Alfred Cortot, at the Château d'eau. Paris was one of the many cities where *Parsifal* was mounted in January 1914 after Bayreuth lost its exclusivity on the work the month before. The First World War, to be sure, put a temporary halt to French Wagnerolatry – German music was de facto banned – but performances of Wagner quickly resumed after 1918. Despite its enormous human cost, the war, from the point of view of operatic history, was an interruption rather than a watershed.

As for *verismo*, Mascagni's *Cavalleria rusticana*, staged with enormous success at the Opéra-Comique in 1892,[1] quickly became a staple of its repertory. Puccini's *La bohème*, first seen on that same stage in 1898, reached its 200th performance within 10 years. *Tosca*, premiered in 1903, also at the Salle Favart, was equally successful, as was *Madame Butterfly* in 1906. Leoncavallo's *Pagliacci* triumphed in Bordeaux in 1894 before it was heard at the Opéra in 1902. But whereas audiences were enthusiastic, French critics and composers were nearly unanimous in denouncing the new Italian School as artistically inferior to the French version. The staging of *Pagliacci* at the Opéra-Comique in 1910 was the pretext for a critical onslaught on *verismo* and an official protest led by a group of librettists and composers (including Bruneau and Lecocq) accusing the Favart directorship of partiality to the Italian repertory.[2] With his customary prudence, Massenet, well aware of the influence he exerted on contemporary Italian music, stayed aloof from the polemic; Saint-Saëns and Charles-Marie Widor also adopted a moderate attitude.

Under Carré's leadership, the Opéra-Comique retained its artistic edge until 1914. There, in addition to *Louise* and *Pelléas*, the most advanced operas of the period – and some of the most popular – were premiered. There d'Indy, Bruneau, Dukas, Ravel, Ropartz, and Magnard could be heard next to less avant-garde works – though not necessarily less dramatically or musically successful – by Massenet, Hahn, Erlanger, Leroux, Rabaud, Lazzari, and Laparra. The core repertory remained distinct from the one of the Opéra and included works with spoken dialogue (*Carmen* for one). Most new works premiered at the Salle Favart, whether they identified themselves as drames lyriques or not, were sung throughout. Inevitably, this led to questions about the future of opéra-comique as a genre. By 1912 most respondents to a survey launched by the magazine *Excelsior* felt that it was moribund.[3] Massenet was one of the rare dissenting voices but – by a symbolic coincidence – he was himself dead by the time his response was published.

At the Opéra, meantime, the decade preceding the First World War was marked by financial difficulties and artistic indirection. The situation changed in 1914 with the appointment of Jacques Rouché, who after a successful business career had taken on with equal success the directorship of the Théâtre des Arts in Rouen in 1910.[4] Rouché went a long way towards restoring the Opéra's fortunes, commissioning new works from modernist composers like Albert Roussel and Maurice Emmanuel, and opening the Palais Garnier to more up-to-date styles of production. By the 1920s the Opéra had recovered its artistic edge over the Opéra-Comique.

While Massenet's late works and the careers of Dukas, Fauré, Magnard, Bloch, Ravel, and Roussel deserve special consideration, French operas of the period can also be examined according to the three broader themes of *verismo*, regionalism, and the return to classical antiquity. Four prominent Belle Époque composers – Erlanger, Pierné, Février, and Rabaud – are less easily classifiable.

Messager and Hahn made the finest contributions to operetta, which flowered throughout the Belle Époque and the 1920s – a flowering that, in retrospect, was also a twilight. Finally, we will survey the involvement with French opera of two inescapable figures in the Paris of the period, Satie and Stravinsky.

Late Massenet

Behind his affable, almost obsequious façade, Massenet went through frequent mood swings. After *Cendrillon* (1899), he apparently considered giving up composition. As it turned out, the last 12 years of his life were remarkably creative. *Grisélidis* (1901), oddly, was his last work premiered at the Opéra-Comique, where he totaled more performances than any other living composer.[5] This setting of the tale of the patient Griselda was adapted by Eugène Morand and Armand Silvestre from their play, staged at the Comédie-Française in 1891. A serious fairy tale, it mixes sinister and farcical elements in its depiction of the Devil, in the tradition of Berlioz and Gounod, except that the Devil here is partnered by his wife. The title role was premiered by Bréval, while Fugère sang the Devil and Dufranne (the original Golaud) the Marquis de Saluces, Grisélidis's husband. This beautiful work has not had an international exposure on a par with its merit, despite stagings in New York in 1910 and in Chicago in 1917.[6]

Le jongleur de Notre-Dame (1902) began Massenet's association with the Monte Carlo opera, where six more of his works were first staged. Maurice Léna's libretto, inspired by a short tale by Anatole France, might have seemed an unfashionable, even provocative choice in the context of the anticlerical laws that followed the Dreyfus Affair. It is the deceptively simple story, set in fourteenth-century Cluny, of a poor juggler bullied by the abbot of the great Benedictine monastery into becoming a monk. There he is scorned by his learned brothers (with musical shades of *Die Meistersinger*) but decides to offer the Virgin all he has – a private performance of his songs and dances in the chapel. As the scandalized monks are about to stop him, the statue of the Virgin miraculously comes alive and the juggler dies in ecstasy. For this opera without women[7] – save for the opening chorus and two angelic voices at the end – Massenet has produced a score of utmost refinement[8] and almost uncanny emotional power, especially in the Act 2 "Romance" in which Boniface, the monastery cook, consoles Jean with the medieval legend extolling the humble sage at the expense of the haughty rose. Long popular at the Opéra-Comique, the work has not been heard in Paris in decades, but its episodic revivals (in Boston for its centenary, in Saint-Étienne at the 2005 Massenet festival) have demonstrated that its appeal remains intact.

There could hardly be a greater contrast between *Le jongleur* and *Chérubin*, loosely adapted by the popular playwright Francis de Croisset, in collaboration with Henri Cain, from Croisset's play focusing on the sentimental education of a 17-year old aristocrat, loosely based on Beaumarchais's character. Unlike the play, the opera (at Massenet's insistence) takes place in Spain, but it is not a sequel to *Le Mariage de Figaro*. Premiered at Monte Carlo in 1905, with Mary Garden *en travesti*, the work is a high-spirited musical comedy, occasionally tinged with melancholy. The musical language harks back both to the eighteenth century of *Manon* and to the Spain of the ballet of *Le Cid*. Less popular at first than other Massenet operas, the work was recently revived for Frederica von Stade and Susan Graham.[9]

Massenet showed his versatility again the following year with the mythological tragedy *Ariane*. Mendès, the librettist, was a longtime Wagnerian, but here he deliberately returned to the Quinault tradition, as if to follow Nietzsche's plea for Mediterranean counter-models to Wagner's Nordic mythology.[10] We follow the story of the Greek heroine from Theseus's victory over the Minotaur until her abandonment by Theseus on the island of Naxos and her suicide attempt by drowning after Theseus and Phaedra have sailed away. Act 4 is set in Hell, where Aridane, like a female Orpheus, wins the heart of Persephone with a gift of roses in order to bring back her sister to earth. With *Ariane* Massenet produced one of his most luscious scores, which seems to anticipate late Strauss. Bréval starred in the demanding title role, partnered by the heroic tenor Lucien Muratore and Louise Grandjean, the Opéra's first *Götterdämmerung* Brünnhilde, as Phaedra. The short part of Persephone was sung by the young contralto Lucy Arbell. Granddaughter of Sir Richard Wallace, the British collector and philanthropist, she was never popular with critics. Massenet was fascinated by her acting abilities and capacity for combining speech and singing. *Ariane* thus represented the first time that a few spoken words were heard at the Opéra.

Arbell starred the following year at Monte Carlo in *Thérèse*. The two acts of this "drame musical" are set during the French Revolution. The heroine, torn between her affection for her husband André and her love for the aristocrat Armand, eventually resists the latter's entreaties and joins André in death when he is led to the guillotine. In the opera's closing moments, as she watches with horror the cart carrying her husband away, Thérèse suddenly shifts from singing to spoken declamation – one of Massenet's most intense and dramatic melodramas, its violence contrasting with the melancholy, autumnal color of the first act. When the work reached the Opéra-Comique in 1911, it was presented in a double bill with Ravel's *L'heure espagnole*.

Massenet suffered a setback in May 1909 with *Bacchus*, the sequel to *Ariane*. Withdrawn after five performances at the Opéra, it has never been revived nor staged anywhere else.[11] Critics were particularly (one would argue unjustly) harsh with Mendès's philosophical, poetic libretto, set in India, and pitting Bacchus's celebration of wine and love against Buddhist asceticism.[12] They also objected to the Prologue, in which the text was spoken throughout – not by singers, remarkably, but by three Comédie-Française actors. Conservative Opéra audiences were evidently not ready for such innovations.

The composer took his revenge in 1910 with *Don Quichotte*, premiered at Monte Carlo with Fedor Chaliapine in the title role and Arbell as Dulcinée – not a simple peasant girl but a coquettish belle in this version, based by Cain not directly on Cervantes but on the 1904 play by Jacques Le Lorrain, *Le chevalier de la longue figure*. The Spanish setting gave Massenet one more opportunity for colorful, festive music in Acts 1 and 4, contrasting with the pastoral Act 2 and a death scene treated with great sobriety. Equally remarkable is Massenet's skill in fashioning miniature forms, such as the exquisitely crafted trio between Dulcinée and her suitors in Act 4. Highly successful at the time, but comparatively neglected in the decades immediately following the Second World War, the work has been restored to the repertory by basses, from Boris Christoff to Samuel Ramey.[13]

The last work premiered in Massenet's lifetime was *Roma* (1912), a stark tragedy adapted by Cain from Alexandre Parodi's play *Rome vaincue* (1876), set at the time of the Punic Wars. The heroine, the vestal Fausta, has forsaken her vows of chastity and is sentenced to die. Less lucky than Spontini's heroine in *La vestale* (1807), she is nonetheless spared being buried alive by her blind mother, Posthumia (Arbell at the Monte Carlo premiere), who, out of mercy, stabs her. The work's classical sobriety will surprise anyone who associates Massenet with the sensuous phrases of *Hérodiade* and *Manon*. The patriotic flavor, no doubt related to the tensions that preceded the First World War, is also surprisingly restrained.

When Massenet died in August 1912,[14] he left three completed works that received posthumous premieres. *Panurge*, staged at the Gaîté-Lyrique in Paris in 1913 with the great bass Vanni-Marcoux in the title role and Arbell as his wife Colombe, is one of the rare French operas based on Rabelais, as well as Massenet's single overtly comic work – belying the acute suffering caused by his cancer when he composed it. *Cléopâtre* was mounted at Monte Carlo in 1914, not with Arbell as the composer had intended, but with the contralto role transposed up for the handsome soprano Maria Kouznetzoff – originally trained as a ballet dancer in St Petersburg – who subsequently married a member of the Massenet family. Despite a production at Chicago in 1916, the work, which loosely follows Shakespeare's *Antony and Cleopatra*, is among Massenet's least performed. This is even more true of *Amadis*, a medieval tale of twin brothers (one a tenor, one a contralto) fighting for the hand of the same woman. Massenet had worked on the opera off and on since 1902, completing it shortly before he died in August 1912. Premiered at Monte Carlo in 1922, and staged in Bordeaux and Geneva, it has never been seen in Paris.

Massenet's late career, as we have seen, demonstrates the versatility (often unfairly dismissed as eclecticism) and almost obsessive quest for self-renewal of a composer whose place in the history of French opera – comparable to a Puccini or a Strauss – has yet to be fully acknowledged in his own country.

Paul Dukas

Although his place in the history of French music is secure, Paul Dukas (1865–1935) owes it to an unusually small body of works: only 12 compositions published in his lifetime. His one opera, *Ariane et Barbe-Bleue*, unquestionably numbers among the outstanding works of its decade.

Dukas was born in Paris to an Alsatian Jewish family (the original name was Dockes).[15] He entered the Conservatoire in 1880, studying harmony with Dubois and composition with Guiraud. Having lost the Prix de Rome to Erlanger in 1888, he became a music critic. The success of his symphonic poem *L'apprenti sorcier* in 1897 suddenly propeled him to the front rank among French composers of the younger generation. In 1899 he approached Maeterlinck about *Ariane et Barbe-Bleue*, which the Belgian writer had conceived from the outset as a play to be set to music and a vehicle for his wife Georgette Leblanc, a wish Dukas loyally respected, while making suggestions to Maeterlinck about the revision of the text.[16] The music was completed in 1906 and Carré, despite misgivings about Leblanc, accepted it for the Opéra-Comique where the premiere, delayed by various illnesses,[17] finally took place on 10 May 1907.

Freely drawn from the Perrault tale, already treated by Grétry and Offenbach, the opera begins as Bluebeard, to the ominous grumbling of peasants in the neighborhood, leads into his castle his new wife Ariane. She and her nurse are alone for most of the act, during which Ariane opens in succession the first six chambers. The one filled with diamonds, while highlighting Dukas's métier as an orchestrator, is followed by the passage that comes closest to an aria, "Ô mes clairs diamants." The underground song of Bluebeard's previous wives, heard when the forbidden chamber is opened, is another unforgettable moment in the score. When Bluebeard – who has little to sing throughout the opera – reappears and threatens Ariane, the peasants rush in to her defense but she dismisses them. In the second act Ariane meets the imprisoned wives, all named after the heroines of other plays by Maeterlinck – Mélisande among them. In the vault Ariane discovers huge shutters and opens them, liberating a great gush of light and leading the wives to their freedom. In Act 3, while the wives adorn themselves with diamonds found in the castle, Bluebeard's return is announced. The peasants capture him and bring him, bound, for his victims to avenge themselves. But Ariane sets him free and, leaving him with his wives, departs, alone, towards a new future.

This philosophical allegory of liberation (the subtitle is "La délivrance inutile") perplexed contemporary critics. They generally praised the music, even though Leblanc's performance was not universally admired. Inevitable comparisons were drawn with *Pelléas*. Debussy's own view, expressed in a conversation with the Italian conductor Vittorio Gui, was that *Ariane* was a masterpiece, but not French music.[18] To put it more positively, Dukas's full-blooded music and rich orchestration perhaps sounded more like Rimsky-Korsakov, Strauss or Stravinsky than music from a French tradition, while the work's message – which explored issues that came to the fore only decades later – was universal. The opera's international success seemed to prove the point. Within the next few years, *Ariane* was staged in Vienna (under Zemlinsky), Brussels, New York (with Geraldine Farrar, under Toscanini), Buenos Aires (also under Toscanini), Madrid, Milan, Turin, and Bologna. In 1935, the year of Dukas's death, the work entered the repertory of the Opéra, with Germaine Lubin as Ariane.

Dukas toyed with other projects, but *Ariane et Barbe-Bleue* remained his single opera. In 1928 he was appointed professor of composition at the Paris Conservatoire, where his pupils included Olivier Messiaen.

Gabriel Fauré

Gabriel Fauré (1845–1924) came to opera at an unusually late stage in his career.[19] Originally from Pamiers, in the foothills of the Pyrenees, he was educated from 1854 until 1865 at the music school founded in Paris by Niedermeyer in 1853; his teachers included Saint-Saëns. He then embarked on a career as organist and choirmaster, first in Rennes (1866–70), then at various Parisian churches, especially the Madeleine as of 1877. Introduced by Saint-Saëns to Pauline Viardot, he was briefly engaged to her daughter Marianne but eventually married the daughter of the sculptor Emmanuel Frémiet.

Fauré's theatrical debut was stage music for a revival of Alexandre Dumas's 1837 tragedy *Caligula* at the Odéon in 1888. For the same theater the following year he supplied music for Edmond de Haraucourt's adaptation of *The Merchant of Venice*, entitled *Shylock*. In 1898, after Debussy had been approached and declined, Fauré also wrote music for the London premiere of Maeterlinck's *Pelléas et Mélisande*, deriving from it the suite that is generally considered his symphonic masterpiece. Having succeeded Massenet as professor of composition at the Paris Conservatoire in 1896, he became its director in 1905, a position he kept for 19 years.

Fauré engaged in several operatic projects, notably after plays by Flaubert's friend Louis Bouilhet, or, in 1893, with Mendès, about the affair between Louis XIV and Louise de La Vallière.[20] Fascinated by Wagner, Fauré went to Germany several times in 1879–81 to attend performances of his works, and heard the *Ring* in London in 1882.

Fauré moved closer to opera with *Prométhée*, written for the open-air festival recently founded at Béziers by a local landowner and amateur musician, Fernand Castelbon de Beauxhostes.[21] One of several manifestations of the contemporary revival of interest in classical antiquity, it was also meant as a form of popular theater (local forces were used for the chorus) while introducing an element of cultural decentralization in a country dominated by its capital. Following the success of his *Déjanire* in 1898, Saint-Saëns recommended Fauré, who conducted the revival of his colleague's work the following summer. The text of *Prométhée* was adapted from Aeschylus by André-Ferdinand Herold – grandson of the composer of *Zampa* – and the decadent writer Jean Lorrain (1855–1906).[22] Fauré wrote the music in a few months and received help from Charles Eustace, conductor of the military band at Montpellier, for the orchestration – which includes 13 harps (18 when the work was revived the following year) and large woodwind and brass sections. *Prométhée* combines spoken roles played by actors (Prometheus himself and Pandora), sung roles, dancers, and elaborate choral parts.

Prométhée was premiered in late August 1900 – one day after the scheduled date, when a violent storm had interrupted the proceedings – with as many as 800 performers and before an audience of 10,000. It was also heard at the Paris Hippodrome in 1907, under acoustically disastrous conditions. Fauré reorchestrated it during the First World War and it was heard in this new form at the Opéra in 1917.

Despite the appellation "tragédie lyrique," *Prométhée* was not strictly speaking an opera. Fauré's filled the gap with *Pénélope*, a project born at a dinner at Monte Carlo in 1907 with Bréval, who suggested both the topic and the librettist, the playright René Fauchois (1882–1962),[23] while Gunsbourg, director of the Mante-Carlo opera, offered to host the premiere. Fauré composed the music during his leisure over six consecutive summers. Pressed for time, he realized about two-thirds of the orchestration; the remainder was completed under his supervision by Fernand Pécoud, a student of d'Indy's. Subtitled "poème lyrique," Fauchois's free-verse libretto follows the *Odyssey* narrative but eliminates Telemachus (a casualty of Fauré's requirement that the work be cut down to three acts). The dramatic structure is simple, but effective: the arrival of the disguised Ulysses on Ithaca in Act 1; his long encounter, still disguised, with Penelope in Act 2; the contest with Penelope's suitors, their massacre, and a brief recognition scene in Act 3. Musically, Fauré built the work on a small number of recurrent themes, the two main ones, heard at once in the Prelude, being associated with Penelope and Ulysses respectively. From Wagner, Fauré also retained the principle of continuous musical writing. The vocal lines differ both from the Wagnerian declamation and from Debussy's musical conversation (Fauré, in any event, felt ambivalent about *Pelléas*). There are no arias or ensembles as such, and the musical texture is closer to arioso than recitative. On the other hand, intensely lyrical passages place the work firmly within the great tradition, while the large orchestra and rich instrumentation give the work a symphonic, post-Wagnerian flavor.

The three Monte Carlo performances in March 1913, with Bréval as Penelope and as Ulysses the heroic tenor Charles Rousselière (the Opéra's resident Siegfried), were, by all contemporary accounts, underpowered. The work was well received at the newly opened Théâtre des Champs-Élysées in May of

the same year, with Lucien Muratore as Ulysses, in a production designed by
the Nabi painter Ker-Xavier Roussel. After the First World War, *Pénélope* was
mounted at the Opéra-Comique with Rousselière and Lubin, who also sang
the title role when the work was transferred to the Opéra in 1943. Among
notable stagings was one at the Orange Roman theater in 1923. From Brussels
(in 1913) to Buenos Aires (1962), there have been productions outside France,
but many important opera houses both in Europe and in America have yet to
stage *Pénélope*. Not lacking in dramatic and musical strengths, it may have
suffered from the assumption that Fauré, a great song and chamber-music
composer, was no man of the theatre.[24]

Albéric Magnard

The question of theatrical viability has also been raised in the case of Albéric
Magnard (1865–1914), one of the leading symphonists of his generation but
whose three works for the stage never gained a foothold in the repertory.[25]
A native Parisian (his father was editor of *Le Figaro*), he graduated in law
but turned to music after hearing *Tristan* at Bayreuth in 1886. At the
Conservatoire he joined Massenet's composition class, but a more important
influence was Franck whom he met via his fellow student and friend Guy
Ropartz, who also introduced him to Chausson. Magnard also took instruction from d'Indy, under whose tutelage Magnard wrote the words and music
of his first opera, *Yolande*, in 1888–91. A one-act "drame en musique," it was
staged (with financial backing from Magnard's father) at the Théâtre royal dela
Monnaie in 1893, without much success.

Having completed his Third Symphony in 1896, Magnard turned to the
composition of his second and most ambitious opera, *Guercoeur*. Act 1 takes
place in heaven[26] where the hero, dead for two years, yearns for his former
existence as a democratic political leader. Despite warnings from Truth,
Goodness, and Suffering, Guercoeur is allowed by the heavenly powers to
return to earth. In Act 2, whose setting is left open to the imagination
(medieval Italy or Flanders), those warnings are verified: Guercoeur's wife
Giselle has taken up with his former disciple Heurtal, who, betraying his
master's democratic principles, plans to seize power. In the act's final tableau,
Guercoeur is massacred by his former people and Heurtal becomes dictator. In
Act 3 Truth welcomes back to heaven the twice-dead Guercoeur, consoling
him with the distant prospect of mankind's betterment – the final word of the
opera is "hope." Called by its author "tragédie en musique," *Guercoeur* is a
personal philosophical statement by the high-minded composer whose
Hymne à la justice (1902) was written as a pro-Dreyfus gesture.[27] *Guercoeur* is
an often beautiful – evoking Bruckner rather than Wagner – but static work,
more oratorio perhaps than an opera. Magnard published the piano-vocal
score in 1904 but never heard the work whole in his lifetime. Ropartz, by then

head of the Nancy Conservatoire, arranged for a performance of the third act
in 1908, while the first was heard in Paris in 1910 (under Pierné). It was also
Ropartz who reconstituted the lost orchestration of these two acts after
Magnard's death. In this version *Guercoeur* was mounted at the Opéra in 1931,
with the Franco-American baritone Arthur Endrèze (1893–1975) in the
title role.[28]

More than *Guercoeur*, Magnard's last opera, *Bérénice*, would deserve
modern stagings.[29] The story of the separation between Titus and the Queen
of Judaea he loves had been told by Racine in his 1670 play. But Magnard's
"tragédie en musique" departs significantly from this model, eliminating the
character of Antiochus altogether and adding characters not in Racine's original. Act 1 begins earlier, showing the lovers at Titus's villa while his father
Vespasian is dying. In Act 2 the decision to separate is made and conveyed to
the queen. Act 3 shows the lovers' farewell and Berenice's departure. By a deliberate conflation with her namesake, the heroine of Callimachus's third-century
BC poem "The Lock of Berenice", she dedicates a lock of her hair and her
lost youth to Venus. Contrasting with the heavy symbolism of *Guercoeur*,
Magnard's score introduces a playful note with its use of musical forms: Titus's
Act 2 monologue is built as a fugue, the love scenes are canons, and (by the
composer's own admission) Act 3 is structured like a sonata finale. The work
was politely received when premiered at the Opéra-Comique in 1911.[30]

Magnard's end was in keeping with his uncompromising personality. When,
in early September 1914, German soldiers invaded his Oise village of Baron,
one of them was shot dead. Magnard's house was set on fire in retaliation and
the composer perished in the conflagration, together with the manuscript of
Yolande and the full score of two acts of *Guercoeur*.

Maurice Ravel

Limited in quantity – barely two hours of music – the contribution of Maurice
Ravel (1875–1937) to twentieth-century French opera is among the most
enduring, both *L'heure espagnole* (1911) and *L'enfant et les sortilèges* (1924)
having gained a permanent place in the repertory.[31] At first, the Basque-born
composer hardly seemed to be destined for an operatic career. His leaving the
Paris Conservatoire, where he studied with Fauré and André Gédalge, without
a piano prize in 1895, his similar failure, five years later, to win either a fugue
or composition prize, his five successive rejections for the Prix de Rome – the
ensuing scandal, in 1905, resulted in charges of cronyism – obviously designated him as the opposite of the *bon élève* composer to whom the doors of the
Opéra or Opéra-Comique were open. Yet, paradoxically, by the same year he
was already considered the leading composer of the younger generation and
Debussy's natural heir. Nor did he repudiate the prestige attached to success in
the theater. Only the overture survives from his first operatic project,

Schéhérazade, after which he contemplated adapting Gerhart Hauptmann's play *Die versunkene Glocke*[32] and E.T.A. Hoffmann's tale *Der Sandmann*; as for his decision to tackle *L'heure espagnole* in 1907, it has been attributed to the desire to gratify his ailing father, who died the following year, by showing him he could achieve success in the theater.

Ravel's first opera is a musical setting, with no modification of the text save for a few cuts, of a one-act verse play by Franc-Nohain (1873–1934), pseudonym of Maurice Legrand,[33] whose *L'heure espagnole*, staged at the Odéon in 1904, is a mixture of bawdy and cool irony. The plot, which recalls both Hérold's *Le muletier* and Rossini's *Comte Ory*, revolves on the attempts of a Spanish clockmaker's wife to arrange a tryst with her usual lovers (a lawyer and a poet) in her husband's absence. Frustrated by their failure to perform, she takes advantage of the availability of a serviceable, handsome (if slightly dumb) muleteer. Ravel's music exquisitely parallels the deadpan detachment of Franc-Nohain's text. After accepting the work for the Opéra-Comique in 1908, Carré had cold feet over the risqué overtones and kept postponing the production, even though the piano-vocal score had appeared and the orchestration was ready. Finally, *L'heure espagnole* was premiered on 19 May 1911, paired with Massenet's *Thérèse*, which ironically had also long been waiting for its Parisian premiere. In an open letter to *Le Figaro* two days previously,[34] Ravel, without naming Rossini, claimed that his "musical comedy" (as the work was labeled) was intended in the spirit of Italian opera buffa rather than that of the French operetta in the Offenbach-Lecocq tradition.[35] He further explained that he had been attracted by the opportunity to render musically the "atmosphere of unusual and amusing noises" that permeates the clockmaker's shop[36] and to indulge the taste (shared by Bizet, Massenet, Lalo, and Debussy) for Spanish color and rhythms. The reception was mixed. Many listeners and critics – perhaps unprepared for irony by the prevailing earnest Naturalism of the operatic stage – were puzzled by what they saw as a jarring contrast between the refined musical language and the crude subject matter, and further disconcerted (as they had been in the *Histoires naturelles*) by Ravel's deliberately informal prosody, eliding the sacrosanct "e" mute of conventional poetic diction. Despite an excellent cast headed by Jean Périer[37] and Geneviève Vix, the work disappeared from the Opéra-Comique repertory after nine performances, to be resurrected at the Opéra in 1921. Similarly, it was only in the 1920s and 1930s that *L'heure espagnole* began to be mounted by opera houses internationally.

Shortly after his appointment in 1914 as Opéra director, Rouché commissioned a ballet libretto from Colette (1873–1954), then famous for her *Claudine* series, written jointly with her then husband the music critic Henry Gauthier-Villars (a.k.a. Willy). Colette had met Ravel in the salon of the hostess Marguerite de Saint-Marceaux, and he was enthusiastically nominated as the composer, but the First World War (in which Ravel served in the automobile division) delayed the project. When he received the libretto in 1918, Ravel was in a state of despair and depression caused by the death, in the previous year, of his mother, his single greatest emotional attachment. Only in 1920 did he begin to write the music. The following year, he moved to a house named Le Belvédère in Montfort l'Amaury, on the outskirts of the forest of Rambouillet, filling it with miniatures and bibelots which, as has been noted,[38] call to mind the fairy-tale world of his "fantaisie lyrique" – as the work was now called. The title *L'enfant et les sortilèges* was chosen at a late stage, while the venue for the opening production shifted from Paris to Monte Carlo. Ravel was in attendance for the rehearsals in the early months of 1925, while putting the last touches to the score. The premiere on 21 March, under the baton of the great Italian conductor Victor de Sabata, was an unqualified success, but at the Opéra-Comique the following year opinions were divided. Like *L'heure espagnole*, the work made its way into the Opéra repertory in 1939. Like its predecessor also, the work has taken several decades to be staged internationally – the first Metropolitan Opera production occurred only in 1981[39] – but is now rightly viewed as one of its author's masterpieces.

Whereas *L'heure espagnole* could claim to be derived from a certain operatic tradition, *L'enfant et les sortilèges* can almost be described as *sui generis*, Ravel himself claiming that it was conceived "in the spirit of an American operetta."[40] Yet, unlike the dominant parlando style of *L'heure espagnole*, the vocal lines are more intensely lyrical – closer to Massenet than to Debussy – including coloratura displays in the Fire aria. Similarly, the predominance of dance rhythms (even though they include a ragtime and foxtrot) may evoke the world of nineteenth-century opéra-comique – as well as Ravel's own fascination with the waltz. Above all, as Arbie Orenstein has noted, the work is a compendium of Ravel's styles, from the melancholy nostalgia of the *Pavane* to the humor of the *Histoires naturelles*, from the modernism of *Jeux d'eau* to the neo-classical pastiche of *Le tombeau de Couperin*, from the cool detachment of *L'heure espagnole* to the sense of wonder conveyed by the enchanted garden of *Ma mère l'oye*.

Albert Roussel

One primarily thinks of Albert Roussel (1869–1937) as a composer of symphonic music – including his superb two ballets, *Le festin de l'araignée* (1913) and *Bacchus et Ariane* (1931). He nonetheless contributed to French opera one of the most original works of the period, *Padmâvatî* (1923), and a little-known operetta.[41]

Born to a prosperous family of carpet manufacturers in Tourcoing, northern France, Roussel lost both his parents at an early age – a personal tragedy that affected him deeply. Though he had received a solid musical education, he decided to become a naval officer and spent several years as a midshipman traveling around the world. Yet his frail health, combined with his desire to pursue a musical career, led him to submit his resignation in 1894. He studied with d'Indy at the Schola Cantorum, where he subsequently taught counterpoint.

Padmâvatî originated from a long trip Roussel and his wife Blanche, whom he married in 1908, took to the Orient the following year. In Rajasthan they were impressed with the ruins of the old city of Chitor (now Chittogahr), whose inhabitants, three times in their history, had chosen collective immolation rather then subjugation to Mogul invaders.[42] In 1912 the success of *Évocations*, a symphonic poem with voices and chorus, also inspired by India, attracted Rouché's attention. On his appointment as Opéra director two years later, he approached Roussel with a commission. Roussel chose as a librettist his orientalist friend Louis Laloy (1874–1944), who based his text on a French source, Théodore Pavie's *La légende de Padmani, reine de Tchitor* (1869). Roussel completed the vocal score by the summer of 1914 when he received the news of the declaration of war. Though past the age limit for conscription, he enlisted, serving – like Ravel – in the automobile division until put on medical leave on account of his poor health in March 1918. He then resumed work on his opera, completing the orchestration the following year. The premiere took place on 1 June 1923 (as a double bill with Ravel's *L'heure espagnole*), with the Wagnerian tenor Paul Franz as Ratan-Sen (a part that, closer to our time, was sung by Jon Vickers at the Teatro Colon in Buenos Aires in 1968).

Padmâvatî has an unusual subject and an unusual form. Subtitled "opéra-ballet" by reference to the eighteenth-century tradition,[43] it closely combines in each of its two acts sung passages and dances and pantomime. The plot is set around 1300. Having defeated Ratan-Sen, king of Chitor, the Mogul Alaouddin is smitten by the beauty of his enemy's wife and demands that she be delivered to him, otherwise the city will be destroyed. The ultimatum is rejected. In Act 2, set in the temple of Shiva, Ratan-Sen, vanquished and wounded, vainly tries to persuade Padmâvatî to yield to the Sultan's demand. She chooses instead to join her husband in death, stabs him and places herself on the funeral pyre. Alaouddin arrives at the scene as she is dying. Roussel, who dedicated this longest and most ambitious of his works to his beloved Blanche, clearly saw it as an allegory of the power of conjugal love. His richly evocative score, drawing from oriental musical traditions and including ancient Hindu phrases in choral passages, is still under-appreciated – a fate it shares with many works making demands on both ballet and opera troupes.[44]

Two years after *Padmâvatî*, Roussel returned to the lyric theater with *La naissance de la lyre*, a "conte lyrique" on an ancient Greek subject – the invention of the lyra by the god Hermes. Classical antiquity was in fashion in the 1920s, in the visual arts as well as in music, and opera in particular, but Roussel's work is, once again, original in not being a conventional opera. The librettist, the Greek scholar Théodore Reinach (1860–1928), based his text on the Homeric hymn to Hermes, incorporating into it, in his own translation, the long fragment from the incomplete play by Sophocles, *Ichneutae* (*The Trackers*), which was discovered in 1907.[45] The form adopted by Roussel is also unconventional: like Fauré's *Prométhée*, the work uses both actors and singers, while giving a prominent role to the chorus in imitation of ancient Greek theater. It also features dances – another nod to the world of opéra-ballet – while quoting ancient Greek modes, in the same spirit of authenticity as *Padmâvatî*.

Responding to the *Excelsior* survey in 1912, Roussel had expressed skepticism about the survival of the genre of opéra-comique, expressing his preference instead for opera buffa in the Chabrier tradition.[46] True to his word, he labeled as "operetta" *Le testament de la tante Caroline*, the short three-act work he composed in 1931–2 to a libretto by the librettist, lyricist, and singer Nino (pseudonym of Michel Veber, 1896–1965). The plot, as the title indicates, revolves on the large will of an eccentric aunt, the beneficiary of which is to be the first child born to a niece of hers within a year, failing which the money goes to the Salvation Army. Unfortunately for this institution, the family driver turns out to be the illegitimate son of one of the unmarried nieces. Premiered, in Czech translation, in the historical Moravian city of Olomouc in 1936, the work, owing to its cool critical reception when given at the Opéra-Comique the following year, has seldom been seen since, even in its subsequent one-act revision.

French *verismo*

Few operas premiered in France before *Louise* could be compared to the Italian works characterized under the label *verismo*: works set in or near the contemporary period, realistic in their subject matter and dramaturgy, and eschewing virtuosity in favor of a forthright, naturalistic vocal style.[47] From this point of view, the closest approaches were Massenet's *La Navarraise* and, perhaps even more so, *Sapho*, whereas Bruneau's Zola-inspired works all retain a strong symbolic, even allegorical element.[48] After the success of *Louise*, a number of operas produced before the First World War adopted a naturalistic outlook.[49] Thus an attempt to paint a musical picture of Paris, as Charpentier had done, was made by Arthur Coquard (1846–1910) in *La troupe Jolicoeur*, a "comédie musicale" based on a story by Henri Cain: the first act shows a funfair on 14 July, with snatches from the *Marseillaise* and musical citations from popular opéras-comiques.[50] A student of Franck, Coquard had collaborated with his teacher on the latter's own operas and had completed Lalo's unfinished *La Jacquerie*. In spite, or perhaps because, of its originality, *La troupe Jolicoeur* lasted only 10 performances at the Opéra-Comique in 1902.

Few French operas came closer to actual *verismo* than *La cabrera*, the two-act "drame lyrique" by Gabriel Dupont (1878–1914): it was the only French work to win, in 1904, the first prize at the fourth and last competition organized by the Milanese publisher Edoardo Sonzogno – the same competition that had revealed Mascagni's *Cavalleria rusticana* 14 years before. Cain's libretto, set in the Basque country, is the story of a poor goat-keeper who, to win back the heart of her fiancé on his return from war, kills the child she had in his absence after being seduced. Gemma Bellincioni (1864–1950), the original Santuzza in 1890, premiered the work in Italian at La Scala in 1904 and in the original French at the Opéra-Comique the following year. A student of Massenet, Dupont also scored a success with *La glu* (1910), adapted by Jean Richepin, with Cain's help, from his 1881 novel of the same title, a brutal story of a coquettish Parisienne whose affair with a Breton fisherman ends with her being murdered by the young man's mother. The work was quickly staged in other French theaters. Dupont died of tuberculosis four years later, on the day of the German ultimatum to Belgium that triggered the hostilities of the First World War. His last work, the orientalist fantasy *Antar*, posthumously premiered at the Opéra in 1921, was seen 40 times until 1946.

Richepin, previously mentioned in conjunction with Massenet and Chabrier's *Le roi malgré lui*, was one of the driving forces behind French verismo.[51] He himself adapted his 1883 novel *Miarka, la fille à l'ourse*, a love story set in a romany camp in the Île-de-France, into the "drame lyrique" *Miarka*, set to music by Alexandre Georges (1850–1938), once Franck's assistant at Saint-Clotilde. With Marguerite Carré and Jean Périer in the work, it was one of the successes of the 1905 season at the Opéra-Comique. In 1925 it was transferred to the Opéra in a revised, two-act version.

Richepin's most regular operatic collaborator was Xavier Leroux (1863–1919). Born in the Lazio town of Velletri to a French father and an Italian mother, he studied with Massenet at the Paris Conservatoire and won the Prix de Rome in 1885. His first opera, *Astarté*, lasted 19 performances at the Opéra in 1901. Two years later the "conte dramatique" *La reine Fiammette*, adapted by Mendès from his 1898 melodrama set during the Italian Renaissance, was a hit at the Salle Favart, with Mary Garden in the title role; it was staged internationally and was regularly revived until the late 1930s. Leroux's most enduring success, however, was *Le chemineau*, drawn by Richepin from his 1897 verse play. The unnamed hero of this "drame lyrique" set in rural France ("between Burgundy and the Île-de-France") is a vagrant who follows the dictates of his nomadic nature. Having seduced Toinette, a local girl, he returns, many years later, and meets the son she had by him. Yet, despite her entreaties, he departs once more, following his destiny. Not a modernist, Leroux is capable of stirring and memorable melodies, and his score – from the Chemineau's offstage song heard from the third measure of Act 1 – translates effectively the poignancy of Richepin's drama. Premiered at the Opéra-Comique in 1907 with Dufrane in the title role, the work was widely staged until the late 1930s and has occasionally been revived in recent years. Leroux and Richepin further collaborated on *Le carillonneur* (1913), a "pièce lyrique" adapted from the 1897 novel by the Belgian writer Georges Rodenbach, and on *La plus forte*, drawn (in collaboration with Paul de Choudens) from Zola's *La terre*, the opera being posthumously premiered at the Opéra-Comique in 1924.

Another notable figure in French *verismo*, Raoul Laparra (1876–1943) was born in Bordeaux to a family of Spanish origin. A student of Fauré at the Paris Conservatoire, he won the 1903 Prix de Rome. His Opéra-Comique debut took place in 1908 with *La habañera*, for which he wrote the libretto. The plot is set in a Castillian village, where two brothers, Pedro and Ramón, are in love with Pilar. While Pilar and the peasants are dancing a habañera, Ramón kills Pedro. In the following two acts, the rhythm of the dance, associated with hallucinations in which his dead brother appears to him, eventually drives Ramón mad. Laparra's fascination with Spanish popular music also inspired his next opera, *La jota*, a comparably powerful story set in Aragon during the Carlist Wars (1833–76). This time, the sentimental rivalry involves the village priest, Mosén Jago, who is in love with Soledad, whose fiancé Juan leaves to fight on the Carlist side. The second act – in eerie prefiguration of episodes from the later Spanish Civil War (1936–9) – shows the fight around the church, which collapses on Soledad and her fiancé while the priest himself is tied to the crucifix, during which scene the obsessive dance rhythms rage on. In the end Laparra himself was a war casualty: he died when an aerial bombardment destroyed his Suresnes home during the Second World War.

Regionalism

Other early twentieth-century French operas fall under a category that can be labeled "regionalist," in the sense that their subject, and often their musical style, are rooted in a particular province or region. There was already such a tradition in French opera: we might recall Mondonville's Languedocian pastorale, or Meyerbeer's *Pardon de Ploërmel*, or even Gounod's *Mireille* and Lalo's *Le roi d'Ys*. During the Belle Époque period, the phenomenon can be related in part to some aspects of contemporary nationalism, as expressed in Maurice Barrès's 1897 novel *Les déracinés* – one of the key works of the period – which extols the virtues of local *enracinement* (roots) and excoriates "rootless" cosmopolitanism.

Such preoccupations were certainly shared by d'Indy – whose *Fervaal* is in some ways a regionalist opera – as they were by Déodat de Séverac (1872–1921). A native of the village of Saint-Félix in the Lauragais region near Toulouse, he studied with d'Indy and Magnard at the Schola Cantorum. An early proponent of cultural decentralization, he advocated drawing from folk tradition to rejuvenate a French national style and, true to what he preached, left Paris for good in 1907, first returning to Saint-Félix and eventually settling in the foothills of the Pyrenees in the picturesque Roussillon village of Céret, where he died. Although he is remembered above all for his colorful piano music – notably the suites entitled, significantly, *En Languedoc* and *Cerdaña* – Séverac also wrote for the theater. By 1902 he had begun work on his first and most important opera, *Le coeur du moulin*, premiered at the Opéra-Comique in 1909. Labeled a "pièce lyrique," it has a libretto by Maurice Magre (1877–1941), a Toulouse-born poet, himself involved in the Occitan revival.[52] The plot, set in eighteenth-century Languedoc, deals with the return of a local boy, Jacques, who finds his fiancée Marie married to another man – his impossible dream of recapturing things as they once stood symbolized by the ruined windmill of his childhood. The work is permeated with references to local dance rhythms and popular songs, while invisible choristers represent the "voices of nature"; there is even a friendly owl (a soprano voice), who tries to console Jacques as he prepares to leave again for ever. Dedicated to Misia Godebska, the Polish-born Ballets russes patron and friend of Ravel, the work proved both appealing and disconcerting to Parisian audiences. Séverac's other notable work, *Héliogabale*, performed in home territory at the Béziers arena, was of a totally different kind – pitting the decadence of the sun-worshiping third-century emperor against the pure faith of early Christians, an opposition manifested musically by the mixing of oriental modes with Gregorian chant.

Another composer whose main opera can be categorized as regionalist is Guy Ropartz (1864–1955), whose friendship with Magnard has already been mentioned. Born in the northern Breton town of Guingamp, he studied with Massenet and Franck at the Paris Conservatoire. After heading the Nancy Conservatoire, he became director of the one in Strasbourg, taking over from Hans Pfitzner (the composer of *Palestrina*) when Alsace became French again in 1918. His deep attachment to his Breton roots, despite this exile, is powerfully expressed in *Le pays*. It is based on a short story, "L'Islandaise," by the Breton writer Charles Le Goffic (1863–1932), who adapted it himself into a prose libretto.[53] Set in Iceland, the plot, which involves three characters only (and no chorus), focuses on the irrepressible homesickness felt by Tual, a shipwrecked Breton fisherman rescued by Kaethe, whom he marries. When Kaethe's father, drunk on gin, reveals that a boat from his native Paimpol has arrived at the harbor, Tual rushes away to join it but is swallowed by the quicksands before the eyes of his anguished wife. The intensity of the emotions is expressed in tense vocal writing for the soprano and tenor, while Ropartz's richly orchestrated score combines four principal themes; the main one, evoking a stylized folksong, represents Tual's nostalgia for his home country. The work, premiered at Nancy in 1912, was staged the following year at the Opéra-Comique. Germaine Lubin, in her debut season, sang the role of Kaethe.

Brittany also provides the setting for three of the five operas of Sylvio Lazzari (1857–1944), who, though a native of the Tyrolian city of Bolzano (then Austrian), settled in France in 1882, studying with Gounod and Guiraud at the Paris Conservatoire. The first, *Armor*, a three-act "drame lyrique" premiered in Prague in 1898, is based on a Breton legend (Armor being the Celtic name of Brittany), with strong Wagnerian overtones. More original, *La lépreuse*, a "tragédie légendaire," was composed in the first years of the century but staged at the Opéra-Comique only in 1912. It is based directly on the text of the first play by Henry Bataille (1872–1922), one of the foremost play-wrights of the Belle Époque with his psychological dramas on daring social subjects.[54] The parents of Evroanik, a young Breton, are convinced that Aliette, the girl he loves, is a leper, a claim he vehemently denies to the point of cursing them. But the claim is true, except that Aliette, who loves him, has resolved to do everything not to contaminate him while hoping that the Virgin will cure her. In the dramatic second act her mother, the witch-like Tili (a role premiered by Marie Delna), manipulates her daughter jealously to the point where she lets Evroanik drink out of Aliette's glass.[55] In the third act the young man, now a leper himself, asks for the forgiveness of his parents before being solemnly expelled from the community and led away, with Aliette, to their new life in the leper colony. Lazzari's powerful score makes abundant use of Breton motifs. A sensation at its 1912 Opéra-Comique premiere, the work was performed more than 70 times in that theater until the 1930s. Its shocking subject matter may have hampered its career outside France. Lazzari's next work, *Le sautériot*, was heard first in Chicago and New York in 1918 before it was staged at the Opéra-Comique in 1920. Based on *Ein Frühlingsopfer*, the play by Eduard von Keyserling, it is set in Lithuania and uses folk music from that country. Lazzari returned to a Breton theme with the "drame lyrique" *La tour de feu*, premiered at the Opéra in 1925, and for which he was his own librettist. On an island off the southern coast of Brittany, Naïck, a girl of myste-rious origin, falls under the spell of the captain of a newly arrived Portuguese boat on the day of her wedding to Yves, the lighthouse keeper – a role premiered by Georges Thill. She agrees to follow the captain but her signal is intercepted by her husband, who causes the boat to crash on the reefs while Naïck tries to catch his attention by singing. Naïck throws herself from the lighthouse and, in his grief, Yves sets the lighthouse on fire. Like *La lépreuse*, the work quotes Breton motifs.[56]

The two most notable operas by Charles-Marie Widor (1844–1937) are also rooted in regional folklore. Widor is remembered chiefly as an organist, asso-ciated for many decades with the church of Saint-Sulpice in Paris for which he wrote his 10 organ symphonies, and Franck's successor as organ professor at the Conservatoire.[57] Premiered at the Opéra-Comique in 1905, *Les pêcheurs de Saint-Jean*, subtitled "Scènes de la vie maritime en quatre actes," takes place in the Basque port of Saint-Jean-de-Luz. It is the story of a poor fisherman who, after being denied the hand of his beloved by her father, obtains it at last when he rescues the latter when his boat is caught in a tempest. Local color is provided by sea shanties and even a picturesque "ballet des sardinières." Despite critical praise, the work's Opéra-Comique career was brief – reportedly because of the rivalry between Marguerite Carré, the director's wife, and Claire Friché, Widor's choice for the part of Marie-Jeanne[58] – but it was staged in a few theaters abroad. Widor was less successful with his adaptation of Frédéric Mistral's verse epic *Nerto*, a tale of possession set during the Avignon papacy, which he composed in the early 1890s on a libretto by his fellow Lyonnais Maurice Léna (1859–1928). It was poorly received when finally mounted at the Opéra in 1924.

Classical themes

Unfashionable in the mid-nineteenth century – except, significantly, in comedies like Gounod's *Philémon et Baucis* or satirical parodies like Offenbach's *Orphée aux enfers* and *La belle Hélène* – classical antiquity came back into favor in the late nineteenth and early twentieth century. Saint-Saëns, Massenet, Fauré, Roussel, and Magnard all contributed to this revival, as did Ravel in his 1912 ballet *Daphnis et Chloé*. Even the label "tragédie lyrique" came back into favor.[59]

Forgotten today, Isidore de Lara's *Messaline* was a major Belle Époque success and one of the rare works set to a French text by an anglophone composer since the days of Michael William Balfe. Born Isidore Cohen in London, Lara (1858–1935) had studied with Lalo in Paris. After a few works set to English libretti,[60] he set Gallet's "drame lyrique" *Moïna*, which was premiered at Monte Carlo in 1897. The co-librettists of *Messaline* were Morand and Silvestre, Massenet's collaborators for *Grisélidis* – Silvestre also wrote the text of many of Fauré's and Massenet's mélodies. As the title promises, *Messaline* is a mouthful of Roman decadence that would make Hollywood green with envy: gladiators, an ancient brothel, a vengeful poet thrown into the Tiber, a promiscuous empress, rival brothers. Rapturously received at its 1899 Monte Carlo premiere, this "tragédie lyrique" was quickly staged in London, Bordeaux, Algiers, Antwerp, and The Hague, reaching Paris in 1903 (not the Salle Favart but the Gaîté). In Italian translation it was the first opera by an English composer to be mounted at La Scala.[61] The continued popularity of the work into the late 1930s would suggest that it may not deserve the oblivion into which it then fell. Lara's subsequent operas were set to French texts. Though none rivaled the success of *Messaline*, *Les trois mousquetaires*, adapted by Cain and Louis Payen from Dumas's own dramatization of his novel, had a respectable career in England following its 1921 Cannes premiere.

Another forgotten figure is the Bordeaux-born Jean Nouguès (1875–1932). Following the premiere of the "drame lyrique" *La mort de Tintagiles*, after Maeterlinck, in Paris in 1905 (starring Georgette Leblanc), he was immensely successful with *Quo Vadis?*, adapted by Cain from Henryk Sienkiewicz's 1896 novel (which earned its author the 1905 Nobel Prize for literature). Premiered in Nice in 1909, the opera was staged in Paris the same year and, given the novel's celebrity, soon afterwards in innumerable theaters around the world, retaining its popularity till the 1930s.[62] Excoriated by the critical establishment, *Quo Vadis?* was nevertheless an efficient piece of music theater, the operatic equivalent of a Cecil B. de Mille cinematic epic, well suited to surroundings like the Roman theater at Orange where it was mounted in 1931. One more of Nouguès's 15-odd works inspired by antiquity was the opéra-ballet *La danseuse de Pompéi*, staged at the Opéra-Comique in 1912.[63]

The *Salomé* of Richard Strauss, which opened in Dresden in December 1905, was set to Hedwig Lachmann's translation of Oscar Wilde's play. First staged in Paris in German at the Châtelet in May 1907, it was mounted at the Opéra in 1910 in a French version reset by Strauss himself, with the help of his friend Romain Rolland, to accommodate Wilde's original French version.[64] Almost simultaneously, the Gaîté premiered the *Salomé* by Antoine Mariotte (1875–1944). Like Roussel, the Avignon-born Mariotte had begun a naval career and, also like him, was trained at the Schola Cantorum. Though his *Salomé* was undertaken before Strauss's, its production was nearly blocked by Strauss's German publisher, Fürstner, claiming exclusive rights to the play (whereas Mariotte had, in fact, previously secured permission from the Wilde Estate). A press campaign convinced Fürstner to relent and allow Mariotte's "tragédie lyrique" to be staged in 1908 at Lyons, where the composer taught the piano at the Conservatoire. Soon eclipsed by its rival, Mariotte's *Salomé* is nonetheless an interesting, attractively orchestrated score. It was well received, especially in Paris, where Bréval sang the title role, with Périer as the baritone Herod. Music critics detected the influence of *Pelléas* – by then an inescapable reference.[65] Mariotte's other significant work was the biblical tragedy *Esther, princesse d'Israël*, staged at the Opéra in 1925. He was director of the Opéra-Comique from 1936 until 1939.

Unlike Mariotte and Roussel, the Breton composer Jean Cras (1879–1932) never abandoned his naval career, rising to the rank of rear admiral.[66] A student of Duparc, whose influence can be detected in his music, he set his "drame lyrique" *Polyphème* to the verse play by the symbolist poet Albert Samain (1858–1900), posthumously published in 1901. Unlike Lully's and Handel's more familiar versions, Samain's "drame antique" is a sympathetic portrait of the cyclops. Cras's only opera, it was awarded the first prize in the 1921 competition sponsored by the City of Paris and was staged at the Opéra-Comique in 1923.[67]

Nearly at the same time, the Opéra was preparing the premiere of Charles Tournemire's (1870–1939) "drame lyrique" *Les dieux sont morts*, which, despite five well-received performances in 1924 (and subsequent stagings in Strasbourg and Nantes), was not revived, a fate shared by many new French works of the period. Like Widor – his *bête noire* – Tournemire was a celebrated organist and was among Franck's successors at Sainte-Clotilde.[68] *Les dieux sont morts* was his only published opera – he also wrote one on the Tristan legend and another on St Francis of Assisi – and initially he called it *Chriséis* when he wrote it in 1910–11. A devout Roman Catholic, Tournemire obviously responded on a deep personal level to Eugène Berteaux's libretto, which deals with the disappearance of ancient gods ("The great Pan is dead") and their replacement by Christianity.

The influence of antiquity on French opera in the twentieth century cannot be discussed without mentioning Maurice Emmanuel (1862–1938).[69] Born in Champagne but raised in Burgundy, he studied composition with Delibes at the Paris Conservatoire but ran into a conflict with his teacher over his use of ancient modes and was barred from competing for the Prix de Rome. Yet he persisted, writing a doctoral dissertation on dance in classical Greece and eventually teaching music history at the Conservatoire, where Messiaen was among his students. Emmanuel's lifelong interest in early Greece – a country he never visited – and his knowledge of ancient Greek musical traditions are reflected both in his choice of topics and the musical style of his two operas, both based on Aeschylus. The three-act *Prométhée enchaîné* was composed during the First World War, to Emmanuel's own libretto. Act 1 was performed in a concert in 1919, but the work was heard for the first time in its entirety only 40 years later. Emmanuel's other opera, *Salamine*, also a "tragédie lyrique," was composed in 1921–4 to a libretto adapted from *The Persians* by Reinach, Roussel's collaborator for *La naissance de la lyre*. Completed in 1924, published in 1926, it was subsequently revised and staged in this new version at the Opéra in 1929. The seven performances were well received but the run was interrupted by one of the singers falling ill, and *Salamine* was never staged again. Widely compared after the First World War with the defeat of Germany – a convenient parallel being drawn between the Kaiser and Xerxes[70] – perhaps the subject had by 1929 lost its topicality.

Ernest Bloch

The *Macbeth* of Ernest Bloch (1880–1959), his only opera, unquestionably counts among the distinguished works premiered in France before the First World War.[71] Bloch had studied composition in his native Geneva with Émile Jaques-Dalcroze (1865–1950), himself the author of 25-odd works for the stage.[72] Bloch also spent two years in Brussels, where he was a pupil of the famous violinist Eugène Ysaÿe and of the Belgian composer and Franck disciple François Rasse, whose "drame lyrique" *Déïdamia*[73] was staged in Brussels in 1906. Bloch also studied in Munich and in Paris, but returned to Geneva in 1904 and, instead of embracing a musical career, joined his father's clockmaking business while working on his opera, which he completed in 1910. Unlike his compatriot Gustave Doret (1866–1943), whose "légende dramatique" *Les Armaillis* was staged with some success at the Opéra-Comique in 1906, he had no interest in regionalism, deciding instead to tackle a major work of world literature. His librettist Edmond Fleg (real name Flegenheimer, 1874–1963), also Geneva-born, came from an Alsatian Jewish family. Horrified by the anti-Semitism unleashed by the Dreyfus Affair, he abandoned a promising academic career – he was a graduate of the École normale supérieure – to become a writer and journalist. He devoted most of his literary and critical work to Jewish themes and issues[74] – with the two exceptions of his libretto for Bloch and the one he wrote for George Enesco's *Œdipe*.

Like Piave and Maffei's libretto for Verdi's *Macbeth* (1847–65), Fleg's follows Shakespeare's play fairly closely. The one crucial episode he omitted is Banquo's murder. On the other hand, the murder of Lady Macduff and her children is included, at least in the original version. There Fleg and Bloch depart most significantly from their model, since Malcolm and Macduff come onstage afterwards and discover the murders. The scene, which ends with a developed choral ensemble, was cut in 1938 when the work received its first revival in Naples.[75]

Macbeth is in many respects a post-*Pelléas* opera, even if the violent atmosphere of the Shakespearean tragedy has little in common with the stifling, *demi-teinte* world of Maeterlinck's play. Bloch's use of recurrent motives is also different from Debussy, Bloch deliberately refraining from associating a musical theme with each of his characters. On the other hand, the continuous declamation, which eschews the traditional separation between recitative and arias, while letting every word be heard, is unmistakably indebted to *Pelléas*, as are the bold, modernist harmony and the impressive sense of orchestral color throughout. As in Verdi, but in a very different way, Lady Macbeth's Sleepwalking Scene (treated here as a pure monologue, without the physician and gentlewoman) is one of the work's summits, with its disjointed utterances conveying the character's lapse into insanity.

Premiered in November 1910 at the Salle Favart with Albers and Bréval – to whom the score is dedicated – in the leading roles, *Macbeth* was warmly received by audiences, by then largely familiar with Debussy's idiom. Yet the critical reception was more mixed, and the work left the Opéra-Comique repertory after 15 performances.

Fleg and Bloch also contemplated collaborating on a biblical opera, *Jézabel*, but the project was abandoned in 1918.[76] By then Bloch had moved to America, where he remained until 1930 (having become an American citizen in 1926), and again from 1940 until his death in 1959.

Camille Erlanger

No Belle Époque opera composer combined Wagnerian and *verismo* elements more ambitiously and successfully than Camille Erlanger (1863–1919). A

Parisian, he came from an Alsatian Jewish family.[77] At the Conservatoire he studied with Delibes, winning the Prix de Rome in 1888. His first success, premiered at the Opéra-Comique in 1900, was *Le Juif polonais*, based on a tale by the then famous team of Alsatian writers Émile Erckmann and Alexandre Chatrian, who had themselves adapted the story for the stage in 1869.[78] The main character, Mathis, the last role premiered by Victor Maurel (Verdi's original Iago and Falstaff), is a respectable Alsatian haunted by remorse for having murdered a Jewish peddler many years before. It has been suggested that Erlanger, not being particularly observant, had distanced himself from his Jewish identity;[79] yet the choice of such a subject (and title), like the Dreyfus Affair which had just brought the issue of French anti-Semitism to the fore, can hardly have been insignificant. The work remained Erlanger's longest-lasting success and was revived in France until the 1930s. The composer also chose a Jewish theme – and a Jewish librettist, Mendès – for his next opera, *Le fils de l'étoile*, premiered at the Opéra in 1904. Its subject is the revolt of the Jews of Judea against their Roman occupants in 132–5 CE, led by Bar Kokhba: the title of the opera is based on the Aramaic meaning of his name, "son of the star." Mendès treated the topic freely, less as a historical than as a mythological and allegorical fresco. Bar Kokeba, as he is called in the libretto, abandons his wife Sephora, daughter of the prophet Akiba, in favor of the magician Lilith, while Sephora herself fails in her Judith-like attempt to slay the emperor. As in *Le Juif polonais*, Erlanger's musical language is based on a complex web of leitmotifs (which he called "musical subjects") and earned him plaudits from Wagnerian critics like Destranges and Bruneau, while others found the result heavy-handed and insufficiently lyrical. Strongly cast, *Le fils de l'étoile* was performed 26 times but was not revived after the First World War.

Erlanger undertook an equally ambitious project with *Aphrodite*, a "drame musical" adapted from Pierre Louÿs's 1896 novel. The writer was actively involved in the preparation of the libretto, officially credited to the sole Louis de Gramont (1854–1912).[80] Premiered at the Salle Favart in 1906, *Aphrodite* starred Mary Garden in the role of Chrysé, the Alexandrine courtesan who forces her lover, the sculptor Démétrios, to commit crimes to prove his love, but is forced by him to reveal her guilt and ends up being sentenced to death. For its ancient setting, the work contains *verismo* elements, such as the (offstage) crucifixion of the slave Corinna, falsely accused of the theft committed by Démétrios. The work climaxes with a long duet between Chrysé and Démétrios, unmistakably recalling Act 2 of *Tristan*, as does Erlanger's use of leitmotifs. Yet the work treats its classical subject with originality and sensitivity. It opens with an atmospheric description of an evening on the Alexandria jetty, while the final tableau, a late addition suggested by Albert Carré, shows the burial of Chrysé, mourned by her two lesbian flute-player friends. *Aphrodite* was a major pre-1914 hit at the Salle Favart, reaching 182 performances until it was dropped from the repertory in the mid-1920s.

Erlanger's subsequent work includes the "rêve lyrique" *Hannele Mattern*, adapted by Jean Thorel and Gramont from Hauptmann's *Hannele Himmelfahrt*. Completed in 1910, it was not staged in Erlanger's lifetime, receiving its first performance in Strasbourg in 1950. *L'aube rouge*, a "drame lyrique" set in Russian anarchist milieus, went no further than its Rouen premiere in 1911. *La sorcière* was based on a Sardou play, set in Portugal in the days of the Inquisition and starring Sarah Bernhardt. Sardou's son André adapted it as a "drame musical." Mounted at the Opéra-Comique in 1912 with a brilliant cast that included the young Ninon Vallin (1886–1961) in her debut season, it lasted 26 performances.

Erlanger's last opera, *Forfaiture*, staged posthumously at the Opéra-Comique in 1921 and withdrawn after three performances, was an unusual project, its source being Cecil B. de Mille's 1915 film *The Cheat*. Hector Turnbull's scenario involves a Japanese villain (Sessue Hayakawa) who black-mails an American woman and even brands her between the shoulders with a red-hot iron. Perhaps, despite Erlanger's much-admired métier, the violence that had earned the film such a success in France could not be transferred happily to the operatic stage, especially since *verismo* had been by then upstaged by the horrors of the First World War.

Gabriel Pierné, Henry Février, Henri Rabaud

Gabriel Pierné (1863–1937) came from Metz, like Ambroise Thomas, thanks to whom he entered the Paris Conservatoire at the age of nine.[81] He studied composition with Massenet, winning the Prix de Rome at 19. An exceptionally versatile musician – he succeeded Franck at Sainte-Clotilde but was also an excellent pianist – he became, along with Pierre Monteux, the leading French conductor of his generation while being a respected composer. His operatic output was relatively modest: a light opéra-comique, *La coupe enchantée*, premiered at the Royan casino in 1895 and mounted with success at the Salle Favart in 1905; a Revolutionary historical drama, *Vendée*, staged at Lyons in 1897. His most ambitious work, *La fille de Tabarin*, on a libretto by Sardou and Ferrier which depicts the life of a theatrical troupe in the seventeenth century, in the tradition of Gautier's *Le capitaine Fracasse*, was moderately successful at the Salle Favart in 1901 (with Mary Garden). So was his adaptation of Musset's *On ne badine pas avec l'amour*, which was performed only 10 times on the same stage in 1910, though it was praised by connoisseurs. His best works, the ones arguably most attuned to his affinity with neo-classicism, came after the war: the one-act *Sophie Arnould* (1927), a melancholy homage to eighteenth-century opera, and, especially, *Fragonard*, premiered at the Porte-Saint-Martin in 1934 and revived at the Salle Favart in 1946.

One of the notable operas of the pre-1914 period, Henry Février's *Monna Vanna* was adapted from Maeterlinck's Renaissance tragedy, staged at the

Opéra in 1909. A pupil of Massenet and Fauré – but more obviously influenced by the former and by *verismo* composers – Février (1875–1957) made his debut at the Opéra-Comique with *Le roi aveugle* in 1906. *Monna Vanna*, with Bréval in the title role, was among the more successful new works of the decade and was staged in various opera houses in Europe and America, as well as being revived in Paris until the late 1930s. *Gismonda*, also a Renaissance costume drama after Sardou, received a Chicago premiere in 1919, with Mary Garden in the Sarah Bernhardt role. The work was produced in several theaters, including the Opéra-Comique in the same year, but was not revived.

In an entirely different genre, Henri Rabaud's *Mârouf, savetier du Caire* was the first major French work based on the *Arabian Nights* since Cherubini's *Ali Baba* in 1833. Rabaud (1873–1949), also a pupil of Massenet at the Paris Conservatoire, won the Prix de Rome in 1894. His first opera, the "tragédie musicale" *La fille de Roland*, after Henri de Bornier's heroic play, was staged at the Opéra-Comique in 1904 (and transferred to the Opéra in 1922). Lucien Népoty's *Mârouf* libretto is the story of the poor cobbler who flees from Cairo and marries a princess by pretending to be a rich merchant waiting for the arrival of his caravan – an event that eventually materializes thanks to the intervention of a genii after Mârouf has confessed the truth to the princess and won her heart. Premiered at the Salle Favart in May 1914, the work was among the most widely staged French operas of the period – including productions at La Scala and the Met. A 2001 revival in Marseilles has testified to its continuing popularity.[82] Its originality and charm are due to a blend of unmistakable oriental color and continuous, *Pelléas*-like arioso vocal line, which lets the text speak. Rabaud's other significant work was *L'appel de la mer*, set to his own libretto after J.M. Synge's *Riders to the sea*. It was staged at the Opéra-Comique in 1937, thus coinciding exactly with the premiere of Ralph Vaughan Williams's more famous setting. By then Rabaud had succeeded Fauré as director of the Paris Conservatoire, where he remained until 1941.

André Messager

André Messager (1853–1929), who came from Montluçon in central France, studied at the École Niedermeyer with Fauré and Saint-Saëns.[83] He became an organist to earn a living but it was as a conductor that he made his reputation, becoming music director at the Opéra-Comique where he premiered *Pelléas et Mélisande* in 1902, and he held similar positions at Covent Garden and the Opéra. His first work, the operetta *François les bas bleus*, completed from the score the Lyonnais composer Firmin Bernicat (1843–1883) had left unfinished at his death, was successful at the Folies-Dramatiques in 1883. Although *Le bourgeois de Calais*, an opéra-comique in three acts, flopped at the same theater in 1887, *Isoline*, a "fairy tale in three acts and ten tableaux" on a libretto by Mendès, was well received at the Théâtre de la Renaissance until the bankruptcy of the theater interrupted the run after 60 performances. The strange libretto revolves on two instances of sex-change: Isoline is changed into a boy, Isolin into a girl (both are soprano parts).

International success came to Messager with *La Basoche*,[84] premiered at the Opéra-Comique in 1890, and quickly staged throughout Europe. Albert Carré's only full-fledged libretto, it is set under the reign of Louis XII in the early sixteenth-century and its hero is the poet Clément Marot. It remained for several decades one of Messager's most popular works. Premiered at the Théâtre de la Renaissance in 1893, *Madame Chrysanthème* was based on Pierre Loti's eponymous novel, which also inspired David Belasco's *Madame Butterfly*. A score of considerable refinement, *Madame Chrysanthème* recovered from its unsuccessful initial run and was eventually staged in Chicago and New York in 1920. Also staged in 1893, Messager's *Miss Dollar* is notable above all as one the first French operettas featuring an American heroine. Further discouraged by the failure, in 1896, of *Le chevalier d'Harmental*, based on the novel by Alexandre Dumas set during the Regency, Messager nearly abandoned composition, but was repaid for his change of mind by the success of the operetta *Les P'tites Michu* at the Bouffes-Parisiens the following year, on a libretto by Vanloo and Georges Duval (1847–1919). Set during the First Empire, whose music is cleverly pastiched, this story of two girls raised as sisters and almost identically named (Marie-Blanche and Blanche-Marie) had more than 150 performances. Messager was by then regarded as the successor to Lecocq's "bourgeois" style of French operetta, elegant and refined, and more sentimental than satirical. With the same librettists, Messager confirmed this standing in 1898 with *Véronique*, one of his most enduring successes, with Périer (the future Pelléas) in the role of a flighty Vicomte pursuing a romance with a woman he believes to be a *grisette* (coquettish working girl) and who turns out to be his aristocratic fiancée in disguise. Their two duets – the Donkey Duet and Swing Duet – number among Messager's most popular pages, but the score contains other gems, such as Véronique's letter at the end of Act 2. *Fortunio* (1907), adapted from Musset's comedy *Le chandelier* by the playwrights Robert de Flers and Gaston Arman de Caillavet,[85] also numbers among Messager's masterpieces. Entirely sung, this "musical comedy" is another evidence of the long way the Opéra-Comique had come since the time when it was under the obligation to perform works including at least *some* spoken dialogue.[86]

After a hiatus of several years, Messager returned to the stage with *Béatrice*, also on a Flers and Caillavet libretto. Premiered at Monte Carlo in 1914, and successfully revived as far away as Buenos Aires and Rio de Janeiro, this "légende lyrique" on a religious theme is now among Messager's least-known works. After the First World War, Messager, an anglophile married to an Englishwoman, composed *Monsieur Beaucaire*, a "romantic opera" based by André Rivoire (1872–1930) and Pierre Veber (1869–1942) (brother of Nino) on Booth Tarkington's 1900 novella of the same title (and the basis for a 1924 film with Rudolph Valentino). Set in eighteenth-century London, Messager's operetta was premiered in its English version at Birmingham in 1919. Before the original French was staged in Paris in 1925, the work had a run of 221 performances in London and was applauded in New York and Montreal.

Messager's last works reflect the shift of operettas towards a style closer to the modern musical and incorporating contemporary dance rhythms. Significantly, none had its premiere at the Opéra-Comique but mostly in "straight" theaters. After *La petite fonctionnaire* (1921) Messager produced one of his masterpieces, *L'amour masqué* (1923), a witty comedy by Sacha Guitry, who starred in it with Yvonne Printemps, his second wife. Together they typi-fied a new generation of operetta singers – actors who could sing rather than singers who could act.[87] *Passionnément*, premiered in 1926, also has a most amusing libretto by Maurice Willemetz (1887–1964), a prolific songwriter and lyricist of the interwar period. Partly set on a yacht off the Deauville shore on the Normandy coast, it shows the gradual conversion of an improbable American puritan named Stevenson from Prohibitionist to champagne enthu-siast. In the process, he happily grants his wife a divorce so that she can marry the Frenchman from whom he had tried to acquire an undiscovered oilfield for a small sum of money. Willemetz also wrote the libretto of Messager's final work, *Coup de roulis* (1928), also set on a boat and premiered with the famous stage and film actor Raimu (1883–1946). The infectious high spirits of the music belie the fact that it was written when the composer was very sick: he died a few months later, in February 1929.

Reynaldo Hahn

One of the greatest French operetta composers, Reynaldo Hahn (1874–1947) in fact wrote in a great variety of operatic genres.[88] Born in Caracas to a Venezuelan mother and a German father, he moved to Paris with his family at the age of four and became a naturalized French citizen in 1909. At the Conservatoire, he studied composition with Massenet. By the age of 21, when Heugel published his collection of 20 songs, Hahn was already famous as a composer of mélodies. His first opera, *L'île du rêve*, premiered at the Opéra-Comique in 1898, was inspired by Loti's novel *Le mariage de Loti* (already the source for *Lakmé*). Set, like the original, in the South Seas, it is subtitled "idylle polynésienne." The part of Loti was sung in 1898 by the great lyric tenor Edmond Clément, while the name of the Tahitian heroine was altered from Rarahu to the more singable Mahénu. Critics deplored the (no doubt delib-erate) lack of musical exoticism, while finding the score too overtly indebted to Massenet.[89]

A more ambitious undertaking, *La carmélite*, staged in 1902, also at the Opéra-Comique, was based by Mendès, its librettist, on the story of the liaison between Louis XIV and Louise de La Vallière, though, curiously, they are not formally identified but simply called The King and Louise, while Bossuet is "The Bishop" and Mme de Montespan "La marquise Athénaïs." With Emma Calvé in the title role, the work was a success, even causing a mini-scandal because of the scrupulous stage reconstitution of a religious ceremony (Louise's formal admission into the Carmel) in the fourth act.[90] As Philippe Blay has perceptibly argued, Hahn's music, with its pronounced neo-classical flavor, was almost ahead of its time, dominated by blockbuster *verismo* and symbolist works, and this may explain why the work left the repertory after 27 performances.

Following this relative disappointment, Hahn focused on his career as conductor (and singer) and did not return to the operatic stage until after the war. *Nausicaa*, an opéra-comique set to a libretto by Fauchois and based on Homer's *Odyssey*, had a brief career after its Monte Carlo 1919 premiere.[91] On the other hand, *Ciboulette*, which opened at the Théâtre des Variétés in 1923, is not only one of the finest operettas of the period, it also became Hahn's most successful work for the stage.[92] Set towards the end of the Second Empire, Flers and Croisset's libretto gives Hahn opportunities for parody and pastiche, including a literal quotation of the beginning of the Saint-Sulpice Duet from Massenet's *Manon* in Act 1. The popular composer Olivier Métra (1830–1889), the author of the proverbial "Quadrille des Lanciers," features as a (spoken) character. The part of Ciboulette, a market-girl at Les Halles like Clairette in Lecocq's *La fille de Madame Angot*, was sung at the premiere by Edmée Favart (1885–1941), while Périer found his last great role as the aging Bohemian Duparquet.

Hahn's gift for neo-classical pastiche is also in evidence in his musical comedy *Mozart* (1925), premiered at the Théâtre Édouard VII with Yvonne Printemps in the title role. The play by Guitry, who himself appeared as the cynical Baron Grimm, deals with Mozart's unsuccessful second Parisian visit of 1778. Hahn and Guitry collaborated on one more musical comedy, *Ô mon bel inconnu* (1933), the plot of which recalls Jerry Bock's Laszlo-based musical *She Loves Me*. The most important work of Hahn's later period, however, was *Le marchand de Venise*, adapted by Michel Zamacoïs from Shakespeare's comedy *The Merchant of Venice*. Hahn had begun to work on the project during the First World War (in which he fought), originally intending the role of Portia for Mary Garden.[93] A full-fledged opera, premiered at the Palais Garnier in 1935, with the distinguished bass André Pernet as Shylock, the work is nevertheless conceived in a Mozartian spirit. Half-Jewish on his father's side, though he successfully petitioned for "Aryan" status, Hahn spent the years of the Nazi Occupation of France quietly in the South, eventually moving to Monte Carlo.[94] After the Liberation, he was briefly appointed head of the Opéra. An individualist with no ties to musical cliques or movements, he has paid the price for his aloofness by being unjustly neglected by the operatic establishment since his death (with the exception of a revival of

Le marchand de Venise at the Opéra-Comique in 1979). Yet it can only be a matter of time before his work for the stage catches up with his reputation as a songwriter.

The twilight of classical operetta

French operetta continued to flourish in the first three decades of the twentieth century. Dominated by the masterpieces of Messager, especially in the earlier period, and Hahn in the 1920s and 1930s, the genre underwent a significant evolution in the years following the First World War. Whereas the production of Lecocq, Varney, Audran, Planquette, and Ganne, discussed in the previous chapter, is clearly rooted in the opéra-comique tradition, works produced after 1918, perhaps as a result of the gradual disappearance of opéra-comique as a living genre, came to resemble more and more the kind of musical comedy pioneered at the same time on the other side of the Atlantic, with reduced orchestral forces and a vocal style closer to popular song than to classical music. This evolution can also be seen as a return to the traditional, café-concert French operetta of the kind illustrated by Hervé, very different dramatically and musically from the sentimental, "bourgeois" kind in favor since the 1870s, with waltz and polka rhythms giving way to foxtrot and charleston. By the same token, operetta now tended to be performed by actors who could sing – very well in cases like Printemps – rather than by classically trained vocalists.

Along with Messager and Ganne, who was still active until the war, the leading French operetta composer of the early twentieth century was Claude Terrasse (1867–1923). He was from the small town of Le Grand-Lemps[95] in the Isère, near Berlioz's native La Côte-Saint-André. An organist, Terrasse was one of Olivier Messiaen's predecessors at the Trinité church in Paris. He was in this position when – in a situation that brings to mind Hervé's *Mam'zelle Nitouche* – he supplied stage music in 1896 for the premiere of Alfred Jarry's *Ubu roi*, which marked the birth of the modern French comic theater. As operetta composer, Terrasse worked with several distinguished librettists: the great humorist Tristan Bernard (1866–1947) for *La petite femme de Loth* (1898); Franc-Nohain for *La fiancée du scaphandrier* (1901); Maurice Donnay (1859–1945) for *Le mariage de Télémaque* (1910); Herold for *La farce du poirier* (1916), one of his last (and best) works; and, especially, Flers and Caillavet, with whom he collaborated on *Les travaux d'Hercule* (1901), *Le sire de Vergy* (1903), and *Monsieur de La Palisse* (1904), three of his greatest successes. Reviewing *Le sire de Vergy* for the periodical *Gil Blas* in 1903, Debussy praised Terrasse's métier, while regretting the absence of a certain "unbuttoned" quality he admired in Offenbach and Hervé.[96]

Perhaps Debussy, had he not died in 1918, might have welcomed the evolution of operetta in the following decade, and not just the later works of Messager and Hahn but also the uproarious creations of Christiné and Yvain.

The Geneva-born Henri Christiné (1867–1941) was largely self-taught as a composer. He first wrote songs for his wife, a café-concert singer, which made him already famous by 1914. His first important commission came during the First World War. Originally intended for a tiny theater installed by the impresario Gustave Quinson in such a way that it would withstand aerial bombings (and thus called "L'Abri"), *Phi-Phi* was instead premiered at the Bouffes-Parisiens on 12 November 1918, one day after the Armistice, and was an instantaneous hit. The libretto by Willemetz and the humorist Fabien Sollar can be described as a modern take on Offenbach's mythological farces of the 1860s. Phi-Phi is the sculptor Phidias, looking for a model who could pose for a statue of Virtue, while his wife's lover ingratiates himself by offering to pose for a statue of Love. The model turns out to be Aspasia, who, by the end of the work, is ready to "move in" with a rising statesman named Pericles. This rapid summary may sound unpromising, but the text's outrageous anachronisms are actually very funny and Christiné's music, originally scored for an orchestra of 12 musicians, matches it in vivacity and verve. The work lasted three years at the Bouffes-Parisiens and was also widely popular abroad. In 1921 Willemetz and Christiné collaborated again on *Dédé*, starring Maurice Chevalier. The setting this time is modern – a Parisian shoe-store, with a riotous visit from a trade-union delegation in Act 2. Other notable Christiné operettas were *Madame* (1923), with Willemetz and Yves Mirande, and *P.L.M.* (acronym for Paris-Lyon-Méditerranée, the train line going from Paris to the Côte d'azur), on a libretto by Rip (pseudonym of Georges-Gabriel Thenon, 1884–1941). Christiné's later collaborations with the operetta composer Tiarko Richepin, the writer's son – *Au temps des merveilleuses* (1934), *Yana* (1936) – were lavish spectacles of the kind in which the Châtelet came to specialize in the decades immediately following the Second World War, and are no match for the gaiety and freshness of his early work.

The other composer who came of age in the 1920s was Maurice Yvain (1891–1965). A student of Xavier Leroux at the Paris Conservatoire, he served as a soldier for seven consecutive years (the First World War having started when his military service was about to end). His first work, characteristic of the escapist climate of the Années folles, was for Casino de Paris revues.[97] In 1922 *Ta bouche*, on a libretto by Willemetz and Mirande, brilliantly launched his career in operetta. The three acts, each set in a different casino (easily identifiable as Trouville, Deauville, and Évian), are a lively social satire of the leisured classes, with louche aristocrats and easy divorces (a relatively new phenomenon, especially in operetta). Musically, the gem of the work is the quartet "Puisqu'un heureux hasard." Two years later, Yvain, echoing the title of his debut work, gave *Pas sur la bouche* at the Théâtre des Nouveautés. The title of André Barde's libretto refers to the abhorrence of a French kiss displayed by the work's American hero, Eric Thomson – a principle he happily sheds at the end of the work, the pretext for a hilarious duet with his new admirer, Mlle de Poumaillac.

Like Christiné, Yvain gave a star part to Maurice Chevalier in *Là-haut* (1923), a fantasy partly set in heaven – with the hero Évariste being granted a return to earth in the manner of Alim in *Le roi de Lahore* – until it all turns out to have been a dream. Among Yvain's other successes are *Gosse de riche* (1924), *Un bon garçon* (1927), and *Bouche à bouche* (1936), the final instalment of his "bouche" trilogy. Like Christiné's work, Yvain's later output was of the Châtelet superproduction kind – *Au soleil du Mexique* (1945) or the highly popular *Chanson gitane* (1946) – and never recaptured the charm of his earlier operettas.

Erik Satie

Strictly speaking, Erik Satie (1866–1925) has left no opera. Yet he contemplated operatic projects, going back to his brief association with the Rosicrucian "Sâr" Joséphin Péladan in the early 1890s.[98] Debussy's *Pelléas et Mélisande* was for him an "absolutely astounding" revelation. Tantalizingly, only a few sketches survive of the unpublished play with music, *Pousse l'amour* – a title referring to an aphrodisiac drink – on a text (also lost) by Maurice de Féraudy and Jean Kolb. Commissioned by Satie's friend the cabaret singer Paulette Darty, it was performed in 1907 at the Comédie royale in Paris and revived at Monte Carlo in 1913 under a different title (*Coco chéri*), this time as a full-fledged operetta.[99]

Although the label "comédie lyrique" attached to *Le piège de Méduse* (1913) can be interpreted as a typical Satie joke, since no singing is involved, a real question arises concerning the genre of *Socrate*, widely considered Satie's masterpiece and, in the words of Ornella Volta, "a high point in Western music of the twentieth century."[100] Commissioned in 1917 by the American Singer sewing-machine heiress and art patron Winnaretta, princesse de Polignac, for performance in her salon, it was initially planned as a sort of melodrama (spoken text on a musical background) and first entitled *Vie de Socrate*. It then became a sung work, with the libretto (Satie's own term) assembled from extracts from Plato's *Symposium*, *Phaedrus*, and *Phaedo* in Victor Cousin's mid-nineteenth century translation: a "Portrait of Socrates" in a form of a dialogue between Alcibiades and Socrates, followed by a conversation between Socrates and Phaedrus on the banks of the Illissus, and a final monologue, the narrative of Socrates's death in *Phaedo*. Although the characters are all male, it is scored for a quartet of women's voices (two sopranos, two mezzo-sopranos), one of whom has a solo part. The subtitle "drame symphonique" suggests a concert opera. After extracts had been performed at the princess's salon in 1918, Part 1 was heard at Adrienne Monnier's bookstore "La Maison des amis des livres" the following year, before an audience that included André Gide and James Joyce. The first public performance with orchestra took place in 1920 with Marya Freund in the solo part, and the first staging occurred in Prague in May 1925.[101]

Another tantalizing project that came to nothing was the opéra-comique *Paul et Virginie* on a libretto by Jean Cocteau and his young friend Raymond Radiguet (1903–1923). Planned in the spring of 1920, it was supposed to be staged, first at the Champs-Élysées, then at Diaghilev's Ballets russes, with sets and costumes by André Derain, and Satie envisaged "Rossini-style" music.[102] But the project was abandoned and little music written towards it has surfaced.

Satie did, however, make a distinguished contribution to French opera with the new music he wrote for the Ballets russes production of Gounod's *Le médecin malgré lui*, staged at Monte Carlo in January 1924. By design or by accident, his name was omitted from the program.[103]

Igor Stravinsky

The presence of Igor Stravinsky (1882–1971) in a history of French opera may seem incongruous. To be sure, Stravinsky would not be discussed in a history of French *music*. Yet the fact that two of his stage works were conceived to a French text justify including him in this study. What *kind* of opera they are is another issue, which in fact gives Stravinsky an interesting position vis-à-vis the evolution of the genre in France.[104]

Though Stravinsky's first opera, *The Nightingale*, actually received its first performance at the Opéra in May 1914 (which explains why it is more commonly referred to by its French title, *Le rossignol*, than as *Solovey*), it was composed on a Russian libretto by Stepan Mitusov and presented – under Pierre Monteux, but in Russian – as part of the Ballets russes season. At the same time, Stravinsky was issuing statements such as "I dislike opera" or "Opera does not attract me at all" that seem to preclude any future involvement in the genre. Accordingly, his next operatic venture, *Bayka pro lisu, petukha, kota da barana* (*Fable of the Vixen, the Cock, the Cat, and the Ram*), composed in Switzerland in 1915–16 and better known under its French title *Renard*, is an opera only in an unconventional sense, anticipating post-1945 forms of musical theater, with its cast of 4 animal characters and an orchestra of 15. Though the manuscript presented to Stravinsky's Chilean patron Eugenia Errazuriz has both Stravinsky's Russian and Charles-Ferdinand Ramuz's (1878–1947) French text superimposed, the work was conceived in Russian.

Musical theater – rather than opera – is also an appropriate description for *L'histoire du soldat*, Stravinsky's second collaboration with Ramuz, this time conceived directly in French. As Eric Walter White has noted, its inclusion in Alfred Loewenberg's *Annals of Opera* may seem odd since it features no sung role.[105] The published score carries no generic labeling, save for the adjectives "lue, jouée et dansée," which do not suggest opera either. In his *Souvenirs sur Igor Strawinsky*, Ramuz refers to it as a "play," while the composer, much later, referred to the text as a "libretto" and spoke of a "dramatic spectacle."[106] On the other hand, the peculiar kind of declamation involved and the way text and music interplay put the work in a different category from plays with stage music, evoking the melodramas of nineteenth-century French opera.

"Melodrama" was the label Stravinsky used to characterize *Perséphone*, which he subsequently discussed as belonging to his operatic output. This might make it his only "French opera," albeit in an unconventional sense.[107] The work originated as a commission from the Russian-born dancer Ida Rubinstein (1885–1960), who recommended Gide's pre-1914 poem based on the Homeric Hymn to Demeter.[108] The three parts deal successively with Persephone's descent into hell (in this version by her own free will), her life in the Elysian Fields, and her return to earth. It was the first time that Stravinsky was actually setting a French text to music since the songs he composed in 1910 on Verlaine texts.[109] As in Debussy's *Le martyre de saint Sébastien*, her most famous creation, Rubinstein both mimed and recited; on the rare occasions when the work has been staged since, the two functions have frequently been allotted to different persons, a solution Stravinsky himself preferred. At the composer's request, a tenor role, Eumolpus, had been added, formally the most overtly "operatic" aspect of the score even though it is essentially a narrator's role. *Perséphone* was performed only three times at the Opéra in 1934 and is among the least frequently staged of his theatrical works. Stravinsky later made negative comments on Gide's incapacity to appreciate his setting of the libretto, as well as on the very principle of melodrama, while maintaining he loved the music of *Perséphone*, emphasizing, in fact, its essentially Russian character.[110] One can only speculate on the kind of opera that might have resulted from a collaboration between Stravinsky and Louis-Ferdinand Céline, which went no further than the discussion stage.[111]

Stravinsky expressed his opinions on various occasions about the French operatic tradition. Equally repelled by *verismo* and the "drame lyrique," he loved to surprise (and shock) modernists by proclaiming his genuine respect for Lecocq, whom he ranked even above Messager.[112] His admiration for *Pelléas* was qualified by reservations about Maeterlinck's text, while the work's Wagnerian elements bored him. He retained a lifelong admiration for Chabrier and he blamed the French for their failure to appreciate *Une éducation manquée* when Diaghilev revived it in Paris.[113] Of Gounod's works he liked above all *Le médecin malgré lui*, and the passages from *Carmen* that appealed to him most, such as the quintet in Act 2, were the ones that, for their inventiveness, were firmly rooted in the opéra-comique tradition.

CHAPTER 10
CRISIS AND RENEWAL

French opera in the 1930s

It is in the nature of things that all forms of art, even at their most successful, are constantly felt at the time to be going through one crisis or another. Such feelings are easily exacerbated in periods of economic or political difficulties. Opera, arguably the most expensive of all art forms, is all the more exposed in times of economic downturns. The Great Depression, which began in 1929 but started to hit France seriously in 1931, resulted in a sharp decline in ticket sales, both in Paris and elsewhere. The financial emergency had obvious artistic implications for French opera: it remained possible to fill houses with the popular repertory – *Faust, Carmen, Manon, Werther, Louise* – but it was much more difficult to attract audiences to hear new works. Naturally, composers and cultural administrators wondered whether opera itself was in crisis.

Since Lully's days, opera had dominated the French musical scene. This preeminence had been officially sanctioned in the training of composers at the Paris Conservatoire. The country's top honor for a budding composer was the Prix de Rome in music, which was established by Bonaparte in 1803 and was intended to launch operatic careers: whereas its first round assessed the student's musical competence in harmony and counterpoint, the final contest, a dramatic cantata (originally for one voice, but for three voices as of 1839) was essentially a mini-opera.[1] At the Conservatoire composition students were typically trained by teachers – Cherubini, Halévy, Delibes, Massenet, to name four of the most prominent – who were first and foremost opera composers, while the longest-serving directors in the nineteenth century, Auber and Ambroise Thomas, were also primarily associated with the theater. Composers, like Chabrier and Lalo, who won a hard-earned place in the lyric repertory without having followed this route, were exceptions that proved the rule. And this orientation remained in place even as the French musical landscape was undergoing major transformations. In the decades following the Franco-Prussian War of 1870–71, opera found itself having to compete for the favor of the public with other musical genres in which the most gifted French composers of their generation distinguished themselves – the symphony, chamber music, instrumental music, symphonic poems, and the mélodie. Success in the theater remained desirable but was no longer the only way to succeed. Massenet – who wrote much, in many genres, besides his 25 operas – was the last major French composer to be, above all, an opera composer. Although some of his gifted pupils – Erlanger, Février, Laparra, Rabaud, among others – followed the same path, none of them achieved a comparable status as an opera composer, save for Charpentier – with one opera. This was also a new trend. For composers like Fauré, Chausson, Debussy, or Dukas – all of whom wrote "their" opera and never completed a second – opera no longer represented, quantitatively at least, the major part of their output. Although Ravel produced two operas, they are, significantly, short works, and more remote from the operatic tradition than *Pelléas* or *Pénélope*. More tellingly, a growing number of composers, even after submitting to the grueling Prix de Rome routine, eschewed opera altogether. Charles Koechlin (1867–1950), a pupil of Massenet and Fauré, wrote ballets – a genre that gained considerably in prestige in the wake of the artistic achievement of the Ballets russes – but no opera. The same is true of Florent Schmitt (1870–1958), who had the same teachers and, luckier than Ravel, won the Prix de Rome at his fifth attempt in 1900. As for Satie, his interest in musical theater notwithstanding, he never became an opera composer in the traditional sense.

This relative disaffection for opera among younger French composers became even more pronounced in the second quarter of the twentieth century. Francis Poulenc, the greatest French opera composer of his generation, stayed away from the genre until his mid-forties. Of his fellow members of *Six, Les* Arthur Honegger and Darius Milhaud, to be sure, achieved prominence as opera composers in the 1930s, but the other three never did. Georges Auric (1899–1983) and Louis Durey (1888–1979) completed only one one-act work each,[2] whereas Germaine Tailleferre (1892–1983) turned to opera, late and briefly, in the 1950s.

Whether as a cause or a consequence, Paris – once the world capital of opera – had by the 1930s lost this position. Its decline had in fact begun long before, caused by or coinciding with the defeat of France by Prussia in 1871: ironically, it was already well underway when the Palais Garnier – the very magnificence of which was intended to underscore Paris's preeminence – opened its doors in 1875. Although it ostensibly remained the world's most glamorous opera house, its importance gradually declined as that of others – La Scala, the Vienna State Opera, Covent Garden, and, as of 1883, the Metropolitan Opera – increased in the first decades of the new century. This trend had inevitable long-term implications for the international standing and dissemination of

French opera. It also meant that fewer non-French composers were tempted or encouraged to write operas in French. There were, of course, exceptions. Lord Berners set an adaptation of Mérimée's *Le carosse du Saint-Sacrement*, premiered in 1923 at the Trianon-Lyrique, Versailles;[3] Franco Alfano's *Cyrano de Bergerac*, though premiered in Rome and in Italian, in 1936, before its Paris premiere in May of the same year, was set to a French text by Henri Cain that left Edmond Rostand's verse largely intact; and arguably the greatest French opera of the 1930s, Enesco's *Œdipe* (1936), was the work of a Romanian composer.

A parallel phenomenon which may partly explain the greater difficulty French works faced in entering the repertory, even at home, was that of the increased internationalization – and standardization – of the operatic repertory. Once mostly French, the programming of French opera houses now had to take into account the public's appetite for Mozart, Verdi, Wagner, Puccini, Strauss, and Mussorgsky. France, in this respect, fell in line with all other countries where operas were presented: the more public demand there was for an international repertory, the more difficult it became to mount contemporary works or, once mounted, to maintain them in the repertory. What Carré and Messager had achieved for *Pelléas* – impose by sheer will a relatively difficult work, admittedly well publicized by a carefully controlled *succès de scandale*, but hardly one of the opera house's top money-makers – became an increasingly difficult proposition.

Before 1914, as we have seen, the Opéra-Comique under Carré's leadership had enjoyed a distinct artistic edge over the Opéra. After the First World War, the trend was largely reversed, and the Opéra even staged a number of works premiered at the Salle Favart in the previous period: *L'heure espagnole*, *Mârouf*, *Ariane et Barbe-Bleue*, *Le roi d'Ys*, *Esclarmonde*, *Grisélidis*. Rouché, the longest-serving Opéra director ever (1915–44), was determined to restore its predominance. Major premieres, in addition to the aforementioned *Œdipe*, took place during his tenure: d'Indy's *La légende de saint Christophe* (1920), Dupont's *Antar* (1921), Roussel's *Padmâvatî* (1923) – which achieved a respectable 39 performances by 1947 – Lazzari's *La tour de feu* (1928), Magnard's *Guercoeur* (1931), Hahn's *Le Marchand de Venise* (1935). There were failures – Widor's *Nerto* and Tournemire's *Les dieux sont morts* in 1924, Philippe Gaubert's *Naila* and Jules Mazellier's *Les matines d'amour* in 1927. Despite critical praise, Joseph Canteloube's *Le mas* and Emmanuel's *Salamine* only achieved eight performances each in 1929. Two operas that received particular publicity failed to keep their promises. The first, Alfred Bachelet's *Un jardin sur l'Oronte*, after the orientalist novella by the nationalist writer Maurice Barrès (President Albert Lebrun attended the gala premiere on 3 November 1932), disappeared from the repertory after 12 performances in 1934.[4] Expectations were similarly disappointed by Canteloube's *Vercingétorix*, a "lyrical epic" in four acts based on the legendary leader of the Gauls defeated by Caesar in 52 BC. "The libretto of *Vercingétorix*, is exactly what Richard Wagner, the author of *Siegfried*, would have written if he had been a Frenchman," wrote the critic Émile Vuillermoz.[5] Despite such lofty claims, the work did not survive the departure of its male lead, Georges Thill, and vanished from the repertory after nine performances. Its instrumentation, remarkably, features the ondes martenot (the electronic instrument Messiaen was to make his own) in the more contemplative sections.[6]

While few new French works premiered at the Opéra in the 1930s succeeded in attracting large audiences, the situation was no better at the Opéra-Comique.[7] If one looks at the number of performances, the most successful recent French work was Omer Letorey's *Le Sicilien ou L'amour peintre*, a neo-classical opéra-comique adaptation of Molière's comedy of the same title. Premiered in 1930 as a double bill with another Molière-based work, Max d'Ollone's *George Dandin*, it had received 66 performances by 1939.[8] Jacques Ibert's *Angélique* – first staged in a different theater in 1927 – came second (33 performances). It was followed by Jean Roger-Ducasse's *Cantegril* – which, however, lasted only one season in 1932 (18 performances)[9] – Février's *La femme nue*[10] and Ibert's *Le roi d'Yvetot* (15 performances each), and Manuel Rosenthal's "department store" comedy *Rayons des soieries* (12 performances), while Mariotte's Rabelais-based *Gargantua* achieved 17 performances only in a version quickly reduced to its first act.[11] With the exception of Février's opera, all the works cited suggest that the public taste, perhaps in reaction to the difficulties of the time, favored comedy and escapism, also embracing neo-classicism at a time when the first debates on the future of tonality were being aired in the musical press.[12]

The Salle Favart tried to remedy its financial crisis by cutting the number of performances. At the Palais Garnier, Rouché, a wealthy man, was able for a while to absorb the shortfall, but in the 1930s he obtained a substantial raise in the State subsidy – it reached 9 million francs by 1939.[13] Yet, seeing no hope for a recovery, Rouché started lobbying for a State takeover: in 1936 Jean Zay, Minister of National Education and Fine Arts in the Popular Front government, appointed him head of a newly created Direction des théâtres lyriques nationaux. Three years later it became the Réunion des théâtres lyriques nationaux – an umbrella organization gathering the Opéra and Opéra-Comique, headed by Rouché as administrator general, though each theater remained financially and administratively autonomous. This system – in effect, a nationalization of the country's two principal opera houses – remained in place until 1972.

It has been suggested that the crisis of French opera in the 1930s was accompanied, if not exacerbated, by a crisis in French singing.[14] To be sure, the troupes of the Opéra and Opéra-Comique could not count on the plethora of outstanding French singers active in the 1870–1914 period. Still, there were first-rate French singers available in Paris in the 1930s: the Opéra had the "two

Germaines" (Hoerner and Lubin), and the mezzo-soprano Ketty Lapeyrette, (the first Padmâvatî). Tenors included Thill and the Belgian José de Trevi, baritones Endrèze and Martial Singher, and bass Pernet. In Louis Musy, the baritone who premiered *Le roi d'Yvetot* as well as Milhaud's *Le pauvre matelot*, the Opéra-Comique had one of the finest singing actors of the day. It is true that the size of the Opéra troupe had shrunk significantly, from 95 in 1908 to 75 in 1938, a diminution affecting especially the women.[15] If French singing experienced a decline during that period, it was probably in that department.[16]

It would be a mistake, in fact, to regard French opera in the 1930s in excessively bleak terms. The economic difficulties of the period should certainly not be underestimated. At the time, understandably, they led musicians and commentators to emphasize negative elements and downplay artistic achievements. Following the 1940–1944 Occupation and in the aftermath of the Second World War, there was another understandable tendency in France to reinterpret the previous decade in the light of the disaster that followed, not least of all in the cultural sphere.[17] As the following sections will show, a decade that nurtured the development of opera composers like Honegger, Ibert, Martinu, and Milhaud, that made it possible to hear Magnard's *Guercoeur*, and that saw the premiere of a work of the caliber of *Œdipe* was not a period of artistic crisis. The real crisis would come later.

Darius Milhaud

With his 16 operas, Darius Milhaud (1892–1974) contributed more to the lyric theater than any other major French composer in the twentieth century.[18] Born in Marseilles to a French father and an Italian mother, he grew up in nearby Aix-en-Provence. On his paternal side he was a member of the Avignon Jewish community, French since the Revolution, a milieu he strongly identified with and of which his memoirs contain a memorable description.[19] He received his musical education in Provence, becoming an excellent violinist. In 1909 he enrolled at the Paris Conservatoire, where his teachers included Dukas, Gédalge, Leroux, and Widor; but Debussy, Satie, Stravinsky, and Magnard were other, major musical influences.

Following a youthful attempt, *Les Saintes-Maries-de-la-Mer*, which he destroyed, Milhaud's first opera proper, *La brebis égarée*, was composed in 1910–14. It was based on a play by the Roman Catholic poet Francis Jammes (1868–1938), then at the height of his fame. This psychological drama deals with an adulterous affair, ending with the betrayed husband forgiving his wife. Owing to the unabashed modernism of Milhaud's writing, the work had a tumultuous premiere at the Opéra-Comique in 1923 but was not revived.

Another prominent Catholic poet, Paul Claudel (1868–1955), played a large part in Milhaud's life and inspiration.[20] He and Milhaud met in 1912 and Milhaud served as Claudel's secretary in Brazil in 1917–18. One of Milhaud's most ambitious stage project was the stage music he wrote for Claudel's version of Aeschylus's *Oresteia*. Like Fauré's *Prométhée*, it falls halfway between a play with music and an opera.[21] *Agamemnon*, composed in 1913, was the first work in which Milhaud experimented with polytonality – the simultaneous use of different keys – which became the hallmark of his musical style. The second part, *Les Choéphores*, followed in 1915–16, and the third, *Les Euménides* – the closest to an actual opera – in 1917–23. *Les Choéphores* was staged in Brussels in 1935; the other two plays had to wait until 1963, when the entire trilogy was mounted by the Berlin Deutsche Oper. Milhaud's other major collaboration with Claudel, *Christophe Colomb*, a vast fresco in two parts and 27 scenes, was commissioned by Max Reinhardt. Rather than a grand opéra in the manner of Meyerbeer's *L'Africaine* – the other French opera inspired by voyages of discovery – it is a symbolist, poetic meditation, emphasizing the role of Columbus as the bringer of Christianity to the New World (Claudel and Milhaud, both deeply religious, were equally respectful of each other's faith). Premiered at the Berlin Staatsoper in 1930, in translation, under the great German conductor Erich Kleiber,[22] it was not heard in Paris until 1936, in concert. Disappointed with the less than enthusiastic reception, Claudel ungenerously attributed it to Milhaud's music, subsequently even trying to convince Honegger to rewrite the work.[23] *Christophe Colomb* admittedly presents a formidable challenge, on account both of its technical complexity – not least the elaborate choral participation – and its staging demands (which include film). Revised by the composer after Claudel's death, with the order of the two parts reversed, it was revived in its new form at Graz in 1968, though a 1984 production at Marseilles (the French stage premiere) made a strong case for the original version. Milhaud's last operatic project, *Saint-Louis, roi de France*, composed in 1970, also used Claudel texts, with additions by Henri Doublier. Though an official French commission, it was not performed in France. First staged at Rio de Janeiro in 1972, this "opéra-oratorio," as it was published, remains one of Milhaud's least-known works.

The poet Armand Lunel (1892–1977), a lifelong friend of Milhaud and like him a Provençal Jew, was his other major operatic collaborator. Their first stage project, *Les malheurs d'Orphée*, a concise retelling of the Orpheus legend in a Camargue setting, was premiered at Brussels in 1926. Staged in Paris and Buenos Aires in 1927 and in Munich in 1931, it was also given in concert from in Amsterdam and New York.[24] In the opera buffa *Esther de Carpentras*, Milhaud and Lunel celebrated their common Jewish heritage: the plot, set during the times when the Provençal town of Carpentras was still controlled by the Pope, evokes one of the sporadic attempts at forced conversions of the Jews, thwarted by a performance of the story of Esther as part of a Purim celebration. Plans for a Monte Carlo production having fallen through over disagreements with Gunsbourg, *Esther* had to wait until 1938 to be produced at the Salle Favart. Many years later Milhaud and Lunel resumed their collaboration on the biblical opera *David*, a commission by Serge Koussevitzky in honor of the 3000th anniversary of the founding of Jerusalem. Following the 1954 concert premiere in Israel, the opera was staged at La Scala in 1955.

Jean Cocteau – under whose umbrella *Les Six* were gathered – wrote the libretto of Milhaud's *Le pauvre matelot*, a tragic tale (subtitled "complainte") of a sailor returning after a 15-year absence, only to be murdered by his faithful wife who fails to recognize him. Premiered at the Opéra-Comique in 1927, the work has been Milhaud's most widely staged, especially in the new version with reduced orchestra: this was issued by Milhaud in 1934 at the request of the conductor Hermann Scherchen so that it could be performed jointly with Stravinsky's *L'histoire du soldat*.

In a completely different register, Milhaud attempted to rejuvenate the genre of historical opera of a kind not seen since the previous century. *Maximilien*, premiered at the Opéra in 1932, was based on Franz Werfel's 1924 play *Juarez und Maximilian*. The libretto was written in German by R.S. Hoffmann and set in Lunel's translation. The work, which received only seven performances, was a critical failure and has seldom been revived. The librettist of Milhaud's second historical opera, *Bolivar*, composed in the 1940s, was his wife (and first cousin) Madeleine (1902–2008). She adapted the play of the same title by the Montevideo-born poet Jules Supervielle (1884–1960), for which Milhaud had supplied stage music when it was premiered at the Comédie-Française in 1936. Milhaud's closest approach to the grand opéra form, it was premiered at the Opéra in 1950, with sets by Fernand Léger. Unlike *Maximilien* it was warmly received, but it has been seldom seen in recent decades.

Milhaud displayed his virtuosity in his trilogy of mythological "opéras-minute," each a witty parody lasting between nine and twelve minutes of a "tragédie en musique," with casts of four or five and a mini-chorus. The libretti are by Milhaud's friend, the diplomat Henri Hoppenot (1891–1977). *L'enlèvement d'Europe* was premiered first at Baden-Baden in 1927 (paired with short operas by Ernst Toch and Paul Hindemith) and repeated, together with the other two, *L'abandon d'Ariane* and *La délivrance de Thésée*, at Wiesbaden in 1928. Milhaud's other major foray into Greek mythology, *Médée*, is, by contrast, a "straight," full-fledged opera, taking as its source Euripides's play, made into a libretto by Milhaud's wife Madeleine. Premiered at Antwerp in 1939, the work was staged at the Opéra the following year. The opening night, on 12 May, took place two days after Hitler's armies invaded France and Belgium. Aware of the danger that would have awaited them, the Milhauds spent the years of the Nazi Occupation in California, where the composer taught at Mills College in Oakland.

Milhaud's late operatic production displays the same versatility. The one-act *Fiesta* is a *humour noir* (black comedy) set on a tropical island, its libretto by the novelist and lyricist Boris Vian (1920–1959) from Saint-Germain-des-Prés. A chamber opera, scored for 13 instruments, it was premiered at Berlin in 1958. *La mère coupable*, Milhaud's penultimate opera, was set to a libretto by Madeleine Milhaud after Beaumarchais's play, the third of his Figaro trilogy. Premiered in Geneva in 1966 with the American soprano Phyllis Curtin, to whom it is dedicated, it is generally considered his least successful work.

Like Massenet, whom he otherwise hardly resembles, Milhaud could be described as fundamentally eclectic. This applies not simply to the form and subject matter of his operas, but also to their music, which has been characterized as in turn "euphonious and cacophonous, tender and violent, spiritual and earthy, sensuous and austere, pastoral and urban, colourful and monochrome."[25] Perhaps lacking the instinctive theatrical sense and feeling for the voice of his fellow member of *Les Six*, Poulenc, he does not deserve the relative neglect into which his works have fallen.

Arthur Honegger

Arthur Honegger (1892–1955) once declared that his dream "would have been to compose nothing but operas". Less prolific than Milhaud, he had more trouble being recognized as an opera composer and has suffered from even greater neglect.[26] He was born in Le Havre to Swiss Protestant parents, ultimately choosing Swiss citizenship.[27] After two years at the Zurich Conservatory, he entered the Paris Conservatoire in 1911. Like Milhaud, he studied with Gédalge and Widor, also taking instruction from d'Indy and Emmanuel.

As Harry Halbreich has pointed out,[28] Honegger's writing for the stage shows a certain generic uncertainty that is characteristic of the period. The work that made him famous, *Le roi David*, conceived in 1921 as incidental music to the biblical play by René Morax for his Théâtre du Jorat, was recast two years later as a "psaume dramatique" – a phrase suggesting more an oratorio than an opera. *Amphion*, premiered at the Opéra in 1931 with Ida Rubinstein and labeled "melodrama" (like Stravinsky's *Perséphone*, which it resembles), is part ballet, part cantata. *Judith* was first cast as an oratorio to a libretto by Morax in 1925, recast into an opera the following year, and revised a third time in 1927 as an "action musicale" (that is oratorio) – the form in which it is now most familiar. Honegger's best-known and most frequently performed work, *Jeanne d'Arc au bûcher*, is called "dramatic oratorio," which suggests that it can be staged or not. Commissioned from both Claudel and Honegger by Ida Rubinstein, it was composed in 1935, initially to be staged at the Opéra. In the event, neither the commissioner nor the Opéra followed through and it was premiered in concert version in Basel in 1938, the first staging occurring in Zurich in 1942 under Paul Sacher.[29] The same ambiguity characterizes the dramatic legend *Nicolas de Flue*, on a libretto by the essayist and philosopher Denis de Rougemont: completed in 1939 and premiered (in concert) in 1940, it was first staged the following year, though, unlike *Jeanne au bûcher*, it includes no sung roles.

Other than incomplete or lost youthful projects, Honegger's first opera was the aforementioned *Judith*, commissioned in this form by Gunsbourg for Monte Carlo, where it was premiered in 1926 under the composer. As Geoffrey K. Spratt has noted, the work shows Honegger's indebtedness both to the delicate lyricism of Debussy and Fauré and to the severe, classical language advocated by his teacher d'Indy.

In 1922 Honegger had supplied incidental music to Cocteau's one-act adaptation of Sophocles's *Antigone* – the first chapter in the poet's lifelong fascination with the Oedipus myth. In 1924–7 the composer made it into an opera, setting the entire prose text to music. Premiered in Brussels in 1927, the work was respectfully rather than enthusiastically received. The reception was more positive at Essen the following year. The Opéra premiere had to wait until 1943, in a production directed and designed by Cocteau. It was hailed then as a great modernist masterpiece by critics and audiences which the atmosphere of occupied Paris no doubt rendered more responsive to the tragic subject.[30] Sadly, the paucity of productions since the war has not confirmed the work's standing. Yet *Antigone*, arguably Honegger's operatic masterpiece, bears comparison, in its tautness and violence – if not in the austerity of its vocal writing – with Strauss's *Elektra*, with atonal passages recalling Berg's *Wozzeck* or Schoenberg's *Erwartung*. The play's dark, desperate quality is emphasized by the unexpected vocal distribution, with the three principal roles – Antigone, Creon, and Haemon – given to low voices.[31] As in *Pelléas*, high notes are avoided in order not to interfere with the intelligibility of the text.

It is ironical that the success which had eluded Honegger with serious works like *Judith* and *Antigone* was instead earned with the boisterous, bawdy operetta *Les aventures du roi Pausole*, which ran for more than 400 performances at the Bouffes-Parisiens after its December 1930 premiere and was also successful in the provinces and abroad. Willemetz's libretto, adapted from the 1901 novel by Pierre Louÿs, is full of sexual jokes and innuendos, and Honegger's music combines robustness and refinement in a way that recalls the Chabrier of *L'Étoile*.[32] A similar playful mood permeates *La belle de Moudon*, another, less memorable foray into the world of operetta, written for the Jorat theater in 1931 to a libretto by Morax.

The "drame musical" *L'Aiglon*, adapted from Rostand's immensely popular 1901 drama by Cain (who, as noted, had performed a similar service for Alfano's *Cyrano*), was composed in tandem by Honegger and his friend Ibert for Monte Carlo, where it was premiered in 1937. The two composers had first declined the commission before agreeing to this unusual arrangement. Honegger wrote Acts 2, 3, and 4, Ibert wrote Acts 1 and 5. As in Rostand's original, where Sarah Bernhardt played the Duke of Reichstadt, the part of Napoleon's son was given to a soprano (Fanny Heldy in both Monte Carlo and Paris). Well received at the time, *L'Aiglon* remained in the Opéra repertory until 1953, but the naïve nationalistic tone of the Rostand play – matched in the music, which cites the Marseillaise in Act 4 – has not aged well, as sporadic revivals in France have demonstrated. Ibert and Honegger also collaborated on the operetta *Les petites Cardinal*, adapted by Willemetz and Paul Brach from Ludovic Halévy's novel about the daughters of a respectable bourgeois couple joining the ballet troupe of the Opéra. Closer, according to Harry Halbreich, to Lecocq than to Delibes,[33] the work was staged in January 1938 at the Bouffes-Parisiens, but, in the tense international climate of that year, met only with moderate success.

Jacques Ibert

Although Jacques Ibert (1890–1962) is less familiar today than other French musicians of his generation, the contribution he made, over a brief period, to twentieth-century opera should not be forgotten.[34] A Parisian, he received his initial musical instruction from his mother, an excellent pianist trained at the Conservatoire. After considering an acting career, he himself entered this institution, where he studied counterpoint with Gédalge, at whose class he became acquainted with Honegger and Milhaud, and composition with Vidal. After serving with distinction during the First World War, he further distinguished himself by winning the Prix de Rome at his first attempt in 1919. He spent the years 1920–23 at the Villa Médicis, where he was to serve as director in 1937–40 and again in 1944–60. During this Italian stay, he composed the music of his first opera, *Persée et Andromède, ou Le plus heureux des trois*, on a libretto by his brother-in-law Nino,[35] drawn from Jules Laforgue's *Moralités légendaires*. In his satirical retelling of Andromeda's rescue by Perseus – the subtitle is an allusion to a play by Labiche – Andromeda is a coquettish young woman, Perseus an insufferable macho bore, and the "monster," Cathos, a likeable creature, who easily conquers Andromeda's heart. Ibert's sparkling music is a perfect match for Nino's tongue-in-cheek humor. In keeping with the tradition of hospitality given to Prix de Rome winners at the Opéra, the work was premiered at the Palais Garnier in 1929 under Henry Busser, with Heldy and Pernet as Andromeda and Cathos, and, as Perseus, the gifted Opéra-Comique singer Miguel Villabella.[36]

Ibert and his brother-in-law continued their collaboration with a work that was to be one of the most popular and widely performed French operas of the interwar period, *Angélique*. Written in 1926, it is a farce à la Boccaccio on the theme of the henpecked husband who decides to put up his wife (the ironically named Angélique of the title) for sale; an Italian, an Englishman, and an African prince show interest, but give up, as does the Devil himself, until a supposedly contrite Angélique is returned to her skeptical husband. Ibert's comic masterpiece in the tradition of Chabrier includes pastiches of various musical styles as well as bitonal passages that recall Milhaud. An unusual effect is the "spoken-sung" interventions of the chorus. Premiered in 1927 in the

small Théâtre Fémina by the troupe of Marguerite Bériza, who had commissioned the work (and who sang the title role), it was staged three years later at
the Opéra-Comique, where it was regularly revived until the early 1960s. It
ranks as one of the most widely performed French operas of the period
worldwide.[37]

Ibert's affinity with the opéra-comique tradition was also illustrated by his
third opera, Le roi d'Yvetot, whose libretto by Jean Limozin and André de La
Tourrasse (1904–19?) is based on the popular Béranger song (already the
inspiration for Adam's similary titled opéra-comique). First staged at the Salle
Favart in 1930, it was cast with two of the company's finest singers, Emma
Luart and Louis Musy, but despite a warm public and critical reception it was
not kept in the repertory.[38]

Ibert's appointment as director of the Villa Médicis by the Popular Front
government in 1937 ruffled feathers at the Institut, since the position was
traditionally reserved for its members. Ibert made further enemies in 1940 by
siding with members of the French parliament opposed to capitulation.
Summarily fired by the Vichy authorities, he spent the Occupation in semi-
disgrace in the south of France, to be immediately reinstated in his function by
De Gaulle at the Liberation.[39] His last opera, Barbe-Bleue, was composed for
the Swiss radio, which broadcast it in 1943 (with the young Hugues Cuénod in
the cast).

Georges Enesco

Not only did Georges Enesco (1881–1955) write the greatest French opera of
the period, he was also one of the most accomplished musicians of his time.[40]
Born in Romanian Moldavia, he received his musical training in Vienna – he
saw the original production of Werther in 1892 – and in Paris, where he
studied with Massenet, Gédalge, and Fauré. Even before completing his studies
in 1899,[41] he had embarked on a triple career as violinist – by all accounts one
of the most brilliant of the first half of the twentieth century – conductor, and
composer.

The genesis of Enesco's only opera Œdipe[42] began in or around 1909 when
the composer attended a performance of Sophocles's Oedipus Rex at the
Comédie-Française with the famous Jean Mounet-Sully in the title role. By
January 1910 Enesco had started jotting down musical ideas. After the
premiere of Bloch's Macbeth later that year, he was introduced by Dukas and
the music critic Pierre Lalo (son of the composer of Le roi d'Ys) to its librettist,
Edmond Fleg, who immediately agreed to become Enesco's collaborator. Fleg
based his text (originally much longer and to be performed on two consecutive evenings) on both Oedipus Rex and Oedipus at Colonus. Enesco worked on
the project in Romania during the First World War. By then his mature
musical style evolved from the Brahmsian and Wagnerian influences charac-

teristic of his early work towards a more personal idiom, where austere forms of modernism blend with subtle references to Romanian folklore. The definitive version of the libretto was delivered in 1921 and Enesco completed the short score in 1922; the orchestration, slowed down by his career as soloist, took eight more years. Summing up the chronology of the project, the composer noted that the work occupied his mind for a quarter of a century and its composition took 10 years.[43]

Fleg's libretto, written in rhymed free verse, was the first modern treatment of the Oedipus myth to represent, in its first two acts, events that in Sophocles are only evoked retrospectively: the abandonment of Oedipus by Laios and Jocasta, terrified by Tiresia's predictions regarding their son; Oedipus's flight from Corinth, where he was raised by the king and queen, whom he believed to be his parents; the brief, accidental murder of Laios at the crossroads; Oedipus's encounter with the Sphinx – another moment of extreme intensity, to which Enesco brings eerie, surreal touches. Act 3 corresponds to the events of *Oedipus Rex*, while the final act is an abbreviated version of *Oedipus at Colonus*. At a few key moments, Fleg departs from Sophocles to reinterpret the myth along his own humanistic lines: thus, the Sphinx's riddle is reduced to one question ("Name someone or name something that is greater than Destiny!"), the answer to which is "Man! Man is greater than Destiny"; and at the very end Oedipus, after his final confrontation with Creon, dies "a conqueror of Destiny," miraculously recovering his eyesight, in a kind of transfiguration that is absent from Sophocles.

Enesco's score, while conveying an impression of dramatic and musical unity, offers a dazzling compendium of types of declamation – including quarter-tones and spoken utterances – and styles, from moments of quiet or passionate lyricism that betray the student of Massenet and Fauré to a percussive brutality recalling Stravinsky. Particularly poignant passages draw from Romanian popular music, such as the shepherd's plaintive flute melody, inspired by the traditional lament called "doïna." Based on a few leitmotifs, and treated in a manner more reminiscent of Debussy than Wagner, the orchestral writing, which never obscures the words, shows Enesco's sensitivity to variety of color and timbre.

Œdipe was premiered at the Opéra on 13 March 1936, with Pernet in the title role and Trévi as the shepherd, with Philippe Gaubert conducting. The critical reception was almost unanimously enthusiastic. Yet, after being revived the following season, the work was dropped from the repertory after 11 performances. It was only after the war that its reputation slowly spread. The Brussels premiere (1956) preceded the first production in Bucharest, in Romanian (1958); this was seen in Paris in 1963, in Athens in 1966, and in Berlin in 1975. The Vienna premiere took place in 1997 and the American one in 2005 (at Urbana). Yet *Œdipe* is still awaiting its first staging at Covent Garden, La Scala, and the Met.

In the words of Enesco's disciple Yehudi Menuhin, summarizing the importance of *Œdipe* in its composer's oeuvre, "it can truly be said, as Elgar did of his violin concerto, 'Acqui está encerrada el alma de' – 'Here lies the very soul and heartblood of Georges Enesco.' "[44]

Bohuslav Martinu

Bohuslav Martinu (1890–1959) is not a name one associates with French opera. But the Czech composer was a longtime resident of France and four of his 14 completed operas were set to French libretti and one more was projected.[45] Having first visited Paris in 1919, he made the city his home until 1940, and after his American exile in 1941, returned again to France in 1953. Debussy and Roussel were strong influences – he studied with the latter. Unlike his teacher, however, Martinu did not turn to exotic or classical subjects but to the avant-garde poet Georges Ribemont-Dessaignes (1884–1974), then associated with the surrealist movement (whose leader André Breton had a notorious aversion to opera, as to music and the theater in general). As the title indicates, the one-act *Les larmes du couteau*, which Martinu composed in nine days in 1928, is a gruesome Dalí-like fantasy. Subtitled "opéra macabre," it features Satan, a hanged man, a young woman named Eleanor, and her mother; but the music, with its references to popular dances like foxtrot, tango, and charleston, retains a light touch. Rejected by Baden-Baden, the work was posthumously premiered at Brno in 1968. Martinu and Ribemont-Dessaignes collaborated next on *Les trois souhaits, ou Les vicissitudes de la vie*, another experimental work in three acts. Dealing with the making of a film, the plot takes one back and forth between the world of the cinema and the surrounding reality. Again, no theater was interested and *Les trois souhaits* was premiered at Brno in 1971, to critical acclaim.[46] Martinu was no luckier with the opera buffa he wrote in 1937, *Alexandre bis*: the production planned within the Paris International Exposition of that year, with sets by Jean Lurçat, was canceled and the first staging was at Mannheim in 1964. André Wurmser's libretto deals with the ironic consequences of a husband's jealousy.

Martinu's masterpiece, *Julietta*, premiered in Prague in 1938, was adapted by the composer, in Czech, from a surrealist play by the Ukraine-born Georges Neveux (1900–1982). Another Neveux adaptation, *Plainte contre inconnu*, was considered and abandoned in 1953. Martinu's last French work, *Ariane*, was undertaken in 1958 as a diversion from the composition of his final opera, *The Greek Passion* (1961), after Nikos Kazantsakis's *Christ Recrucified*. *Ariane* is derived from yet another play by Neveux, *Le voyage de Thésée*, staged during the Occupation. Martinu set to music a condensed version, reduced from four acts to three scenes. It is a symbolic retelling of the Aridane myth, set not on Naxos but on Crete. When Theseus, at the end of the second scene, calls for the Minotaur, he thus faces a young man exactly like to him, who explains that he is the image of his own happiness, which he is about to shatter by abandoning the young woman. Left alone on the island, Ariane, in a beautiful final monologue (written by Martinu with the voice of Maria Callas in mind) bids farewell to her own dream. Unlike Martinu's experimental operas of the 1920s, the work is neo-classical in style, with three "sinfonias" connecting the scenes. Like all of them, however, it was premiered posthumously, at Gelsenkirchen in 1961.

French opera during the Nazi Occupation

The four years during which France was occupied by Adolf Hitler's forces hardly represent a major moment in French operatic history. At the Opéra, where Rouché remained in charge as administrator, no new French works were presented. The only notable premiere was Honegger's *Antigone* in 1943. Another, P.-L. Hillemacher's forgotten "opéra féerique" *Le Drac* (first staged at Karlsruhe in 1896), appears to have been motivated by political cronyism: the wife of Roman historian Jérôme Carcopino, Marshal Pétain's education minister, was related to the Hillemacher brothers.[47] Of the three new works staged by the Opéra-Comique in 1942, two at least had been commissioned and completed before the war: Paul Le Flem's "fantaisie lyrique" *Le rossignol de Saint-Malo* and Marcel Delannoy's *Ginevra*, after Boccaccio, which incorporated French Renaissance songs. The position of Delannoy (1898–1962) is characteristic of the ambiguities of the period. A protégé of Honegger, partly self-taught (he had originally contemplated a career as an architect), he had made his name with his opéra-comique *Le poirier de misère*, staged at the Salle Favart in 1927. Based on a Flemish legend, it adopted a "popular" idiom in the style of traditional songs, earning the composer accusations of vulgarism and "Bolshevist tendencies."[48] Delannoy's second opera, *Le fou de la dame*, also based on a medieval subject, was well received at the Opéra-Comique in 1929. During the Occupation, Delannoy took advantage of the circumstances to advance his career. Along with Rouché, Bachelet, and Honegger – the latter having at least the excuse of not being a French national[49] – he participated in a Nazi-sponsored trip to Vienna in 1941 to mark the 150th anniversary of Mozart's death. He also contributed to the ultra-collaborationist journal *Les nouveaux temps*, whose founder and editor Jean Luchaire was executed for high treason in 1946.[50] Coincidentally, the libretto of *Ginevra* was written by the latter's father, Julien Luchaire (1876–1962), an Italian Renaissance scholar and, by one of those tragic paradoxes typical of the period, a member of the Resistance.[51] Delannoy was not the only musician behave less than honorably. Max d'Ollone was happy to step in as head of the Opéra-Comique in 1941 after the Nazi authorities demanded the firing of Busser. He was himself replaced, in April 1944, by the tenor Lucien Muratore (who proved an inept administrator). At the Opéra, within weeks of the Liberation of Paris the great bass

Vanni-Marcoux successfully intrigued with the government of Pierre Laval –
by then dominated by out-and-out Nazis – to be given control of all artistic
matters.[52] Meanwhile, the anti-Semitic laws promulgated by the Vichy regime
as early as October 1940 were in full force. Halévy's and Meyerbeer's busts
remained in place on the Opéra façade, but their works – by then routinely
vilified by music historians – were not revived.[53] Offenbach and Milhaud,
among others, were kept out of the repertory, while Jewish singers and musicians were banned from public performance and, as of 1942, faced arrest and
deportation or had to go into hiding.

The Vichy years – if one strives to find something positive to say about
them – were at least marked by laudable initiatives with a view to rediscovering
and preserving the French operatic heritage, albeit in the narrow definition
then current. The ministerial department in charge of fine arts thus sponsored
a series of recordings, among which was the first complete one of *Pelléas*,
under Roger Désormière, made in 1941 with Soprano Irène Joachim and baritone Jacques Jansen – a performance that, more than 65 years later, has lost
little of its power.[54] Honegger and Claudel's *Jeanne au bûcher* was recorded in
the summer of 1941, followed by Berlioz's *Damnation de Faust*, conducted by
Jean Fournet, in 1942, and (remarkably) Chabrier's *L'Étoile* in 1943. In addition
to *Jeanne au bûcher* the contemporary repertory was represented by excerpts
from Lazzari's *La tour de feu* and Henri Rabaud's *Rolande et le mauvais garçon*
(the latter sung by Thill).[55]

The post-war crisis

Whatever loss of prestige France may have suffered as a nation due to the 1940
defeat and the Occupation, French culture – which, in any event, extends
beyond France – can be said to have largely recovered after the Liberation. The
post-war period was, in fact, marked by a remarkable flowering in French literature, photography, the cinema, and the theater. In the visual arts, the presence
in the country of such towering figures as Pierre Bonnard, Henri Matisse,
Georges Braque, Alberto Giacometti, and Pablo Picasso was a source of enormous prestige, even though the center of gravity was gradually shifting to the
other side of the Atlantic. French opera, however, had entered a long period of
decline.

No doubt this decline was tied to some extent to the decline of the Opéra.
Its prominence during the Occupation – often at the service of the Nazis or
their cultural propaganda – had left it tainted in the eyes of the public and
suspect in those of the political power of the day. Rouché was summarily
dismissed (he was 82 in 1944), though in the end no charges were leveled
against him. Germaine Lubin, the main star of his troupe, was less fortunate:
having sung at Bayreuth in 1938 and 1939 and been introduced to Hitler, she
was made to pay for her conspicuous wartime Germanophilia. She was

arrested, her property was confiscated, and her civil rights suspended. Such settlings of accounts – and there were others, where personal rivalries intervened – were obviously detrimental to the Opéra's morale. But French singers were also affected by the historical circumstances in another, broader sense: cut off during five years from international circuits, most of them found themselves in the following decades confined to Paris and French provincial theaters, and ignored outside the French borders. By the same token, singers from other countries frequently built their international careers without appearing regularly – if ever – at the Opéra. This situation continued for many years after the war, causing a largely unjust perception that French singing itself was in decline, even though an outstanding generation of artists was reaching maturity. This absence of native French (or Francophone) singers on the international scene had an indirect consequence in the general decline of the quality of the singing of French internationally, which in turn inevitably affected the status of the French operatic repertory.[56]

The day-to-day activities of the Opéra in the late 1940s and throughout the 1960s were plagued like other branches of activity then and since, by an increasing number of strikes. They occurred every year between 1944 and 1948, in 1950–51, and again in 1953.[57] Unsurprisingly, the number of French works premiered during that period fell to an all-time low. After the failure of Henry Barraud's Cervantes-based Numance in 1955 (despite a cast that included Rita Gorr, Alain Vanzo, Ernest Blanc, and Robert Massard), one had to wait until Charles Chaynes's Erszebet and Daniel-Lesur's Ondine in 1982.[58] And it surely says something about the status of France as a country with a long operatic tradition that the most important and successful French opera of the post-war era, Poulenc's Dialogues des carmélites, was premiered not in Paris but Milan, not in French but in Italian translation. Apart from Numance, the only Palais Garnier premieres of the period were Milhaud's Bolivar, one of his more successful operas, performed 22 times between 1950 and 1955, and Samuel-Rousseau's one-act Kerbeb, danseuse berbère. One of the few French operas with an Algerian theme, it was premiered in 1951 and reached its twenty-sixth performance in 1958 – by which time the Algerian War was in full swing.[59] At the Opéra-Comique, the only unqualified post-war successes were Poulenc's Les mamelles de Tirésias (1947) and La voix humaine (1959). Other works premiered were half-successes or failures: among the earlier were Busser's Le carosse du Saint-Sacrement (1948) and Emmanuel Bondeville's Madame Bovary (1951);[60] on the other hand, Germaine Tailleferre's Il était un petit navire, which poked fun at operatic conventions, memorably flopped at its tumultuous 1951 premiere.[61] The last new work presented at the Salle Favart before it was closed in 1972 was Henri Tomasi's Princesse Pauline in 1962.

Whether a consequence of this decline or a contributing factor, more French composers than ever stayed away from opera in the post-war period. André

Jolivet (1905–1974), with several important ballet scores to his credit, wrote only a one-act opéra-comique with a Spanish setting, *Dolorès ou le miracle de la femme laide*, composed during the war and staged at the Salle Favart only in 1961. He did accept a commission from the Opéra at the very end of his life but died before completing his *Bogomilé, ou Le lieutenant perdu*.[62] Henri Dutilleux (1916–), the 1939 Prix de Rome winner, never contributed to the genre; and Olivier Messiaen, no doubt the dominant figure in French music after the Second World War, might not have written *Saint François d'Assise* but for coaxing from both the Opéra and the Presidency of the Republic. The musical avant-garde of the 1950s and 1960s, led by Pierre Boulez – notwithstanding his magnificent performances as conductor at Bayreuth and elsewhere – tended to view opera, explicitly or implicitly, along Marxist or pseudo-Marxist lines: a genre tied to the rise of the bourgeoisie and doomed to extinction (as a living form) since the bourgeoisie itself was doomed.[63] No such arguments, interestingly, were heard about the ballet, which continued to attract French composers, as attested by the long collaboration between choreographer Maurice Béjart and composer Pierre Henry (1927–), the leading name in *musique concrète*. The Greek-Romanian born Iannis Xenakis (1922–2001), along with Boulez the most prominent musician of his generation active in France in the 1960s and 1970s, had a strong interest in the theater, but not in the operatic form: his *Oresteia* (1965–6), *Kassandra* (1987), and *La déesse Athéna* (1992) are more along the lines of "spectacles" with music, stemming from a reflection on ancient Greek theater and incorporating elements from non-Western traditions.

Another major composer who, in a different period, might have contributed to French opera was the Swiss Frank Martin (1890–1974). His most famous work, *Le vin herbé* (1942) – a retelling of the Tristan story based on Joseph Bédier's version of the medieval poems – was conceived and published as an "oratorio," even though – beginning in 1948 at the Salzburg Festival – it has regularly been presented in staged versions. The subtitle of his sacred work *Le mystère de la Nativité* (1959), "oratorio spectacle," is more ambiguous: on the one hand it suggests that it is intended to be staged, on the other hand that it is an oratorio, not an opera. Martin's first opera proper, *Der Sturm*, premiered in Vienna under Ernest Ansermet in 1956, was set to Friedrich Schlegel's German version of Shakespeare's *The Tempest*. Martin's first and only real French opera, *Monsieur de Pourceaugnac*, after the Molière comedy that inspired Hugo von Hoffmansthal for Strauss's *Der Rosenkavalier*, was premiered in Geneva in 1963.

This neglect by prominent composers unfortunately went along with a neglect of the French repertory, especially in Paris, where it dwindled to eight or ten works at best. The seventeenth and eighteenth centuries were largely ignored, even though two of the brightest spots of the 1950s were a sumptuous production of Rameau's *Les Indes galantes* at the Opéra and a staging of *Platée*

at the recently founded Aix-en-Provence festival. The opéra-comique tradition, from Boieldieu to Ambroise Thomas, was left untapped. Grand opéra
was openly despised and its practitioners written off in French music histories
as *italianisants*.[64] When the Opéra revived Verdi's *Don Carlos* for the first time
since 1867, it did so in Italian.[65] Berlioz suffered from similar neglect.
Benvenuto Cellini was first staged at the Palais Garnier in 1972 and not until
1990 was an uncut *Les Troyens* mounted in Paris. Lip service was paid to
Chabrier, but his works were not performed. Massenet, whose standing in
French operatic history ought to be that of a Verdi or a Richard Strauss, was
treated with contempt.[66] Even Bizet's *Les pêcheurs de perles* became a rarity. A
parallel phenomenon was the virtual disappearance of classical French
operetta after the Second World War. With rare exceptions, the lavish shows
produced at the Châtelet (under Francis Lopez) or at Mogador were of a stan-
dardized, international variety that – for their polish and savoir-faire – had
little to do with the tradition of Offenbach, Lecocq, Messager, Hahn, and their
successors, and appealed to audiences with limited if any interest in opera.[67]

One major exception to this dispiriting picture of the operatic scene in Paris
from 1945 till the early 1970s was the work done by the French national radio
throughout the period to keep the French repertory alive, by commissioning
new works and, especially, by performing seldom heard ones. Weekly concert
performances, broadcast live, sung by some of the finest singers active in
France – Blanc, Jacqueline Brumaire, Christiane Eda-Pierre, Massard, Michel
Sénéchal, Vanzo, to name a few – made it possible for an entire generation to
hear works by Cherubini, Hérold, Auber, Meyerbeer, Massé, Reyer, or Terrasse
– and many lesser-known composers – not otherwise performed throughout
that period.[68]

The decline of Paris as an operatic center had one salutary consequence: it
stimulated operatic activity in the rest of the country. In 1956 a Réunion des
théâtres lyriques de province was established to facilitate sharing of new
productions of contemporary works. Many were thus premiered at Bordeaux,
Lyons, Marseilles, Rouen, or Strasbourg before being mounted in other French
houses, and, as often as not, were never seen in Paris. The career of Claude
Arrieu (1903–1990) is characteristic of this evolution:[69] having studied with
Dukas at the Paris Conservatoire, she had her first opera *Noé*, an "imagerie
musicale" after a play by André Obey, staged in Strasbourg in 1950, and her
other major works were all premiered in the provinces where they were invari-
ably well received: *Cadet Roussel* at Marseilles in 1953; *La princesse de Babylone*
(an adaptation of Voltaire's tale) at Strasbourg in 1960; the opera buffa *Un
clavier pour un autre*, on a libretto by the noted playwright Jean Tardieu, at
Avignon in 1971; and *Les amours de don Perlimpin et dona Bélise en leur jardin*,
after the play by Federico García Lorca, at Tours in 1980.

Outside France, Brussels and Geneva saw their prestige increase as that of
Paris diminished. Under normal circumstances, *Le serment* by Alexandre

Tansman (1897–1986), in retrospect one of the strongest French operas of the period, would have been staged at the Salle Favart or Palais Garnier: its Polish-born composer, a disciple of Ravel, was one of several gifted Eastern European composers who had settled in Paris before the war.[70] In the event, his two-act opera adapted from *La Grande Bretêche*, the horror story by Balzac, after receiving its radio premiere in Paris in 1954 (under André Cluytens) was staged at la Monnaie the following year. When it was finally produced in Paris, in 1963, it was by a visiting German company, and in German.[71] Geneva, while giving pride of place to works by Francophone Swiss composers – Honegger, Martin, and even Doret, whose *Les Armaillis* was revived in 1956 – also hosted the premiere of Milhaud's *La mère coupable*. As for Monte Carlo, which went through a slump in the 1930s and 1940s after its heyday earlier in the century, it premiered with much success in 1973 the opera by the Roman-born Renzo Rossellini after the play by Henry de Montherlant (1896–1972), *La reine morte*.[72]

While Poulenc towers above all other French opera composers of this disappointing period, it is fair to add that he was not alone: Sauguet, Landowski, Tomasi, Daniel-Lesur, and Damase all deserve credit for carrying the flag of French opera under such difficult circumstances, while other composers, beginning in the 1960s, turned to new, more experimental forms labeled "théâtre musical."

Francis Poulenc

Unlike his colleagues Milhaud and Honegger from *Les Six*, Francis Poulenc (1899–1963) came to opera relatively late: he was 48 when his first work was staged at the Opéra-Comique. His operatic output is also small compared to theirs. But, unlike theirs, not only were his three operas immediate successes, they have also earned a permanent place in the international repertory, a unique case among French composers active after the Second World War.

Poulenc was born a rich Parisian.[73] His father and uncles owned a prosperous pharmaceutical business which was to develop into the conglomerate Rhône-Poulenc. Instead of entering the Conservatoire, he studied the piano with Ricardo Viñes (1875–1943), the Catalan pianist and friend of Debussy and Ravel, through whom he also became acquainted with Satie, another major influence. In 1921, having had by then several compositions publicly performed with success, Poulenc took composition lessons with Koechlin. However, his literary friendships – with Cocteau or Paul Éluard especially – were equally important for his artistic development and, ultimately, influential on his approach to opera, especially his mellifluous setting of the French language.

Poulenc does not appear to have contemplated an operatic project seriously until 1939. By the time he composed the music of *Les mamelles de Tirésias*, however, he already had a solid experience of the stage, with several ballets to his credit, the recitatives he had written at Diaghilev's request for Gounod's *La colombe* upon its 1924 revival at Monte Carlo, and (not least, though some of it is lost) the incidental music he wrote for several major plays in that brilliant period for the French theater – Jean Giraudoux's *Intermezzo* (1933), Jules Romains's *Monsieur Le Trouhadec saisi par la débauche* (1933), and Jean Anouilh's *Léocadia* (1940) and *Le voyageur sans bagage* (for its 1943 revival).

Poulenc had attended the premiere of Guillaume Apollinaire's "drame surréaliste" (the adjective was Apollinaire's own coinage) *Les mamelles de Tirésias* at a small Montmartre theater on 24 June 1917. Though actually drafted much earlier, it paralleled, in its deliberate outrageousness, the anti-war posture of the Dada movement launched in Switzerland the previous year: a woman shedding her breasts (the "mamelles" of the title) and growing a beard (Thérèse becoming Tirésias); a man procreating 40,000 babies; a police officer strangled by a clairvoyant who turns out to be the heroine in disguise; and the whole thing, located in a fanciful Zanzibar,[74] presented as a plea for the country's repopulation (a message Apollinaire took seriously). Poulenc decided on the play as early as 1939. Having prepared his own libretto, which is basically Apollinaire's text with a few cuts, he wrote most of the music in his house in Touraine in the dramatic weeks that followed the Allied landing in June 1944, completing the orchestration in August of the following year. Ravel's *L'heure espagnole* was a particularly admired model, but Poulenc added purely personal touches, such as virtuoso piano playing in the Entr'acte and musical allusions to the world of early twentieth-century "café concert." Subtitled "opéra-bouffe," the work includes few spoken passages; nor is there a clear separation between recitatives and arias, but rather a fluid treatment of a text with constant attention to the clarity of words. Instead of trying to replicate the humor of the text by musical means, a variety of musical styles (some recalling operetta, others liturgical music) are called for, letting the listeners decide what is serious and what is not. Dedicated to Milhaud, to celebrate his return to France from his wartime American exile, *Les mamelles de Tirésias* was premiered in June 1947 at the Opéra-Comique in a production by Max de Rieux, himself an operetta singer, and with a cast headed by the soprano Denise Duval (1921–), who immediately became Poulenc's favorite performer.[75] Disconcerting conservative members of the Opéra-Comique audience and some critics,[76] the work attracted much attention, but its international career did not take off at once: although Leonard Bernstein conducted its American premiere at Brandeis in 1953, Milan had to wait until 1963 and London until 1968.

Having contemplated another Apollinaire-based project on the life of Casanova, Poulenc took a completely different route when he was approached to write an opera for La Scala. Guido Valcarenghi, head of the music publisher Ricordi, proposed Georges Bernanos's (1888–1948) *Dialogues des carmélites*, which, staged at the Théâtre Hébertot in 1952 (after performances in Germany the previous year), had immediately been hailed as a masterpiece. Written at the very end of the life of the great French Catholic novelist and essayist, it had actually been commissioned from him as a screenplay for a film which remained unrealized, based on a scenario by a Dominican friar, Raymond Brückberger (1907–1998), in collaboration with Philippe Agostini.[77] Bernanos adapted his screenplay from the 1931 novella by Gertrud von Le Fort, *Die letzte am Schafott* – a fictionalized account of the historical guillotining of 16 Carmelite nuns from Compiègne in 1794. (Acute problems of literary rights arose when it turned out that the American playwright Emmet Lavery had secured exclusivity for stage adaptations of the Le Fort novella.)[78] As for *Les mamelles*, Poulenc himself prepared his libretto: he managed the tour-de-force of reducing the long text (5 tableaux, 60 scenes) into a structure of three acts comprising four scenes each.[79] The composition of the music, between August 1953 and August 1955, coincided with one of the bleakest periods in his life – the illness and death from lung cancer of his lover Lucien Roubert. Throughout, Poulenc sought the advice of his performing partner and confidant, the baritone Pierre Bernac, on issues of vocal writing.[80] A genuine opera fan and lover of beautiful voices – among his favorites were Leonie Rysanek and Renata Tebaldi – Poulenc wrote the main parts of this opera, where male voices play only a minor role, with specific vocal types and colors in mind. He settled for a Thaïs voice for Blanche, an Amneris or Azucena for Mother Marie, a Sophie (*Rosenkavalier*) or Blondchen (*The Abduction from the Seraglio*) for Constance, an Aida for the Second Prioress. The emotionally wrenching scene of the death of Mme de Croissy, the first prioress, arguably the emotional high point of the opera, turned out to be the most difficult to write. Another problem, brilliantly solved in the *Salve regina* that closes the work, was how to handle the tempo – musically and dramatically – of the nuns' execution. The orchestration, begun in 1954, was completed by Poulenc in the summer of 1956.

The premiere of *Dialogues des carmélites*, in Italian translation, took place at La Scala on 26 January 1957, under Nino Sanzogno, with a Romanian Blanche (Virginia Zeani) and a Turkish Mme Lidoine (Leyla Gencer). The French premiere followed in June at the Opéra, with Duval (for whom the part of Blanche had been intended), Crespin as Mme Lidoine, and Rita Gorr as Marie.[81] The first American production took place in San Francisco the following September, under Erich Leinsdorf, with Dorothy Kirsten as Blanche and the young Leontyne Price as Mme Lidoine.[82] For the Covent Garden premiere in January 1958, Rafael Kubelik conducted a cast headed by his wife Elsie Morrison as Blanche and Joan Sutherland as Mme Lidoine. Within 10 years the work had also been staged in Argentina, Austria, Belgium, Brazil, Germany, Greece, Holland, Mexico, Portugal, Spain, and Switzerland, and was on its way to becoming the most widely staged French opera since *Pelléas*. Yet, paradoxically, it took a generation for its true greatness to be understood. In 1957 both the religious subject matter and the unapologetically tonal character of the music were at odds with the fashion of the day, and indeed some of the patronizing early reviews make for embarrassing reading today. Fifty years later the work – like Benjamin Britten's *Peter Grimes* and *Billy Budd* – has reached the undisputed status of a modern classic.[83]

Hardly had the *Dialogues* been premiered than Poulenc embarked on the composition of his third and final opera, *La voix humaine*. The subject was first proposed to him by his friend Hervé Dugardin, but it turned out that Hans Werner Henze had reserved the rights, which he relinquished in the fall of 1957. Cocteau's play, staged at the Comédie-Française in 1930, is a long mono-logue by an unnamed young society woman ("Elle") talking on the telephone to her lover, who has just left her, and gradually breaking down. Its operatic adaptation seemed to present formidable challenges, prompting Poulenc to refer to it as a "monstrous" work.[84] With the support of Cocteau, a friend of more than four decades, Poulenc solved the difficulty by organizing the play into "phases," like the movements of a symphony. The music was written between March and June 1958, and orchestrated in August and September of that year. Despite its classical appellation of "tragédie lyrique," it includes snatches of jazz and popular music from the 1920s and is more outwardly "modern," as well as more tonally ambiguous than the *Dialogues*. Duval, for whom the part was destined (Poulenc also hoped that Callas, with whom he was on friendly terms, might do it at La Scala), premiered *La voix humaine* at the Opéra-Comique in February 1959, under Georges Prêtre, in a production directed by Cocteau (it was given as a double bill with Messager's *Isoline*).[85] While its chamber-opera quality – and the fact that the voice is often unsup-ported by any accompaniment – designates it for smaller houses than the *Dialogues*, this "French *Erwartung*" (in Hervé Lacombe's felicitous phrase)[86] quickly established its place in the international repertory.

Henri Sauguet

Though his works are seldom revived now, Henri Sauguet (1901–1989) deserves more than a passing mention in a survey of mid-twentieth-century French opera.[87] He was born Henri Poupard in Bordeaux and studied with Canteloube, among others, but the strongest influences were those of *Les Six* – he became especially close to Poulenc – and Stravinsky. A Satie admirer, he joined Henri Cliquet-Pleyel, Maxime Jacob, and Roger Désormière to form the École d'Arcueil, named after the Paris suburb where Satie lived. Sauguet's first stage work was the "opéra bouffe militaire" *Le plumet du colonel*, commis-sioned by the Bériza Company and performed at the Champs-Élysées under Ernest Ansermet in 1924. After writing several successful ballets – *La chatte*, premiered by George Balanchine in 1927, is still regularly revived, as is *Les forains* (1945), written for the dancer Roland Petit – Sauguet returned to opera in 1930 with *La contrebasse*, an opera buffa based on Chekhov, with a libretto by the popular novelist Henri Troyat (1911–2007), then a high-school student. Sauguet's third opera and his most ambitious work was *La chartreuse de Parme*, a full-fledged adaptation of Stendhal's novel by Armand Lunel. Sauguet's 1990 autobiography contains an illuminating account of the difficulties of having a new work staged at the Opéra.[88] Planned as early as 1927, the work, recommended to Rouché by Julien Cain, head of the Bibliothèque nationale and his fellow Institut member, was finally premiered in March 1939 with Germaine Lubin as Gina Sanseverina and Raoul Jobin as Fabrice del Dongo; Jacques Dupont, Sauguet's lifelong companion, designed the sets and costumes. Anticipating the style of Poulenc, Sauguet mixed a variety of vocal styles and forms, from the opéra-comique manner of the insouciant early scenes (one of them, set at La Scala, is a delightful "opera within the opera") to the melancholy tone of the last two tableaux, leading to Fabrice's retirement in the Carthusian monastery of the title.[89] Sauguet's opera, which includes a ballet in the third tableau, can be considered the last successful French "number opera." Received warmly by the public, tepidly by critics, the war ended its Parisian career.

The tone of *La gageure imprévue*, written by Sauguet during the Second World War, belies the circumstances under which it was composed. Pierre Bertin's (1891–1984) libretto was adapted from a comedy by Sedaine[90] and, accordingly, the work evokes the world of eighteenth-century opéra-comique. This appealing piece, premiered with success at the Salle Favart in July 1944, remained in its repertory until 1969. Sauguet's next opera – his last major work for the stage – *Les caprices de Marianne*, was written for the 1954 Aix-en-Provence festival, where it was premiered with the Italian soprano Graziella Sciutti in the title part. Musset's dark comedy is based on a love triangle that resolves itself tragically: Coelio, whose love for Marianne is unrequited, dies at the hand of her jealous husband, after which she declares her love for Octave, Coelio's friend, who rejects her. Sauguet set Jean-Pierre Grédy's (b. 1920) libretto in the mode of a through-composed musical conversation, with an idiom more ostensibly modern than his previous works. Revived at Aix-en-Provence the following seasons, the work numbers among the more successful French operas of the decade.[91]

Notable post-war opera composers

The career of Marcel Landowski (1915–1999) shows the close ties that, under the Fifth Republic – three centuries after Lully – could still exist in France between culture and the political power of the day.[92] He was born in Brittany, the son of the sculptor Paul Landowski, whose Christ dominates the Bay of Rio de Janeiro. At the Paris Conservatoire, Landowski studied composition with

Busser, but the main influence he acknowledged was Honegger. His first work for the stage, *Le rire de Nils Halerius*, premiered at Mulhouse in 1951, was subtitled "légende lyrique et chorégraphique" – a testimony to the continued interest of French composers in the alliance between dance and opera. It also reflected his preference for serious, even philosophical subjects, as did his second opera *Le fou*. The composer wrote the libretto in collaboration with the poet Patrice de La Tour du Pin (1911–1975). The plot of this "drame lyrique" is set in a besieged city where a scientist named Peter Bell has devised an absolute weapon. Fearing the consequences of his invention, he refuses to divulge it and dies under torture. Premiered at Nancy in 1956 and staged shortly afterwards at the Théâtre des Champs-Élysées in Paris, the work was immediately interpreted as an allegory of the atomic bomb – a claim Landowski disputed, since the libretto was written in 1942–3. *Le fou* was also notable for using electromagnetic tape in addition to the standard orchestra. One of the most widely performed post-war French operas, it was mounted in many French theaters (Lyons, Strasbourg, Marseilles, Avignon, Mulhouse, Reims, Metz, Lille, Rouen, Montpellier etcetera) but has also been seen in Liège, Warsaw, Leningrad, and Rio. By the early 1960s, Landowski had embarked on an administrative career that led to his appointment, in the mid-1960s, as director of music at the Ministry of Culture – a position created by de Gaulle and held by André Malraux until 1969. This position, which Landowski kept until 1974 (he then became head of music for the city of Paris), made him the most important person in musical affairs in France, controlling state subventions and commissions. He resumed his operatic career in his retirement with *Montségur*, a historical opera in 11 scenes based on the brutal repression of the Cathar heresy in the early thirteenth century. Calling for a substantial cast and large orchestral and choral forces, the work was highly successful at its Toulouse premiere in 1985 but less so at the Opéra two years later. Landowski's late work also included the "conte musical" *La vieille maison*, premiered at Nantes in 1988, and an opera for children, *La sorcière du placard à balai* (Colmar, 1992). His final work, *Galina*, first seen at Lyons in 1995, is based on Galina Vishnevskaya's autobiography. The music quotes Verdi and Puccini roles sung by the Russian soprano, while her husband, Mstislav Rostropovich, is represented by a dancer holding a cello.

The Marseilles-born Henri Tomasi (1901–1971), a student of Vidal at the Paris Conservatoire, won the Prix de Rome in 1927.[93] Like Gaubert, his other teacher, he had a double career as conductor and composer. *Miguel Mañara*, Tomasi's most ambitious – and arguably greatest – opera is symptomatic of the difficulties faced by a French opera composer after the Second World War. It is based on the 1914 play *Don Juan de Mañara* by the Franco-Lithuanian Oscar Milosz (1877–1939),[94] an account of the seventeenth-century Spanish saint who, after a dissolute early life, devoted himself to God. Tomasi wrote his own prose libretto, completing the score in 1949. The work was received at the

Opéra but never produced there. Instead it was premiered in Munich in 1956, in German, under Cluytens. Its success led to further productions: Brussels in 1958, Lisbon (with Duval) and Naples in 1965, Mulhouse in 1967, Tours in 1981, and Marseilles in 1988; but the work has yet to be staged in Paris. Tomasi's next (but first staged) opera, *L'Atlantide*, was based on the legend of the submerged city of Atlantis as told in the 1919 bestseller by Pierre Benoît. Antinéa, the heroine of this "drame lyrique et chorégraphique," like that in Auber's *La muette de Portici* and Rimsky-Korsakov's *Mlada*, is not sung but danced by a ballerina. Premiered at Mulhouse in 1954 and soon afterwards presented in Lyons, Marseilles, and Gelsenkirchen, *L'Atlantide* was given at the Opéra in 1959 – a production delayed by strikes for months. Tomasi's own Corsican background provided the setting for *Sampiero Corso*, premiered at Bordeaux in 1956, with Crespin as Vannina, and revived at Marseilles as recently as 2005. The hero of this "drame lyrique" is a patriot with an uncompromising sense of honor who strangles his wife after learning that she pleaded for his life with their Genoese enemy. Tomasi also wrote operas on Joan of Arc and (before Messiaen) St Francis of Assisi – adaptations of Alphonse Daudet and Jean Giono – and an operatic version of the clandestinely published Resistance classic by Vercors, *Le silence de la mer*. As in the original novella, where a man and his daughter respond with total silence to the presence of a German officer billeted in their house, the opera has only one singing role. It was premiered in Toulouse in 1964.

Daniel-Lesur (1908–2002) – born Daniel-Jean-Yves Lesur – was trained as composer and organist at the Paris Conservatoire, becoming a professor at the rival Schola Cantorum. In 1936, together with Messiaen and Yves Baudrier, he formed a group which took on the name "Jeune France." Like Landowski, Daniel-Lesur occupied important administrative functions, notably at the French radio and at the Opéra, serving as its co-director in 1971–3.[95] The first of his two operas, an adaptation of Musset's drama *Andrea del Sarto*, occupied him for more than two decades: first he wrote stage music to the play, then a tone poem on the same subject, and finally an opera, set directly to Musset's prose text. Dedicated to the memory of Poulenc – one of its models, along with Debussy and Dukas – the work was premiered in Marseilles in 1969 (with Gabriel Bacquier in the title role). Daniel-Lesur's second opera, *Ondine*, was based on Jean Giraudoux's 1939 poetic version of the German romantic legend that had inspired E.T.A. Hoffmann, among others. Like *Andrea del Sarto*, it is written in the tradition of Poulenc and with scrupulous attention to the clarity of the text. Well received when presented by the Opéra at the Théâtre des Champs-Élysées in 1982, it merits a revival.[96]

Jean-Michel Damase (1928–) was a child prodigy. After receiving tuition from Samuel-Rousseau at an early age, he studied composition with Busser at the Paris Conservatoire, winning the Prix de Rome in 1947. Like the composers just mentioned, his career as an opera composer has taken place largely outside Paris. His first work, an adaptation of Jean Anouilh's dark comedy *Colombe*, set directly to the original prose, was premiered in Damase's native Bordeaux in 1961 with the composer conducting; it was staged at the Opéra-Comique in 1970. The same Anouilh (1910–1987) was Damase's librettist for the equally successful *Madame de . . .*, adapted from the Louise de Vilmorin story on which Max Ophüls based his film *The Earrings of Madame de. . . .* Subtitled "roman musical" (like *Louise*), Damase's version was premiered at Monte Carlo in 1970 and has received several productions since, most recently at Geneva in 2001. Anouilh's modern retelling of the Orpheus story, *Eurydice*, was also adapted by Damase into an opera for Bordeaux in 1972. Two years later Nancy premiered his *L'héritière*, an adaptation of *The Heiress*, Augustus and Ruth Goetz's stage version of Henry James's *Washington Square*. Renée Auphan, heroine of the original production, revived it with success in 2004 at Marseilles, where she was by then director of the opera. In recent years Damase has written an opera for children, and *Ochelata's Wedding*, a witty "comic opera" on an English libretto by Jaston Williams and Joe Sears, written for the OK Mozart Festival in Bartlesville, Oklahoma.

Another opera of the post-war period that deserves mention is Jean Françaix's *La princesse de Clèves*. Apparently turned down by the Ministry of Culture for a state-subsidized Paris production,[97] this adaptation of Madame de La Fayette's classic novel was produced to general acclaim at Rouen in 1965 and has been heard at the 1987 Schwetzingen Festival. A pupil of Nadia Boulanger, Françaix (1912–1998) also wrote a musical comedy after Balzac, *L'apostrophe*, first staged in Amsterdam in 1951 and revived at Strasbourg. Like Daniel-Lesur and Damase, his style is influenced by Poulenc.

An exception to the lack of interest in opera among the musical avant-garde of the period was the Romanian-born Marcel Mihalovici (1898–1985), who lived in Paris as of 1919. becoming a close friend of Martinu in the 1920s and 1930s. Following his modernist adaptation of Racine's *Phèdre* in 1949, on a libretto by the poet Yvan Goll, he tried to convince his friend Samuel Beckett (1906–1989) to collaborate on an opera. Beckett being reluctant, Mihalovici obtained instead the Irish playwright's permission to set to music his play *Krapp's Last Tape*: by an interesting twist the operatic version, entitled *Krapp, ou la dernière bande*, involves electromagnetic tape – except that this time it is specifically called for by the play. Premiered at Bielefeld, Germany, in 1961, it was finally staged in the original French in Paris in 2006.[98]

Théâtre musical

While the composers we have just discussed remained essentially faithful to operatic tradition, a number of younger musicians working in France, beginning in the 1960s, began to explore new, experimental forms that came to be grouped under the heading "théâtre musical," to distinguish those productions from traditional opera.[99] Since the lyric theater was widely perceived to be in crisis, "théâtre musical" practitioners created works that differed markedly from the kinds of work typically performed at the Opéra or at the Opéra-Comique: usually short, requiring small, often unconventional instrumental forces; frequently dispensing with a chorus; calling for actors who could sing rather than for conventional operatic voices; freely mixing spoken and sung text; mounted on a reduced budget and in small theaters – and, preferably, in unconventional venues. Several of Claude Prey's works were thus performed by a barge-based company called the "Péniche-Opéra." Its models, rather than *Carmen* or *Louise* – or even *Pelléas* – were the Stravinsky of *L'histoire du soldat* or the Satie of *Le piège de Méduse*. Like the so-called "nouveau roman" of the 1950s and 1960s, which "deconstructed" the form of the novel, the "théâtre musical" produced works that could more appropriately be described as "anti-operas": Michel Butor, the prominent "new novelist," thus collaborated with the Belgian composer Henri Pousseur (1929–) on a "Fantaisie variable genre opéra" entitled *Votre Faust*, a collage-like work assembled from previous versions of the Faust myth.[100] Written for a cast of five actors and a non-standard instrumental ensemble (including electromagnetic tape), it was premiered at the Piccola Scala in 1969. A comparable "work in progress" quality characterizes Jean-Pierre Rivière's (1896–1987) earlier *Pour un Don Quichotte*, which was awarded the Ricordi Prize for a chamber opera and was premiered, also at the Piccola Scala, in 1961 (with Bacquier and Duval in the leading roles).

Born in the 1960s, the "théâtre musical" can be seen in retrospect as being part of the revolutionary, iconoclastic spirit of the time expressed in the events of May 1968 – which influenced both "théâtre musical" and the avant-garde theater of the period in general.[101] It also received an official consecration in 1969 when the Avignon Festival – the leading theater festival in France, launched in the late 1940s – included "théâtre musical" among its annual activities. Among the works mounted at Avignon during the following decade were *Ubu à l'opéra* (1974) by Antoine Duhamel (1925–); *Le pavillon au bord de la rivière* (1975) by the Franco-American composer Betsy Jolas (1926–), based on a medieval Chinese play; *Trois contes de l'honorable fleur* (1978) by Maurice Ohana (1913–1992), influenced by Japanese theater (one singer playing nine different parts). Also in 1978 *Le nom d'Œdipe*, subtitled "protocole musical," brought together the Bulgarian-born composer André Boucourechliev (1925–1997) and the feminist scholar and writer Hélène Cixous: the parts of Oedipus and Jocasta are each divided between a singer and an actor (there are also two Tiresiases, actors both).[102] In 1981 *Opéras-Instantanés* was a collaborative venture between nine composers (among whom Françoise Barrière, François-Bernard Mache, Yutaka Makino, Yves Prin, Pascal Dusapin, and Félix Ibarrondo). It called for three singers, five instrumentalists, electromagnetic tape, and seven TV sets. Reviewing it for the London-based magazine *Opera*,

Tony Mayer wrote: "The show is so original, so strong, so compact, so imaginative [. . .] that at the end of the performance one steps out brimming with confidence in the future of contemporary opera."[103]

One of the consequences of the "théâtre musical" in the 1970s and 1980s was to focus the attention on the vitality (and viability) of French provincial theaters. Lyons, under the dynamic leadership of Louis Erlo, and Strasbourg, with its "Atelier lyrique du Rhin," were particularly active in this respect, but so were Tours and Rennes, hitherto not particularly notable operatic centers. Rouen gave the 1980 premiere of Prodromidès's *Les traverses du temps*, a complex work whose plot unfolds on multiple time levels (the Jews' exile to Babylon, sixteenth-century Cyprus, French Revolutionary Terror, Auschwitz) and whose music invites comparison with such avant-garde composers as Xenakis, Ligeti, Berio, or Penderecki.[104]

The names of two composers are especially linked to "théâtre musical": Georges Aperghis and Claude Prey. Aperghis, born in Athens in 1945, moved to Paris at the age of 18.[105] His long association with Avignon began with *La tragique histoire du nécromancien Hiéronimo et de son miroir* in 1971, but he also founded his own music theater workshop in the eastern Paris suburb of Bagnolet in 1976. The writer of more than 20 works that can be labeled "théâtre musical," he has also authored large-scale works that, while closer to the world of avant-garde opera, are also influenced by the "théâtre musical": among them are *Pandaemonium*, adapted from Jules Verne's fantastic novel *Le château des Carpathes* (1973); *Jacques le fataliste*, after Diderot's highly experimental novel, staged in Lyons, also in 1973;[106] and *Je vous dis que je suis mort*, after Edgar Allan Poe's *Narrative of Arthur Gordon Pym*, staged at the Opéra-Comique in 1979.[107]

Claude Prey (1925–1998), a student of Messiaen and Milhaud at the Paris Conservatoire, was a rare case of a French contemporary composer who worked almost exclusively for the theater.[108] The labels he has given to his works show his sense of humor and gift for parody: "opéra radiophonico-épistolaire" (*Lettres perdues*, 1961); "mono-mimo-mélodrame" (the "opéra-minute" *Métamorphose d'Écho, ou Réponse à tout*, premiered in Prague in 1967); "opéra-test" (*La noirceur du lait, ou Le testeur testé*, whose protagonist is an analyst, staged at Strasbourg, also in 1967); "opera con variazioni" (*L'homme occis ou Un tunnel sous le Mont-Blanc*, 1963–78); "opéra-parodie en 2 procès" (*On veut la lumière Allons-y*, 1968, a satirical work on the Dreyfus Affair), etcetera. Prey's most admired work is his 1973 "opéra épistolaire" *Les liaisons dangereuses*, after the novel by Choderlos de Laclos. Subtitled "Éros et révolution" (extracts from Sade's *La philosophie dans le boudoir* are worked into the libretto), it features the novel's five principal characters, each associated with a particular instrument, while additional instrumental players, on stage, double as some of the minor characters. A musical *intermède* – deliberately archaic vis-à-vis the date of the novel (1782) – is provided by a shortened version of Rousseau's *Le devin du village*. Prey's final contribution to the "théâtre musical," *Sitôt le septuor ou beauté du ciel un soir d'alerte en 1917*, subtitled "opera opus Proust," was the first opera inspired by *À la recherche du temps perdu*.

First signs of renewal

The "théâtre musical" could have given the impression, for a while, that it was about to supplant other forms of contemporary opera. In fact a renewal was already underway, prompted – as usual in France – by a sense on the part of the political authorities that the decline of Paris as an operatic center was deleterious to the nation's prestige.[109] Radical measures were taken, including the closing of the Opéra-Comique in 1972, the disbanding of most of the Opéra troupe, and the highly publicized appointment of the Swiss composer Rolf Liebermann (longtime manager of the Hamburg Opera) as director of the Paris Opera. Liebermann's brief tenure (1973–80) had no immediate effect on contemporary creation – his commissions, *Erszebet*, *Ondine*, *Saint François d'Assise*, were all produced after his departure – but it went a long way towards restoring the luster of the institution. Luxury casts and conductors were brought to Paris,[110] and – even more importantly – prominent stage directors were recruited to raise the theatrical level of new productions: Giorgio Strehler staged *Le nozze di Figaro*, Jorge Lavelli *Faust* and *Pelléas*, Patrice Chéreau *Les contes d'Hoffmann* and the world premiere of Friedrich Cerha's completion of Alban Berg's *Lulu*. Meanwhile the Opéra-Comique was given to a newly created "Opéra-Studio," headed by Louis Erlo, for the training and development of young French singers. Though its existence was brief, the Opéra-Studio nurtured artists of the caliber of Colette Alliot-Lugaz, François Le Roux, and Jean-Philippe Lafont. After it was closed in 1978, the Opéra-Comique then became a second stage for the Opéra, recovering its autonomy only in 1990.

The new appetite for opera in the French capital, fostered by the State's financial largesse, resulted in the opening of a third opera theater, this time under the auspices of the city of Paris. Initial plans for the creation of an "Opéra municipal de Paris" collapsed in political intrigue – provoking the resignation of Landowski, among others – but the project was resurrected in the late 1970s when the Châtelet was turned from a venue for grand spectacle operettas into a third opera theater, which took the name "Théâtre musical de Paris."

Paris was not alone in benefiting from this restoration of prestige. Provincial opera houses, which arguably had done more than the capital since 1945 to keep opera alive, received additional attention and funding – especially in the 1980s, when the Socialist governments actively took up the cause of cultural decentralization. Another development was the proliferation of music festivals throughout the country, which offered additional venues and encouraged original programming choices. The French, after neglecting their own operatic tradition, thus became more curious about it. Soon it was possible to hear Dalayrac's *Maison à vendre* at Saint-Céré, Dupont's *Farce du cuvier* at Caen, Leroux's *Chemineau* at Reims, and Méhul's *L'irato* at Tours. Spurred perhaps by those provincial initiatives, the Salle Favart began to restage forgotten gems such as Gounod's *Médecin malgré lui*, Hahn's *Marchand de Venise*, and Philidor's *Tom Jones*. This broadening of the repertory was bolstered by the rediscovery and popularization of authentic baroque performance style which began in the early 1970s. Long ignored, or inadequately served, the operas of Lully, Charpentier, Campra, Rameau, and their contemporaries began to emerge from purgatory. Two important dates were the first staging ever of Rameau's *Les Boréades*, under John Eliot Gardiner, at the 1982 Aix-en-Provence Festival, and Jean-Marie Villégier's 1987 production of Lully's *Atys* by William Christie's company *Les arts florissants*, which revealed the theatrical potential of the work in a musically impeccable realization.

The enormous attention received by two very different works staged in Paris in the early 1980s shows that the life of French opera had come a long way since its post-1945 doldrums: one was *La tragédie de Carmen*, a "théâtre musical" reworking of *Carmen* by the Romanian-born avant-garde composer Marius Constant (1925–2004), directed by Peter Brook, which ran for many seasons in the Bouffes du Nord theater, where it opened in 1981;[111] the other one, in 1983, was the long-awaited premiere of Messiaen's *Saint François d'Assise*.

Olivier Messiaen

The involvement of Olivier Messiaen (1908–1992) with opera provides yet another instance of the political dimension that cultural matters often take in France. Even before his tenure at the Paris Opéra began in 1973, Liebermann – himself a notable opera composer[112] – was determined to commission an opera from France's most prominent and respected living composer. Messiaen was first approached that summer and the request was officially reiterated – and accepted – at a dinner hosted at the Élysée Palace by President Georges Pompidou.[113] Reinforcing the official character of the commission, Messiaen's opera was to be premiered in 1975 to mark the centenary of the opening of the Palais Garnier.

Messiaen, to be sure, had always been interested in opera. A student of Dukas at the Paris Conservatoire, he held *Ariane and Barbe-bleue* in high regard. The discovery of *Pelléas et Mélisande* in his adolescence had been a defining event in his decision to become a composer. Wagner too was the object of his lifelong admiration: his classes at the Conservatoire, where he taught composition from 1966 to 1978, involved detailed analyses of Wagner's works. An unspecified operatic project was apparently on his mind in the late 1940s, though by the 1960s – the lowest ebb in French operatic history – no such plans resurfaced. Having accepted Liebermann's offer, Messiaen – in an unsurprising Wagnerian gesture – decided to be his own librettist and made it clear that he intended to be involved in all aspects of the staging. Interestingly, his initial conception was a work with spoken rather than sung parts, more in the manner of Stravinsky's *Perséphone* and Honegger's *Amphion*, before he embarked on a "real" opera, with roles worthy of attracting major singers of the day.

Given the religious inspiration of much of Messiaen's music, the choice of the life of St. Francis as a subject seems, in retrospect, a perfectly logical one,[114] all the more so considering this saint's special association with birds, bird songs being Messiaen's other great source of inspiration. Indeed the score of *Saint François*, beginning with the motifs associated with the principal characters, is literally permeated with bird songs. But as the work's dramatic and musical scope expanded, it became clear that the initial target of 1975 was not to be met: it was only, in fact, in 1976 that the libretto took shape. Rather than giving a biographical account of the saint, the eight episodes (the opera is subtitled "scènes franciscaines"), arranged in three acts, focus each on a symbolic event of his spiritual journey, as reported in early accounts of his life, or the so-called *Fioretti* compiled by his first disciples: the first episode, "La Croix," is a philo-sophical, Socratic conversation with the naive, easily terrified Brother Leo; the second, "Lauds," is based on Francis's Canticle of Brother Sun; the third, "The kissing of the leper," introduces the figure of the angel – the only feminine vocal presence in the opera (apart from the chorus). The angel figures prominently in the next two scenes, "L'ange voyageur," the only scene in which Francis does not appear, and "L'ange musicien," in which, in a musical tour-de-force of indescrib-able beauty, the music of the heavenly spheres is revealed to Francis. The following scene, "The sermon to the birds," is the longest and the one Messiaen composed last; it features bird songs from lands as distant as the South Pacific. The first scene of the last act is devoted to Francis receiving the Stigmata; the second and final one, which moves from poignant sadness to triumphant exal-tation, deals with his last moments and resurrection, with a final chorus ending on the word "joy" in a terrific blaze of sound.

The short score of *Saint François* was completed by the autumn of 1977 and plans were made for a 1980 premiere, though the announcement of the opera's title, which Messiaen had kept a secret even from his wife, the pianist Yvonne Loriod, upset him greatly. In the event, orchestration was delayed by the composer's health problems and its completion, in August 1983, was achieved only once Messiaen recovered from a period of deep depression and in no small part thanks to Loriod's own involvement in the final stages of the project.

A work of vast proportions, *Saint François d'Assise* is scored for an orchestra of 119 – including three ondes martenot and a large percussion section – and a chorus reduced to 100 from the intended 150 (divided into 10 groups). Such massive forces severely tested the resources of the Palais Garnier when the opera was premiered in November 1983, though the sensation caused by the 11 performances vindicated the enormous efforts they required. Seiji Ozawa, assisted by Kent Nagano, conducted. The cast, which Messiaen had chosen himself, was headed by José Van Dam as Francis and Christiane Eda-Pierre as the angel. Sandro Sequi's production faithfully translated the intentions of the composer – who had wisely given up his initial intention to direct the work himself. Admittedly, however, it was only when the work was seen in other stagings – such as Peter Sellars's at Salzburg and Paris in 1992, or Nicolas Brieger's at San Francisco for the 2002 American stage premiere[115] – that *Saint François d'Assise* confirmed its musical greatness and dramatic effectiveness as one of the most demanding operas of the modern age. As the composer himself acknowledged shortly before he died in 1992, it is at once his most ambitious achievement and a synthesis of his work.[116]

French opera since Messiaen

In 1989, to mark the bicentenary of the French Revolution, a new opera house opened in Paris. Located, appropriately, where the Bastille once stood, it closed its doors after the inaugural gala, to reopen them the following year with the first complete staging in France of Berlioz's *Les Troyens*. In keeping with the monarchical character of the Fifth Republic, the design of the new Opéra-Bastille had been chosen in 1983 by President François Mitterrand and a handful of close advisers. The surprise winner of the international contest – reportedly on the superficial resemblance of the entrance to a Richard Meier building – was a young Canadian architect of Uruguayan birth, Carlos Ott. The Bastille has not been uncontroversial, but the fact was that, for the first time since the mid nineteenth century, Paris now had four opera theaters running concurrently.

In certain respects, the situation of French opera at the dawn of the twenty-first century looks like the return to an earlier age, when most composers wrote operas. By contrast with the dispiriting situation of the 1960s and 1970s, a respectable number of French works were staged in Paris. Since 1983 operatic world premieres hosted by the French capital have included Edison Denisov's *L'écume des jours* (Opéra-Comique, 1986); Ohana's *La Célestine* (Palais Garnier, 1988); Philippe Fénelon's *Le chevalier imaginaire* (Châtelet, 1992); and Philippe Manoury's *60ᵉ Parallèle* (Châtelet, 1997). For its part, the Opéra-Bastille has boasted an unprecedented string of world premieres in the past 10 years: Fénelon's *Salammbô* (1998); Manoury's *K* (2001), based on Kafka's *The Trial*; Pascal Dusapin's *Perelà, uomo di fumo* (2003); Matthias Pintscher's *L'espace dernier* (2004), inspired by the life and works of Rimbaud; and Kaija Saariaho's *Adriana Mater* (2006). Many new works were also mounted in the provinces, with Lyons confirming its leading role: it thus presented the first stagings of Duhamel's *Quatrevingt-treize* (1989), after Hugo's novel; Fabio Vacchi's Goldoni-based *La station thermale* (1994); Jolas's *Schliemann* (1995); Gilbert Amy's *Le premier cercle* (1999), after Aleksandr Solzhenitsyn; Michèle Reverdy's *Médée* (2003); and Michaël Levinas's *Les nègres* (2004), after Jean Genet. Montpellier premiered Philippe Hersant's *Le château des Carpathes* (1993), based on the same Jules Verne novel that had inspired Aperghis's *Pandaemonium*; and Rouen Chaynes's *Jocaste* (1993). Strasbourg premiered Levinas's *Go-Gol* and Aperghis's *Tristes Tropiques* (both in 1966); Nancy, Prodromidés's *La noche triste* (1989), which deals with Hernán Cortez and the conquest of Mexico; Levinas's *Go-Gol* and Aperghis's *Tristes tropiques* (both in 1996); and Georges Boeuf's *Verlaine Paul* (1997). Fénelon's *Les rois* (after Julio Cortázar) was premiered in Bordeaux in 2004 and his *Faust* at Toulouse in 2007, while Peter Eötvös's *Le balcon* – another Genet-based opera – was first seen at the 2002 Aix-en-Provence Festival. However, what is perhaps the most significant event in recent French operatic history did not take place in France, or in a French-speaking country: it was the 2000 premiere, at the Salzburg Festival, of Saariaho's *L'amour de loin*. The composer (b. 1952) was Finnish, the French libretto was by a Lebanese writer, Amin Maalouf (b. 1949). The work was performed in its original language at a prestigious international festival in Austria under a Finnish conductor (Esa-Pekka Salonen), in a production by an American director (Peter Sellars) without a native French speaker in the cast.[117]

As emblematized by *L'amour de loin*, the cosmopolitan character of recent French opera might appear to be a return to its oldest tradition – which it never totally abandoned, even if the post-1945 decades, may convey, in retrospect, an impression of cultural isolationism. Of the other composers just listed, Denisov (1929–1996) – who wrote his own libretto after Boris Vian's cult novel *L'écume des jours* – was Russian; Pintscher (born 1971) is German, and Vacchi (born 1949) Italian. Eötvös was born in 1944 in a part of Transylvania that was then Hungarian and is now Romanian. Yet the international character of French opera has also taken, in recent years, more complex forms: Dusapin's *Perelà*, premiered in Paris, was set to an Italian libretto by the composer after Aldo Palazzeschi's 1911 Futurist novel *Il codice di Perelà*. Of the five operas Dusapin has written so far, only the first, *Roméo et Juliette*, on a libretto by Olivier Cadiot, is in French. *Medeamaterial*, premiered at Brussels in 1992, is set to a text by the German playwright Heiner Müller; the third, *To be sung* (after Gertrude Stein) and fifth (*Faustus, the Last Night*, premiered at the Berlin Staatsoper in 1996), both on libretti by the composer, are in English. Can one still call Dusapin a French opera composer, or have we entered a period when such national – or cultural – distinctions make little sense? Dusapin's exceptional – but not unique – case is paralleled by that of Philippe Boesmans. One of today's foremost opera composers, Boesmans, born in 1936 in Flemish Belgium, wrote his first work *La passion de Gilles*, premiered at

Brussels in 1983, to a French libretto, but has since ceased to set French texts to music and considers the kind of limpid prosody Debussy used in *Pelléas* as "impracticable"[118] today: all his subsequent works for the stage – *Die Reigen* (1993), after Arthur Schnitzler's play; *Wintermärchen* (1999), based on *The Winter's Tale, Julie* (2005), after Strindberg; *Yvonne* (2009), after the play by Witold Gombrowicz – have been on German libretti. Similarly, Eötvös, who was raised in Hungary but also studied in Germany, set his most famous stage work *Die Drei Schwestern*, after Chekhov, in German – its 1998 world premiere in Lyons was in French translation – while his setting of Tony Kushner's *Angels in America*, premiered at the Châtelet in 2004 (and produced since in Boston and Fort Worth), is in English.

To be sure, such phenomena are not unprecedented in operatic history. Balfe wrote operas in Italian, French, and English, and Meyerbeer in German, Italian, and French; and Wagner himself, after excoriating Meyerbeer for having no "mother tongue," was happy to reset *Tannhaüser* to a French text. Yet one is also tempted to interpret the recent forms of cosmopolitanism in terms of cultural globalization – a phenomenon that affects music like everything else. Another recent development has been works whose text is in several languages – one of which may be French.[119] Ohana's *La Célestine* (after Fernando de Rojas's classic tragicomedy) included passages in Spanish, Latin, and English. Fénelon's *Don Quichotte* opera, *Le chevalier imaginaire*, mixes French, Spanish, and Italian. *Paysage avec parents éloignés* (*Landschaften mit entfernten Verwandten*), the opera by Heiner Goebbels (born 1952), staged at Geneva in 2002, goes even further by being in five different languages (English, French, German, Hindi, and Italian), gathering texts by Giordano Bruno, T.S. Eliot, Michel Foucault, Henri Michaux, Gertrude Stein, among others. This heterogeneity, often matched on a musical level by a refusal to settle on one particular style, may be an essential characteristic of the postmodern age, in which fragmented, multiple perspectives are favored over attempts at a unified, coherent vision.

Yet it is equally striking, after two decades dominated by the "théâtre musical," to see composers return to the grand genre, and, by contrast with early twentieth-century composers writing only one opera, return to it regularly: full-fledged operas rather than short works; large-scale compositions for full symphonic forces rather than chamber pieces scored for unusual instrumental combinations; roles written for opera stars rather than for contemporary music specialists. The case of Fénelon – a student of Messiaen – is telling: his *Salammbô*, the first new work to be staged at the Opéra-Bastille, is based on the Flaubert novel that had already inspired Reyer (not to mention Mussorgsky's unfinished project); *Salammbô* further conforms to the tradition with its structure in identifiable solos, duets, and full-scale choral passages. It is also significant that two French composers, within one year, unveiled their own version of the *Faust* story – another subject in the grand French tradition:

Dusapin, whose English text is mostly inspired by Christopher Marlowe, while Fénelon's libretto (his own) is based on Nikolaus Lenau's tragedy rather than on Goethe.

It is also paradoxical, after decades during which the musical avant-garde tended to regard opera as a dying form, to see among the leading French opera composers active today names long associated with IRCAM,[120] the state-sponsored musical laboratory established under Boulez's aegis within the Centre Georges Pompidou with a view to developing the most advanced forms of contemporary music. Eötvös, who conducted the inaugural IRCAM concert in 1978, was for many years music director of its affiliate formation, the Ensemble intercontemporain; Manoury, Saariaho, Dusapin even (briefly in his case) were all associated with IRCAM. There is no better indication of the current vitality of French opera in recent years than this determination of musicians from the younger generation to contribute to a genre illustrated by the greatest composers of the past.

Will any of the works premiered since the mid-1980s find their place in the permanent repertory, in France and elsewhere? One should refrain from trying to answer the question. The so-called judgments of posterity, in any event, can be arbitrary and unfair. Will it regard Saariaho's *L'amour de loin* as a modern classic, one to which future generations may turn to as a defining work in the early twenty-first century, as ours does to *Louise* or *Pelléas* for the early twentieth century? No contemporary French opera has received such international acclaim since Messiaen's *Saint François d'Assise*.[121] Its subject – Saariaho's own choice – may seem at first sight as undramatic as that of Messiaen's. The legend surrounding the life of the twelfth-century troubadour poet Jaufré Rudel, who is assumed to have died in the Second Crusade around 1149, had already inspired an opera, Georges Witkowski's *La princesse lointaine*, which had only the briefest run at the Paris Opera in 1934.[122] Based on Edmond Rostand's 1895 verse tragedy of the same title, it was set directly on the original. In the two operas, Jaufré, having sailed across the Mediterranean to meet the faraway princess about whose beauty and virtue he has sung in his love poetry, becomes fatally sick at sea and dies in her arms on his arrival at Tripoli. But the two libretti could not be more contrasted. Rostand's play is a mildly jingoistic pageant. Saariaho, by contrast, commissioned her libretto (at the suggestion of Peter Sellars) from Amin Maalouf a writer born in Lebanon of mixed Arab and Christian parentage (Arabic was his mother tongue), who had, obviously, a different perspective on the Crusades.[123] Reducing the story to its essential, spiritual dimension, Maalouf's version rests on three characters: Jaufré (baritone), Clémence de Tripoli (soprano), and an unnamed pilgrim (a male character, sung by a mezzo-soprano), who acts as a sort of go-between: it is he who first tells Jaufré about Clémence, and then reports to her his infatuation. The chorus is used sparingly, assuming different roles – Jaufré's companions, Clémence's friends, inhabitants of Tripoli – as it dialogues with the principals in the manner of the ancient Greek theater; at other moments the chorus assumes a purely instrumental function in the tapestry of sound. The plot unfolds slowly, almost hieratically, over its five acts, from Jaufré's initial monologue to the heartbreaking episode – reminiscent of Act 3 in Wagner's *Tristan* – in which Jaufré and his beloved are in the presence of each other for a few anguished moments before he dies. In the extended final scene Clémence begins by accusing God of injustice, but eventually sublimates her grief and recognizes the spiritual side of the feeling that bound her and Jaufré together.

Kaija Saariaho, while making sure that the text is intelligible throughout, emphasizes its poetical, oneiric dimension by adopting a style of declamation halfway between recitative and chant. The references to medieval music do not take the form of musical archaism, as in previous "medieval" French operas of the twentieth century, but of a more refined, subtle subtext. Similarly, the motifs associated with the three characters are not of the obvious, Wagnerian kind (which Debussy likened to calling cards), but are more discreet and insinuating, in the manner of *Pelléas*. Saariaho's musical idiom, neither tonal nor completely dissonant, impresses itself on the listener's attention by an extraordinary palette of timbres. The vocal writing, unlike so many modernist works of the 1950s and 1960s, goes neither against the text nor against the voice: it is both challenging and rewarding. As in *Pelléas* and *Louise* – or, indeed, *Saint-François d'Assise* – it is of the kind that promises to continue attracting great singing actors of today and tomorrow. To summarize this achievement one is tempted to quote Dusapin, deploring, on the subject of his own opera *Perelà*, that "in the evangelical world of contemporary music, you can't talk of love, emotion, expression," and announcing that his work, in contrast, was meant to be "a study of expression."[124] Saariaho's work shows that it is the musical realization of the emotional power of a text wherein lies the future not just of French opera, but of opera itself.

NOTES

Chapter 1: From the Origins to Lully

1. On the ballet de cour in general, see McGowan 1963, McGowan 2008, and Isherwood 1973, 77–113. On "geometric" dancing, also called "horizontal," see McGowan 1963, 36–7 and plates VI-VII, which reproduce some of the figures, supposedly derived from a lost Druidic alphabet, from the *Ballet de Monsieur de Vendosme* (1610).
2. Among them was the *Paradis d'amour*, words by Pierre de Ronsard, music by Claude Le Jeune and Thibault de Courville, staged four days before the St. Bartholomew Massacre; see Isherwood 1973, 60–1, and McGowan 2008, 87–90. The first work to be actually called "ballet" was the *Ballet des Polonais*, performed in 1573 to celebrate the election of the Duc d'Anjou (the future Henri III) as king of Poland (Isherwood 1973, 63).
3. On the *Balet comique*, see in particular Isherwood 1973, 79–87, and McGowan 2008, 114–18.
4. McGowan 1963, 265, lists 19 ballets just for the year 1607.
5. The main name, in addition to Guédron, being his son-in-law Antoine Boësset (1585–1643).
6. The music and choreography of the *Ballet de la Merlaison*, performed at Chantilly in March 1635, were his work.
7. See McGowan 1963, 117–31. One of the victims of Concini's downfall was the brilliant court poet Estienne Durand, author, among other works, of the *Ballet de la délivrance de Renaud*: accused of having written a pamphlet hostile to the king, he was broken on the wheel, at the age of 28, in 1618 (*ibid.*, 114–15).
8. On this ballet, see Isherwood 1973, 107–12.
9. On Colletet and the ballet de cour, see McGowan 1963, 155–67.
10. *Ibid.*, 217.
11. McGowan in Lewis and Fortune 1975, 169.
12. On Mazarin and Italian opera in Paris, see Isherwood 1973, 117–34, and Anthony 1997, 64–71.
13. It may be recalled that "comédie" here means play, not comical in tone, but without a tragic ending.
14. A capacity as large as 7,000 has been suggested. More realistic estimates put it at *c.*6,000 or even 4,000; see Wild 1989, 406, and Wood and Sadler 2000, 23. In the eighteenth century, the theater was redesigned by Soufflot and Gabriel, who reduced its size by half. It was used by several political assemblies during the Revolution. The Tuileries Palace burned down during the Paris Commune in 1871 and was subsequently demolished.
15. On Benserade, see Christout 1967; Isherwood 1973, 134–41; and the entry by Margaret McGowan in *The New Grove Dictionary of Music and Musicians*, ed. by Stanley Sadie. 2nd ed. London: Macmillan, 2001. Hereafter cited as *New Grove 2*.
16. See La Gorce 2002, especially 59–62.
17. Corneille, however, resorted to mixed meters in one of his later plays (without music), *Agésilas* (1666).
18. Cited from Isherwood 1973, 126.
19. See especially Powell 2000, 23–8.
20. Labeled "tragédie-ballet" in the 1671 libretto, *Psyché* in fact exhibits all the features of the "tragédie à machines," while coming "close to being a full-fledged opera" (see Isherwood 1973, 180).

21. On pastorals in general, see especially Powell 2000, 160–242; see also Anthony 1997, 84–92.
22. Henri-Jean Martin's phrase, in *Histoire de l'édition française*, Paris: Promodis, 1982, 1:548. Guarini's *Il pastor fido* appeared in French in 1622 in the wake of the success of d'Urfé's novel.
23. The libretto was published in 1654 (a copy is recorded in the online catalogue of the Bibliothèque nationale de France).
24. The Jesuit polygraph Claude-François Menestrier, in his *Des représentations en musique anciennes et modernes* (Paris: Guignard, 1681, 177–8), reports that a certain Abbé Mailly, secretary to Cardinal Bigi, set several scenes sung in recitative throughout, accompanied by a "symphonie," performed with the play *Achebar, roi du Mogol* in Carpentras in 1646. See Pougin 1881, 14, and Anthony 1997, 86. Though neither words or music have been traced, it is clear from Menestrier's description, however, that Mailly's experiment, limited to a few passages, did not constitute a full opera.
25. On Pougin's chauvinism, one quotation suffices: "One can justly note, in this context, that the destinies of the Opéra have always been the same since its origin, and from the birth of this 'palace of harmony,' French musicians have repeatedly been sacrificed to outsiders" (Pougin, 1881, 201; see also 205, n1: "with Cambert we would also have had a French music, and really French at that"). On Perrin generally, see also Nuitter and Thoinan 1886; Auld 1986; La Gorce 1992, 11ff.; Anthony 1997, 86–90.
26. Cited by Christina Bashford in her entry on Cambert in *New Grove 2*. The text (not by Perrin) and music of *La muette ingrate* are lost.
27. The text of Perrin's letter is in Auld, 1:102–8. On this important document, see especially Kintzler 1990, 191ff., and Isherwood 1973, 171–2.
28. Interestingly, the same reproach was to be leveled at French opera throughout the eighteenth century by Italian and other visitors to Paris.
29. See Christina Bashford, "Perrin and Cambert's 'Ariane, ou Le mariage de Bacchus' re-examined," *Music and Letters* 72:1 (February 1991), 1–26.
30. Cited from Isherwood 1973, 174–5, and La Gorce 1992, 14–15. As La Gorce notes, Perrin's wording echoes earlier attempts during the French Renaissance around Antoine de Baïf; on Baïf's "Académie de musique et de poésie", see Isherwood 1973, 29–32.
31. It also participated in a similar Franco-Italian debate. An important step, in 1666, the year Perrin approached Colbert, was the creation of the French Academy in Rome.
32. The Académie des sciences morales et politiques, the fifth of the academies that together form the Institut de France, was established during the French Revolution. The fact that musicians were never given an academy of their own – music was simply added to the constituencies of the Académie des beaux-arts under Napoleon – is to be understood in the context of these early debates and of Lully's subsequent monopoly.
33. One of the leitmotifs of Friedrich Melchior Grimm's pamphlet, *Le petit prophète de Boehmischbroda* (1753), is that the official name of the Opéra ("Académie royale de musique") is absurd, since it is not an "académie." Yet the term has stood.
34. Cited from McGowan 1975, 202.
35. See Howard Mayer Brown and Iain Fenlon's entry "Academy" in *New Grove 2*. The phrase "Royall Academy of Musick" appeared in London in 1674 in connection with the staging of Perrin and Cambert's *Ariane* (see Bashford, "Perrin and Cambert's 'Ariane,' " 1).
36. The point is made by Beaussant 1992, 462.
37. See Bashford, *op. cit.*, "Perrin and Cambert's 'Ariane,' " 2.
38. A colorful portrait of Sourdéac can be found in the "Extravagans, visionnaires, fantasques, bizarres, etc." section of Tallemant des Réaux's contemporary *Historiettes*, ed. Antoine Adam, Paris: Gallimard, Bibliothèque de la Pléiade, 1961, 2:727–8.
39. See Pierre Perrin, *Pomone. Opéra, ou Représentation en musique*. Pastorale. Paris: Le Mercier, 1671, 7–9.
40. See Nuitter and Thoinan 1886, 118, and Pougin 1881, 117–21. Beaumavielle, in particular, sang Cadmus in Lully's *Cadmus et Hermione* (1673) and the title role in his *Roland* (1685).
41. This first home of the Paris Opera was destroyed in 1688 (Nuitter and Thoinan 1886, 147).
42. On *Pomone*, see especially Powell, 296–304.
43. Ballard, the music printer, began engraving the score but stopped in the middle of Act 2, scene 5. The surviving music can be heard on Hugo Reyne's 2004 recording (Accord 476 2437).
44. The figure makes *Pomone* one of the most successful works performed in Paris until the nineteenth century. By comparison, the greatest theatrical triumph of the seventeenth century, Thomas Corneille's *Timocrate*, ran for about 80 performances in 1656–7.
45. See La Gorce 1992, 21.
46. A revised version with additional dances, *Le triomphe de l'Amour*, was performed before the court at Saint-Germain-en-Laye in February 1672. See La Gorce 1992, 25.

47. Only a portion of the music survives.

48. Sourdéac continued to design stage machinery, notably for Thomas Corneille's tragedy *Circé* at the Comédie-Française in 1675.

49. See Bashford, *op. cit.*, "Perrin and Cambert's 'Ariane.' " The work had a new, topical prologue. The music (now lost) was not credited to Cambert but to the Catalan musician Louis (Luis) Grabu, Master of the King's Violins, whose exact involvement in the London *Ariane* is not clear.

50. On Lully's life, see especially La Gorce 2002, which has superseded all previous studies, and the same author's entry in *New Grove 2*.

51. Probably with Nicolas Métru and Nicolas Gigault, organists at the Jesuit church of Saint-Paul on the rue Saint-Antoine; see la Gorce 2002, 39–41.

52. Molière's actual name was Jean-Baptiste Poquelin. On Lully and Molière, see Powell 2000, 323–81 and 398–415.

53. The king's presence is mentioned in the libretto printed before the premiere, which has led most historians to believe it took place (see La Gorce 2002, 156).

54. Lully's monopoly on musical matters after 1673 may also, to be sure, have been a factor in discouraging potential followers.

55. Cited by La Gorce 2002, 175. Brossard (1655–1730), himself a composer, wrote the first French dictionary of music (1703). His collections, donated to the Royal Library, form the nucleus of the music department of the Bibliothèque nationale de France.

56. Cited from Isherwood 1973, 181; see also Beaussant 1992, 457, and La Gorce 2002, 184–5.

57. The theater, which was also called "de Bel Air," is described by La Gorce 2002, 188–9.

58. The work, recorded by Hugo Reyne, is available on the same set as *Pomone* (Accord 476 2437).

59. Molière's troupe was relocated on the Left Bank – in the very theater where *Pomone* had been performed, now called Théâtre Guénégaud – to be eventually merged with the Hôtel de Bourgogne in 1680 to form the Comédie-Française.

60. The performance has been immortalized by the engraver Jean Le Pautre.

61. The privilege was never officially registered and the Académie des spectacles had only a brief existence; see Isherwood 1973, 202.

62. On the Guichard affair, see La Gorce 2002, 224–40. Lully responded with charges of sodomy.

63. On Berain, see La Gorce, *Berain, dessinateur du Roi Soleil*, Paris: Herscher, 1986.

64. On the Brunet scandal, see La Gorce 2002, 306–15. As late as 1729, Antoine I Grimaldi, prince of Monaco, who had known Lully, tried to obtain a copy of a painting once in Lully's house, showing Brunet singing, accompanied by Lully on the harpsichord and the Comte de Fiesque on the theorbo. The painting has since disappeared.

65. The Vendôme brothers were notorious, according to Saint-Simon, for their bisexuality.

66. According to a song cited by La Gorce 2002, 334, he fully shared his employer's sexual propensities. He is remembered above all for Victor Hugo's unkind gibe in *Les contemplations*, "Sur le Racine mort le Campistron pullule" ("Réponse à un acte d'accusation").

67. Most of Lully's tragédies en musique have been recorded. At the time of writing, there are still no complete recordings available of *Cadmus et Hermione* (only a DVD) or *Bellérophon*. *Alceste* has been recorded by Jean-Claude Malgoire (Montaigne 782012); *Thésée* (CPO 777 240–2) and *Psyché* (CPO 777 367–2) by Paul O'Dell and Stephen Stubbs; *Atys* by William Christie (HM 901257); *Isis* (Accord 4768048) by Hugo Reyne, who has also recorded *Amadis* (Accord 442 8549); *Persée* (Astrée 8874) and *Roland* (ABM 9949) by Christophe Rousset; *Proserpine* by Hervé Niquet (GES 921615); *Phaéton* (4509–91737–2) by Marc Minkowski, who has also recorded the pastorale *Acis et Galatée* (DGG 453497); and *Armide* by Philippe Herreweghe (HM 901456).

68. On this issue, see Graham Sadler's entry on "tragédie en musique" in *New Grove 2* and *Opera Grove*. On the tragédie en musique in general, see, especially Girdlestone 1972 and Kintzler 1990.

69. The main study of Quinault remains Étienne Gros, *Philippe Quinault, sa vie et son oeuvre*, Paris: Champion, 1926. See also Buford 2001 and the entries by James R. Anthony in *New Grove 2* and Lois Rosow in *The New Grove Dictionary of Opera*, ed. by Stanley Sadie. London: The Macmillian Press, 1992. Hereafter cited as *Opera Grove*.

70. See La Gorce 2002, 143–4.

71. *Ibid.*, 659.

72. *Ibid.*, 639.

73. In his preface to *Pomone*, Perrin had already argued that the marvelous played the central role in all types of opera; on the theory of the *merveilleux*, see especially Kintzler 1990, 270–77.

74. Jean de La Bruyère, no. 47 in "Des ouvrages de l'esprit," in *Les caractères ou les moeurs de ce siècle*.

75. *Ibid.*

76. See La Gorce 2002, 582–3.

77. See Kintzler 1990, *passim*, especially 172–8. See also Kintzler 2004, 13–15.

78. In his Letter to Della Rovere, Auld 1986, 1:107–8.

79. See La Gorce 2002, 584.
80. That Lully was not an easy person to work with is evidenced by his difficult relationship with La Fontaine, from whom he commissioned a libretto, *Daphné*, which he rejected. La Fontaine avenged himself in the satirical poem "Le Florentin." Yet the two men were reconciled and La Fontaine penned the two verse dedications to Louis XIV that appeared in the printed scores of *Amadis* and *Roland*. See La Gorce 1992, 72, and La Gorce 2002, 205–8.
81. La Gorce 2002, 396–7.
82. On the *ouverture à la française*, see especially Anthony 1997, 129–31.
83. See Lois Rosow's discussion of the Lullian recitative in her entry "Lully" in *Opera Grove* and Anthony 1997, 123–4.
84. See James R. Anthony entry "Le Rochois, Marie" in *Opera Grove*.

Chapter 2: From Lully to Rameau

1. See chapter 1, p. 6.
2. Edmond-Jean-François Barbier, *Journal historique et anecdotique du règne de Louis XV*, April 1763, cited from Wood and Sadler (2000), 20–21.
3. Marshal Vauban's figure, cited in Anthony 1997, 28.
4. Lully's music was known, besides, to people who were unlikely to attend performances at the Académie royale. According to Le Cerf de La Viéville, Arcabonne's aria in *Amadis*, "Amour, que veux-tu de moi?," was "sung by every woman cook in France" (cited by La Gorce 2002, 676).
5. Joseph Addison, *The Spectator*, 3 April 1711; see Girdlestone 1969, 124.
6. *Trois siècles d'opéra à Lyon*, 9.
7. See Anthony 1997, 140, and La Gorce 2002, 295–302.
8. See La Gorce 2002, 255–6. The work was performed with spoken *intermèdes* in the course of which actors disputed the respective merits of Italian and French opera. Lorenzani, not Charpentier as one might assume, was perceived as Lully's main rival. See Cessac 2004, 50n1.
9. According to La Gorce in *New Grove*, entry "Lully, (3) Jean-Louis Lully."
10. The repertory of the Académie royale de musique from the origin until 1715 is in La Gorce 1992, 197–203. For details of Francine's financial woes, see especially 95–100, 111–22.
11. "What a wretched thing opera has become since we lost Baptiste . . ." cited by Isherwood 1973, 239.
12. An edition of Raguenet's work appeared in English in 1709, with the addition of an anonymous "Critical discourse upon operas in England."
13. On Collasse (often spelled Colasse), see the entries by James R. Anthony in *New Grove* and Caroline Wood in *Opera Grove*.
14. Collasse's predecessor, Jean-François Lalouette (1651–1728), had been fired by Lully in 1677 for hinting publicly that the best music of *Isis* was his; see Isherwood 1973, 241.
15. The work was performed at Brussels; see La Gorce 1992, 119.
16. Cited from Anthony 1997, 154. The Parfaict brothers, in their *Histoire de l'Académie royale de musique* (*c*.1750), claim that Collasse developed an obsession with finding the philosophical stone (see Fajon 1984, 96).
17. See Isherwood 1973, 327–32, and Kintzler 1990, 109–10ff.
18. On this important woman composer, see especially Cessac 1995.
19. See the entry by Robert Fajon in *New Grove*.
20. On Maupin, see Julie Anne Sadie in *New Grove 2*. Maupin's colorful life, which served as a basis for Théophile Gautier's 1835 novel, *Mademoiselle de Maupin* included lesbian affairs.
21. See Montagnier 2001, especially 5 and 93–130, and the entry on Gervais by the same author in *New Grove 2*.
22. Heard in concert in Paris in 2007, the work has been recorded by Hugo Reyne (Vendée 605003).
23. On Charpentier's life, see especially Cessac 1995 (as well as the revised 2004 French edition). As Cessac points out, the rediscovery of Charpentier owes much to American musicology, especially to the work of Patricia Ranum and that of H. Wiley Hitchcock, author of the catalogue raisonné of Charpentier (1982) and the entry on Charpentier in *New Grove 2*.
24. Whether Charpentier could actually have received private tuition from Carissimi has been questioned by recent scholarship: see Jean Lionnet, "Charpentier à Rome," in Cessac 2005, 71–2, 74, and Hitchcock in *New Grove 2*.
25. A revised prologue was subsequently set by Charpentier; on *Le malade imaginaire*, see Cessac 2004, 76–87. The music to *Le malade imaginaire* has been recorded, especially, by William Christie (HMC 901336).
26. All four works have been recorded by William Christie and his ensemble, Les Arts florissants (named after Charpentier's work): *Les plaisirs de Versailles* on 0630–147742; *Les arts florissants* on 1901–083; *Actéon* on 1951–095; and *La descente d'Orphée aux enfers* on 0630–119132.

27. See Isherwood 1973, 320–24.
28. Based on the Philidor copy, *David et Jonathas* was first published in 1981 in a reconstituted version by Jean Duron; it has been recorded by William Christie (HM 1901–28990).
29. An extended analysis of the work can be found in Cessac 2004, 230–43. That Charpentier's work had produced a considerable impression is evidenced by the unusual fact that it was revived in other French Jesuit schools, and as late as 1741 (Cessac 2004, 228).
30. To borrow David Richards's telling image in his review of Diana Rigg's performance of Euripides's tragedy ("Amid Pain and Din, A Mighty Medea," *The New York Times*, 8 April 1994).
31. See La Gorce 1992, 199.
32. In the monologue that follows Creusa's death in Act 5, scene 4.
33. Cessac 2004, 428.
34. One might even read a faint echo of Seneca's overtly atheistic treatment of the Medea story in the Act 5 offstage chorus of the horrified Corinthians: "Refusons notre encens, notre hommage / À ces dieux inhumains."
35. The strength of Corneille's libretto becomes even more apparent when compared to the one supplied by the Abbé Pellegrin (his first effort, under the pseudonym La Roque) for Salomon's *Médée et Jason*. The human side of Medea is given less prominence, whereas Creusa and Jason are treated more sympathetically. As for the poisoned wedding gown, it disappears altogether: Creusa perishes, along with Creon, when Medea sets the palace on fire.
36. Like Lully's *Atys*, in a production by J.-M. Villégier conducted by William Christie, with Lorraine Hunt Lieberson in the title role. This production has been preserved on disc (4509–96558–2).
37. See Cessac 2004, 410–12.
38. *Tous les matins du monde*, Alain Corneau's 1991 film based on the novel by Pascal Quignard (who wrote the screenplay), with music selected and performed by Jordi Savall.
39. On Marais, see especially Milliot and La Gorce 1991, as well as the entry by the same authors in *New Grove 2*.
40. Milliot and La Gorce 1991, 178–9.
41. *Ibid.*, 198.
42. *Ibid.*, 234. *Alcyone* was recorded in 1990 under Marc Minkowski (Erato 45522–2).
43. See Milliot and La Gorce 1991, 250–51. *Sémélé* was published without intermediate parts, but these have been reconstituted and the work, revived for the first time in 2006–7, is now available on CD (Glossa 921614).
44. On Campra, see Barthélémy 1995; see also James R. Anthony in *New Grove 2*.
45. As was the collection of short stories by Paul Morand of the same title (1925) when published by Boni and Liveright in 1927.
46. Barthélémy 1995, 84.
47. The phrase "opéra-ballet" became standard only after 1750. See James R. Anthony, "The French Opéra-Ballet in the Early 18th Century: Problems of Definition and Classification," *Journal of the American Musicological Society* 18:2 (Summer 1965), 197–206.
48. Turkey, which controlled part of southeastern Europe, could thus evidently be casually grouped with other "European" countries in 1697, whereas by 1735, the date of Fuzelier and Rameau's *Les Indes galantes*, it was treated as "Indian" (in this case Asian).
49. The more than 31 dance numbers constitute a record for the period. See Barthélémy 1995, 100.
50. *Le carnaval de Venise* was revived with great success at the 1975 Aix-en-Provence Festival in an imaginative production by Jorge Lavelli.
51. On the evidence of the score, the work is a strong candidate for revival; see Barthélémy, 104–10.
52. The same episode also inspired an important ballet de cour (the *Ballet de Tancrède*) in 1619; cf. McGowan 1963, 117–31.
53. See Barthélémy 1995, 122–33; *Tancrède* was recorded at the Aix-en-Provence Festival in 1986 (Erato 2292–45001–2).
54. See Jean-Louis Le Cerf de La Véville, *Comparaison de la musique italienne et de la musique françoise*, Brussels: Foppens, 1704, 1–2.
55. *Les fêtes vénitiennes* was performed 66 times in its first year, in several versions; "L'opéra" appeared at the 51st performance. On the different versions, see Barthélémy 1995, 202–3. The work was revived at Wuppertal and Schwetzingen in 1970.
56. On the many differences between Danchet's and Varesco's treatments, see "Les Idoménée: infanticide et théâtre classique," in Kintzler 2004, 73–102.
57. *Idoménée* has been recorded under William Christie (HMC 901396/8).
58. See the chronology of Destouches's life in Renée P.-M. Masson, "André-Cardinal Destouches, surintendant de la musique du roi, directeur de l'Opéra 1672–1749," *Revue de Musicologie* 43 (1959), 81–98; see also the entries by Caroline Wood in *Grove Opera* and by James R. Anthony in *New Grove 2*.

59. Satirical songs later lampooned him as "the musketeer-musician" (see La Gorce 1992, 107–8; see also Isherwood 1973, 344).

60. This revised version, based on an edition by Françoise Escande, is featured in Hervé Niquet's 2007 recording (GCD 921612) which, unfortunately, omits the prologue (discussed in Isherwood 1973, 348–9).

61. On Desmarets's life, see Antoine 1965.

62. Titon du Tillet, *Supplément au Parnasse françois* (1743), quoted by Antoine 1965, 34.

63. Or Xaintonge. Her mother, Louise-Geneviève Gomez de Vasconcelle, was a prominent novelist.

64. By the Abbé Bordelon, cited by Antoine 1965, 51.

65. See Bordelon's critique, cited *ibid.*, 53.

66. Through most of the eighteenth century "Rousseau" meant Jean-Baptiste. The author of *Émile* and *La nouvelle Héloïse* was usually called simply "Jean-Jacques" not to be confused with his illustrious namesake.

67. See Jean Duron and Yves Ferraton, *Vénus & Adonis, tragédie en musique de Henry Desmarest (1697)*, Liège: Mardaga, 2006. The work, in a critical edition by Jean Duron, was revived in 2006 by Christophe Rousset and recorded, minus the prologue (AM 127).

68. Not in 1696 as indicated by Antoine 1965, 65.

69. The work was revived in Paris until 1762 and mounted in Lyons, Dijon, Grenoble, Marseilles, and at Baden-Durlach and Brussels; it was also frequently heard at the court of Louis XV. See Antoine 1965, 193.

70. Some scholars doubt that the play was actually mounted (see Maurice Barthélémy in Vendrix, *L'opéra-comique*, 27), but others dispute this claim; see William Brooks, "Louis XIV's Dismissal of the Italian Actors," *Modern Language Review* 91:4 (October 1996), 840–47.

71. By Barry Russell in his hypertext website on the "Théâtre de la foire" (as of December 2009: www.theatrales.uqam.ca/foires/).

72. See Mary Hunter's entry "Gillier" in *New Grove 2*.

73. The figure may be exceptional but other contemporary shows featured 10–12 players (Barthélémy in Vendrix, *L'opéra-comique*, 37).

74. La Gorce 1992, 141.

75. Barthélémy in Vendrix 1992, 34–5.

76. The premiere and publication of this work precede those of *Télémaque*, which Barthélémy, *ibid.*, 10–11, claims was the first to be called "opéra-comique," but which was in fact issued under the appellation "parodie" according to the BnF online catalogue.

77. On little operas, see, especially, Nathalie Berton's *Les petits opéras*, PhD, University of Tours, 1996.

78. The recording, conducted by Hervé Niquet, is available on Naxos 8.554455. On Clérambault, see the entry by David Tunley in *New Grove 2*; there is no mention of *Le triomphe d'Iris*, however, in *Opera Grove*.

79. On Sceaux and the Duchesse du Maine, see especially Cessac and Couvreur 2003.

80. On Mouret, see especially Viollier 1950; see also James Anthony's entry in *New Grove 2* and Cessac, "La duchesse du Maine et la musique," in Cessac and Couvreur 2003, 97–107.

81. See the 1999 recording under Frédérique Chauvet (AAOC 94202).

82. One of them was the divertissement *Le mystère ou les fêtes de l'inconnu*, on a text by Destouches, not listed in *New Grove 2* (see Cessac, "La duchesse du Maine," in Cessac and Couvreur 2003, 101).

83. The libretto printed in 1714 labels it "comédie en musique."

84. *Le mariage de Ragonde* was recorded in 1992 by Marc Minkowski (WE 810 ZK).

85. Durey de Noinville 1753, 2:31. Mouret also occupies a minor place in the history of the ballet, since he wrote the music (now lost) for the "danse caractérisée de Camille et d'Horace" (based on Pierre Corneille's tragedy), performed at the fourteenth "Grande Nuit," and now considered the first ballet. See Nathalie Lecomte, "Un maître à danser à la cour de Sceaux: Claude Balon," in Cessac and Couvreur 2003, 133.

Chapter 3: The Age of Rameau

1. Toussaint Bertin de La Doué (*c.*1680–1743) collaborated with Bouvard on the tragédie en musique *Cassandre* (1706) and wrote two on his own: *Diomède* (1710) and *Ajax* (1716); he also composed an opéra-ballet, *Les plaisirs de la campagne* (1719).

2. Born in Leghorn, Jean-Baptiste (or Giambattista) Stuck (1680–1755), a virtuoso cellist, had a tragédie en musique, *Méléagre* (1709), and a fantastic opera featuring the enchanter Merlin, *Manto la fée* (1711), performed at the Académie royale, with little success; both were Italianate in style – the latter includes an aria in Italian in its Act 5 divertissement.

3. The Concert Spirituel remained in existence until 1790. See Constant Pierre, *Histoire du Concert Spirituel 1725–1790* [1900], Paris: Société française de musicologie, 1975.

4. Of the 59 tragédies en musique premiered between 1687 and 1733, only 14 were revived at least once (Anthony 1990, 36).

5. See Mary Grace Swift, "The Three Ballets of the Young Sun," *Dance Chronicle* 3:4 (1979–80), 361–72.

6. In the allegorical prologue, Melpomene – the muse of tragedy and, thus, of the tragédie en musique – rejects the input of magic, preferring to rely on history and on love. The story of Skanderbeg had been treated by Vivaldi in 1718.

7. Rebel was also the Opéra's "administrateur général" from 1772 until his death. See Lois Rosow's entry "Francoeur," *New Grove 2*.

8. See Jérome de la Gorce, "L'orchestre de l'opéra et son évolution de Campra à Rameau," *Revue de musicologie* 76:1 (1990), 23–43.

9. On Montéclair, see the entries by James R. Anthony in *New Grove 2* and by Jean Duron in *Opera Grove*.

10. As usual, it was published with the subtitle "ballet"; the third of the three original entries (later expanded to four) is called "Les nuits d'été", like Berlioz's famous song cycle on poems by Théophile Gautier.

11. On Pellegrin, see especially Sylvie Bouissou, Introduction, in Jean-Philippe Rameau, *Hippolyte et Aricie*, 1757 version, Bonneuil-Matours: Société Jean-Philippe Rameau, 2007 (Opera Omnia Rameau, IV:6).

12. Mme de Maintenon and religious authorities thus considered that the excitement caused by the lavishly produced *Esther* had taken a frivolous turn. Even though *Athalie* was done more soberly, the practice, at Saint-Cyr, was put to an end.

13. Desmarets's *tragédie en musique*, completed by Campra (1704), dealt with the later episode of Iphigenia's story, her quasi-miraculous reunification with her brother Orestes in Tauris. Of course, a sacrifice is also involved, except that the siblings' mutual recognition interrupts it.

14. This preface is reproduced in the booklet accompanying William Christie's 1992 recording (HMX 2901424).

15. Similarly, Racine had spared Iphigenia in *Iphigénie* (1674).

16. According to the *Mercure de France* for June 1761, cited by Jean Duron and Fannie Vernaz, entry "*Jephté*," *Opera Grove*.

17. The standard study remains Girdlestone 1969; a more accurate and up-to-date historical background, however, is provided by Graham Sadler's entry in *New Grove 2*.

18. A separate work also called *Anacréon*, on a libretto by Gentil-Bernard, was incorporated in 1757 in a revision of *Les surprises de l'amour*, which also contained *Les Sibarites*.

19. Cited by Sadler, "Rameau," *New Grove*. A vivid picture of Rameau at a rehearsal of *Les fêtes de Polymnie* can be found in a 1745 letter by Françoise de Graffigny; see *Correspondance de Mme de Graffigny*, ed. J.A. Dainard, vol. 7, Oxford: Voltaire Foundation, 2002, 45 (letter of 10 October 1745).

20. Diderot's unfavorable portrait of the composer in his posthumous *Le neveu de Rameau* (first published in German, in Goethe's translation, 1805) should be interpreted in the context of the cooling of their relations.

21. Sadler, in his entry on *Les Boréades* in *Opera Grove*, indicates that the work may have been given in concert at Lille in the 1770s; the pianist and harpsichordist Louis Diémer also arranged for a performance of large excerpts in Paris in 1896.

22. Cited in Wood and Sadler 2000, 146–7.

23. Rameau does not appear to have been a Freemason, but his librettist was; see Sadler, entry "Cahusac," *New Grove 2*.

24. Another common feature with Quinault, Gentil-Bernard is not averse to using unusual meters, such as the five-syllable lines of the Demons' chorus "Brisons tous nos fers" in Act 3 of *Castor et Pollux*. The point is made in Girdlestone 1969, 169.

25. The point is made in Girdlestone 1969, 169.

26. On this "Trio des Parques" (the second of the two sung by the Fates at the end of this act), see *ibid.*, 149–54. The horror of the prediction is conveyed in a modulation by semitone steps from G minor to D minor, characterized as "enharmonic" as it involves quarter-tones.

27. These potentialities were wonderfully exploited in Robert Carsen's 2003 production of *Les Boréades*, seen, among other venues, in Paris and at the Brooklyn Academy of Music, and captured on DVD (OA 0899).

28. It may even have been felt as inappropriate for a royal wedding, especially given the Infanta's ungainly physique (she was compared by a contemporary to a botched marble statue); see Girdlestone 1969, 438 n1.

29. See M. Elizabeth Bartlett, Introduction, in Rameau, *Platée*, Bonneuil-Matours, 2005 (Rameau Opera Omnia, IV:10).

30. Girdlestone 1969, 348–9.
31. The ariette "L'objet qui règne dans mon âme" was actually lifted – and transposed up a semitone – from the 1728 secular cantata *Le berger fidèle* (see Sadler, "*Les fêtes d'Hébé*," *Opera Grove*). Jelyotte can be seen playing the guitar, next to the seven-year-old Mozart, in Michel Barthélémy Ollivier's painting *Le thé à l'anglaise chez le prince de Conti* at the Louvre (see Jacques-Gabriel Prodhomme, "Pierre de Jélyotte [1713–1797], *Sammelbände der Internationalen Musikgesellschaft* 3:4 [August 1902], 714–15).
32. See Prodhomme, "A Pastel by La Tour: Marie Fel," *The Musical Quarterly* 9:4 (October 1923), 482–507.
33. Graham Sadler, "Foreword," in Rameau, *Zoroastre, version 1749*, Paris: Gérard Billaudot, 1999 (Opera Omnia Rameau, IV:19), XLIV.
34. See Sadler, "Rameau," *New Grove 2*.
35. Girdlestone 1969, 447.
36. As Girdlestone puts it, French baroque opera from Lully to Rameau "consists in a succession of tensions and relaxations obtained by pathetic scenes alternating with festivity" (Girdlestone 1969, 139).
37. See Louis de Cahusac, *La danse ancienne et moderne, ou Traité historique de la danse*, The Hague: Neaulme, 1754, vol. 3, VII:4, especially 119–21.
38. See Girdlestone 1969, 347.
39. That is, of course, the view adopted by the ongoing critical edition of Rameau's complete works, which will include different volumes for the 1737 and 1754 *Castor et Pollux*, the 1739 and 1744 *Dardanus*, the 1749 and 1756 *Zoroastre*, and even the 1733 and 1757 *Hippolyte et Aricie*. The Rameau discography, unfortunately, has yet to adopt the same principle. Both versions of *Castor et Pollux* have benefited from excellent recordings, the 1737 under William Christie (HMC 901435/7) and the 1754 under Charles Farncombe (Erato 95311/2); but complete – or near complete – recordings of other works are often based, silently or overtly, on conflations of different versions, with the exception of *Zoroastre*, which both Sigiswald Kujiken (HM 77144-2) and William Christie (Erato 43182-2) have recorded in its revised 1756 version.
40. A sample of late eighteenth- and nineteenth- century misguided opinions on Rameau can be found in Girdlestone 1969, 516–17.
41. According to Girdlestone 1969, 234, La Bruère's libretto earned praise from Voltaire. The characters in Act 3 ("La cour") are Ovid and Augustus's daughter Julia; an alternative version features an unidentified Roman emperor.
42. A recording of *Don Quichotte* has been made by Hervé Niquet (Naxos 8.553647).
43. *Daphnis et Chloé* has also been recorded by Niquet (GCD 921605).
44. On Mondonville, see especially Machard 1980.
45. The work has been recorded by Marc Minkowski (Erato 45715-2).
46. For her Mondonville had written a concerto for violin and human voice, now lost, performed at the Concert Spirituel in 1747 (see Marc Signorile's entry, "Mondonville," *New Grove 2*).
47. *Les fêtes de Paphos* was recorded in 1997 under Christophe Rousset (OL 455 084-2); see Graham Sadler's illuminating assessment of the work in *Early Music* 26:4 (November 1998), 695–7.
48. See Neal Zaslaw entry on Leclair in *Grove Music 2*. On Leclair generally, see also Marc Pincherle, *Jean-Marie Leclair, l'aîné*, Paris: La Colombe, 1952; and Graham Sadler's entry on Leclair and *Scylla and Glaucus* in *Grove Opera*.
49. See Neal Zaslaw, " 'Scylla and Glaucus': A Case Study," *Cambridge Opera Journal* 4:3 (November 1992), 199–228, especially 227–30. *Scylla et Glaucus* was staged at Lyons and Aix-en-Provence in 1986 and subsequently recorded under James Eliot Gardiner (Erato 75340/2).
50. See Fabiano 2006, 23–25, and Graham Sadler, entry "*Scylla et Glaucus*," *Grove Opera*. Serpina was Laura Monti, who had premiered the role in Naples in 1733 (Fabiano 2005, 12).
51. *The Collected Writings of Rousseau*, edited by Christopher Kelly, Roger D. Masters and Peter G. Stillman, translated by Christopher Kelly, Hanover and London: University Press of New England, 1990–[2006], 5:321–2.
52. Fabiano 2006, 26–32.
53. Sixty-one are published in Launay 1973.
54. The last argument is particularly stressed by Elisabeth Cook in her entry "Querelle des Bouffons" in *New Grove 2*.
55. Girdlestone 1969, 463.
56. Rousseau's retrospective account in *Les confessions*, however, exaggerates the radical character of this revelation (see Fabiano 2005, 18).
57. By contrast, for instance, with the soothsayer featured in Act 2 of La Bruère and Boismortier's *Les voyages de l'Amour* (1736).

58. *Bastien et Bastienne*, set by the 12-year-old Mozart in 1768, is a Gernan version of Favart's adaptation of Rousseau's work.
59. See in particular Kintzler 1990, especially 418–91, and her entry on Rousseau in *New Grove*; a much less sympathetic account will be found in Girdlestone 1969, *passim*, especially 145–7.
60. See Kintzler 1990, 481–7.
61. On *Pygmalion* and melodrama in general, see in particular Waeber 2005, especially 17–28.
62. When *Pygmalion* was reviewed in the *Mercure de France*, Coignet's participation was not acknowledged, which caused some friction. In Germany, *Pygmalion* was mounted with music by other composers, notably Georg Anton Benda (see Waeber 2005, 18–21).
63. See Jean-Jacques Rousseau, *Essay on the Origin of Languages and Writings Related to Music*, ed. John T. Scott, Hanover and London: University Press of New England, 1998, xxxix–xlii.
64. From a letter (in French) to Pierre Guy of 28 February 1771. See *The Letters of Dr Charles Burney*, Vol. 1, 1751–1784, ed. by Alvaro Ribeiro, SJ, Oxford: Clarendon Press, 1991, 74. Burney arranged *Le devin du village* in English as *The Cunning-Man* (1766).
65. See his autobiography *Supplément au roman comique* (1772).
66. *La chercheuse d'esprit* was written in collaboration with Antoine-René de Voyer d'Argenson, marquis de Paulmy, a statesman and famous bibliophile (his collections formed the nucleus of what is now the Bibliothèque de l'Arsenal in Paris). Favart's standing as the father of the modern opéra-comique was consecrated in 1783 when the theater devoted to the genre was named the Salle Favart – a name the present building still carries.
67. See Barthélémy in Vendrix, *L'opéra-comique*, 55–6.
68. See Girdlestone 1969, 440 and 502. *Les troqueurs* has been recorded by William Christie (HM 901454).
69. On *Les troqueurs*, see Charlton, "Continuing Polarities," in Charlton 2000, II/14–25.
70. See Elizabeth Cook and Stanley Sadie, "Parody," *New Grove 2*; the parodies are listed in Fabiano 2005, 35.
71. Fabiano 2005, 43.
72. The popularity of the work is attested by its ballet adaptation by Dauberval in 1789, better known today in its 1828 reworking by Aumer and Hérold.
73. On the "Goldoni project," see Fabiano 2006, 45 ff.

Chapter 4: Gluck to Revolution

1. It is described in Pitou, I:26–7.
2. Burney 1959, 18.
3. Milliot and La Gorce 1991, 213.
4. Burney 1959, 277.
5. Goldoni (1783), cited by Anthony 1997, 111.
6. See Martin Cooper in Wellesz and Sternfeld 1973, 207.
7. Described by Cooper in Wellesz and Sternfeld 1973, 221; see also Charlton 1986, 130–31.
8. See Charlton 1986, 215.
9. On Gossec, see especially Role 2000.
10. Charlton 1986, 15.
11. *Ibid.*, 210.
12. After Jean-Blaise Martin (?1768/9–1837), whose distinguished opéra-comique career lasted from 1789 to 1823.
13. Fétis 1860, 2:147.
14. The four servants in *Les contes d'Hoffmann* and Guillot in *Manon* are typical "trial" parts.
15. On Philidor, see *Philidor, musicien et joueur d'échecs*, Paris: Picard, 1995 (Recherches sur la musique française classique, 28).
16. *Tom Jones* is the only work by Philidor that has been regularly revived in the twentieth century. It is available on CD (Dynamic 509) and on DVD (33509), both versions conducted by Jean-Claude Malgoire.
17. Berlioz, *Critique musicale*, 4:237.
18. Julian Rushton, Introduction, in Philidor, *Ernelinde, tragédie lyrique*, Stuyvesant, New York: Pendragon Press, 1992 (French Opera in the 17th and 18th Centuries, LVI), xv.
19. *Ibid.*, viii.
20. On Monsigny, see in particular Karin Pendle, "L'opéra comique à Paris de 1762 à 1789," in Vendrix, *L'opéra-comique*, and Michel Noiray's entry in *New Grove 2*.
21. As many as 26 opéra-comique adaptations of La Fontaine for the years 1714–61 are listed by Charlton, "Continuing Polarities," in Charlton 2000, II/18–19.

22. As Noiray notes in his entry on the work in *Opera Grove*, Sedaine and Monsigny significantly refrained from having the king participate in the concluding vaudeville, which might have conveyed a perilous whiff of egalitarianism.

23. The wedding procession, with spoken exchanges on a musical background between the reluctant bride and her father, is also one of the earliest examples of opéra-comique melodrama.

24. Sadly, no recording exists of the opera – or of any other by Monsigny for that matter – save for a 1960 Radio France broadcast, conducted by Louis de Froment (Charlton, "Continuing Polarities," in Charlton 2000, II/5 n16). *Le déserteur* was revived at the Théâtre Impérial in Compiègne as recently as 1996.

25. Fétis 1861, 6:177.

26. On Grétry, see especially Charlton 1986.

27. It was thus sung in 1814 to welcome the exiled Louis XVIII back to France. More recently, André Gide used it as a sort of anti-family manifesto by suggesting that the rhetorical question ("Where could one better be than within one's family?") should be answered "anywhere else."

28. See Charlton's entry on her in *New Grove 2*.

29. Statistics given in Charlton 1986, 65, show that in the 1770s the combined figure for performances of his works at the Comédie-Italienne was twice that for his closest rival, Monsigny, himself well ahead of Duni and Philidor.

30. *Ibid.*, 100.

31. There is one complete recording of *Zémire et Azor*, conducted by Edgar Doneux (7243-5-75290-2).

32. See Charlton 1986, 114–15.

33. Grétry, *Mémoires*, 1:374. Rather than with this tune, however, or even the long popular romance sung by Blondel, "O Richard, ô mon roi," modern opera audiences will be familiar with Laurette's air "Je crains de lui parler la nuit," sung by the Countess in Act 2 of Tchaikovsky's *The Queen of Spades*. Two complete recordings of *Richard Coeur-de-lion* are available, one conducted by Edgard Doneux (EMI 75266), the other by Francesco Vizioli (Nuova Era 7327, with *Denys le tyran*).

34. See Charlton 1986, 162. Highlights of *Le jugement de Midas* have been recorded under Ronald Zollman (Koch 3-1090-2).

35. There exists a complete recording under Edgard Doneux (EMI 75263).

36. Charlton 1986, 175.

37. Mozart wrote a set of piano variations (K. 352) in 1781 based on the Act 1 chorus "Dieu d'amour."

38. It should be noted that the phrase "opéra-ballet" here applies to a work based on a unified plot, as opposed to the "ballet à entrées" created by Collasse and Campra.

39. Cited in Charlton 1986, 291.

40. On Gluck's career, see especially Brown 1991, Howard 1995, and Bruce Alan Brown and Julian Rushton, "Gluck," *New Grove 2*.

41. See Brown 1991.

42. *Ibid.*, 229–31.

43. *Ibid.*, 410. Mozart based a set of piano variations (K. 455), composed in 1784, on the Calender's Act 1 aria "Les hommes pieusement."

44. *Les pèlerins de la Mecque*, in its original version, is the only Gluck opéra-comique to have been recorded in French, under John Eliot Gardiner (Erato 45516); a recording of *Le cadi dupé* is available in German (CPO 999-552-2).

45. See Howard 1995, 62.

46. Cited in its entirety, *ibid.*, 102–5. The composer's name was spelled "Glouch."

47. *Ibid.*, 106–7.

48. Sophie Arnould premiered the title role.

49. Howard 1995, 115.

50. The 1774 French edition, dedicated to Marie-Antoinette, is labeled both "tragédie" and "opéra." For a comparison between the Vienna and Paris texts, see Patricia Howard, *C.W. Von Gluck, Orfeo*, Cambridge [etc.]: Cambridge University Press, 1981, 74–83 and 127–34.

51. Castrati appeared in concert in Paris but not (since Cavalli's *Xerse* in 1660) on stage. See Grétry's revealingly horrified comments on them in *Mémoires*, 1:440–41.

52. In 1777 Legros became head of the Concert Spirituel, a position he kept until the end of this institution in 1790.

53. The accusation is discussed and refuted in Howard 1995, 202–3.

54. As reported by Jean-François de La Harpe, cited in *ibid.*, 125.

55. See Julian Rushton, " 'Royal Agamemnon': The Two Versions of Gluck's *Iphigénie en Aulide*," in Boyd 1992, 15–36.

56. On the two versions of *Alceste*, see F.W. Sternfeld, "Expression and Revision in Gluck's *Orfeo* and *Alceste*," in Westrup, Jack, ed., *Essays Presented to Egon Wellesz*, Oxford: Clarendon Press, 1966,

114–29; Julian Rushton, "In Defence of the French 'Alceste'," *Musical Times* 122:1,665 (November 1981), 738–40; Michel Noiray, "Genèse de l'oeuvre," "Les éléments d'une réforme," and "Commentaire littéraire et musical," *L'Avant-Scène Opéra* 73 (*Alceste* issue), 7–11, 20–25, and 32–79; and the entry "*Alceste*" by Jeremy Hayes, including a comparative table, in *Opera Grove*, 1:62–70.

57. Brown 1991, 258.
58. The comparison is suggested by Jeremy Hayes, "*Armide*: Gluck's most French Opera?", *Musical Times* 123:1,672 (June 1982), 409.
59. See his only surviving letter to Guillard in Howard 1995, 187–90.
60. See Michel Noiray, "Commentaire musical et littéraire," *L'Avant-Scène Opéra* 62 (*Iphigénie en Tauride* issue), 45.
61. A recording, conducted by René Jacobs, was made at the Schwetzingen Festival in 1987 (HM 905201–02).
62. On his contribution to Antonio Salieri's *Les Danaïdes*, see below, p. 88.
63. See the testimonies of Du Roullet and Salieri cited in Howard 1995, 237 and 238–9.
64. See Vignal 1997, 265–71. The one complete recording, under Helmut Rilling, is sung in German translation (Hännsler 98963).
65. On Piccinni generally, see especially Rushton 1970; M. Liggett, *A Biography of Piccinni and a Critical Study of his "La Didone" and "Didon,"* PhD, Washington University, 1977; and Rushton, Introduction, in Piccinni, *Atys* (Stuyvesant, New York: Pendragon Press, 1991).
66. *New Grove 2* lists 98 works before Piccini's arrival in Paris.
67. Howard 1995, 172.
68. *Roland* was recorded at the 2000 Martina Franca Festival, under David Golub (Dynamic 367-1/3), unfortunately with the part of Médor arranged for a mezzo.
69. On Vismes's Italian seasons, see Fabiano 2006, 74–87 and 97–103.
70. See Rushton, Introduction, and Mary Hunter, entry "*Atys*," *Grove Opera*.
71. On the two *Iphigénies* see Julian Rushton, " 'Iphigénie en Tauride': The Operas of Gluck and Piccinni," *Music & Letters* 53:4 (October 1972), 411–30.
72. The first modern revival at Bari in 1986, under Donato Renzetti, has been recorded (Fonit Cetra CDC 32). It was also staged at the Paris Châtelet in 1987, with Katia Ricciarelli in the title role.
73. According to Pitou 2:163; *Didon* was recorded at Bari in 2001 under Arnold Bosman (Dynamic 406/1–2).
74. See Martin Cooper in Wellesz and Sternfeld 1973, 240.
75. On Salieri's career and works, see especially Rice 1998.
76. Rice 1998, 313–15; see also Howard 1995, 236–7. The published libretto mentions both Gluck and Salieri as authors.
77. See Berlioz, *Memoirs*, 47.
78. *Les Danaïdes* was recorded at Perugia in 1983, with Montserrat Caballé as Hypermnestra (Dynamic 489).
79. Calpigi's comic couplets in Act 3, "Je suis né natif de Ferrare," accompanied by mandolin-like pizzicati, and evoking his fate, constitute another chapter in the history of the French revulsion towards castrati.
80. A DVD of *Tarare* was made, under the direction of Jean-Claude Malgoire, at the 1988 Schwetzinger Festival (Arthaus 100557).
81. Rice 1998, 403–20.
82. On Sacchini in Paris, see Rushton 1970.
83. *Il Cidde*, premiered in Rome in 1767; Baptistin (a.k.a. Jean-Baptiste Stuck) had previously given *Il Cid* (Leghorn, 1715) and Piccinni *Il gran Cid* (Naples, 1766).
84. Berlioz, *Memoirs*, 84–5. A great admirer of Sacchini's work, Berlioz nevertheless stopped short of putting it on the same level as Gluck's masterpieces.
85. Julian Rushton, entry "*Oedipe à Colone*," Opera Grove.
86. See David Charlton, "Dalayrac," *New Grove*, and "Motif and Recollection in Four Operas of Dalayrac," in Charlton 2000, VIII/38–61.
87. Long attributed to Élisabeth Vigée-Lebrun, *Mme Dugazon as Nina* is now in a private collection in Switzerland.
88. Berlioz, *Memoirs*, 32.
89. Martin Cooper, in Wellesz and Sternfeld 1973, 254–5.
90. Loewenberg 1978, 385.
91. On Montansier and Italian opera, see Di Profio 2003, 28 ff., and Fabiano 2006, 105 ff.
92. "Monsieur" was the title traditionally given at court to the king's younger brother.
93. Di Profio 2003, 66–70.
94. *Ibid.*, 85.

Chapter 5: Revolution to Romanticism

1. Role 2000, 179–81. Incorporating verses from the recently composed *Marseillaise*, the work – the greatest success among such occasional Revolutionary pieces – did much to establish the song's status as a national anthem in 1795 (it lost it subsequently until it was reinstated in 1879).

2. See Jean-Louis Jam, "Marie-Joseph Chénier and François-Joseph Gossec: Two Artists in the Service of Revolutionary Propaganda," in Boyd 1992, 222.

3. Described in Pitou 1983–1990, 2:467–8.

4. *Denys le tyran* has been recorded under the direction of Francesco Vizioli (Nuova Era 7327, with *Richard Coeur-de-lion*).

5. On Revolutionary works performed at the Opéra, see M. Elizabeth C. Bartlet, "The New Repertory at the Opéra during the Reign of Terror: Revolutionary Rhetoric and Operatic Consequences," in Boyd 1992, 107–56.

6. On this apparent paradox, see Mongrédien 1996, 51.

7. See Charlton 1986, 300–308. The work has been recorded both on CD, under the direction of Olivier Opdebeeck (Cascavelle 3062), and on DVD, under Sergei Stadler (Arthaus 101097) – the former, however, with a modernized libretto.

8. According to Loewenberg 1978, 489, it was performed in New York, in French, as late as 1831.

9. Joseph Barra (or Bara, 1779–1793), a young volunteer in the Revolutionary armies fighting the Vendée insurgents, was killed in battle near Cholet. He was immediately hailed as a Republican martyr and plans were made to bury him in the Panthéon.

10. See the figures quoted in Mongrédien 1996, 139–40, and the impressive list of provincial cities where Dalayrac's works were mounted in 1793–5.

11. Charlton, "On Redefinitions of 'rescue opera,'" in Boyd 1992, 175–7. See *ibid.*, *passim*, Charlton's reasons for rejecting the phrase "rescue opera" as vague and misleading.

12. The list given in Mongrédien 1996, 139, includes Calais, Carcassonne, Douai, Saint-Quentin, and Valenciennes.

13. According to Loewenberg 1978, 480.

14. On Devienne and *Les visitandines*, see Sherwood Dudley, Introduction, in Devienne, *Les visitandines*, Stuyvesant, NY: Pendragon Press, 1992.

15. Winton Dean, in Abraham 1982, 64.

16. Frank Dawes, Karen A. Hagberg, and Stephan D. Lindeman, entry "Steibelt," *New Grove*.

17. See David Galliver, "*Léonore ou L'amour conjugal*: A Celebrated Offspring of the Revolution," in Boyd 1992, 157–68.

18. Conversely, Simon Mayr's *L'amor coniugale* (Padua, 1805), on a libretto by Gaetano Rossi, reduces the action to one act and sets it in Poland.

19. Di Profio 2003, 96–7.

20. The classic study of Méhul is by Bartlet 1999; see also her entries in *New Grove* and *Opera Grove* and her introductions to Méhul, *Mélidore et Phrosine* and *Stratonice* (Stuyvesant, New York: Pendragon Press, 1990 and 1997).

21. It was the first opera featuring Napoleon (then aged 27), but the part is spoken.

22. That is, not so much pro-monarchy as sympathetic to the Austrian emperor; see Bartlet 1999, 1:242–3.

23. *Ibid.*, 1:212–28.

24. Winton Dean, in Abraham 1992, 48.

25. It is one of the few Méhul operas to have been recorded (Capriccio 60128).

26. Cited by Bartlet in her entry "Méhul," *New Grove 2*.

27. See Bartlet's detailed analysis in her edition of *Stratonice*, xxvii–xxxi. The opera has been recorded under William Christie (Erato 127–14–2).

28. Entry "*Mélidore et Phrosine,*" *Opera Grove*.

29. See Winton Dean in Abraham 1982, 50.

30. The only complete recording (two different versions) available are in German (GL 173).

31. See Mongrédien 1996, 103.

32. The best introduction to Cherubini is Michael Fend's entry "Cherubini" in *New Grove 2*; the fact that only four of Cherubini's works are given individual entries in *Opera Grove* (*Les Abencérages* not among them) is symptomatic of his still vastly undervalued reputation.

33. According to Fétis 1860, 2:265.

34. *Ibid.*, and Winton Dean in Abraham 1982, 38, 44.

35. Di Profio 2003, 187–91.

36. According to Pitou 1983–1990, 2:40, it was the first time in the Opéra's recent history that a work was hissed during the performance.

37. See the anecdote reported by Fétis 1860, 2:267.

38. Berlioz's sneering comments in his *Memoirs* see above, 316, nn77, 88, 237 are to be understood in the context of his difficult personal relations with Cherubini. For a much more positive assessment, see Fétis 1960, 2:271. *Ali-Baba* was revived at La Scala in 1963, in Italian, starring Alfredo Kraus in the title role.

39. Lorenzo Tozzi, in his notes to the complete performance recorded under Ricardo Muti (Sony 2450).

40. It goes without saying that this effect disappears in Lachner's version.

41. Hoffmann's libretto, contrary to what has occasionally been suggested, is a fine literary achievement.

42. As noted by Charlton 1986, 276, the plot is not without similarities to Grétry's *Le comte d'Albert*.

43. Regrettably, the recent "complete" recording under Christoph Spering (Naïve 30306) omits all spoken dialogue, which is as disfiguring as, and perhaps even more than it would be in *The Magic Flute, Fidelio,* or *Der Freischütz*.

44. See Pitou 1983, 2:306–7 and the entry on Jouy in the *Dictionnaire de biographie française*.

45. Florian's novel is also a source of Chateaubriand's novel *Les aventures du dernier Abencérage*, contemporary with Cherubini's opera but published only in 1826.

46. A recording of *Les Abencérages* in the original French was made by Italian Radio under Peter Maag (Arts Music 43066).

47. On Napoleon and music, see Chaillou 2004, as well as David Charlton and M. Elizabeth C. Bartlet, entry "Napoleon," *New Grove 2*.

48. On the other hand, Haselmayer, a Westphalian theatre director, failed to establish a German Theater in Paris; on his "Mozart Theater," which gave three performances of *The Abduction from the Seraglio* in 1801, with Aloysia Weber as Contanze, see Mongrédien 1996, 326–31.

49. This is suggested by Michael F. Robinson, entry "Paisiello," *New Grove 2*.

50. Winton Dean, "German Opera," in Abraham 1982, 458.

51. Pitou 1983–1990, 2:101.

52. See Dean's appraisal, 95–6.

53. Robert L. Pounder, "Antiquité fin-de-siècle," in Branger and Giroud 2008, 26.

54. According to Loewenberg 1978, 616.

55. Mongrédien 1996, 52.

56. *Ibid.*, 60–61.

57. See Elizabeth C. Bartlet, "Opera as Patriotic Ceremony: The Case of *L'Oriflamme*," in Marc Honegger and Christian Meyer, eds, *La musique et le rite sacré et profane*, Strasbourg: Association des Publications près les Universités de Strasbourg, 1986 (Actes du XIIIe Congrès de la Société Internationale de Musicologie), 1:327–38. Not only did *L'Oriflamme* receive a respectable 12 performances in Paris, it was staged in eight provincial cities, Caen and Cherbourg among them.

58. On Le Sueur, see especially Mongrédien 1980, as well as Mongrédien's entries on Le Sueur in *New Grove 2* and *Opera Grove*.

59. See Jean Mongrédien, Introduction, Jean-François Le Sueur, *La caverne*, Stuyvesant, NY: Pendragon Press, 1985, xvii.

60. According to Loewenberg 1978, 582, the subject was first recommended for operatic treatment by Johann Georg Sulzer in his *Allgemeine Theorie der schönen Künste* (1771–4).

61. The painting is at the Musée Ingres in Montauban.

62. Dean, in Abraham 1982, 73, and see 84–8.

63. Mongrédien 1996, 78–9.

64. Mongrédien, Introduction to *La caverne*, x–xi.

65. On Le Sueur's influence on Berlioz, see Winton Dean, "French opera," in Abraham 1982, 88–92.

66. *Ibid.*, 75.

67. Hector Berlioz, *Evenings in the Orchestra*, translated by Charles E. Roche, New York: Knopf, 1929, 154.

68. *La vestale* has been recorded in the original French under Ricardo Muti (Sony 66–357).

69. See Loewenberg 1978, 605–6.

70. Dean 1982, 81–2.

71. In 1785 the Opéra had staged, without much success, *Pizarre, ou La conquête du Pérou*, a tragédie lyrique in five acts by Pierre Candeille. The imperial commission derailed Spontini's plans for an opera on the Electra-Orestes story.

72. The plot summary by Anselm Gerhard, in his entry "Fernand Cortez, ou La conquête du Mexique" in *Opera Grove* corresponds to the 1809 version. The three available recordings, on the other hand, notably the one in French under Jean-Paul Penin (Accord 206612), are all based on the 1817 text, as is the facsimile edition published by Garland in 1980.

73. See Fabiano 2006, 198–202.

74. Mongrédien 1996, 62–3; Pitou 1983–1990, 2:412.

75. Born in Germany, Christian Kalkbrenner (1755–1806), active in Italy as of 1796 and in Paris as of 1799, had written several French operas for the Prussian court and was the author of a French adaptation of *Don Giovanni* performed at the Opéra in 1805. His son Friedrich Kalkbrenner (1785–1849) completed his opera *Oenone* (1812). No entry on the elder Kalkbrenner can be found in *New Grove 2* or *Opera Grove*. See Fétis 1860, 4:467–9.

76. See the costume designs reproduced in Charles Bouvet, *Spontini*, Paris: Rieder, 1930, plates xxxvi–ix.

77. The main study of Boieldieu remains Favre 1944; see also Favre's entry, with Thomas Betzwiezer, in *New Grove 2*, and Elizabeth Forbes's entry in *Opera Grove*. The popularity of *La dame blanche* is made fun of in Delibes' operetta *L'Écossais de Chatou* (1869), whose hero claims to have seen it 600 times and is obsessed about it.

78. On the popularity of the letter Z (as in Zétulbe below) in eighteenth-century France as the non plus ultra of exoticism, see Jean Starobinski, *The Invention of Liberty, 1700–1789*, translated by Bernard C. Swift, Geneva: Skira, 1964, 23.

79. The role of Henri, in Boieldieu's *La fête du village voisin* (1816), is written in the bass clef yet the Act 3 cavatine goes up to high C (which would, of course, have been sung in falsetto at the time).

80. The work has been recorded under Antonio de Almeida, with excellent accompanying notes by David Charlton (Sonpact 93007).

81. Unfortunately, the one recording (Philips 456–655–2) omits spoken dialogues and is grievously cut.

82. See Robert-Aloys Mooser, *L'opéra-comique français en Russie au XVIIIe siècle*, Geneva: R. Kister, 1954.

83. For copyright reasons, neither work could be staged in Paris. Boieldieu recycled some of the music in some of his later operas.

84. Quoted by Elizabeth Forbes, entry "Jean de Paris," *Opera Grove*.

85. See Favre 1944, 2:85. Two decades later, Felice Romani adapted the libretto for Donizetti, whose *Gianni di Parigi* was premiered at La Scala in 1839.

86. Rodolphe was another Martin role, written alternatively in the F and G clefs, that can be sung by both tenors and baritones.

87. The libretto by Alexandre Guiraud, François Ancelot, and Alexandre Soumet presents obvious similarities with *Norma*, the tragedy the last wrote in 1831 – and the souce of Bellini's 1833 opera; see Favre 1944, 2:143–4.

88. On *La dame blanche*, see especially Damien Colas's analysis in *L'avant-scène opéra* 176 (*La dame blanche* issue), as well as the essays by Patrick Taïeb and Jean-Claude Yon in the same issue; see also Pendle 1979, 274–311.

89. According to the anecdote reported in Favre 1944, 2:116, this was a theme Boieldieu had long intended to treat.

90. Actually adapted from "La belle chose qu'un tournoi" from the collaborative work *Les trois genres* (1824), where it was scored for baritone; see Favre 1944, 122.

91. Damien Colas, *L'avant-scène opéra* 176, 10.

92. Cosima Wagner, *Diaries*, ed. Martin Gregor-Dellin and Dietrich Mack, translation Geoffrey Skelton, New York and London: Harcourt Brace Jovanovich, 1980, 2:66, 349.

93. Favre 1944–5, 249–50.

94. In his entry "Boieldieu," *New Grove 2*.

95. On Nicolo, see the entry "Isouard" by Marie Briquet and David Charlton, revised by Hervé Lacombe, in *New Grove 2*.

96. The Parisian street named after him in the 16th arrondissement is, thus, the rue Nicolo.

97. See Favre 1944, 1:289n3.

98. Large extracts were recorded at a French radio concert (Musidisc/INA 201832).

99. There exists a complete recording of *Cendrillon*, under Richard Bonynge (Olympia 661).

100. As noted by Dean in Abraham 1982, 100.

101. Entry "Isouard," *New Grove 2*.

102. See, among others, Richard Osborne, "Rossini's Life"; Benjamin Walton, "Rossini and France"; and Paolo Fabbri, "Librettos and Librettists," in Senici 2004, 11–24, 25–36, and 63–7; and Philip Gossett, "Rossini," *New Grove*.

103. A shorter version had first appeared in London, when Rossini was there, in January 1824. See Stendhal, *Life of Rossini*, translation Richard N. Coe, London: John Calder, 1956.

104. See Philip Gossett's introductions to Gioacchino Rossini, *Le siège de Corinthe*, New York: Garland, 1980; and *Maometto II*, New York: Garland, 1981; as well as *L'avant-scène opéra* 81 (*Le siège de Corinthe* issue).

105. See the example given by Dean in Abraham 1982, 106–7.

106. The only complete recording in French was made at the Teatro Carlo Felice in Genoa under Paolo Olmi (Nuova Era 7372); the Italian version used by Beverly Sills as a vehicle for her Scala and Met debuts, a dubious conflation of *Maometto II* and *Le siège de Corinthe*, is not recommendable – see Gossett 2006, especially 119–22.

107. See Philip Gossett, "Introduction," Gioacchino Rossini, *Moïse*, New York: Garland, 1980.
108. See Charles S. Brauner, "Prefazione," Gioachino Rossini, *Mosè in Egitto*, Pesaro: Fondazione Rossini, 2004, 1:xxxiii.
109. Loewenberg 1978, 658. *Le siège de Corinthe* was staged 103 times in Paris between 1826 and 1844.
110. See Philip Gossett, "Introduction," Gioachino Rossini, *Le comte Ory*, New York and London: Garland, 1978; see also *L'avant-scène opéra* 140 (*Le voyage à Reims/Le comte Ory* issue).
111. The success of the play also inspired the three-volume novel by Louis-François Raban published in 1824; see Fabbri in Senici 2004, 66.
112. See Loewenberg 1978, 719–20, and Dean in Abraham 1982, 105. On *Guillaume Tell* generally, see especially M. Elizabeth C. Bartlet, "Prefazione," in Gioachino Rossini, *Guillaume Tell*, Pesaro, Fondazione Rossini, 1992, 1:xxi–lvi; Gerhard 1998, 63–121; and Cormac Newark, "*Guillaume Tell*," in Senici 2004, 175–85.
113. See the letter quoted by Bartlet, *Guillaume Tell*, 1:xxiv.
114. According to Loewenberg 1978, 719, the work totaled 832 performances at the Paris Opéra, but the figure for the four-act version would be about 770. On the fortunes of *Tell* in Paris and in France, see Bartlet, "Prefazione," xxxviii–xlvi and xlix–liv.

Chapter 6: The Age of Grand Opéra

1. Walter Benjamin, "Paris – the Capital of the Nineteenth Century," translated by Quintin Hoare, in Benjamin, *Charles Baudelaire: A Lyric Poet in the Era of High Capitalism*, London: Verso Editions, 1983.
2. In keeping with current scholarly practice, we favor the French spelling, in order to avoid confusion with the ill-defined English phrase "grand opera."
3. On grand opéra, see especially Fulcher 1987; Dahlhaus 1989, especially 124–34; David Charlton, "Romantic Opera: 1830–1850", in Abraham 1990, 85–140; Gerhard 1998; Charlton 2003, especially Part I; and M. Elizabeth C. Bartlet, "Grand opéra," *New Grove 2*.
4. Massenet's *Le roi de Lahore* (1877) and Saint-Saëns' *Henry VIII* (1883) are among the last successful such works.
5. *La Fronde* (1853) by the Swiss composer Louis Niedermeyer (1802–1861) takes place in the mid-seventeenth century. Auber's *Gustave III* (1833) was an extreme case: the widow of the king's murderer, Anckarström, one of the opera's main characters, was still alive when it was premiered.
6. Meyerbeer, however, supplied an additional aria for the tenor Mario in *Robert le diable*.
7. *La muette de Portici* and *Guillaume Tell* include dances in their first acts, but in neither case do they constitute the only divertissement in the opera. On dance in grand opera, see Marian Smith, "Dance and Dancers" in Charlton 2003, 93–107.
8. It should be added that those ballets featured some of the legendary dancers of the time and were therefore major attractions in themselves: Marie Taglioni (1804–1884) thus appeared as the Prioress in the Act 3 ballet of *Robert le diable*.
9. Significantly, the first French opera to be based on one of Shakespeare's great tragedies, the tragédie lyrique *Macbeth* by Hippolyte Chélard (1789–1861), was premiered in that year at the Opéra. Its librettist, Claude-Joseph Rouget de l'Isle (author of the *Marseillaise*) used as his main source Jean-François Ducis' 1784 adaptation.
10. On *La Esmeralda*, see Gerhard 1998, 215–46.
11. See *ibid.*, 140–45.
12. Karin Pendle, "The Boulevard Theaters and Continuity in the French Opera of the 19th Century," in Bloom 1987, 526.
13. *Ibid.*, 514–15 and 528–30.
14. Quoted in Pougin 1906, 54. "Director" refers to the director of the opera, but specifically in his capacity as stage director. The two functions were often combined: as recently as the first decade of the twentieth century, Albert Carré was both manager of the Opéra-Comique and responsible for its *mises en scène*.
15. Compare to Verdi writing in 1848 from Paris: "Here the *mise-en-scène* is perhaps the most important element" (quoted by M. Elizabeth Bartlet in Charlton 2003, 268).
16. See Thomas Grey, "Richard Wagner and the Legacy of French Grand Opera," in Charlton 2003, 321–43.
17. Similarly, Carafa's *Le nozze di Lammermoor*, premiered at the Théâtre-Italien in 1829, preceded Donizetti's *Lucia* by six years. See Julian Budden, "Carafa," *New Grove 2*.
18. The work is discussed in Pendle 1979, 237–74.
19. See the tables in Pendle 1979, 569–96.
20. On this concept, see Pendle 1979, 85ff., and Gerhard 1998, 134–40.
21. Pendle 1979, 94.

22. *Ibid.*, 94–8 and 390–93.
23. See Philip Gossett, "Music at the Théâtre-Italien," in Bloom 1987, 327–64.
24. See Mary Ann Smart, "Roles, Reputations, Shadows: Singers at the Opéra, 1828–1849," in Charlton 2003, 108–28.
25. The main source on Hérold remains Pougin 1906; see also Elizabeth Forbes, "Herold," *Grove Opera*. See also France-Yvonne Bril, "Ferdinand Herold ou 'la raison ingénieuse' " in Prévost 1995.
26. The same subject, adapted from a play by Alexandre Duval, was treated in 1817 by Giuseppe Mosca (1772–1839).
27. Later in the nineteenth century the role was arranged for baritone; see Pougin 1906, 91n1.
28. Subsequently retitled *Chronique du règne de Charles IX*.
29. His given name was Esprit, not Daniel as often seen in recent publications.
30. On Auber, see Rey Morgan Longyear, *Daniel-François-Esprit Auber (1782–1871): A Chapter in French Opéra-Comique*, PhD Dissertation, Cornell University, 1957, and Herbert Schneider, "Auber," *New Grove 2*.
31. On their partnership, see especially Herbert Schneider, "Scribe and Auber: Constructing Grand Opera," in Charlton 2003, 168–88, and Eugène Scribe et Daniel-François-Esprit Auber, *Correspondance*, ed. Herbert Schneider, Liège: Mardaga, 1998.
32. See in particular Pendle 1979, 102–39.
33. On *La muette de Portici*, see especially Sarah Hibberd, "La Muette and her Context," in Charlton 2003, 149–67, as well as Fulcher 1987, 11–46, and Gerhard 1998, 122–57.
34. See Charlton, in Abraham 1990, 435, n1.
35. See Sonia Slatin, "Opera and Revolution: *La Muette de Portici* and the Belgian Revolution of 1830 Revisited," *Journal of Musicological Research* 3:1/2 (1979), 45–62.
36. The point is made by Hibberd, "La Muette," 436 n13. The fact that Fenella is a handicapped person renders her seduction even more odious and makes her more sympathetic to the audience.
37. Rimsky-Korsakov used the same device in *Mlada* (1892).
38. Into the burning lava below, but there is no suggestion in the libretto or the staging manual that she is leaping into the volcano's crater nine miles away, as has been absurdly claimed by some modern critics (e.g. Winton Dean, "French Opera", in Abraham 1982, 113). See the *mise en scène* directions in Cohen 1991, 47.
39. Richard Wagner, "Reminiscences of Auber" (1871) in *Prose Works*, translated by William Ashton Ellis, London: Kegan Paul, Trench, Trübner & Co, 1896, 5:40, 42; see also Schneider, "Scribe and Auber," 180. A complete (or nearly complete) recording of *La muette de Portici* was made under Thomas Fulton (EMI 7492842).
40. See especially Schneider, "Scribe and Auber," 180–84.
41. The one number in *Un ballo in maschera* with no equivalent in Auber is Renato's "Eri tu" in Act 3.
42. *Gustave III* was recorded at Compiègne in 1991, under Michel Swierczewski (Arion 368220).
43. See Schneider, "Scribe and Auber," 178–9 and 187–8.
44. See Pendle 1979, 139–72, and Schneider, "*Fra Diavolo*," *Opera Grove*.
45. Particularly in evidence in *Fra Diavolo* in the aria "Je vois marcher sous ma bannière" at the beginning of Act 3, where, to give only one example, the line "Le bel état que celui de brigand" is an obvious parody of Scribe's own "Le bel état que celui de soldat" in Boieldieu's *La dame blanche*.
46. There is one complete recording in French, under Marc Soustrot (EMI 54810).
47. As noted by Charlton, in Abraham 1990, 124.
48. A French radio broadcast of *Le cheval de bronze* has been released on CD (Gala 714).
49. *Le domino noir* has been recorded under Richard Bonynge (London 440646). A curiosity of the set is that it includes a selection of the recitatives composed by Tchaikovsky in 1869 when the work was staged in Moscow with the Russian composer's one-time fiancée Désirée Artot in the role of Angèle.
50. *Les diamants de la couronne* was recorded at Compiègne in 1999 under Edmon Colomer (Mandala 5003/5).
51. See Pendle 1979, 222–5. The source is incorrectly listed in *New Grove 2*.
52. Or more, but the text of the piano-vocal score extenuates the implication present in the libretto, whose text is "Je viens de me donner à lui."
53. See Charlton, in Abraham 1990, 127–8. *Haydée* is available on a DVD filmed at Compiègne, under Michel Swierczewski (Cascavelle D4244).
54. There are two complete recordings of *Manon Lescaut*, one under Jean-Pierre Marty (EMI 763252), the other under Patrick Fournillier (CDM 2781054/5).
55. See Herbert Schneider, *Chronologisch-thematisches Verzeichnis sämtliche Werke von Daniel François Esprit Auber*, Hildesheim and New York: G. Olms, 1994.
56. On Meyerbeer's French operas, see in particular Fulcher 1987; Gerhard 1998; Charlton 2003; Letellier 2006; and Steven Huebner's and Matthias Brzoska's respective entries on Meyerbeer in

Opera Grove and *New Grove 2*. Meyerbeer's diaries, now available in English in a translation by Letellier, are an invaluable document on his Parisian years.

57. This source, not recorded in *New Grove 2*, was identified by Mark Everist, "Meyerbeer's *Il Crociato in Egitto: Mélodrame*, Opera, Orientalism," *Cambridge Opera Journal* 8:3 (1996), 215–49.

58. On *Robert le diable*, see especially Pendle 1979, 427–55; Hugh Macdonald, "*Robert le diable*," in Bloom 1987, 457–69; Charlton, in Abraham 1990, 93–100; Letellier 2006, 107–31; and Matthias Brzoska, "Meyerbeer: *Robert le Diable* and *Les Huguenots*," in Charlton 2003, 189–207.

59. See Pendle 1979, 437.

60. Loewenberg 1978, 736–8, records French-language performances in Calcutta (1836), New Orleans (1840), New York (1845), Batavia (1850), and Buenos Aires (1854).

61. See Brzoska, "Meyerbeer: *Robert le Diable* and *Les Huguenots*," in Charlton 2003, 191–2.

62. See, for example, *Histoire de Robert le diable, duc de Normandie*, Paris: Fournier, 1783; on the original legend, see Élisabeth Gaucher, *Robert le diable: histoire d'une légende*, Paris: Champion, 2003.

63. Designed by Ciceri in 1831 after the cloisters of Montfort l'Amaury.

64. The action thus takes place in the twelfth century, well past the period of the "historical" Robert the Devil.

65. The Paris Opera staged it with great success in 1985 (the broadcast, conducted by Thomas Fulton, has been released on Gala 622), a production marred, alas, by the absurd choreography.

66. On *Les Huguenots*, see in particular Pendle 1979, 465–93; Charlton "Romantic Opera" in Abraham 1990, 97–100; Gerhard 1998, 158–214; Brzoska, "Meyerbeer: *Robert le Diable* and *Les Huguenots*," in Charlton 2003 198–207; and Letellier 2006, 131–64.

67. Dezède's *Péronne sauvée* (Opéra, 1783) and Carafa's *Jeanne d'Arc, ou La délivrance d'Orléans* (Feydeau, 1821), to mention only two examples.

68. In the same scene, the call of the nightwatchman obviously served as a model for Wagner in Act 2 of *Die Meistersinger*.

69. Meyerbeer expanded the part in 1848 with a rondo in Act 2, written for the star contralto Marietta Alboni.

70. See Brzoska, "Meyerbeer," 203–4.

71. "I have written the whole of Marcel's part for my musical needs," Meyerbeer wrote to Scribe on 2 July 1834 (Meyerbeer, *Briefwechsel und Tagebücher*, ed. Heinz Becker, Berlin: Walter de Gruyter, 1959–2006, 2:377, cited from Charlton, in Abraham 1990, 99 n29). See also Brzoska, "Meyerbeer," in Charlton 2003, 206.

72. See Loewenberg 1978, 778–9.

73. On *Le prophète*, see Pendle 1979, 495–520; Gerhard 1998, 247–317; John H. Roberts, "Meyerbeer: *Le Prophète* and *L'Africaine*," in Charlton 2003, especially 208–22; and Letellier 2006, 181–210.

74. This is suggested by Letellier 2006, 188–92.

75. On Stoltz, see Mary Ann Smart, "The Lost Voice of Rosine Stoltz," *Cambridge Opera Journal* 6 (1994), 31–50.

76. See Pendle 1979, 502–4.

77. Marilyn Horne, who sang the work at the Met and has recorded it under Henry Lewis (CBS 79400) has told the present writer that Fidès was the most arduous role she ever attempted.

78. On *Ein Feldlager in Schliesen* and *Vielka*, see Letellier 2006, 164–81.

79. On *L'étoile du nord*, see especially Letellier 2006, 210–26. A complete recording was made at the Wexford Festival in 1996 (Marco Polo 8-223829).

80. See Gerhard 1998, 340–41.

81. On *L'Africaine*, see especially John H. Roberts in Charlton 2003, 222–32, and Letellier 2006, 245–70; see also Roberts 1977 dissertation, "The Genesis of Meyerbeer's *L'Africaine*" (PhD, University of California at Berkeley).

82. Long presumed lost, the manuscript was acquired by Yale in 2001 (it can be consulted in its entirety, in digital form, on the Beinecke Library's website).

83. This was correctly surmised by Roberts based on the similarity of words and meter (Charlton 2003, 219), though he assumes the manuscript to be lost.

84. Roberts in Charlton 2003, 229–31.

85. See Letellier 2006, 258–60. Only in the 1940s are there no performances recorded.

86. The main reference work on Adam remains Pougin 1877; see also Elizabeth Forbes's entries in *New Grove 2* and *Opera Grove*.

87. See Pendle 1979, 196–213.

88. *Ibid.*, 200–2.

89. The libretto was reset by Donizetti, who adapted the text himself, under the title *Betly* (1836). Adam, in turn, adapted Donizetti's work for the Opéra in 1853.

90. A complete recording in French was made under Thomas Fulton (EMI 74106). There are others in German.

91. The work has been recorded under Richard Bonynge (London 455 664).
92. On Halévy, see especially Hallman 2002 as well as Jordan 1994, and Claudon, de Van, and Leich-Galland 2003.
93. The Zürich opera revived the work for Cecilia Bartoli in 2008.
94. As Diana Hallman points out (Charlton 2003, 235) this is historically incorrect since Sigismund was then king of Hungary and Germany and became emperor only in 1433.
95. The issue is discussed at length in Hallman 2002, especially 210–52.
96. See Steven Huebner's table in Charlton 2003, 301.
97. See, for example, the references to the aria in Proust's À la recherche du temps perdu, where it is used as the nickname of Robert de Saint-Loup's mistress, herself called Rachel.
98. See the discussion of the work by Gilles de Van and Gérard Condé in Claudon, de Van, and Leich-Galland 2003, 131–8 and 193–204.
99. The libretto, in an Italian version by Giacomo Sacchero, was also set by Donizetti in 1844.
100. See Hallman in Charlton 2003, 240–45.
101. The role has an unusually low tessitura, going down in Act 4 to a low F sharp.
102. See Hallman in Charlton 2003, 245–8. Halévy toned down the patriotic element in his 1848 revision.
103. The work is discussed by Béatrice Prioron-Pinelli in Claudon, de Van, and Leich-Galland 2003, 139–47; see also Hallman in Charlton 2003, 248–50.
104. Writing just before the Second World War, Loewenberg 1978, 774, describes it as "still popular in France."
105. See A. Jacobshagen, "L'Éclair," in Fauquet 2003.
106. See Hervé Lacombe's discussion of the work in Claudon, de Van, and Leich-Galland 2003, 72–92.
107. Or rather, as the score has it, "Wales, England."
108. Possibly the first instance of operatic ergotherapy, as suggested by Karl Leich-Galland in Fauquet 2003.
109. See Karl Leich-Galland in Fauquet 2003.
110. See Hallman 2002, 85–6.
111. Noé, premiered in German at Karlsruhe in 1885, was first staged in France at Compiègne in 2004; see Karl Leich-Galland, "Noé," in Fauquet 2003.
112. A complete list of French works by Italian composers staged at the Opéra between 1820 and 1870 is supplied by M. Elizabeth Bartlet in Charlton 2003, 260–63.
113. The work's exotic title was attributed to Scribe's desire to have titles beginning with every single letter of the alphabet.
114. On Donizetti's Parisian career, see especially Asbrook 1982, and Mary Ann Smart, "Donizetti," New Grove 2.
115. A testimony to the opera's fame in France is its choice by Gustave Flaubert as the work that Emma Bovary and her husband see in Rouen in Chapter 15 of Madame Bovary (1856).
116. Its latest major revival in 1840 featured the great tragic actress Rachel (1821–1858) as Pauline.
117. Poliuto was finally staged in Naples in 1848 in the different political climate created by the introduction of a constitution.
118. Contrary to what Steven Huebner assumes in Charlton 2003, 294; see the exchange between Polyeucte and his wife in Act 4, scene 4.
119. According to Ashbrook, "Poliuto," Opera Grove.
120. Not F as claimed in Ashbrook 1982, 433 (E is the dominant of the piece, written in A major). There is one recording available, of a live performance in Venice in 1978 under Gianluigi Gelmetti (LS 1128).
121. On La fille du régiment, see especially L'avant-scène Opéra 179, which is entirely devoted to the work.
122. On the historical background, see Jean-Claude Yon in L'avant-scène Opéra 179, 68–73.
123. The theme, oddly, was lifted by Donizetti from his 1830 biblical opera Il diluvio universale. See Asbrook 1982, 437.
124. Cited from Mary Ann Smart, "Donizetti," New Grove 2.
125. Berlioz was above all furious over what he called Donizetti's "invasion" of Paris, suggesting that the Florentines would be equally unhappy if their theaters were suddenly flooded with works by Adam.
126. On La favorite, see Ashbrook 1982, 440–47, and Rebecca Harris-Warwick, "Introduzione storica," Donizetti, La favorite, Milan, Ricordi, 1997, I:xi–xxxii.
127. This 1912 recording, which even features a shortened version of the ballet, has been reissued by Marston Records (52010–2).
128. The play was itself based on a 1735 novel by Mme de Tencin, d'Alembert's mother. Pacini had set it as an opera in 1817 as Adelaide e Comingio, on a libretto by Rossi.
129. Similarly, "Rayons dorés," Inès's graceful aria with chorus in Act 1, scene 2, comes from Pia da Tolomei (1837).

130. It is also known as *Deux hommes et une femme*. See Ashbrook 1982, 454–6. Both the piano-vocal score and the orchestral score published in Paris in 1860 use, however, the title *Rita*.
131. Significantly, the work is not even mentioned in Fauquet 2003.
132. Not the Académie française as claimed in Ashbrook 1982, 176 (no musician was ever elected to that body), but the Académie des beaux-arts.
133. *Le duc d'Albe*, in its unfinished form, was eventually premiered in 1882.
134. See Ashbrook 1982, 183–9 and 510–32, and Mary Ann Smart, "Introduzione storica" in Donizetti, *Dom Sébastien, roi de Portugal*, Milan: Ricordi, 2003, 1:xi–xxiv; see also Jeremy Commons's notes accompanying the first complete recording of the work in French (Opera Rara 33). As Mary Ann Smart indicates, the libretto had originally been intended for Felix Mendelssohn.
135. Camoens was to make another, indirect, appearance in Scribe's work in *L'Africaine*, in which Nelusko's Adamastor song in Act 3 is inspired by the famous episode in his epic *The Lusiads*.
136. In his entry "*Dom Sébastien*," *Opera Grove*.
137. It has also been suggested that the royal funeral in Act 3 recalled painful memories of that of the Duke of Orléans, heir to the throne, who had died in a carriage accident the previous year. See Jean-Claude Yon, *Eugène Scribe*, 209.
138. There were performances in the provinces, however, and a major production in Vienna in 1845 (in German), for which Donizetti made changes to the score. The Italian premiere was at La Scala in 1847. New Orleans heard it in French in 1875.
139. The story is told in Mary Ann Smart, "The Lost Voice of Rosine Stoltz," *Cambridge Opera Journal* 6/1 (1994), 31–50.

Chapter 7: French Opera under the Second Empire

1. Reynaldo Hahn, "La musique au théâtre sous le Second Empire," *Conferencia*, 15 February 1925, cited from Lacombe 2001, 9–10.
2. On the Théâtre-Lyrique, see especially Walsh 1981. Jules Verne was for a while the Théâtre-Lyrique secretary (*ibid.*, 38).
3. Acquired by Sarah Bernhardt in 1899, it subsequently bore her name and reopened in 1968 as Théâtre de la Ville.
4. See Nicole Wild, "Théâtre-Lyrique," Fauquet 2003.
5. Hector Berlioz, "Les dilettanti en blouse et la musique sérieuse" (1853), in *Les grotesques de la musique*, ed. Léon Guichard, Paris: Gründ, 113–16.
6. The name "Théâtre-Lyrique" was subsequently used by other ephemeral companies, usually performing at the Gaîté theater on the Right Bank.
7. His real name was Count Adolphe de Ribbing.
8. The relations between Wagner and France are summarized by Joël-Marie Fauquet, "Wagner," in Fauquet 2003.
9. On the influence of French forms on Wagner's works, see Thomas Grey, "Richard Wagner and the Legacy of French Grand Opera" in Charlton 2003.
10. The circumstances of the premiere are summarized by Ulrich Drüner, "La version parisienne du *Tannhäuser* de Richard Wagner ou l'introduction du psychologique dans le grand opéra," in Prévost 1995, 163–4.
11. On the Saint-Simonians, see Ralph P. Locke, *Music, Musicians, and the Saint-Simonians*, Chicago and London: The University of Chicago Press, 1986.
12. Quoted by Hugh Macdonald, "David, Félicien," *New Grove 2*.
13. See Jean-Pierre Bartoli, "David, Félicien-César," in Fauquet 2003.
14. Quoted by Walsh 1981, 137.
15. This undated work, which is only known in short score and may never have been orchestrated, has been recorded complete (ORR 212) with Nicolas Koh playing the piano and conducting.
16. See Budden 1973, 1:247.
17. De Van 1998, 59.
18. Verdi, who clearly was of that opinion, vainly objected to *I Lombardi* being staged by the Théâtre-Italien in 1863.
19. This is reflected in the paucity of recordings, not to mention that some of them are in the inadequate Italian translation.
20. Alessandro di Profio, "Verdi," Fauquet 2003.
21. See M. Elizabeth Bartlett in Charlton 2003, 282.
22. See the letter to Scribe quoted by Budden 1973, 2:171–2.
23. Delavigne had written a well-known play with that title. On *Les vêpres siciliennes* see especially Budden 1973, 2:167–242, and Gerhard 1998, 335–9 and 342–87.
24. From a 1855 letter to François Crosnier, director of the Opéra, quoted by Budden 1973, 2:180.

25. See Gerhard 1998, 350–52.
26. Quoted in Budden 1973, 2:187.
27. *Ibid.*, 2:239.
28. *Ibid.*, 2:242. There is still no complete recording in French. The French, of course, are largely to be blamed for this state of affairs. When the Opéra staged the work in 1974 (to much public success), it did so in Italian translation – though the principal, Placido Domingo, admitted he found the word-setting awkward to sing and he would have been happy to do it in French. Even worse, when the usually better-inspired journal *L'avant-scène opéra* devoted a special issue (no. 75) to *Les vêpres siciliennes* in 1985, it used as its primary text the faulty Italian translation, *retranslating it into French* instead of printing the original, with the astounding claim that it would be an "absurdity" to cling to the latter.
29. The genesis of *Don Carlos* has been reconstructed by Ursula Günther; see "La genèse de *Don Carlos*," *Revue de musicologie* 58 (1972), 16–64, and 60 (1974), 87–158, and "La genèse du *Don Carlos* de Verdi: nouveaux documents," *Revue de musicologie* 72 (1986), 104–77. See also Budden 1973, 3:3–157, and Bartlett in Charlton 2003, 282–9.
30. It was more recently in the possession of Elizabeth Taylor.
31. See Pierre Véron's review cited by Bartlett in Charlton 2003, 289.
32. Is it by chance that *Don Carlos* has the same number of principals as *Les Huguenots*?
33. Budden 1973, 3:32.
34. In the absence of a biography of this unjustly neglected composer, see the entries by Bril in Fauquet 2003 and by Andrew Lamb in *New Grove 2* and *Opera Grove*.
35. The popularity of *Galathée* is attested by its inclusion among the complete opera recordings made by Pathé before the First World War.
36. Like *Galathée*, *Les noces de Jeannette* was included in the Pathé project. Made just after the First World War, the recording stars Ninon Vallin.
37. According to Charles Darcourt in the *Journal illustré* for 20 July 1884; cited by J.G. Ropartz, *Victor Massé*, Paris: Ed. Sagot, 1887, 10.
38. Based on its inclusion in Kreutzer's 1816 ballet of that title (it was the work performed at the Opéra on the night when the Duc de Berry was assassinated). See Walsh 1981, 76–8.
39. An unashamedly showy – and highly diverting – piece of virtuosity, the aria can be heard on Sumi Jo's recital of French coloratura arias (Phillips 317202).
40. The standard biography of Berlioz in English is Cairns 2000.
41. The edition of his collected music criticism, 5 large volumes of which have been published to date by Buchet-Chastel, will eventually run to 10.
42. See Ric Graebner and Paul Bancs, "Foreword," Hector Berlioz, *New Edition of the Complete Works*, 4, *Incomplete Operas*, Kassel et al.: Bärenreiter, 2002.
43. On the complex genesis of the opera, see especially Hugh Macdonald, "Foreword," Hector Berlioz, *New Edition of the Complete Works*, 1a, *Benvenuto Cellini*, Kassel et al.: Bärenreiter, 1994, as well as Cairns 2000, especially 2:157–75.
44. Then famous for his verse collection *Iambes*, he was the brother of the now better-known co-librettist of *Faust* and other Gounod operas, as well as *Le pardon de Ploërmel* and *Les contes d'Hoffmann*.
45. The former (recycled in 1841 as the *Rêverie et caprice* for violin and orchestra), as well as the original version of the overture, can be heard on John Nelson's recent complete recording, which restores the work to its pre-premiere stage (Virgin Classics 7243-5-45706-2-9).
46. His exculpations in his memoirs, written much later, sound particularly lame and self-serving; see Cairns 2000, 2:166.
47. Only in 1972 did the Opéra restage *Benvenuto Cellini*.
48. Queen Victoria wrote in her diary: "We saw and heard one of the most absurd and unattractive operas I suppose anyone could have written."
49. The next Parisian staging was for the inauguration of the Théâtre des Champs-Élysées in the spring of 1913.
50. Cited by Hugh Macdonald, "Foreword," XXII.
51. See Julian Rushton, "Foreword," *New Edition of the Complete Works*, 8b, *La damnation de Faust*, Supplement, Kassel et al.: Bärenreiter, 1986, 457.
52. On the genesis of *Les Troyens*, see Hugh Macdonald, "Foreword," *New Edition of the Complete Works*, 2c, *Les Troyens*, Supplement, Kassel et al.: Bärenreiter, 1970, and Cairns 2000, 2:591–627 and 688–708.
53. An abbreviated reconstitution of this original denouement can be seen on the DVD of the Berlioz bicentenary production at the Châtelet, conducted by John Eliot Gardiner (OA 0900 D).
54. The 1899 edition, evidently prepared in ignorance of Virgil, mistakenly placed this number at the end of Act 4.

55. On *Les Troyens à Carthage* at the Théâtre-Lyrique, see Walsh 1981, 165–71.
56. As D. Kern Holoman notes in his entry for *Grove Opera*, it lacked the ballets.
57. See Hugh Macdonald, "Foreword," *New Edition of the Complete Works*, 3, *Béatrice et Bénédict*, Kassel et al.: Bärenreiter, 1980; Cairns 2000, 2:666–71 and 681–3; and Gérard Condé, "Commentaire littéraire et musical," *L'avant-scène opéra* 214 (*Béatrice et Bénédict* issue), 8–44.
58. Walsh 1981, 145.
59. See Joël-Marie Fauquet, "Somarone ou l'ivresse de soi," *L'avant-scène opéra* 214, 60–63.
60. The music by Berlioz heard most often at the Opéra was the recitatives he composed for a new French version of Weber's *Der Freischütz* staged in 1841 (with his orchestration of *L'invitation à la valse* serving as ballet).
61. Hugh Macdonald, "Berlioz," *New Grove 2*.
62. On Gounod generally, see Huebner 1990, Condé 2009, and the entries on the individual operas in Honegger and Prévost 1991 and Fauquet 2003.
63. Sand eventually collaborated with Michel Carré on the libretto of *La petite Fadette* (1869), an opéra-comique by Théophile Semet (1824–1888), who had set an earlier version of the theme in 1850 (see Éric Kocevar, "Semet," in Fauquet 2003).
64. Among recent commentators, Paul Prévost makes a case for a modern revival (see his entry in Honegger and Prévost 1991).
65. See Gérard Condé, "Genèse et transformations" and "Création et accueil," *L'avant-scène opéra* 231 (*Faust* issue), 98–104 and 110–13.
66. For instance, the text of the Act 2 tenor aria "Est-on sage?" comes from the prologue of *Psyché*, the play by Molière, Corneille, and Quinault, and the Fabliau originates from Molière's *La princesse d'Élide*.
67. See Robert Orledge, ed., Erik Satie, *Scènes nouvelles pour* Le médecin malgré lui *de Charles Gounod*, Liverpool: Aeriel Kites Press, 2001.
68. On the *Faust* premiere, see Walsh 1981, 97–106.
69. Notably towards the end of the Duel Trio in Act 4, one of the rare passages where one can sense that something is missing in the music as it now stands.
70. All these passages are included in the appendix to the complete recording made under Michel Plasson (EMI 7-54228).
71. These early versions of the duets can be heard on Richard Bonynge's complete recording (London 421-240/3).
72. Huebner 1990, 65–6.
73. See especially Gérard Condé, "Introduction et guide d'écoute" and "*Mireille* en toutes lettres" in *L'avant-scène opéra* 251 (*Mireille* issue), 8–53 and 68–75. Although Condé's musical commentary follows the Hahn-Busser version, he gives as variants the text of the original libretto.
74. The differences between the various versions are outlined by Joël-Marie Fauquet in *L'avant-scène opéra* (*Roméo et Juliette* issue), 66–9. The complete music can be heard on Michel Plasson's 1995 recording (EMI 5-56123-2).
75. See Condé 2009, 158–84. On Georgina Weldon, see Brian Thompson, *The Disastrous Mrs. Weldon: The Life, Loves, and Lawsuits of a Legendary Victorian*, New York: Doubleday, 2001 (published in the UK in 2000 under the title *A Monkey Among Crocodiles*).
76. See my *Catalogue of the Frederick R. Koch Collection at Yale University*, New Haven: Beinecke Rare Book and Manuscript Library, 2006, 78–9.
77. At his death in 1893, Gounod was awarded "funérailles nationales," the first non-political figure to be treated to such an honor since Victor Hugo in 1885 (and the only composer ever).
78. Though Ben-Saïd, acting out of love, can be described to some extent as the villain of the work, his brother Hadjar (the bass role) is sympathetically treated, while a saying from the Koran on the sanctity of holy fools serves as a kind of motto.
79. Quoted by Masson 1996, 7, and Rogeboz-Malfroy 1994, 7. On Thomas, see also the entries by Richard Langham Smith in *New Grove 2* and Annegret Fauser in Fauquet 2003.
80. Masson 1996, 13.
81. It later became one of Fauré's favorite roles, but collectors of early recordings will be familiar with his aria through Pol Plançon's interpretation.
82. Compiègne revived it to mark the opening of the Channel Tunnel, a performance issued on DVD (Cascavelle D 4014) in 1994.
83. See the 2008 complete recording under Andrew Litton, with accompanying notes by Richard Langham Smith (ORC 37).
84. On *Mignon* generally, see especially Rogeboz-Malfroy 1994, 200–18.
85. The 2,000th performance was reached in 1955; see Rogeboz-Malfroy 1994, 201.
86. This is not clear from Elizabeth Forbes's entry on *Mignon* in *Opera Grove*.

87. In *Manon Lescaut*'s case, it would have been difficult to distort the denouement of such a classic of French literature. The reasoning, clearly, did not apply with the same strength to Provençal (in the case of *Mireille*) or German sources.
88. Details are provided in Rogeboz-Malfroy 1994, 204–6.
89. On *Hamlet*, see especially Rogeboz-Malfroy 1994, 219–35, and Masson 1996, 90–109.
90. This was also the case in Dumas' 1847 adaptation; see Masson 1996, 97.
91. Both can be heard on the 1993 complete recording with Thomas Hampson, conducted by Antonio de Almeida (EMI 7-54820-2).
92. Rogeboz-Malfroy 1994, 229. The Ghost Scene (Act 1, scene 2) is particularly remarkable for its orchestral effects, including a long solo for the trombone.
93. It was, for instance, used by the musical weekly *Le Ménestrel* when announcing the opening of the Bouffes-Parisiens in May 1855 (see Yon, *Offenbach*, 137).
94. The first work to be called "opérette" without any qualifier was apparently Jules Bovery's *Madame Mascarille* in 1856.
95. According to a famous dictum by Henry Lecomte (quoted by Jean-Claude Yon, "Opérette," Fauquet 2003), Hervé was the Columbus of the operetta whereas Offenbach was its Amerigo Vespucci.
96. On Hervé, see Cariven-Galharret and Ghesquière 1992, and Rochouse 1994.
97. As pointed out by Rochouse 1994, 29.
98. Not to be confused with the eighteenth-century Opéra, it is the theater still called Théâtre du Palais-Royal, built in 1831.
99. The building – subsequently called Théâtre Déjazet – is still standing.
100. Real name Joseph Cahen (b. 1807).
101. The former was called "anthropophagie musicale" and the latter "asphyxie musicale."
102. He was arrested after soliciting sexual favors from a 12-year-old boy. See Yon, *Offenbach*, 184–5. Cariven-Galharet and Ghesquière and Rochouse both draw a veil over the episode, while Bruyas 1974, 56, suggests that Hervé had fallen ill as a result of overwork. This circumstance notwithstanding – to which should be added Hervé's second, bigamous marriage during his years in England – the composer was clearly an affectionate father and his son Emmanuel, who himself became a composer of popular music under the name Gardel-Hervé (1847–19??), was devoted to his memory.
103. The original Marguerite in Hervé's work, Blanche d'Antigny, was the model for Émile Zola's Nana (see Rochouse 1994, 278–9).
104. *La veuve du Malabar* was the title of a 1770 tragedy by Lemierre about an Indian widow rescued from a sutee by the intervention of a French general. It remained proverbial even after the play had fallen into oblivion.
105. *Mam'zelle Nitouche* has been filmed twice, by Marc Allégret in 1931 (with Raimu) and by Yves Allégret, Marc's son, in 1954 (with Fernandel).
106. The best biography of Offenbach is Yon 2000.
107. Little is known about this work, whose title evokes Donizetti's abandoned *Duc d'Albe*, and of which only a few fragments have been recovered.
108. That second theater is the one still called Bouffes-Parisiens.
109. See Yon 2000, 210–12.
110. The work's most famous number, known in the English-speaking world as the Gendarmes Duet, was adopted at the end of the nineteenth century by the US Marines, reset to the words "From the Halls of Montezuma . . ." (see Yon, *Offenbach*, 363).
111. Despite being thoroughly revised by librettists and composer in 1874, the work established itself as one of Offenbach's masterpieces only after his death.
112. Recently reprinted, in an English translation by Gwenda David and Eric Mosbacher, as *Jacques Offenbach and the Paris of His Time* (New York: Zone Books; Cambridge: MIT Press, 2002).
113. Dahlhaus, for one, dismisses the suggestion that there was anything subversive about Offenbach's operettas; see Dahlhaus 1989, 228.
114. Yon 2000, 397–8.
115. Admittedly, the notoriously thin-skinned Wagner had never forgiven Offenbach's own satire of the "music of the future" in his 1860 *Tyrolienne de l'avenir* (see Yon 2000, 229).
116. Yon's phrase, *ibid.*, 469.
117. Not the theater where Donizetti's *Lucie* had been premiered, but a different theater of the same name, built in 1873 next to the Porte Saint-Martin.
118. On the genesis of *Les contes d'Hoffmann*, see especially Michael Kaye's notes to the complete recording under Kent Nagano (Erato 0630-14330-2); see also Jean-Christophe Keck, "Commentaire littéraire et musical," *L'avant-scène opéra* 235 (*Les contes d'Hoffmann* issue).

119. For the remainder of the work, Guiraud, following Offenbach's own practice, noted the orchestration on the same sheets as the short score: the manuscript, now split between the Bibliothèque nationale de France and Yale University, is clearly in two different hands.

120. The bulk of the Gunsbourg manuscript, acquired by Frederick R. Koch in 1984, is part of his outstanding collection of Offenbach manuscripts; see my *Catalogue of the Frederick R. Koch Collection at the Beinecke Library, Yale University*, New Haven: Beinecke Rare Book and Manuscript Library, 2006, 185–8. The manuscript from the end of the Venice act is currently (2007) in the possession of the Offenbach scholar Jean-Christophe Keck. The edition of *Les contes d'Hoffmann* by M. Kaye and J.-C. Keck (Mainz: Schott, forthcoming) will at last present an authoritative text.

Chapter 8: From Carmen to Pelléas

1. See Huebner 1999, 11–21.
2. See the list in Patureau, 449–53.
3. Though her parents were Irish, she was born in Paris, becoming a French citizen after the Franco-Prussian War. See Jann Pasler, *Writing Through Music*, Oxford; Oxford University Press, 2008, 213–48.
4. In this work premiered two years after the arrest and condemnation of Alfred Dreyfus, Cahen and his librettists altered Dumas's play, which features Jewish characters and even a discussion of Zionism, transposing the action to 1792 and eliminating the Jewish theme. On the composer Albert Cahen (full name Cahen d'Anvers, 1846–1903), a nephew of Meyerbeer and briefly associated with the Franck circle, see Joël-Marie Fauquet's entry in Fauquet 2003.
5. The phrase "Théâtre-Italien" remained in use to describe Italian seasons organized from time to time at the Gaîté or at the Théâtre des Nations in the 1880s and 1890s.
6. By an uncanny coincidence, Act 2 of the opera ends with the fire of a theater.
7. Among the survivors was the young Henri Matisse; see Hilary Spurling, *A Life of Henri Matisse, 1. The Unknown Matisse, 1869–1908*, London: Hamish Hamilton, 1998, 39–40.
8. Called Théâtre des Nations until it took the name Théâtre Sarah-Bernhardt in 1899.
9. At least in the original version; see the section on Bruneau below.
10. See Branger 1999, 25–9.
11. See Josiane Mas's entry on the work in Fauquet 2003.
12. On Bizet's life and career, see especially Lacombe 2000, as well as Curtiss 1958, Dean 1975, and Hugh Macdonald's entry in *New Grove 2*.
13. Lacombe 2000, 309–10.
14. Recent appraisals of *Ivan IV* are mixed (see Hugh Macdonald in *Opera Grove* and Lacombe 2000, 335, or, for a more sympathetic view, Lesley Wright in Fauquet 2003). The recent recording under Michaël Schoenwandt (Naïve 4940), based on a new reconstitution by Howard Williams, makes a persuasive case for the opera.
15. A lively altercation is recorded in Lacombe 2000, 350–51.
16. It is savagely taken apart in Dean 1975, 177–80; for a more nuanced appraisal, see Lacombe 2000, 399.
17. Michel Poupet summarizes some of the complex textual issues posed by the work in his essay "Trials and Tribulations of a Score" in the booklet accompanying the complete recording under Georges Prêtre (EMI 747598).
18. On this exceptional woman, who later married the banker Émile Straus, see especially Françoise Balard, *Geneviève Straus: Biographie et correspondance avec Ludovic Halévy 1855–1908*, Paris: CNRS-Éditions, 2002. Geneviève Straus was greatly admired by Proust (a schoolmate of her son Jacques Bizet), and her wit and stylishness have partly inspired the character of the Duchesse de Guermantes.
19. Diaz's work was the last new work to be staged, with Faure, at the Salle Le Peletier before it burned down in 1873.
20. From the sketches for the last named came the motif of Don José's aria, "La fleur que m'avais jetée"; see Lacombe 2000, 468.
21. See especially the extensive discussion of *Djamileh* in Lacombe 2000, 511–86.
22. In 1862 Bizet had composed a one-act opera, now lost, adapted by Halévy from Mérimée's *La guzla*.
23. See Lacombe 2000, 641–5, and 666–7 on Halévy's own early misgivings about the appropriateness of the subject and its treatment.
24. The original version of the aria was recently discovered in Choudens's archives and recorded for the first time in Michel Plasson's recording (EMI 57434); see Hervé Lacombe, "La version primitive de l'air d'entrée de Carmen: réflexion sur la dramaturgie et 'l'autorialité' d'un opéra," in Branger and Giroud 2009, 35–55.

25. See Walsh 1981, 81.

26. See Lacombe 2000, 504–7.

27. This is the way it was recorded by Pathé in 1911 in a fine performance conducted by François Ruhlmann (recently remastered by Ward Marston on Marston 52019), with the odd exception of one short Guiraud recitative, the one preceding Micaëla's aria in Act 3.

28. See Lacombe 2000, 677.

29. On Delibes, see Studwell 1987 and Hugh Macdonald's entry in *New Grove 2*.

30. It was subsequently the source of Reynaldo Hahn's *L'île du rêve* (1898). *Lakmé* is also inspired by three stories by Théodore Pavie (see Wild and Charlton 2005, 299).

31. Its vocal writing seems to anticipate the trio between the Marshallin, the disguised Octavian, and Baron Ochs in Act 1 of Richard Strauss's *Der Rosenkavalier*.

32. On Massenet's life, see Irvine 1994, as well as Hugh Macdonald's entry in *New Grove 2*.

33. With a corpus of more than 260 works, Massenet was by far the most prolific song-writer of his generation in France.

34. Jules Duprato (1827–1892), Prix de Rome in 1848, composer of opéras-comiques and operettas. His *La fiancée de Corinthe*, after Goethe, failed at the Opéra in 1867.

35. On the genesis of *Hérodiade*, see especially Jean-Christophe Branger, "Genèse d'*Hérodiade* de Massenet: le manuscrit Koch de la Beinecke Library," in Branger and Giroud 2009, 57–93. The tableau set in Phanuel's Observatory was added for the Milan premiere.

36. See Huebner 1999, 40–43.

37. See Alban Ramaut, "La création d'Hérodiade à Lyon," in Branger and Ramaut 2006, 147–72.

38. On *Manon*, see especially Branger 1999 and Huebner 1999, 45–72.

39. On this feature, which the Massenet scholar Jean-Christophe Branger considers the work's most striking innovation, see Branger 1999, 385–419.

40. These recitatives can be heard on a 1967 Scala performance, in Italian and in a somewhat abridged version, with Mirella Freni and Luciano Pavarotti (OPD 1164).

41. As her biographer recently revealed, she was for a while engaged to William Randolph Hearst; see Jack Winsor Hansen, *Requiem for a Diva*, Portland, OR: Amadeus Press, 2005, 15–22.

42. It can be heard as an appendix in the complete recording under Julius Rudel (DGG B0002470–02).

43. As pointed out by Steven Huebner in Charlton 2003, 291–7.

44. See Huebner 1999, 76.

45. *Ibid.*, 78, and, on *Esclarmonde* generally, 82–101.

46. Their complete recording (London 425–651–2) makes a strong case for the work.

47. See Huebner 1999, 45.

48. On this subject, see Jean-Christophe Branger, "*Werther* de Jules Massenet: un 'drame lyrique' français ou germanique?", *Revue de musicologie* 87/2 (2001), 419–83.

49. In the late 1890s Massenet himself prepared a version with the title role transposed for baritone, intended, not for Mattia Battistini as usually claimed, but for Victor Maurel. This version has recently been rediscovered, thanks in particular to Thomas Hampson.

50. On *Thaïs*, see Huebner 1999, 135–59.

51. Thus Athanaël's aria "Voilà donc la terrible cité" opens with what in poetry would be a highly irregular nine-foot line, while Thaïs's scene at the mirror freely combines even and odd meters.

52. Calvé has left an impressive recording of the Act 4 aria, "Pendant un an je fus ta femme" (reissued on Marston 52013–2).

53. See Jean-Christophe Branger and Sylvie Douche, eds, *Massenet et ses pairs: de Castillon à Humperdinck, Correspondances inédites*, Paris: Observatoire musical français, 2003.

54. It goes without saying that such finely calibrated effects are ruined when the part of the Prince is given to a tenor, singing an octave lower, as in the 2007 production at the New York City Opera, or, lamentably, on the only complete commercial recording under Julius Rudel (CBS MZK79323).

55. Madame Angot herself is not a real character, but the proverbial type of plain-speaking, working-class Parisian woman of the kind one would encounter at the Halles, where Acts 1 and 3 are set.

56. Théodore Dubois (1837–1924), who succeeded Thomas as director of the Paris Conservatoire, was himself the author of *Xavière*, an "idylle dramatique" set in the Auvergne, on a libretto by Gallet, premiered at the Opéra-Comique in 1895.

57. On Reyer, see especially Huebner 1999, 169–94, and Hugh Macdonald's entry in *New Grove 2*.

58. See Walsh 1981, 133–5.

59. On *Sigurd*, see Huebner 1999, 178–94.

60. See Hervé Lacombe's entry on "motif conducteur" in Fauquet 2003.

61. Caron can be heard on a brief recorded extract (reissued on Malibran CDRG 151).

62. In his entry on the work in Fauquet 2003.

63. The lack of a commercial recording is compensated by the existence of a strongly cast, if awkwardly cut, radio performance under Manuel Rosenthal (BJR 5141).
64. See Christian Goubault, 'Salammbô', in Fauquet 2003.
65. The parody of the scene in Act 2 of Jean Giraudoux's play *Ondine* (1939) is an indication of the opera's celebrity, while suggesting that it was considered rather old hat by then.
66. In the absence of a modern biography of Lalo, see Joël-Marie Fauquet's edition of his *Correspondance*, Paris: Aux amateurs de livres, 1989, as well as Huebner 1999, 231–51; *L'avant-scène opéra* 65 (*Le roi d'Ys* issue); and Hugh Macdonald's entry in *New Grove 2*.
67. See Hugh Macdonald, "A Fiasco Remembered: *Fiesque* Dismembered," *Slavonic and Western Music: Essays for Gerald Abraham*, Ann Arbor: Michigan University Press, 1985, 163–85. *Fiesque* received its world premiere, in concert, at the 2006 Montpellier Festival and its stage premiere at Mannheim in June 2007.
68. See Huebner 1999, 236.
69. Quoted by Joël-Marie Fauquet in his entry on Lalo in Fauquet 2003.
70. See his letter to Adolphe Jullien quoted and discussed in Huebner 1999, 242–5.
71. On Saint-Saëns's life, see especially Rees 1999; see also Hugh Macdonald's entry in *New Grove 2*. On Saint-Saëns as an opera composer, see Huebner 1999, 195–230.
72. As noted by Hugh Macdonald in his entry on the work in *Opera Grove*.
73. See Walsh 1981, 237.
74. On *Étienne Marcel*, see Huebner 1999, 213–15.
75. *Henry VIII* is discussed at length in *ibid.*, 215–30.
76. As pointed out by Huebner, *ibid.*, 222.
77. See Rees 1999, 295–8. The work was, however, not labeled operetta but opéra-comique.
78. Contrary to what is implied in Loewenberg 1978, 1,235 (he also lists stagings in Algiers and Barcelona), the 1913–14 revivals were of the single second act; see Wolff 1983, 46.
79. On Melba and Saint-Saëns, see Rees 357–9.
80. On Franck, see especially Fauquet 1999.
81. Never orchestrated, *Stradella* was premiered in a version with two pianos at the Opéra-Comique in 1985.
82. See Fauquet 1999, 255–60.
83. On *Hulda*, see *ibid.*, 769–95.
84. See Fauquet 1999, 795–809.
85. See Chabrier, *Correspondance*, eds Roger Delage and Franz Durif, with Thierry Bodin. Paris: Klincksieck, 1994. On Chabrier generally, see Delage 1999; Huebner 1999, 255–300, and Huebner's entry in *New Grove 2*.
86. The existing music for both has been recorded under Delage, together with *Une éducation manquée* (Arion 68252).
87. See Delage 1999, 201.
88. John Eliot Gardiner's classic 1984 performance, recorded in conjunction with a Lyons Opera staging (EMI 58688), has also been released on DVD.
89. See his comments in *Stravinsky: An Autobiography*, New York: Simon and Schuster, 1936, 174.
90. On *Gwendoline*, see especially Huebner 1999, 269–85.
91. Delage 1999, 317.
92. A complete performance of *Gwendoline* was recorded in 1996 under Jean-Paul Penin (Empreinte digitale 13059).
93. Plays published under the name Ancelot were the work of either François Ancelot or his wife Virginie, and occasionally resulted from their collaboration; Wild and Charlton 2005, 394, attribute *Le roi malgré lui* to her.
94. The complete recording under Charles Dutoit (Erato 45792) is serviceable but lacks the spoken dialogues.
95. Fugère, who had an exceptionally long career, has left recordings, but none unfortunately from *Le roi malgré lui*.
96. *Briséis* was recorded under Jean-Yves Ossonce at the 1994 Edinburgh Festival (Hyperion 66803).
97. On Chausson and *Le roi Arthus*, see Gallois 1994, in particular 373–410, and Huebner 1999, 351–92.
98. A list of operatic projects quoted in Gallois 1994, 375, also mentions Pushkin, Schiller, Shakespeare, Mickiewicz, Cervantes, and Calderón.
99. See Huebner 1999, 361–3.
100. Summarized in Gallois 1994, 383–5.
101. Huebner 1999, 381.
102. A point made by Gallois 1994, 408–9.
103. See *ibid.*, 580–82.

104. Two complete recordings are now available, one conducted by Armin Jordan (Erato 88213), the other by Leon Botstein (Telarc 80645).
105. On d'Indy, see Thomson 1996, Schwartz 2006, as well as the entry by Thomson and Robert Orledge in *Grove Music 2*; on d'Indy as an opera composer, see Huebner 1999, 308–50, and Robert Orledge's entries on the composer and his works in *Opera Grove*.
106. The connection is discussed at length by Anya Suschitzky in "*Fervaal, Parsifal*, and the French National Identity," *19th Century Music* 25:2–3 (November 2001), 237–65.
107. On *L'étranger*, see especially Huebner, " 'Le Hollandais fantôme': Ideology and Dramaturgy in *L'étranger*," in Schwartz 2006, 263–81.
108. On this work, see Jane Fulcher, "Vincent d'Indy's 'Drame Anti-Juif' and its meaning in Paris, 1920," *Cambridge Opera Journal* 2:3 (1990), 295–319, as well as Huebner, "Vincent d'Indy et le 'drame sacré': de *Parsifal* à *La Légende de Saint-Christophe*," in Branger and Ramaut 2006, 227–55; the work is also discussed in Fulcher 2005, 97–105.
109. On Bruneau, see especially Huebner 1999, 395–425, and Branger 2003, as well as Richard Langham Smith's entry in *New Grove 2*.
110. Bruneau eventually wrote stage music for a theatrical adaptation of the novel, staged at the Odéon in 1907.
111. The parallel with *Pelléas* is explored in detail by J.-C. Branger in his essay "*Le rêve* d'Alfred Bruneau: un opéra pré-debussyste," in *Pelléas et Mélisande 1902–2002: un centenaire*, ed. Jean-Christophe Branger, Sylvie Douche, and Denis Herlin, Lyons: Symétrie, forthcoming; see also Richard Langham Smith, "Quelques aspects du langage musical d'Alfred Bruneau," in Branger and Ramaut 2004, 81–93.
112. The second edition of the piano-vocal score indicates that the cut was sanctioned by the composer. However, when the work was revived at the Opéra-Comique in 1899, the original denouement was restored; see Branger 2003, 119.
113. On *L'attaque du moulin*, see especially Huebner 1999, 412–25.
114. And not his wife, as indicated by mistake in the entry on the work in *Opera Grove*.
115. See the sets costumes as reproduced by Kelkel 1984, 1,122–7.
116. The chauvinistic aspect of the Gaîté production was further enhanced by a move of the locale from Lorraine to Alsace. See my article "Bruneau et Delna," in Branger and Giroud 2009, 95–135.
117. In the French Revolutionary calendar, Germinal was the first month of spring, whereas Messidor corresponded to the harvest season.
118. See the analysis of the work in Kelkel 1984, 319–25.
119. Loewenberg 1978, 1,234, mentions a 1905 Russian production.
120. Recent research favors the assassination theory; see Henri Mitterand, *Zola*, Paris: Fayard, 1999–2002.
121. He also composed an oratorio (wrongly listed as an opera in *New Grove 2*) on a text by Zola, *Lazare*, premiered posthumously in 1954.
122. Adapted from a 1866 short story by Zola, the work was updated to include an episode situated in 1914 during the Battle of the Marne; see Kelkel 1984, 69.
123. On Charpentier, see especially Huebner 1999, 426–67, and the Robert Orledge entry in *New Grove 2*.
124. The issue is explored in detail in Huebner 1999, 426–35, while Charpentier's bohemianism is discussed in Fulcher 1999, 77 ff.
125. After *Louise* was performed, Saint-Pol-Roux, by then leading a reclusive and impecunious existence in Brittany, asked Charpentier for a share in the royalties. Although the French Society of Authors ruled unequivocally in the composer's favor, Charpentier, of a generous, disinterested nature (he subsequently founded a conservatory for the musical education of young working-class women), arranged for a portion to go to Saint-Pol-Roux's son, whose godfather he was. A controversy resurfaced towards the end of Charpentier's life, leading several sources (including the recent edition of Debussy's correspondence) to present Saint-Pol-Roux flatly as "the author of the libretto of *Louise*." On this issue, see Kelkel 1984, 176–8; see also Huebner 1999, 431–3. The issue is discussed at length by Michela Niccolai, to whom I am grateful for sharing information, in *La dramaturgie de Gustave Charpentier: contribution à l'étude de* "Le couronnement de la muse" – *Louise*, PhD Dissertation, Université de Saint-Étienne, 2008.
126. The parallel with Puccini's *Bohème* and Leoncavallo's *Bohème* (both 1896) is obvious, but one should recall that the plot of Henri Murger's novel takes us back to the 1840s.
127. Sixty according to Kelkel 1984, cited in Huebner 1999, 441.
128. See Barbara Kelly, "Vies parasites du poète: art et recyclage dans *Julien* de Charpentier," in Branger et Ramaut 2004, 271–83.
129. On Debussy's life and personality, see Lesure 1977, 2003, as well as Lesure's entry in *New Grove 2*; see also Robert Orledge, "Debussy the Man," in Trezise, 9–24.

130. See David Grayson, "Debussy on Stage," in Trezise 2003, 67–9.
131. Mendès had initially approached the Belgian composer and musicologist François-Auguste Gevaert (1828–1908), the eminent theoretician of ancient and medieval music, who, before 1870, had had a respectable career at the Opéra-Comique, where his Scott-based *Quentin Durward* was staged in 1858.
132. See Richard Langham Smith, Foreword, Claude Debussy, *Rodrigue et Chimène*, ed. Richard Langham Smith, Paris: Durand, 2003, xxi–xxx.
133. Maurice Barrès, Jacques-Émile Blanche, Léon Blum, Mallarmé, Henri de Régnier, James McNeill Whistler were in the audience for that single performance; see Grayson 1986, 15.
134. On the genesis of *Pelléas*, see Grayson 1986; Orledge 1982, 48–101; and Grayson in Nichols and Langham Smith 1989, 30–61.
135. On the performance history and reception of *Pelléas*, see Nichols in Nichols and Langham Smith 1989, 140–83.
136. Mary Garden, cited in Nichols and Smith 1989, 143.
137. *Ibid.*, 168.
138. The question of *Pelléas*'s Wagnerism came to the fore again when Pierre Boulez conducted the work at Covent Garden in 1966; on this issue, see Grayson, 225–75, and Nichols and Langham Smith, 163–5.
139. It entered the Opéra repertory in 1977.
140. Quoted in Nicholls and Langham Smith 1989, 156.
141. See Orledge 1982, 102–27. Other projects – including one with Saint-Pol-Roux – are discussed in his chapter 12, 257–78.
142. See Orledge, "L'opéra perdu de Debussy: *La Chute de la maison Usher* (1908–1917). Édition et reconstruction d'un chef-d'oeuvre macabre," in Branger and Giroud 2009, 171–91.

Chapter 9: From the Belle Époque to the Années Folles

1. The French version was by Paul Milliet, co-librettist of Massenet's *Hérodiade* and *Werther*. He also prepared the French version of *Andrea Chénier*, premiered in Lyons in 1897.
2. See Jean-Christophe Branger, "Les compositeurs français et l'opéra italien: la crise de 1910," in Branger and Ramaut, 2004, 315–42.
3. See Branger 1999, 421–3.
4. On Rouché, see especially Garban 2007.
5. In the 1908–9 season alone, the Salle Favart programmed six Massenet operas – *Manon*, *Werther*, *La Navarraise*, *Sapho*, *Cendrillon*, and *Le jongleur de Notre-Dame*. If one adds that *Thaïs* and *Bacchus* were on the Opéra schedule, it is difficult to think of a composer who, in his lifetime, had so many works performed within one year in the same city.
6. On *Grisélidis*, see especially Gérard Condé's "commentaire littéraire et musical" in *L'avant-scène opéra* 148 (*Esclarmonde/Grisélidis* issue).
7. Perversely, Mary Garden coaxed a reluctant Massenet into letting her assume the part of Jean at the New York premiere in 1908, but her example has seldom been imitated.
8. See Jean-Pierre Bartoli, "Le langage musical du *Jongleur de Notre-Dame* de Massenet," in Branger and Ramaut 2006, 305–33.
9. See the two complete recordings, the first made in 1991 under Pinchas Steinberg (RCA 60593), the more recent one under Emmanuel Villaume (Dynamic 508).
10. See Timothée Picard, "Mendès librettiste à la lumière de son wagnérisme," in *Catulle Mendès: l'énigme d'une disparition*, eds Patrick Besnier, Sophie Lucet, and Nathalie Prince, Rennes: La Licorne, Presses Universitaires de Rennes, 2005, 89–103.
11. On this unhappy episode of Massenet's career, see my chapter "Le désastre de Bacchus" in Branger and Giroud 2005, 155–84.
12. Mendès's accidental death, a few weeks before the premiere, was an additional blow, depriving Massenet of a collaborator for any last-minute changes.
13. See Gérard Condé's "commentaire littéraire et musical" in *L'avant-scène opéra* 93 (*Don Quichotte* issue).
14. The date was Friday the 13th, a fact worth recording in view of the fact that Massenet had become superstitious to the point of avoiding the fateful number in the foliation of his manuscripts.
15. On Dukas's life, see especially Perret and Ragot 2007, as well as Manuela Schwartz's entry in *New Grove 2*. On *Ariane et Barbe-Bleue*, see Perret and Ragot 2007, 453–516, and *L'avant-scène opéra* 149–50 (*Bluebeard Castle/Ariane et Barbe-Bleue* issue).
16. The first version of the text was published in German in the periodical *Wiener Rundschau* in 1899.
17. According to Perret and Ragot 2007, 177–8, Leblanc suddenly found herself forced to have an abortion.

18. Quoted by Perret and Ragot 2007, 172.
19. On Fauré's life, see Orledge 1979 and Nectoux 1991, as well as Jean-Michel Nectoux's entry in *New Grove 2*.
20. This project, in a modified version, was realized with Reynaldo Hahn as *La carmélite* (1902).
21. On *Prométhée*, see especially Nectoux 1991, 192–214.
22. Famous for his duel with Proust in 1897 (over references he had made to Proust's homosexuality), Lorrain is best-known for his novel *Monsieur de Phocas* (1901), which has been compared to *The Portrait of Dorian Gray*.
23. On *Pénélope*, see Orledge 1979, 150–62 and 219–26, and Nectoux 1991, 313–36. Besides *Pénélope*, Fauchois's name is linked to the play *Boudu sauvé des eaux*, which inspired one of Jean Renoir's cinematographic masterpieces.
24. A complete studio recording was made in 1980 under Charles Dutoit (Erato 88205).
25. On Magnard, see especially Perret and Halbreich 2001.
26. A secular heaven since Magnard was a confirmed agnostic.
27. See Fulcher 1999, 74–7.
28. Born Arthur Kraeckman, Endrèze recorded two extracts of *Guercoeur* (reissued on Malibran CDRG 157). A complete recording of the opera was made in 1986 under Michel Plasson (EMI 7491938).
29. In his entry on the work in *Opera Grove*, Malcolm Macdonald even argues that the work has the strongest claim among all early twentieth-century French operas.
30. It received its first modern staging at Marseilles in 2001.
31. On Ravel generally, see especially Orenstein 1975. On the operas, see Richard Langham Smith, "Ravel's Operatic Spectacles: *L'Heure* and *L'Enfant*," in Mawer 2000.
32. The subject was eventually treated by Ottorino Respighi in *La campana sommersa* (1927).
33. Born in Corbigny, Franc-Nohain – Nohain being a local river – was thus from the same area as Jules Renard, born in nearby Chitry-les-Mines, whose *Histoires naturelles* were the inspiration for Ravel's 1907 song cycle.
34. Cited by Orenstein 1975, 55–6.
35. The final quintet, however, recalls the traditional vaudeville of eighteenth-century opéra-comique.
36. As Roger Nichols points out in his entry on the work in *Opera Grove*, the clock sounds were recycled from Ravel's projected Hoffmann-based opera, where they were associated with the character of Coppélius.
37. Premiered by a baritone, the part of Ramiro calls for that traditional opéra-comique voice known as "baryton Martin"; similarly, Torquemada, the clockmaker, is written for the French character tenor voice called "trial."
38. See Orenstein 1975, 81. The house is now the Maison-Musée Maurice Ravel, a national museum.
39. Lavishly designed by David Hockney, it did not capture the spirit of the work as empathetically as Maurice Sendak did in Frank Corsaro's production, first seen at Glyndebourne in 1987 and mounted at the New York City Opera in 1990.
40. Cited by Orenstein 1975, 194.
41. On Roussel, see especially Deane 1961, as well as the entries by Nicole Labelle in *New Grove 2* and Richard Langham Smith in *Opera Grove*.
42. Their traveling companions on this expedition were an English couple who turned out to be the future Labour Prime Minister Ramsay MacDonald and his wife.
43. See Deane 1961, 87.
44. A complete recording, under Michel Plasson, was issued in 1983 with Marilyn Horne in the title role (EMI 47891).
45. Deane 1961, 91, dismisses the text as inadequate; for a more positive appraisal, see Christophe Corbier, "*La Naissance de la lyre* d'Albert Roussel," in Branger and Giroud 2008, 311–46. Reinach had initially offered his libretto to Fauré and to Charles Koechlin.
46. See Branger 1999, p. 422.
47. See Matteo Sansone's entry "Verismo" in *New Grove 2* and *Opera Grove*.
48. It is worth recalling that Zola's own work as an operatic librettist substantially departs from the theories he expressed in 1881 in *Le naturalisme au théâtre*.
49. Most of them are listed in Kelkel 1984, 40–44.
50. See the discussion of this musical collage in Kelkel 1984, 419–23.
51. See Sylvie Douche, "Jean Richepin et le théâtre lyrique naturaliste," in Branger and Ramaut 2004, 285–313.
52. After the First World War, under the influence of Mme Blavatsky, his interests moved towards theosophy.
53. See Mathieu Feret and Benoît Menut, *Joseph-Guy Ropartz, ou le pays inaccessible* (Geneva: Papillon, 2005), and the essay by Michel Fleury in the booklet accompanying the complete recording made in 2001 under Jean-Yves Ossonce (Timpani 2C2065).

54. His best-known play, *La femme nue* (1908), was said to be based on Debussy's sensational divorce from Lilly Texier and her subsequent suicide attempt. The program of the original production of *La lépreuse* was illustrated by Toulouse-Lautrec.

55. A prolonged kiss in the play, but the change, though medically improbable, was insisted upon by Albert Carré.

56. Large extracts, recorded in 1944 under François Ruhlmann, have been re-released on CD (Malibran 155).

57. On Widor, see Thomson 1987.

58. See *ibid.*, 59.

59. On the general subject of classical themes in French operas of the period, see Branger and Giroud 2008.

60. His *Amy Robsart*, however, adapted from Walter Scott's *Kenilworth*, received its premiere in French translation at Covent Garden in 1893; see the entry on the composer by Nigel Burton and Susan Thach Dean in *Opera Grove*, and Lara's autobiography, *Many Tales of Many Cities* (London: Hutchinson & Co, 1928).

61. See Loewenberg 1978, 1,218, and Nigel Burton's entry on the work in *Opera Grove*.

62. See Renata Suchowiejko, "*Quo Vadis?* de Jean Nouguès," in Branger and Giroud 2008, 295–309.

63. Nouguès also wrote the "discographic opera" in two acts (apparently unpublished and not listed in *New Grove 2* or *Opera Grove*), *Les frères Danilo*, whose plot is set in a circus. Evidently commissioned by Pathé for release as part of its "Théâtre chez soi" series of complete operas, it was recorded under the composer. It has been recently re-released on CD (Marston Records 52043-2).

64. This French version of *Salomé* has been recorded under Kent Nagano (Virgin 91477).

65. See Fiona Maddocks in *Opera 2006/3*, 303–4. Mariotte's *Salomé* was recorded at Montpellier in 2004 under Friedemann Layer (Accord 442 8553).

66. On Cras, see Paul-André Bempéchat's entry in *New Grove 2*.

67. A complete recording was made in 2003 under Bramwell Tovey (Timpani 3078).

68. On Tournemire, see Ianco 2002.

69. On Emmanuel, see Corbier 2007, and Robert Orledge's entry on the composer in *New Grove 2*. See also the *Revue musicale* 206 (1947, special Emmanuel issue).

70. See Christophe Corbier, "*Salamine*, une tragédie lyrique en 1929," in Sylvie Douche, ed., *Maurice Emmanuel, compositeur français*, Paris: Université de Paris-Sorbonne (Paris V); Prague: Bärenreiter, 2007, 137–8.

71. On Bloch, see Strassburg 1977, as well as Kushner 2002 and Kushner's entry in *New Grove 2*.

72. Most were mounted in Switzerland, with the notable exception of the two-act opéra-comique *Les jumeaux de Bergame*, on a libretto by Maurice Léna, premiered in Brussels in 1908.

73. Based, like Puccini's *Edgar*, on Musset's *La coupe et les lèvres*.

74. See his four-volume poetic cycle *Écoute Israël* (1913–48) and his pamphlet *Pourquoi je suis juif* (1928), translated into many languages.

75. See David Z. Kushner's entry on *Macbeth* in *Opera Grove*. The recording made in 1997 under Friedemann Layer (Actes Sud 34100) is of this shorter, revised version.

76. Drafts are preserved at the Library of Congress, Washington, DC.

77. Erlanger is not to be confused with the Paris-born British composer Frédéric d'Erlanger, author of *Tess* (1904), adapted from Thomas Hardy's novel.

78. The same tale inspired, the following year, *Der polnische Jude* by the Prague composer Karel Weis (1862–1944), who, after Bruneau, also wrote an opera based on Zola's *L'attaque du moulin* (1912). As Elizabeth Forbes points out in her entry on Erlanger's work in *Opera Grove*, the Erckmann-Chatrian story was also the basis for Leopold Lewis's play *The Bells*, in which Sir Henry Irving scored one of his biggest successes.

79. See Jacques Tchamkerten, "Démons antiques et moines maudits: les avatars du sentiment religieux dans l'oeuvre lyrique de Camille Erlanger," in Branger and Ramaut 2006, 181–200 (here 183).

80. See Lesley A. Wright, "*Aphrodite* (1906) and Camille Erlanger: Antiquité, imagination et volupté," in Branger and Giroud 2008, 259–94.

81. On Pierné, see Masson 1987.

82. A 1964 French radio broadcast, conducted by Pierre-Michel Leconte, has been released on CD (Gala 100.587).

83. On Messager, see especially Wagstaff 1991; see also Duteurtre 2003.

84. The medieval term, derived from "basilica," referred to courts of justice and, by extension, the whole legal profession.

85. Two of the foremost comic playwrights of the period, they notably authored *L'habit vert* (1912), a satire of the Académie française, also featuring an uproarious figure of a musician named Parmeline.

86. It has been recorded under John Eliot Gardiner (Erato 75390–2).
87. One should add that the extracts recorded by Printemps, in impeccable style, are among the finest examples of classic French operetta singing (recently re-released on CD as part of the compilation *Hommage à André Messager*, Cascavelle 3074).
88. In the absence of a scholarly biography of Hahn, see Gavoty 1976 and Depaulis 2007.
89. See the exhaustive study by Philippe Blay, *"L'Île du rêve" de Reynaldo Hahn: contribution à l'étude de l'opéra de l'époque fin-de-siècle*, Lille: ANRT, Université de Lille III, 1999.
90. See Blay, "Grand Siècle et Belle Époque: *La Carmélite* de Reynaldo Hahn," in Branger and Giroud 2009.
91. After being staged at Liège, it reached the Opéra-Comique in 1923 but was eclipsed by the triumph of *Ciboulette* in the same year.
92. See Patrick O'Connor's entry in *Opera Grove* and the complete recording made in 1983 under Cyril Diederich (EMI 49874/5).
93. See Patrick O'Connor's entry on the work in *Opera Grove*.
94. See Simon 2009, 40–1.
95. Pronounced "lins" and perhaps best remembered for being the country residence of the painter Pierre Bonnard, who was in fact Terrasse's brother-in-law.
96. See Lesure and Langham Smith 1977, 182–4.
97. In this capacity he authored the song "Mon homme," immortalized in English by Billie Holiday.
98. See the list of stage works in Robert Orledge's entry in *New Grove 2*, as well as in Orledge 1990, Appendix.
99. See Ornella Volta, *Satie Seen through his Letters*, translated by Michael Bullock, London and New York: Marion Boyars, 1989, 79–81.
100. *Ibid.*, 156.
101. See Loewenberg 1978, 1,383–4.
102. See Orledge 1990, 323.
103. See *Infra*, p. 275.
104. On Stravinsky and opera, see especially Richard Taruskin's entry in *Opera Grove* as well as his entries on the individual works.
105. See White 1979, 263–75 (here 269). The work is not included in *Opera Grove*.
106. See Charles-Ferdinand Ramuz, *Souvenirs sur Igor Strawinsky*, Lausanne: Mermod, 1946, 114, 116, 119, etc.; and Igor Stravinsky and Robert Craft, *Memories and Commentaries*, London: Faber and Faber, 1960, repr. 2002, 130–31.
107. He also called it a "masque or danced pantomime co-ordinated with a sung and spoken text" (*ibid.*, 177).
108. See White 1979, 374–88.
109. The sung parts of *Oedipus Rex* (1925) were set to a Latin translation of Cocteau's text – with only the Narrator speaking in the vernacular.
110. See White 1979, 379, and *Memories and Commentaries*, 178–9.
111. *Ibid.*, 181.
112. *Ibid.*, 276–7.
113. See his *Chronicle of My Life*, London: Victor Gollancz Ltd, 1936, 182–4.

Chapter 10: Crisis and Renewal

1. See Lesley A. Wright's entry, "Prix de Rome," in Fauquet 2003.
2. According to Madeleine Milhaud (cited in Pistone 1987, 298), Cocteau's libretto for Milhaud's *Le pauvre matelot* was initially destined for Auric.
3. Berners's work is not to be confused with the comédie lyrique based on the same source by Henri Busser, premiered at the Opéra-Comique in 1948.
4. The librettist, oddly, was the same Franc-Nohain who supplied the text for Ravel's rambunctious *L'heure espagnole*. On *Un jardin sur l'Oronte*, see Fulcher 2005, 105–6.
5. Cited by Nigel Simone, "France and the Mediterranean," in Cooke 2005, 137.
6. *Ibid.*, 136–8. Named "ondes musicales" by its inventor Maurice Martenot (1898–1980), the instrument had been unveiled at a concert at the Opéra in 1928.
7. See Jean-Christophe Branger, "Répertoire lyrique et politique de création à l'Opéra-Comique dans les années trente," in Pistone 2000, 135–49.
8. A student of Massenet, the Burgundian Omer Letorey (1873–1938) won the Prix de Rome in 1895. He served as music director at the Comédie-Française. His and d'Ollone's works were not the only Molière adaptations staged at the Opéra-Comique in the 1930s: Emmanuel Bondeville's *L'école des maris*, premiered in 1935, was sufficiently well received to be revived as late as 1940.

9. A disciple of Fauré, Jean Roger-Ducasse (1873–1954), who succeeded Dukas as professor of composition at the Conservatoire in 1935, was the author of a "mimodrame lyrique," *Orphée*, staged at the Opéra in 1926, with Ida Rubinstein.
10. On the play by Henry Bataille, see p. 334, n54.
11. See Wild and Charlton 2005, 267.
12. In 1935 a polemic centering on the notion of musical "banality" opposed Poulenc and Koechlin on one side and, on the other, the Austrian avant-garde composer Ernst Krenek, who had recently completed an opera, *Karl V*, based on the 12-tone system; see Branger, "Répertoire lyrique et politique de création," Pistone 2000 136.
13. The figures are quoted from Garban 2007, 162–3. The 1925 subsidy of 800,000 francs, a fairly large sum before 1914 (a successful performance brought 20,000 in receipts), was quickly eroded by inflation in the 1920s (the franc was "stabilized" at a lower level by Poincaré in 1929).
14. This has been suggested by critics like Roland Mancini. See, for example, his highly polemical "Autour du chant français: rappel, questions, perpectives", *L'avant-scène opéra* 65 (July 1984), 61 and 63–4.
15. See Jean Gourret, *Dictionnaire des chanteurs de l'Opéra de Paris*, Paris: Éditions Albatros, 1982, 29.
16. Sadly, two of the most gifted French singers of the period, the soprano Ninon Vallin (1886–1961) and the tenor César Vezzani (1886–1951), seldom sang in Paris. Although both appeared at the Opéra-Comique at the beginning of their careers, she was heard only three times at the Opéra and he *never*.
17. This tendency was deliberately exploited by the Vichy regime to deflect attention away from the responsibilities of some of its leaders in the military defeat and to suggest instead that its real causes lay with the country's moral and cultural decadence.
18. On Milhaud, see especially Collaer 1988, Drake 1989, and Drake's entries in *New Grove 2* and *Grove Opera*.
19. *My Happy Life*, translated by Donald Evans, George Hall, and Christopher Palmer, London and New York: Marion Boyars, 1995.
20. Their correspondence was published as a volume of the *Cahiers Paul Claudel* in 1961. A career diplomat, Claudel eventually became French ambassador to the United States. On Claudel and opera, see especially Lécroart 2004.
21. Not classified as operas in *New Grove 2* and *Grove Opera*, the works are treated as such in Madeleine Milhaud's catalogue of her husband's work; see Collaer 1988, 316–17.
22. The cast included the legendary Delia Reinhardt in the soprano part of Queen Isabella.
23. See Claudel 2007, 95, 169, 170–71 n163, 172.
24. A complete recording, made under the composer, has been reissued on CD (Adès 650, with *Le pauvre matelot*).
25. Christopher Palmer, entry "Milhaud," *Grove Opera*.
26. Save for one reference in passing, he does not figure, for instance, in *New Kobbé's*. On Honegger, see especially Halbreich 1999 (the quotation is on p. 393).
27. When he was elected to the Institut de France in 1952 (not in 1938 as claimed by Geoffrey K. Spratt in *New Grove 2* and other sources), it was as a foreign correspondent.
28. See Halbreich 1999, 393.
29. Claudel, for one, maintained that the work made a greater impact as an oratorio.
30. On the ambiguities surrounding this 1943 production, see Jane F. Fulcher, "French Identity in Flux: Vichy's Collaboration and Antigone's Operatic Triumph," *Journal of Interdisciplinary History* 36:4 (2006), 649–74.
31. The soprano role, sung by the young Régine Crespin at the 1952 Opéra revival, is Ismène, Antigone's sister.
32. A parallel noted in Halbreich 1999, 553. A complete recording was made in 1992 under Mario Venzago (MGB 6115).
33. Halbreich 1999, 561.
34. On Ibert, see Laederich 1998 and her entry in *New Grove 2*.
35. Nino (Michel Veber) later wrote the libretto to Roussel's *Le testament de La tante Caroline*.
36. A recording was made in 2002, conducted by Jan Latham-Koenig (AV 0008).
37. Several recordings have been made, the most recent in Palermo under Yoram David (HOM 701833).
38. A 1958 radio broadcast conducted by Manuel Rosenthal, with Musy as the king, exists in the INA archives in Paris. The work was staged with success at Strasbourg in 1961 (see the review by André Tubeuf in *Opera 12* [1961], 657).
39. Ironically, the Nazi authorities urged a revival of *L'Aiglon* in late 1940 as part of the propaganda following Hitler's "gift" of the Duke of Reichstadt's ashes to be buried next to Napoleon at the Invalides in Paris.

40. On Enesco and *Œdipe*, see in particular Cophignon 2006, especially 349–91.
41. Not being a French national, he was barred from competing for the Prix de Rome.
42. An early project on a Romanian subject, *Prin Carpati*, remained incomplete.
43. Cited in Cophignon 2006, 283.
44. In his foreword printed in the booklet to the 1990 complete recording of *Œdipe* under Lawrence Foster (EMI 7540112).
45. On Martinu, see Large 1975.
46. A planned third collaboration with Ribemont-Dessaignes, *Jour de bonté*, was left incomplete.
47. See Sandrine Grandgambe, "La Réunion des Théâtres Lyriques nationaux," in Chimènes 2001, 119.
48. See Fulcher 2005, 107.
49. It can be added that his music, considered too modern, was little performed in Nazi Germany.
50. See Leslie Sprout, "Les commandes de Vichy, aube d'une ère nouvelle," *ibid.*, 167–71; the librettist of *Ginevra* is mistakenly identified as Jean Luchaire, 180–81.
51. See his autobiography, *Confession d'un Français moyen* (1943).
52. See the correspondence preserved in the "Dossier d'artiste" in the Bibliothèque-musée de l'Opéra.
53. It is worth mentioning in this context that Lucien Rebatet (1903–1972), whose virulently anti-Semitic memoir *Les décombres* (1942) was one of the bestsellers of the Vichy years, subsequently published an *Histoire de la musique* (1969, and still in print in 2009) in which value judgments representative of the period abound, especially on French opera.
54. This classic version of Debussy's work has seldom been absent from the catalogue since. It is currently available on EMI 45782.
55. See Philippe Morin, "Une mouvelle politique discographique pour la France," in Chimènes 2001, 253–68."
56. It is revealing to compare the quality of the French pronunciation on the Metropolitan Opera broadcasts of *Faust* in 1936, with Richard Crooks, and in 1959 with Björling (not to mention the latter's ugly downward transposition, from A flat to G, of the end of the Cavatine).
57. See Nigel Simeone, "France and the Mediterranean," in Cooke 2005, 142–5.
58. The other "new" work staged in the 1950s – Henri Tomasi's *L'Atlantide* – had been premiered in Mulhouse. Daniel-Lesur's *Ondine* was premiered at the Théâtre des Champs-Élysées in an Opéra production.
59. *Kerkeb* was based on a story by "Elissa Rhaïs," ostensibly the Blida-born Leila Bou Mendil (1882–1940), a woman of mixed Arab and Jewish parentage, though her books are now known to have been penned by her nephew (and lover) Raoul Tabet (1899–1968). On this little-known literary hoax, see the semi-fictionalized account by Paul Tabet (Raoul's son), *Elissa Rhaïs*, Paris: Grasset, 1982.
60. The libretto is by Fauchois, Fauré's collaborator for *Pénélope*.
61. See the spirited account by its librettist, Henri Jeanson, in Pistone 1987, 294–6.
62. Extracts, arranged by Michel Philippot, were given posthumously at the Palais Garnier in 1982.
63. Much – far too much – has been made of Boulez's sarcastic statement, made in the 1960s, that the "most elegant solution" to the problems faced by opera houses would be to blow them up.
64. See, for example, Émile Vuillermoz's *Histoire de la musique* Paris: Fayard, 1949.
65. The persistence of this prejudice can be gauged from some of the comments made in 2008 in *L'avant-scène opéra* 244 (*Don Carlos* issue), see especially 11. One suspects the same critics who claim they prefer *Don Carlos* in Italian translation would hesitate to suggest, say, that Kaija Saariaho's *L'amour de loin* sounds better in Finnish.
66. Negative reactions were thus heard when Rolf Liebermann scheduled productions of *Don Quichotte* and *Manon* at the Opéra in the 1973–4 season.
67. An exception worth mentioning is Jean-Michel Damase's witty *Eugène le mystérieux*, based by its librettist Marcel Achard on Eugène Sue's *Les mystères de Paris*, premiered at the Châtelet in 1964.
68. Pistone 1987, 23–6, gives the list, not without grievous misattributions: Massenet is no more the author of *La basoche* and *Fortunio* than Messager that of *Sappho*. Those French radio broadcasts were not, of course, limited to the French repertory, but this is the one that concerns us here. It is to be hoped that these recordings – which often constitute the only execution preserved of the work in question – will some day be made permanently available by the Institut national de l'audiovisuel, keeper of the French radio archives. (A few were briefly issued on CD by Le chant du monde.)
69. See Françoise Masset, "Le théâtre lyrique de Claude Arrieu," in Pistone 1987, 193–202.
70. Tansman's wife was a daughter of Jean Cras. A naturalized French citizen as of 1938, he spent the war years in exile in the United States to avoid the fate of French Jews of foreign birth, many of whom were arrested by the French police and handed over to the Nazis.
71. The work has recently been recorded under Alain Altinoglu (FRF 001-HM90).

72. Brother of the film director Roberto Rossellini, Renzo Rossellini (1908–1982) also wrote an opera based on Claudel's *L'annonce faite à Marie*, premiered in Paris in 1970.

73. On Poulenc, see Schmidt 2001, as well as the entry by Myriam Chimènes and Roger Nichols in *New Grove 2*. See also the relevant sections in Schmidt 1995.

74. In the opera Zanzibar is relocated "somewhere between Nice and Monte Carlo."

75. On this singer, and especially on her relationship with Poulenc, see Bruno Berenguer, *Denise Duval*, Lyons: Symétrie, 2003.

76. See Schmidt 2001, 328–9.

77. This explains the work's somewhat cryptic title: "dialogues" means screenplay in French, and the title carefully chosen by Bernanos's publisher – literally "Screenplay for [the unrealized film] *The Carmelites*" – acquired, so to speak, a life of its own.

78. The score was published with the mention "with the authorization of Emmet Lavery."

79. The initial structure, in two acts, was modified in 1955.

80. Many, but by no means all, of their letters are published in Chimènes 1994. The originals are in the Koch Collection at Yale.

81. It was transferred to the Opéra-Comique, in a different production, in 1964, before returning to the Opéra in 1972, and was heard at the Salle Favart again in the 1980s.

82. Angered at being preempted by California, Rudolf Bing, the Met's director, canceled plans for a New York production and the work had to wait until his departure to be staged in that theater. See Schmidt 2001, 417.

83. An interesting discussion of this change of perspective on the work is provided by Crespin – who, for the 1977 Metropolitan Opera premiere, traded the part of Mme Lidoine for that of the First Prioress – in *L'avant-scène opéra* 52 (*Dialogues des carmélites* issue), 104–7.

84. Letter to Pierre Bernac of 11 August 1958, cited by Schmidt 1995, 479.

85. Duval has recorded the three Poulenc roles she premiered in Paris: *Les mamelles de Tirésias* under André Cluytens; *Dialogues des carmélites* with the Paris premiere cast, under Pierre Dervaux; and *La voix humaine* under Prêtre. All three are available on EMI 7243-5-6684-3-2-4).

86. In his entry on *La voix humaine* in Honegger and Prévost 1991, 3:2,205.

87. See Bril 1967 and Sauguet 2001.

88. See Sauguet 2001, especially 307–20.

89. See Bril's entry in Honegger and Prévost, I:351–2.

90. Actually deriving from Scarron's *la précaution inutile* (itself referred to in Beaumarchais's *Le barbier de Séville*, which is subtitled after it). See Bril in Honegger and Prévost 1991, 2:769.

91. See Bril's entry in Honegger and Prévost 1991, 1:298–9. The opera was recorded in 1959 under Manuel Rosenthal (SOCD 98-9).

92. See Françoise Andrieux, "Marcel Landowski et le théâtre lyrique," in Pistone 1987, 243–53, and *Opéra aujourd'hui 2* (special Landowski issue) as well as Bruno Serrou's entry in *New Grove 2*.

93. See Frédéric Ducros, "Les opéras d'Henri Tomasi, musicien appassionato et méditatif," in Pistone 1987, 299–308, and "Hommage à Henri Tomasi," in *L'avant-scène opéra* 109, 109–39.

94. A diplomat as well as a poet, Milosz (who used as a nom de plume Oscar-Vladislav de Lubicz-Milosz) was the uncle of the Polish writer and 1980 Nobel Prize winner Czeslaw Milosz.

95. His co-director being Bernard Lefort (a former singer), Parisian wits immediately came up with the motto: "Lefort n'est pas sûr et Lesur n'est pas fort" ("Lefort is not reliable and Lesur is not very smart").

96. It is inexplicably omitted from the list of Daniel-Lesur's works in *New Grove 2*.

97. According to Stéphane Wolff in *Opera* 17 (1966), 231.

98. A production in Prague in 2003 presented the work as a double bill with Beckett's play.

99. On the "théâtre musical" generally, see Robert Aldington, "Music Theatre since the 1960s" in Cooke 2005, 225–43.

100. Its title recalls the device Butor used in his own 1957 novel *La modification*, written throughout in the phural second person, as if the events described were happening to the reader.

101. Thus, in the "enquête lyrique" *La passion selon nos doutes* (1971) by Jean Prodromidès (b. 1927), a pupil of Messiaen and René Leibowitz, actors shout questions at the audience. See *Opéra aujourd'hui 1* (Jean Prodromidès issue), 16.

102. The work is discussed in *L'avant-scène opéra* 18 (*Dido and Aeneas* issue), 87–101.

103. *Opera* 33:1 (January 1982), 78.

104. See the review by Kevin Stephens in *Opera* 32: (1981), 284–5.

105. See the entry on Aperghis in *New Grove 2*. Aperghis's own views on "théâtre musical" are expounded in his article "Quelques réflexions sur le théâtre musical," in *Acanthes An XV: composer, enseigner, jouer la musique d'aujourd'hui* (Paris, 1991), 180–82.

106. See Tony Mayer's review in *Opera* 25:1 (January 1974), 25–7.

107. His more recent work – *L'écharpe rouge* (1984), *Tristes tropiques* (1996), *Avis de tempête* (2004) – is more along the lines of avant-garde opera, and he himself characterizes it as such (see his website, www.aperghis.com).
108. On Prey, see especially *Opéra aujourd'hui* 5 (1993); see also Nigel Simeone, "France and the Mediterranean," in Cooke 2005, 144–5.
109. As early had 1962 Malraux had appointed a commission to look into the "crisis of music in France."
110. The opening production of *Le nozze di Figaro* in 1973 was conducted by Georg Solti and sung by Gundula Janowitz, Mirella Freni, Frederica von Stade, Jane Berbié, Michel Sénéchal, Gabriel Bacquier, José Van Dam, and Kurt Moll – as strong a cast as could then be assembled.
111. Also in collaboration with Peter Brook, Constant subsequently wrote a similar work based on Debussy, *Impressions de Pelléas* (1992).
112. After his retirement, he wrote one opera to a French libretto, *La forêt*, on a libretto by his wife Hélène Vida after Aleksandr Ostrovsky's play. Its world premiere was given at Geneva in 1987.
113. On Messiaen in general and his opera, see in particular Hill and Simeone 2005, especially 304–41, and Dingle 2007, especially 188–219. See also *Opéra aujourd'hui*, *L'avant-scène opéra*, hors série 4 (1992), *Saint François d'Assise* issue.
114. It had previously inspired an oratorio dy Pierné (1912), an unpublished opera (*c*.1938) by Tournemire – one of Messiaen's admired teachers – on a libretto by the Rosicrucian Joséphin Péladan, entitled *Il poverello di Assisi*; and a "drame lyrique" by Tomasi, *François d'Assise (Le petit pauvre)*.
115. See Alex Ross, "Sacred monster," *The New Yorker*, 28 October 2002.
116. See "Entretien avec Olivier Messiaen," *Opéra aujourd'hui* 4, 8.
117. Another recent French opera premiered in French in a non-French-speaking country is *Joseph Merrick, dit Elephant Man*, the four-act opera by Laurent Petitgirard (born 1950) on a libretto by Éric Nonn, first staged in Prague in 2002, and subsequently recorded by Naxos (8557–608/9).
118. Quoted from Lamantia 2005, 332.
119. It may be recalled that Campra had included a mini Italian opera in *Le carnaval de Venise* and that Rameau introduced an Italian air in the Persian act of *Les Indes galantes*.
120. The acronym stands for Institut de recherche et coordination acoustique/musique.
121. A spiritual affiliation can be seen between the two works, since Saariaho has admitted that it was the success of Messiaen's opera that prompted her to turn her attention to the genre. Rather than a studio recording of *L'amour de loin*, there exists, fortunately, a DVD of the original production, filmed in Helsinki (DGG B0004721–09). The cast is that of the Salzburg premiere: Dawn Upshaw as Clémence, Gerald Finley as Jaufré, and Monica Groop as the Pilgrim.
122. A pupil of d'Indy, Witkowski (1867–1943) became head of the Lyons Conservatoroise.
123. Having come to prominence by winning the Goncourt Prize in 1993 for his novel *Le rocher de Tanios*, he has published a book on Arab perspectives on the Crusades.
124. Cited by Alan Riding, "Unafraid to Wear His Opera On His Sleeve; The Emotions of the Classics Drive Composer's New Work," *The New York Times*, 6 March 2003.

BIBLIOGRAPHY

Abraham, Gerald, ed. *The Age of Beethoven, 1790–1830*. London and New York: Oxford University Press, 1982 (New Oxford History of Music, 8).

Abraham, Gerald, ed. *Romanticism, 1830–1890*. London and New York: Oxford University Press, 1990 (New Oxford History of Music, 9).

Adam, Adolphe. *Lettres sur la musique française (1836–1850)*. Introduction by Joël-Marie Fauquet. Geneva: Minkoff, 1996.

Anthony, James R. *French Baroque Music from Beaujoyeulx to Rameau*. Rev. ed., Portland, OR: Amadeus Press, 1997.

Antoine, Michel. *Henry Desmarets (1661–1741): Biographie critique*. Paris, 1965.

Ashbrook, William. *Donizetti and his Operas*. Cambridge et al.: Cambridge University Press, 1982.

Auld, Louis E. *The Lyric Art of Pierre Perrin, Founder of French Opera*. Henryville, PA: Institute of Mediaeval Music, 1986, 3 vols.

Bacilly, Bénigne de. *A Commentary upon the Art of Proper Singing*. Translated and edited by Austin B. Caswell. New York: The Institute of Mediaeval Music, 1968 (Musical Theorists in Translation, VII).

Barthélémy, Maurice. *André Campra (1660–1744): étude biographique et musicologique, sa vie et son oeuvre*. Arles: Actes Sud, 1995.

Bartlet, M., Elizabeth C. *Étienne-Nicolas Méhul and Opera: Source and Archival Studies of Lyric Theatre during the French Revolution, Consulate and Empire*. Heilbronn: Musik-Edition Lucie Galland, 1999, 2 vols.

Beaussant, Philippe. *Lully ou Le musicien du Soleil*. Paris: Gallimard/Théâtre des Champs-Élysées, 1992.

Berlioz, Hector. *Critique musicale, 1823–1863*, eds H. Robert Cohen, Yves Gérard et al. Paris: Buchet/Chastel, 1996–.

Berlioz, Hector. *Memoirs*. Translated and edited by David Cairns. London: Victor Gollancz Ltd, 1977.

Bloom, Peter, ed. *Music in Paris in the Eighteen-Thirties*. Stuyvesant, NY: Pendragon Press, 1987.

Boyd, Malcolm, ed. *Music and the French Revolution*. Cambridge et al.: Cambridge University Press, 1992.

Branger, Jean-Christophe. *Manon de Jules Massenet ou le crépuscule de l'opéra-comique*. Metz: Serpenoise, 1999.

Branger, Jean-Christophe. *Alfred Bruneau, un compositeur au coeur de la bataille naturaliste: lettres à Étienne Destranges, Paris-Nantes, 1891–1915*. Paris: Honoré Champion, 2003.

Branger, Jean-Christophe, and Alban Ramaut, eds. *Le naturalisme sur la scène lyrique*. Saint-Étienne: Publications de l'Université de Saint-Étienne, 2004.

Branger, Jean-Christophe, and Vincent Giroud, eds. *Figures de l'Antiquité dans l'opéra français des* Troyens *de Berlioz à l'Œdipe d'Enesco*. Saint-Étienne: Publications de l'Université de Saint-Étienne, 2008.

Branger, Jean-Christophe, and Vincent Giroud, eds. *Aspects de l'opéra français de Meyerbeer à Honegger*. Lyons: Symétrie, 2009.

Branger, Jean-Christophe, and Alban Ramaut, eds. *Religion et opéra sous la IIIe République*. Saint-Étienne: Publications de l'Université de Saint-Étienne, 2006.

Bril, France-Yvonne. *Henri Sauguet*. Paris: Seghers, 1967.

Brown, Bruce Alan. *Gluck and the French Theatre in Vienna*. Oxford: Clarendon Press, 1991.

Bruyas, Florian. *Histoire de l'opérette en France 1855–1965*. Lyon: Emmanuel Vitte, 1974.

Budden, Julian. *The Operas of Verdi*. London: Cassell, 1973–81, 3 vols.

Buford, Norman. *Touched by the Graces: The libretti of Philippe Quinault in the Context of French Classicism*. Birmingham, AL: Summa Publications, 2001.

Burney, Charles. *An Eighteenth-Century Musical Tour in France and Italy*, ed. Percy A. Scholes. London et al.: Oxford University Press, 1959.

Cairns, David. *Berlioz*. London: Allen Lane, The Penguin Press, 1989, 2 vols; 2nd ed. Berkeley: University of California Press, 2000.

Cariven-Galharet, Renée, and Dominique Ghesquière. *Hervé: un musicien paradoxal (1825–1892)*. Paris: Éditions des Cendres, 1992.

Cathé, Philippe. *Claude Terrasse*. Ouverture d'Ornella Volta. Paris: L'Hexaèdre, 2004.

Cessac, Catherine. *Marc-Antoine Charpentier*. Translated by E. Thomas Glasow. Portland, OR: Amadeus Press, 1995.

Cessac, Catherine. *Marc-Antoine Charpentier*. Paris: Fayard, 1988; rev. ed., Paris: Fayard, 2004.

Cessac, Catherine. *Élisabeth Jacquet de la Guerre: une femme compositeur sous le règne de Louis XIV*. Arles: Actes Sud, 1995.

Cessac, Catherine, ed. *Marc-Antoine Charpentier: un musicien retrouvé*. Sprimont: Mardaga, 2005.

Cessac, Catherine, and Manuel Couvreur, eds. *La duchesse du Maine (1676–1753): Une mécène à la croisée des arts et des siècles*. Brussels: Éditions de l'Université de Bruxelles, 2003.

Chaillou, David. *Napoléon et l'opéra: la politique sur la scène, 1810–1815*. Paris: Fayard, 2004.

Charlton, David. *Grétry and the Growth of opéra-comique*. Cambridge and New York: Cambridge University Press, 1986.

Charlton, David. "Romantic Opera: 1830–1850," in Abraham, 1990, pp. 85–140.

Charlton, David. *French Opera 1730–1830: Meaning and Media*. Aldershot; Brookfield, USA: Ashgate Variorum, 2000.

Charlton, David, ed. *The Cambridge Companion to Grand Opera*. Cambridge and New York: Cambridge University Press, 2003.

Chimènes, Myriam. *Correspondance, 1910–1963*, ed. Francis Poulenc. Paris: Fayard, 1994.

Chimènes, Myriam, ed. *La vie musicale sous Vichy*. Brussels: Éditions Complexe, 2001.

Christensen, Thomas. *Rameau and Musical Thought in the Enlightenment*. Cambridge: Cambridge University Press, 1993.

Christout, Marie-Françoise. *Le ballet de cour de Louis XIV, 1643–1672: mises en scène*. Paris: Picard, 1967.

Claudel, Paul. *Correspondance musicale*, ed. Pascal Lécroart. Drize, Geneva: Papillon, 2007.

Claudon, Francis, ed. *Dictionnaire de l'opéra-comique français*. Bern, Berlin, Paris.: Peter Lang, 1995.

Claudon, Francis, Gilles de Van, and K. Leich-Galland. *Actes du colloque Fromental Halévy*, Paris, Novembre 2000. Weinsberg: Musik-Edition Lucie Galland, 2003.

Cohen, H. Robert. *The Original Staging Manuals for Twelve Parisian Operatic Premières*. Stuyvesant, NY: Pendragon, 1991.

Collaer, Paul. *Darius Milhaud*. Translated and edited by Jane Hohfeld Galante. San Francisco CA: San Francisco Press, Inc., 1988.

Condé, Gérard. *Charles Gounod*. Paris: Fayard, 2009.

Cooke, Mervyn, ed. *The Cambridge Companion to Twentieth-Century Opera*. Cambridge: Cambridge University Press, 2005.

Cophignon, Alain. *Georges Enesco*. Paris: Fayard, 2006.

Corbier, Christophe. *Maurice Emmanuel*. Paris: Bleu Nuit, 2007.

Curtiss, Mina. *Bizet and His World*. New York: Knopf, 1958.

Dahlhaus, Carl. *Nineteenth-Century Music*. Translated by J. Bradford Robinson. Berkeley and Los Angeles, CA: University of California Press, 1989.

Dean, Winton. *Bizet*. London: J.M. Dent, 1948; new ed., 1975.

Deane, Basil. *Albert Roussel*. London: Barrie and Rockliff, 1961.

Delage, Roger. *Emmanuel Chabrier*. Paris: Fayard, 1999.

Dent, Edward J. *The Rise of Romantic Opera*. Edited by Winton Dean. Cambridge et al.: Cambridge University Press, 1976.

Depaulis, Jacques. *Reynaldo Hahn*. Biarritz: Atlantica, 2007.

Dingle, Christopher. *The Life of Messiaen*. Cambridge: Cambridge University Press, 2007.

Di Profio, Alessandro. *La révolution des Bouffons: L'opéra italien au Théâtre de Monsieur 1789–1792*. Paris: CNRS Éditions, 2003.

Drake, Jeremy. *The Operas of Darius Milhaud*. New York and London: Garland Publishing, Inc., 1989.

Durey de Noinville, Jacques-Bernard. *Histoire du théâtre de l'opéra en France depuis l'établissement de l'Académie royale de musique, jusqu'à présent*. Paris: Barbou, 1753.

Duteurtre, Benoît, ed. *André Messager*. Paris: Klincksieck, 2003.

Ewans, Michael. *Opera from the Greek: Studies in the Poetics of Appropriation*. Burlington, VT: Ashgate, 2007.

Fabiano, Andrea. *Histoire de l'opéra italien en France (1752–1815): héros et héroïnes d'un roman théâtral*. Paris: CNRS Éditions, 2006.

Fabiano, Andrea, ed. *La "Querelle des Bouffons" dans la vie culturelle française du XVIIIᵉ siècle*. Paris: CNRS Éditions, 2005.

Fajon, Robert. *L'opéra à Paris du Roi-Soleil à Louis le Bien-aimé*. Geneva: Slatkine, 1984.

Fauquet, Joël-Marie. *César Franck*. Paris: Fayard, 1999.

Fauquet, Joël-Marie, ed. *Dictionnaire de la musique en France au XIXᵉ siècle*. Paris: Fayard, 2003.

Favre, Georges. *Boïeldieu: sa vie, son oeuvre*. Paris: Droz, 1944–1945.

Fétis, François-Joseph. *Biographie universelle des musiciens et bibliographie générale de la musique*, 2nd ed. Paris: Firmin Didot frères, fils et Cⁱᵉ, 1860.

Fulcher, Jane. *The Nation's Image: French Grand Opera as Politics and Politicized Art*. Cambridge et al.: Cambridge University Press, 1987.

Fulcher, Jane. *French Cultural Politics & Music: From the Dreyfus Affair to the First World War*. New York and Oxford: Oxford University Press, 1999.

Fulcher, Jane. *The Composer as Intellectual: Music and Ideology in France 1914–1940*. Oxford and New York: Oxford University Press, 2005.

Gallois, Jean. *Ernest Chausson*. Paris: Fayard, 1994.

Garban, Dominique. *Jacques Rouché, l'homme qui sauva l'Opéra de Paris*. Paris: Somogy, 2007.

Gavoty, Bernard. *Reynaldo Hahn, le musicien de la Belle Époque*. Paris: Buchet/Chastel, 1976.

Gerhard, Anselm. *The Urbanization of Opera: Music Theater in Paris in the Nineteenth Century*. Translated by Mary Whittal. Chicago, IL, and London: The University of Chicago Press, 1998.

Girdlestone, Cuthbert. *Jean-Philippe Rameau: His Life and Work*, rev. ed. New York: Dover, 1969.

Girdlestone, Cuthbert. *La tragédie en musique (1673–1750) considérée comme genre littéraire*. Geneva and Paris: Droz, 1972.

Gossett, Philip. *Divas and Scholars: Performing Italian Opera*. Chicago, IL, and London: The University of Chicago Press, 2006.

Grayson, David A. *The Genesis of Debussy's* Pelléas et Mélisande. Ann Arbor, MI: UMI Research Press, 1986.

Grétry, André-Modeste. *Mémoires ou essais sur la musique.* 1/1797. New York: Da Capo Press, 1971, 3 vols.

Gros, Étienne. *Philippe Quinault, sa vie et son oeuvre.* Paris: Champion, 1926.

Grout, Donald Jay, and Hermine Weigel Williams. *A Short History of Opera,* 4th ed. New York: Columbia University Press, 2003.

Halbreich, Harry. *Arthur Honegger.* Translated by Roger Nichols. Portland, OR: Amadeus Press, 1999.

Hallman, Diana. *Opera, Liberalism, and Antisemitism in Nineteenth-Century France: The Politics of Halévy's* La Juive. Cambridge and New York: Cambridge University Press, 2002.

Hill, Peter, and Nigel Simeone. *Messiaen.* New Haven, CT, and London: Yale University Press, 2005.

Honegger, Marc, and Paul Prévost, eds. *Dictionnaire des oeuvres de l'art vocal.* Paris: Bordas, 1991, 3 vols.

Howard, Patricia. *Gluck and the Birth of Modern Opera.* London: Barrie and Rockliff, 1963.

Howard, Patricia. *Gluck: An Eighteenth-Century Portrait in Letters and Documents.* Oxford: Clarendon Press, 1995.

Huebner, Steven. *The Operas of Charles Gounod.* Oxford: Clarendon Press, 1990.

Huebner, Steven. *French Opera at the Fin de Siècle: Wagnerism, Nationalism, and Style.* Oxford: Oxford University Press, 1999.

Ianco, Pascal. *Charles Tournemire ou le mythe de Tristan.* Geneva: Papillon, 2002.

Irvine, Demar. *Massenet: A Chronicle of his Life and Times.* Portland, OR: Amadeus Press, 1994.

Isherwood, Robert M. *Music in the Service of the King: France in the Seventeenth Century.* Ithaca, NY, and London: Cornell University Press, 1973.

Jordan, Ruth. *Fromental Halévy: His Life and Music, 1799–1862.* London: Kahn and Averill, 1994.

Kelkel, Manfred. *Naturalisme, vérisme et réalisme dans l'opéra de 1890 à 1930.* Paris: Vrin, 1984.

Kintzler, Catherine. *Poétique de l'opéra français de Corneille à Rousseau.* Paris: Minerve, 1991.

Kintzler, Catherine. *Théâtre et opéra à l'âge classique: une familière étrangeté.* Paris: Fayard, 2004.

Kushner, David Z. *The Ernest Bloch Companion.* Westport, CT: Greenwood Press, 2002.

Lacombe, Hervé. *The Keys to French Opera in the Nineteenth Century.* Translated by Edward Schneider. Berkeley: University of California Press, 2001.

Lacombe, Hervé. *Géographie de l'opéra au XXᵉ siècle.* Paris: Fayard, 2007.

Lacombe, Hervé. *Georges Bizet: naissance d'une identité créatrice.* Paris: Fayard, 2000.

La Gorce, Jérôme de. *L'Opéra à Paris au temps de Louis XIV: Histoire d'un théâtre.* Paris: Desjonquères, 1992.

La Gorce, Jérôme de. *Jean-Baptiste Lully.* Paris: Fayard, 2002.

Laederich, Alexandra. *Catalogue de l'oeuvre de Jacques Ibert (1890–1962).* Hildesheim and New York: Georg Olms Verlag, 1998.

Lamantia, Frédéric. *L'opéra dans l'espace français.* Paris: Connaissances et savoirs, 2005.

Large, Brian. *Martinu.* London: Duckworth, 1975.

Launay, Denise, ed. *La Querelle des Bouffons: texte des pamphlets.* Geneva: Minkoff Reprints, 1973.

Le Cerf de la Viéville, Jean-Laurent. *Comparaison de la musique italienne et de la musique françoise.* Brussels: F. Foppens, 1705–6.

Lécroart, Pascal. *Paul Claudel et la rénovation du drame musical.* Liège: Mardaga, 2004.

Lesure, François. *Claude Debussy: biographie critique, suivie du catalogue de l'oeuvre.* Paris: Fayard, 2003.

Lesure, François, and Richard Langham Smith. *Debussy on Music.* Translated by Richard Langham Smith. New York: Alfred A. Knopf, 1977.

Letellier, Robert Ignatius. *The Operas of Giacomo Meyerbeer*. Madison, WI, and Teaneck: Fairleigh Dickinson University Press, 2006.

Lewis, Anthony, and Nigel Fortune, eds. *Opera and Church Music 1630–1750*. London, New York, Toronto: Oxford University Press, 1975 (New Oxford History of Music, V).

Loewenberg, Alfred. *Annals of Opera 1597–1940*, 3rd ed. Totowa, NJ: Rowman and Littlefield, 1978.

Machard, Roberte. *Jean-Joseph Cassanéa de Mondonville, virtuose, compositeur et chef d'orchestre*. Béziers: Centre international de documentation occitane; Société de musicologie du Languedoc, 1980.

Masson, Georges. *Gabriel Pierné, musicien lorrain*. Nancy: Presses universitaires de Nancy; Metz Éditions Serpenoise, 1987.

Masson, Georges. *Ambroise Thomas: un compositeur lyrique au XIXe siècle*. Metz: Serpenoise, 1996.

Mawer, Deborah, ed. *The Cambridge Companion to Ravel*. Cambridge: Cambridge University Press, 2000.

McGowan, Margaret M. *L'art du ballet de cour en France, 1581–1643*. Paris: Éditions du CNRS, 1963.

McGowan, Margaret M. *Dance in The Renaissance: European Fashion, French Obsession*. New Haven, CT, and London: Yale University Press, 2008.

Meyerbeer, Giacomo. *Diaries*. Translated and edited by Robert Ignatius Letellier. Madison, WI, and Teaneck: Fairleigh Dickinson University Press; London: Associated University Presses, 1999–2004, 4 vols.

Milliot, Sylvette, and Jérôme de La Gorge. *Marin Marais*. Paris: Fayard, 1991.

Mongrédien, Jean. *Jean-François Le Sueur: contribution à l'étude d'un demi-siècle de musique française: 1780–1830*. Berne and Las Vegas: Peter Lang, 1980.

Mongrédien, Jean. *French Music from the Enlightenment to Romanticism, 1879–1830*. Translated by Sylvain Frémaux. Portland, OR: Amadeus Press, 1996.

Montagnier, Jean-Paul. *Charles-Hubert Gervais: Un musicien au service du Régent et de Louis XV*. Paris: CNRS Éditions, 2001.

Nectoux, Jean-Michel. *Gabriel Fauré: A Musical Life*. Translated by Roger Nichols. Cambridge and New York: Cambridge University Press, 1991.

New Grove 2: The New Grove Dictionary of Music and Musicians, ed. by Stanley Sadie. 2nd ed. London: Macmillan, 2001.

Nichols, Roger, and Richard Langham Smith, eds. *Claude Debussy*. Pelléas et Mélisande. Cambridge: Cambridge University Press, 1989.

Nuitter, Charles, and Ernest Thoinan. *Les origines de l'opéra français d'après les minutes des notaires, les registres de la Conciergerie et les documents originaux*. Paris: Plon, Nourrit et Cie, 1886.

Ochsé, Fernand. *Histoire du théâtre lyrique en France*. Paris: Radio-Paris Éditeur, 1938.

Opera Grove: The New Grove Dictionary of Opera, ed. by Stanley Sadie. London: The Macmillan Press, 1992.

Orenstein, Arbie. *Ravel: Man and Musician*. New York and London: Columbia University Press, 1975.

Orledge, Robert. *Gabriel Fauré*. London: Eulenburg Books, 1979.

Orledge, Robert. *Debussy and the Theatre*. Cambridge and New York: Cambridge University Press, 1982.

Orledge, Robert. *Satie the Composer*. Cambridge: Cambridge University Press, 1990.

Patureau, Frédérique. *Le Palais Garnier dans la société parisienne (1875–1914)*. Liège: Mardaga, 1991.

Pendle, Karin. *Eugène Scribe and French Opera of the Nineteenth Century*. Ann Arbor, MI: UMI (*Studies in Musicology*, 6), 1979.

Perret, Simon-Pierre, and Harry Halbreich. *Albéric Magnard*. Paris: Fayard, 2001.

Perret, Simon-Pierre, and Marie-Laure Ragot. *Paul Dukas*. Paris: Fayard, 2007.

Pistone, Danièle, ed. *Le théâtre lyrique français 1945–1985*. Paris: Champion, 1987.

Pistone, Danièle, ed. *Musique et musiciens à Paris dans les années trente*. Paris: Champion, 2000.

Pitou, Spire. *The Paris Opéra: An Encyclopedia of Operas, Ballets, Composers, and Performers.* Westport, CT, and London: Greenwood Press, 1983–, 3 vols.

Pougin, Arthur. *Albert Grisar.* Paris: Hachette; Brussels: Schott frères, 1870.

Pougin, Arthur. *Adolphe Adam: sa vie, sa carrière, ses mémoires artistiques.* Paris: Charpentier, 1877.

Pougin, Arthur. *Les vrais créateurs de l'opéra français, Perrin et Cambert.* Paris: Charavay frères, 1881.

Pougin, Arthur. *Hérold: Biographie critique.* Paris: Laurens [1906].

Poulenc, Francis. *Correspondance 1910–1963,* ed. Myriam Chimènes. Paris: Fayard, 1994.

Powell, John S. *Music and Theatre in France, 1600–1680.* Oxford and New York: Oxford University Press, 2000.

Prévost, Paul, ed. *Le théâtre lyrique en France au XIXᵉ siècle.* Metz: Serpenoise, 1995.

Prunières, Henri. *L'opéra italien en France avant Lully.* Paris, 1913. Paris: Champion, 1975.

Pure, Michel de. *Idées des spectacles anciens et nouveaux.* 1/1668. Geneva: Minkoff, 1972.

Raguenet, François. *Parallèle des Italiens et des Français en ce qui regarde la musique et les opéras.* 1/1702. Geneva: Minkoff, 1976.

Rees, Brian. *Camille Saint-Saëns: A Life.* London: Chatto & Windus, 1999.

Rice, John A. *Antonio Salieri and Viennese Opera.* Chicago, IL, and London: University of Chicago Press, 1998.

Rochouse, Jacques. *Cinquante ans de folies parisiennes: Hervé (1825–1892), le père de l'opérette.* Paris: Éditions Michel de Maule, 1994.

Role, Claude. *François-Joseph Gossec (1734–1829): un musicien à Paris de l'Ancien Régime à Charles X.* Paris: L'Harmattan, 2000.

Rushton, Julian. *Music and Drama at the Académie Royale de Musique, Paris, 1774–1789.* PhD, Oxford University, 1970.

Sadie, Stanley, ed. *History of Opera.* New York and London: W.W. Norton & Company, 1990.

Sauguet, Henri. *La musique, ma vie.* 1/1990. Paris: Séguier/Archimbaud, 2001.

Schmidt, Carl B. *The Music of Francis Poulenc (1899–1963): A Catalogue.* Oxford: Clarendon Press, 1995.

Schmidt, Carl B. *Entrancing Muse: A Documented Biography of Francis Poulenc.* Hillsdale, NY: Pendragon Press, 2001.

Schneider, Herbert, ed. *Correspondance d'Eugène Scribe et de Daniel-François-Esprit Auber.* Sprimont, Belgium: Mardaga, 2000.

Schneider, Louis. *Les maîtres de l'opérette française: Hervé, Charles Lecocq.* Paris: Librairie académique Perrin et Cⁱᵉ, 1924.

Schwartz, Manuela, and Myriam Chimènes, ed. *Vincent d'Indy et son temps.* Liège: Mardaga, 2006.

Senici, Emanuele. *The Cambridge Companion to Rossini.* Cambridge and New York: Cambridge University Press, 2004.

Simon, Yannick. *Composer sous Vichy.* Lyons: Symétrie, 2009.

Spies, André. *French Opera during the Belle Époque: A Study in the Social History of Ideas.* PhD Dissertation, University of North Carolina at Chapel Hill, 1986.

Strassburg, Robert. *Ernest Bloch, Voice in the Wilderness: A Biographical Study.* Los Angeles, CA: Trident Shop, California State University, Los Angeles, 1977.

Studwell, William Emmett. *Adolphe Adam and Léo Delibes: A Guide to Research.* New York: Garland, 1987.

Thomson, Andrew. *Widor: The Life and Times of Charles-Marie Widor, 1844–1937.* Oxford and New York: Oxford University Press, 1987.

Thomson, Andrew. *Vincent d'Indy and His World.* Oxford: Clarendon Press, 1996.

Trezise, Simon, ed. *The Cambridge Companion to Debussy.* Cambridge and New York: Cambridge University Press, 2003.

Trois siècles d'opéra à Lyon. Lyons: Bibliothèque de la Ville de Lyon, 1982.

Van, Gilles de. *Verdi's Theater: Creating Drama Through Music.* Translated by Gilda Roerts. Chicago, IL: University of Chicago Press, 1998.

Vendrix, Philippe, ed. *Grétry et l'Europe de l'opéra-comique*. Liège: Mardaga, 1992.

Vendrix, Philippe, ed. *L'opéra-comique en France au XVIIIe siècle*. Liège: Mardaga, 1992.

Vignal, Marc. *Les fils Bach*. Paris: Fayard, 1997.

Viollier, Renée. *Jean-Joseph Mouret, le musicien des grâces 1682–1738*. Paris: Floury, 1950.

Waeber, Jacqueline. *En musique dans le texte: le mélodrame, de Rousseau à Schoenberg*. Paris: Van Dieren, 2005.

Wagstaff, John. *André Messager: A Bio-Bibliography*. New York: Greewood Press, 1991.

Walsh, T.J. *Second Empire Opera: The Théâtre Lyrique, Paris, 1851–1870*. London: John Calder; New York: Riverrun Press, 1981.

Wellesz, Egon, and Frederick Sternfeld. *The Age of Enlightenment 1745–1790*. London and New York: Oxford University Press (*New Oxford History of Music*, VII), 1973.

White, Eric Walter. *Stravinsky: The Composer and his Works*. London and Boston, MA: Faber and Faber, 1966, repr. 1979.

Wild, Nicole. *Dictionnaire des théâtres parisiens au XIXe siècle*. Paris: Aux Amateurs de livres, 1989.

Wild, Nicole, and David Charlton. *Théâtre de l'Opéra-Comique, Paris: Répertoire 1762–1972*. Liège: Mardaga, 2005.

Wolff, Stéphane. *L'Opéra au Palais-Garnier (1875–1962)*. 1/1962. Geneva: Slatkine, 1983.

Wood, Caroline. *Music and Drama in the "tragédie en musique," 1673–1715: Jean-Baptiste Lully and His Successors*. New York: Garland, 1996.

Wood, Caroline, and Graham Sadler. *French Baroque Opera: A reader*. Aldershot, Burlington: Ashgate, 2000.

Yon, Jean-Claude. *Eugène Scribe: la fortune et la liberté*. Saint-Genouph: Nizet, 2000.

Yon, Jean-Claude. *Jacques Offenbach*. Paris: Gallimard, 2000.

INDEX